APPROPRIATIONS LAW
Principles and Practice

APPROPRIATIONS LAW
Principles and Practice

Steven N. Tomanelli

MANAGEMENTCONCEPTS
Vienna, Virginia

MANAGEMENTCONCEPTS
8230 Leesburg Pike, Suite 800
Vienna, Virginia 22182
Phone: (703) 790-9595
Fax: (703) 790-1371
Web: www.managementconcepts.com

Copyright © 2003 by Management Concepts, Inc.

All rights reserved. No part of this book may be reproduced or utilized in any form or by any means, electronic or mechanical, including photocopying, recording, or by an information storage and retrieval system, without permission in writing from the publisher, except for brief quotations in review articles.

Printed in the United States of America

Library of Congress Cataloging-in-Publication Data

Tomanelli, Steven N.
  Appropriations law: principles and practice / Steven N. Tomanelli.
    p. cm.
  Includes index.
  ISBN 1-56726-121-3 (hb)
  1. Budget—Law and legislation—United States. 2. United States—Appropriations and expenditures. I. Title.

KF6225 .T66 2003
343.73'034—dc21

2002043108

About the Author

Steven N. Tomanelli is an attorney who provides training and consulting services pertaining to all aspects of government procurement. He teaches a broad variety of courses to contracting personnel, attorneys, financial managers, support staff, and program office personnel.

Steve has served as a Judge Advocate in the United States Air Force and has held numerous high-level positions, including Chief of Acquisition and Fiscal Law for the Air Force's Air Mobility Command and Senior DoD Counsel for the National Reconnaissance Office (NRO) in Chantilly, Virginia. He has provided consulting services and legal advice in support of highly classified major system acquisitions and has been a member of various source selection boards, advisory councils, and "red teams." Steve has also served as a Professor of Contract and Fiscal Law at the Army Judge Advocate General's School in Charlottesville, Virginia, where he provided instruction in a wide variety of procurement and fiscal law topics. In 2001, he was selected as the Outstanding Career Judge Advocate of the Air Force.

While obtaining his Master of Laws degree in Procurement, Steve worked as an intern at the Armed Services Board of Contract Appeals. He received his B.A. (cum laude) and J.D. at Hofstra University, and his Master of Laws in federal procurement law at George Washington University (highest honors).

Steve has authored more than 30 course books and written numerous articles for national publications in federal procurement and fiscal law. He is a member of the Public Contract Law Section of the American Bar Association, the National Contract Management Association, and the Advisory Board of *Government Contractor*.

Dedication

For my girls, Susan, Lauren, and Lisa

Table of Contents

Preface xix

Acknowledgments xxiii

Chapter 1. Overview of Appropriations Law 1
The Constitution and the Separation of
   Powers Doctrine 1
   The Power to Tax and Spend 2
   The Appropriations Clause 2
   Congressional Exercise of the "Power of the Purse" 3
   Evolution of the Appropriations Process 5
The Language of Federal Appropriations Law 6
The Federal Budget Process 8
   The President's Budget 9
   Congressional Action 9
   Budget Execution 12
Agency Management of Appropriations 12
   Administrative Subdivision of Funds 13
   Accounting Classification Codes 14
   Impoundment Actions 15
      Deferrals 16
      Rescissions 16
      The Role of the Comptroller General 16
Overview of Congressional Limitations on the
   Use of Appropriated Funds 19
Purpose Limitations 19
Time Limitations 19
Amount Limitations 20

Key Appropriations Law Concepts 20
Specific vs. General Appropriations 20
Two Appropriations Available for the Same Purpose:
  The Rule of Election 22
Permanent vs. Transitory Legislation 23
The Doctrine of Ratification by Appropriation 27
The Rule against Repeal by Implication 30
Appropriated Amount Exceeds Previously
  Authorized Amount 34
Appropriated Amount Is Less Than Previously
  Authorized Amount 36
Funds Appropriated Prior to Enactment of
  Authorization Act 38
Effect of the Failure to Enact an Authorization Act 40

Chapter 2. Commitment and Obligation of Funds 43
Definitions 43
Commitment of Funds 44
  Purpose of Commitment 45
  Responsibilities 46
  Determining How Much to Commit 47
    Contingent Liabilities 47
    Other Contractual Liabilities 50
Obligation of Appropriations 51
  Statutory Requirement for Recording
    Obligations 53
  Contract Obligations 55
    The Requirement for a Binding Agreement 56
    The Requirement That the Contract Be
      "in Writing" 58
    The Requirement of Specificity 61
Determining How Much to Obligate 62
  Fixed-Price Contracts 62
    Firm Fixed-Price Contracts 62
    Fixed-Price with Economic Price Adjustment
      Contracts 63
    Fixed-Price Incentive Contracts 64
    Fixed-Price Award Fee Contracts 65
  Cost-Reimbursement Contracts 66
    Cost-Plus Fixed Fee Contracts 68
    Cost-Plus Incentive Fee Contracts 68
    Cost-Plus Award Fee Contracts 69

    Variable Quantity Contracts 70
        Indefinite-Delivery/Indefinite-Quantity Contracts 71
        Requirements Contracts 71
    Letter Contracts 73
    Purchase Orders 75
    Options 76
    Rental Agreements 76
    Interagency Transactions 77
        Voluntary Interagency Agreements 78
        Interagency Agreements Required by Law 81
    Orders from Stock 83
Specific Obligations Situations 83
    Ratification of Unauthorized Commitments 84
    Liquidated Damages 85
    Litigation 86
    Obligations Subject to the Availability of Funds..................... 88
Deobligations 89

Chapter 3. Availability of Appropriations:
    Purpose 93
The Purpose Statute 93
Application of the Purpose Statute 94
How to Determine the Purpose of an
    Appropriation 97
    Consider the Plain Meaning of the
        Appropriation Act 98
    Use of Legislative History to Determine Purpose 100
        Meaning of "Legislative History" 101
        Types of Legislative History and Their
            Significance 102
    The Effect of Items Included in the Agency's
        Budget Request 107
    Termination of a Program with Funds
        Appropriated for That Program 110
The Necessary Expense Doctrine 112
    Relationship of the Expenditure to the
        Appropriation 113
        Specifically Stated Purpose... 113
        The Role of Agency Discretion 114
    The Expenditure Must Not Be Prohibited by Law 121
    The Expenditure Must Not Be Otherwise
        Provided For 123

Specific Examples 124
　Attendance at Meetings and Conventions 124
　　Meetings and Conventions Sponsored by
　　　Nongovernment Entitites 124
　　Meetings and Conventions Sponsored by
　　　the Federal Government 127
　　Attendance by Military Personnel 128
　　Expenses of Nongovernment Personnel 128
　Payment of Attorneys' Fees Incurred during
　　Contract Litigation 131
　　Bid Protests 131
　　Contract Disputes 133
　Clothing 134
　　Statutory Authorities for the Purchase
　　　of Clothing 135
　　Application of the Necessary Expense Doctrine 138
　Entertainment 141
　　The Definition of "Entertainment" 142
　　Food 143
　Official Representation Funds 159
　Fines and Penalties 165
　　Fines Incurred by Employee to Protect
　　　Government's Interests 166
　　Fines Levied Directly against an Agency 169
　Gifts and Awards 170
　Rewards 175
　　Rewards Paid to Informants 176
　　Rewards Relating to Missing Government
　　　Employees 179
　　Rewards As a "Necessary Expense" 180
　　Rewards to Finders of Lost Government Property 180
　　Contractual Bases for Rewards 181
　Telephones in Private Residences of
　　Government Employees 183
　　Application of the Rule 184
　　Exceptions 185
　Membership Fees 191
　　Individual Membership 191
　　Agency Membership 193
　Business Cards for Government Employees 196
　Office Decorations 197

**Chapter 4. Limitations on the Use of
   Appropriated Funds: Time** 201
Definitions 202
Determining the Period of Availability 203
   Presumption of One-Year Period of Availability 204
   Congressionally Specified Periods of Availability 206
      Multiple-Year Appropriations 206
      No-Year Appropriations 207
      The Effect of Authorization Acts and Enabling
         Legislation on the Period of Availability 210
The Bona Fide Needs Rule 211
   Statutory Basis of the Bona Fide Needs Rule 212
   Bona Fide Needs Determinations Are Highly
      Fact-Sensitive 212
   Application of the Bona Fide Needs Rule to
      Multiple-Year Appropriations 213
   "Continuing" Needs 215
   Application of the Bona Fide Needs Rule to
      Supply Contracts 218
      The Lead-Time Exception 220
      The Stock-Level Exception 221
   Application of the Bona Fide Needs Rule to
      Service Contracts 222
      Severable vs. Nonseverable Services 223
      Statutory Exception 225
   Application of the Bona Fide Needs Rule to
      Training Contracts 226
   Application of the Bona Fide Needs Rule to
      Construction Contracts 226
Use of Expired Appropriations 228
   Bid Protests 228
   Terminations for Default 230
      Requirements 231
      General Continuing Needs Distinguished 232
      Mandatory vs. Discretionary Use of Expired
         Funds after Default Termination 233
   Terminations for Convenience of the
      Government 234
      Fiscal Effect of Termination for Convenience 235
      Requirements 236
   Contract Modifications That Reduce Scope 237

Contract Modifications That Increase
　Amount Obligated 239
　Situations in Which Modifications May Be
　　Charged to Expired Appropriations 239
　Situations in Which Modifications May
　　Not Be Charged to Expired Appropriations 243
Closed Appropriations 247

Chapter 5. Limitations on the Use of Appropriated Funds: Amount 251
Overview of the Antideficiency Act 252
Apportionment of Appropriations 255
　Requirement to Avoid Apportionments That
　　Indicate a Need for Additional Appropriations 257
　　Implementing the Statutory Requirement 258
　　Exceptions 261
　Requirement to Avoid Obligations or Expenditures
　　That Exceed the Amount Available in an
　　Apportionment 263
　　Overview 263
　　Statutory Requirement 265
Administrative Subdivision of Appropriations 268
Antideficiency Act Violations at the
　Appropriations Level 273
　Scope of the Statutory Limitation 274
　Obligations in Excess of Appropriations 276
　　Determining the Amount Available in an
　　　Appropriation 277
　　Determining if an Obligation or Expenditure
　　　Exceeds the Amount Available 282
　　Exhausted Appropriations 285
　　Examples of Violations of 31 U.S.C. § 1341 (a)(1)(A) 286
　Obligations in Advance of Appropriations 292
　　Obligations Citing Future Year's
　　　Appropriations 292
　　Multi-year Contracts 294
　　Unlimited Indemnification Clauses 305
　　Obligations in Advance of Apportionments 319
Voluntary Services Prohibition 321
　Employment of Personal Services 324
　Acceptance of Voluntary Services 329

Exceptions 335
　The Emergency Exception 335
　Statutorily Authorized Waivers of Compensation
　　Fixed by Statute 341
　Experts and Consultants 342
　Services in Support of Alternative Dispute
　　Resolution 343
　Student Intern Programs 344
　Medical Care, Museums, Natural Resources Programs,
　　and Family Support Programs 345
　Red Cross Volunteers 346
　Reserve Officers 346
　Statutory Training Programs 347
　Other Statutory Exceptions 350
Reporting Antideficiency Act Violations 350
Consequences of Antideficiency Act Violations 352
　Criminal Penalties 353
　Administrative Sanctions 354
Effect of Exhaustion of Appropriation on Contractors'
　Right to Payment 354
Attachment 5-1 359

**Chapter 6. Fiscal Law Issues Related to Interagency
　Transactions 367**
The Economy Act 367
　Overview of the Economy Act 367
　Scope of the Economy Act 375
　Fiscal Issues Related to Implementation of the
　　Economy Act 377
　　Making and Accounting for Payments 378
　　Calculating the "Actual Cost" To Be
　　　Reimbursed 383
　　Obligation and Deobligation of Funds 392
　　Applicability of General Restrictions and
　　　Limitations 397
　　Exception to the Requirement for Certification
　　　in Advance of Payment 403
　Authorized Services 406
　　Details of Personnel 406
　　Loans of Personal Property 415
　　Common Services 423

Services Not Authorized under the Economy Act 425
Use of Contractors to Perform Economy
  Act Orders 432
Amendments to the Economy Act 432
Applicability of the Competition in
  Contracting Act 434
Economy Act Abuses and "Off-Loading" 435
Other Interagency Transactions 437
The Project Order Statute 437
The Government Employees Training Act 440
The Clinger-Cohen Act of 1996 441
The Federal Property and Administrative Services
  Act of 1949 443
The Tennessee Valley Authority 444
District of Columbia 444
National Academy of Sciences 445

Chapter 7. Funding Gaps and Continuing
Resolution Authority 447
Funding Gaps 447
  Legal Framework for Agency Operations
    during a Funding Gap 448
    The 1980 Attorney General Opinion 449
    The 1980 Comptroller General Opinion 450
    The 1995 Attorney General Opinion 451
    OMB Bulletin No. 80-14 461
  Problems Associated with Operating during a
    Funding Gap 462
  Permissible Activities during a Funding Gap 464
  Impact of Funding Gaps on Agency Operations 467
Continuing Resolutions 471
  Definitions 472
  Key Aspects of Continuing Resolutions 473
    Amount Provided by a Continuing Resolution 473
    Duration of a Continuing Resolution and the
      Pattern of Obligation 485
    Agency Actions under a Continuing Resolution 487
Attachment 7-1 495

Chapter 8. Liability and Relief of Accountable Officers 511
Historical Perspective 511
   Historical Bases of Accountable Officer Liability 511
   Historical Bases for Relief of Liability 514
Accountable Officer Defined 515
   Certifying Officers 517
   Disbursing Officers 519
   Cashiers 520
   Collecting Officers 523
   Other Custodians of Federal Funds 525
Funds for Which Accountable Officers Are Responsible 528
   Appropriated Funds 528
      Imprest Funds 529
      Flash Rolls 529
      Travel Advances 529
   Funds Received from Nongovernment Sources 531
   Funds Held in Trust for Others 532
Events That Can Result in Accountable Officer Liability 533
   Physical Loss or Deficiency 534
   Illegal, Improper, or Incorrect Payment 534
   Comparison of the Two Bases for Liability 535
Relief from Liability 538
   Relief in Physical Loss or Deficiency Cases 538
      Civilian Agency Accountable Officers 540
      Department of Defense Disbursing Officers and Certifying Officers 542
   Officials Authorized to Grant Relief 544
      Civilian Agency Accountable Officers 544
      Department of Defense Disbursing and Certifying Officers 546
   Standard for Granting Relief in Physical Loss or Deficiency Cases 547
      Absence of Negligence 547
      The Concept and Application of Proximate Cause 552

Unexplained Losses 554
Effect of Regulatory Violations 557
Earthquakes, Fires, and Other Unfortunate
    Events 559
Theft by Third Parties 560
Embezzlement 565
Adequacy of Security Measures 566
Standard for Granting Relief in Improper
    Payments Cases 570
Impact of Automated Disbursing Systems
    on Relief from Liability 574
Relief of Certifying Officers 575
Relief of Disbursing Officers 583

Student Exam 593

Index 605

Preface

Federal appropriations law, often referred to as fiscal law, is fundamental to the operation of the federal government's numerous and varied agencies. An understanding of federal appropriations law is therefore essential to the daily operations and functioning of the federal government. The aim of this book is to identify, discuss, and explain the various sources of fiscal law so that anyone involved in the use or management of appropriated funds can better understand his or her responsibilities and maximize the effective use of the funds available.

This book was written with two audiences in mind. First, it was written for the practitioner who needs a practical fiscal law reference book that can be consulted to get concise answers to a broad spectrum of fiscal problems. Although this book deals with the subject of fiscal law, it is not a law book in the traditional sense and is intended for practitioners in all disciplines affected by the law of federal appropriations. This group includes contracting officers, accountable officers, resource managers, program managers, and budget personnel. Second, the book was written for students interested in learning the complex subject of fiscal law, whether by attending formal classes or by initiating a program of self-study. The first chapter starts out at a basic level so that the student can establish a solid foundation upon which the subsequent chapters build.

The term "fiscal law" may suggest that one could go to a reference library and find a book of laws passed by Congress that constitute the universe of fiscal law. Unfortunately, there is no such book. "Fiscal law" is generally used to refer to a broad variety of rules affecting the use of public funds, including statutes, implementing regulations, decisions issued by the General Accounting Office (GAO), bulletins and circulars issued by the Office of Management and Budget (OMB), the Treasury Financial Manual, and agency policy directives. This book attempts to pull together the relevant sections from these many references and organize them based on subject matter. Thus, when reading about the scope of an agency's authority under a continuing resolution (Chapter 7), the reader will find authoritative and relevant references from a variety of sources that are explained and interrelated.

Historically, one of the primary fiscal law references has been the *Principles of Federal Appropriations Law* (a.k.a. the "Redbook"), published by the Office of General Counsel of the United States General Accounting Office. Consisting of five large volumes, this reference offers depth and breadth that are more than what most practitioners and students need. While it is an excellent reference, the Redbook is used primarily by attorneys and some people in the budget policy business, but not usually by those involved with contracting, program management, or the certification and disbursement of funds. My objectives in writing this book were to combine what I consider to be the most practical sections of the Redbook with every other relevant reference I could identify, and then to present the results in an easily readable format geared for lawyers and non-lawyers alike.

The key points made in the text are illustrated with dozens of practical illustrations and discussion problems designed to have the student apply the principles addressed in the text. Also, since nineteen years have passed between publication of the first edition of the Redbook and Volume 5 of the second edition, I wanted to provide practitioners and students with a reference that is as current as possible.

Chapter 1 introduces the subject of fiscal law by explaining key terms and concepts, especially the complementary roles of Congress and the executive branch of the federal government. Chapter 2 discusses the many rules applicable to the commitment and obligation of funds, especially in the context of specific types of contractual agreements. Chapters 3, 4, and 5 address the critically important rules pertaining to congressional limitations on the use of funds. Specifically, Chapter 3 discusses the purposes for which appropriated funds may be used. Chapter 4 discusses when appropriated funds may be used to create new obligations and modify contracts, addresses the applicability of the bona fide needs rule in various contexts, and explains the consequences of the closure of appropriations accounts. Chapter 5 provides an in-depth explanation of the Antideficiency Act. Chapters 6, 7, and 8 deal with specialty topics and build upon the core concepts addressed in Chapters 1–5. Chapter 6 discusses the various types of interagency transactions, with particular emphasis on the Economy Act. Chapter 7 explains how agencies may operate when there is a lapse in appropriations or a continuing resolution. Finally, Chapter 8 addresses the bases for liability of accountable officers and how they may be relieved of liability.

The text of this book is followed by a 50-question exam that can be used in a classroom setting or as a self-study tool. For answers to the exam, send an e-mail to publications@managementconcepts.com. Answers to the discussion problems interspersed throughout the text are also available to instructors upon request, also from publications@managementconcepts.com.

This book does not necessarily represent the current policies of the Air Force, the Department of Defense, or any other federal agency.

It is my hope that readers will find that this book provides a concise, easily understandable, and useful reference. Please send any questions or comments to me at: stomanel@aol.com.

Steve Tomanelli
February 2003

Acknowledgments

Three people provided valuable assistance that contributed greatly to the final product. First, I would like to thank Rick Hurley for the time he spent reviewing the initial drafts and for his valuable substantive inputs. Second, thanks to Myra Strauss, who edited the drafts and provided expert assistance in structuring and formatting the text. Last, but not least, thanks to Mike Brown, who worked with me to develop the overall concept of the book and provided helpful inputs throughout the writing and editing process.

CHAPTER 1
Overview of Appropriations Law

Federal appropriations law affects virtually every aspect of a federal agency's operations. Also referred to as "fiscal law," federal appropriations law comprises a broad variety of rules, including statutes, implementing regulations, decisions issued by the General Accounting Office (GAO), bulletins and circulars issued by the Office of Management and Budget (OMB), and agency policy directives. A thorough understanding of fiscal law must begin with an understanding of the constitutional relationship among the three branches of the federal government, particularly between Congress and the executive branch.

THE CONSTITUTION AND THE SEPARATION OF POWERS DOCTRINE

To ensure that no single branch of the newly formed republic became so powerful that it could dominate the other branches, the Founding Fathers deemed it necessary to establish a system of checks and balances whereby each branch was, to some extent, dependent on the other branches. This philosophy is evident in several sections of the United States Constitution.

The Power to Tax and Spend

Article I, § 8, grants to Congress the power to "lay and collect Taxes, Duties, Imports, and Excises, to pay the Debts and provide for the common Defense and general Welfare of the United States. . . ." Further, this section gives Congress the power "[t]o make all laws which shall be necessary and proper for carrying into Execution the foregoing Powers, and all other Powers vested by this Constitution in the Government of the United States, or in any Department or Officer thereof." Under this broad authority, Congress may establish executive branch agencies and can limit the range of activities that such agencies can perform. Thus, when Congress creates an executive agency through the enactment of "enabling legislation," it defines the agency's mission and, therefore, the range of the agency's permissible activities. As discussed more fully in Chapter 3, analysis of an agency's enabling legislation is a very useful starting point in determining what an agency can and cannot do with appropriated funds.

The Appropriations Clause

In addition to the power to create executive branch agencies, Congress has the power to provide (or not provide) funding to the agencies it has created. Article I, § 9, provides that "no Money shall be drawn from the Treasury but in Consequence of an Appropriation made by Law." This constitutional provision, commonly referred to as the congressional "power of the purse," is the cornerstone of federal appropriations law. It means that "no money can be paid out of the Treasury unless it has been appropriated by an act of Congress." *Cincinnati Soap Co. v. United States*, 301 U.S. 308, 321 (1937). This rule applies to all types of payments, including federal salaries, payments under a contract, and payments ordered by a court. A federal agency may not make a payment from the United States Treasury unless Congress has made the funds available. As the Supreme Court stated well over a century ago: "However much money may be in the Treasury at any one time, not a dollar of it can be used in the payment of any thing not previously sanctioned [by Congress]." *Reeside v. Walker*, 52 U.S. (11 How.) 272, 291 (1850).

Through the authority conferred by the appropriations clause, Congress has exerted fiscal control over agencies by enacting permanent legislation and annual appropriations and authorization acts that determine how and when federal agencies may use appropriated funds.

Congressional Exercise of the "Power of the Purse"

These constitutional provisions authorize Congress to decide whether or not to provide funds for a particular program or activity and to fix the level of that funding. In exercising its appropriations power, however, Congress is not limited to these basic functions. Congress can also, within constitutional limits, determine the terms and conditions under which an appropriation may be used. See, e.g., *Cincinnati Soap Co.*, 301 U.S. at 321; *Oklahoma v. Schweiker*, 655 F.2d 401,406 (D.C. Cir. 1981); *Spaulding v. Douglas Aircraft*, 60 F. Supp. 985,988 (SD. Cal. 1945), aff'd, 154 F.2d 419 (9th Cir. 1946). Thus, Congress can specify, either in the appropriation itself or by separate statutory provisions, what will be required to make the appropriation "legally available" for any expenditure.

Most commonly, these restrictions describe the purposes for which the funds may be used, the length of time the funds may remain available for these uses, and the maximum amount an agency may spend on particular elements of a program. However, Congress has also imposed various administrative-type restrictions on an agency's authority to use funds. This type of restriction may require certain high levels of approval prior to the award of certain contracts. See, e.g., *AT&T v. United States*, 177 F.3d 1368 (Fed. Cir. 1999) (DoD's FY 1987 Appropriations Act required that the Under Secretary of Defense for Acquisition determine that risk had been reduced and realistic pricing is possible prior to award of a fixed-price weapons development contract over $10 million). In this manner, Congress may, and often does, use its appropriations power to accomplish policy objectives and to establish priorities among federal programs.

The current approach, in which Congress uses the appropriations process to exercise varying degrees of control (depending on the agency) over budget execution, is quite different from the practice in earlier times. For example, during the period after the adoption of the Constitution, executive agencies exerted little fiscal control over the funds appropriated to them. During these years, agencies often would obligate funds in advance of appropriations, commingle funds, use funds for purposes other than those for which they were appropriated, and obligate all available funds early in the fiscal year and then ask Congress for additional appropriations to continue operations. To curb these abuses, Congress passed the Antideficiency Act (ADA). The ADA consists of several statutes that mandate administrative and criminal sanctions for the unlawful use of appropriated funds. *See* 31 U.S.C. §§ 1341, 1342, 1350, 1351, and 1511-1519.

The effect of the constitutional power of Congress is that an agency cannot expend appropriated funds unless it has authority to do so. The Supreme Court described this rule as follows:

> The established rule is that the expenditure of public funds is proper only when authorized by Congress, not that public funds may be expended unless prohibited by Congress.

United States v. MacCollom, 426 U.S. 317, 321 (1976). Personnel involved in the acquisition process must always bear in mind that the level of discretion applicable to fiscal matters is much more restrictive than the level of authority enjoyed by federal agencies when conducting acquisitions. For example, in the context of federal acquisitions, the Federal Acquisition Regulation (FAR) states:

1.102-4 Role of the Acquisition Team.
. . .
(e) The FAR outlines procurement policies and procedures that are used by members of the Acquisition Team. If a policy or procedure, or a particular strategy or practice, is in the best interest of the Government and is not specifically addressed in the FAR, nor prohibited by law (statute or case law), Executive order or other regulation, Government members of the Team should not assume it is prohibited. Rather, absence of direction should be interpreted as permitting the Team to innovate and use sound business judgment that is otherwise consistent with law and within the limits of their authority.

Thus, when conducting acquisitions, an agency may assume that if an action is not specifically prohibited, it is authorized. Since this rule is essentially the opposite of the rule applicable to the expenditure of appropriated funds, federal acquisitions personnel must be cognizant of the difference. An agency may legitimately develop and implement an innovative and unprecedented acquisition strategy, but the obligation and expenditure of funds would have to be authorized and would have to comply with all applicable fiscal rules.

Evolution of the Appropriations Process

In the earliest days of the republic, the appropriations process was relatively simple. The general appropriations act enacted by Congress in 1789 appropriated a total of $639,000 for all federal agencies. The full text stated:

> Be it enacted by the Senate and House of Representatives of the United States of America in Congress assembled, That there be appropriated for the service of the present year, to be paid out of the monies which arise, either from the requisitions heretofore made upon the several states, or from the duties on impost and tonnage, the following sums, viz. A sum not exceeding two hundred and sixteen thousand dollars for defraying the expenses of

the civil list, under the late and present government; a sum not exceeding one hundred and thirty-seven thousand dollars for defraying the expenses of the department of war; a sum not exceeding one hundred and ninety thousand dollars for discharging the warrants issued by the late board of treasury, and remaining unsatisfied; and a sum not exceeding ninety-six thousand dollars for paying the pensions to invalids.

In contrast, the appropriations act for the Department of Defense alone is typically more than 35 pages long; authorization acts typically exceed 200 pages. The annual appropriations acts and authorizations acts exist against a backdrop of permanent legislation that fills two volumes of the United States Code at Title 31, as well as numerous statutes located in other titles, most notably Title 10 (DoD agencies) and Title 41 (civilian agencies). This increase in the complexity of the appropriations process can be attributed, at least in part, to a series of agency actions and congressional reactions. Over the years, a federal agency would circumvent some restriction on the use of its appropriations, Congress would enact a law to prevent further abuses, the agency would find a way to circumvent the new law, Congress would pass another law, and the process would continue—and it continues to the present time.

THE LANGUAGE OF FEDERAL APPROPRIATIONS LAW

Like many specialized subject areas, federal appropriations law has its own unique language that one must understand to be able to interpret and apply the myriad of applicable rules. An excellent fiscal law definitional resource is GAO's manual *A Glossary of Terms Used in the Federal Budget Process* (GAO/AFMD-2.1.1, 1993, available at http://161.203.16.4/t2pbat6/148403.pdf). The most important general definitions are provided below. Specific terms will be defined in the sections of this book that introduce and discuss them.

Appropriations Act: A statute that provides budget authority that enables federal agencies to incur obligations and make payments out of the Treasury. An appropriations act fulfills the requirements of Article I, section 9 of the Constitution which, as noted above, states that "no Money shall be drawn from the Treasury but in Consequence of an Appropriation made by Law."

Authorization Act: Legislation that sets up or continues the operation of a federal program or agency either indefinitely or for a specific period of time or that authorizes a particular type of obligation or expenditure within a program. Authorizing legislation is generally a prerequisite for appropriations. Authorizing legislation may limit the amount of budget authority to be included in an appropriations act, or it may authorize "such sums as may be necessary" and leave it to the appropriations committees to determine the specific amount. The authorization act itself does not provide budget authority.

Budget Authority: Congress finances federal programs and activities by granting budget authority. Budget authority is also called obligational authority. Budget authority is "authority provided by law to enter into obligations which will result in immediate or future outlay involving government funds. . . ." 2 U.S.C. § 622(2). Examples of budget authority include appropriations, borrowing authority, contract authority, and spending authority from offsetting collections. OMB Circular A-34, § 11.2. (Circulars issued by OMB may be downloaded at http://www.whitehouse.gov/omb/circulars/index.html).

Contract Authority: A limited form of budget authority that permits agencies to obligate funds in advance of appropriations but not to pay or disburse those funds absent some additional appropriations authority. *See, e.g.*, 41 U.S.C. § 11 (Feed and Forage Act).

Fiscal Year: The fiscal year for the federal government begins on October 1 and ends on September 30 of the following year. The fiscal year is designated by the calendar year in which it ends. For example, fiscal year 2000 began on October 1, 1999, and ended on September 30, 2000.

Multiple-Year Appropriation: An appropriation that is available for obligation for a definite period of time in excess of one fiscal year.

No-Year Appropriation: An appropriation that is available for obligation for an indefinite period. A no-year appropriation is usually identified by language such as "to remain available until expended."

One-Year Appropriation: An appropriation that is available for obligation only during a specific fiscal year. This is the most common type of appropriation. It is also known as a "fiscal year" or "annual" appropriation.

Obligation: An obligation is any act that legally binds the government to make payment. Obligations represent the amounts of orders placed, contracts awarded, services received, and similar transactions during an accounting period that will require payment during the same or a future period.

THE FEDERAL BUDGET PROCESS

To fully understand federal appropriations law, one must have some understanding of the federal budget process. For most agency personnel and government contractors, the critical point is the enactment of the appropriation, since that is the event that confers budget authority and allows the agency to obligate funds. However, the enactment of an appropriation is the culmination of a lengthy and complex process.

The first step in the life cycle of an appropriation is the long and exhaustive administrative process of budget preparation and review, a process that may take place several years before the budget for a particular fiscal year is ready to be submitted to Congress. The primary participants in the process at this stage are the agencies and individual organizational units, which review current operations, program objectives, and future plans. Overseeing the entire process is the Office of Management and Budget (OMB), which is charged with broad oversight, supervision, and responsibility for coordinating and formulating a consolidated budget submission.

Throughout this preparation period, there is a continuous exchange of information among the various federal agencies, OMB, and the President, including revenue estimates and economic outlook projections from the Treasury Department, the Council of Economic Advisers, the Congressional Budget Office, and the Departments of Commerce and Labor. The major objective of this process is for each agency to acquire the personnel and resources necessary to fulfill its long-term strategic plan within any known budget constraints. Agencies must carefully prioritize their requirements to ensure that the most important items are funded.

The President's Budget

The President's budget must be submitted to Congress on or before the first Monday in February of each year, for use during the following fiscal year. 2 U.S.C. § 631. Numerous statutory provisions, the most important of which are 31 U.S.C.§§ 1104–1109, prescribe the content and nature of the materials and justifications that must be submitted with the President's budget request. A comprehensive listing is contained in GAO'S report *Budget Issues: The President's Budget Submission*, GAO/AFMD-90-35 (October 1989). Specific instructions and policy guidance are contained in OMB Circular No. A-11, *Preparation and Submission of Budget Estimates* (November 8, 2001).

Congressional Action

In exercising the broad discretion granted by the Constitution, Congress can approve funding levels contained in the President's budget, increase or decrease those levels, eliminate proposals, or add programs not requested by the Administration. Before considering individual appropriations measures, however, Congress must, under the Congressional Budget Act, first agree on government-wide budget totals.

The goal of this part of the process is to ensure that expected revenues match expected budget requirements as closely as possible. If there is a shortfall, funds must be borrowed (usually by issuing savings bonds or through international transactions). If expected revenues exceed expected budget requirements, the federal government will have a surplus. (In 1998, the federal budget reported its first surplus—$69 billion—since 1969. In 1999, the surplus nearly doubled to $124 billion. As a result of these surpluses, federal debt held by the public has been reduced from $3.8 trillion at the end of 1997 to $3.6 trillion at the end of 1999. The events of September 11, 2001, and various tax cuts have reduced the size of the surplus somewhat.) A timetable for congressional action is set forth in 2 U.S.C. § 631, with further detail provided in sections 632–656.

By February 15, the Congressional Budget Office (CBO) submits to the House and Senate Budget Committees its annual report required by 2 U.S.C. § 602(f). The report contains the CBO's analysis of fiscal policy and budget priorities. (For more information on the role of CBO, see www.cbo.gov/respon.shtml.)

Within six weeks after the President's submittal of the budget, each congressional committee with legislative jurisdiction submits to the appropriate budget committee its views and estimates on spending and revenue levels for the following fiscal year on matters within its jurisdiction. 2 U.S.C. § 632(d), as amended by section 13112(a)(5) of the Omnibus Budget Reconciliation Act of 1990, 104 Stat. 1388-608. The House and Senate Budget Committees then hold hearings and prepare their respective versions of a concurrent resolution, which is intended to be the overall budget plan against which individual appropriation bills are to be evaluated. By April 15, both the House and the Senate must adopt a single compromise budget resolution, which includes a breakdown of estimated outlays by budget function. 2 U.S.C. § 632(a). In practice, however, Congress does not generally pass its budget resolution until May or June.

The concurrent resolution establishes the appropriate levels of budget authority, outlays, budget surplus or deficit, and federal revenues. The resolution may also include "reconciliation directives," which are directives to individual committees to recommend legislative changes in revenues or spending to meet the goals of the budget plan. 2 US.C. § 641(a). The conference report on the concurrent resolution allocates the totals among individual committees. 2 U.S.C. § 633(a). Because the budget resolution is designed solely to guide Congress in its detailed deliberations on the budget, it is in the form of a concurrent resolution, which is agreed to by both houses but is not signed by the President.

By June 10 the House Appropriations Committee completes the process of reporting the individual appropriation bills to the full House. By June 30 the House must complete action on all of the annual appropriations bills. Prior to this time, each of the appropriations subcommittees studies the appropriations requests of the agencies within its jurisdiction. Typically, each subcommittee will conduct hearings at which federal officials give testimony concerning both the costs and achievements of the various programs administered by their agencies, and provide detailed justifications for their funding requests. During this process, the committees may decide to increase or decrease funding, or to drop a program entirely. Eventually each subcommittee reports a single appropriation bill for consideration by the entire committee and then the full House membership. As individual appropriation bills are passed by the House, they are sent to the Senate. As in the House, each appropriation measure is first considered in subcommittee and then reported by the full appropriations committee to be voted upon by the full Senate.

In the event of variations in the Senate and House versions of a particular appropriation bill, a conference committee including representatives of both Houses of Congress is formed. It is the function of the conference committee to resolve all differences, but the full House and Senate (in that order) must also vote to approve the conference report. Following either the Senate's passage of the House version of an appropriation measure, or the approval of a conference report by both bodies, the enrolled bill is then sent to the President for signature or veto. The Congressional Budget Act envisions completion of the process by October 1.

Budget Execution

Budget execution refers to the agency's obligation, expenditure, and management of the funds appropriated to it by Congress. The appropriation and authorization acts enacted by Congress, as augmented by the legislative history and the agency budget submissions, serve as the government's financial plan for that fiscal year. The "execution and control" phase refers generally to the period of time during which the budget authority made available by the appropriations acts remains available for obligation. An agency's task during this phase is to spend the money Congress has given it to carry out the objectives of its program legislation.

AGENCY MANAGEMENT OF APPROPRIATIONS

Congress, apparently motivated by past fiscal mismanagement by federal agencies, has enacted legislation that requires agencies to establish administrative processes to effectively manage appropriated funds. 31 U.S.C. §§ 1513(d), 1514. For example, section 1514 of Title 31 of the United States Code requires agency heads to establish administrative controls that restrict obligations or expenditures to the amount of apportionments and enable the agency to fix responsibility for exceeding an apportionment. This law is implemented by OMB Circ. A-34, *Instructions on Budget Execution*, which applies to all agencies. OMB exercises a leadership role in executive branch financial management; this role was strengthened, and given a statutory foundation, by the Chief Financial Officers Act of 1990, Pub. L. No. 101-576 (November 15, 1990), 104 Stat. 2838. The "CFO" Act also enacted a new 31 USC Chapter 9, which (1) establishes a Chief Financial Officer in the cabinet departments and several other executive branch agencies to work with OMB and to develop and oversee financial management plans, programs, and activities within the agency, and (2) requires OMB approval of fund control systems. Individual federal agencies issue regulations that establish their fund control systems and provide guidance on how they are to be implemented. For example, the fund control system used by the Department of Defense is set forth at DOD Dir. 7200.1, Administrative Control of Appropriations; DOD 7000.14-R, vol. 14, app. A.

Administrative Subdivision of Funds

Once Congress enacts and the President has signed an appropriations act, the agency must have an orderly means of distributing the budget authority conferred by the act throughout the agency so it can be effectively used. Thus, consistent with 31 U.S.C. §§ 1513 and 1514, appropriations are subdivided by the executive branch departments and agencies so that funds are available to all levels of the organization. These formal subdivisions of funds are referred to as apportionments, allocations, and allotments. As will be discussed more fully in Chapter 5, making or authorizing an obligation or expenditure that exceeds one of these formal subdivisions of funds violates the Antideficiency Act. 31 U.S.C. § 1517(a)(2). Agencies may also subdivide funds at lower levels, such as within a particular branch of the organization, without creating an absolute, formal limitation on obligational authority. These subdivisions are considered funding targets. These limits are not formal subdivisions of funds, and exceeding them will not automatically violate the Antideficiency Act.

Accounting Classification Codes

Accounting classifications are codes used to manage appropriations. They are used to implement the administrative fund control system and to help ensure that funds are used correctly. Accounting classification codes are essential tools that agencies use to keep track of funds.

An accounting classification is commonly referred to as a "fund cite." Each digit in a fund cite provides useful information regarding the funds being cited. For example, assume that a funding document contains the following fund cite:

97 01 0100 37 4569 P720000 4738 S23478

The first two digits (97) identify the agency, in this case the Department of Defense. The next two digits (01) identify the fiscal year of the funds being cited; these would be FY 2001 funds. The next four digits (0100) represent the code assigned to the funds by the United States Treasury; this code identifies these funds as operations and maintenance funds of the Department of Defense. The next two digits (37) identify the operating agency code, and the subsequent four digits (4569) are the allotment number. The "P" number (P720000) refers to the budgetary program element.

The next four digits (4738) identify the element of expense, and finally, the last series of characters (S23478) identifies the fiscal station number.

This system of accounting classifications enables an agency to trace the distribution of funds from the headquarters level down to the lowest levels of the organization. It also enables the agency to identify precisely where and when an overobligation or overexpenditure occurred. In the event of a suspected violation of the Antideficiency Act, an agency should be able to use its fund control system and accounting codes to identify the responsible parties.

> **Discussion Problem 1-1**
>
> A federal agency's fiscal year (FY) 02 appropriations act states: "None of the funds appropriated by this act shall be available to purchase computers manufactured in a foreign country." The agency's procurement regulations state: "Procurement of computers manufactured in a foreign country is not authorized unless approved in writing by the agency head." During FY 02, the agency is able to get a great price on computers manufactured in a foreign country, and the agency head, always interested in saving taxpayer dollars, approves the purchase in writing. The agency awards a contract for the computers citing FY 02 funds.
>
> Is this purchase authorized under the FY 02 appropriations act? Would it make a difference if the purchase request was approved by the President of the United States?

Impoundment Actions

Article II, Section 3 of the Constitution requires that the President (and the agencies of the executive branch of government) "take care that the laws be faithfully executed." Since an appropriations act is a law enacted by Congress, executive agencies are generally required to obligate and expend the funds appropriated. While an agency's basic mission is to carry out its programs with the funds Congress has appropriated, there is also the possibility that, for a variety of reasons, the agency does not expend or obligate the full amount appropriated by Congress. Under the Impoundment Control Act of 1974, an impoundment is an action or inaction by an officer or employee of the United States that precludes the obligation or expenditure of budget authority provided by Congress. The Act applies to "salaries and expenses" appropriations as well as program appropriations. 64 Comp. Gen. 370, 375-76 (1985). There are two types of impoundment actions: deferrals and rescission proposals.

Deferrals

A deferral is a postponement of budget authority by which an agency temporarily withholds or delays obligation or expenditure. The President is required to notify Congress of any deferral of budget authority. Deferrals are authorized only to provide for contingencies, to achieve savings made possible by changes in requirements or greater efficiency of operations, or as otherwise specifically provided by law. A deferral may not be proposed for a period beyond the end of the fiscal year in which the special message reporting it is transmitted. In the case of multiple-year funds, a new deferral message may apply to the same funds in the following fiscal year. 2 U.S.C. §§ 682(l), 684.

Rescissions

A rescission involves the cancellation of budget authority previously provided by Congress (prior to when that authority would otherwise expire). Since a rescission has the effect of partially repealing an appropriations act, it can be accomplished only through legislation. The President must advise Congress of any proposed rescissions in a special message and is authorized to withhold the budget authority that is the subject of a rescission proposal for a period of 45 days of continuous session following receipt of the proposal. Unless Congress approves the proposed rescission within that time, the President (through OMB) must make the appropriation available for obligation, and the funds must be obligated by the agency to which the funds had been appropriated. 2 U.S.C.§§ 682(3), 683, 688.

The Role of the Comptroller General

The Impoundment Control Act requires the Comptroller General to monitor the performance of the executive branch in reporting proposed impoundments to the Congress. A copy of each message reporting a proposed deferral or rescission must be delivered to the Comptroller General, who then must review each message and present his views to the Senate and House of Representatives. 2 U.S.C. § 685(b). If the

Comptroller General finds that the executive branch has established a reserve or deferred budget authority and failed to transmit the required special message to Congress, the Comptroller General must report this to Congress. The Comptroller General also reports to Congress on any special message transmitted by the executive branch that has incorrectly classified a deferral or a rescission. 2 U.S.C. § 686.

Agencies must ensure that the timing of a deferral request (e.g., late in the fiscal year) is not tantamount to a rescission. GAO will construe a deferral as a de facto rescission if the timing of the proposed deferral is such that "funds could be expected with reasonable certainty to lapse before they could be obligated, or would have to be obligated imprudently to avoid that consequence." 54 Comp. Gen. 453, 462 (1974).

If, under the Impoundment Control Act, the executive branch is required to make budget authority available for obligation (for example, if Congress does not pass a rescission bill) and fails to do so, the Comptroller General is authorized to bring a civil action in the United States District Court for the District of Columbia to require that the budget authority be made available. 2 U.S.C. § 687.

The Impoundment Control Act is not violated if budget authority expires as a result of ineffective or unwise program administration. These situations are not regarded as impoundments unless the agency acted with the intention to withhold the budget authority. B-229326, August 29, 1989. There is also a distinction between deferrals, which must be reported, and "programmatic" delays, which GAO does not regard as reportable under the Impoundment Control Act. A programmatic delay is one in which operational factors unavoidably impede the obligation of budget authority, notwithstanding the agency's reasonable and good faith efforts to implement the program. For example, if a contractor working on a complex project for the National Aeronautics and Space Administration (NASA) encounters technical difficulties that impact the program schedule, the funds available for the next phase of the program may expire before they can be obligated. In such a case, the agency would have preferred to have begun the next phase promptly and was not intentionally delaying use of the funds.

Since intent is a relevant factor, the determination requires a case-by-case evaluation of the agency's justification in light of all of the surrounding circumstances. Delays resulting from the following factors may be programmatic, depending on the facts and circumstances involved:

- Uncertainty as to the amount of budget authority that will ultimately be available for the program (B-203057, September 15, 1981; B-207374, July 20, 1982, noting that the uncertainty is particularly relevant when it "arises in the context of continuing resolution funding, where Congress has not yet spoken definitively")
- Time required to set up the program or to comply with statutory conditions on obligating the funds (B-96983/B-225110, September 3, 1987)
- Compliance with congressional committee directives (B-221412, February 12, 1986)
- Delay in receiving a contract proposal requested from the contemplated sole source awardee (B-115398, February 6, 1978)
- Historically low loan application level (B-115398, September 28, 1976)
- Late receipt of complete loan applications (B-195437.3, February 5, 1988)
- Delay in awarding grants pending issuance of necessary regulations (B-171630, May 10, 1976)
- Administrative determination of allowability and accuracy of claims for grant payments (B-115398, October 16, 1975).

A programmatic delay may become a reportable deferral if the programmatic basis ceases to exist and the agency does not initiate a formal deferral action.

OVERVIEW OF CONGRESSIONAL LIMITATIONS ON THE USE OF APPROPRIATED FUNDS

In exercising its constitutionally granted "power of the purse," Congress has placed three limitations on the authority of executive agencies to obligate and expend appropriated funds. An agency: (1) may obligate and expend appropriations only for a proper purpose; (2) may obligate only within the time limits applicable to the appropriation (e.g., most operations and maintenance funds are available for obligation for one fiscal year); and (3) must obligate and expend funds within the amounts appropriated by Congress and formally distributed to or by the agency.

Purpose Limitations

The "purpose statute" requires agencies to apply appropriations only to the objects for which the appropriations were made, except as otherwise provided by law. *See* 31 U.S.C. § 1301. The number of appropriations Congress provides to an agency will vary depending on the size and complexity of the agency. Smaller agencies may have only one general appropriation for all of their activities, whereas other agencies have literally hundreds of appropriations. When an agency has many appropriations, it must be especially careful to ensure that each appropriation is being used in a manner that is consistent with the congressional intent. Obviously, this task is much easier when an agency has only one or just a few appropriations.

Time Limitations

Appropriations are generally available only for limited periods. An agency must incur the legal obligation to pay money within this period of availability. If an agency fails to obligate funds before they expire, the funds are no longer available for new obligations. Expired funds retain their "fiscal year identity" for five years after the end of the period of availability. This means, for example, that an FY 00 "salary and expense" appropriation will continue to be identified as FY 00 funds, even after the funds expire. During this time, the funds are available to adjust existing obligations or to liquidate prior valid obligations, but are not available for new obligations.

Amount Limitations

Limitations on amount are set forth in the various statutory provisions of the Antideficiency Act, 31 U.S.C. §§ 1341-42, 1511-19. The ADA prohibits any government officer or employee from: (1) making or authorizing an expenditure or obligation in excess of the amount available in an appropriation [31 U.S.C. § 1341(a)(1)(A)]; (2) making or authorizing expenditures or incurring obligations in excess of formal subdivisions of funds, or in excess of amounts permitted by regulations prescribed under 31 U.S.C. § 1514(a) [31 U.S.C. § 1517(a)(2)]; (3) incurring an obligation in advance of an appropriation, unless authorized by law [31 U.S.C. § 1341(a)(1)(B)]; and (4) accepting voluntary services, unless otherwise authorized by law (31 U.S.C. § 1342).

KEY APPROPRIATIONS LAW CONCEPTS

Several basic concepts permeate the law of federal appropriations. It is critical to understand how these core concepts apply in various contexts.

Specific vs. General Appropriations

An appropriation may be either general or specific. Sometimes the general appropriation and the specific appropriation overlap so that a particular item is covered by both. The applicable rule in this situation is that an appropriation for a specific object is available for that object to the exclusion of a more general appropriation that might otherwise be considered available for the same object. It does not matter that the amount available in the specific appropriation has been depleted. Exhaustion of the more specific appropriation does not authorize charging any excess payment to the more general appropriation, unless there is language in the general appropriation making it available in addition to the specific appropriation. In other words, if an agency has a specific appropriation for a particular item and also has a general appropriation broad enough to cover the same item, it does not have an option as to which to use—it must use the specific appropriation. If this were not the case, agencies could easily evade or exceed congressionally established spending limits.

Many GAO decisions illustrate this rule. Generally, the fact patterns and the specific statutes involved may differ, but the agency does not have an option in selecting which appropriation to use. If a specific appropriation exists for a particular item, then that appropriation must be used, and it is improper to charge the more general appropriation (or any other appropriation) or to use it as a "back-up." For example, in B-255979, October 30, 1995, the Coast Guard asked whether it could reimburse natural resources trustees directly from a general fund or whether such reimbursements may only be made under the more specific authority of subsection 1012(a)(2), which required compliance with the annual appropriations process. GAO applied the rule that a specific appropriation is available to the exclusion of a general appropriation and concluded that reimbursement was authorized only under the more specific provision and was, therefore, subject to the annual appropriations process. Similarly, a State Department appropriation for "publication of consular and commercial reports" could not be used to purchase books because the agency also had a specific appropriation for "books and maps." 1 Comp. Dec. 126 (1894). In another case, the Navy could not use a general appropriation to augment a specific appropriation for the construction of an additional wing on the Navy Department building. 20 Comp. Gen. 272 (1940). The rule that a general appropriation cannot supplement a specific appropriation also applies when the specific appropriation is included as an earmark within a general appropriation. 20 Comp. Gen. 739 (1941).

> ### Discussion Problem 1-2
>
> The National Forest Service has two appropriations available for obligation in FY 1999, one titled "construction and acquisition of buildings and facilities" and another titled "salary and expenses." In FY 1999, the Forest Service wants to use its "salary and expenses" appropriation to construct three buildings to be used for administrative offices. The three buildings are not specifically referenced in the FY 1999 "Construction and Acquisition of Buildings and Facilities" appropriation. Can the National Forest Service use either of its appropriations to construct the three administrative office buildings?

Two Appropriations Available for the Same Purpose: The Rule of Election

There are situations in which more than one appropriation can be construed as available for a particular object, but none can reasonably be considered the *most* specific appropriation. The rule in this situation is: Where more than one appropriation may reasonably be construed as available for expenditures that are not specifically mentioned under any appropriation, the agency's determination as to which appropriation to use will not be questioned. (This rule is often referred to as the "rule of election.") However, once the election has been made, the agency must continue to use the appropriation selected for the remainder of the fiscal year to the exclusion of any other for the same purpose, unless Congress changes the appropriation acts. 68 Comp. Gen. 337 (1989); 23 Comp. Gen. 827 (1944); 10 Comp. Gen. 440

(1931); 5 Comp. Gen. 479 (1926); 15 Comp. Dec. 101 (1908); 5 Op. Off. Legal Counsel 391 (1981).

For example, in 59 Comp. Gen. 518 (1980), the Environmental Protection Agency (EPA) received separate lump-sum appropriations for "research and development" and "abatement and control." A contract entered into in 1975 could arguably have been charged to either appropriation, but EPA had elected to charge it to research and development. Applying the rule of election, the Comptroller General concluded that a 1979 modification to the contract had to be charged to research and development funds, and that the abatement and control appropriation could not be used. Thus, in this type of situation (i.e., where there are two available appropriations, but neither specifies the object in question), the agency may make an initial election regarding which appropriation to use. However, once it has made that election and has in fact used the selected appropriation, the agency cannot thereafter, because of insufficient funds in the selected appropriation or for other reasons, change its election and use the other appropriation.

However, if Congress specifically authorizes the use of two accounts for the same purpose, the agency is not required to make an election between the two and is free to use both appropriations for the same purpose. See, e.g., *Funding for Army Repair Projects*, B-272191, Nov. 4, 1997 (statute provided that "funds appropriated to the Secretary [of the Army] for operation and maintenance" in the FY 1993 Defense Appropriations Act are "[i]n addition to. . .the funds specifically appropriated for real property maintenance under the heading [RPM,D]" in that appropriation act).

Permanent vs. Transitory Legislation

An issue that frequently arises is whether provisions in an appropriation act are applicable only during the fiscal year in which the appropriation was enacted ("transitory" legislation) or are applicable beyond the fiscal year in which the appropriation was enacted ("permanent" legislation). Since an appropriation act is made for a particular fiscal year, the starting presumption is that everything contained in the act is effective only for the fiscal year covered. Thus, the general rule is that a provision contained in an annual appropriation act is not to be construed to be permanent legislation unless the language used therein or the nature of the provision makes it clear that Congress intended it to be permanent. The presumption can be overcome if the provision uses language indicating futurity, such as "hereafter," or if the provision is of a general character bearing no relation to the object of the appropriation. 65 Comp. Gen. 588 (1986); 62 Comp. Gen. 54 (1982); 36 Comp. Gen. 434 (1956); 32 Comp. Gen. 11 (1952); 24 Comp. Gen. 436 (1944); 10 Comp. Gen. 120 (1930); 5 Comp. Gen. 810 (1926); 7 Comp. Dec. 838 (1901).

In analyzing a particular statutory provision, the starting point in determining congressional intent is always the language of the statute itself. The researcher must determine whether the provision uses "words of futurity." The most common word of futurity is "hereafter," and the courts and GAO have generally construed provisions using this term as permanent. For specific examples, see *Cella v. United States*, 208 F.2d at 790; 70 Comp. Gen. (B-242142, March 22, 1991); 26 Comp. Gen. 354,357 (1946); 2 Comp. Gen. 535 (1923); 11 Comp. Dec. 800 (1905); B-108245, March 19, 1952; B-100983, February 8, 1951; B-76782, June 10, 1948. In some cases, the precise location of the word "hereafter" may be an important indicator of congressional intent. It may not be sufficient, for example, if the word appears only in an exception clause and not in the main portion of the provision. B-228838, September 16, 1987.

Words of futurity other than "hereafter" have also been deemed sufficient. Thus, GAO has determined that there is no significant difference in meaning between "hereafter" and "after the date of approval of this act." 65 Comp. Gen. 588,589 (1986); 36 Comp. Gen. 434,436 (1956); B-209583, January 18, 1983. Using a specific date rather than a general reference to the date of enactment produces the same result.

B-57539, May 3, 1946. "Henceforth" has also been considered sufficient to indicate futurity. B-209583, January 18, 1983. Finally, if the appropriation provision makes specific references to future fiscal years, the provision will be deemed to survive the fiscal year covered by the appropriation. B-208354, August 10, 1982. Similarly, the phrasing of a provision as positive authorization rather than a restriction on the use of an appropriation is an indication of permanence, but usually has been considered in conjunction with a finding of adequate words of futurity. In 36 Comp. Gen. 434 (1956), GAO held:

> The language of the proviso is not, in its phraseology, a restriction on the use of the appropriation but a substantive provision prohibiting the public housing administration from authorizing, "after the date of approval" of the act, the construction of housing projects in certain instances. Its language, standing alone, appears permanent in nature. Also, while not controlling, it is noted that the codifiers have included the proviso as permanent law in the [United States Code] (42 U.S.C. 1411a, 1946 edition).

See also, 24 Comp. Gen. 436 (1944).

As the preceding paragraphs indicate, the language of the statute is the crucial indicator of congressional intent. However, other factors should also be considered. For example, as noted by GAO in 36 Comp. Gen 434 (1956), the inclusion of a provision in the United States Code is relevant as an indication of permanence but is not controlling. Legislative history is also relevant, but has been used for the most part to support a conclusion based on the presence or absence of words of futurity. See 65 Comp. Gen. 588 (1986); B-209583, January 18, 1983; B-208705, September 14, 1982; B-108245, March 19, 1952; B-57539, May 3, 1946; *Cella v. United States*, 208 F.2d at 790 n.l; *NLRB v. Thompson Products*, 141 F.2d at 798. In B-192973, October 11, 1978, a general provision requiring the submission of a report "annually to the Congress" was not considered permanent in view of conflicting expressions of congressional intent.

The point being made in all these cases is that legislative history by itself is insufficient to find futurity where it is missing in the statutory language.

Another factor that should be considered is the degree of relationship between a given provision and the object of the appropriation act in which it appears or the appropriating language to which it is appended. For example, if the provision bears no direct relationship to the appropriation act in which it appears, this is an indication of permanence. In one case, a provision prohibiting the retroactive application of an energy tax credit provision in the Internal Revenue Code was found sufficiently unrelated to the rest of the appropriation act in which it appeared to support a conclusion of permanence. B-214058, February 1, 1984. See also 62 Comp. Gen. 54, 56 (1982); 26 Comp. Gen. 354,357 (1946); 32 Comp. Gen. 11 (1952); B-37032, October 5, 1943; A-88073, August 19, 1937. Conversely, the closer the relationship, the less likely it is that the provision will be viewed as permanent.

Finally, a provision may be construed as permanent if construing it as temporary would render the provision meaningless or produce an absurd result. 65 Comp. Gen. 352 (1986); 62 Comp. Gen. 54 (1982); B-200923, October 1, 1982. These decisions dealt with a general provision designed to prohibit cost-of-living pay increases for federal judges except as specifically authorized by Congress. The provision appeared in a continuing resolution that expired on September 30, 1982. The next applicable pay increase would have been effective October 1, 1982. Thus, if the provision were not construed as permanent, it would have been completely meaningless "since it would have been enacted to prevent increases during a period when no increases were authorized to be made." 62 Comp. Gen. at 56-57. Similarly, a provision was held permanent in 9 Comp. Gen. 248 (1929) although it contained no words of futurity, because it was to become effective on the last day of the fiscal year, and interpreting the provision to be transitory would have rendered it effective for only one day, which was clearly not the legislative intent.

In sum, these various factors are all relevant as evidence of whether a given provision was intended by Congress to be permanent or transitory. However, the presence or absence of words of futurity remains the crucial factor, and the additional factors have been used for the most part to support a conclusion based primarily on this presence or absence. For example, the occurrence or non-occurrence in subsequent appropriation acts, inclusion in United States Code, legislative history, and phrasing as positive authorization have never been used as the sole basis for finding permanence in a provision without words of futurity. The two remaining factors discussed above (the relationship to the rest of the statute and avoidance of a meaningless or absurd result) have been used to find permanence in the absence of words of futurity, but the conclusion is almost always supported by at least one of the other factors, such as legislative history.

The Doctrine of Ratification by Appropriation

"Ratification by appropriation" is the doctrine by which Congress can, through the appropriation of funds, legitimize an agency action that may have been questionable when initially taken. This is a logical and intuitive rule, since Congress can ratify that which it could have authorized. *Swayne & Hoyt, Ltd. v, United States*, 300 U.S. 297, 301-02 (1937). It is also a well-established rule that Congress can indicate its ratification by the appropriation of funds. *Greene v. McElroy*, 360 U.S. 474, 504-06 (1959); *Ex Parte Endo*, 323 U.S. 283, 303 n.24 (1944); *Brooks v. Dewar*, 313 U.S. 354, 360-61 (1941). However, "ratification by appropriation" is not favored by GAO or the courts and will not be applied where it cannot be clearly demonstrated that Congress had prior knowledge of the specific disputed agency action. *D.C. Federation of Civic Associations v. Airis*, 391 F.2d 478, 482 (D.C. Cir. 1968); *Associated Electric Cooperative, Inc. v. Morton*, 507 F.2d 1167, 1174 (D.C. Cir. 1974), cert. denied, 423 LJ.S. 830. Thus, a simple lump-sum appropriation, without more, will generally not provide a sufficient basis to find a ratification by appropriation. *Endo,* 323 U.S. at 303 n.24; *Airis,* 391 F.2d at 481-82; *Wade v. Lewis,* 561 F. Supp. 913, 944 (N.D. Ill. 1983); B-213771, July 10, 1984. The appropriation "must plainly show a purpose to bestow the precise authority which is claimed." *Endo,* 323 U.S. at 303 n.24.

The doctrine of ratification by appropriation has been applied in a variety of contexts over the years. Presidential reorganizations have generated perhaps the largest number of cases. As discussed above in Section I.A., Congress creates agencies and defines the scope of their mission through "enabling legislation." Thus, when an executive branch official alters the scope of the agency's mission, questions often arise regarding the official's authority to take such action in the absence of specific congressional direction. Generally, when the President has created a new agency or has transferred a function from one agency to another, and Congress subsequently appropriates funds to the new agency or to the old agency for the new function, the courts have found that the appropriation ratified the Presidential action. *Fleming v. Mohawk Wrecking & Lumber Co.,* 331 U.S. 111, 116 (1947); *Isbrandtsen-Moller Co. v. United States,* 300 U.S. 139, 147 (1937).

The transfer to the Equal Employment Opportunity Commission (EEOC) in 1978 of enforcement responsibility for the Age Discrimination in Employment Act and the Equal Pay Act resulted in litigation of a multitude of cases. A clear majority of the decisions concluded that the subsequent appropriation of funds to the EEOC ratified the transfer. *EEOC v. DaWon Power & Light Co.,* 605 F. Supp. 13 (S.D, Ohio 1984); *EEOC v. Delaware Dept. of Health & Social Services,* 595 F. Supp. 568 (D. Del, 1984); *EEOC v. New York,* 590 F. Supp. 37 (N. D.N.Y. 1984); *EEOC v. Radio Montgomery, Inc.,* 588 F. Supp. 567 (W.D. Va. 1984); *EEOC v. City of Memphis,* 581 F. Supp. 179 (W.D. Term. 1983).

In another group of cases, the courts have refused to find ratification by appropriation for proposed construction projects funded under lump-sum appropriations where the effect would be either to expand the scope of a prior congressional authorization or to supply an authorization required by statute but not obtained. *Libby Rod and Gun Club v. Poteat,* 594 F.2d 742 (9th Cir. 1979); *National Wildlife Federation v. Andrus,* 440 F. Supp. 1245 (D.D.C. 1977); *Atchison, Topeka and Santa Fe Ry Co. v. Callaway,* 382 F. Supp. 610 (DD.C. 1974); B-223725, June 9, 1987.

Finally, the following cases illustrate other situations in which ratification by appropriation was found. In *Young v. TVA,* 606 F.2d 143 (6th Cir. 1979), cert. denied, 445 U.S. 942, the Tennessee Valley Authority (TVA) had asserted the authority to construct power plants. TVA's position was based on an interpretation of its enabling legislation. Although the legislation did not explicitly authorize or prohibit construction of power plants, the court found that the enabling legislation was consistent with TVA's proposed actions. However, the legislation itself was somewhat vague and ambiguous, and the court concluded that it was the specific appropriation of funds to TVA for power plant construction that ratified TVA's actions.

Similarly, the authority of the Postmaster General to conduct a mail transportation experiment was ratified by the appropriation of funds to the former Post Office Department under circumstances showing that Congress was fully aware of the experiment. The court noted that existing statutory authority was broad enough to encompass the experiment, and nothing prohibited it. *Atchison, Topeka and Santa Fe Ry. Co. v. Summerfield,* 229 F.2d 777 (D.C. Cir. 1955), cert. denied, 351 U.S. 926. Lastly, the authority of the Department of Justice to retain private counsel to defend federal officials in limited circumstances, while not explicitly provided by statute, was regarded as ratified by the specific appropriation of funds for that purpose. 2 Op. Off. Legal Counsel 66 (1978).

Note that in all of the cases in which ratification by appropriation was approved, the agency had at least an arguable legal basis for its action. The doctrine has not been used to excuse plain violations of the law.

The Rule against Repeal by Implication

To understand the rule against repeal by implication, one must first understand the general rule that Congress cannot bind a future Congress (or a later action by the same Congress). Under this rule, Congress is free to amend or repeal prior legislation as long as it does so directly and explicitly. Although it is also possible for one statute to *implicitly* amend or repeal a prior statute, it is firmly established that such "repeal by implication" is disfavored, and statutes must be construed to avoid this result whenever reasonably possible.

In the appropriations law context, the leading case addressing repeal by implication is *Tennessee Valley Authority v. Hill*, 437 U.S. 153 (1978). In that case, Congress had authorized construction of the Tellico Dam and Reservoir Project on the Little Tennessee River and had appropriated funds for that purpose. Subsequently, Congress passed the Endangered Species Act of 1973. Under the provisions of that Act, the Secretary of the Interior determined that the "snail darter," a three-inch fish, was an endangered species. Since the Little Tennessee River was considered to be the snail darter's critical habitat, it was determined that completion of the dam would result in extinction of the species. Consequently, environmental groups filed a lawsuit to halt further construction of the Tellico Project, and the case was eventually appealed all the way to the Supreme Court. In its decision, the Supreme Court held in favor of the environmental groups and ruled that the Tellico Project had to be halted, notwithstanding the fact that construction was well under way and that, even after the Secretary of the Interior's determinations regarding the snail darter, Congress had continued to make yearly appropriations for the completion of the dam project. The appropriation involved was a lump-sum appropriation that included funds for the Tellico Dam but made no specific reference to it. However, passages in the reports of the appropriations committees indicated that those committees intended the funds to be available notwithstanding the Endangered Species Act. The Court held that this was not enough. The doctrine against repeal by implication, the Court said, applies with even greater force when the claimed repeal rests solely on an appropriation act, since they are generally considered to be transitory legislation. The Court stated: "When voting on appropriations measures, legislators are entitled to operate under the assumption that the funds will be devoted to purposes which are lawful and not for any purpose forbidden." 437 U.S. 153, at 190. Noting that "[e]xpressions of committees dealing with requests for appropriations cannot be equated with statutes enacted by Congress" (437 U.S. 153, at 191), the Court held that the unspecified inclusion of the Tellico Dam funds in a lump-sum appropriation was not sufficient to constitute a repeal by implication of the Endangered Species Act insofar as it related to that project.

TVA v. Hill is an important case because it is a clear and forceful statement from the Supreme Court. The rule in *TVA v. Hill* is consistent with numerous lower court decisions that likewise applied the rule against repeal by implication. One group of cases, for example, had established the rule that the appropriation of funds does not excuse non-compliance with the National Environmental Policy Act. See, e.g., *Environmental Defense Fund v. Froehlke*, 473 F.2d 346 (8th Cir. 1972); *Committee for Nuclear Responsibility v. Seaborg*, 463 F.2d 783 (D.C. Cir. 1971); *National Audubon Society v. Andrus*, 442 F, Supp. 42 (D.D.C. 1977); *Environmental Defense Fund v. Corps of Engineers*, 325 F. Supp. 749 (ED. Ark. 1971).

Discussion Problem 1-3

In Section D, the Doctrine of Ratification by Appropriation states that Congress can, by the appropriation of funds, legitimize an agency action that may have been questionable when initially taken. Since the determination by the Secretary of the Interior rendered TVA's continuation of the Tellico Project "questionable," could TVA have successfully argued that the subsequent appropriation of funds by Congress for the project constituted a ratification by appropriation?

The rule against repeal by implication has also been applied in many Comptroller General decisions. In B-277905, March 17, 1998, the agency contended that its general authority to conduct water conservation activities authorized it to build pipelines on an Army golf course, even though there was specific statutory language prohibiting such use of the funds. The Comptroller General upheld the prohibition, stating:

> This presumption [against repeal by implication] is particularly strong where, as with 10 U.S.C. sec. 2246 and 2866, Congress considered and enacted the two provisions in the same Act, namely, the National Defense Authorization Act for Fiscal Year 1994, Public Law 103-160, 107 Stat. 1618 and 1884 (1993). Their location in the same Act is forceful evidence that Congress intended the two provisions to stand separately. . . .One section generally authorizes the use of appropriated funds for water conservation activities at military installations; the other specifically prohibits the use of appropriated funds to equip, operate or maintain a golf course. Had Congress intended to allow the use of appropriated funds for water conservation projects on military golf facilities it would have done so. Instead it enacted a broad statutory prohibition prescribing the use of appropriated funds for any activity to "equip, operate, or maintain" military golf courses.

B-277905.

Similarly, in a 1993 case, the Treasury Department determined that 1941 legislation enacted by Congress to provide a source of funds to pay victims of forged federal checks was obsolete and superseded by the more general Competitive Equality Banking Act of 1987, Pub. L. No. 100-86, 101 Stat. 657 (1987). The Comptroller General disagreed and held:

> It is a cardinal principle of statutory construction that repeals by implication are not favored. . . .This principle carries special weight when it is urged that a specific statute has been repealed by a more general one. *United Con-*

tinental Tuna, supra. at 169; *Morton v. Mancari,* 417 U.S. 535, 550-551, 41 L. Ed. 2d 290, 94 S. Ct. 2474 (1973). Where there is no clear intention otherwise, a specific statute will not be controlled or nullified by a general one, regardless of the priority of enactment. The Supreme Court also has held that agencies have no license to pick and choose among congressional enactments, and when two statutes are capable of co-existence, it is the duty of the courts, absent a clearly expressed congressional intention to the contrary, to regard each as effective. In this case neither the text nor the legislative history of the Act reflect an intent by the Congress to [repeal the prior legislation]. The statute governing the payment of forged checks is a specific provision of law, applying to a very specific set of circumstances. The Act, on the other hand, is a statute of general application, which does not address the payment of claims on forged checks. The Act is silent regarding the treatment of forged check claims.

Department of the Navy—Settling Claims on Fraudulently Endorsed Checks and Claims on Checks Subject to Limited Payability Provisions of the Competitive Equality Banking Act of 1987, B-242666, 72 Comp. Gen. 295, August 31, 1993. See also, B-258163, September 29, 1994; 64 Comp. Gen. 282 (1985); B-208593.6, December 22, 1988; B-213771, July 10, 1984; and B-193307, February 6, 1979.

As indicated by the decisions discussed above, the general rule is that a lump-sum appropriation, without more, is not sufficient to overcome a statutory requirement. If, however, instead of an unrestricted lump sum, the appropriation in *TVA v. Hill* had provided a *specific* line-item appropriation for the Tellico project, together with the words "notwithstanding the provisions of the Endangered Species Act," it is difficult to see how a court could fail to give effect to the express mandate of the appropriation. Thus, the message is not that Congress cannot legislate in an appropriation act. The real message is that, if Congress wants to use an appropriation act as the vehicle for amending or repealing a provision of existing law, it must do so directly and explicitly.

Appropriated Amount Exceeds Previously Authorized Amount

Appropriation acts are generally enacted based upon limits and authority contained in authorization acts. GAO has held, as a general proposition, that appropriations made to carry out authorizing laws "are made on the basis that the authorization acts in effect constitute an adjudication or legislative determination of the subject matter." B-151157, June 27, 1963. Thus, except as specified otherwise in the appropriation act, appropriations to carry out authorizing acts must be expended in strict accord with the original authorization both as to the amount of funds to be expended and the nature of the work authorized. 36 Comp. Gen. 240, 242 (1956); B-220682, February 21, 1986; B-204874, July 28, 1982; B-125404, August 31, 1956; B-151157, June 27, 1963. Thus, the requirements contained in an authorization act must be followed unless changed by subsequent legislation.

Since an appropriation act enacted after an authorization act is "subsequent legislation," the effect of an appropriation in a larger amount than authorized creates an apparent conflict that must be resolved. The standard rule of statutory construction is that statutes should be construed harmoniously so as to give maximum effect to both wherever possible. E.g., *Posadas*, 296 U.S. at 503; 53 Comp. Gen. at 856; B-208593.6, December 22, 1988. For example, if NASA received an authorization act stating that "$10 million shall be available to conduct biological studies in space," and a subsequent appropriations act stating that "$10 million is hereby appropriated to conduct biological studies in space, of which not to exceed $2 million shall be available for space-based research to study the effects of zero gravity on cancer cells," both statutes can be read harmoniously. The effect would be that NASA has $10 million to conduct biological studies in space, but can spend no more than $2 million to study the effects of zero gravity on cancer cells.

However, if an appropriation act directly conflicts with a previously enacted authorization act, the more recent statute, as the latest expression of Congress, governs. This situation would occur, for example, if in the above example the authorization stated, "Not more than $2 million shall be available to conduct space-based research to study the effects of zero gravity on cancer cells" and the subsequent appropriations act provided $4 million for the exact same purpose. As one court concluded: "The statutes are thus in conflict, the earlier permitting and the later prohibiting. The later statute supersedes the earlier." *Eisenberg v. Corning*, 179 F.2d 275, 277 (D.C. Cir. 1949). Consequently, Congress is generally free to appropriate more money for a given object than the amount previously authorized. The Comptroller General has stated: "While legislation providing for an appropriation of funds in excess of the amount contained in a related authorization act apparently would be subject to a point of order under Rule 21 of the Rules of the House of Representatives, there would be no basis on which we could question otherwise proper expenditures of funds actually appropriated." B-123469, April 14, 1955. (Rule 21 of the Rules of the House of Representatives states: "2. (a)(1) An appropriation may not be reported in a general appropriation bill, and may not be in order as an amendment thereto, for an expenditure not previously authorized by law, except to continue appropriations for public works and objects that are already in progress.")

A "point of order" is an objection that a pending matter or proceeding is in violation of a rule of the House. A bill may be susceptible to various points of order that may be made against its consideration, including that an amount proposed to be appropriated exceeds that which has been authorized.

Similarly, the Comptroller General has held that: "It is fundamental that one Congress cannot bind a future Congress and that the Congress has full power to make an appropriation in excess of a cost limitation contained in the original authorization act. This authority is exercised as an incident to the power of the Congress to appropriate and regulate expenditures of the public money." 36 Comp. Gen. 240, 242 (1956).

The "last in time" rule is easy to apply when one is dealing with a line-item appropriation or a specific earmark in a lump-sum appropriation, since the irreconcilable conflict with the authorization act is readily identifiable. However, the issue becomes more complex where the authorization for a given item is specific and a subsequent lump-sum appropriation contains legislative history indicating an intent to fund the item at a higher amount. Does the lump-sum appropriation provide funding at the higher level based on the legislative history? To answer this question, one must apply the rule against repeal by implication. This rule holds that a subsequent law will not be considered to repeal a preexisting law unless that intent is clear in the subsequent legislation. Since legislative history is not legislation, it generally cannot repeal an existing statute. Thus, the limitation in the authorization act will generally control.

Appropriated Amount Is Less Than Previously Authorized Amount

Just as Congress is free to appropriate *more* than it had previously authorized, it is likewise free to appropriate *less* than it had previously authorized. However, as in the case of exceeding an authorization, the congressional intent to amend or repeal the prior legislation must be clear and direct. See, e.g., 53 Comp. Gen. 695 (1974). Under this authority, Congress may decide not to fund a program at all, i.e., to appropriate no funds. *United States v. Dickerson*, 310 U.S. 554 (1940). Another case in point is *City of Los Angeles v. Adams*, 556 F.2d 40 (DC. Cir. 1977). The Airport and Airway Development Act of 1970 authorized airport development grants "in aggregate amounts not less than" specified dollar amounts for specified fiscal years, and provided an apportionment formula. Subsequent appropriation acts included specific limitations on the aggregate amounts to be available for the grants, less than the amounts authorized. The court concluded that both laws could be given effect by limiting the amounts available to those specified in the appropriation acts, but requiring that they be distributed in accordance with the formula of the authorizing legislation. In holding the appropriation limits controlling, the court said: "According to its own rules, Congress is not supposed to use appropriations measures as vehicles for the amendment of general laws, including revision of expenditure authorization. Where Congress chooses to do so, however, we are bound to follow Congress's last word on the matter even in an appropriations law." 556 F.2d 40, at 48-49.

Even where the amount authorized to be appropriated is mandatory rather than discretionary, Congress can still appropriate less, or can suspend or repeal the authorizing legislation, as long as the intent to suspend or repeal the authorization is clear. The power is considerably diminished, however, with respect to entitlements that have already vested. The distinction is made clear in the following passage from the Supreme Court's decision in *United States v. Larionoff*, 431 U.S. 864, 879 (1977): "No one disputes that Congress may prospectively reduce the pay of members of the Armed Forces, even if that reduction deprived members of benefits they had expected to be able to earn. It is quite a different matter, however, for Congress to deprive a service member of pay due for services already performed, but still owing. In that case, the congressional action would appear in a different constitutional light."

Several earlier cases provide concrete illustrations of what Congress can and cannot do in an appropriation act to reduce or eliminate a non-vested mandatory authorization. In *United States v. Fisher*, 109 U.S. 143 (1883), permanent legislation set the salaries of certain territorial judges. Congress subsequently appropriated a lesser amount, "in full compensation" for that particular year. The Court held that Congress had the power to reduce the salaries and had effectively done so. "It is impossible that both acts should stand. No ingenuity can reconcile them. The later act must therefore prevail. . . ." 109 U.S. 143, at 146.

In these cases, the "reduction by appropriation" was effective because the intent of the congressional action was unmistakable. In contrast, if Congress simply appropriates less than the amount required in the authorization act, the authorization act will control. In a case involving the authorized salaries of federal officials, the Court refused to find a repeal by implication in "subsequent enactments which merely appropriated a less amount . . . and which contained no words that expressly or by clear implication modified or repealed the previous law." *United States v. Langston*, 118 U.S. 389 (1886), at 394. A similar case is *United States v. Vulte*, 233 U.S. 509 (1314). Thus, appropriating less than the amount of a non-vested mandatory authorization, including not appropriating any funds at all for it, will be effective under the "last in time" rule, if the intent to suspend or repeal the authorization is clear. However, by applying the rule against repeal by implication, a mere failure to appropriate sufficient funds will not be construed as amending or repealing prior authorizing legislation.

Discussion Problem 1-4

An appropriations act includes two provisions pertaining to payments to current and former civil service employees. One states: "For the period covered by this appropriation, the salary of all employees of the federal civil service shall be reduced by 3% from the prior fiscal year rates." The other provision states: "For the period covered by this appropriation, the amounts paid to retired civil service employees shall be reduced by 3% from the prior fiscal year rates." If challenged, is it likely that either or both of these provisions will be upheld by a court?

Funds Appropriated Prior to Enactment of Authorization Act

Generally, Congress will enact the authorization act prior to enactment of the corresponding appropriation act. As indicated, this sequence provides the appropriating committees with a framework and enables agencies to better understand the purposes for which the appropriated funds may be used. Sometimes, however, consideration of the authorization act is delayed, and it is not enacted until after the appropriation act. Determining the relationship between the two acts involves application of the same general principles that are applied when the acts are enacted in the normal sequence.

The first step is to try to construe the statutes together in some reasonable fashion. To the extent this can be done, there is no conflict, and the reversed sequence will not matter. For example, in November 1978, the Justice Department authorization act authorized a lump-sum appropriation to the Immigration and Naturalization Service (INS) and provided that $2 million "shall be available" for the investigation and prosecution of certain cases involving alleged Nazi war criminals. The 1979 appropriation act, enacted in October, made a lump-sum appropriation to the INS but contained no specific mention of the Nazi war criminal item. In response to a question as to the effect of the November authorization provision on the October appropriation, the Comptroller General advised that the two statutes could be construed harmoniously, and that the $2 million earmarked in the authorization act could be spent only for the purpose specified. It was further noted that the $2 million represented a minimum but not a maximum. B-193282, December 21, 1978. This is the same result that would have been reached if the normal sequence had been followed.

Similarly, in B-226389, November 14, 1988, a provision in the 1987 Defense appropriation act prohibited the Navy from including certain provisions in ship maintenance contracts. The 1987 authorization act, enacted after the appropriation, amended a provision in Title 10 of the United States Code to require the same provisions prohibited by the 1987 Defense appropriation act. Application of the "last in time" rule would have negated the appropriation act provision. However, it was possible to give effect to both provisions by construing the appropriation restriction as a temporary exemption from the permanent legislation in the authorization act. Again, this is the same result that would have been reached if the authorization act were enacted first.

However, if the authorization and appropriation acts cannot be reasonably reconciled, the "last in time" rule will apply just as it would under the normal sequence, except here the result will be different because the authorization is the later of the two. For example, the 1989 Treasury Department appropriation act contained a provision prohibiting the placing of certain components of the department under the oversight of the Treasury Inspector General. A month later, Congress enacted legislation placing those components under the Inspector General's jurisdiction and transferring their internal audit staffs to the Inspector General "notwithstanding any other provision of law." If the "notwithstanding" clause were not included, it might have been possible to conclude that the appropriation restriction was only a temporary exemption from the new permanent legislation. In view of the "notwithstanding" clause, however, GAO found that the two provisions could not be reconciled and concluded that the Inspector General legislation, as the later enactment, superseded the appropriation act provision. B-203900, February 2, 1989. Just as with any other application of the "last in time" rule, the later enactment prevails only to the extent of the irreconcilable conflict. B-61178, October 21, 1946 (specific limitations in appropriation act not superseded by after-enacted authorization absent indication that authorization was intended to alter provisions of prior appropriation).

Effect of the Failure to Enact an Authorization Act

Although there is no general statutory requirement that appropriations be preceded by specific authorizations, they are required in some instances. Where authorizations are not required by law, Congress may, subject to a possible point of order, appropriate funds for a program or object that has not been previously authorized or that exceeds the scope of a prior authorization, in which case the appropriation act, in effect, carries its own authorization and is available to the agency for obligation and expenditure. 67 Comp. Gen. 401 (1988); B-219727, July 30, 1985; B-173832, August 1, 1975.

It has also been held that, as a general proposition, the appropriation of funds for a program whose funding authorization has expired, or is due to expire during the period of availability of the appropriation, provides sufficient legal basis to continue the program during that period of availability, unless there is some indication of contrary congressional intent. 65 Comp. Gen. 524 (1986); 65 Comp. Gen. 318,320-21 (1986); 55 Comp. Gen. 289 (1975); B-131935, March 17, 1986; B-137063, March 21, 1966. The result in these cases follows in part from the fact that the total absence of authorization legislation would not have precluded the making of valid appropriations for the programs. B-202992, May 15, 1981. In addition, the result is based on the conclusion, derived either from legislative history or at least the absence of legislative history to the contrary, that Congress did not intend for the programs to terminate.

> This chapter provided an overview of the constitutional underpinnings of federal appropriations law and discussed the roles of the legislative and executive branches of government in the budgetary process. The constitutional relationship between the legislative and executive branches permeates all aspects of federal appropriations law and serves to explain many rules that may, at first, be counterintuitive (e.g., the requirement that agencies obligate annul funds prior to September 30).
>
> This chapter also introduced and defined key terms used in discussing federal appropriations law. These terms will be used throughout the remaining chapters, and the reader should be familiar with them before proceeding to the following chapters. Similarly, this chapter discussed several core concepts that will reappear in the following chapters in more specific contexts (e.g., repeal by implication, ratification by appropriation). This chapter can be used as a reference regarding those core concepts and should be consulted whenever questions arise in the more specific contexts that follow.

CHAPTER 2
Commitment and Obligation of Funds

The timing of obligations is critical in determining whether an agency has complied with the time, purpose, and amount restrictions established by Congress for each appropriation. For example, the determination of whether an obligation exceeds the amount available in the appropriation is based on the unobligated balance in the appropriation account on the day the obligation is created. It does not matter that there was a sufficient amount on the preceding day or that there will be an additional amount available on the next day. Therefore, it is important to know when an obligation is created, as well as how much must be obligated, when analyzing a fiscal law issue. A commitment protects funds to ensure that they will be available when needed to fund an anticipated obligation.

In this chapter, we will discuss the definitions applicable to commitments and obligations, the purpose and use of commitments, what constitutes an obligation, and how much must be obligated in various situations.

DEFINITIONS

Certifying Officer. An individual who is authorized to certify the availability of funds on any documents or vouchers submitted for payment and/or who indicates payment is proper.

Fund Managers. Individuals who manage financial resources, include major activity or subactivity directors and their representatives who are delegated fund certification responsibility.

Certification of Fund Availability. A certification by a funds-certifying official that funds are available in the proper subdivision of funds to cover the obligation to be incurred. This certification authorizes the obligating official to make the obligation.

Commitment. An administrative reservation of an allotment or of other funds in anticipation of their obligation. An obligation equal to or less than the commitment may be incurred without further approval of a certifying official.

Initiation. Allows for the preliminary negotiation of procurement actions; however, one must obtain certification of fund availability before making a commitment or incurring an obligation. Initiations are entered into memorandum accounts to ensure that precommitment actions, such as approved procurement programs and procurement orders, are maintained within the available subdivision of funds.

Obligation. Any act that legally binds the government to make payment. Obligations represent the amounts of orders placed, contracts awarded, services received, and similar transactions during an accounting period that will require payment during the same or a future period.

COMMITMENT OF FUNDS

The commitment of funds in anticipation of a particular obligation protects those funds from being obligated for other purposes. For example, if an agency is preparing to award a contract and estimates that it will need $1 million, the fund certification official will determine if sufficient funds are available and, if they are, will commit $1 million so funds will remain available at the time of contract award. In most agencies, the office that generated the requirement will obtain the commitment from the fund certifying officer.

Once funds are committed, the office that generated the requirement will take the commitment document to an agency contracting officer, who will then determine the best method for acquiring the goods or services. Funds may be committed only to acquire goods and services that meet the bona fide needs of the period for which Congress appropriated funds, or to replace stock used during that period. Agencies must cancel outstanding commitments when the committed funds expire for obligation.

Purpose of Commitment

Most federal agencies have established a system of commitment accounting to manage their appropriations. For example, the DoD Financial Management Regulation states:

> Commitment accounting is required by agreement with the OMB for the procurement appropriation accounts; military construction appropriation accounts; and the research, development, test and evaluation appropriation accounts. However, commitments need not be recorded for small purchases if, in the aggregate, they are not significant in the management of funds. Commitment accounting is not required for the operation and maintenance appropriation accounts, revolving fund accounts, or the military personnel appropriation accounts, but may be used if cost effective.

DOD 7000.14-R, vol. 3, ch. 15, para. 150202A5.

Commitment accounting "fences" funds and helps ensure that the subsequent entry of an undelivered order or accrued expenditure will not exceed available funds. Commitments generally do not have to be recorded for purchases below the simplified acquisition threshold if, in the aggregate, they are insignificant in the management of funds.

Commitment accounting is also a useful financial management tool because it provides information on the pattern of obligations, whether too much or too little is being committed, the time between commitment and obligation of funds, and other related information. For example, the NASA Financial Management Manual states:

> **9031-4 NEED FOR COMMITMENT DATA**
>
> It is necessary in the management of resources to have data available on commitments, the authorizations issued to incur obligations. Commitment data, including information on obligations actually incurred, is necessary to know the balance of allotments and resources authority available to finance further program accomplishment. It is also desirable that financial reports to all levels provide full information on the status of available resources authority in terms of uncommitted as well as unobligated balances. These data are necessary for management to evaluate monthly financial progress in carrying out programmed procurement activities. They are also helpful in the review and justification of budgets, apportionment requests, reprogramming actions and financial plans; and in the administration of funding programs.

NASA FMM 9031-4.

Responsibilities

The fund certifying official responsible for administrative control of funds for the affected subdivision of the appropriation is generally the individual authorized to sign the commitment document. The DoD Financial Management Regulation specifies that:

> A commitment document shall be signed by a person authorized to reserve funds; that is, the official responsible for administrative control of funds for the affected subdivision of the appropriation. This helps ensure that the subsequent entry of an undelivered order or accrued expenditure will not exceed available funds.

DoD 7000.14-R, vol. 3, ch. 15, para. 150202.

To ensure that funds are not overcommitted or overobligated, the fund manager should maintain commitment registers and is responsible for processing, recording, and performing the oversight function for commitment accounting.

Determining How Much to Commit

When an agency must use commitment accounting, it will generally commit funds according to certain rules. Since a commitment has the effect of making the committed funds unavailable for purposes other than the obligation for which they have been committed, agencies should commit only the amount that it thinks is necessary. The fund certification official will record as a commitment the cost estimate set forth in the commitment document. It is, therefore, critically important that the estimated amount of the anticipated obligation be as accurate as possible. The date the commitment document is signed by an authorized official determines the accounting period in which the commitment is to be recorded.

Contingent Liabilities

A "contingent liability" is a potential liability that may become an actual liability if some particular event happens or does not happen. If and when the contingency materializes, the liability becomes a recordable obligation. GAO, Policy and Procedures Manual for Guidance of Federal Agencies, Title 7, § 3.4.C. See also, 62 Comp. Gen. 143, 145 (1983). An example of a contingent liability that would generally require a commitment of funds is discretionary award fee amounts. For example, under a fixed-price award fee type of contract, the contracting agency expects that it will have to pay some amount of award fee in the future. However, since the contractor has not yet earned the award fee (and it is not certain how much award fee will be earned), the agency does not have a firm liability and cannot, therefore, record an obligation for the as-yet-unearned award fee. Nevertheless, since it is very likely that *some* amount will eventually be earned, the agency should commit or reserve an amount so that it will be available when the authorized fee determination official makes the fee award and the contract is modified.

The contingent liability creates a fiscal dilemma. On the one hand, it is by definition not sufficiently definite or certain to support the formal recording of an obligation. Yet on the other hand, sound financial management (as well as Antideficiency Act considerations) dictates that it somehow be recognized. The middle ground between recording an obligation and doing nothing is the "administrative reservation" or "commitment of funds." A contingent liability that is less than an obligation but nevertheless sufficiently important to warrant recognition should be reflected in a footnote to pertinent financial statements (e.g., the fund certification document). See 37 Comp. Gen. 691,692 (1958); see also 62 Comp. Gen. 143, 146 (1983).

The treatment of contingent liabilities is largely a matter of sound judgment. "No hard and fast rule can be laid down as to the circumstances that would require disclosure. Judgment would have to be exercised with respect to the possible financial implications." 37 Comp. Gen. at 694. The general question to ask in this context is whether a given situation is sufficiently probable to justify recognition or is little more than a mere possibility. If the contingent liability should be recognized, as in the award fee example above, the agency should commit an amount that is conservatively estimated to be sufficient to cover the additional obligations that probably will materialize, based upon judgment and experience.

The DoD Financial Management Regulation provides what is probably the most extensive guidance on the treatment of contingent liabilities:

> 080202. Special Provisions for Determining the Amounts of Commitments
> A. Contingent Liabilities Remaining under Outstanding Contracts. There are contingent liabilities for price or quantity increases or other variables that cannot be recorded as valid obligations in the cases of (1) outstanding

fixed-price contracts containing escalation, price redetermination, or incentive clauses, or (2) contracts authorizing variations in quantities to be delivered, or (3) contracts where allowable interest may become payable by the U.S. Government on contractor claims supported by written appeals pursuant to the "Disputes" clause contained in the contract... Amounts to cover these contingent liabilities should be carried as outstanding commitments pending determination of actual obligations. The amounts of such contingent liabilities, however, need not be recorded at the maximum or ceiling prices under the contracts. Rather, amounts should be committed that are estimated conservatively to be sufficient to cover the additional obligations that probably will materialize, based upon judgment and experience. In determining the amount to be committed, allowances may be made for the possibility of downward price revisions and quantity underruns. Each contingent liability shall be supported by sufficient detail to facilitate audit.

DoD Financial Management Regulation, Ch. 3, para 080202A.

Note that the guidance cautions against taking a "worst case" approach and committing the maximum potential liability. This is because a commitment makes the committed funds unavailable for other purposes. Additional guidance may be found in GAO's Accounting Principles and Standards (1984) and in 37 Comp. Gen. 691.

One example of a contingent liability that should be recognized and recorded as a commitment is a pending claim under the "changes" clause of a contract. 37 Comp. Gen. 691 (1958). However, the amount of the claim would not be a recordable obligation until adjudicated and allowed. Another example is an authorized indemnification provision limited to appropriations available at the time of a loss. 54 Comp. Gen. 824, 826–27 (1975).

Termination liability under a renewal option or similar contract is another type of contingent liability. As a general proposition, "an amount equal to the maximum contingent liability of the Government [must be] always available for obligation from appropriations current at the time the contract is made and at the time renewals thereof are made." 37 Comp, Gen. 155, 160 (1957). See also 43 Comp. Gen. 657 (1964); 8 Comp. Gen. 654 (1929).

Other Contractual Liabilities

There are many contractual situations in which an agency is fairly certain that it will have to adjust the cost or price of a contract, but cannot precisely quantify the amount of the adjustment at the time of contract award. The following contracts illustrate this situation: fixed-price contracts with price escalation, price redetermination, or incentive clauses; contracts authorizing variations in quantities to be delivered; cost-reimbursable contracts; and time-and-material contracts. In each of these situations, the agency knows that it is very likely that it will have to make an adjustment to the cost or price of the contract, but must wait until it has additional information to determine the amount of the adjustment.

The standard practice relating to cost-plus-fixed-fee contracts is to commit the estimated cost and the fixed fee. Under cost-plus-incentive-fee contracts, the agency should commit the estimated cost plus the target fee. Under cost-plus-award-fee contracts, the agency should commit the estimated cost, the base fee, and an estimated amount based on judgment and experience for the award fee. When using a letter contract (see FAR 16.603), the agency should commit funds to cover the difference between the maximum legal liability of the government under the interim agreement and the maximum estimated cost of the definitized contract.

Discussion Problem 2-1

An agency plans to award a cost-plus-award-fee contract. The estimated cost is $1 million, the base fee is $30,000, and the maximum award fee available is $70,000. Historically, the agency has paid approximately 80% of the maximum available award fee, which would be $56,000 in this case (.8 x $70,000). How much should the agency commit?

There are some contractual situations in which the agency is not required to commit any amount prior to award of the contract. For example, since a requirements contract and a blanket purchase agreement (BPA) do not create an obligation at the time of award or agreement, there is no need to commit funds until an actual obligation is anticipated, for example, when an order will be placed under the requirements contract or BPA.

Similarly, an agency is not required to commit funds when the contingent liability is too speculative. For example, every government contract contains numerous clauses that could be the basis for government liability to the contractor. Common examples of such clauses are the government property clause (e.g., FAR 52.245-2), the changes clauses (e.g., FAR 52.243-4), and the suspension of work clause (FAR 52.242-14). Although such clauses could provide the basis for government liability, many preconditions to this liability render it too speculative to justify commitment of funds. Under the government property clause, for example, the contractor must prove that the government provided it property for use under the contract that is defective and must provide notice to the contracting officer. The contractor must also prove that the defective property increased its performance costs. Since it is unknown at the time of contract award whether all of these preconditions will be satisfied (or even whether the property will be defective), an agency should not commit funds for this type of contingent liability.

OBLIGATION OF APPROPRIATIONS

It is an essential aspect of sound financial management for any institution to have accurate and current information regarding the extent of its financial obligations. Accordingly, federal agencies must have procedures that ensure that obligations are recorded promptly and accurately. Both the overrecording and the underrecording of obligations are improper. Agencies occasionally overrecord (i.e., record as obligations items that are not) to prevent appropriations from expiring at the end of a fiscal year. Underrecording (failing to record legitimate obligations) is problematic because it makes it impossible to determine the precise status of the appropriation and may result in violation of the Antideficiency Act.

A 1953 Comptroller General decision stated:

> In order to determine the status of appropriations, both from the viewpoint of management and the Congress, it is essential that obligations be recorded in the accounting records on a factual and consistent basis throughout the Government. Only by the following of sound practices in this regard can data on existing obligations serve to indicate program accomplishments and be related to the amount of additional appropriations required.

32 Comp. Gen. 436, 437 (1953).

It is important to emphasize the relationship between the existence of an obligation and the act of recording. Recording evidences the obligation but does not create it. If a given transaction is not sufficient to constitute a valid obligation, recording it will not make it one. B-197274, February 16, 1982 ("reservation and notification" letter held not to constitute an obligation, act of recording notwithstanding, where letter did not impose legal liability on government and subsequent formation of contract was within agency's control). Conversely, failing to record a valid obligation does not affect the validity of the obligation or the fiscal year to which it is properly chargeable. B-226782, October 20, 1987 (letter of intent, executed in FY 1985 and found to constitute a contract, obligated FY 1985 funds, notwithstanding agency's failure to treat it as an obligation); 63 Comp. Gen. 525 (1984); 38 Comp. Gen. 81, 82-83 (1958).

> ## Discussion Problem 2-2
>
> A contracting officer settles a claim with a contractor and the contracting officer modifies the contract on June 15, 2002. However, funding will not be available until the start of the next quarter, i.e., on July 1, 2002. The contracting officer wants to avoid an Antideficiency Act violation and works out an arrangement with the agency comptroller whereby the modification would not be recorded as an obligation until after July 1, 2002. Discuss the merits of this arrangement.

The precise amount of the government's liability should be recorded as the obligation where that amount is known. However, where the precise amount is not known at the time the obligation is incurred, the obligation should be recorded on the basis of the agency's best estimate. 56 Comp. Gem 414, 418 (1977) and cases cited therein; 21 Comp. Gen. 574 (1941). See also OMB Circular No. A-34, §§ 22.1, 22.2. Where an estimate is used, the basis for the estimate must be shown on the obligating document. As more precise data on the liability become available, the obligation must be periodically adjusted. See GAO, *Policy and Procedures Manual for Guidance of Federal Agencies*, Title 7, § 3.4.D (1990).

Statutory Requirement for Recording Obligations

The standards for the proper recording of obligations are found in 31 U.S.C. § 1501(a). A Senate committee has described the origin of the statute as follows:

> [31 U.S.C. § 1501(a)] resulted from the difficulty encountered by the House Appropriations Committee in obtaining reliable figures on obligations from the executive agencies in connection with the budget review. It was not uncommon for the committees to receive two or three different sets of figures as of the same date. This situation, together with rather vague explanations of cer-

tain types of obligations, particularly in the military departments, caused the House Committee on Appropriations to institute studies of agency obligating practices.

. . . .

The result of these examinations laid the foundation for the committee's conclusion that loose practices had grown up in various agencies, particularly in the recording of obligations in situations where no real obligation existed, and that by reason of these practices the Congress did not have reliable information in the form of accurate obligations on which to determine an agency's future requirements. To correct this situation, the committee, with the cooperation of the General Accounting Office and the Bureau of the Budget, developed what has become the statutory criterion by which the validity of an obligation is determined. . . .

Subsection (a) of 31 U.S.C. § 1501 lists specific criteria for recording obligations. The subsection states that "[a]n amount shall be recorded as an obligation of the United States Government only when supported by documentary evidence of. . . ." Subsection (a) then goes on to list nine criteria for recording obligations. If a given transaction does not meet at least one of the criteria, then it is not a proper obligation and must not be recorded as one. Once one of the criteria is met, however, the agency not only may but *must* record the transaction as an obligation. This section will analyze those obligations that arise in the context of federal acquisitions.

While 31 U.S.C. § 1501 does not explicitly state that obligations must be recorded as they arise or are incurred, it follows logically from an agency's responsibility to comply with the Antideficiency Act. GAO has made the point in reports and decisions in various contexts. See, e.g., *Substantial Understatement of Obligations for Separation Allowances for Foreign National Employees*, B-179343, October 21, 1974, at 6; FGMSD-75-20, February 13, 1975, at 3 (letter report); 65 Comp. Gen. 4,6 (1985); B-226801, March 2, 1988; B-192036, September 11, 1978; and A-97205, February 3, 1944, at 10.

Agency regulations also require prompt recording of obligations. For example, the DoD Financial Management Regulation states:

> Ten-Day Rule. Obligations shall be recorded in the official accounting records at the time a legal obligation is incurred, or as close to the time of incurrence as is feasible. In no instance shall obligations be recorded any later than 10 calendar days following the day that an obligation is incurred (to include obligations incurred when invoices are overpaid or duplicate payments are made). Every effort shall be made to record an obligation in the month incurred. Notwithstanding the 10-day rule, obligations of $100,000 or more—per fund citation or accounting line on the obligation document—shall be recorded and included in the official accounting records in the same month in which the obligation is incurred. If an obligation is not recorded within the specified timeframe, the guidance in section 0814 of this chapter shall be followed.

DoD Financial Management Regulation, Ch. 3, para 080301A.

If an agency fails to promptly record an obligation, it creates the inaccurate perception that the appropriation that should have been charged has a greater unobligated balance than is warranted. Consequently, funds needed to liquidate the unrecorded obligation could be diverted to other obligations, resulting in an overobligation of the cited appropriation.

Contract Obligations

The first criterion discussed in 31 U.S.C. § 1501 deals with contracts and states that a recordable obligation exists if there is documentary evidence of:

> (l) a binding agreement between an agency and another person (including an agency) that is–
> (A) in writing, in a way and form, and for a purpose authorized by law; and

> (B) executed before the end of the period of availability for obligation of the appropriation or fund used for specific goods to be delivered, real property to be bought or leased, or work or service to be provided.

This subsection imposes several different requirements: (1) it requires the existence of a binding agreement; (2) the agreement must be "in writing"; (3) the agreement must be for a purpose authorized by law; (4) the agreement must be executed before the expiration of the period of availability of the appropriation charged; and (5) the agreement must be for specific goods, real property, or services.

The Requirement for a Binding Agreement

While the agreement must be legally binding under the traditional concepts of contract law (i.e., offer, acceptance, consideration, made by authorized official), it does not have to be the final "definitized" contract. The legislative history of subsection (a)(1), as contained in the Conference Report, states:

> It is not necessary, however, that the binding agreement be the final formal contract on any specific form. The primary purpose is to require that there be an offer and an acceptance imposing liability on both parties. For example, an authorized order by one agency on another agency of the Government, if accepted by the latter and meeting the requirement of specificity, etc., is sufficient. Likewise, a letter of intent accepted by a contractor, if sufficiently specific and definitive to show the purposes and scope of the contract finally to be executed, would constitute the binding agreement required.

HR Rep. No. 2663, 83d Cong., 2d Sess. 18 (1954).

Essentially, agency officials must use judgment to determine whether a recordable obligation exists. In 42 Comp. Gen. 733, 734 (1963), the Comptroller General noted that:

> The question whether Government funds are obligated at any specific time is answerable only in terms of an

analysis of written arrangements and conditions agreed to by the United States and the party with whom it is dealing. If such analysis discloses a legal duty on the part of the United States which constitutes a legal liability or which could mature into a legal liability by virtue of actions on the part of the other Party beyond the control of the United States, an obligation of funds may generally be stated to exist.

In a 1980 decision, the Comptroller General provided a three-part test to determine whether a binding contract exists. First, each bid/proposal must have been in writing. Second, the acceptance of each bid/proposal must have been communicated to the bidder in the same manner as the bid was made. If the bid was mailed, the contract must have been mailed before the close of the fiscal year. If the bid was delivered other than by mail, the contract must have been delivered in like manner before the end of the fiscal year. Finally, each contract must have incorporated the terms and conditions of the respective bid/proposal without qualification. 59 Comp. Gen. 431 (1980).

Most agency financial management regulations include these requirements. For example, the NASA Financial Management Manual states:

> b. The amount evidenced by a contractual document is not recordable as an obligation until the document is:
> (1) Signed by the contractor or other performing agency when required,
> (2) Signed by an authorized representative of NASA,
> (3) Approved administratively when required, and
> (4) Mailed or otherwise delivered to the contractor or other performing agency.

NASA Financial Management Manual, para. 9041-6(b).

The NASA Manual also provides useful guidance regarding what must happen for a document to be considered "[m]ailed or otherwise delivered":

> "Mailed or otherwise delivered" means the documents have been placed in United States (or other Government)

official postal channels, placed with a publicly recognized messenger service, or handed to the recipient. Placing documents in administrative services' mail or messenger channels is not sufficient. Special postal arrangements may be necessary to ensure that obligating documents processed at fiscal year-end are deposited in official mail channels before the close of the fiscal year.

For example, where the agency notified the successful bidder of the award by telephone near the end of FY 1979, but did not mail the contract document until FY 1980, there was no valid obligation of FY 1979 funds. 59 Comp. Gen. 431 (1980). See also 35 Comp. Gen. 319 (1955).

A document is considered "mailed" when it is placed in the custody of the Postal Service (given to a postal employee or dropped in a mailbox or letter chute in an office building). However, merely delivering the document to an agency messenger with instructions to mail it is insufficient. 59 Comp. Gen., at 433. The critical difference in these two cases is that in the latter case, the document was still within the agency's control, whereas in the former case, control had been relinquished to the postal service. Similarly, a binding agreement will not be created if the agency erroneously mailed the notice of award to the wrong bidder and did not notify the successful bidder until the first day of the new FY. 40 Comp. Gen. 147 (1960). Applying this rule to the current business environment, no binding agreement would be created if the agency erroneously sent an electronic transmission (e.g., e-mail, fax) to the wrong bidder.

It is important to note that, in these cases, the obligation was invalid only with respect to the fiscal year the agency wanted to charge. The agency could still finalize the obligation, but it would have to charge funds current in the subsequent fiscal year. 59 Comp. Gen. at 433; 40 Comp. Gen. at 148.

The Requirement That the Contract Be "in Writing"

Although the binding agreement under 31 U.S.C. § 1501(a)(l) must be "in writing," the "writing" is not necessarily limited to words on a piece of paper. The traditional mode of contract execution is to manually sign the document (paper) setting forth the contract terms. Contracts, purchase orders, rental agreements, travel orders, bills of lading, civilian payrolls, and interdepartmental requisitions are common contractual documents supporting obligations. However, the dominance of electronic data transmission has altered this traditional approach. In 1983, GAO's legal staff, in an internal memorandum, took note of modern legal trends and advised that the "in writing" requirement could be satisfied by computer-related media that produce tangible recordings of information, such as punch cards, magnetic cards, tapes, or disks. B-208863 (2)-O. M., May 23, 1983.

Eight years later, the Comptroller General issued his first formal decision on the topic, B-245714, 71 Comp. Gen. 109 (1991). In that opinion, the National Institute of Standards and Technology (NIST) asked whether federal agencies could use certain Electronic Data Interchange (EDI) technologies to create valid contractual obligations for purposes of 31 U.S.C. § 1501(a). The Comptroller replied in the affirmative, as long as there are adequate safeguards and controls to provide no less certainty and protection of the government's interests as under a "paper and ink" method. The decision states:

> We conclude that EDI systems using message authentication codes which follow NIST'S Computer Data Authentication Standard (Federal Information Processing Standard (FIPS) 113) [footnote omitted] or digital signatures following NIST'S Digital Signature Standard, as currently proposed, can produce a form of evidence that is acceptable under section 1501.

The Federal Acquisition Regulation also recognizes the equivalence between a writing and electronic data transmission methods. FAR 2.101 states: "In writing," "writing," or "written" means any worded or numbered expression that can be read, reproduced, and later communicated, and includes electronically transmitted and stored information."

While there may be some room for interpretation as to what constitutes a "writing," the writing, in some acceptable form, must exist. Under the plain terms of the statute, an oral agreement may not be recorded as an obligation. In *United States v. American Renaissance Lines, Inc.*, 494 F.2d 1059 (D.C. Cir. 1974), cert. denied, 419 U.S. 1020, the court found that 31 U.S.C. § 1501(a)(l) "establishes virtually a statute of frauds" for the government and held that neither party can judicially enforce an oral contract in violation of the statute. Thus, for example, the DoD Financial Management Regulation states in pertinent part:

> 080302. . . . A verbal order or agreement shall be reduced to writing and conform to the applicable provisions of this section before the obligation may be recorded. When the amount is not known or cannot be ascertained feasibly at the time that it is to be recorded, the best estimate shall be used. The best estimate should be based on a thorough analysis of the transaction that actually occurred.

DoD Financial Management Regulation, Ch. 3, para 080302.

However, the Court of Federal Claims and its predecessors have held that 31 U.S.C. § 1501(a)(l) does not bar recovery "outside of the contract" where sufficient additional facts exist for the court to infer the necessary "meeting of minds" (contract implied-in-fact). *Narva Harris Construction Corp. v. United States*, 574 F.2d 508 (Ct. Cl. 1978); *Johns-Manville Corp. v. United States*, 12 Cl. Ct. 1, 19–20 (1987). Cf. *Kinzley v. United States*, 661 F.2d 187 (Ct. Cl. 1981). Thus, for example, it is possible to have a binding oral contract if the required elements are present, i.e., "mutuality of intent to be bound, definite offer, unconditional acceptance, and consideration," and if the government official involved had actual authority to bind the government. *Edwards v. United States*, 22 Cl. Ct.411, 420 (1991). See also *Northrup Grumman Corp. v. United States*, 47 Fed. Cl. 20 (2000), No. 97-276C (Jun 16, 2000).

These would be examples of subsequently imposed liability where the agency did not record (and lawfully could not have recorded) an obligation when the events giving rise to the liability took place. However, if the contractor submits a claim and is successful in demonstrating entitlement under an implied-in-fact theory of liability, the contracting agency would be required to record an obligation. If a contractor received a judgment based on a claim filed under the authority of the Contract Disputes Act, the judgment would be paid initially from the permanent judgment appropriation (31 U.S.C. § 1304) and would have to be reimbursed by the agency from appropriations current when the judgment was rendered. This scenario could arise where an authorized agency official, e.g., a contracting officer, arranged to have a contractor perform work based on an oral agreement. If the contractor performs and the government receives a benefit, the contractor may be able to file a claim based on an implied-in-fact theory of liability. If the contractor receives a judgment in its favor, a legally recordable obligation would arise.

Even when dealing with written documents, it is important that *all* aspects of the agreement be in writing (or equivalent electronic form). In B-118654, August 10, 1965, GAO concluded that a notice of award signed by the contracting officer and issued before the close of the fiscal year did not satisfy the requirements of 31 U.S.C. § 1501(a)(1) where it incorporated modifications of the offer as to price and other terms that had been agreed to orally during negotiations. The reason is that there was no evidence in writing that the contractor had agreed to the modifications.

The Requirement of Specificity

The statute (31 U.S.C. § 1501) requires documentary evidence of a binding agreement for *specific* goods or services. An agreement that fails this test is not a valid obligation. For example, a State Department contract under the Migration and Refugee Assistance Program establishing a contingency fund "to provide funds for refugee assistance by any means, organization or other voluntary agency as determined by the Supervising Officer" did not meet the requirement of specificity and therefore was not a valid obligation. B-147196, April 5, 1965. Similarly, a purchase order that lacks a description of the products to be provided is not sufficient to create a recordable obligation. B-196109, October 23,

1979. In the cited decision, a purchase order for "regulatory, warning, and guide signs based on information supplied" on requisitions to be issued did not validly obligate FY 1978 funds where the requisitions were not sent to the supplier until after the close of FY 1978.

DETERMINING HOW MUCH TO OBLIGATE

In this section, the guiding principles of obligations will be applied to specific contract situations to determine how much to obligate in each situation. Since the government must record the full amount of its liability and the contract type will determine the extent of the government's liability, the type of contract involved will determine how much to obligate and when to record the obligation.

Fixed-Price Contracts

In these types of contracts, the contractor promises to perform at a fixed price and bears the responsibility for (and risk of) increases in the cost of performance. In other words, the price is fixed at contract award. So, if a contract is awarded at $5,000, the contractor only gets $5,000, regardless of the actual cost of performance, and the government's maximum liability is fixed on the date of contract award at $5,000.

Firm Fixed-Price Contracts

Under a firm fixed-price (FFP) contract, the government must obligate the amount of the firm fixed price on the date the government entered into a binding contract. This would generally be the date of contract award. However, as noted in section II.B.1., above, a contract does not become binding until the contracting officer properly notifies the awardee of the award. Thus, if the government entered into a binding FFP contract on September 30 for $100,000, it must record an obligation against the appropriation cited on the funding document in the amount of $100,000.

Once it is determined how much to obligate, the agency must compare that amount with the amount that was previously committed. If the funding document indicates that more than $100,000 was committed, then the excess funds must be credited to the appropriation cited. If the funding document indicates that less than $100,000 was committed, then the contracting officer must obtain additional funds prior to awarding the contract. If additional funds are not available, the contracting officer may have to cancel the solicitation.

Fixed-Price with Economic Price Adjustment Contracts

Another type of fixed-price contract is the fixed-price with economic price adjustment (FP/EPA) contract. An agency may use this type of contract when it wants to use an FFP contract but expects that there may be large fluctuations in the prices of raw materials or labor involved in the contract performance. The EPA clause, FAR 52.216-2, provides that the government assumes a portion of the cost risk of certain unforeseeable price fluctuations, such as material or wage increases. The EPA provision permits contractors to eliminate contingencies for these potential costs, thereby enabling them to offer lower prices to the government. Under this type of contract, the contract price will be adjusted when the specified contingency occurs.

For example, contracts to purchase oil may include EPA clauses, as would contracts requiring the use of precious metals or any other material likely to fluctuate significantly in price. Depending on the fluctuation, the government may pay more or less for the same goods or services. Basically, the government and the contractor enter into a fixed-price contract, but the price of the contract may change if a specified indicator changes. For example, if the EPA clause is based on the price of silver, and the price of silver increases by 3 percent or more, the price of the items procured under the contract will be adjusted. In this case, the government has a contingent liability that is triggered if the price of silver rises by more than 3 percent.

Many EPA clauses include maximum adjustments (e.g., 10 percent). For FP/EPA contracts, agencies obligate the fixed or target price on the date of award. While an amount may be administratively reserved for any potential adjustments, the contingent nature of the liability precludes recording the potential EPA adjustment as an obligation at the time of award. However, the agency will have to record an obligation when the price of the specified indicator fluctuates and the contract price is adjusted in accordance with the EPA clause.

Fixed-Price Incentive Contracts

A fixed-price incentive (FPIF) contract provides for adjusting profit and establishing the final contract price by application of a formula based on the relationship of the total final negotiated cost to the total target cost. The final price is subject to a price ceiling that is negotiated at the time of contract award. The ceiling price is a significant negotiation item because the contractor bears all costs above the fixed ceiling price.

An agency may use an FPIF contract when it is not as certain about the actual costs of performance as it would be when using an FFP contract. For example, if an agency is procuring a fairly new production item, the costs of performance are harder to predict. Generally, this occurs after research and development but before full-scale production. During this initial production period, the contractor generally has the opportunity to identify many ways to make the production process more efficient. Use of an FPIF contract type provides the contractor with an extra incentive to cut costs and identify efficient production methods.

When using this type of contract, the agency and the contractor negotiate the target cost, the target profit, the target price (i.e., target cost + target profit), the price ceiling, and the adjustment formula or share ratio. Essentially, the contractor and the government share the underruns and the overruns. Thus, if the contractor finds a way to perform the contract at a price lower than the target cost, the contractor and the government each share in the savings. Conversely, if the contractor's costs are higher than the target cost, its fee will be reduced by its share of the overrun.

For example, assume that the target cost is $1,000 and the target profit is $60, for a target price of $1,060. Also assume that the parties have agreed to a 50/50 share ratio. If the contractor has an overrun of $100, its target fee will be reduced by 50 percent of the overrun amount, or $50 (.5 x $100 = $50). Thus, start with the contractor's allowable cost ($1,100) and add a reduced fee of only $10 ($60–$50), for a total of $1,110. However, if the FPIF ceiling price is less than $1,110, then the contractor's payment will be limited to the ceiling price. Thus, in the example, if the ceiling price were $1,100, the contractor would receive that amount instead of $1,110. Thus, the contractor would have incurred costs of $1,100 but earned no fee. This is obviously not a desirable return on investment and one that the contractor will be motivated to avoid.

Agencies obligate the target price at the date of award. Thus, in an incentive contract with a target price of $1,060 and a ceiling price of $1,100, the proper amount to record initially as an obligation is the target price of $1,060. 55 Comp. Gen. 812, 824 (1976). Commitments relating to fixed-price incentive fee contracts are recorded in an amount sufficient to cover the target price plus an estimated amount, based upon judgment and experience, for the incentive fee. 34 Comp. Gen. 418 at 420–21; B-206283-O.M., February 17, 1983. As a general rule, agencies should not commit the entire amount up to the price ceiling, because this will unnecessarily tie up funds that could be used for other, perhaps higher-priority, purposes.

Fixed-Price Award Fee Contracts

Under a fixed-price award fee (FPAF) contract, the contractor receives a negotiated fixed price (which includes some amount of profit). This is the target price. In addition, the contractor has the opportunity to receive an additional award fee based on the quality of its performance. The contract must provide for periodic evaluation of the contractor's performance against an award fee plan. Award-fee provisions may be used when the government wants to motivate a contractor and other incentives cannot be used because contractor performance cannot be measured objectively. Agencies frequently use FPAF contracts to implement a performance-based acquisition strategy, since the fee is based on the quality of the contractor's performance against specified performance criteria.

For this type of contract, the agency obligates the target or billing price on the date of contract award, even if the contract has a higher ceiling price. See, e.g., DOD 7000.14-R, vol. 3, ch. 8, para. 080402. When the fee determination official determines that the contractor has earned an additional fee and the contract is modified, the agency will have to record an obligation for the additional amount. Prior to the award fee decision, the agency has a contingent liability for the additional award fee that should be fenced with a commitment. Amounts committed for the award fee need not be at the maximum under the contract, but at an amount that may be conservatively estimated to cover the obligation arising when the award fee is awarded to the contractor.

Commitments for the award amount should be reviewed periodically to make sure that the amount committed is a reasonable estimate of the obligation that will result upon finalization of the award fee. Commitments recorded for award fees should remain until funds expire to ensure that funds will be available when the amount of the award fee is determined.

Cost-Reimbursement Contracts

Cost-reimbursement contracts provide for payment of allowable incurred costs to the extent prescribed in the contract. To be allowable, a cost must be reasonable, allocable, properly accounted for, and not specifically disallowed by either the contract or the cost principles in the Federal Acquisition Regulation (Subpart 31.2).

These contracts establish an estimate of total cost for the purpose of obligating funds and establishing a ceiling that the contractor may not exceed—except at its own risk— without the written approval of the contracting officer. In these contracts, the contractor promises to use its "best efforts" to perform the contract within the contract's estimated cost. The contractor's obligation to perform is limited to the funds available in the contract. Thus, once the funds available in the contract have been used, the contractor has the right to stop working, regardless of whether it has delivered the full amount of goods or services contemplated by the contract.

Since the government assumes the risk of cost growth under a cost-reimbursement contract, such contracts include cost ceilings. Ceilings are imposed through the limitation of cost clause, FAR 52.232-20, or the limitation of funds clause, FAR 52.232-22. The contractor may not recover costs above the ceiling unless the contracting officer authorizes the contractor to exceed the ceiling. *RMI, Inc. v. United States*, 800 F.2d 246 (Fed. Cir. 1986). Thus, at the time of award, the government's obligation is to pay the contractor the estimated cost plus the fee prescribed in the contract.

In addition to the requirement for cost ceilings, to use a cost-reimbursement type of contract, the contracting officer must conclude that the contractor has an adequate cost accounting system [see *CrystaComm, Inc.*, ASBCA No. 37177, 90-2 BCA ¶ 22,692 (contractor failed to set up required cost accounting system)] and that the agency will be able to exercise adequate surveillance over the contractor to ensure a reasonable level of efficiency.

The decision to use a cost-type contract is within the contracting officer's discretion, and GAO will generally not grant protests challenging the contracting officer's choice of contract type. See, e.g., *Crimson Enters.*, B-243193, June 10, 1991, 91-1 CPD ¶ 557 (decision to use cost-type contract reasonable considering uncertainty over requirements causing multiple changes), and *Delco Elec. Corp.*, B-244559, Oct. 29, 1991, 91-2 CPD ¶ 391 (selection of type committed to agency discretion and selection of firm-fixed-price found reasonable).

Cost-Plus Fixed Fee Contracts

A cost-plus fixed fee (CPFF) contract is generally used for research or preliminary studies. The contract amount is the contractor's allowable costs, plus a fixed fee that is negotiated and set prior to award. A CPFF is used frequently because it is the easiest cost-reimbursement contract to administer. Because the fee is fixed regardless of actual cost or the quality of the contractor's performance, no adjustment is required during administration of the contract. However, there is little incentive for the contractor to control costs in a CPFF contract, since the fee is based on the estimated cost at the time of award rather than the actual costs of performance. Under a CPFF contract, the agency obligates the total contract amount, i.e., the estimated cost plus the fixed fee.

Discussion Problem 2-3

An agency awards a cost-plus fixed fee contract consisting of an estimated cost of $1 million and fixed fee of 10%, which amounts to $100,000, for a total contract award amount of $1.1 million. At the end of the period of performance, the contractor's actual costs total $1.5 million. The contractor submits a final payment voucher that would result in a total payment of $1.65 million. The voucher contains the following notation: "The total contract payment of $1.65 million consists of $1.5 million in allowable costs plus the 10% fee, or $150,000 (.10 x $1,500,000 = $150,000). Assuming that the contractor incurred $1.5 million of allowable costs and did not exceed any contract ceilings, how much is the contractor entitled to?

Cost-Plus Incentive Fee Contracts

In cost-plus incentive fee (CPIF) contracts the government wants to provide incentives to the contractor, but costs are not certain enough to use a fixed-price incentive contract.

This contract type shifts some of the risks of performance to the contractor by requiring the contractor to share in the underruns and overruns. Under a CPIF contract, the contracting officer negotiates the target cost, the target fee, the minimum fee, the maximum fee, and the share ratio. The target fee is not fixed and can be increased or decreased based on the actual costs incurred by the contractor. In other words, if the cost of performance exceeds the estimated cost, the contractor receives less fee; if the cost of performance is less than the estimated cost, the contractor receives more fee.

For example, assume that the target cost is $1,000, the target fee is $60, the share ratio is 50/50, and the minimum/maximum fees are $10 and $100, respectively. If the contractor experiences an overrun, the amount of target fee will be reduced, whereas if it experiences an underrun, the amount of fee will be increased. Assume that the contractor's actual cost of performance is $900. One would calculate the allowable costs of $900 plus the target fee of $60, plus 50 percent of the underrun, or $50 (.5 x $100), for a total of $1,110. However, since the maximum fee was set at $100, the contractor will receive $1,000 ($900 + $100). This is a large return on investment of 11.1 percent ($100/$900).

Under a CPIF contract, the agency obligates the target cost plus the target fee. In this example, the agency would have recorded $1,060 and would have committed some amount, up to $40, to cover the difference between the target fee ($60) and the maximum fee ($100). Note that in some cases, as in this example, since the maximum fee would only be payable if the contractor experiences an underrun, there may be sufficient funds already obligated on the contract that would be available to pay some or all of the additional fee.

Cost-Plus Award Fee Contracts

Under a cost-plus award fee (CPAF) contract, the contractor receives its allowable costs; a base fee that is fixed at award; and, possibly, an additional award fee based on the quality of the contractor's performance. Most agencies limit the amount of the base fee to 3 percent of the estimated cost.

The contractor is entitled to the base fee regardless of the quality of its performance. CPAF contracts are commonly used with service contracts to reward achievement of a goal that is difficult to measure objectively. This might include the quality of performance, customer service and satisfaction, or exceeding minimum environmental requirements. The contractor's performance is graded (usually quarterly) by the government; if the contractor exceeds the stated performance levels, it will receive a higher percentage of award fee.

As with fixed-price award fee (FPAF) contracts, commitments relating to cost-plus award fee contracts are recorded in an amount sufficient to cover the estimated cost and the base fee, plus an estimated amount for the award fee. Amounts committed for the award fee need not be the maximum under the contract, but an amount that may be conservatively estimated to cover the obligation arising when the award fee is awarded to the contractor. Agency regulations often prohibit obligating the maximum amount of award fee. For example, the Air Force's regulation on budget guidance and procedures (AFI 65-601, v. 1) states:

> 8.3.1. . . . .Until the determination has been made that a contractor is due an award fee, the award fee funds are committed as a contingent liability, not obligated. (See DoD 7000.14-R, Vol. 3, Chap. 8, Para. 080202.A.)

This rule would apply to FPAF contracts as well as CPAF contracts. Similarly, as with FPAF contracts, commitments for the award amount should be reviewed periodically to ensure that the amount committed is a reasonable estimate of the obligation that will result upon finalization of the award fee.

Variable Quantity Contracts

There are two types of variable quantity contracts in which the quantity is not fixed under the contract. Occasionally, an agency may not know at the time of contracting the precise quantity of goods and services required. When a decision is made to order goods or services under a variable quantity contract, the government issues a delivery order (DO) for supply items or a task order (TO) for services.

Indefinite-Delivery/Indefinite-Quantity Contracts

In an indefinite-delivery/indefinite-quantity (IDIQ) contract, the government is obligated to purchase a guaranteed minimum quantity. It is common for the government to have more than one contractor for the same or similar goods or services. These "multiple award ID/IQ contracts" have grown in popularity in recent years.

Under an ID/IQ contract, the agency obligates the amount of the guaranteed minimum quantity stated in the contract at contract award. When the agency issues DOs or TOs, it obligates the amount of the order. The precise amount obligated will depend on the pricing structure of the order. The agency will apply the rules discussed above, depending on whether the order is fixed-price or cost-reimbursable.

Discussion Problem 2-4

An agency has made three awards under a multiple award ID/IQ contract. The minimum guaranty for each contractor is $10,000. How much must the agency record as an obligation at the time of the awards? Several days later, the agency issues the first task order for a firm fixed price of $50,000 to one of the contractors. How much should be recorded for this task order?

Requirements Contracts

Under a requirements contract, the government agrees to buy from the contractor all of the supplies and services it needs, if any, that are within the scope of the contract. This is the extent of the government's obligation, however, and it is not required to purchase any minimum quantity. For example, in *Cleek Aviation v. United States*, 19 Cl. Ct. 552 (1990), the court determined that the government breached a requirements contract when it bought items available under the contract from another source. The court also noted, however, that if the goods or services were different, there would be no breach. See also *Systems Architects, Inc.*, ASBCA No. 28861, 90-3 BCA ¶ 23,175 (failure to order requirements is a constructive termination for convenience); *Air-Flo Cleaning Sys.*, ASBCA No. 39608, 90-3 BCA ¶ 23,071 (no termination costs for a requirements contract terminated for convenience prior to first order).

The traditional rule that under a requirements contract, the government must satisfy all of its needs from one contractor, may be changing. In *Ace-Federal Reporters, Inc. v. Barram, No.*, 226 F.3d 1329 (Fed.Cir. Sept. 28, 2000), the Court of Appeals for the Federal Circuit held that a multiple-award requirements contract was valid. It is a fundamental rule of contracts law that a contract must be supported by adequate consideration, i.e., each party must perceive a benefit to the agreement. In *Ace-Federal*, the court found that the contract was supported by consideration because: "Rather than vying with 18,000 other transcription services for the government's business, the contractors had to compete with only one to four other contractors."

However, that a prior GAO bid protest decision held that a multiple award requirements contract in which no individual awardee was guaranteed any minimum amount of work was not a binding agreement. In *Satellite Services, Inc.*, B-280945, 98-2 Comp. Gen. Proc. Dec. ¶ 125, December 4, 1998, GAO held:

> [T]he essence of a requirements contract is not only that the government agrees to satisfy all its requirements from one contractor, but also that the contractor agrees to fill all those requirements. *Media Press, Inc.*, 215 Ct. Cl. 985, 986 (1977); *Sea-Land Serv., Inc.*, supra. The contract contemplated here lacks this element as well. As originally issued, the RFP sec. B.1.c required the contractors to submit proposals for task orders on all the locations and in all the dollar ranges specified in their offers. By amendment No. 0003, however, the agency deleted that

requirement. In sum, both parties to the contract here would retain the right to avoid performing; neither will have agreed to be bound in any meaningful way. The absence of valid mutual promises renders the contract unenforceable.

It is arguable that the later decision from the Court of Appeals for the Federal Circuit, in effect, overrules the earlier GAO opinion. However, this result is not certain, given GAO's expertise in contract matters. This situation leaves at least two issues for acquisition personnel to consider. First, if an agency wants to pursue a multiple award requirements contract, it should ensure that it structures the contract as closely as possible to the contract at issue in *Ace Federal*. Second, the agency should avoid clauses such as the one referenced in *Satellite Services*, since such a clause may render the agreement non-binding, and therefore not recordable as an obligation.

Since the government is not required to purchase any minimum quantity under a requirements contract, it incurs no monetary obligation at the time of contract award. Consequently, the agency does not record an obligation upon award of the contract, but obligates the amount of the task or delivery orders as they are issued.

Letter Contracts

Letter contracts are used to expedite performance in emergency circumstances. A letter contract is a written preliminary contractual instrument authorizing the immediate commencement of work under its terms and conditions. Since a letter contract is awarded prior to the definitization of all terms and conditions, such contracts must contain a definitization schedule that includes a date for submission of the contractor's price proposal; a date for the start of negotiations; and a target date for completing definitization, which should be within 180 days after the letter contract date or before completion of 40 percent of the work, whichever occurs first.

The FAR imposes several limitations on an agency's authority to use letter contracts. Specifically, FAR 16.603-3 states:

> 16.603-3 Limitations.
> A letter contract may be used only after the head of the contracting activity or a designee determines in writing that no other contract is suitable. Letter contracts shall not—
> (a) Commit the Government to a definitive contract in excess of the funds available at the time the letter contract is executed;
> (b) Be entered into without competition when competition is required by Part 6; or
> (c) Be amended to satisfy a new requirement unless that requirement is inseparable from the existing letter contract. Any such amendment is subject to the same requirements and limitations as a new letter contract.

These limitations represent an effort to balance the need of agencies to enter into agreements quickly when necessary with the need to ensure that adequate funding is available and letter contracts are not used to circumvent competition requirements.

Letter contracts must contain a "not to exceed" (NTE) amount (which is the ceiling on the contract when definitized) and must specify the government's maximum liability pending definitization (generally 50 percent of the NTE amount). Letter contracts must be approved by the heads of the contracting activity (HCA) or designee prior to award.

Since the government, at the time of award, is liable only for the maximum liability, this is the amount that is recorded as an obligation. When the contract is definitized, then the obligation is adjusted to reflect the definitized price. Agencies will generally commit funds at an amount between the maximum liability and the NTE price to ensure that funds are available when the contract is definitized.

Discussion Problem 2-5

In response to a natural disaster, the Federal Emergency Management Agency (FEMA) must arrange for the transport of electric generators to 10 locations within 48 hours. FEMA enters into a letter contract for an NTE amount of $100,000. How much should FEMA obligate? How much should it keep committed after the initial obligation?

Purchase Orders

The FAR defines a purchase order as "an offer by the Government to buy supplies or services, including construction and research and development, upon specified terms and conditions, using simplified acquisition procedures." FAR 2.101. The purchase order process is generally initiated when a government official issues a request for quotations (RFQ) for an item or service. The commercial firm responds with a price quote, and the government issues a purchase order if it wants to make the purchase. The agency must determine at what point in this process a "binding agreement" is created, since it would have to record an obligation at that time.

Simplified acquisition procedures are located at Part 13 of the FAR. The issue of the legal effect of price quotations is addressed at FAR 13.004:

> **13.004 Legal effect of quotations.**
> (a) A quotation is not an offer and, consequently, cannot be accepted by the Government to form a binding contract. Therefore, issuance by the Government of an order in response to a supplier's quotation does not establish a contract. The order is an offer by the Government to the supplier to buy certain supplies or services upon specified terms and conditions. A contract is established when the supplier accepts the offer.

Thus, when the supplier accepts the government's offer (i.e., the purchase order), a binding agreement is created and must be recorded as an obligation in the amount of the order. If written acceptance is not received from the supplier, delivery under the purchase order is evidence of acceptance to the extent of delivery. See, e.g., DOD 7000.14-R, vol. 3, ch. 8, para. 080510B.

Some purchase orders are issued in response to a binding written offer from a vendor. This type of purchase order is referred to as a unilateral purchase order and creates an obligation when issued in the amount stated. In this case, the government records the obligation upon issuance of the order. Since the order is issued in response to a binding offer from the vendor, no additional manifestation of acceptance is required to create a binding obligation.

Options

An option is an offer from a contractor to a buyer (in this case a federal agency) that is irrevocable for a fixed period. An option gives the government the unilateral right, for a specified time, to order additional supplies or services, or to extend the term of the contract, at a specified price. FAR 17.201. *Fjellestad, Barrett & Short*, B-248391, Aug. 21, 1992, 92-2 CPD ¶ 118; *Young-Robinson Assoc., Inc.*, B-242229, Mar. 22, 1991, 91-1 CPD ¶ 319 (GAO will not consider a protest challenging an agency's decision not to exercise an option because that decision is a matter of contract administration, which GAO has traditionally refused to consider). The option matures into an obligation upon proper exercise of the option by the agency. The agency will obligate funds for each option period after funds become available. In addition, obligations must be consistent with all normal limitations on the obligation of appropriated funds (e.g., bona fide needs rule, period of availability, type of funds). *See Cessna Aircraft Co. v. Dept. of the Navy*, 744 F. Supp. 260 (D. Kan. 1990).

Rental Agreements

The issue that must be resolved when determining how much to obligate under a rental agreement is the amount of government liability created when the agreement is signed. The general rule is that an agency obligates funds for one month at a time throughout the term of the rental agreement. This rule applies if the government may terminate a rental agreement without notice and without obligation for any additional termination costs. However, if the government may terminate a rental agreement without cost only upon giving a specified number of days notice, then it must obligate the monthly amount of the rent plus an amount for the number of days notice the government is required to give. If the rental agreement provides for a specified payment in the event of termination, then the government must obligate the monthly rental amount plus the amount of the termination payment.

Interagency Transactions

It is not uncommon for federal agencies to provide goods or services to other federal agencies. Subsection (a)(1) of 31 U.S.C. §1501 expressly applies to interagency contracts and states:

> (a) An amount shall be recorded as an obligation of the United States Government only when supported by documentary evidence of —
> . . .
> (3) an order required by law to be placed with an agency

This statute, however, does not embrace all interagency transactions. When an agency obtains goods or services from another agency, the obligational treatment of the transaction depends on whether or not the order is "required by law" to be placed with the other agency (e.g., Government Printing Office, Federal Prison Industries). If it is "required by law," the transaction is governed by subsection (a)(3) of 31 U.S.C. § 1501 (above) and must be recorded as an obligation when the order is issued to the performing agency. If it is not "required by law," the general requirements of subsection (a)(1) apply. Interagency orders not required by law are sometimes termed "voluntary orders."

Voluntary Interagency Agreements
The major source of authority for voluntary interagency agreements is the Economy Act, 31 U.S.C. § 1535. An Economy Act agreement (assuming it meets the criteria of subsection (a)(1)) is recorded as an obligation when accepted by the performing agency. However, Economy Act agreements are subject to one additional requirement. Under 31 U.S.C. § 1535(d), the period of availability of funds transferred pursuant to an Economy Act agreement may not exceed the period of availability of the source appropriation. Thus, one-year appropriations obligated by an Economy Act agreement must be deobligated at the end of the fiscal year charged if the performing agency has not performed or incurred valid obligations under the agreement. 39 Comp. Gen. 317 (1959); 34 Comp. Gen. 418, 421-22 (1955). It was, for example, improper for the Library of Congress to use annual funds transferred to it under Economy Act agreements and unobligated by it prior to the end of the fiscal year to provide services in the following fiscal year. *Financial Audit: First Audit of the Library of Congress Discloses Significant Problems*, GAO/AFMD-91-13 (August 1991).

The reason for this requirement is to prevent the Economy Act from being used to extend the obligational life of an appropriation beyond that provided by Congress in the appropriation act. 31 Comp. Gen. 83, 85 (1951). Thus, Military Interdepartmental Procurement Requests (MIPRs) are viewed as authorized by the Economy Act. While an MIPR must be initially recorded as an obligation under 31 U.S.C. § 1501(a)(l), when the performing agency accepts the order, it is subject to the deobligation requirement of 31 U.S.C. § 1535(d) and is thus ultimately chargeable to appropriations current when the performing component incurs valid obligations. 59 Comp. Gen. 563 (1980); 34 Comp. Gen. 418, 422 (1955). The deobligation requirement of 31 U.S.C. § 1535(d) does not apply to obligations of no-year funds. 39 Comp. Gen. 317, 319 (1959).

Where the agreement is based on some statutory authority other than the Economy Act, the recording of the obligation is still governed by 31 U.S.C. § 1501(a)(l). Thus, the obligation would be recorded when the performing agency accepts the order in writing or by equivalent electronic means. However, the deobligation requirement of 31 U.S.C. § 1535(d) does not apply. In this situation, the obligation will remain payable in full from the appropriation initially charged, regardless of when performance occurs, in the same manner as contractual obligations generally (subject, of course, to the bona fide needs rule and to any restrictions in the legislation authorizing the agreement).

Thus, it is necessary to determine the correct statutory authority for any interagency agreement in order to apply the proper obligational principles. If the order is not governed by the Economy Act, it constitutes an obligation only to the extent that the performing agency has accepted the order in writing, has completed the work, or has awarded contracts to fill the order.

Regardless of the statutory basis for the agreement, an obligation is recordable under subsection 1501(a)(1) only if the criteria of that subsection are met, i.e., binding agreement, in writing, and sufficiently specific. In B-193005, October 2, 1978, GAO considered the procurement of crude oil for the Strategic Petroleum Reserve. Under the Federal Property and Administrative Services Act, GSA may procure materials for other federal agencies and may delegate this authority. GSA had delegated the authority to procure fuel commodities to the Secretary of Defense. Thus, the Department of Energy could procure the oil through the Defense Fuel Supply Center in a non-Economy Act transaction. An order placed by the Department of Energy could be recorded as an obligation under 31 U.S.C. § 1501(a)(l) because it constituted a "binding agreement" and the funds would, therefore, remain available for contracts awarded by Defense beyond the original period of obligational availability. This result would not have been permissible if this were an Economy Act transaction, since 31 U.S.C. § 1535(d) would have required deobligation at the end of the period of availability of the funds.

The requirement for a binding agreement in the context of interagency purchases was illustrated in 59 Comp. Gen. 602 (1980). In this case, GAO considered the procedure by which the Bureau of Alcohol, Tobacco, and Firearms (ATF) ordered "strip stamps" (the excise tax stamps pasted across the caps of liquor bottles) from the Bureau of Engraving. GAO reviewed pertinent legislation and concluded that ATF was not "required by law" to procure its strip stamps from the Bureau of Engraving. Since individual orders were not binding agreements, it was essentially immaterial in one important respect whether the order was governed by the Economy Act or some other law; in neither event could ATF's funds remain obligated beyond the last day of a fiscal year to the extent an order remained unfilled. Funds could be considered obligated at the end of a fiscal year only if the stamps were printed or were in the process of being printed or if the Bureau of Engraving had entered into a contract with a third party to provide them.

Thus, a voluntary interagency order, whether authorized by the Economy Act or some other law, is recordable under 31 U.S.C. § 1501(a)(l) only if it constitutes a binding agreement and meets the other criteria of that subsection. If it does, the applicability or non-applicability of the Economy Act (31 U.S.C. § 1535(d)) becomes relevant. If it does not, the order constitutes an obligation only to the extent that the performing agency has completed the work or has awarded contracts to have it done.

> **Discussion Problem 2-6**
>
> It is the end of the fiscal year and an agency (the ordering agency) wants to use its annual appropriation to purchase computer equipment. However, the agency does not have enough time to compete the order or define its requirement and plans to issue an interagency order to another agency that has a multiple-award computer equipment contract already in place. This agency (the performing agency) is authorized to credit funds it receives from other agencies to its revolving fund and then place the order using these funds. The interagency order contains a fund cite for the about-to-expire funds and describes the goods to be purchased as: "Various items of computer equipment." The ordering agency records the obligation before the end of the fiscal year.
>
> After the ordering agency has had a chance to refine its requirement, it discusses with the performing agency the various types of computer equipment available under the multiple award contract and their prices and advises the performing agency that it would like to use the funds cited on the interagency order to purchase: "One hundred Gateway® Computers with Pentium® 4 chips, 1.6 Gb of memory, 512Mb of SRAM, and 17" LCD screens." Did the ordering agency obligate its funds properly?

Interagency Agreements Required by Law

As noted, the third standard for recording obligations, 31 U.S.C. § 1501(a)(3), is an order required by law to be placed with a federal agency. Under this section, an order placed with another government agency is recordable under this subsection only if it is required by statute or statutory regulation to be placed with the other agency. The subsection does not apply to orders that are merely authorized rather than required. 34 Comp. Gen. 705 (1955). This is because orders that are authorized, rather that required, to be placed with another agency are discretionary. Because the ordering agency could decide to place the order through an alternative source, the mere issuance of an order does not create a binding agreement, as required by 31 U.S.C. § 1501(a)(3). Conversely, if an agency *must* place an order with a particular agency for designated goods or services, then the issuance of the order alone is sufficiently binding to justify recording an obligation. Thus, orders required by law to be placed with another U.S. governmental agency, such as the Federal Prison Industries (18 U.S.C. § 4124) or the Government Printing Office (GPO) (44 U.S.C. § 111), are recorded as obligations by the requiring agency in the amount stated in the order when the order is issued.

Since an order required by law to be placed with another agency is not an Economy Act transaction, the deobligation requirement of 31 U.S.C. § 1535(d) does not apply. 35 Comp. Gen. 3,5 (1955). The fact that the work will be performed in the next fiscal year does not defeat the obligation, provided that the general bona fide need rule was met when the order was placed. 59 Comp. Gen. 386 (1980); 35 Comp. Gen. 3 (1955). Also, the fact that the work is to be accomplished and reimbursement made through use of a revolving fund is immaterial. 35 Comp. Gen. 3 (1955); 34 Comp. Gen. 705 (1955).

For example, an order for printing services placed with the GPO is recorded as an obligation when placed if: (1) there is a present need for the printing, and (2) the requisition is accompanied by copy or specifications sufficient for GPO to proceed with the job. Thus, a requisition by the Commission on Fine Arts for the printing of "Sixteenth Street Architecture, Volume I" placed with GPO in FY 1977 and accompanied by a manuscript and specifications obligated FY 1977 funds and was chargeable in its entirety to FY 1977 funds, notwithstanding that the printing would be done in the following fiscal year. 59 Comp. Gen. 386 (1980). However, a requisition for U.S. Travel Service sales promotional literature placed with GPO near the end of FY 1964 did not obligate FY 1964 funds where no copy or manuscript was furnished to GPO until FY 1965. 44 Comp. Gen. 695 (1965). The distinction is that in the latter case, because the order was not sufficiently specific to create an obligation, there was no bona fide need in FY 1964.

Orders from Stock

The obligational rules applicable to orders for items to be delivered from stock of the requisitioned agency are based on 32 Comp. Gen. 436 (1953). An order for items to be delivered from stock is a recordable obligation when the order is issued if: (1) it is intended to meet a bona fide need of the fiscal year in which the order is placed or to replace stock used in that fiscal year, and (2) the order is firm and complete. To be firm and complete, the order must request prompt delivery of specific available stock items for a stated consideration and must be accepted by the supplying agency in writing. "Available" means on hand or routinely on order. Acceptance by the stock fund activity is not required for common-use stock items that are on hand or on order and will be delivered promptly.

Materials that are specially created for a particular purpose are not "stock." 44 Comp. Gem 695 (1965). Consequently, agencies generally should not record an obligation for an order of an item without a standard stock number until the stock fund activity accepts the order in writing. See, e.g., DOD 7000.14-R, vol. 3, ch. 8, para. 080801. This rule is merely the consequence of the statutory requirement for a "binding agreement" and the determination that an order for a non-standard item is less certain than an order for a standard item. The basic rules in this area were established by 34 Comp. Gen. 705 (1955).

SPECIFIC OBLIGATIONS SITUATIONS

The general rules are sometimes applied somewhat differently because of unique circumstances or the application of rules that only apply in particular situations. This discussion addresses the correct application of the rules of obligation in these special cases.

Ratification of Unauthorized Commitments

The FAR defines an unauthorized commitment as "an agreement that is not binding solely because the Government representative who made it lacked the authority to enter into that agreement on behalf of the Government." FAR 1.602-3. Since a nonbinding agreement cannot support disbursement of funds, it cannot be recorded as an obligation. However, if an agency has received a benefit as a result of an unauthorized commitment, it may ratify the agreement to allow for payment to the party rendering performance under the agreement. The FAR defines a ratification as an "act of approving an unauthorized commitment by an official who has the authority to do so."

To properly ratify an unauthorized agreement (and thereby create a recordable obligation), the FAR requires that:

> (1) Supplies or services have been provided to and accepted by the Government, or the Government otherwise has obtained or will obtain a benefit resulting from performance of the unauthorized commitment;
> (2) The ratifying official has the authority to enter into a contractual commitment;
> (3) The resulting contract would otherwise have been proper if made by an appropriate contracting officer;
> (4) The contracting officer reviewing the unauthorized commitment determines the price to be fair and reasonable;
> (5) The contracting officer recommends payment and legal counsel concurs in the recommendation, unless agency procedures expressly do not require such concurrence;
> (6) Funds are available and were available at the time the unauthorized commitment was made; and
> (7) The ratification is in accordance with any other limitations prescribed under agency procedures.

Note that the FAR requires that funds were available at the time the unauthorized commitment was made, without regard to when the ratification action is taken. This is because the ratified agreement is charged against the funds that would have been charged had the obligation been valid from its inception. *Fish & Wildlife Serv.—Fiscal Year Chargeable on Ratification of Contract*, B-208730, Jan. 6, 1983, 83-1 CPD ¶ 75 (ratification relates back to the time of the initial agreement, which is when the services were needed and the work was performed). This rule applies even if the prior year's funds have expired. See *Fish & Wildlife Serv.*, supra.

Discussion Problem 2-7

A contracting officer with authority to award contracts up to $500,000 awards a contract for $750,000, thereby creating an unauthorized commitment. If a ratification action is finalized in the subsequent fiscal year, which year's funds must the agency charge—funds current when the unauthorized agreement is ratified or funds current when the contracting officer created the unauthorized commitment?

Liquidated Damages

Many contracts, particularly construction contracts, contain "liquidated damages" clauses.

These clauses require the contractor to pay the government a stated sum if the contractor's performance fails to meet some contractual requirement. Liquidated damages clauses are generally applied to the timeliness of the contractor's performance and state that the contractor must pay the government a stated amount for every day of lateness. The lateness may relate to the overall completion of the contract, to specific milestones, or both.

The contractor's liability for liquidated damages has the effect of reducing the extent of the government's expenditures under the contract. 44 Comp. Gen. 623 (1965). Since the government's liability under the contract has been reduced, the amount obligated on the contract should be adjusted downward by the amount of the liquidated damages.

Litigation

As in the other situations discussed, the government is always required to record an obligation in the amount of its known liability. An issue arises, however, when the government's liability is the subject of litigation and the government is contending that it is *not* liable for the amount claimed by the contractor. In this situation, no obligation should be recorded until the extent of the government's liability is conclusively determined.

If a judgment will eventually be payable from agency funds but recording is not required, the Comptroller General indicated in 35 Comp. Gen. 185 that the agency should nevertheless administratively reserve sufficient funds to cover the contingent liability to ensure that adequate funds are available to reimburse the Judgment Fund. In that opinion the Comptroller noted that it was unlikely that Congress could have intended to require recording an obligation in every pending case that might or might not result in liability, and concluded that recording an obligation based on pending litigation is required "only in those cases where the Government is definitely liable for the payment of money out of available appropriations and the pending litigation is for the purpose of determining the amount of the Government's liability." 35 Comp. Gen. at 187.

The DoD Financial Management Regulation is consistent with this approach but permits recording an obligation if the government's liability is certain and the purpose of the litigation is merely to quantify the extent of liability. The regulation states:

> 081203. Litigation. As a general rule, the amount of the liability expected to result from pending litigation shall be recorded as an obligation in cases where the government definitely is liable for the payment of money from available appropriations, and the pending litigation is for the purpose of determining the amount of the government's liability. In other cases, an obligation shall not be recorded until the litigation has been concluded or the government's liability finally is determined. A

written administrative determination of the amount of the liability shall serve as documentary evidence of the obligation.

When a contractor's claim results in a final judgment against the government for a specific amount, the government initially pays the claim from a permanent appropriation called the Permanent Indefinite Judgment Fund. 31 U.S.C. § 1304. However, the Contract Disputes Act (CDA) requires agencies to reimburse the Judgment Fund for CDA judgments. 41 U.S.C. § 612(c). Agencies must obligate funds from the appropriation that was available for obligation when the judgment was entered. 63 Comp. Gen. 308 (1984). Thus, if a contract is awarded in FY 1999 and the contractor files a claim in FY 2000 that results in judgment in FY 2001, the agency must determine to which fiscal year the liability should be charged. Under the rule stated, the agency would charge the FY 2001 appropriation because that is the year in which the judgment was entered.

If the agency has insufficient funds available to reimburse the Judgment Fund, the statute authorizes the agency to seek additional appropriations. However, the statute does not require a specific, line-item appropriation, and reimbursement may be made from subsequent lump-sum appropriations available for the agency's procurement. 63 Comp. Gen 308, 312. This is a practical approach, since if a specific appropriation were required, an agency could avoid reimbursement simply by never requesting the funds.

The agency is not expected to disrupt its normal operations by diverting funds for essential activities to reimburse the Judgment Fund. Although reimbursement is a statutory requirement, the statute does not require that it occur within any specified time. The agency has some discretion in the matter. The level of agency discretion was addressed by the Comptroller General in B-217990.25-O.M., October 30, 1987, as follows:

> It is clear that Congress wanted the ultimate accountability to fall on the procuring agency, but we do not think the statute requires the agency to disrupt ongoing programs or activities in order to find the money. If this

were not the case, Congress could just as easily have directed the agencies to pay the judgments and awards directly. Clearly, an agency does not violate the statute if it does not make the reimbursement in the same fiscal year that the award is paid. Similarly, an agency may not be in a position to reimburse in the following fiscal year without disrupting other activities, since the agency's budget for that fiscal year is set well in advance. In our opinion, the earliest time an agency can be said to be in violation of 41 U.S.C. § 612(c) is the beginning of the second fiscal year following the fiscal year in which the award is paid.

The rationale for allowing the agency to wait until the start of the second fiscal year is to allow it to program and budget for the additional funds. Of course, if the agency can reimburse the Judgment Fund from the appropriation that is current when the judgment is entered, then there would be no need to request additional funds for a subsequent fiscal year.

When a contract claim is settled by the parties, however, the general obligation rules apply because the settlement action is treated like any other aspect of contract administration. Thus, under the "relation-back" doctrine, the agency would generally charge the funds that were originally obligated on the contract to pay the settlement. (The relation-back doctrine is discussed in greater detail in Chapter 3.)

For a variety of reasons, the contracting officer may not want to charge the funds originally obligated on the contract to pay the settlement. This situation could arise, for example, if that appropriation does not have a sufficient unobligated balance to pay the settlement. There is a procedure by which an agency could have the cognizant board of contract appeals issue a judgment based on the settlement, which would trigger the applicability of the Judgment Fund and permit the agency to pay the settlement from funds current when the judgment is entered.

Obligations Subject to the Availability of Funds

To ensure the continuity of services, an agency may award contracts at the end of one fiscal year for services to be performed in the subsequent fiscal year. If the agency intends to use funds that will not be available for obligation until the subsequent fiscal year, it must cite those funds on the contract. However, since the cited funds are not yet available for obligation, the agency cannot record an obligation against the unavailable appropriation. Such an obligation in advance of appropriations would violate the Antideficiency Act, specifically 31 U.S.C. 1341(a)(1)(B). To avoid a violation, the contract must state that it is being awarded "subject to the availability of funds" (SAF). The standard SAF clause is located at FAR 52.232-18, Availability of Funds. When an agency uses this clause, it must not accept supplies or services until the contracting officer has given the contractor written notice that funds are available. FAR 32.703-2. Further, the SAF clause may be used only for operation and maintenance and continuing services (e.g., rentals, utilities, supply items not financed by stock funds) that are necessary for normal operations and for which Congress previously had consistently appropriated funds. FAR 32.703-2 (a).

Similarly, FAR 52.232-19, Availability of Funds for the Next Fiscal Year, is used for one-year indefinite-quantity or requirements contracts for services that are funded by annual appropriations that extend beyond the fiscal year in which they begin, provided any specified minimum quantities are certain to be ordered in the initial fiscal year. FAR 32.703-2 (b). When an SAF clause is used, the agency does not record an obligation until the contracting officer has notified the contractor that funds are available.

DEOBLIGATIONS

We have addressed the various rules pertaining to the obligation of appropriated funds. In most situations, the obligated funds are fully expended under the contract. However, in some situations obligated funds must be *de*obligated. A deobligation is defined as a "downward adjustment of previously recorded obligations." GAO, *Glossary of Terms Used in the Federal Budget Process*, PAD-81-27, at 56.

A deobligation may be necessary for a variety of reasons. For example, the terms of the contract may reduce the amount of the government's liability if certain conditions exist. This may occur if there is cost underrun in an adjustable type of contract (B-207433, September 16, 1983) or if the agency required less work than anticipated under a level-of-effort contract (B-183184, May 30, 1975). A deobligation is also generally required if the agency terminates a contract for convenience or deletes work from the contract, if such actions reduce the government's liability. Also, when a contractor must pay liquidated damages for late performance, the effect is to reduce the contract price, which thereby reduces the amount of the agency's obligation. In addition, deobligation may be statutorily required in some instances. As discussed above, 31 U.S.C. § 1535(d) requires deobligation of appropriations obligated under an Economy Act agreement to the extent the performing agency has not incurred valid obligations under the agreement by the end of the fiscal year.

There are no special rules relating to deobligation. Instead, deobligation procedures follow the general rules of obligation. Thus, funds deobligated within the original period of obligational availability are once again available for new obligations just as if they had never been obligated in the first place. Naturally, any new obligations are subject to the same purpose, time, and amount restrictions that were applicable when the funds were initially obligated. Regarding funds deobligated after the source appropriation has expired, the Comptroller General has stated: "Funds deobligated after the expiration of the original period of obligational availability are not available for new obligations." 64 Comp. Gen. 410 (1985); 52 Comp. Gen. 179 (1972). However, such funds may be retained as unobligated balances in the expired account until the account is closed, and are available for adjustments to valid obligations in accordance with 31 U.S.C. 3 1553(a), as amended by Pub. L. No. 101-510, §1404 (1990).

In certain situations funds should *not* be deobligated. Funds should not be deobligated from a valid, unliquidated obligation unless (as discussed) the agency's liability under the contract or order has been reduced. It is not appropriate to deobligate funds solely to "free them up" for new obligations. This would increase the risk of violating the Antideficiency Act because if the deobligated funds were obligated for other purposes, there might not be sufficient funds available in the appropriation to make payments under the contract to which the funds were initially obligated.

In this chapter the terms "commitment" and "obligation" were defined and distinguished. It is important to remember that a commitment reserves funds in anticipation of an eventual obligation and that an obligation ensures that funds are available to make anticipated disbursements. The amount to commit and obligate is based on the expected extent of the government's eventual liability. Since the government's liability will vary based on contract type, this chapter discussed how much should be committed and obligated under a variety of contract types.

CHAPTER 3
Availability of Appropriations: Purpose

For appropriated funds to be "legally available" for obligation, the following three requirements must be satisfied: (1) the *purpose* of the obligation or expenditure must be authorized; (2) the obligation must occur within the *time* limits applicable to the appropriation; and (3) the obligation and expenditure must be within the *amounts* Congress has established. Thus, the three elements of the concept of availability are: purpose, time, and amount. All three must be satisfied for the obligation or expenditure to be legal. This chapter discusses availability as to purpose. Availability as to time and amount will be Chapters 4 and 5.

THE PURPOSE STATUTE

The concise statutory directive, appropriately referred to as the "purpose statute," 31 U.S.C. § 1301(a), states:

> Appropriations shall be applied only to the objects for which the appropriations were made except as otherwise provided by law.

Congress enacted this statutory control in the Act of March 3, 1809, 2 Stat. 535. This act, generally referred to as the "Purpose Statute," was passed as part of a reorganization of the War, Navy, and Treasury Departments to limit the discretion of the Executive Branch in spending appropriations.

Since money cannot be paid from the Treasury except under an appropriation (U.S. Const. art. I, § 9, cl. 7), and since an appropriation can only be enacted by Congress, Congress is empowered to determine the purposes for which an appropriation may be used. Simply stated, 31 U.S.C. § 1301(a) says that public funds may be used only for the purpose or purposes for which they were appropriated. The purpose statute prohibits charging authorized items to the wrong appropriation and charging unauthorized items to any appropriation. One early Comptroller General decision took particular note of the directness of the purpose statute, stating:

> It is difficult to see how a legislative prohibition could be expressed in stronger terms. The law is plain, and any disbursing officer disregards it at his peril.

4 Comp. Dec. 569, 570 (1898).

APPLICATION OF THE PURPOSE STATUTE

The starting point in applying 31 U.S.C. § 1301(a) is that, unless there is a clear indication to the contrary, the common meaning of the words in the appropriation act and the program legislation it funds governs the purposes to which the appropriation may be applied. Thus, at least two statutory references must be considered when trying to determine the proper purpose of an appropriation. First, the legislation authorizing a program will typically describe the scope of the program. Any funds obligated and expended for that program must fall within that program scope. Second, since program legislation does not appropriate funds, an appropriation is necessary. The appropriations act may alter or delete requirements contained in the program authorization or can add completely new requirements.

For example, the Comptroller General held in 41 Comp. Gen. 255 (1961) that an appropriation available for the "replacement" of state roads damaged by nearby federal dam construction could be used only to *restore* those roads to their former condition, not for *improvements* such as widening. Similarly, funds provided for the modification of existing dams for safety purposes could not be used to construct a new dam, even as part of an overall safety strategy. B-215782, April 7, 1986.

If a proposed use of funds is inconsistent with the statutory language, the expenditure is improper, even if it would result in substantial savings or other benefits to the government. Thus, while the Federal Aviation Administration (FAA) could construct its own roads needed for access to FAA facilities, it could not contribute a share "for the improvement of county-owned roads, even though the latter undertaking would have been much less expensive." B-143536, August 15, 1960. See also 39 Comp. Gen. 388 (1959).

It is the duty of federal agencies to comply with the intent of Congress, as manifested in the appropriation act and program legislation, even if there are other, less expensive alternatives. If an agency has identified a more efficient or less expensive way to accomplish its mission than that specified in existing statutes, the agency may consider proposing legislation to obtain necessary congressional approval for the initiative.

From these principles, it follows that the purpose statute may be violated in several different ways. For example, deliberately charging the wrong appropriation for purposes of expediency or administrative convenience, with the intent of later transferring funds from the right appropriation, would violate 31 U.S.C. § 1301(a). 36 Comp. Gen. 386 (1956); 26 Comp. Gen. 902, 906 (1947); 19 Comp. Gem 395 (1939); 14 Comp. Gen. 103 (1934); B-97772, May 18, 1951; B-104135, August 2, 1951. Similarly, the fact that the expenditure would be authorized under some *other* appropriation is irrelevant. Charging the "wrong" appropriation, unless authorized by statute, violates the purpose statute. Finally, the rule prohibiting transfers without congressional approval illustrates the close relationship between 31 U.S.C. § 1301(a) and the Antideficiency Act, 31 U.SC. § 1341. For example, an unauthorized transfer violates 31 U.S.C. § 1301(a) because the transferred funds would be used for a purpose other than that for which they were originally appropriated; if the receiving appropriation is exceeded, the Antideficiency Act is also violated.

Although the purpose statute and the Antideficiency Act are related, not every violation of 31 U.S.C. § 1301(a) is automatically a violation of the Antideficiency Act, and not every violation of the Antideficiency Act is automatically a violation of 31 U.S.C. § 1301(a). For example, if an agency obligates the "wrong" appropriation and sufficient funds are available from the "right" appropriation to cover the obligation, then there would be no Antideficiency Act violation (although there was a violation of the purpose statute). However, many of GAO's appropriations law decisions frequently involve elements of both laws. Thus, an expenditure in excess of an available appropriation violates both statutes. The reason the purpose statute is violated is that, unless the disbursing officer used personal funds, he or she must necessarily have used money appropriated for other purposes. 4 Comp. Dec. 314, 317 (1897).

A 1992 GAO decision, B-248284.2, September 1, 1992, illustrates how strictly the purpose statute can be applied. In that case, the United States Information Agency (USIA) wanted to build exhibits in Seville, Spain, and Genoa, Italy, to commemorate the 500th anniversary of Columbus' voyage to America. Such projects were within the mission of USIA and traditionally would be funded from its salary and expenses appropriation. However, as is common in many purpose violation cases, the unobligated balance of the "right" appropriation was insufficient and USIA wanted to use funds from another appropriation, radio construction. Recognizing that use of the radio construction funds might violate the purpose statute, the agency sought and obtained reprogramming approval from the chairmen of the subcommittees on Commerce, Justice, State, and the Judiciary and Related Agencies, as well as the House and Senate appropriations committees. Based on this approval, USIA obligated funds to commence construction of the exhibits.

In a subsequent audit, GAO questioned USIA on its use of the radio construction funds for this purpose and eventually issued B-248284.2, in which it stated:

> The language in the Radio Construction appropriation evidences no relationship between its purposes and the construction expenditures for the Seville and Genoa expositions, nor do the accompanying congressional committee reports show an intention to broaden the purposes beyond that described by the quoted language. Although the House and Senate appropriations subcommittees did not object to the reprogramming, informal congressional approval of an unauthorized transfer of funds between appropriation accounts does not have the force and effect of law.

In this case, the agency's purpose violation also resulted in a violation of the Antideficiency Act because, as often happens, the reason the agency used the "wrong" money in the first place was because it lacked sufficient funds in the "right" appropriation.

Finally, it is also important to recognize that GAO has consistently held that an agency cannot do indirectly what it is not permitted to do directly. Thus, an agency cannot use the device of a contract or grant to accomplish a purpose it could not accomplish by direct expenditure. See 18 Comp. Gen. 285 (1938) (contract stipulation to pay wages in excess of Davis-Bacon Act rates held unauthorized). Similarly, a grant of funds for unspecified purposes would be improper. 55 Comp. Gen. 1059, 1062 (1976). Such expenditures violate the purpose statute just as if the agency had made the improper expenditures directly.

HOW TO DETERMINE THE PURPOSE OF AN APPROPRIATION

The effect of the purpose statute is to hold the agency responsible for determining the proper purpose of the appropriation it intends to obligate. To discharge this responsibility properly, agencies use several well-established rules of interpretation. In this section, we will discuss those various rules of statutory interpretation and how they should be applied in the context of fiscal law.

Consider the Plain Meaning of the Appropriation Act

The most obvious reference available for determining the purpose of an appropriation is the language of the appropriation act itself. This approach is sometimes referred to as the "plain meaning" rule. Principles of Federal Appropriations Law, 2d ed., vol. 1,GAO/OGG91-5 (July 1991), pp. 2–60. B-288658, Nov. 30, 2001("It is a fundamental canon of statutory construction that words, unless otherwise defined by the statute, will be interpreted consistent with their ordinary, contemporary, common meaning."). One commonsense way to determine the plain meaning of a word is to consult a standard dictionary. E.g., *Mallard v. United States Dist. Court*, 490 U.S. 296 (1989), at 301; *American Mining Congress v. EPA*, 824 F.2d 1177, 1183-84& n.7 (D.C. Cir. 1987). The "plain meaning" will be the ordinary, everyday meaning rather than some obscure usage. *Mallard*, 490 U.S. at 301; 38 Comp, Gen. 812 (1959). For example, if an appropriation provides funds "to demolish Building 100 at Federal Agency X," a standard dictionary could provide a useful reference. "Demolish" is a verb meaning "to tear down (a building or other structure); raze." *The Random House College Dictionary*, rev. ed. (1980), p. 353. This definition should dissuade Agency X from considering whether it could use the funds to renovate, repair, or replace Building 100. If a word has more than one ordinary meaning and the context of the statute does not make it clear which is being used, there may well be no "plain meaning" for purposes of that statute. In such cases it may become necessary for the agency to consult the legislative history associated with the statute to determine the intent of Congress.

The plain language of an appropriation act can be very general (which affords the agency great discretion) or very specific (which limits the agency's discretion in proportion to the level of specificity). An example of a very general appropriation is the following excerpt from the Fiscal Year 2002 Department of Transportation and Related Agencies Appropriations Act:

> For necessary expenses, not otherwise provided for, for applied scientific research, development, test, and evaluation; maintenance, rehabilitation, lease and operation of facilities and equipment, as authorized by law, $20,222,000, to remain available until expended . . .

Under this language, the agency has broad discretion to conduct research and development (R&D) over a wide range of areas as it considers necessary. The agency is free to prioritize the R&D work between the various areas and has discretion to determine the specific nature of the R&D projects it will fund.

Compare the following excerpt from the Fiscal Year 2002 Department of Defense Appropriations Act:

> SEC. 8016. None of the funds in this Act may be available for the purchase by the Department of Defense (and its departments and agencies) of welded shipboard anchor and mooring chain 4 inches in diameter and under unless the anchor and mooring chain are manufactured in the United States from components which are substantially manufactured in the United States. . .

The specificity of this paragraph restricts DoD's authority to purchase, from nondomestic sources, chains of the designated sizes and classes. In another example, an appropriation for topographical surveys in the United States was held not available for topographical surveys in Puerto Rico. 5 Comp. Dec. 493 (1899). Similarly, an appropriation to install an electrical generating plant in the custom-house building in Baltimore could not be used to install the plant in a nearby post office building, even though the plant would serve both buildings and thereby reduce operating expenses. 11 Comp. Dec. 724 (1905). This case illustrates a point that is very often overlooked when analyzing a fiscal law issue, i.e., it does not matter whether a particular expenditure makes good business sense or will save taxpayer dollars. If the expenditure is not within the purpose of the appropriation to be charged, then the agency may not apply the funds to that purpose.

Between the two extremes of very general and very specific appropriations are many variations. A common form of appropriation provides funds to implement statutes referenced in the appropriation. The following is an example from the Fiscal Year 2002 Health and Human Services (HHS) Appropriations Act:

> GENERAL DEPARTMENTAL MANAGEMENT
> For necessary expenses, not otherwise provided, for general departmental management, including hire of six sedans, and for carrying out titles III, XVII, and XX of the Public Health Service Act, and the United States-Mexico Border Health Commission Act, $341,703,000...

This appropriation authorizes the agency to use the funds for any lawful purposes it deems necessary to implement the referenced statutes. In situations such as this, where the appropriation references other statues, it becomes necessary to look beyond the appropriation language and examine the referenced statutes to determine whether particular expenditures are authorized. In this case HHS would have to review the test of the Public Health Service Act and the United States–Mexico Border Health Commission Act to fully determine the scope of the appropriation.

Use of Legislative History to Determine Purpose

When the language of the statute is clear, there is no need to resort to legislative history to determine congressional intent. *United States v. Ron Pair Enters., Inc.*, 489 U.S. 235 (1989) ("plain meaning" rule); *Tennessee Valley Authority v. Hill*, 437 U.S. 153 (1978); *LTV Aerospace Corp.*, B–183851, Oct. 1,

1975, 55 Comp. Gen. 307, 317, 75-2 CPD ¶ 203. However, if the statutory language is unclear, or will lead to an absurd result, then one may have to consult the statute's legislative history to determine congressional intent. See *Mallard v. United States Dist. Court*, 490 U.S. 296 (1989); *Federal Aviation Admin.—Permanent Improvements to a Leasehold*, B–239520, 69 Comp. Gen. 673 (1990) (conference report clearly indicated that $5.7 million was available for a permanent improvement to a leasehold). Legislative history is often used when the appropriations act language is general (e.g., "$10 million is available to upgrade agency laboratories") and the agency wants to know if a particular obligation is appropriate (e.g., whether the preceding statutory language would allow for *expansion* of the agency's laboratories). Often the legislative history will reveal what Congress had in mind when it enacted the legislation, which would enable the agency to assess the propriety of its planned obligation or expenditure.

Meaning of "Legislative History"

The term "legislative history" refers to the body of congressionally generated written documents relating to a bill from the time of introduction to the time of enactment. It is never improper for an agency to consider legislative history to seek guidance on the purpose of a statute (to see, for example, what kinds of problems Congress wanted to address), to confirm the apparent plain meaning, or to resolve ambiguities. It is improper, however, to use legislative history to override the clear language of the statute. The Comptroller General has stated:

> [A]s a general proposition, there is a distinction to be made between utilizing legislative history for the purpose of illuminating the intent underlying language used in a statute and resorting to that history for the purpose of writing into the law that which is not there.

55 Comp. Gen. 307, 325 (1975).

For example, if an appropriation act provided funding to an agency for the acquisition of imagery reconnaissance satellites (i.e., satellites that take pictures), the agency could not use the funds to acquire satellites that collect signals intelligence (e.g., cell phone calls), even if the legislative history stated that the funds *could* be used to acquire imagery satellites, signals satellites, or both. The once-burdensome task of searching through hundreds of pages of legislative history has been greatly simplified by the ability to perform word searches of electronic versions of the relevant documents. (The various types of legislative history are available on several websites, including: http://thomas.loc.gov; http://www.access.gpo.gov/su_docs/aces/aaces200.html; http://ublib.buffalo.edu/libraries/units/law/guides_handouts/legis1.html; http://www.lib.umich.edu/govdocs/legchart.html; and http://www.law.berkeley.edu/library/services/legis.html#bills. Some sites that provide guidance on how to research legislative history are: http://www.llsdc.org/sourcebook/fed-leg-hist.htm; and http://www.lib.ohio-state.edu/refweb/govdocs/leghis.htm.)

Types of Legislative History and Their Significance

Legislative history falls generally into three categories: committee reports, floor debates, and hearings. These different types of legislative history vary in their degree of helpfulness in the quest to ascertain the meaning of ambiguous statutory language. In general, the evidentiary value of any piece of legislative history depends on its relationship to other available legislative history and, most importantly, to the language of the statute itself. This section will discuss the three principal types of legislative history and their significance.

Committee Reports. The most authoritative single source of legislative history is the conference report. E.g., *Squillacote v. United States,* 739 F.2d 1208, 1218 (7th Cir. 1984); B-142011, April 30, 1971. This is especially true if the statutory language in question was drafted by the conference committee. This may happen if the Senate and House versions of a bill differ and the conference committee members draft a compromise version. The reason the conference report is so authoritative is that it must be voted on and adopted by both Houses, and thus is the only legislative history document that reflects the will of both Houses. *Commissioner v. Acker,* 361 U.S. 87,94 (1959) (Frankfurter, J., dissenting).

Next in the sequence are the reports from the Senate and House committees that considered the bill. The Supreme Court has consistently been willing to rely on committee reports when there is no more authoritative reference. E.g., *U.S. v. Cleveland Indians Baseball Co.,* 121 S.Ct. 1433 (2001); *Duplex Printing Press Co. v. Deering,* 254 U.S. 443,474 (1921); *United States v. St. Paul, Minneapolis & Manitoba Ry. Co.,* 247 U.S. 310, 318 (1918); *Lapina v. Williams,* 232 U.S. 78,90 (1914).

However, as mentioned, material in committee reports, even a conference report, generally cannot be used to controvert clear statutory language. *Squillacote,* 739 F.2d at 1218; *Hart v. United States,* 585 F.2d 1025 (Ct. Cl. 1978); B-33911/B-62187, July 15, 1948. Committee reports, as with all legislative history, must be used with caution. Agencies must be careful not to elevate legislative history to the status of a statute. This point is made by the following excerpt from the opinion of the Court of Claims in *Hart v. United States,* 585 F.2d at 1033, quoted in *Conlon v. United States,* 8 Cl. Ct. 30,33 (1985):

> We note that with the swiftly growing use of the staff system by Congress, many congressional documents may be generated that are not really considered fully by each or perhaps by any legislator. Thus, committee reports and the like are perhaps less trustworthy sources of congressional intent than they used to be, and less than the actual wording of the legislation, which one would hope received more thorough consideration prior to enactment. If there is inadvertent error either in the statute or in the committee report, the offender is more likely to be the latter, surely.

Although some caution should always be exercised, in those cases where there is a need to resort to legislative history, committee reports remain generally recognized as the best source.

Floor Debates. Somewhat less persuasive than committee reports are records of floor debates discussing the legislation in question. Statements made in the course of floor debates have traditionally been regarded as suspect because they are "expressive of the views and motives of individual members" and, therefore, do not provide direct evidence of the will of the entire Congress. *Duplex Printing Press Co. v. Deering*, 254 U.S. 443, 474 (1921); *Garcia v. United States*, 469 U.S. 70, 76 (1984); *Zuber v. Allen*, 396 U.S.168, 186 (1969); *United States v. O'Brien*, 391 U.S. 367, 385 (1968); *United States v. United Automobile Workers*, 352 U.S. 567, 585 (1957). As expected, floor debates will not be regarded as persuasive if they conflict with explicit statements in more authoritative portions of legislative history such as committee reports. *United States v. Wrightwood Dairy Co.*, 315 U.S. 110, 125 (1942); B-114829, June 27, 1975. Another concern, as expressed by the Supreme Court, is that:

> [I]t is impossible to determine with certainty what construction was put upon an act by the members of a legislative body that passed it by resorting to the speeches of individual members thereof. Those who did not speak may not have agreed with those who did; and those who spoke might differ from each other.

United States v. Trans-Missouri Freight Ass'n, 166 U.S. 290,318 (1897).

Some of the earlier cases, such as *Trans-Missouri Freight* quoted above, suggest that floor debates should never be taken into consideration. More recent cases (discussed below) have held that floor debates can properly be considered. The real issue concerns the weight they should receive when trying to determine the meaning of statutory language.

When there is no more persuasive evidence, courts have frequently considered floor debates to ascertain congressional intent, especially in the more recent cases. See, e.g., *United States v. H.*, 2001 U.S. Dist. LEXIS 21295 (E.D.N.Y., 2001) ("The court of appeals for the Second Circuit recently examined the legislative history in detail, including the floor debate, to determine that the Child Support Recovery Act does not create a private right of action"); *Yolanda Burton v. City of Alexander City, Alabama*, 2001 U.S. Dist. LEXIS 6651 (DC ALA, 2001) ("The 2000 Act speaks to federal superintendence of construction and safety standards. See 42 U.S.C. § 5401(b)(1) (amended). The floor debates confirm this point"). In *Preterm, Inc. v. Dukakis*, 591 F.2d 121, 128 (lst Cir. 1979), cert. denied, 441 U.S. 952, the court suggested that "heated and lengthy debates" in which "the views expressed were those of a wide spectrum" of members might be more valuable in discerning congressional intent than committee reports "which represent merely the views of [the committee's] members and may never have come to the attention of Congress as a whole." *Preterm*, 591 F.2d at 133.

The weight to be given statements made in floor debates will even vary with the identity of the speaker. Thus, statements by legislators in charge of a bill, such as the pertinent committee chairperson, have been regarded as "in the nature of a supplementary report" and receive somewhat more weight. *United States v. St. Paul, Minneapolis & Manitoba Ry. Co.*, 247 U.S. 310, 318 (1918). See also *McCaughn v. Hershey Chocolate Co.*, 283 U.S. 488, 493-94 (1931) (statements by members "who were not in charge of the bill" were "without weight"); *Duplex v. Deering*, 254 U.S. at 474-75; *National Labor Relations Board v. Thompson Products. Inc.*, 141 F.2d 794, 798 (9th Cir. 1944). Statements by the sponsor of a bill are also entitled to somewhat more weight. E.g., *Schwegmann Brothers v. Calvert Distillers Corp.*, 341 U.S. 384, 394-95 (1951); *Ex Parte Kawato*, 317 U.S. 69, 77 (1942). Conversely, statements by the opponents of a bill expressing their "fears and doubts" generally receive little, if any, weight. *Shell Oil Co. v. Iowa Dept. of Revenue*, 488 U.S. 19, 29 (1988); *Schwegmann*, 341 U.S. at 394. However, even the statements of opponents may be "relevant and useful," although not authoritative, in certain circumstances, such as, for example, where the supporters of a bill make no response to opponents' criticisms. *Arizona v. California*, 373 U.S. 546, 583 n.85

(1963); *Parlane Sportswear Co. v. Weinberger,* 513 F.2d 835,837 (lst Cir. 1975).

Hearings. Hearings are the least persuasive type of legislative history of the three types discussed in this section, yet they can prove useful when no more authoritative source exists. For example, hearings often help define the problem Congress is addressing because they present opposing viewpoints for Congress to consider. Nevertheless, the researcher should bear in mind that hearings reflect only the personal opinion and motives of the witness providing testimony. It is impossible to attribute these opinions and motives to anyone in Congress, let alone Congress as a whole, unless more authoritative forms of legislative history have expressly adopted them. As one court has stated, an isolated excerpt from the statement of a witness at hearings "is not entitled to consideration in determining legislative intent." *Pacific Ins. Co. v. United States,* 188 F.2d 571, 572 (9th Cir. 1951). "It would indeed be absurd," said another court, "to suppose that the testimony of a witness by itself could be used to interpret an act of Congress." *SEC v. Collier,* 76 F.2d 939, 941 (2d Cir. 1935).

While hearings are generally not a very effective means to determine legislative intent, there is one significant exception. Testimony by the government agency that recommended the bill or amendment in question, and that often helped draft it, is entitled to special weight. *Shapiro v. United States,* 335 U.S. 1, at 12 n.13 (1948); *SEC v. Collier,* 76 F.2d at 941. Frequently, a federal agency will propose legislation that addresses a matter within the scope of the agency's mission jurisdiction. Since the agency proposing the legislation typically has special expertise in the subject matter, testimony of the agency's senior management is often accorded great weight.

Also, testimony at hearings can be more valuable as legislative history if the language of a bill was revised in direct response to that testimony. Relevant factors include the presence or absence of statements in more authoritative history linking the change to the testimony; the proximity in time of the change to the testimony; and the precise language of the change as compared to that offered in the testimony. See *Premachandra v. Mitts*, 753 F.2d 635, 640-41 (8th Cir. 1985). See also *Allen v. State Board of Elections*, 393 US. 544, 566-68 (1969); *SEC v. Collier*, 76 F.2d at 940, 941. For example, if the conference report indicates that a particular change was made in response to testimony of the head of the agency that will implement the legislation, such testimony should be accorded significant weight. Cases in which congressional testimony was found significant by the courts include *Navegar, Inc. v. United States*, 338 U.S. App. D.C. 213; 192 F.3d 1050 (DC Cir., 1999) ("The congressional testimony behind the 1994 Act demonstrated that the previous federal firearms regulation scheme and state law were being widely circumvented and were thus inadequate to allow states to control the flow of semiautomatic assault weapons across their borders."); *United States v. Schaffer*, 337 U.S. App. D.C. 214; 183 F.3d 833 (DC Cir., 1999) (congressional testimony used to determine scope of agency program).

The Effect of Items Included in the Agency's Budget Request

The relationship of an appropriation to the agency's budget request is another important factor in determining purpose availability. If a budget submission requests a specific amount of money for a specific purpose, and Congress makes a specific line-item appropriation for that purpose, then the appropriation is legally available only for the specific object described. This type of situation rarely causes any interpretational problems since the appropriation is quite clear regarding what Congress intended.

However, the trend in recent decades, at least for some agencies, has been for Congress to enact lump-sum appropriations, which are stated in terms of broad object categories such as "salaries and expenses," "operations and maintenance," or "research and development," without further breakdown. In analyzing the relationship of a lump-sum appropriation to its corresponding budget request from the perspective of purpose availability, there are two basic rules.

First, when an amount to be expended for a specific purpose (that is not otherwise prohibited) is included in a budget estimate, the appropriation is legally available for the expenditure even though the appropriation act does not specifically refer to it. B-278968 May 28, 1998; B-278121 November 7, 1997; 35 Comp. Gen. 306, 308 (1955); 28 Comp. Gen. 296, 298 (1948); 26 Comp. Gen. 545, 547 (1947); 23 Comp. Dec. 547 (1917); B-125935, February 7, 1956; B-125404, September 16, 1955; B-51630, September 11, 1945. For example, in preparing its budget request for a salaries and expenses appropriation, an agency will typically include such items as employee salaries, travel, training, incentive awards, contributions to health insurance and retirement, and other similar expenses. The lump-sum appropriation enacted based on this budget request, stating "For Salaries and Expenses, $X," would be legally available for all the items specified in the budget request.

A corollary to this rule is that the lack of a specific budget request for an item does not mean that an agency is prohibited from making an expenditure for that item from a lump-sum appropriation, if the appropriation is otherwise available for items of that type. E.g., B-149163, June 27, 1962. See also 20 Comp. Gen. 631 (1941); B-198234, March 25, 1981. Thus, in the example above pertaining to the "salary and expense" appropriation, if the agency neglected to budget specifically for incentive awards for FY 2002, it would still be able to use the appropriation for this purpose. This is because incentive awards are sufficiently related to the general purpose of a salaries and expenses appropriation and do not require specific appropriation language. Thus, the agency's 2002 salary and expense appropriation would be legally available for payment of the incentive awards, even though not specifically mentioned in the budget request. This is because when Congress enacts a lump-sum appropriation, it intends to confer on the agency receiving the appropriation a considerable degree of discretion to decide how best to use the funds appropriated.

The second basic rule is that the inclusion of an item in an agency's budget request for an expenditure that is otherwise prohibited, and the subsequent appropriation of funds without specific reference to the item, does not constitute authority for the proposed expenditure or make the appropriation available for the prohibited purpose. 26 Comp. Gen. 545, 547 (1947); 6 Comp. Gen. 573 (1927); B-76841, August 23, 1948. See also 18 Comp. Gen. 533 (1938). In other words, authority to use funds for an otherwise prohibited purpose is not inferred simply because the agency buried the prohibited item in its budget request and Congress appropriated funds without objecting. Thus, if an agency's budget request seeks funds to dispose of hazardous materials in violation of applicable environmental laws, the enactment of a lump-sum appropriation without objection does not authorize the agency to obligate or expend funds for the illegal disposal.

An appropriation is available for an otherwise prohibited item only if it makes specific reference to the item. Congress can, in effect, "waive" a statutory prohibition, but it must do so explicitly. This is because of the rule against repeals by implication. Thus, a reference to the prohibition in the appropriation's legislative history is insufficient, standing alone, to authorize the prohibited expenditure. Between these two extremes (clear prohibition specifically waived in the appropriations act and no mention in the appropriations act but mention in the legislative history), there is a middle ground: When an item is questionable but not clearly prohibited, and legislative history indicates that Congress intended to include that item in a lump-sum appropriation, GAO has determined that the appropriation is available for the expenditure. E.g., A-30714, March 1, 1930.

> **Discussion Problem 3-1**
>
> The 1967 legislation that established a medical research agency states: "No appropriated funds shall be obligated or expended for experimentation on animals likely to result in the death of the animal, unless specifically authorized by law." The agency's budget request for FY 02 includes: "For testing the effects of bomb blast damage on chimpanzees to develop anti-terrorism protective measures in federal buildings—$500,000." The agency receives a research and development appropriation stating: "For research and development, including experimentation using animals—$5,000,000." The appropriation does not preclude use of the funds for the blast damage experiment. Can the funds be used for this purpose?

Termination of a Program with Funds Appropriated for That Program

Can an agency use funds appropriated by Congress to implement a program to cancel that program and pay necessary termination costs? (When an agency terminates a contract for convenience, the contractor will generally be entitled to reimbursement for various costs such as performance costs incurred prior to the termination, costs incurred to terminate subcontracts, and legal and administrative costs associated with preparing the termination settlement proposal. The termination for convenience clauses identifying the costs that may be paid are at FAR 52.249-1 thru 52.249-5.) If implementation of the program is mandatory, the answer is no. In 1973, for example, the President's administration attempted to terminate certain programs funded by the Office of Economic Opportunity (OEO), relying in part on the fact that it had not requested any funds for OEO for the next fiscal year. The programs in question were funded under a multiple-year authorization that directed that the programs be carried out during the fiscal years covered by the authorization. The United States

District Court for the District of Columbia held that funds appropriated to carry out the programs could not be used to terminate them. *Local 2677, American Federation of Government Employees v. Phillips*, 358 F. Supp. 60 (D.D.C. 1973). The court cited 31 U.S.C. § 1301(a) as a basis for its holding. Id. at 76 n. 17. See also 63 Comp. Gen. 75,78 (1983).

Is important to note that in *Local 2677*, implementation of the terminated programs was *specifically* directed in the authorizing legislation, and the District Court determined that this constrained the agency's authority to terminate the program. Where the program is not mandatory, the agency has more discretion, but there are still limits. For example, in B-115398, August 1, 1977, the Comptroller General advised that the Air Force could terminate B-1 bomber production, which had been funded under a lump-sum appropriation but was not mandated by any statute. Later cases have stated that an agency may use funds appropriated for a program to terminate that program where: (1) the program is not mandatory, and (2) the termination would not result in curtailment of the overall program to such an extent that it would no longer be consistent with the scheme of applicable program legislation. 61 Comp. Gen. 482 (1982) (Department of Energy could use funds appropriated for fossil energy research and development to terminate certain fossil energy programs); B-203074, August 6, 1981. Several years earlier, GAO had held that the closing of all Public Health Service (PHS) hospitals would exceed the Surgeon General's discretionary authority because a major portion of the Public Health Service Act would effectively be inoperable without the PHS hospital system. B-156510, February 23, 1971; B-156510, June 7, 1965.

The concepts are further illustrated in a series of cases involving the Clinch River Nuclear Breeder Reactor. In 1977, the administration proposed using funds appropriated for the design, development, construction, and operation of the reactor to terminate the project. Construction of a breeder reactor had been authorized, but not explicitly directed, by statute. As contemplated by the program legislation, the agency had submitted program criteria for congressional approval. GAO reviewed the statutory scheme, found that the approved program criteria were "as much a part of [the authorizing statute] as if they were explicitly stated in the statutory language itself," and concluded that use of program funds for termination was unauthorized. B-115398, June 23, 1977. However, by 1983 the situation had changed. Congressional support for the reactor had eroded considerably, no funds were designated for it for fiscal year 1984, and it became apparent that further funding for the project was unlikely. In light of these circumstances, GAO revisited the termination question and concluded that the agency now had a legal basis to use 1983 funds to terminate the project in accordance with the project justification data, which provided for termination in the event of insufficient funds to permit effective continuation. 63 Comp. Gen. 75 (1983). This series of decisions suggests that an agency's authority to use program funds to terminate the program is related to the general sense of Congress regarding support for the program. The agency can often assess the sense of Congress in this regard by analyzing the committee reports and the transcripts of hearings and testimony.

THE NECESSARY EXPENSE DOCTRINE

The necessary expense doctrine is a rule that has evolved through decisions of the Comptroller General in recognition that it is impossible for Congress to specifically identify every authorized expenditure in every appropriation act. In addition to the sheer volume of information this would involve, such micromanagement would greatly constrain the discretion of agencies to reprioritize expenditures based on changes that arise after they have submitted their budget requests.

The Comptroller General has never established a precise formula for determining the application of the necessary expense rule; in light of the vast differences among agencies, any such formula would almost certainly be unworkable. Rather, the determination of whether or not an expenditure is "necessary" must be made essentially on a case-by-case basis.

Under the necessary expense doctrine, for an expenditure to be justified it must meet the following three conditions:

1. The expenditure must bear a logical relationship to the appropriation to be charged. In other words, it must make a direct contribution to carrying out either a specific appropriation or an authorized agency function for which more general appropriations are available.
2. The expenditure must not be prohibited by law.
3. The expenditure must not be otherwise provided for, that is, it must not be an item that falls within the scope of some other more specific appropriation or statutory funding scheme.

See 63 Comp. Gen. 422,427-28 (1984); B-230304, March 18, 1988.

Relationship of the Expenditure to the Appropriation

The first test—the relationship of the expenditure to the appropriation—is the one that generates the majority of issues and GAO decisions. On the one hand, the rule does not require that a given expenditure be "necessary" in the strict sense that the object of the appropriation could not possibly be fulfilled without it. Thus, the expenditure does not have to be the only way to accomplish a given object, nor does it have to reflect GAO'S perception of the best way to do it. On the other hand, however, it has to be more than merely desirable or even important. E.g., 34 Comp. Gen. 599 (1955); B-42439, July 8, 1944.

Specifically Stated Purpose

When an appropriations act specifically makes funds available for a particular purpose, all three elements of the necessary expense test are met, and it is rarely necessary to perform any additional analysis. For example, in response to the terrorist attacks on the World Trade Center on September 11, 2001, the FY 2002 Department of Labor Appropriations Act (Pub. L. No. 107-117, Chapter 8) contained a provision stating:

$125,000,000 shall be for payment to the New York State Workers Compensation Review Board, for the processing of claims related to the terrorist attacks: Provided further, That, of such amount, $25,000,000 shall be for payment to the New York State Uninsured Employers Fund, for reimbursement of claims related to the terrorist attacks.

Based on this provision, expenditure of the $125 million is within the purpose of the appropriation, and, therefore, satisfies the first part of the three-part test. Since the expenditure is not prohibited by law and there is no more specific appropriation available for the same purpose, the necessary expense rule is satisfied.

As a general rule, the amount of analysis required to ensure compliance with the necessary expense rule will vary in inverse proportion to the level of specificity of the appropriation language. Thus, very specific appropriation language, such as the Department of Labor example, requires very little analysis to determine that the necessary expense rule is satisfied. Conversely, a very general appropriation, such as "operations and maintenance," imposes upon an agency the duty to perform sufficient analysis to ensure that the specific expenditure satisfies the three-part necessary expense test. Since very general appropriations do not provide specific direction, the agency has the opportunity to exercise some discretion to determine the appropriateness of expenditures.

The Role of Agency Discretion

An expenditure is permissible if it is reasonably necessary to carry out an authorized function or will contribute materially to the effective accomplishment of that function, and is not otherwise prohibited by law. See, e.g., B-280440, February 26, 1999. Within these broad parameters, agencies have discretion to determine the most effective way to use the funds that Congress has appropriated to them. However, an obligation or expenditure cannot be justified merely because some agency official thinks it is a good idea. The important thing is not the significance of the proposed expenditure itself or its value to the government or to some social purpose in abstract terms, but the extent to which it will contribute to accomplishing the purposes of the appropriation the agency wants to charge. For example, the Forest Service can use its appropriation for "forest protection and utilization" to buy plastic litter bags for use in a national forest, since the bags advance the general purpose of the appropriation. 50 Comp. Gen. 534 (1971). However, an agency could not use appropriated funds to purchase prescription eyeglasses for its employees. Although the agency would clearly benefit by the improved vision of its employees, GAO determined that such an expense is personal to the employee and was not a necessary expense for the agency. B-286137, Feb. 21, 2001.

The "necessary expense" rule is not, and cannot, be absolute, but must be applied based on the relationship between the expenditure and the purpose of the appropriation. In other words, the concept is a relative one. As stated in 65 Comp. Gen. 738, 740 (1986):

> We have dealt with the concept of 'necessary expenses' in a vast number of decisions over the decades. If one lesson emerges, it is that the concept is a relative one: it is measured not by reference to an expenditure in a vacuum, but by assessing the relationship of the expenditure to the specific appropriation to be charged or, in the case of several programs funded by a lump sum appropriation, to the specific program to be served. It should thus be apparent that an item that can be justified under one program or appropriation might be entirely inappropriate under another, depending on the circumstances and statutory authorities involved.

The difficulty involved in stating an absolute rule is attributable to the role and importance of agency discretion. Administrative agencies have the responsibility to initially determine that a given item is reasonably necessary to accomplish an authorized purpose. Once the agency makes this determination, GAO and agency auditors will normally not substitute their own judgment for that of the agency. Since the agency presumably knows how best to perform its mission, GAO will give considerable deference to the agency's determination of necessity. The standard GAO uses were summarized in B-223608, December 19, 1988:

> When we review an expenditure with reference to its availability for the purpose at issue, the question is not whether we would have exercised that discretion in the same manner. Rather, the question is whether the expenditure falls within the agency's legitimate range of discretion, or whether its relationship to an authorized purpose or function is so attenuated as to take it beyond that range.

In the exercise of its legitimate discretion, the agency must analyze its appropriations and other relevant statutory authority to determine if an obligation or expenditure is for an authorized purpose and must justify its determination to use the particular funds to be charged. In most cases, when the agency has used the same fund source for the same purpose over many years, a specific written determination of appropriateness for each obligation is unnecessary. (Of course, agency regulations may require justifications in such cases even if not required as a matter of fiscal law.) However, when an agency intends to use funds for a new purpose or if there are some questions concerning the appropriateness of an expenditure, the agency should research the appropriations act, relevant statutes, and the legislative history and prepare a written justification for the proposed use of the funds.

The role of discretion in assessing whether an expenditure is "necessary" is complicated by the fact that not all federal entities have the same range of discretion. For example, a government corporation with the authority to determine the character and necessity of its expenditures has, by virtue of its legal status, a broader measure of discretion than a "regular" agency. But even this discretion is not unlimited and is bound at least by considerations of sound public policy. See 14 Comp. Gen. 755 (1935), affirmed upon reconsideration in A-60467, June 24, 1936.

The following two decisions involving the Bonneville Power Administration (BPA) illustrate this point. In 1951, the Interior Department asked whether funds appropriated to BPA could be used to enter into a contract to conduct a survey to determine the feasibility of "artificial nucleation and cloud modification" (i.e., rainmaking) for a portion of the Columbia River drainage basin. If the amount of rainfall during the dry season could be significantly increased by this method, the amount of marketable power for the region would be enhanced. Naturally, BPA did not have an appropriation specifically available for rainmaking. However, in view of BPA's statutory role in the sale and disposition of electric power in the region, GAO concluded that the expenditure to conduct a survey was authorized. B-104463, July 23, 1951.

The Interior Department then asked whether, assuming the survey results were favorable, BPA could contract with the rainmakers. GAO thought this was going too far and questioned whether BPA's statutory authority to encourage the widest possible use of electric energy really contemplated artificial rainmaking. GAO emphasized that the expenditure would be improper for a department or agency with the "ordinary authority usually granted" to federal agencies. However, the legislative history of BPA's enabling statute indicated that Congress intended that it have a degree of freedom similar to public corporations and that it be largely free from "the requirements and restrictions ordinarily applicable to the conduct of Government business." Therefore, while the Comptroller General expressly refused to "approve" the rainmaking contract, he felt compelled to hold that BPA's funds were legally available for it. B-105397, September 21, 1951.

These cases illustrate the importance of considering the unique authority and mission of each agency when making a "necessary expense" analysis. Simply stated, what may be necessary for one agency would be outside the legitimate purpose of another agency's appropriation. Each agency's enabling legislation, i.e., the legislation by which Congress creates a federal agency, is always a significant reference point for defining the parameters of what an agency may and may not fund under the necessary expense rule. For example, while it may be appropriate for the Navy to contract for systems engineering services for the design of a battleship, it would be inappropriate for any of the National Institutes of Health to do so. Similarly, the Immigration and Naturalization Service could use its "salaries and expenses" appropriation to purchase and install lights, automatic warning devices, and observation towers along the boundary between the United States and Mexico. 29 Comp. Gen. 419 (1950). It would be more difficult for NASA or the FAA to justify the same expenditure.

> **Discussion Problem 3-2**
>
> The enabling legislation that created the Department of Energy (DOE), 42 U.S.C. § 7112 states, in part:
>
> The Congress therefore declares that the establishment of a Department of Energy is in the public interest and will promote the general welfare by assuring coordinated and effective administration of Federal energy policy and programs. It is the purpose of this chapter:
>
> . . .
>
> (4) To create and implement a comprehensive energy conservation strategy that will receive the highest priority in the national energy program.
>
> DOE would like to conduct research to develop a new type of windowpane that collects sunlight and converts it into electrical power. Would this be a "necessary expense" under DOE's enabling legislation?

Cases involving fairs and expositions provide further illustration. In general, since the mission of most agencies does not include sponsoring and participating in fairs and expositions, when Congress seeks federal participation in such events, it will provide specific legislation. See, e.g., B-160493, January 16, 1967, discussing legislation that authorized federal participation in HemisFair 1968 in San Antonio. Another example is that U.S. participation in the 1927 International Exposition in Seville, Spain, was specifically authorized by statute. See 10 Comp. Gen. 563,564 (1931).

However, specific statutory authority is not essential. If participation is directly connected with and is in furtherance of the purposes for which a particular appropriation has been made, and an appropriate administrative determination is made to that effect, the appropriation is available for the expenditure. 16 Comp. Gen. 53 (1936); 10 Comp. Gen. 282 (1930); 7 Comp. Gen. 357 (1927); 4 Comp. Gen. 457 (1924). Authority to disseminate information will generally provide adequate justification. E.g., 7 Comp. Gen. 357; 4 Comp. Gen. 457. Such determinations are within the agency's discretion under the necessary expense doctrine. However, specific congressional approval is required if the agency wants to use an appropriation other than the one it has used historically for fairs and expositions.

In B-248284.2, September 1, 1992, USIA wanted to use its radio construction appropriation for construction work on exhibits in Seville, Spain, to commemorate the 500th anniversary of Columbus' voyage to America. Although this type of project was within the scope of USIA's mission, USIA had historically used its salary and expenses appropriation. USIA officials realized that its plan raised potential issues under the purpose statute, so they consulted with various members of the agency's appropriation and authorization committees, and the members gave their approval. GAO concluded, however, that these informal approvals were not enough to effect a transfer of funds from the proper appropriation (salary and expenses) and the one proposed for use (radio construction), stating:

> The language in the Radio Construction appropriation evidences no relationship between its purposes and the construction expenditures for the Seville and Genoa expositions, nor do the accompanying congressional committee reports show an intention to broaden the purposes beyond that described by the quoted language. Although the House and Senate appropriations subcom-

mittees did not object to the reprogramming, informal congressional approval of an unauthorized transfer of funds between appropriation accounts does not have the force and effect of law.

The decision went on to state that if there were insufficient funds available in the salary and expenses appropriation, the agency could be in violation of the Antideficiency Act. See 31 U.S.C. § 1341(a).

In the absence of either statutory authority or an adequate justification under the necessary expense doctrine, the expenditure, like any other expenditure, is illegal. Thus, the Department of Housing and Urban Development (HUD) had no authority to finance participation at a trade exhibition in the Soviet Union where HUD's primary purpose was to enhance business opportunities for American companies. 68 Comp. Gen. 226 (1989); B-229732, December 22, 1988. Regardless of whether it may or may not have been a good idea, commercial trade promotion is not one of the purposes for which Congress appropriates money to HUD.

Although a written determination that a particular use of funds is justified is always a good idea, it will not ensure that GAO will find the agency's justification to be reasonable. In another case involving HUD, B-285066, May 19, 2000, HUD wanted to use its lump-sum appropriation to purchase guns in the vicinity of public housing projects (the "buyback program"). Its rationale was that part of HUD's general mission was to provide for safe housing in a drug-free environment under the Public Housing Drug Elimination Act of 1988. [Pub. L. No. 100-690, Title V, §§ 5121-5129, 102 Stat. 4181, 4301 (Nov. 18, 1988), codified at 42 U.S.C. §§ 11901-11908.] GAO held that HUD's lump-sum appropriation was not available for the gun buyback program because there was not a sufficient connection between that program and the statutory objective of reducing drug use around public housing. GAO stated:

> [T]here must be a reasonable showing that the program has the means of accomplishing the statutory purpose,

namely, to reduce drug use. While HUD relies upon evidence of a relationship between guns and violence and guns and drug dealing, this does not support a relationship between reduction of guns and reduction of drug-use. In fact, none of the studies cited by HUD find any direct correlation between the impact of reducing violence or weapons used for violent crime to a reduction in drug use.

Thus, while an agency may have broad discretion to determine whether an expense is "necessary" under the necessary expense doctrine, it still must demonstrate a connection between the expenditure and the scope of its authorized activities.

The Expenditure Must Not Be Prohibited by Law

The second test under the necessary expense doctrine is that the expenditure must not be prohibited by law. The prohibition would most commonly be stated in statutory law, but may also be a matter of constitutional law. See, e.g., B-240365.2 March 14, 1996 (GAO considered whether particular expenditures violated the establishment clause of the United States Constitution). As a general proposition, neither a necessary expense rationale nor the necessary expense language in an appropriation act can be used to overcome a statutory or a constitutional prohibition. E.g., 38 Comp. Gen. 758 (1959); 4 Comp. Gen. 1063 (1925). In the two cited decisions, the Comptroller General held that the necessary expense language did not overcome the prohibition in 41 U.S.C. § 12 against contracting for public buildings or public improvements in excess of appropriations for the specific purpose. This rule is merely another example of the more general rule against repeals by implication discussed in Chapter 1.

There is an exception where applying the rule would make it impossible to carry out a specific appropriation. A very small group of cases holds that, where a specific appropriation is made for a specific purpose, an expenditure that is "absolutely essential" to accomplish the specific objective may be incurred, even though the expenditure would violate another law. This is a narrowly construed exception, and it will be applied only if the objective of the appropriation could not be accomplished without the particular obligation and expenditure. Also, the rule would not apply to the use of a more general appropriation.

For example, in 2 Comp. Gen. 133 (1922), modifying 2 Comp. Gen. 14 (1922), GAO determined that an appropriation to provide airmail service between New York, Chicago, and San Francisco was available to construct hangars and related facilities at a landing field in Chicago, even though another statute (41 U.S.C. § 12) required a *specific* appropriation for such construction projects. The reason was that it would have been impossible to provide the service, and thereby accomplish the purpose of the appropriation, without constructing the facilities. See also 17 Comp. Gen. 636 (1938) and 22 Comp. Dec. 317 (1916).

An 1899 case, 6 Comp. Dec. 75, provides another good illustration of the concept and is still applicable today. The building housing the Department of Justice had become unsafe and overcrowded. Congress enacted legislation to authorize and fund the construction of a new building for the Department. The statute specifically provided that the new building be constructed on the site of the old building, but did not address the question of how the Department would function during the construction period. The obvious solution was to rent another building until the new one was ready, but a statute (40 U.S.C. § 34) prohibits the rental of space in the District of Columbia except under an appropriation specifically available for that purpose, and the Department had no such appropriation. Because any other result would be absurd, the Comptroller of the Treasury held that the Department could rent interim space notwithstanding the statutory prohibition. While the decision was not couched in terms of the expenditure being "absolutely essential," it said basically the same thing. Since the Department of Justice could not simply cease to function during the construction period, the appropriation for construction of the new building could not be fulfilled without the expenditure for interim space.

The Expenditure Must Not Be Otherwise Provided For

The third test is that an expenditure cannot be authorized under a necessary expense theory if it is otherwise provided for under a more specific appropriation or fund. This test is the specific application of the general rule that an appropriation for a specific object is available for that object to the exclusion of a more general appropriation that might otherwise be considered available for the same object. The fact that the more specific appropriation or fund may be exhausted is immaterial. Thus, in B-139510, May 13, 1959, the Navy could not use its shipbuilding appropriation to deepen a channel in a river to permit submarines then under construction to move to deeper water. The reason was that this function had traditionally been funded from appropriations of the Army Corps of Engineers, not the Navy. The fact that appropriations had not been made in this particular instance was irrelevant. Similarly, the Navy could not use appropriations made for the construction or procurement of vessels and aircraft to provide housing for civilian employees engaged in defense production activities because funds for that purpose were otherwise available. 20 Comp. Gen. 102 (1940).

In another case, Federal Prison Industries could use its revolving fund to build industrial facilities incident to a federal prison, or to build a residential camp for prisoners employed in federal public works projects, but could not use that fund to construct other prison facilities because such construction was statutorily provided for in other fund sources. B-230304, March 18, 1988.

In these cases, the existence of a more specific source of funds, or a more specific statutory means of getting them, is the governing factor and overrides the "necessary expense" considerations.

SPECIFIC EXAMPLES

This section will discuss application of the purpose statute to specific types of expenses. The analysis used to determine the propriety of these expenses can be applied to any expenses. As will be illustrated in the examples that follow, the first step is to determine whether an expense is specifically identified in an appropriations act or other statute. The purpose statute and the necessary expense doctrine have a common objective, which is to ensure that executive agencies obligate and expend funds in accordance with the intent of Congress. This objective is most easily satisfied when the obligation or expenditure is for a purpose that is specifically identified in an appropriations act. In such cases, the agency will not have to apply the three-part necessary expense test. In other words, an agency may consider an expense "necessary" if that expense is specifically identified in the agency's appropriations act and is otherwise authorized. If the expense is not specifically identified, then the agency must apply the three-part necessary expense test to determine if the expense will satisfy the requirements of the purpose statute.

Attendance at Meetings and Conventions

The rules governing the use of appropriated funds to attend meetings and conventions differ somewhat depending on whether the meeting or convention is sponsored by the federal government or by a nongovernment entity.

Meetings and Conventions Sponsored by Nongovernment Entities

As noted, the first step in assessing the propriety of an obligation or expenditure is to determine whether it is specifically identified in an appropriations act or other statute. Thus, a government employee may attend a nongovernment sponsored meeting at government expense if the meeting is authorized under either of two key provisions of the Government Employees Training Act. Section 10 of the act, now codified at 5 U.S.C. § 4109, authorizes payment of certain expenses in connection with authorized training. The types of expenses authorized by this statute include tuition and matriculation fees; library and laboratory services; purchase or rental of books, materials, and supplies; and other services or facilities directly related to the training of the employee. The other key provision, section 19(b) of the act, now codified at 5 U.S.C. § 4110, makes travel appropriations available for expenses of attendance at meetings "which are concerned with the functions or activities for which the appropriation is made or which will contribute to improved conduct, supervision, or management of the functions or activities."

For example, the Labor Department could use its salaries and expenses appropriation to pay the attendance fees of its Director of Personnel at a conference of the American Society of Training Directors since the meeting qualifies under the broad authority of 5 U.S.C. § 4110. 38 Comp. Gen. 26 (1958). Of course, the expenses of attendance may not be paid if the employing agency refuses to authorize attendance, even if authorization would have been permissible under the statute. B-164372, June 12, 1968.

To fully understand which meetings and conventions are authorized and which are not, it is necessary to review the background of sections 4109 and 4110 of Title 5 of the United States Code. Those sections are actually exceptions to a statute that prohibits the use of appropriated funds for the expense of attending meetings or conventions of a "society or association." That statute, 5 U.S.C. § 5946, states:

> Sec. 5946. Membership fees; expenses of attendance at meetings.
> Except as authorized by a specific appropriation, by express terms in a general appropriation, or by sections 4109 and 4110 of this title, appropriated funds may not be used for payment of -
> (1) membership fees or dues of an employee as defined by section 2105 of this title or an individual employed by

the government of the District of Columbia in a society or association; or

(2) expenses of attendance of an individual at meetings or conventions of members of a society or association.

This statute was at issue in several early cases. Since the statute is directed at meetings of a "society or association," other types of meetings were not prohibited (and would not be prohibited today). Thus, the Federal Power Commission could, if it was determined to be in the furtherance of authorized activities, send a representative to the World Power Conference (in Basle, Switzerland) since it was not a meeting of a "society or association." 5 Comp. Gen. 834 (1926). Similarly, the statute did not prohibit travel by United States Attorneys "to attend a conference of attorneys not banded together into a society or association, but called together for one meeting only for conference in a matter bearing directly on their official duties." 1 Comp. Gen. 546 (1922).

However, if GAO considered the gathering to be a meeting or convention of a society or association, it consistently disallowed the expenses. E.g., 16 Comp. Gen. 252 (1936); 5 Comp. Gen. 599 (1926), affirmed by 5 Comp. Gen. 746 (1926); 3 Comp. Gen. 883 (1924). In these decisions, GAO often told agencies that if the attendance would be in the interest of the government, they should seek statutory authorization from Congress. The statutory exceptions provided by the Government Employees Training Act are examples of Congress' recognition that attendance at certain meetings or conventions can serve a useful public purpose. Agencies may also seek specific appropriation language authorizing attendance at meetings that would otherwise be prohibited by 5 U.S.C. § 5946. To satisfy the rule that disfavors repeals by implication, the agency budget request should be as specific as possible, should reference 5 U.S.C. § 5946, and should request that Congress include specific language in the appropriations act itself.

> **Discussion Problem 3-3**
>
> A federal agency responsible for generation of electric power is interested in learning more about wind-generated power technology (windmills). It would like to send a team of its electrical engineers to attend an annual conference sponsored by the "Society for Wind-Generated Power." The conference focuses on new technologies pertaining directly to wind-generated power. The agency included in its budget request for the current fiscal year the following line item: "For expenses and fees of attending conferences pertaining to training on new wind-generated power technologies—$100,000." If Congress appropriates a lump-sum appropriation, what argument could be made in support of obligating and expending funds to attend the conference?

Meetings and Conventions Sponsored by the Federal Government

Federally sponsored meetings for employees (intra-agency or inter-agency), such as management or planning seminars, are not prohibited by 5 U.S.C. § 5946 since they are not meetings of a "society or association." Since there is no applicable statutory prohibition, specific statutory authority to attend government-sponsored meetings is unnecessary. Thus, the determination of whether appropriated funds may be used to pay the expenses of attending a government-sponsored meeting will generally be based on application of the necessary expense rule.

One of the recurring questions in this area is the use of appropriated funds for "retreat type" conferences. In this situation, an authorized agency official determines that the participants should get away from their normal work environment and its associated interruptions (e.g., telephones, e-mails, faxes). Oddly, it seems that the appropriate distance is often just far enough away to justify the payment of per diem allowances and reimbursement of lodging expenses. While this type of meeting may create perception problems and be criticized as extravagant, it is not illegal per se and under proper circumstances may be justified under the necessary expense rule. See B-193137, July 23, 1979.

Agency meetings at or near the participant's normal duty station may present special problems with respect to reimbursement for meals. In many cases, the use of appropriated funds to pay for meals or snacks will be not be authorized even though there is nothing improper about conducting the meeting itself.

Attendance by Military Personnel

Attendance at meetings by military personnel is specifically authorized by 37 U.S.C. § 412, which states:

> Appropriations of the Department of Defense that are available for travel may not, without the approval of the Secretary concerned or his designee, be used for expenses incident to attendance of a member of an armed force under that department at a meeting of a technical, scientific, professional, or similar organization.

This statute provides a broad exception for the Defense Department from 5 U.S.C. § 5946. The administrative approval required by the statute is a prerequisite to the availability of the appropriation and has the effect of removing the appropriation from the prohibition of 5 U.S.C. § 5946 to the extent of such approval. 34 Comp. Gen. 573, 575 (1955). Oral approval, if satisfactorily established by the record, is sufficient to meet the requirement of the statute. B-140082, August 19, 1959. However, where implementing departmental regulations establish more stringent requirements, such as advance approval in writing, the regulations will control. B-139173, June 2, 1959. The administrative approval requirement of 37 U.S.C. S412 does not apply to meetings sponsored by a federal department or agency. 50 Comp. Gen. 527 (1971).

Expenses of Nongovernment Personnel

Issues pertaining to the use of appropriated funds to pay the travel expenses of nongovernment personnel may be subdivided into two categories. One category involves payment of the expenses related to attendance by nongovernment personnel at government meetings. The other category involves payment of the expenses related to attendance by nongovernment personnel at government awards ceremonies. Different rules apply to each category.

Nongovernment Personnel Attendance at Meetings. In general, appropriated funds are not available to pay for travel, transportation, and subsistence expenses of nongovernment personnel. This prohibition has a statutory basis, 31 U.S.C. § 1345, which states:

> Sec. 1345. Expenses of meetings
> Except as specifically provided by law, an appropriation may not be used for travel, transportation, and subsistence expenses for a meeting. This section does not prohibit-
> (1) an agency from paying the expenses of an officer or employee of the United States Government carrying out an official duty;

In 14 Comp. Gen. 638 (1935), the Comptroller applied this statute and held that the Federal Housing Administration (FHA) could not pay the travel and lodging expenses for attendance at meetings of private citizens who were cooperating with FHA in a campaign to encourage the repair and modernization of real estate. GAO reasoned:

> There seems very little if any room for doubt as to the reasonable meaning and legal effect of [31 U.S.C. § 1345]. Simply stated, it is that no convention or other form of assemblage or gathering may be lodged, fed, conveyed, or furnished transportation at Government expense unless authority therefor is specifically granted by law.

Similarly, in a 1993 case, GAO found that the Environmental Protection Agency (EPA) could not use its appropriated funds to pay the travel expenses of 16 private citizens to attend a United Nations–sponsored conference at which

EPA was a participant., concluding that, "[a]bsent specific statutory authority or a direct benefit to the agency, the expenditures questioned are improper." If the gathering qualifies as a "meeting," then the use of appropriated funds for the stated purposes would be prohibited—unless specifically authorized by law. An example of such authority is language in an appropriation act making the appropriation available for "expenses of attendance at meetings" or similar language. See 34 Comp. Gen. 321 (1955); 24 Comp, Gen. 86 (1944); 17 Comp. Gen. 838 (1938); 16 Comp. Gen. 839 (1937); B-117137, September 25, 1953.

Similarly, any other statute that specifically authorizes payment of travel, transportation, or subsistence in conjunction with a meeting should suffice to overcome the prohibition of 31 U.S.C. § 1345. If the gathering does not qualify as a "meeting," then the statutory prohibition would not apply and an agency could use its appropriated funds for attendance expenses if the general "necessary expense" test is satisfied. Thus, in B-252551, May 28, 1993, 72 Comp. Gen. 229, the Comptroller General determined that DoD may expend appropriated funds for the travel and lodging costs of public school recruiters attending "job fairs" for teachers at DoD Dependent Schools if DoD determines that the proposed payments reasonably further the purpose of the appropriation charged.

In summary, an agency cannot use appropriated funds to pay for travel, transportation, and subsistence expenses of nongovernment personnel to attend a meeting unless statutorily authorized, or the gathering does not qualify as a "meeting" and the use of appropriated funds satisfies the "necessary expense" test.

Nongovernment Personnel Attendance at Award Ceremonies. Another statute that may grant an exception is the Government Employees' Incentive Awards Act, 5 U.S.C. §§ 4501-4506, which authorizes the use of appropriated funds for award ceremonies and related expenses. In addition, individual agencies often have specific authority to make awards. In B-235163.11, February 13, 1996, the Comptroller

General was asked whether appropriated funds could be used to fund the travel of the spouse of a recipient of a statutorily authorized award issued by the National Science Foundation. (The award in this case was the Waterman Award, specifically authorized by 42 U.S.C. § 1881a.) GAO allowed the proposed use of the funds and concluded:

> We have previously recognized that the authority to make an award carries with it the authority to incur necessary expenses that will contribute to effectively achieving the purpose of the award. 65 Comp. Gen. 738. In this regard, we have concluded that the travel expenses for an awardee, 32 Comp. Gen. 134 (1957), and for an awardee's spouse, 69 Comp. Gen. 38, 39 (1989), are appropriate expenses of an awards ceremony.

In response to this GAO decision, the Office of Personnel Management issued FPM Letter 451-7 (July 25, 1990), extending the exception to "any individual related by blood or affinity." Travel and miscellaneous expenses may also be paid to a surviving spouse to receive an award on behalf of a deceased recipient. B-111642, May 31, 1957. Where a recipient is handicapped and cannot travel unattended, the travel and miscellaneous expenses of an attendant, whether or not a family member, may be paid. 55 Comp. Gen. 800 (1976).

Payment of Attorneys' Fees Incurred during Contract Litigation

Attorneys' fees in the context of contract litigation may be incurred during bid protests, claims, and requests for equitable adjustment and may be incurred by the contractor, the government, or both. In this section, we will discuss whether appropriated funds may be used to pay attorney's fees under these various circumstances.

Bid Protests

Prior to 1984, a protester could not recover the attorneys' fees it incurred to file a bid protest with GAO. 57 Comp.

Gen. 125, 127 (1977); B-197174, August 25, 1980; B-192910, April 11, 1979. When the Equal Access to Justice Act (EAJA) was passed in 1980, authorizing payment of attorneys' fees in actions resulting in an "adversary adjudication" against the government under the Administrative Procedures Act (APA), a question arose regarding payment of a successful protester's attorneys' fees. Since a bid protest at GAO is not considered an adversary adjudication that is governed by the APA, the EAJA did not apply to a protester's attorneys' fees. 63 Comp. Gen 541 (1984); 62 Comp. Gen. 86 (1982); B-211105.2, January 19, 1984. (The APA defines an "adversary adjudication" as an adjudication in which the United States is represented, either by counsel or otherwise. See 5 U.S.C. § 504(a)(l), (b)(l)(C). (However, the necessary authority was provided in 1984 with enactment of the Competition in Contracting Act (CICA). (Title VII of the Deficit Reduction Act of 1984, Pub. L. No. 98-369, 98 Stat. 494, 1175 (1984).) Under CICA, upon determining that a solicitation or contract award violates a statute or regulation, the Comptroller General "may declare an appropriate interested party to be entitled to" bid and proposal preparation costs and the costs of filing and pursuing the protest, including reasonable attorney's fees. The costs and fees are payable from the contracting agency's procurement appropriations. (The use of the term "procurement appropriations" refers generally to the appropriation used to fund the protested procurement and is not a reference to a particular category of appropriation received by some agencies titled "procurement.") 31 U.S.C. § 3554(c). That section states:

> (c)(1) If the Comptroller General determines that a solicitation for a contract or a proposed award or the award of a contract does not comply with a statute or regulation, the Comptroller General may recommend that the Federal agency conducting the procurement pay to an appropriate interested party the costs of -
> (A) filing and pursuing the protest, including reasonable attorneys' fees and consultant and expert witness fees; and
> (B) bid and proposal preparation.

GAO'S approach under 31 U.S.C. § 3554(c) is to determine the entitlement to fees and costs and leave it to the protester and the agency to negotiate the appropriate amount. If the parties cannot agree, then GAO will determine the amount. 4 C.F.R. § 21.6(d) and (e). Sample cases involving awards under section 3554(c) are B-289139.2, March 6, 2002 and B-289332, February 19, 2002.

GAO has pointed out that the recovery of protest costs is neither an "award" to the protester nor is it a "penalty" imposed upon the agency, but is "intended to relieve protesters of the financial burden of vindicating the public interest." *Defense Logistics Agency—Recon.*, B-270228, Aug. 21, 1996, 96-2 CPD ¶ 80. The amount of attorney's fees and protest costs is determined by reasonableness. See, e.g., *JAFIT Enters., Inc. Claim for Costs*, B-266326.2, Mar. 31, 1997, 97-1 CPD ¶ 125 (GAO allowed only 15 percent of protest costs and fees). Attorneys' fees are limited to not more than $150 per hour.

GAO'S bid protest authority is not exclusive. A protester may seek resolution with the contracting agency, may go directly to court in lieu of filing a protest with GAO, or may seek judicial review of a GAO decision. 31 U.S.C. § 3556. Once a case is in court, 31 U.S.C. § 3554(c) no longer applies, and the court may consider a fee application under the judicial portion of EAJA. (28 U.S.C. § 2412(d)(1)(A).) E.g., *Crux Computer Corp. v. United States*, 24 Cl. Ct. 223 (1991); *Essex Electro Engineers, Inc. v. United States*, 757 F.2d 247 (Fed. Cir. 1985); *Laboratory Supply Corporation of America v. United States*, 5 Cl. Ct. 28 (1984); *Bailey v. United States*, 1 Cl. Ct. 69 (1983). The traditional rule is that only those attorneys' fees associated with the litigation are recoverable. *Cox v. United States*, 17 Cl. Ct. 29 (1989).

Contract Disputes

The Contract Disputes Act of 1978 (41 U.S.C. §§ 601-613) authorized agency boards of contract appeals to adjudicate disputes arising under or related to performance of government contracts. Under the original (1980) version of the Equal Access to Justice Act, the Court of Appeals for the Federal Circuit held that (1) a court, reviewing a decision of an agency board of contract appeals, could, under the judicial portion of EAJA, make a fee award covering services before both the board and the court, but that (2) boards of contract appeals were not authorized to independently make EAJA fee awards. *Fidelity Construction Co. v. United States*, 700 F.2d 1379 (Fed. Cir. 1983), cert. denied, 464 U.S. 826. The 1985 EAJA amendments legislatively overturned Fidelity to the extent that it held 5 U.S.C. 9504 inapplicable to boards of contract appeals.

Specifically, the law amended the definition of "adversary adjudication" to expressly include appeals to boards of contract appeals under the Contract Disputes Act. Thus, under the current law, agency boards of contract appeals may award attorneys' fees. See *The Green Shack Marketplace*, PSBCA No. 4557, March 14, 2002; *J.C. Equipment Corporation*, ASBCA No. 51321, March 4, 2002; *Hughes Moving & Storage, Inc.*, ASBCA No. 45346, 00-1 BCA ¶ 30,776 (award decision in T4D case); *Oneida Constr., Inc.*, ASBCA No. 44194, 95-2 BCA ¶ 27,893 (holding that the contractor's rejection of the agency settlement offer, which was more than the amount the board subsequently awarded, did not preclude recovery under the EAJA); *cf. Cape Tool & Die, Inc.*, ASBCA No. 46433, 95-1 BCA ¶ 27,465 (finding rates in excess of the $75 per hour guideline rate reasonable for attorneys in the Washington, D.C., area with government contracts expertise) and *Q.R. Sys. North, Inc.*, ASBCA No. 39618, 96-1 BCA ¶ 27,943 (rejecting the contractor's attempt to transfer corporate assets so as to fall within the EAJA ceiling).

The 1985 amendments also added language, at 28 U.S.C. § 2412(d), to make it clear that fee awards are authorized when a contractor appeals a contracting officer's decision directly to court instead of to a board of contract appeals, as authorized by the Contract Disputes Act.

Clothing

Clothing for federal employees is generally considered a personal expense and cannot, therefore, be purchased with appropriated funds. See, e.g., B-240271, Oct 15, 1990, where GAO held that, "[g]enerally, the cost of clothing or personal equipment to enable a federal employee to qualify himself to perform his official duties constitutes a personal expense of the employee and, as such, is not payable from appropriated funds." The long-standing rationale for this general rule was stated by the GAO as follows: "[E]very employee of the Government is required to present himself for duty properly attired according to the requirements of his position. 63 Comp. Gen. 245, 246 (1984), quoting from B-123223, June 22, 1955.

Statutory Authorities for the Purchase of Clothing
If, however, the purchase of clothing is specifically authorized by statute or can otherwise be justified under the necessary expense doctrine, then appropriated funds may be used for the purchase. Three statutes authorize the use of appropriated funds to purchase clothing.

5 U.S.C. § 7903. An example of statutory authorization for the use of appropriated funds to purchase clothing is 5 U.S.C. § 7903, which states:

> Appropriations available for the procurement of supplies and material or equipment are available for the purchase and maintenance of special clothing and equipment for the protection of personnel in the performance of their assigned tasks. For the purpose of this section, 'appropriations' includes funds made available by statute [to wholly-owned government corporations].

For an item to be authorized by 5 U.S.C. § 7903, three tests must be met: (1) the item must be "special" and not part of the ordinary and usual furnishings an employee may reasonably be expected to provide for himself; (2) the item must be for the benefit of the government, that is, essential to the safe and successful accomplishment of the work, and not solely for the protection of the employee, and (3) the employee must be engaged in hazardous duty. See 32 Comp. Gen. 229 (1952); B-193104, January 9, 1979.

Applying 5 U.S.C. § 7903, the Comptroller General has held that raincoats and umbrellas for employees who must frequently go out in the rain are not special equipment but are personal items that the employee must furnish. B-193104, January 9, 1979; B-122484, February 15, 1955. Similarly unauthorized are ordinary prescription eyeglasses (B-286137, February 21, 2001), coveralls for mechanics (B-123223, June 22, 1955) and running shoes for Department of Energy nuclear materials couriers (B-234091, July 7, 1989). Nor does 5 U.S.C § 7903 authorize reimbursement for ordinary clothing and toiletry items purchased by narcotics agents on a "moving surveillance." B-179057, May 14, 1974.

An illustration of the type of apparel authorized by 5 U.S.C. § 7903 is found in 63 Comp. Gen. 245 (1984), in which GAO advised the Office of Surface Mining that the purchase of down-filled parkas for Office of Surface Mining employees temporarily assigned to Alaska or the high country of the Western states was authorized by the statute. The purchase of clothing in this case was justified because the employee was required to work in weather conditions that were more severe than that in which the employee normally works or resides. See B-230820, April 25, 1988. For example, it is not reasonable to expect an employee who normally lives and works in Florida to own clothing suitable for Alaska in January.

5 U.S.C. § 5901. The second statute authorizing the purchase of clothing is 5 U.S.C. § 5901, the so-called Federal Employees Uniform Act. This provision authorizes annual appropriations to each agency, on a showing of necessity or desirability, to provide a uniform allowance of up to $400 a year (or more if authorized under Office of Personnel Management regulations) to each employee who wears a uniform in the performance of official duties. The agency may pay a cash allowance or may furnish the uniform.

Note that 5 U.S.C. § 5901 is merely an authorization of appropriations. An appropriation is still required for payments to be made or obligations incurred. In 35 Comp. Gen. 306 (1955), GAO stated that specific appropriation language is preferable, but recognized that the inclusion of an item for uniforms in an agency's budget request that is then incorporated into a lump-sum appropriation would be legally sufficient. An example of an item that could properly be required under 5 U.S.C. § 5901 is frocks for Department of Agriculture meat grader employees. 57 Comp. Gen. 379, 383 (1978). Another example is robes for administrative law judges of the Occupational Safety and Health Review Commission. B-199492, September 18, 1980 (the decision concluded merely that the expenditure would be legal, not that it was an especially good idea, pointing out that federal judges pay for their own robes).

An employee is not limited to only one uniform allowance per year, if changes in the employee's duties require a different type of uniform. For example, in 48 Comp. Gen. 678 (1969), a National Park Service employee was given a uniform allowance but, in less than a year, was promoted to a position that required a substantially different uniform. The Comptroller General held that the employee could receive the uniform allowance of his new position even though the sum of the two allowances would exceed the statutory annual ceiling. To hold otherwise would have been inconsistent with the statutory purpose.

While the uniform allowance under 5 U.S.C. § 5901 may be in cash or in kind, there is no similar option for "special clothing or equipment" under 5 U.S.C. § 7903. The latter statute authorizes the furnishing of covered items in kind only. 46 Comp. Gen. 170 (1966).

29 U.S.C. § 668. The third statute authorizing the purchase of clothing with appropriated funds is the Occupational Safety and Health Act of 1970 (OSHA). Section 19 of OSHA, 29 U.S.C. § 668, requires each federal agency to establish an occupational safety and health program and to acquire necessary safety and protective equipment. Thus, protective clothing may be furnished by the government if the agency head determines that it is necessary under OSHA and its implementing regulations.

Under the OSHA authority, GAO determined that the purchase of snowmobile suits, mittens, boots, and crash helmets was permissible for Department of Agriculture employees required to operate snowmobiles over rough and remote terrain. 51 Comp. Gen. 446 (1972). Similarly, GAO upheld the purchase of down-filled parkas for Interior Department employees temporarily assigned to colder weather areas away from their normal places of duty. 63 Comp. Gen. 245 (1984). See also, B-187507, December 23, 1976 (protective footwear for Drug Enforcement Administration agents assigned to temporary duty in jungle environments; the footwear remains the property of the United States and must be disposed of in accordance with the Federal Property Management Regulations); 57 Comp. Gen. 379 (1978) (special "cooler" coats and gloves for Department of Agriculture meat grader employees); B-191594, December 20, 1978 (ski boots for Forest Service snow rangers, where determined to be necessary protective equipment in a job-hazard analysis); 67 Comp.Gen, 104 (steel-toe safety shoes for an Internal Revenue Service supply clerk whose work includes moving heavy objects (1987). The discretion of federal agencies to determine what is necessary for safety and health is not unlimited, however. For example, GAO determined that 29 U.S.C. § 668 did not authorize the purchase of ordinary prescription eyeglasses (B-286137, February 21, 2001).

Application of the Necessary Expense Doctrine

If there is no specific statutory authority to purchase clothing, the agency must determine if the expenditure may be justified under the necessary expense doctrine. GAO described the analysis that should be used in 3 Comp. Gen. 433 (1924), stating:

> In the absence of specific statutory authority for the purchase of personal equipment, particularly wearing apparel or parts thereof, the first question for consideration in connection with a proposed purchase of such equipment is whether the object for which the appropriation involved was made can be accomplished as expeditiously and satisfactorily from the Government's standpoint, without such equipment. If it be determined that use of

the equipment is necessary in the accomplishment of the purposes of the appropriation, the next question to be considered is whether the equipment is such as the employee reasonably could be required to furnish as part of the personal equipment necessary to enable him to perform the regular duties of the position to which he was appointed or for which his services were engaged. Unless the answer to both of these questions is in the negative, public funds cannot be used for the purchase. In determining the first of these questions there is for consideration whether the Government or the employee receives the principal benefit resulting from use of the equipment and whether an employee reasonably could be required to perform the service without the equipment. In connection with the second question the points ordinarily involved are whether the equipment is to be used by the employee in connection with his regular duties or only in emergencies or at infrequent intervals and whether such equipment is assigned to an employee for individual use or is intended for and actually to be used by different employees.

Id. at 433-34.

Under the rule set forth in this case, GAO considered most items of apparel to be the personal responsibility of the employee. For example, in B-234091, July 7, 1989, GAO held that the "[p]urchase of running shoes by the Department of Energy (DOE) for Nuclear Materials Couriers who are required to pass fitness tests and to meet certain physical requirements is not authorized . . .[and] such a purchase [would not] be considered a necessary expense of DOE's activities." See also, B-240001, 70 Comp. Gen. 248 (1991) (Combined Federal Campaign T-shirts for employees who donated five dollars or more per pay period not authorized); 5 Comp. Gen. 318 (1925) (rubber boots and coats for custodial employees in a flood-prone area not authorized); 2 Comp. Gen. 258 (1922) (coats and gloves for government drivers not authorized).

There are limited exceptions, however, if the agency can justify the expenditure of clothing under the necessary expense doctrine. Thus, in 2 Comp. Gen. 652 (1923), caps and gowns for staff workers at Saint Elizabeth Hospital in Washington were viewed as for the protection of the patients rather than the employees and could therefore be provided from appropriated funds as part of the hospital equipment. See also, B-247683, 71 Comp. Gen. 447 (1992) (tuxedo rental or purchase for employees authorized based on requirement to be formally attired as part of job); B-229085, 67 Comp. Gen. 104 (1987) (safety shoes authorized). Similarly, aprons for general laboratory use were held permissible in 2 Comp. Gen. 382 (1922). Another exception was wading trousers for Geological Survey engineers as long as the trousers remained the property of the government and were not for the regular use of any particular employee. 4 Comp. Gen. 103 (1924).

Discussion Problem 3-4

Determine whether or not an agency could properly use appropriated funds to purchase each of the following items of clothing. If you determine that the use of appropriated funds is proper, identify the basis (5 U.S.C. § 7903, 5 U.S.C. § 5901, 29 U.S.C. § 668, or the necessary expense doctrine).

1. A radiation suit for the Environmental Protection Agency (EPA) employees who must conduct soil samples at nuclear test sites in the Nevada desert
2. Polarized sunglasses and sunscreen for the same EPA employees
3. Uniforms for agency security personnel
4. Insulated snow boots for Federal Emergency Management Agency (FEMA) employees while assigned to temporary duty in Alaska away from their normal place of duty at the Miami, Florida, FEMA office.
5. Insulated snow boots for FEMA employees assigned to the Northern North Dakota FEMA office
6. Anthrax filtration masks for agency personnel working in the mailroom during periods of heightened anthrax alerts.

Entertainment

The general rule regarding entertainment is that appropriated funds may not be used to purchase entertainment except when specifically authorized by statute and authorized or approved by proper administrative officers. E.g., 43 Comp. Gen. 305 (1963). The basis for the rule is that entertainment is essentially a personal expense even where it occurs in some business-related context.

Statutory authority is required because, in most cases, it would be difficult to justify the use of appropriated funds for entertainment under the necessary expense doctrine. Such expenses will generally not be necessary to carry out the purpose of an appropriation. It should be apparent that the government views the use of appropriated funds for entertainment much more restrictively than private industry views the use of corporate funds for similar purposes.

Entertainment is generally considered a cost of business development and, therefore, a "necessary expense" for corporate growth. Even though federal agencies have been encouraged to conduct their business more like the private sector over the past few years, the use of appropriated funds for entertainment is one of several areas where distinctions are likely to remain. The difference, and the policy underlying the rule for the government, is summarized in B-223678, June 5, 1989:

> The theory is not so much that these items can never be business-related, because sometimes they clearly are. Rather, what the decisions are really saying is that, because public confidence in the integrity of those who spend the taxpayer's money is essential, certain items which may appear frivolous or wasteful—however legitimate they may in fact be in a specific context—should, if they are to be charged to public funds, be authorized specifically by the Congress.

Thus, the underlying basis for the different approaches to entertainment expenses taken by private industry and the federal government is based on public trust and the government's concern with avoiding the appearance of impropriety.

The Definition of "Entertainment"

The term "entertainment," as used in decisions of the Comptroller General and the Comptroller of the Treasury, is an "umbrella" term that includes food and drink (either as formal meals or as snacks or refreshments); receptions, banquets, and the like; music, live or recorded; live artistic performances; and recreational facilities. The definition also includes one other category that, even though not "entertainment" in the same sense as the other examples, is closely related to the entertainment cases. The additional category pertains to facilities for the welfare or morale of employees.

One of the favorite topics in the entertainment cases seems to involve liquor and other alcoholic beverages. In some circumstances, GAO has found it appropriate for an agency to purchase alcoholic beverages. In B-20085, September 10, 1941, it held: "Where an appropriation expressly provides in general terms for entertainment of officials and others, the selection of form of entertainment must of necessity rest largely within the sound discretion of the administrative officer concerned." In that case, the Coordinator of Inter-American Affairs asked whether authorized entertainment could include such items as cocktail parties, banquets and dinners, theater attendance, and sightseeing parties. The Comptroller General, recognizing that an appropriation for entertainment conferred considerable discretion, replied, in effect, "all of the above." Similarly, responding to an inquiry from the Navy, a Comptroller of the Treasury decided that: "Entertainments . . . without wines, liquors or cigars, would be like the play of Hamlet with the melancholy Dane entirely left out of the lines." 14 Comp. Dec. 344, 346 (1907). Of course, the critical factor in both cases is that the agency was specifically authorized to provide entertainment; the purchase of alcoholic beverages was considered a reasonable implementation of that authority.

Food

Perhaps the most common misapplication of appropriated funds is their use to purchase food for government employees at their normal duty location. Although there are exceptions, as a general rule, appropriated funds are not available to pay for food for government employees at their official duty stations. Food is considered a personal expense and government salaries are presumed adequate to enable employees to eat regularly. See 65 Comp. Gen. 738, 739 (1986). In addition, furnishing free food might violate 5 U.S.C. § 5536, which prohibits an employee from receiving compensation in addition to the pay and allowances fixed by law. See, e.g., 68 Comp. Gen. 46, 48 (1988); 42 Comp. Gen. 149, 151 (1962); B-140912, November 24, 1959.

The "no free food" rule applies to snacks and refreshments as well as meals. For example, in 47 Comp. Gen. 657 (1968), the Comptroller General held that Internal Revenue Service appropriations were not available to serve coffee to either employees or private individuals at meetings. Similarly prohibited was the purchase of coffeemakers and cups. Although serving coffee or refreshments at meetings may be desirable, it is not a "necessary expense" in the context of appropriations availability. See also B-159633, May 20, 1974.

The question of food for government employees arises in many contexts, and there are certain well-defined exceptions to the general prohibition on the use of appropriated funds to purchase food. For example, the government may pay for the meals of civilian and military personnel in travel status because there is specific statutory authority to do so. 5 U.S.C. § 5702 (civilian employees); 37 U.S.C. § 404 (military personnel). The rule and exception are illustrated by 65 Comp. Gen. 16 (1985), in which the issue was whether the National Oceanic and Atmospheric Administration could provide in-flight meals, at government expense, to persons on extended flights on government aircraft engaged in weather research. The Comptroller General determined that meals could be purchased for government personnel in travel status, but not for anyone else, including government employees not in official travel status.

While feeding employees at their normal duty locations may not be regarded as a "necessary expense" as a general proposition, it may qualify as such when the agency is carrying out some particular statutory function where the agency can establish the necessary relationship between the statutory function and the purchase of food. Thus, in B-201186, March 4, 1982, it was a permissible implementation of a statutory accident prevention program for the Marine Corps to set up rest stations on highways leading to a Marine base to serve coffee and doughnuts to Marines returning from certain holiday weekends. The agency was able to demonstrate the relationship between the coffee and doughnuts and the statutory safety program.

Exceptions of this type once again make the point that the necessary expense doctrine is highly fact specific and what may be necessary in one context may not be necessary in another. For example, in B-230382, Dec. 22, 1989, the Comptroller General held that coffee and donuts at the employee's normal duty location were an unauthorized entertainment expense and could not, therefore, be purchased with appropriated funds. Thus, it is not the type of food purchased that is determinative; the key issue is the connection between the food and either the agency's mission or some statutory objective.

There are exceptions, however. These include:

Unusual Conditions at the Employee's Usual Duty Location. When a government employee must work under severe conditions, it may be permissible to purchase food for the employee with appropriated funds. This is a narrow exception, and some element of an emergency must be present. For example, in 53 Comp. Gen. 71 (1973), the unauthorized occupation of a building in which the Bureau of Indian Affairs was located necessitated the assembling of a team of General Services Administration special police, who had to remain in the building overnight. Agency officials purchased and brought in sandwiches and coffee for the team. GAO concluded that it would not question the agency's determination that the expenditure was incidental to the protection of government property during an extreme emergency and approved reimbursement. The decision emphasized, however, that it was an exception and that the general rule would still apply in less urgent circumstances.

A similar exception was permitted in B-189003, July 5, 1977, where agents of the Federal Bureau of Investigation had been stranded in their office during a severe blizzard in Buffalo, New York. The area was in a state of emergency and was later declared a national disaster area. GAO agreed with the agency's determination that the situation presented a danger to human life. The rationale of 53 Comp. Gen. 71 and B-189003 was applied in B-232487, January 26, 1989, for government employees required to work continually for a 24-hour period to evacuate and secure an area threatened by the derailment of a train carrying toxic liquids.

The exception, however, is limited. The requirement to remain on duty for a 24-hour period, without more, is not enough. In B-185159, December 10, 1975, for example, the cost of meals was denied to Treasury Department agents required to work more than 24 hours investigating a bombing of federal offices. The Comptroller General pointed out that dangerous conditions alone are not enough. Under the exception established in 53 Comp. Gen. 71, it is necessary to find that the situation involves imminent danger to human life or the destruction of federal property. Also, in that case, the agents were investigating a dangerous situation that had already occurred, and there was no suggestion that any further bombings were imminent.

A similar case is B-217261, April 1, 1985, involving a Customs Service official required to remain in a motel room for several days on a surveillance assignment. See also 16 Comp. Gen. 158 (1936); B-202104, July 2, 1981; and, more recently, B-272985, December 30, 1996 (CIA may not use appropriated funds to pay all or part of the cost of meals purchased by members of the Director of Central Intelligence's security detail while providing 24-hour security to the Director or Deputy Director at their normal duty station because there was no evidence of an emergency situation involving danger to human life or destruction of federal property).

Short of the emergency situation described in B-189003, July 5, 1977 (severe blizzard), inclement weather is not enough to support an exception. There are numerous cases in which employees have spent the night in motels rather than returning home in a snowstorm in order to be able to get to work the following day. Reimbursement for meals has consistently been denied in these cases. See, e.g., 68 Comp. Gen. 46 (1988); 64 Comp. Gen. 70 (1984); B-226403, May 19, 1987; B-200779, August 12, 1981; B-188985, August 23, 1977. It does not matter that the employee was directed by his or her supervisor to rent the room (B-226403 and B-188985) or that the federal government in Washington was shut down (68 Comp. Gen. 46) because of a heavy snowstorm. The rationale for this rule is that a supervisor does not have the authority to direct an employee to spend the night in a hotel room. See B-226403 (The erroneous exercise of authority does not bind the government).

As in all other potentially suspect expenses, statutory authority will overcome the prohibition. Thus, since the Veterans Administration (VA) had statutory authority to accept uncompensated services and to contract for related "necessary services, " the VA could, upon an administrative determination of necessity, contract with local restaurants for meals to be furnished without charge to uncompensated volunteer workers at VA outpatient clinics when their scheduled assignment extended over a meal period. B-145430, May 9, 1961. There is also statutory authority to make subsistence payments to law enforcement officials and members of their immediate families when threats to their lives force them to occupy temporary accommodations. 5 U.S.C. § 5706a.

> **Discussion Problem 3-5**
>
> Employees of the United States Information Agency (USIA) who serve as "escort officers" for the agency's International Visitors Program are issued travel orders authorizing them to travel from Washington, D.C. (their official duty station) to various cities and return. Under the International Visitors Program, the designated escort officers are with the visitors or on call around the clock throughout their visit and are responsible for making the visitors' experience as meaningful as possible. As such, the escort officers incur the expenses of staying in the same hotels and eating at the same restaurants as the visitors. Since the employees incur the costs in pursuit of their duties, the agency contends that they may be reimbursed with appropriated funds. Is the agency correct? (Based on B-233130, May 19, 1989)

Food in Conjunction with Meetings and Conferences. For meetings sponsored by nongovernment organizations, the attendee will commonly be charged a fee, often referred to as a registration or conference fee. If a single fee is charged covering both attendance and meals and no separate charge is made for meals, the government may pay the full fee (assuming, of course, that funds are otherwise available for the cost of attendance). 38 Comp. Gen. 134 (1958); B-66978, August 25, 1947. The same is true for an evening social event where the cost is a mandatory nonseparable element of the registration fee. 66 Comp. Gen. 350 (1987). The key element in such situations is that the meal charge is not severable from the conference or registration fee.

If a separate charge is made for meals, the authority of the government to pay for the meals is somewhat more limited. In these circumstances, the government may pay for the meals only if there is a showing that (1) the meals are incidental to the meeting, (2) attendance of the employee at the meals is necessary to full participation in the business of the conference, and (3) the employee is not free to take the meals elsewhere without being absent from essential formal discussions, lectures, or speeches concerning the purpose of the conference. B-160579, April 26, 1978; B-166560, February 3, 1970. If one or more of these factors is missing, the government may not pay for the meals. B-154912, August 26, 1964; B-152924, December 18, 1963; B-95413, June 7, 1950; B-88258, September 19, 1949.

The GAO cases in this area indicate that these rules apply regardless of whether the conference takes place within the employee's duty station area or someplace else. Where the government is authorized to pay for meals under the above principles, the employee normally cannot be reimbursed for purchasing alternate meals. See B-193504, August 9, 1979; B-186820, February 23, 1978.

The cases make clear that personal taste is irrelevant in determining the availability of appropriated funds to purchase food. Thus, if the meal provided under the all-inclusive conference fee is liver and onions with sour cream, an employee who dislikes this offering will either have to eat it anyway, pay for a substitute meal from his or her own pocket, or go without. For an employee on travel or temporary duty status, which is where this rule usually applies, per diem is reduced by the value of the meals provided. E.g., 60 Comp. Gen. 181, 183-84 (1981). The rule will not apply, however, where the employee is unable to eat the meal provided (and cannot arrange for an acceptable substitute) because of bona fide medical or religious reasons. B-231703, October 31, 1989 (per diem not required to be reduced where the employee, an Orthodox Jew who could not obtain kosher meals at the conference, purchased substitute meals elsewhere).

In contrast, attendance at *agency*-sponsored meetings and conferences will generally be subject to the prohibition on furnishing free food to employees at their official duty stations. Thus, the cost of meals and coffee breaks could not be provided for government officials attending a one-day conference on implementation of the Speedy Trial Act. B-188078, May 5, 1977. Similarly, meals could not be provided at a conference of field examiners of the National Credit Union Administration. B-180806, August 21, 1974. Use of appropriated funds was prohibited for coffee breaks at a management seminar, B-159633, May 20, 1974; meals served during "working sessions" at Department of Labor business meetings, B-168774, January 23, 1970; and meals at monthly luncheon meetings for officials of law enforcement agencies, B-198882, March 25, 1981. See also 47 Comp. Gen. 657 (1968); B-45702, November 22, 1944 and B-270199, Aug. 6, 1996. In B-137999, December 16, 1958, the commissioners of the Outdoor Recreation Resources Review Commission had statutory authority to be reimbursed for actual subsistence expenses. This was held to include the cost of lunches during meetings at a Washington hotel. However, the cost of lunches for *staff members* of the Commission could not be paid.

The relevant GAO decisions indicate that form will not prevail over substance. Thus, merely calling the cost of meals a "registration fee" will not avoid the prohibition. In B-182527, February 12, 1975, the cost of meals was disallowed for Army employees at an Army-sponsored "operations and maintenance seminar." The charge had been termed a registration fee but covered only luncheons, dinner, and coffee breaks. See also B-195045, February 8, 1980. In B-187150, October 14, 1976, grant funds provided to the government of the District of Columbia under the Social Security Act for personnel training and administrative expenses could not be used to pay for a luncheon at a four-hour conference of officials of the D.C. Department of Human Resources. The conference could not be reasonably characterized as training and did not qualify as an allowable administrative cost under the program regulations. Thus, the general rule applicable to the purchase of food in conjunction with agency-sponsored meetings is that, absent statutory authority, appropriated funds are not available.

This is not to say that the rules for meals at nongovernment meetings and conferences will *never* apply to government-sponsored meetings at the employee's duty station.

There have been cases in which GAO applied the three-part test applicable to meals at nongovernment sponsored meetings. For example, in 1980, the President's Committee on Employment of the Handicapped held its annual meeting in the Washington Hilton Hotel. The meeting was to last for three days and included a luncheon and two banquets. There was no registration fee for the meeting, but there were charges for the meals. GAO'S Equal Employment Opportunity Office planned to send three employees to the meeting and asked whether the agency could pick up the tab for the meals. The three employees were to make a presentation at the meeting, and it seemed clear that attendance was authorized under 5 U.S.C. § 4110. Also, if a nonseverable registration fee were involved, under the decisions discussed above, payment would have presumably been authorized. The Comptroller General applied the three-part test applicable to nongovernment meetings and held that the GAO could pay for the meals if administrative determinations were made that (1) the meals were incidental to the meeting, (2) attendance at the meals was necessary for full participation at the meeting, and (3) the employees would miss essential formal discussions, lectures, or speeches concerning the purpose of the meeting if they took their meals elsewhere. B-198471, May 1, 1980.

As a result of this decision, many agencies attempted to justify the use of appropriated funds to purchase food in conjunction with government meetings. GAO determined that it was necessary to issue several additional decisions to clarify B-198471 to explain precisely what that decision does and does not authorize. In 64 Comp. Gen. 406 (1985), the Comptroller General held that the cost of meals could not be reimbursed for employees attending monthly meetings of the Federal Executive Association within their duty station area. The meetings were essentially luncheon meetings at which representatives of various government agencies could discuss matters of mutual interest. The decision stated:

> What distinguishes [B-198471] is that the President's annual meeting was a 3-day affair with meals clearly inci-

dental to the overall meeting, while in [the cases in which reimbursement has been denied] the only meetings which "took place were the ones which took place during a luncheon meal. . . .In order to meet the three-part test [of B-198471], a meal must be part of a formal meeting or conference that includes not only functions such as speeches or business carried out during a seating at a meal but also includes substantial functions that take place separate from the meal. [W]e are unwilling to conclude that a meeting which lasts no longer than the meal during which it is conducted qualifies for reimbursement.

Id. at 408.

A similar case the following year, 65 Comp. Gen. 508 (1986), reiterated that the above-quoted test of 64 Comp. Gen. 406 must precede the application of the three-part test of B-198471. The three-part test, and hence the authority to reimburse, relates to a meal that is incident to a meeting, not a meeting that is incident to a meal. 65 Comp. Gen. at 510; 64 Comp. Gen. at 408. In other words, if the meeting consists of nothing more than discussions over a meal, then appropriated funds cannot be used to pay for the meal and application of the three-part test is not triggered.

Two other decisions, 68 Comp. Gen. 604 and 68 Comp. Gen. 606, provided further clarification of the "food at government meetings" rules, holding that 5 U.S.C. § 4110 (which makes travel appropriations available for expenses of attendance at meetings "which are concerned with the functions or activities for which the appropriation is made or which will contribute to improved conduct, supervision, or management of the functions or activities") and B-198471 do not authorize purely internal business meetings or conferences sponsored by government agencies. Both decisions explained the rationale for this holding as follows:

> We think . . . that there is a clear distinction between the payment of meals incidental to formal conferences or meetings, typically externally organized or sponsored, involving topical matters of general interest to govern-

mental and nongovernmental participants, and internal business or informational meetings primarily involving the day-to-day operations of government. With respect to the latter, 5 U.S.C. § 4110 has little bearing.

68 Comp. Gen. At 605 and 608.

One of the decisions specifically stated that the claim "should have been summarily rejected based on the application of the general rule." 68 Comp. Gen. at 609. In a more recent case, however, GAO has held that appropriated funds may be used to pay for meals if the meals are part of an all-inclusive facility rental fee. See *Payment of a Non-Negotiable, Non-Separable Facility Rental Fee that Covered the Cost of Food Service at NRC Workshops*, B-281063, Dec. 1, 1999, (unpub.) (payment of fee was proper because fee was all-inclusive, not negotiable, and competitively priced to those that did not include food). In summary, appropriated funds may be used to purchase food at government-sponsored meetings if: (1) authorized by statute, (2) authorized as a "necessary expense" under the three part test applied in B-19847, or (3) the food is included in an all-inclusive facility rental fee.

Agencies should also check applicable travel regulations, which may authorize payment for "light refreshments" as part of the agency's overall administrative costs of hosting government-sponsored conferences. See, e.g., Federal Travel Regulation, Part 301-74. See also Joint Federal Travel Regulation (JFTR), Part G: Conference Planning, ¶ 2550; Joint Travel Regulation (JTR), Part S: Conference Planning, ¶ 4950. The conference must involve attendee travel. JFTR, ¶ U2550, D; JTR ¶ 4950, D. A "conference" is defined as a "meeting, retreat, seminar, symposium or . . . training activities that are conferences . . ." *Id.*

Of course, if the meeting or conference does not have the necessary connection with official agency business, the cost of meals may not be paid regardless of who sponsors the meeting or where it is held. Thus, a registration fee consisting primarily of the cost of a luncheon was disallowed for three Community Services Administration employees attending a Federal Executive Board meeting at which Combined Federal Campaign awards were to be presented. B-195045, February 8, 1980. Similarly, an employee of the Department of Housing and Urban Development could not be reimbursed for meals incident to meetings of a local business association. B-166560, May 27, 1969.

Food in Conjunction with Training. Under the Government Employees Training Act, an agency may pay, or reimburse an employee for, necessary expenses incident to an authorized training program. 5 U.S.C. § 4109. The Comptroller General has held that the government can provide meals under this authority if the agency determines that providing meals is *necessary* to achieve the objectives of the training program. 48 Comp. Gen. 185 (1968); 39 Comp. Gen. 119 (1959); B-193955, September 14, 1979; B-244473, Jan. 13, 1992. The government may also furnish meals to nongovernment speakers as an expense of conducting the training. 48 Comp. Gen. 185. In 50 Comp. Gen. 610 (1971), the Training Act was held to authorize the procurement of catering services for a Department of Agriculture training conference where government facilities were deemed inadequate in view of the nature of the program.

If providing the meals is not "necessary" to achieve the objectives of the training, then GAO is likely to find the purchase of meals improper. In B-270199, August 6, 1996, GAO determined that although providing the meals achieved objectives that were "desirable," the meals were not "necessary," and therefore could not be purchased with appropriated funds. GAO explained its rationale as follows:

> At the senior executive breakfast seminars, the food was provided during a preliminary social gathering of seminar attendees or at coffee breaks. The stated purpose of providing the food was not the training itself, but rather "to maximize the time of these busy executives," "to get the participants acquainted and interacting," and to improve the "on time attendance" of the participants. Although all of these objectives clearly were desirable from the perspective of those who managed the seminars,

they were not "necessary" to the training. Had no food been provided, i.e., had the employees obtained breakfast or beverages with their own resources, the training would have occurred as planned and the objectives of the training would have been achieved nonetheless.

This case provides a useful indication of which purported justifications the GAO will *not* find persuasive.

As in the cases involving meals at meetings and conferences, GAO has not allowed form to rule over substance, and the fact that an agency characterizes its meeting as "training" is not controlling. In other words, for purposes of authorizing the government to feed participants, something does not become training simply because it is *called* training. In B-168774, September 2, 1970, headquarters employees of the (then) Department of Health, Education, and Welfare met with consultants in a nearby hotel at what the agency termed a "research training conference." However, the conference consisted of little more than "working sessions" and included no employee training as defined in the Government Employees Training Act. Therefore, the cost of meals could not be paid using appropriated funds. See also B-247563.4, December 11, 1996; 68 Comp. Gen. 606 (1989); B-208527, September 20, 1983; B-187150, October 14, 1976; B-140912, November 24, 1959.

If, however, the training is legitimate, the fact that it takes place near the attendee's duty station will not affect the agency's ability to pay for meals in support of the training. In 65 Comp. Gen. 143 (1985), GAO held that a Social Security Administration employee who had been invited as a guest speaker at the opening day luncheon of a legitimate agency training conference in the vicinity of her duty station could be reimbursed for the cost of the meal.

Food in Conjunction with Award Ceremonies. An agency may use its general operating appropriations to provide refreshments at award ceremonies authorized under the Government Employees Incentive Awards Act. 65 Comp. Gen. 738 (1986). This result is consistent with guidance from the Office of Personnel Management contained in the Federal Personnel Manual. Similarly, in 65 Comp. Gen. 738, the Social Security Administration asked whether it could use operating appropriations, apart from its limited entertainment appropriation, to provide refreshments at its annual awards ceremony. GAO observed that the Incentive Awards Act (5 U.S.C. § 4503) authorizes agencies to "pay a cash award to, and incur necessary expense for the honorary recognition of" employees. The decision reasoned that the concept of a necessary expense is, within limits, a relative one based on the relationship of the expenditure to the particular appropriation or program involved. Thus, while the necessary expense rule would generally not permit the purchase of refreshments in an agency's normal day-to-day operations, it would be within an agency's discretion to determine that refreshments would materially enhance the effectiveness of a statutorily authorized award ceremony.

This 1986 decision essentially followed B-167835, November 18, 1969, which had concluded that the Incentive Awards Act authorized NASA to fund part of the cost of a banquet at which the President was to present the Medal of Freedom to the Apollo 11 astronauts. See also B-270327, March 12, 1997 (agency may spend $20.00 per person for luncheons provided at awards ceremonies pursuant to the Government Employees Incentive Awards Act).

An interesting twist on this line of cases was presented in B-271511, March 4, 1997, in which the National Security Agency (NSA) wanted to use appropriated funds to purchase food vouchers to be used as nonmonetary awards under the Government Employees Incentive Awards Act. The Office of Personnel Management (OPM), which is the agency responsible for establishing the policies and instructions for carrying out the act, had no objection to NSA's purchase of food vouchers as nonmonetary awards. Relying on OPM's opinion, NSA requested a formal opinion from GAO. GAO permitted NSA's proposed use of funds, reasoning that:

> Nothing in the Act prohibits OPM, or agencies generally with OPM's concurrence, from authorizing award programs under which merchandise is used as a form of

award. Nor does anything compel treating food differently from other merchandise for purposes of the Act. Accordingly, given the views expressed by OPM, we have no basis to object to NSA's use of its appropriations for food or food vouchers of nominal value as informal recognition awards pursuant to the Act.

Of course, the ceremony at which the government-purchased food is provided must be a legitimate award ceremony under the act. The act does not authorize expenditures for food or for "light refreshments" in connection with an event or function designed to achieve other objectives simply because the agency distributes awards as part of the event or function. For example, in B-247563.4, December 11, 1996, the agency used appropriated funds to purchase a buffet breakfast for its employees who were being recognized with a special performance award. GAO determined that the expenditures were improper because the breakfast buffet was not a legitimate award ceremony. GAO based its determination on the fact that no employees other than the 45 specifically recognized and the agency director participated in the event and there was no evidence that the awards were publicized within the agency. Noting that one of the purposes of the Incentive Awards Act is to facilitate public recognition of award recipients, GAO found that this purpose is not served where the award recipients and the donor are the only participants at the event and concluded that the agency's use of appropriated funds for the breakfast refreshments was improper.

However, since the Incentive Awards Act applies only to federal employees, GAO has disallowed the cost of refreshments at an awards ceremony for persons who were not federal employees (and therefore not authorized under the Incentive Awards Act nor governed by the "necessary expense" language of that statute). Presumably, this inapplicability of the Incentive Awards Act to nonfederal employees also means that the act does not authorize the use of appropriated funds to purchase food vouchers as nonmonetary awards for nonfederal employees, as was permitted in the case of federal employees in B-271511, March 4, 1997.

Finally, although the Incentive Awards Act does not apply to members of the armed forces, the uniformed services have similar authority, including the identical "necessary expense" language, in 10 U.S.C. § 1124. Therefore, the rule applied in the Social Security Administration case (65 Comp. Gen. 738) applies equally to military award ceremonies conducted under the authority of 10 U.S.C. § 1124. 65 Comp. Gen. at 739 n.2. (There is another statute, 10 U.S.C. § 1125, that authorizes the Secretary of Defense to award medals, trophies, badges, etc., to members/units of armed forces for accomplishments. However, since this statute does not have the express "incur necessary expense" language of 5 U.S.C. § 4503 or 10 U.S.C. § 1124, appropriated funds could not be used to pay for meals under the rationale discussed here.)

Food in Conjunction with Cultural and Ethnic Programs. Agencies may use appropriated funds to pay for entertainment (including food) in furtherance of equal opportunity training programs. In B-200017, 60 Comp. Gen. 303 (1981), GAO overruled several prior cases and approved funding for meals in support of a National Black History Month ceremony. In that case, the IRS asked whether it could certify a voucher covering payments for a performance by an African dance troupe and lunches for guest speakers at a ceremony observing National Black History Month. The Comptroller General determined that the expenditure was proper and held:

> [W]e now take the view that we will consider a live artistic performance as an authorized part of an agency's EEO effort if, as in this case, it is part of a formal program determined by the agency to be intended to advance EEO objectives, and consists of a number of different types of presentations designed to promote EEO training objectives of making the audience aware of the culture or ethnic history being celebrated.

Id. at 306. See also B-278805, July 21, 1999 (GAO held that the agency reasonably concluded that a program commemorating Irish-American Month that included musicians playing and explaining the history and meaning of Irish songs furthered EEO objectives by expanding employees' cultural understanding and awareness).

The rule in the IRS case (60 Comp. Gen. 303) was expanded in B-199387, March 23, 1982, to include small "samples" of ethnic foods prepared and served during a formal ethnic awareness program as part of the agency's equal employment opportunity program. In the particular program being considered, the attendees were to pay for their own lunches, with the ethnic food samples of minimal proportion provided as a separate event. Thus, the samples could be distinguished from meals or refreshments, which remain unauthorized.

Many agencies have issued regulatory guidance on this topic, and these regulations should be consulted prior to the obligation or expenditure of funds under the ethnic food exception. For example, the Air Force's Budget Guidance Manual states:

> 4.26.1.2. Sponsoring Air Force activities may use appropriated funds to purchase small "samples" of ethnic foods prepared and served during a formal ethnic awareness program. The samples should be of minimal proportion and are not intended to serve as meals or refreshments.

AFI 65-601, vol. 1, para. 4.26.1.2.

Of course, a multitude of samples can become a meal and this will no doubt be the subject of a future GAO opinion.

> **Discussion Problem 3-6**
>
> On March 8, 2002, the President proclaims March 2002 as Irish-American Heritage Month, urging Americans to observe the month with appropriate ceremonies and activities. On March 9, 2002, the Director, Office of Equal Employment Opportunity, United States International Trade Commission, submits a "Requisition for Supplies, Equipment, or Services" to procure the services of an Irish band to perform for Commission employees on St. Patrick's day. The musicians are to be part of a program presenting factual information about the Irish culture, including an explanation by the musicians of the history of each song. The event will include "traditional Irish meals." The total expense for the band and the food will be $1,500. Can the agency use its appropriated funds for this purpose?

Official Representation Funds

Representation funds are appropriations made available to executive branch agencies that may be expended without the normal statutory controls and are appropriated for "emergency and extraordinary expenses." Congress recognizes that many agencies have a legitimate need for items that otherwise would be prohibited as entertainment, and has historically provided representation funds for such purposes—within limitations. See Act of March 3, 1795, 1 Stat. 438.

Representation funds originated from the need to permit officials of agencies whose activities involve substantial contact with foreign officials to reciprocate for courtesies extended to them by foreign officials. For example, the State Department would find it difficult to accomplish its mission if it could not spend any money entertaining foreign officials. In fact, some of the early representation funds were limited to entertaining non-U.S. citizens, and some could only be spent overseas. However, such restrictions are rarely seen today.

Representation funds may take various forms. Some agencies have their own well-established structures, which may include permanent legislation. For example, the State Department has permanent authorization to pay for official entertainment. 22 U.S.C. § 4085. See also 22 U.S.C. § 2671, which authorizes expenditures for "unforeseen emergencies" (which may include official entertainment in certain contexts). The authority of 22 U.S.C. § 4085 is implemented by means of annual appropriations under the heading "representation allowances." Pub. L. No. 107-77 (2002). Agencies may use representation funds for a broad variety of purposes, provided the use is consistent with the general purpose of such funds. For example, State Department representation allowances have been found available for rental of formal evening wear by embassy officials accompanying the Ambassador to the United Kingdom in presenting his credentials to the Queen, 68 Comp. Gen. 638 (1989); hiring extra waiters and busboys to serve at official functions at foreign posts, 64 Comp. Gen. 138 (1984); and meals for certain embassy officials at Rotary Club meetings in Tanzania, if approved by the local Chief of Mission, B-232165, June 14, 1989.

The Defense Department also has its own structure. Under 10 U.S.C. § 127, the Secretary of Defense, or of a military department, within the limitations of appropriations made for that purpose, may use funds to "provide for any emergency or extraordinary expense which cannot be anticipated or classified." When so provided in an appropriation, the official may spend the funds "for any purpose he determines to be proper." Annual operation and maintenance appropriations include amounts for "emergencies and extraordinary expenses." Although the title is not particularly revealing, it has long been understood that official representation expenses are charged to this account. See Internal Controls: Defense's Use of Emergency and Extraordinary Funds, GAO/AFMD-86-44 (June 4, 1986); DoD Use of Official Representation Funds to Entertain Foreign Dignitaries, GAO/ID-83-7 (December 29, 1982); 69 Comp. Gen. 197 (1990) (reception for newly assigned commander at U.S. Army School of the Americas); B-221257-O.M., February 6, 1986.

For DoD, the language typically used to provide representation funds reads as follows:

> For expenses, not otherwise provided for, necessary for the operation and maintenance of the Air Force, as authorized by law; and not to exceed $7,998,000 can be used for emergencies and extraordinary expenses, to be expended on the approval or authority of the Secretary of the Air Force.

DoD Fiscal Year 2002 Appropriations Act, Pub. L. No. 107-117.

Aside from these two major exceptions for the State Department and DoD, most agencies receive their entertainment funds, if they receive them at all, simply as part of their annual appropriations. The appropriation may specify that it will be available for "entertainment." See, e.g., B-20085, September 10, 1941. More commonly, however, the term used in the appropriation is "official reception and representation." This has come to be the technical "appropriations language" for entertainment. When the "official reception and representation" funds are appropriated as a subaccount of a more general appropriation, the funds are available for the same period as the more general appropriation. Thus, if the representation funds are a subaccount of an annual appropriation, their period of availability for obligation is one year. If the representation funds are a subaccount of a "no-year" appropriation, they are available until expended.

> **Discussion Problem 3-7**
>
> Each fiscal year, the Department of Energy (DOE) receives a no-year appropriation titled: "departmental administration." In each such appropriation, Congress authorizes DOE to use a specified, "not to exceed" portion of its departmental administration appropriation for official reception and representation (R&R) activities. For the last several years, the "not to exceed" amount has been $50,000 per year. However, DOE has only obligated half of this amount for each year of the past three years and now has an unobligated balance of $125,000 ($75,000 carried forward from the prior three years plus $50,000 appropriated for the current fiscal year).
>
> If the current appropriation contains the "not to exceed" $50,000 language, how much can DOE obligate and expend in the current fiscal year? Is it $50,000, $125,000, or some other amount? (Based on *Availability of Department of Energy Reception and Representation Funds*, B-274576 January 13, 1997)

The GAO cases addressing representation funds make clear that use of these funds is not limited to the entertainment of foreign nationals, unless the appropriation language states such a limitation. The experience of the former HEW provides further evidence that, absent some indication to the contrary, Congress does not intend that an "official R&R" appropriation be limited to entertaining foreign nationals. The Secretary of HEW first received an entertainment appropriation in HEW's FY 1960 appropriation act, but it was limited to certain foreign visitors. The language was changed to "official reception and representation" in HEW's FY 1964 appropriation. The conference report on the 1964 appropriation explained that the change was intended to expand the scope of the appropriation to include U.S. citizens as well as foreign visitors. H.R. Conf. Rep. No. 774, 88th Cong., 1st Sess 11 (1963).

The scope of permissible entertainees is often specified in an agency's regulations pertaining to representation funds. For example, the applicable DoD directive states:

> 3. POLICY
> It is DoD policy that:
> 3.1. ORFs shall be used to maintain the standing and prestige of the United States by extending official courtesies to guests of the Department of Defense. Authorized guests include distinguished and prominent citizens who have made a substantial contribution to the United States or the Department of Defense, including individuals who are recognized leaders in their fields of expertise; dignitaries and officials of local, county, State, and Federal Governments; and dignitaries and officials from foreign governments.

DoD Directive 7250.13, *Official Representation Funds* (23 February 1989).

It is clear that representation funds have traditionally been sought, justified, and granted in the context of an agency's need to interact with various nongovernment individuals or organizations. Precisely who these individuals or organizations might be will vary with the agency. Of course, the fact that the thrust of the appropriation is the entertainment of nongovernment persons does not mean that government persons are excluded. For example, it has long been recognized that persons from other agencies (and by necessary implication members of the host agency as well) may be included incident to an authorized entertainment function for nongovernment persons. E.g., B-84184, March 17, 1949. Since the use of representation funds is so agency-specific, one must consult the applicable agency regulations to fully understand what can and cannot be properly purchased. See, e.g., DoD Directive 7250.13, *Official Representation Funds* (23 February 1989), AR 37-47, *Representation Funds of the Secretary of the Army* (31 May 1996); AFI 65-603, *Official Representation Funds: Guidance and Procedures* (1 Nov 1997); SECNAV 7042.7, *Guidelines for Use of Official Representation Funds* (5 Dec 1998) for the rules applicable to DoD agencies.

An agency has wide discretion in the use of its representation funds. 61 Comp. Gen. 260, 266 (1982); B-212634, October 12, 1983. As a general proposition, "official agency events, typically characterized by a mixed ceremonial, social and/or business purpose, and hosted in a formal sense by high level agency officials" and relating to a function of the agency will not be questioned. B-223678, June 5, 1989. Accordingly, R&R funds have been found available for a Christmas party for government officials and their spouses held by the Secretary of the Interior, 61 Comp. Gen. 260 (1982); a party for various government officials and their families or guests held on July 4 by the Secretary of the Interior to celebrate Independence Day, B-212634, October 12, 1983; a luncheon incident to a "graduation ceremony" for Latin American students being trained by the Bureau of Labor Statistics, B-84184, March 17, 1949; and entertainment of British war workers visiting various American cities as guests of the British Ministry of Information, B-46169, August 18, 1945. More recently, GAO has held that the State Department may use representation funds to reimburse the Ambassador and Deputy Chief of Mission for the costs of renting formal morning dress required by protocol for official occasions, B-256936, June 22, 1995.

Representation funds may be an authorized fund source in situations where the agency's more general appropriation would not be available. For example, in the case of award ceremonies, an agency may not be able to use its general appropriations to provide refreshments at an awards ceremony for volunteers, but it may be able to use its representation funds. See, e.g., 43 Comp. Gen. 305 (1963). An agency may also use its R&R funds, although it is not required to, for refreshments at award ceremonies under the Government Employees' Incentive Awards Act. 65 Comp. Gen. 738, 741 n.5. Similarly, in B-250450, May 3, 1993, GAO held that, although an invoice for food and entertainment provided at the grand opening of a government cafeteria could not be paid from the construction appropriation used to fund the project, the invoice could be paid from unobligated representation funds available at the time the expenses were incurred, provided the event otherwise qualifies as an "official reception."

Notwithstanding the discretion it confers, representation funds are not intended to permit government officials to feed themselves and one another incident to the normal day-to-day performance of their jobs. Thus, GAO has held that representation funds may not be used to provide food or refreshments at intra-government work sessions or routine business meetings, even if held outside of normal working hours. B-223678, June 5, 1989.

Finally, another significant limitation on the use of representation funds stems from the appropriation language itself, i.e., representation funds are made for the expenses of official reception and representation activities. There must be some connection with official agency business. Thus, it would be improper to use representation funds for a social function hosted and attended by private parties, such as a breakfast for the spouses of Cabinet members. 61 Comp. Gen. 260 (1982), affirmed upon reconsideration, B-206173, August 3, 1982. Similarly, representation funds may not be used for entertainment incident to an activity that is itself unauthorized. 68 Comp. Gen. 226 (1989) (entertainment incident to trade show in the Soviet Union that the agency had no authority to sponsor). The impropriety of the underlying activity necessarily "taints" the entertainment expenditures.

Fines and Penalties

The general rule is that an agency may not use its appropriated funds to pay fines or penalties incurred as a result of its activities or those of its employees. A common situation involves a fine that is assessed against a government employee for some action taken in the course of performing official duties, such as receiving a speeding ticket while on the way to an important meeting. The rule is that appropriated funds are not available to pay the fine or reimburse the employee. The rationale for this rule is that, while an employee may have certain discretion as to precisely how to perform a given task, the range of permissible discretion does not include violating the law. If the employee chooses to violate the law, he is acting beyond the scope of his authority and must bear any resulting liability as his personal responsibility.

The earliest case stating this rule seems to be B-58378, July 31, 1946. Holding that a government employee ticketed for parking a government vehicle in a "no parking" zone could not be reimbursed, the Comptroller General stated:

> [T]here is not known to this office any authority to use appropriated moneys for payment of the amount of a fine imposed by a court on a Government employee for an offense committed by him while in the performance of, but not as a part of, his official duty. Such fine is imposed on the employee personally and payment thereof is his personal responsibility.

The same rationale prohibits the use of appropriated funds to compensate a government employee who must forfeit property as part of the punishment for an offense. B-102829, May 8, 1951.

The case most cited for the general rule prohibiting the use of appropriated funds to pay fines and penalties incurred by an employee is 31 Comp. Gen. 246 (1952). In that case, a government employee double-parked a government vehicle to make a delivery. While the employee was inside the building, the inner vehicle drove away, leaving the government vehicle unattended in the middle of the street, whereupon it was ticketed. Citing B-58378 and B-102829, the Comptroller General held that the employee could not be reimbursed from appropriated funds for the amount of the fine. See also, 57 Comp. Gen 270 (1978); B-147420, April 18, 1968; B-168096-O.M, August 31, 1976; B147420, July 27, 1977; B-173783.188, March 24, 1976.

In B-251228, July 20, 1993, GAO held that the Forest Service was not authorized to use appropriated funds to pay penalties and interest assessed by Nevada County, California, against a Forest Service employee for delayed payment of a tax arising from the employee's occupation of government-owned quarters. In reaching its conclusion, GAO found that the penalties and interest were personal liabilities of the employee and not the federal government.

There are, however, limited exceptions that would allow an agency to pay a fine or penalty incurred by a government employee.

Fines Incurred by Employee to Protect Government's Interests

This exception was recognized in 44 Comp. Gen. 312 (1964). In connection with the case of *Sam Giancana v. J. Edgar Hoover*, 322 F.2d 789 (7th Cir. 1963), an agent of the Federal Bureau of Investigation (FBI) was ordered by the court to answer certain questions. The Justice Department believed that answering the questions would compromise sensitive ongoing undercover investigations. Based on Justice Department regulations and specific instructions from the Attorney General, the FBI agent refused to testify and was fined for contempt of court. Finding that the employee had incurred the fine by reason of his compliance with Justice Department regulations and instructions and that he was without fault or negligence, GAO held that the FBI could reimburse the agent from its salaries and expenses appropriation under the "necessary expense" doctrine."

The basis for this exception is that the fine in the Sam Giancana case (44 Comp. Gen. 312) was "necessarily incurred" in the sense that the employee was following his agency's regulations and the instructions of his agency head. Thus, the actions that gave rise to the contempt fine could be viewed as a necessary part of the employee's official duties.

In the cases applying the general rule (e.g., 31 Comp. Gen. 246), the offenses were also committed while performing official duties, but they were not a necessary part of those duties. The employees could have performed their duties in a legal manner, e.g., in 31 Comp. Gen. 246 the employee who double-parked could have made the delivery without parking illegally. Applying these concepts, the Comptroller General held in B-205438, November 12, 1981, that the Federal

Mediation and Conciliation Service could reimburse a former employee for a contempt fine levied against him for refusal to testify, pursuant to agency regulations and instructions, on matters discussed at a mediation session at which he was present while an agency employee.

The common factor in the cases in which reimbursement of the fine was authorized was that the employee's compliance with the lawful performance of official duties resulted in liability. If the employee could have performed without violating the law, reimbursement will not be authorized. Thus, reimbursement was denied in B-186680, October 4, 1976, for a Justice Department attorney who was fined for contempt of court for missing a court-imposed deadline. The attorney had been working under a number of tight deadlines and argued that it was impossible to meet them all. However, he had not been acting in compliance with regulations or instructions, had exercised his own judgment in missing the deadline in question, and the record did not support a determination that he was without fault or negligence in the matter. Therefore, the case was governed by 31 Comp. Gen. 246 rather than 44 Comp. Gen. 312.

Reading all these cases together, it seems that the mere fact of compliance with instructions will not by itself be sufficient to authorize reimbursement. There must be some legitimate government interest to protect, such as the protection of undercover FBI investigations in the Sam Giancana case. Thus, it would not be sufficient to instruct an employee to refuse to testify where the purpose is to avoid embarrassment or to avoid the disclosure of government wrongdoing. Similarly, it would follow that the prohibition against reimbursement of traffic fines could not be circumvented merely because some supervisor instructed a subordinate to park illegally.

Finally, employees have been authorized reimbursement for fines even if not acting in direct response to specific agency instructions or directions, provided the employee was acting in the agency's (and not his own) interests. For example, in B-107081, January 22, 1980, the Comptroller General noted that reimbursement of a parking fine could be authorized if incurred by a law enforcement official who illegally parked an unmarked undercover vehicle during a surveillance where there was no other feasible alternative. See also 38 Comp. Gen. 258 (1958) (permitting reimbursement of parking meter fees).

Another situation in which a fine was held reimbursable is illustrated in 57 Comp. Gen. 476 (1978). In that case, Forest Service employees had loaded logs on a truck to transport them from Virginia to West Virginia. In Virginia, the driver was fined for improper loading (overweight on rear axle). The employees had loaded the logs in a forest and there was no way for them to have checked the weight. The fine did not result from any negligent or intentional act on the part of the driver. Under these circumstances, the Comptroller General found that the fine was not for any personal wrongdoing by the employee but was, in effect, a citation against the United States. Therefore, Forest Service appropriations were available to reimburse the fine. This situation is distinguishable from the case of an overweight fine levied against a commercial carrier, which is not reimbursable. 35 Comp. Gen. 317 (1955).

Fines Levied Directly against an Agency

These cases involved fines against individual employees. When a fine is properly levied against the agency, appropriated funds may generally be used for its payment. The initial issue in such cases involves the well-established doctrine of sovereign immunity.

Under the doctrine of sovereign immunity, before a federal agency can be liable for a fine or penalty, Congress must enact a statute that expressly waives sovereign immunity. E.g., *Ohio v. United States Department of Energy*, 904 F.2d 1058 (6th Cir. 1990). For example, the Clean Air Act provides for the administrative imposition of civil penalties for violation of state or local air quality standards. The statute directs the federal government to comply with these standards and makes government agencies liable for the civil penalties to the same extent as nongovernmental entities. Since the Clean Air Act waives sovereign immunity and authorizes fines against federal agencies, the Comptroller General held that agency operating appropriations are available, under the "necessary expense" theory, to pay administratively imposed civil penalties under the Clean Air Act. B-191747, June 6, 1978.

There are many other examples where Congress has waived sovereign immunity and, thereby, subjected federal agencies to fines and penalties. Two of the better known examples are 10 U.S.C. § 2703(f) (Defense Environmental Restoration Account) and 31 U.S.C. § 3902 (interest penalty under the Prompt Payment Act).

However, if there is not a clear statutory waiver of sovereign immunity, the agency's appropriations would not be available to pay a fine or penalty. For example, in 65 Comp. Gen. 61 (1985), appropriated funds were not available to pay a "fee," which was clearly in the nature of a penalty, imposed by a City of Boston ordinance for equipment malfunctions resulting in the transmission of false fire alarms. See also B-227388, September 3, 1987 (no authority to pay false alarm fines imposed by municipality).

Gifts and Awards

As with virtually all expenditures that are of a personal nature, appropriated funds may not be used for personal gifts, unless there is specific statutory authority. 68 Comp. Gen. 226 (1989). If, for example, an agency decided it would greatly improve employee morale to purchase each employee a new sports car, few would argue that the agency could use appropriated funds for this expense (except, perhaps, the employees). Appropriated funds could not be used because the appropriation was not made for this purpose and because giving sports cars to agency employees is not reasonably necessary to carry out the agency's mission.

Most cases, however, are not quite this obvious or simple. The cases generally involve the application of the necessary expense doctrine, and the result is that gifts can rarely be justified. In making the analysis, it makes no difference whether the "gift items" are given to federal employees or to others. Either the expense is necessary or it is not; the identity of the recipient is not controlling. In each of the cases in which GAO found that the funds were unavailable, there was a certain logic to the agency's justification, and the amount of the expenditure in many cases was small. The problem is that, if the justifications were sufficient, there would be no stopping point. If a free ashtray might generate positive feelings about an agency or program or enhance motivation, so would a new car or a deposit of cash into an employee's bank account. The strict rule prohibiting the use of appropriated funds for personal gifts recognizes the clear potential for abuse and the impossibility of drawing a rational line.

In 53 Comp. Gen. 770 (1974), a certifying officer for the Small Business Administration (SBA) asked GAO to rule on the propriety of an expenditure for decorative ashtrays, which were distributed to federal employees participating in a conference sponsored by that agency. The agency attempted to justify the purchase and distribution of the ashtrays by claiming that this would generate conversation concerning the conference and thereby further the agency's objectives by serving as a reminder of the purposes of the conference. GAO determined that the agency's justification was not sufficient because the recipients of the ashtrays were federal officials who were already required by law to cooperate with the objectives of the SBA. Thus, it was not necessary for the agency to give away ashtrays. The ashtrays were considered personal gifts and could not, therefore, be purchased with the agency's appropriations.

Similarly, in 54 Comp. Gen. 976 (1975), specially made key chains, which were distributed to educators who attended seminars sponsored by the Forest Service, were determined to be personal gifts despite the Department of Agriculture's claim that their distribution would generate future responses from participants. That decision stated:

> The appropriation . . . proposed to be charged with payment for the items in question is available for . . . expenses necessary for forest protection and utilization.

Since the appropriation is not specifically available for giving key chains to individuals, in order to qualify as a legitimate expenditure it must be demonstrated that the acquisition and distribution of such items constituted a necessary expense of the Forest Service.

The decision concluded that the key chains were not necessary to implement the appropriation and were, therefore, improper expenditures.

This same rationale was used in 57 Comp. Gen. 385 (1978). In that case, GAO held that novelty plastic garbage cans containing candy in the shape of solid waste, which were distributed by the Environmental Protection Agency to attendees at an exposition, were personal gifts. The agency's argument that the candy was used to attract people to its exhibit on the Resource Conservation and Recovery Act and therefore to promote solid waste management was not sufficient to justify the expenditure. Similarly, in B-195247, August 29, 1979, the Comptroller General held that an expenditure of appropriated funds for the cost of jackets and sweaters as Christmas gifts to corpsmen at a Job Corps Center with the intent of increasing morale and enhancing program support was unauthorized. The Comptroller determined that the purchase of these items was not a necessary and proper use of appropriated funds and therefore constituted personal gifts.

Many examples illustrate the types of items that GAO has determined constituted personal gifts. In B-240001, February 8, 1991, GAO determined that T-shirts stamped with the Combined Federal Campaign logo to be given to employees contributing a certain amount were a personal gift, as were winter caps purchased by NOAA to be given to volunteer participants in weather observation program to create "esprit de corps" and enhance motivation (B-201488, February 25, 1981); baseball caps for personnel recruitment purposes (B-260260, December 28, 1995); photographs taken at the dedication of the Klondike Gold Rush Visitor Center to be sent by the National Park Service as "mementos" to persons attending the ceremony (B-195896, October 22, 1979); "Sun

Day" buttons procured by GSA and given out to members of the public to show GSA'S support of certain energy policies (B-192423, August 21, 1978); agricultural products developed in Department of Agriculture research programs (gift boxes of convenience foods, leather products, paperweights of flowers embedded in plastic) to be given to foreign visitors and other official dignitaries (B-151668, June 30, 1970); and cuff links and bracelets to be given to foreign visitors by the Commerce Department to promote tourism to the United States (B-151668, December 5, 1963; B-151668, June 12, 1963). These cases illustrate that, while the agency's administrative determination of necessity is given considerable weight, it is not controlling.

Nevertheless, some expenditures that resemble personal gifts have been approved because they were found necessary to carry out the purposes of the agency's appropriation. The key seems to be the agency's ability to link what would otherwise be a gift to some significant agency objective. If the agency has a rational basis for making this connection, GAO has demonstrated a willingness to uphold the expenditure. For example, in B-193769, January 24, 1979, it was held that the purchase and distribution of pieces of lava rocks to visitors of the Capulin Mountain National Monument was a necessary and proper use of the Department of the Interior's appropriated funds. The appropriation in question was for "expenses necessary for the management, operation, and maintenance of areas and facilities administered by the National Park Service. . . ." The distribution of the rocks furthered the objectives of the appropriation because it was effective in preserving the monument by discouraging visitors from removing lava rock elsewhere in the monument. Thus, the rocks were not considered to be personal gifts.

Similarly, GAO concluded in B-230062, December 22, 1988, that the Army could use its appropriations to give away framed recruiting posters as "prizes" in drawings at national conventions of student organizations. The students had to fill out cards to enter the drawings, and the cards would be used as leads for potential recruits. Also, the Army is authorized to advertise its recruitment program, and posters are a legitimate form of advertising. Another case in which GAO found adequate justification is 68 Comp. Gen. 583 (1989), concluding that the United States Mint may give complimentary specimens of commemorative coins and medals to customers whose orders have been mishandled. Since customers who do not receive what they paid for may be disinclined to place further orders, the goodwill gesture of giving complimentary copies to these customers would directly contribute to the success of the Mint's commemorative sales program. See also B-257488, November 6, 1995 (FDA could use its salaries and expenses appropriations to purchase buttons printed with the slogan "No Red Tape" for distribution to its employees to remind FDA employees to find ways to work efficiently to satisfy customer needs); B-280440, February 26, 1999 (INS could use its salaries and expenses appropriation to purchase commemorative medals to be worn by Border Patrol agents because the medals serve a legitimate agency interest by reminding the public and agency staff of the Border Patrol's 75 years of hard work and dedication).

In B-286536, November 17, 2000, GSA's Public Buildings Service (PBS) wanted to increase the response rate to customer surveys it distributed to employees of tenant-agencies in GSA-managed buildings by using the Federal Buildings Fund to provide prizes to survey recipients whose names PBS would choose in a drawing connected to the survey. This case provides a useful insight to how GAO will analyze such cases. GAO held:

> While the Federal Buildings Fund does not specifically provide budget authority to GSA to cover the cost of prizes, we see a direct connection between the purpose of the Fund and the use of prizes to increase the response rate to customer satisfaction surveys. Because GSA's statutory mission is to . . . ensure that the building needs of federal agencies are met, it is necessary for GSA to collect valid information about the status of federal buildings and the needs of federal employees. . . . One important way to collect measurable information on performance is through the use of data collection instru-

ments . . . GSA does not control the surveyed employees nor does it have the authority to compel federal employees to return data collection instruments. However, by using incentives, it can encourage federal employees to provide the information it needs. Indeed, GSA has demonstrated, statistically, that conducting a drawing in connection with its customer satisfaction surveys will enhance the response rate to the survey and, thus, the value to GSA of the information that GSA obtains from its customers. We, therefore, have no objection to GSA's use of the Federal Buildings Fund for this purpose.

Although GAO had no objection to the proposed use of appropriated funds, it did caution the agency to ensure that its *method* of awarding the prizes, through a drawing, did not constitute an unauthorized lottery.

As noted in the cases applying the exception to the general prohibition, an agency can purchase gifts and prizes with appropriated funds if it can demonstrate a rational connection between the items purchased and its mission. In the GSA case, GAO found the following factors persuasive: (1) GSA needed certain information to perform an essential part of its mission (i.e., ensuring "that the building needs of federal agencies are met"); (2) GSA's approach to gathering that information was reasonable (i.e., distributing customer surveys); (3) GSA did not control the employees it surveyed and needed a way to increase the return rate; and (4) GSA had statistical evidence to support its determination that prizes would achieve the goal of increasing the return rate. This is a sound approach that agencies could use to satisfy the necessary expense test and justify the purchase of what would otherwise be impermissible gifts. Of course, agency personnel should always check with agency counsel and consult any applicable agency-specific regulations prior to making such a purchase.

Rewards

Although gifts and awards generally cannot be purchased with appropriated funds, there may be situations in which rewards may be paid from appropriated funds. In general, statutory authority is needed for an agency to use appropriated funds to pay rewards. However, the degree of specificity of this statutory authority will depend on the nature of the information or services for which the reward is contemplated and its relationship to the authority of the paying agency. Issues pertaining to rewards arise in several contexts, such as payments to informants, rewards to locate missing government employees or recover missing government property, rewards paid based on a contract, and rewards paid to government employees.

Rewards Paid to Informants

One category of GAO decisions deals with rewards paid to informants for providing information regarding violations of civil and criminal laws. The general rule is that if the information is "essential or necessary" to the effective administration and enforcement of the laws, a reward may be paid if it falls within the purpose of a particular appropriation under the "necessary expense" theory. When the information is "essential or necessary," the statutory authority does not have to expressly provide for the payment of rewards. If, however, the information is merely "helpful or desirable," then more explicit statutory authority is needed.

The Comptroller General addressed the issue in 8 Comp. Gen. 613, 614 (1929), stating:

> An appropriation general in terms is available to do the things essential to the accomplishment of the work authorized by the appropriation to be done. As to whether such an appropriation may properly be held available to pay a reward for the furnishing of information, not essential but probably helpful to the accomplishment of the authorized work, the decisions of the accounting officers have not been uniform. The doubt arises generally because such rewards are not necessarily in keeping with the value of the information furnished and possess elements of a gratuity or gift made in appreciation of helpful assistance rendered.

While the reward in that particular case was permitted, the decision announced that specific legislative authority would be required in the future. See also 9 Comp. Gen. 309 (1930); A-26777, May 22, 1929.

Whether a reward to an informer is "necessary" or merely "helpful" depends largely on the nature of the agency's area of responsibility and its appropriations language. For example, the Forest Service is responsible for protecting the national forests "against destruction by fire and depredations." 16 U.S.C. § 551. It receives appropriations for expenses necessary for "forest protection and utilization." The issue that arose for the Comptroller General to consider was whether the Forest Service could use its "forest protection and utilization" appropriation to pay rewards to informants providing information relating to violations (such as deliberately set forest fires, theft of timber, unauthorized occupancy, and vandalism). The decision would be based on whether the information could be considered necessary rather than just helpful.

If the information could be considered necessary, the Forest Service could offer rewards to informers without more specific statutory authority. The Comptroller General considered that the relationship between the information and the purpose of the appropriation was sufficiently direct that the information could properly be considered "necessary" to implementation of the purposes of the appropriation. Consequently, the Forest Service could use its "forest protection and utilization" appropriation to pay the rewards. B-172259, April 29, 1971. See also, 5 Comp. Gen. Dec. 118 (1898). Similarly, the Commerce Department could pay rewards to informers as a necessary expense under a provision of the Export Control Act of 1949, which authorized the obtaining of confidential information incident to enforcement of the Act, B-117628, January 21, 1954. The rule was also applied in B-106230, November 30, 1951, in which GAO advised the Treasury Department that rewards to informers for information or evidence on violations of the revenue, customs, or narcotics laws could be offered under an appropriation for the necessary expenses of law enforcement. As long as the information was necessary and not just helpful, more specific appropriations language was not needed. The result would be different if the agency did not have specific law enforcement authority. A.D. 6669, May 15, 1922.

Discussion Problem 3-8

EPA is responsible for, among other things, the promulgation and enforcement of rules pertaining to the lawful disposal of hazardous wastes. EPA suspects that several hazardous waste disposal companies are disposing of waste illegally in remote areas. EPA considers establishing field offices in hundreds of remote locations to deter this activity, but the cost is prohibitive. Instead, EPA develops an initiative whereby it will pay a $1,000 reward to any citizen who reports suspicious activity relating to waste dumping in certain designated remote areas.

Although EPA does not have a specific statute authorizing it to pay rewards, it would like to use its "general expense" appropriation for this purpose. What argument could be made to support this initiative?

Several agencies have specific statutory authority to pay rewards; in such cases the "necessary expense" analysis would not be required. Of course, the specific statute may impose various procedural requirements as preconditions to exercise of the reward authority. An example of a statutorily authorized reward program is the reward offered by the IRS for the detection of tax violators. The statute authorizes payment of sums deemed necessary "for detecting and bringing to trial and punishment persons guilty of violating the internal revenue laws." 26 U.S.C. §7623.

The Customs Service also has statutory authority to pay rewards. Under 19 U.S.C. § 1619, a person (other than a government employee) who detects and seizes any vessel, vehicle, aircraft, merchandise, or baggage subject to seizure and forfeiture under the customs or navigation laws, or who furnishes original information leading to a monetary recovery, may be paid a reward of 25 percent of the amount recovered, not to exceed $250,000. Rewards are payable from "appropriations available for the collection of the customs revenue." Id. § 1619(d).

Another example is 33 U.S.C. § 2337, which states:

> (a) In general. The Secretary may carry out a program to reduce vandalism and destruction of property at water resources development projects under the jurisdiction of the Department of the Army.
> (b) Provision of rewards. In carrying out the program, the Secretary may provide rewards (including cash rewards) to individuals who provide information or evidence leading to the arrest and prosecution of individuals causing damage to Federal property.

Note that if the statute only consisted of subsection (a), the Army would have to perform the "necessary expense" analysis. However, the specific authority provided in subsection (b) eliminates the need for that analysis.

Rewards Relating to Missing Government Employees

The only decisions that exist on rewards for locating missing government employees concern military deserters. Statutory authority exists in the form of a provision that has appeared in the annual Defense Department appropriation acts authorizing payment of expenses relating to the apprehension and delivery of deserters, including a reward. In 1984, the provision was made permanent and is now found at 10 U.S.C. § 956(l). The Coast Guard has similar authority to pay rewards for the apprehension of deserters. 14 U.S.C. § 644.

As a result of the existence of specific statutory authority, the Comptroller General decisions concern mainly questions of interpretation under the statutory language and implementing regulations. For example, in one case, the issue was whether a reward could be paid for the "apprehension" of a deserter if the deserter voluntarily surrendered to the person seeking the reward. The Comptroller General interpreted the word "apprehension" broadly and authorized payment. 6 Comp. Gen. 479 (1927).

Rewards As a "Necessary Expense"

The Comptroller General has determined that in certain circumstances, agencies may use appropriated funds to pay rewards under a "necessary expense" theory. For example, in B-242391, September 27, 1991, 70 Comp. Gen. 720, the Comptroller General found that a proposal to pay $5 rewards to members of the public who return fish tags that they might otherwise collect, display, or discard was reasonably necessary to its accomplishment of an authorized purpose and was therefore a permissible expenditure. The justification for the reward was that the agency was authorized to conduct research pertaining to the fish and the tags provided useful information that the agency could use to support this research. Agencies may be able to apply this same rationale if it there is a reasonable connection between the reward and accomplishment of the agency's mission.

Rewards to Finders of Lost Government Property

The Comptroller General has long held that no payment may be made to one who finds lost government property unless a reward has been offered prior to the return of the property. 11 Comp. Dec. 741 (1905); 5 Comp. Gen. 37 (1898); A-23019, May 24, 1928; B-l17297-O.M, February 12, 1954. To offer a reward for the recovery of lost or missing property, an agency must have a statutory basis. Examples of such a statutory basis are 10 U.S.C. § 2252 (Defense, military departments) and 14 U.S.C. § 643 (Coast Guard). While the degree of specificity required cannot be precisely defined, the rules appear to be the same as in the case of rewards for information.

Two early decisions permitted the use of military "contingent expense" appropriations. In the first decision, 6 Comp. Gen. 774 (1927), GAO told the Army that it could offer a reward from its contingent expense appropriation for the recovery of stolen platinum. In the other case, B-33518, April 23, 1943 (decided prior to the enactment of 10 U.S.C.§ 2252), the Navy wanted to use a general appropriation to offer rewards for locating lost aircraft. The Comptroller General advised that the general appropriation could not be used since the reward was not essential to carrying out the purposes of the general appropriation. However, the Comptroller General, relying on 6 Comp. Gen. 774, concluded that the Navy could use its contingent expense appropriation. In a similar case, 41 Comp. Gen, 410 (1961), the Treasury Department asked if the Coast Guard had any general authority beyond 14 U.S.C. § 643 to make reasonable payments to persons who found lost property. The Comptroller General replied that no such authority existed. Based on these decisions, it appears that an agency could not use its general operating appropriation to pay rewards for the recovery of lost property.

The relevant cases seem to be consistent with this conclusion. In B-79173, October 18, 1948, the Civil Aeronautics Administration had an appropriation for the temporary relief of distressed persons. The question presented was whether the appropriation was available to pay a reward to someone who had found a lost airplane four months after it disappeared. The Comptroller General said no, because the passengers could all be presumed dead after four months, but expressly declined to decide whether the appropriation would have been available if the airplane had been found "with such promptness as to afford reasonable hope that survivors might be found and given relief." The reasoning is similar to that in the information cases—the reward might have been considered necessary to carrying out the purpose of the relief appropriation if there was a reasonable chance of survivors, but after the passage of several months it would be merely "helpful," as opposed to "necessary." As with the necessary expense theory in general, "necessary" relates not to the importance of the object itself but to carrying out the purposes of the particular appropriation.

Contractual Bases for Rewards

In this group of reward cases, the basis of the right to a reward is contractual. Consequently, there must be an offer and an acceptance. The rationale is that "no person by his [or her] voluntary act can constitute himself [or herself] a creditor of the Government." 20 Comp. Gen. 767, 769

(1914). Where a reward is based on the "necessary expense" theory rather than on explicit statutory authority, the Comptroller General has held that there must be an offer of reward before a reward can be claimed. Performance of the service constitutes the acceptance. See, e.g., 26 Comp. Gen. 605 (1947); 3 Comp. Gen. 734 (1924). The offer does not have to be specifically related to a particular situation and may be in the form of a "standing offer" promulgated by regulation. See, e.g., B-131689, June 7, 1957, in which a Treasury Decision constituted the offer for an IRS reward. Another example is 28 C.F.R. Part 7, a "standing offer" by the Attorney General for rewards for the capture, or information leading to the capture, of escaped federal prisoners.

As with any contractual relationship, it is also possible for an offer to be implied from practice or course of conduct. For example, a reward was held payable to an informer under the prohibition laws without a specific offer in 4 Comp. Gen. 255 (1924). The informer was a member of a "gang of whiskey thieves," and the Comptroller General noted that "[u]nder such conditions no specific agreement for compensation is generally made, but with a man of such character there is, and practically must be, to obtain the information, an understanding that there will be compensation. " Id. at 256. It is likely that this reward for information could have also been justified under the "necessary expense" concept. The course of conduct and standing offer concepts were combined in A-23019, May 24, 1928, a case involving a reward for finding a lost Navy torpedo. In view of the prevailing understanding in the area and past practice, the Comptroller General determined that the Navy's regulations "implicitly" made a standing offer.

The Comptroller General has not found a "standing offer" where the reward is based on statutory language stating that the reward is either discretionary or authorizes the agency to "offer and pay" a reward. Since such a statute will not constitute a "standing offer," there would have to be an actual offer or reward before payment can be made. 41 Comp. Gen. 410 (1961) (interpreting 14 U.S.C. § 643); 20 Comp. Gen. 767 (1914) (apprehension of a deserter). However, if a statute provides for a reward as a matter of entitlement, the reasons for requiring an offer are less compelling; the terms of the statute and any implementing regulations will determine precisely how and when the "contract" comes into existence.

An issue that sometimes arises in the reward cases is whether the claimant must have knowledge of the offer. The answer seems to depend on whether the case involves apprehension of deserters or the finding of lost property. Cases involving the apprehension of deserters have held that performance of the service creates an obligation on the part of the government to pay the offered reward notwithstanding the claimant's lack of knowledge of the offer when he or she performed the service. 27 Comp. Gen. 47 (1920); 20 Comp. Gen. 767 (1914); B-41659, May 26, 1944. Conversely, in the lost property cases, the Comptroller General has held that knowledge *is* required. Thus, in 26 Comp. Gen. 605 (1947), a reward the Navy had offered for the discovery of a lost airplane was denied where the person discovering the airplane had no knowledge of the offer at the time he performed the service. This ruling was later followed in 41 Comp. Gen. 410 (1961), holding that the Coast Guard could not pay a reward under 14 U.S.C. § 3643 to someone who had no knowledge of the published offer. See also A-35247, April 1, 1931 (escaped prisoner).

Telephones in Private Residences of Government Employees

In 1912, Congress enacted legislation, 31 U.S.C. § 1348(a)(l), to prevent the use of appropriated funds for private telephone service for government officials. The statute provides that:

> Except as provided in this section, appropriations are not available to install telephones in private residences or for tolls or other charges for telephone service from private residences.

Based on this law, appropriated funds are not available to install telephones in private residences or for tolls or other charges for telephone service from private residences. B-262013, Apr. 8, 1996, 96-1 CPD ¶ 180 (appropriated funds may not be used to install telephone lines in Director's residence); B-240276, 70 Comp. Gen. 643 (1991) (agency may not use appropriated funds to pay the phone charges, but may use appropriated funds to investigate). However, there are some exceptions to this general rule.

Application of the Rule

A threshold issue that must be addressed is the scope of the term "private residence." The relevant GAO cases apply a common-sense definition and hold that a private residence is where one lives as opposed to where one works, assuming the two can be distinguished. Cases where the two cannot be distinguished present special problems.

For purposes of 31 U.S.C. S 1348, it makes no difference that the residence is government-owned or on public land. 35 Comp. Gen. 28 (1955); 7 Comp. Gen. 651 (1928); 19 Comp. Dec. 198 (1912). The statute therefore applies to military family housing on a military installation. 21 Comp. Gen. 997 (1942); B-61938, September 8, 1950; A-99355, January 11, 1939. It does not apply, however, to tents or other temporary structures on a military installation that are not available for family occupancy, notwithstanding that military personnel may use them as temporary sleeping quarters. 21 Comp. Gen. 905 (1942). Similarly, the statutory prohibition does not apply to military barracks (today called "dorms") occupied by large numbers of enlisted personnel. 53 Comp. Gen. 195 (1973). Lastly, since the statute uses only the term "residence," in at least one case it has been held not to apply to an "office." Thus, in B-236232, Oct. 25, 1990, GAO approved the installation of a telephone line in a Naval Reserve member's civilian business office so the individual could receive Navy faxes on a Navy-provided fax machine.

Once it has been determined that the location qualifies as a "private residence," the prohibition will (with limited exceptions noted below) apply. The prohibition applies even though the telephones are to be extensively used in the transaction of public business and even though they may be desirable or necessary from an official standpoint. 59 Comp. Gen. 723, 724 (1980). The key factors are whether the telephone will be freely available for the employee's personal use and whether facilities other than the employee's residence exist for the transaction of official business. The employee's personal desires are irrelevant. Thus, it makes no difference that the employee doesn't want the telephone and has asked to have it removed. 33 Comp. Gen. 530 (1954); A-99355, January 11, 1939. The fact that a telephone is unlisted (and therefore presumably less susceptible to receiving incoming personal calls) is also immaterial. 15 Comp. Gen. 885 (1936).

The general rule was illustrated in a 1980 decision in which the District Commander of the Seventh Coast Guard District sought to be reimbursed for a telephone installed in his residence. The Commander was in charge of the Cuban Refugee Freedom Flotilla in the Florida Straits. He was in daily contact with the various federal, state, and local agencies involved and was required to be available 24 hours a day. Since this situation placed a burden on the Commander's immediate family by restricting their personal use of the home telephone, he had another telephone installed for official business. In view of the statutory prohibition, and since the Commander was already provided with an office by the Coast Guard, reimbursement could not be allowed. 59 Comp. Gen. 723 (1980). See also 11 Comp. Gen. 87 (1931).

In B-130288, February 27, 1957, a government employee agreed to list his personal phone number under his agency's name, and the question presented was whether the agency could use appropriated funds to pay the fee charged for the listing. GAO reasoned that this arrangement did not violate 31 U.S.C. § 1348 because the agency would not be paying for installation or use of the telephone.

Exceptions

There are both statutory and nonstatutory exceptions that would permit the use of appropriated funds to purchase, install, and use telephones in private residences. One example of a statutory exception is 31 U.S.C. § 1348(a)(2), for residences owned or leased by the United States in foreign countries for use of the Foreign Service. Another statutory exception is 31 U.S.C. § 1348(c), enacted in 1922, authorizing telephones deemed necessary in connection with the construction and operation of locks and dams for navigation, flood control, and related water uses, under regulations of the Secretary of the Army. Still another is 16 U.S.C. § 580f, for telephones necessary for the protection of national forests. Finally, DoD is authorized to install, repair, and maintain telephone lines in residences owned or leased by the U.S. government and, if necessary for national defense purposes, in other private residences. 31 U.S.C. § 1348(c). Additionally, DoD may install telephone lines in certain volunteers' residences. Such volunteers are those who provide medical, dental, nursing, or other health-care related services; volunteer services for museum or natural resources programs; or programs that support service members and their families. 10 U.S.C. § 1588(f).

There are also nonstatutory exceptions. These fall generally into two categories. The first, dictated by common sense, involves situations where private residence and official duty station are one and the same. Thus, the Comptroller General has recognized an exception where a government-owned private residence was the only location available under the circumstances for the conduct of official business. E.g., 4 Comp. Gen. 891 (1925) (isolated lighthouse keeper); 19 Comp. Dec. 350 (1912) (lock tender); 19 Comp. Dec. 212 (1912) (national park superintendent). Note that in all of these cases the combined residence/duty station was government-owned. GAO has been reluctant to extend the exception to privately owned residences that are also used for the conduct of official business. See, e.g., 26 Comp. Gen. 668 (1947); B-130288, February 27, 1957; B-219084-O.M., June 10, 1985. The concern is that, in a privately owned residence, the risk of personal use is considered so great that a stricter prohibition is required, since there would be no other practical way to control abuse. 53 Comp. Gen. 195, 197-98 (1973).

> **Discussion Problem 3-9**
>
> The Commodity Futures Trading Commission (CFTC) would like to use appropriated funds to pay the costs of installing, maintaining, and removing call forwarding telephone service on an employee's government office telephone so that calls may be forwarded to the employee's telephone in her private residence. Specifically, the CFTC wants to authorize an employee to work part-time from her home for six months to care for her newborn child. The CFTC proposes programming the employee's office telephone to ring at her home and would pay the costs of installing, maintaining, and removing the call forwarding service with appropriated funds.
>
> Is this arrangement prohibited by 31 U.S.C. § 1348? If not, can it be justified under a "necessary expense" theory? [Scenario based on B-254666, November 18, 1993]

It should also be noted that isolation of the government employee is not sufficient to justify an exception. In 35 Comp. Gen. 28 (1955), the Comptroller General held that 31 U.S.C. § 1348(a)(1) prohibited payment for telephones in government-owned residences of Department of Agriculture employees at a sheep experiment station. The employees claimed need for the telephones because they frequently received calls outside of normal office hours from Washington or to notify them of unexpected visitors and shipments of perishable goods, and because they were sometimes stranded in their residences by severe blizzards. Cases like 4 Comp. Gen. 891 (which authorized installation of a telephone for an isolated lighthouse keeper) was distinguished because the telephone in that case was installed in a room equipped and used only as an office and was not readily available for personal use.

The second category of nonstatutory exceptions stems from the recognition that the "evil" 31 U.S.C. § 1348(a)(1) it is intended to prevent is not the physical existence of a telephone in a private residence, but the potential for charging the government for personal use. Thus, a series of cases has approved exceptions where (1) there is an adequate justification of need for a telephone in a private residence, and (2) there are adequate safeguards to prevent abuse. This category seems to have first developed in the context of "military necessity" and national security justifications. For example, an exception was made to permit the installation in the residence of the Pearl Harbor Fire Marshal (a civilian employee) of a telephone extension that was mechanically limited to emergency fire calls. 32 Comp. Gen. 431 (1953). In B-128144, June 29, 1956, GAO approved a proposal to install direct telephone lines from an Air Force Command Post switchboard to the private residences of certain high-level civilian and military officials to ensure communications in the event of a national emergency. Air Force regulations prohibited the use of these lines for anything but urgent official business in the event of a national emergency and authorized the recording of conversations as a safeguard against abuse.

However, a "necessity" that is little more than a matter of convenience is not enough to overcome the prohibition. For example, in A-99355, January 11, 1939, a telephone could not be maintained at government expense in the private quarters of the Officer-in-Charge on a Navy installation because several telephones were available in established offices on the station. This decision was followed in 21 Comp. Gen. 997 (1942) and 33 Comp. Gen. 530 (1954). The statutory prohibition applies equally to internal telecommunications systems that are not connected to outside commercial trunk lines, unless the agency has statutory authority. B-61938, September 8, 1950.

Relying largely on B-128144 (the Air Force case), GAO approved a GSA proposal to install Federal Secure Telephone Service telephones in the residences of certain high-level civilian and military officials certified by their agency heads as having national security responsibilities. 61 Comp. Gen. 214 (1982). The system was designed to provide a secure communications capability to permit the discussion of classified material that could not be discussed over private telephones. As in B-128144, the proposal included a number of safeguards against abuse, which GAO deemed adequate.

The concept established in the military necessity/national security cases was subsequently applied in other contexts. For example, GAO approved the use of appropriated funds for installation of telephone equipment by the IRS in the homes of customer "assistors" who were intermittent, part-time employees. The phones to be installed had no outcall capability and could receive calls only from IRS switching equipment. Separate lines were essential because the employees' personal phones could not be used with the IRS equipment. B-220148, June 6, 1986.

In another IRS case, GAO authorized installation of separate telephone lines in the homes of IRS data transcribers authorized to work at home under a "flexiplace" program, again subject to the establishment of adequate safeguards. 68 Comp. Gen. 502 (1989). Many agencies have adopted similar "flexiplace" arrangements for their employees, and the rationale of this case would apply in those situations.

The justification based on urgency and quickness of response time was upheld by GAO in B-223837, January 23, 1987. That case involved installation of telephones in the homes of certain high-level Nuclear Regulatory Commission (NRC) officials to ensure immediate communication capability in the event of a nuclear accident. The phones would be capable of dialing only internal NRC numbers, with any other calls to be placed through the NRC operator.

A similar rationale was applied in a more recent case involving installation of an Integrated Services Digital Network (ISDN) line in an agency employee's home. In that case, B-280698, Jan. 12, 1999, GAO determined that the agency could use appropriated funds to pay for installation of dedicated ISDN lines to transmit data from computers in private residences of agency's commissioners to agency's local area network.

Note that some of the cases noted earlier in which the prohibition was applied, such as 59 Comp. Gen. 723, also presented strong justifications. However, the primary factor distinguishing these cases from the exceptions is the existence in the latter group of adequate safeguards against abuse.

A related issue involves the use of appropriated funds for cell phones and related charges. Agencies may reimburse their employees for the *actual* costs associated with any official government usage of personal cell phones. B-287524, Oct. 22, 2001 (unpub.) (indicating that the agency may not, however, pay the employees a flat amount each month, unrelated to actual costs, even if the calculation of that flat amount is made using historical data).

In a 1988 case, B-229406, December 9, 1988, an agency official used his own funds to purchase a cellular telephone and have it installed in his personal automobile. GAO considered the relevance of both 31 U.S.C. § 1348(a) and § 1348(b). With respect to § 1348(a), the simple fact is that the statute addresses residences, not automobiles. Concluding that "section 1348 does not apply to cellular phones located in private automobiles, " GAO advised that the agency could reimburse local business calls as long as there were adequate safeguards to prevent abuse. The safeguards existed in this case because all local calls were individually itemized on a monthly basis. The agency could also reimburse necessary long-distance calls provided it makes the certification required by section 1348(b). The decision cautioned, however, that "agency heads should strictly scrutinize automobile telephone calls before certifying them for reimbursement, to ensure that the most economical means of communication are being used."

With respect to the purchase price of the phone itself, the decision found the agency's appropriations unavailable. However, it was clear in that case that the official intended the phone to be his own property. If the agency is the owner of the phone and can make a "necessary expense" justification, the absence of a statutory prohibition would allow the agency to use its appropriated funds for the purchase. Many agencies have specific regulations that provide guidance regarding the conditions in which cellular phones may be purchased with appropriated funds. See, e.g., AFI 33-106, *Managing High Frequency Radios, Land Mobile Radios, Cellular Telephones, and The Military Affiliate Radio System* (September 1, 1997).

Membership Fees

The use of appropriated funds to pay membership fees of an employee of the United States or the District of Columbia in a society or association is prohibited by 5 U.S.C. § 5946, which states:

> Except as authorized by a specific appropriation, by express terms in a general appropriation, or by sections 4109 and 4110 of this title, appropriated funds may not be used for payment of -
> (1) membership fees or dues of an employee as defined by section 2105 of this title or an individual employed by the government of the District of Columbia in a society or association; or
> . . .

The prohibition is subject to the usual exception that it will not apply if an appropriation is expressly available for that purpose, or if the fee is authorized under the Government Employees Training Act. Under the Training Act, membership fees may be paid if the fee is a necessary cost directly related to the training or a condition precedent to undergoing the training. 5 U.S.C. § 4109(b).

Individual Membership

The rule that has evolved under 5 U.S.C. § 5946 is that membership fees for individuals may not be paid even if there is some resulting benefit to the agency. Thus, the fact that membership may result in savings to the government, such as reduced travel rates for members, does not overcome the prohibition against individual memberships. 3 Comp. Gen. 963 (1924).

GAO has upheld the statutory prohibition in numerous cases. For example, in 53 Comp. Gen. 429 (1973), GAO advised EPA that it could not pay the membership fees for its employees in professional organizations (such as the National Environment Research Center and the National Solid Waste Management Association), notwithstanding the allegation that the benefits of membership would accrue more to the agency than to the individuals. EPA could, however, purchase a membership in its own name if it justified the expenditure as being of direct benefit to the agency and sufficiently related to carrying out the purposes of its appropriation.

In another 1973 decision, the Comptroller General held that the Department of Justice could not reimburse an electronics engineer employed by the Bureau of Narcotics and Dangerous Drugs for membership in the Institute of Electrical and Electronic Engineers. The Department had argued that the government benefited from the membership by virtue of reduced subscription rates to Institute publications and because the membership contributed to employee development. These factors were not sufficient to overcome the prohibition of 5 U.S.C.§ 5946. As in the other cases discussed, GAO pointed out that the Bureau could become a member of the Institute in its own name if it determined that it membership served a valid agency purpose. 52 Comp. Gen. 495 (1973). See also B-205768, March 2, 1982 (Federal Mediation and Conciliation Service can purchase agency membership in Association of Labor Related Agencies upon making appropriate administrative determinations).

The prohibition has been applied even in situations in which the membership was directly related to the employee's duties. For example, in B-198720, June 23, 1980, GAO held that the National Oceanic and Atmospheric Administration could not pay the membership fee of one of its employees in Federally Employed Women, Inc., notwithstanding the fact that the agency had designated the employee as the agency's regional representative. The mere fact that membership may be job-related does not overcome the statutory prohibition. See also 19 Comp. Dec. 650 (1913)

(Army could not pay for Adjutant General's membership in International Association of Chiefs of Police).

Agency Membership

Although the payment of individual membership fees is statutorily prohibited, an agency may purchase a membership in its *own name* if it makes an administrative determination that the expenditure would further the authorized activities of the agency. The authority to pay for an agency membership is not affected by any incidental benefits that may accrue to individual employees. Payment for agency membership is not prohibited by 5 U.S.C. § 5946, since the statute applies only to memberships for individual employees.

A case in which an agency was permitted to purchase a membership in its own name is 24 Comp. Gen. 814 (1945). In that case, the Veterans Administration (VA) asked the Comptroller General whether it could pay membership fees for VA facilities in the American Hospital Association. Facility membership would enable individual employees to apply for personal membership at reduced rates. The Comptroller General responded that the facility memberships were permissible if administratively determined necessary to accomplish the objectives of the appropriation to be charged. The indirect benefit to individual officials would not invalidate the appropriateness of the agency's membership. However, the expenditure would be improper if its purpose was merely to enable the officials to obtain the reduced rates for personal memberships. Nor could the VA, under the general prohibition of 5 U.S.C. § 5946, pay for the individual memberships.

The distinction between individual and agency memberships is not a distinction in name only; there are substantive differences. An agency must be able to justify the expenditure for an agency membership as a "necessary expense." To do this, the membership must provide benefits to the agency itself. For example, in 31 Comp. Gen. 398 (1952), the Economic Stabilization Agency was permitted to become a member of a credit association because members could purchase credit reports at reduced cost and the procurement of credit reports was determined to be necessary to the enforcement of the Defense Production Act. In 33 Comp. Gen. 126 (1953), the Office of Technical Services, Commerce Department, was permitted to purchase membership in the American Management Association. The appropriation involved was an appropriation under the Mutual Security Act to conduct programs including technical assistance to Europe, and the membership benefit to the agency was the procurement of association publications for foreign trainees and foreign productivity centers. Citing 31 Comp. Gen. 398 and 33 Comp. Gen. 126, the Comptroller General held in 57 Comp. Gen. 526 (1978) that the Department of Housing and Urban Development could purchase, in the name of the department, air travel club memberships to obtain discount airfares to Hawaii. Similarly, GSA could join a shippers' association to obtain the benefit of volume transportation rates. B-159783, May 4, 1972.

GAO has also approved membership by the Federal Law Enforcement Center in the local Chamber of Commerce, B-213535, July 26, 1984, and by a naval installation in the local Rotary Club, 61 Comp. Gen. 542 (1982). In the latter decision, membership was justified because the Navy operated a facility in a densely populated Philadelphia suburb and joined the Rotary Club to express its concerns regarding the impact of the expanding civilian population on the Navy installation. GAO cautioned, however, that the result was based on the specific justification presented and that the decision should not be taken to mean that "every military installation or regional Government office can use appropriated funds to join the Rotary, Kiwanis, Lions, and similar organizations." Id. at 544.

The acquisition of needed publications for the agency has also been considered a sufficient benefit to justify purchase of an agency membership. 20 Comp. Gen. 497 (1941) (membership of Naval Academy in American Council on Education); A-30185, February 5, 1930 (membership of Phoenix Indian

School in National Education Association). See also 33 Comp. Gen. 126 (1953). Compare 52 Comp. Gen. 495 (1973), holding that acquisition of publications is not sufficient to justify an individual, as opposed to agency, membership.

If no specific agency benefit can be demonstrated, then the membership expense is improper. Thus, in 32 Comp. Gen. 15 (1952), GAO held that it was improper for the agency to pay the cost of membership fees for the New York Ordnance District of the Army in the Society for Advancement of Management because it was actually four separate memberships for individual employees and the primary purpose was to enhance the knowledge of those individuals. Similarly, since the benefit to the agency must be in terms of furthering the purposes for which its appropriation was made, a benefit to the United States as a whole rather than the individual agency may not be sufficient.

For example, in 5 Comp. Gen. 645 (1926), the former Veterans Bureau owned herds of livestock and wanted to have them registered. Reduced registration costs could be obtained by joining certain livestock associations. The benefit of registration would be a higher price if the agency sold the livestock. However, sales proceeds would have to be deposited in the Treasury as miscellaneous receipts and would thus not benefit the agency's appropriations. Membership was therefore improper. (The agency's appropriation language was subsequently changed, and the membership was approved in A-38236, March 30, 1932.)

Several of the decisions have pointed out that an agency may accept a gratuitous membership without violating the Antideficiency Act. 31 Comp. Gen, 398, 399 (1952); A-38236, March 30, 1932, quoted in 24 Comp. Gen. 814,815 (1945). In addition, payment of a membership fee at the beginning of the period of membership does not violate the prohibition on advance payments found in 31 U.S.C. 53324. B-221569, June 2, 1986. What is being purchased is a "membership," and the "membership" is received upon payment.

Business Cards for Government Employees

Under certain circumstances, an agency may use appropriated funds to purchase business cards for its employees. See B-280759, Nov. 5, 1998 (purchase of business cards with appropriated funds for government employees who regularly deal with public or outside organizations is a proper "necessary expense" of the Army Operations and Maintenance account). This case "overturned" a long history of Comptroller General's decisions holding that business cards were generally a personal expense. See, e.g., B-231830, 68 Comp. Gen. 467 (1989). For an agency to justify the purchase of business cards, it would have to demonstrate that an agency mission would be served by distribution of the cards.

In the case authorizing the purchase of business cards (B-280759), the Army wanted to purchase business cards for its personnel specialists. GAO found that primary responsibility of the personnel specialists was to "act as liaisons between Army employing units and their employees, to provide advice and assistance to employers and employees, and to forward personnel actions and related documents to the Army's centralized center." Since the personnel specialists would use the business cards to provide agency customers an accurate reference to the specialist and a precise electronic address for contacting the specialist, GAO found that there was an adequate connection between the purchase of the cards and the mission of the agency.

Even though the purchase of business cards may be authorized as a necessary expense, most agencies strictly limit the purchase of business cards to employees in specific positions. For example, Air Force Instruction 65-601, v. 1, para. 4.36.1.1, limits the purchase of business cards with appropriated funds to personnel involved in recruiting. See, also, AR 25-30, paragraph 11.11 (21 June 1999); AFIC 99-1 to DoDD 5330.3/AFSUP; Department of the Navy memorandum, dated 9 March 1999.

Office Decorations

Under the general "necessary expense" rationale, an agency may use its appropriations to purchase necessary office items, such as desks, filing cabinets, and other ordinary office equipment. However, issues may arise when the item to be procured is decorative rather than utilitarian. Since decorations are a typical element of business offices, GAO has long recognized that agencies may, within certain limits, use appropriated funds to purchase decorative items. For example, in 7 Comp. Dec. 1 (1900), the Comptroller of the Treasury advised the Secretary of the Treasury that "paintings suitable for the decoration of rooms" were within the meaning of the term "furniture." Therefore, an appropriation for the furnishing of public buildings was available to purchase cases and glass coverings for paintings of deceased judges. The paintings had been donated to the government for display in a courtroom.

The Comptroller followed this decision in 9 Comp. Dec. 807 (1903), holding that Treasury appropriations were available to buy portraits as furniture for the Ellis Island immigration station if administratively determined "necessary for the public service." Citing both of these decisions, the Comptroller General held in B-178225, April 11, 1973, that the appropriation for salaries and expenses of the Tax Court was available for portraits of the Chief Judges of the Tax Court, to be hung in the main courtroom. Similarly, the Tax Court could purchase artwork and other decorative items for judges' individual offices. 64 Comp. Gen. 796 (1985). Other decisions approving the use of appropriated funds for decorative items are B-143886, September 14, 1960 (oil painting of agency head for "historical purposes" and public display); B-121909, December 9, 1954 ("solid walnut desk mount attached a name plate"); B-114692, May 13, 1953 (framing of Presidential Certificates of Appointment for display in the appointee's office).

Purchase of decorative items for federal buildings is now addressed in the Federal Property Management Regulations. These regulations authorize expenditures for pictures, objects of art, plants, flowers (both artificial and real), and other similar items. However, such items may not be purchased solely for the personal convenience or to satisfy the personal desire of an official or employee. The regulation was discussed and the rule restated in 60 Comp. Gen. 580 (1981). Thus, decorative items may be purchased if the purchase is consistent with work-related objectives and the items to be purchased are not "personal convenience" items.

As in any other application of the necessary expense rule, the determination of "necessity" is within the agency's discretion, subject to the applicable regulations. The Federal Property Management Regulations apply equally to space leased by an agency in a privately owned building. See also 64 Comp. Gen. 796, (1985); 63 Comp. Gen. 110, 113 (1983).

Discussion Problem 3-10

Milborne Wickersham IV is a federal agency employee who has recently been promoted and moved to a new office. Milborne, a connoisseur of fine art, is appalled at the low artistic quality of the cardboard prints left hanging in "his" new office by his predecessor. Milborne makes a few phone calls to his art dealer pals and is able to locate a set of three watercolor paintings by a well-known artist for the incredibly low price of $12,000 (normally these prints would have commanded at least $25,000, but the economy is in a recession and fine art is not selling that well). Milborne informs the office manager of his find and requests that the agency purchase the prints for his office.

Is this a justifiable expenditure? Can the agency purchase the paintings, later sell them at profit, and use the proceeds to purchase other decorations?

Regarding seasonal decorations, in B-226011, Nov 17, 1987, the Comptroller General changed its position regarding the use of appropriated funds and held that the same rules should apply to seasonal decorations that applied to other types of office decorations. The decision stated:

> We think that if the same standards are used in judging the permissibility of expenditures for permanent office decorations as for seasonal decorations, it is difficult to explain why the result should turn on the relative life of the decoration. Therefore, agency expenditures for seasonal decorations as necessary expenses may be properly payable where the purchase is consistent with work-related objectives, agency or other applicable regulations, and the agency mission, and is not primarily for the personal convenience or satisfaction of a government employee.

However, the decision also pointed out a potential problem that is unique to seasonal decorations. The nature of some of these decorations could raise possible constitutional issues that also must be addressed in determining the appropriateness of these expenditures. In this case, for example, the agency's request included vouchers for menorah candelabra. The Comptroller General stated: "We caution agencies to be sensitive to the possibility that the display of certain seasonal decorations which are primarily religious in character could be viewed as an endorsement of religion lacking any clearly secular purpose and might therefore be challenged as government conduct prohibited by the Establishment Clause of the First Amendment." If an agency's purchase of a religious seasonal item violates the Constitution, then its purchase would be unlawful.

As discussed, to satisfy the purpose statute (31 U.S.C. § 1310), the agency's expenditure must not be prohibited by law. Consequently, such a purchase in violation of the establishment clause of the Constitution would also violate the purpose statute. Finally, since there would be no lawful fund source, the expenditure would also likely violate the Antideficiency Act.

> This chapter addressed the first of the three limitations imposed by Congress on the use of appropriated funds: the purpose limitation. Rules of statutory interpretation and the use of legislative history were discussed to enable the reader to ascertain more accurately the purpose of a given appropriation. Next, the three-part test of the "necessary expense" doctrine was analyzed and applied to various practical situations. Finally, the application of the purpose statute to specific expenditures, such as entertainment, gifts, and awards, was discussed to alert the reader to particular expenses that GAO has questioned in the past.

CHAPTER 4
Limitations on the Use of Appropriated Funds: Time

As discussed in Chapter 1, Congress controls the use of appropriated funds by executive agencies by imposing limitations related to time, purpose, and amount. This chapter will discuss the time limitation and how it affects the availability of funds for obligation and expenditure. Many of the rules that will be discussed are statutory and may be found in the provisions of Title 31 of the United States Code; these are cited throughout this chapter.

Recall that an obligation is a binding commitment against an appropriation that will require an expenditure at some later time. An expenditure is the actual disbursement of funds. When an appropriation is available for a fixed period of time or until a specified date, the general rule is that the period of availability relates to the authority to *obligate* the appropriation and does not prohibit payments for valid obligations after the appropriation has expired. 37 Comp. Gen. 861, 863 (1958); 23 Comp. Gen. 862 (1944); 18 Comp. Gen. 969 (1939); 16 Comp. Gen. 205 (1936). Thus, a time-limited appropriation is available for obligation only during the period for which it is made but remains available beyond that period, within limits, for expenditures to liquidate properly made obligations. In this connection, 31 U.S.C. § 1502(a) provides:

> The balance of an appropriation or fund limited for obligation to a definite period is available only for payment of expenses properly incurred during the period of avail-

ability or to complete contracts properly made within that period of availability and obligated consistent with section 1501 of this title. However, the appropriation or fund is not available for expenditure for a period beyond the period otherwise authorized by law.

The authority of Congress to place limitations on when appropriations may be used has been recognized for many years. In 1870, the Attorney General concluded that: "Congress has the right to limit its appropriations to particular times as well as to particular objects, and when it has clearly done so, its will expressed in the law should be implicitly followed." 13 Op. Att'y Gen. 288, 292 (1870). The placing of time limits on the availability of appropriations is one of the primary means of congressional control. By imposing time limits on the availability of appropriations, Congress can exercise control by periodically reviewing an agency's programs and activities. In addition, if time limits were not placed on the period of availability of agency appropriations, agencies could roll forward unobligated balances and, over time, could amass such large amounts that they would become fiscally independent from the congressional budget process. Since this loss of control is antithetical to Congress' constitutional role, the vast majority of appropriations have limited periods of availability.

DEFINITIONS

Bona Fide Needs. The concept that the balance of an appropriation is available only for payment of expenses properly incurred during the period of availability, or to complete contracts properly made during the period of availability. 31 U.S.C. § 1502(a).

Period of Availability. The period of time during which an appropriation is available for obligation. Most appropriations are available for obligation for a limited period of time, such as one fiscal year. If funds are not obligated during the period of availability, they expire and are generally unavailable for new obligations thereafter.

Current Appropriations. Appropriations whose availability for new obligations has not expired under the terms of the applicable appropriations act.

Expired Appropriations. Appropriations whose availability for new obligations has expired, but that retain their fiscal identity and are available to adjust and liquidate previous obligations. 31 U.S.C. § 1553(a). Appropriations remain "expired" for five years, after which they "close."

Closed Appropriations. Appropriations that are no longer available for any purpose. An appropriation becomes "closed" five years after the end of its period of availability as defined by the applicable appropriations act. 31 U.S.C. § 1552(a).

DETERMINING THE PERIOD OF AVAILABILITY

If an appropriation is available for obligation for a definite period of time, then an agency must obligate the appropriation during its period of availability, or the authority to obligate expires. 31 U.S.C. § 1552. Since agencies may incur new obligations only within the period of availability of the appropriation charged, it is important to ascertain the duration of that period accurately.

The rule that time-limited budget authority ceases to be available for obligation after the last day of the specified time period is well established and has been reconfirmed in many court decisions. See, e.g., *West Virginia Association of Community Health Centers, Inc. v. Heckler,* 734 F.2d 1570, 1576 (D.C. Cir. 1984); *Population Institute v. McPherson,* 797 F.2d 1062, 1071 (D.C. Cir. 1986). See also 18 Comp. Gen. 969, 971 (1939). Unless there is specific statutory authority in the appropriations act itself, agencies may not obligate funds after their period of availability expires. 31 U.S.C. §1502; *National Endowment for the Arts—Time Availability for Appropriations,* B-244241, 71 Comp. Gen.39 (1991). However, appropriations remain available for five fiscal years after they expire to make payments to liquidate liabilities arising from obligations made during the period of availability. 31 U.S.C. § 1553(a), as amended by Pub. L. No, 101-510, § 1405(a), 104 Stat. at 1676 (1990).

The principle that payment is chargeable to the fiscal year in which the obligation is incurred applies even though the funds are not to be disbursed and the exact amount owed by the government cannot be determined until the subsequent fiscal year. E.g., 21 Comp. Gen. 574 (1941). Thus, in a case where the United States entered into an agreement with a state to provide assistance for the procurement of civil defense items for the state and to pay a specified percentage of the cost, the Comptroller General found that the need arose in the year in which the agreement with the state was made. Therefore, appropriations current at that time were to be charged with the cost, notwithstanding the fact that the actual procurement contracts with suppliers, including the exact price, would not be negotiated and executed until a subsequent fiscal year. 31 Comp. Gen. 608 (1952).

Presumption of One-Year Period of Availability

As a starting point, all appropriations are presumed to be annual appropriations unless the appropriation act expressly provides otherwise. Annual appropriations (also called fiscal year or one-year appropriations) are made for a specified fiscal year and are available for obligation only during the fiscal year for which they are made. The federal government's fiscal year begins on October 1 and ends on September 30 of the following year. 31 U.S.C. § 1102. Thus, fiscal year 2001 began on October 1, 2000, and ended on September 30, 2001. Generally, routine activities of the federal government are funded by annual appropriations.

There are several reasons why all appropriations are presumed to be annual appropriations. First, as required by 1 U.S.C § 105, the title and enacting clause of all regular and supplemental appropriation acts specify the making of appropriations "for the fiscal year ending September 30,

19XX." Thus, everything in an appropriation act is presumed to be applicable only to the fiscal year covered unless specified to the contrary. Second, 31 U.S.C. § 1301(c) provides that, with specified exceptions:

> (c) An appropriation in a regular, annual appropriation law may be construed to be permanent or available continuously only if the appropriation
> . . .
> (2) expressly provides that it is available after the fiscal year covered by the law in which it appears.

Third, appropriation acts commonly include the following general provision:

> No part of any appropriation contained in this Act shall remain available for obligation beyond the current fiscal year unless expressly so provided herein.

Under the unambiguous terms of this standard provision, the availability of an appropriation may not be extended beyond the fiscal year for which it is made unless there is an express indication in the appropriation act itself. See 58 Comp. Gen. 321 (1979); B-118638, November 4, 1974.

Similarly, the presumption that the appropriation is effective for one fiscal year also applies to any limitations included in the appropriation act (for example, a lump-sum appropriation with a proviso that not-to-exceed a specified sum shall be available for a particular object), unless the limitation is specifically exempted from the limitation in the appropriation act. 37 Comp. Gen. 246, 248 (1957).

> **Discussion Problem 4-1**
>
> For the last 30 years an agency has received an appropriation titled "Procurement" with a period of availability of three years stated in the appropriation. This year, the agency's procurement appropriation does not specify a period of availability. It does state, however, that, "None of the funds appropriated by this Act shall be used to purchase products containing titanium unless produced in the United States."
>
> What is the period of availability of this appropriation? What is the duration of the limitation regarding products containing titanium?

Congressionally Specified Periods of Availability

If Congress wants to provide for a period of availability in excess of one fiscal year, it has the Constitutional authority to do so. Under this authority, Congress often appropriates multiple-year and no-year appropriations.

The period of availability of an appropriation is presumed to be one fiscal year, unless a contrary intent is clearly indicated. Congress has often specified that funds are available for a multiple-year period, or "until expended." A period of availability that is specifically stated in an appropriations act will generally override conflicting language in enabling legislation or previously enacted authorization acts.

Multiple-Year Appropriations

Multiple-year appropriations are available for obligation for a definite period in excess of one fiscal year. 37 Comp. Gen. 861, 863 (1958). For example, if a fiscal year 2000 appropriation act (effective on October 1, 1999) specifies that it shall remain available until September 30, 2001, it is a two-year appropriation. In this case, this means that the funds appropriated will be available for obligation from October 1, 1999, until September 30, 2001. As a more specific illustration, the Navy's "shipbuilding and conversion" appropriation, found in the annual Defense Department appropriation acts, is typically a five-year appropriation. Congress generally will use language such as the following to create a multi-year appropriation (FY 2000 DoD Appropriations Act, Air Force RDT&E):

> For expenses necessary for basic and applied scientific research, development, test and evaluation, including maintenance, rehabilitation, lease, and operation of facilities and equipment, $13,674,537,000, to remain available for obligation until September 30, 2001.

Apart from the extended period of availability, multiple-year appropriations are subject to the same principles applicable to annual appropriations and do not present any special problems.

Just as Congress can by statute expand the obligational availability of an appropriation beyond one fiscal year, it can also appropriate funds for a fixed period less than a full fiscal year. For example, a fiscal year 1980 appropriation for the now-defunct Community Services Administration included funds for emergency energy assistance grants. Since the program was intended to provide assistance for increased heating fuel costs, and Congress did not want the funds to be used to buy air conditioners, the appropriation specified that awards could not be made after June 30, 1980. Department of the Interior and Related Agencies Appropriation Act, 1980, Pub. L. No. 96-126, 93 Stat. 954, 978 (1979). Appropriations available for obligation for less than a full fiscal year are, however, uncommon.

No-Year Appropriations

A no-year appropriation is available for obligation without fiscal year limitation. For an appropriation to be a no-year appropriation, the appropriating language must expressly so provide. 31 USC. § 1301(c). The standard language used to make a no-year appropriation is "to remain available until expended." 40 Comp. Gen. 694,696 (1961); 3 Comp. Dec.

623, 628 (1897). However, other language will suffice as long as its meaning is unmistakable, such as "without fiscal year limitation." See 57 Comp. Gen. 865, 869 (1978). For example, in the FY 2000 DoD Appropriations Act Congress indicated its intent to make a no-year appropriation with the following language:

> For activities of the [DoD] pursuant to...the Defense Production Act of 1950...$3,000,000 only for microwave power tubes [is appropriated] to remain available until expended.

The appropriations act language will take precedence over other general statutory provisions. For example, in *National Endowment for the Arts—Time Availability for Appropriations*, B-244241, 71 Comp. Gen. 39 (1991), the Comptroller General held that general statutory language making funds available until expended is subordinate to appropriations act language stating that funds are available until a date certain. This rule is a consequence of the application of the general rule that the more specific statute controls the more general statute. This is especially true when the more specific statute is also the last in time to be enacted.

The rules relating obligation and expenditure of no-year appropriations are straightforward. Essentially, all statutory time limits as to when the funds must be obligated and expended are removed, and the funds remain available for their original purposes until expended. 43 Comp. Gen. 657 (1964); 40 Comp. Gen. 694 (1961).

One issue that has arisen with regard to no-year appropriations involves the effect of subsequent congressional action on the availability of a prior year's no-year appropriation. In one case, Congress had made a no-year appropriation to the Federal Aviation Administration for the purchase of aircraft. A question arose as to the continued availability of the appropriation because, in the following year, Congress explicitly denied a budget request for the same purpose. The Comptroller General held that the subsequent denial did not restrict the use of the unexpended balance of the prior no-year appropriation The availability of the prior appropriation could not be changed by a later act "except in such respects and to such extent as is expressly stated or clearly implied by such act." 40 Comp. Gen. 694 (1961). See also B-200519, November 28, 1980. This is a specific example of the application of the rule against repeal by implication that was discussed in Chapter 1.

In another case, a no-year appropriation for the National Capital Park and Planning Commission included a monetary ceiling on non-contract services during the fiscal year. Based on the apparent intent of the ceiling, GAO concluded that the specific restriction had the effect of suspending the "available until expended" provision of prior unrestricted no-year appropriations as far as personal services were concerned, for any fiscal year in which the restriction was included. Thus, unobligated balances of prior unrestricted no-year appropriations could not be used to augment the ceiling. 30 Comp. Gen. 500 (1951).

A similar issue was considered in 62 Comp. Gen. 692 (1983). The Nuclear Regulatory Commission (NRC) received a no-year appropriation that included a prohibition on compensating interveners (an "intervener" is a party who joins a lawsuit after it has commenced). GAO held that the unobligated balance of a prior unrestricted no-year appropriation could be used to pay an Equal Access to Justice Act award to an intervener made in a restricted year, where part of the proceeding giving rise to the award was funded by an unrestricted appropriation. Unlike the situation in the National Capital case (30 Comp. Gen. 500), the restriction in the NRC case was expressly limited to "proceedings funded in *this Act*" (emphasis added). Since the no-year appropriation enacted in the prior year did not prohibit compensating interveners, those funds were available to compensate the interveners.

When no-year funds are deobligated, they remain available for obligation on the same basis as if they had never been obligated. 40 Comp. Gen. 694, 697 (1961); B-211323, January 3, 1984; B-200519, November 28, 1980. For example, if an agency recovers funds under the liquidated damages clause of the contract and the contract was funded from a no-year appropriation, the funds would be treated as unobligated balances available for expenditure in the same manner as the other funds in the account. 23 Comp. Gen. 365 (1943).

No-year appropriations have both advantages and disadvantages. An advantage to the spending agency is that no-year appropriations provide flexibility to use the funds when they will be most effective. Since the no-year funds will not expire, agencies can avoid the tendency to race to incur obligations at the end of the fiscal year. From the legislative perspective, however, a key disadvantage is the loss of congressional control over actual program levels from year to year. GAO has expressed the position that no-year appropriations should not be made in the absence of compelling programmatic or budgetary reasons. See GAO report entitled, *No-Year Appropriations in the Department of Agriculture*, PAD-78-74 (September 19, 1978).

The Effect of Authorization Acts and Enabling Legislation on the Period of Availability

An authorization of appropriations, like an appropriation itself, can be made on a multiple-year, no-year, or fiscal-year basis. A question arises regarding the extent to which the period of availability specified in an authorization or enabling act is controlling. Congress can, in an appropriation act, expand the period of availability beyond that specified in the authorization, but it must do so explicitly. The action must be explicit because of (1) the rule against repeals by implication, (2) the presumption that every appropriation in an annual appropriation act has a one-year period of availability, and (3) the prohibition in 31 U.S.C. § 1301(c) against construing an appropriation to be permanent or available continuously unless the appropriation act expressly so states. Thus, an appropriation of funds "to remain available until expended" (no-year) will override a provision in the authorizing legislation that authorized appropriations on a two-year basis. B-182101, October 16, 1974. See also B-149372/B-158195, April 29, 1969 (two-year appropriation of Presidential transition funds held controlling notwithstanding provision in Presidential Transition Act of 1963, which authorized services and facilities to former President and Vice President only for six months after expiration of term of office).

It also appears to make no difference whether the authorization merely authorizes the longer period of availability or directs it. For example, in 58 Comp. Gen. 321 (1979), the general provision in the appropriation act restricting availability to the current fiscal year, as the later expression of congressional intent, was held to override 25 U.S.C. §13a, which provides that the unobligated balances of certain Indian assistance appropriations "shall remain available for obligation and expenditure" for a second fiscal year. Similarly, in *Dabney v. Reagan*, No. 82 Civ. 2231-CSH (S.D.N.Y. March 21, 1985), 1985 WL 443, the court held that a two-year period of availability specified in appropriation acts would override a "mandatory" no-year authorization contained in the Solar Energy and Energy Conservation Bank Act.

THE BONA FIDE NEEDS RULE

One of the fundamental principles of appropriations law is the "bona fide needs" rule, which provides that a fiscal year appropriation may be obligated only to meet a legitimate, or bona fide, need arising in, or continuing to exist in, the fiscal year for which the appropriation was made. See, e.g., B-286929, April 25, 2001; B-282601, September 27, 1999; 68 Comp. Gen. 170, 171 (1989); 58 Comp. Gen. 471,473 (1979); B-183184, May 30, 1975. Although bona fide need issues arise most frequently in the context of annual appropriations, they can also arise in the context of multi-year appropriations.

Bona fide need questions arise in many contexts. For example, if an agency wants to enter into or modify a contract or make some other obligation or expenditure, it must determine which fiscal year to charge. The question may be whether a previously recorded obligation was charged against the correct appropriation. An agency may have taken certain actions that it should have recorded as an obligation but did not. When the time for payment arrives, the question again is which fiscal year to charge. All these scenarios raise essentially the same basic question: whether an obligation bears a sufficient relationship to the legitimate needs of the period of availability of the appropriation charged or sought to be charged.

Statutory Basis of the Bona Fide Needs Rule

The bona fide needs rule has a statutory basis. As noted in Chapter 1, the first general appropriation act in 1789 made appropriations "for the service of the present year," indicating the intent of Congress that the amount appropriated not be used for needs of the prior year or needs of the year following the expiration of the appropriation. This concept continues to the present time.

This "one-year" concept is also reflected in 31 U.S.C. § 1502(a), sometimes called the "bona fide needs statute," which states that the balance of a fixed-term appropriation "is available only for payment of expenses properly incurred during the period of availability or to complete contracts properly made within that period. . . ." The key word here is "properly," i.e., expenses "properly incurred" or contracts "properly made" within the period of availability. Thus, in B-257617, April 18, 1995, GAO held that the Internal Revenue Service could not use fiscal year 1993 cost underrun money to order additional contract items, reasoning that a contract modification that increases the quantity of items purchased is chargeable only to funds current at the time of the modification. See also, B-207453, Sept. 16, 1983, 83-2 CPD ¶ 401; B-115736, 33 Comp. Gen. 57 (1953); 37 Comp. Gen. 155 (1957).

Bona Fide Needs Determinations Are Highly Fact-Sensitive

Although the bona fide needs rule is applicable to all agency obligations that cite fixed-term appropriations, the determination of what constitutes a bona fide need of a particular fiscal year depends largely on the facts and circumstances of the particular case. 44 Comp. Gen. 399, 401 (1965); 37 Comp, Gen. 155, 159 (1957). In its most elementary form—where the entire transaction (contract or purchase, delivery or other performance, and payment) takes place during the same fiscal year—the rule means simply that the appropriation is available only for the needs of the current year. The corollary to this rule is that an annual appropriation is not available for the needs of a future year.

For example, suppose that on the last day of the fiscal year an agency learns that it can get a great deal on pencils and buys a truckload when it is clear that, based on the current usage rate, it already has in stock enough pencils to last several years. Since the agency does not have a bona fide need for a truckload of pencils for the last day of the fiscal year, it appears that the agency was merely trying to use up its appropriation before it expired. Such a purchase would violate the bona fide needs rule.

This example does not mean, however, that an agency can purchase only those supplies that it will actually use during the fiscal year. Agencies normally maintain inventories of common-use items. The bona fide needs rule does not prevent maintaining a legitimate inventory at reasonable and historical levels—the "need" being to maintain the inventory level so as to avoid disruption of operations. The problem arises when the inventory crosses the line from reasonable to excessive.

Application of the Bona Fide Needs Rule to Multiple-Year Appropriations

The bona fide needs rule applies to multiple-year as well as fiscal year appropriations, 68 Comp. Gen. 170 (1989); 55 Comp. Gen. 768, 773-74 (1976); B-235678, July 30, 1990. See also 64 Comp. Gen. 163, 166 (1984). During the last year of availability of a multiple-year appropriation, the bona fide needs rule applies in much the same way as it applies to an annual appropriation. Thus, if an agency is obligating funds from a two-year appropriation in September of the last year of the appropriation's period of availability, the agency must ensure that the obligation satisfies a bona fide need of the current fiscal year and not the subsequent fiscal year. If this analysis indicates that the obligation is intended to satisfy a bona fide need of the subsequent fiscal year, then the agency must obligate funds that will be available for obligation in that year.

In the case of multiple-year appropriations, the agency may have a choice regarding which appropriation to charge. For example, if an agency receives a two-year appropriation each year, it should be able to charge a new obligation to either of two appropriations. It could charge the obligation to the first year of newly appropriated two-year funds or to the second (and last) year of the appropriation that was enacted last year, since both are legally available for obligation.

> **Discussion Problem 4-2**
>
> An agency has received a three-year procurement appropriation. It must use this appropriation to purchase capital investment items with a purchase price over $100,000. On September 30 of the last year of the appropriation's period of availability, the agency obligates the funds to procure a $500,000 power generator that will be installed in a building. The agency wants to ensure that it uses this money prior to its expiration (at the end of the day). Although the site of the building has been identified, construction will not commence until March of the following year. Does this obligation comply with the requirements of the bona fide needs rule?

Although an agency may use a multiple-year appropriation for needs arising at any time during the period of availability, it may take a more restrictive approach and determine that a multiple-year appropriation can be obligated at any time during its availability, but only to meet a bona fide need of the year in which the funds were appropriated. Suppose, for example, that an agency receives a two-year appropriation every year. For FY 2000, it received an appropriation available through the end of FY 2001; for FY 2001, it received an appropriation available through the end of FY 2002, and so on. An agency may establish a policy that requires that the FY 2000 appropriation be used only for needs arising in FY 2000, although the appropriation act would allow the agency to create new obligations until the end of FY 2001. Thus, although an agency may elect to take this restrictive approach to impose strict control over its appropriations, the Comptroller General has held that such an approach is not legally required by the bona fide needs rule. In 68 Comp. Gen. 170, January 4, 1989, the Comptroller General determined that the Defense Logistics Agency could use its FY 1987 two-year research and development appropriation for a need arising in FY 1988. "There is no requirement that two-year funds be used only for the needs of the first year of their availability." 68 Comp. Gen. 170, at 172.

Thus, an agency can use its multiple-year appropriations to incur obligations to satisfy a bona fide need arising at any time during the period of availability of the multiple-year appropriation. Based on this rationale, it follows that the bona fide needs rule does not apply to no-year funds. 43 Comp. Gen. 657, 661 (1964). Since the period of availability of a no-year appropriation is indefinite (funds are available until expended), an agency may use no-year funds to satisfy any bona fide need arising prior to exhaustion of the appropriation.

"Continuing" Needs

When a need arises in one fiscal year and continues to exist in a subsequent fiscal year, the need may be a bona fide need of both fiscal years, and an issue arises regarding which year's appropriation should be charged. If a need arises during a particular fiscal year and the agency chooses not to satisfy it during that year, perhaps because of insufficient funds or higher priority needs, and the need continues to exist in the following year, the obligation to satisfy that need is properly chargeable to the later year's funds. "An unfulfilled need of one period may well be carried forward to the next as a continuing need with the next period's appropriation being available for funding." B-197274, September 23, 1983. For example, if a building develops a leaky roof in one fiscal year that is not repaired, there is a bona fide need for roof repair that arose in the first fiscal year and continues into subsequent fiscal years. Whenever the agency decides to fix the roof, it must use funds current when the obligation is created.

Thus, an important corollary to the bona fide needs rule is that a continuing need is chargeable to funds current for the year in which the obligation is made, regardless of the fact that the need may have originated in a prior year. The essential requirements of the "continuing need" corollary are that: (1) the need, unmet in the year in which it arose, must continue to exist in the subsequent fiscal year; (2) the decision of whether or not to incur the obligation must be within the agency's discretion; and (3) no obligation was in fact incurred during a prior year.

A good illustration of this rule is B-207433, September 16, 1983. In this case, the Army determined that it needed 150 thermal viewers. However, at the time of contract award, it only had funds to purchase 100 and entered into a contract for that number. The contract provided for a downward adjustment in the contract price if the contractor was able to perform at less than the contract price. After the appropriation charged with the contract had expired, the contractor incurred an underrun and proposed to use the excess funds to supply 50 additional viewers. It was undisputed that the Army had a need for the additional viewers at the time it entered the contract, and that the need continued to exist. The issue in the case was whether the Army could use the prior year funds to purchase the additional viewers, since there was an established bona fide need in the prior fiscal year and because the funds were already obligated on the contract.

GAO determined that the proper course of action was to deobligate the excess funds on the contract and credit the now-expired appropriation. If the Army still wanted to purchase the 50 additional viewers, it would have to charge current funds since they represent an additional quantity. GAO provided the following explanation:

> The essence of the [bona fide needs] rule is simply that an appropriation may be validly obligated only to meet a legitimate need existing during the period of availability. Under this concept, payments are chargeable to the year in which the obligation took place, even though not actually disbursed until a later year, as long as the need existed when the funds were obligated. Certainly the Army could have used underrun funds to procure additional viewers at any time during the period those funds remained available for obligation. Also, we are of course aware that an unmet need does not somehow evaporate merely because the period of availability has expired. However, nothing in the bona fide needs rule suggests that expired appropriations may be used for an item for which a valid obligation was not incurred prior to expiration merely because there was a need for that item during that period. . . Once the obligational period has expired, the procurement of an increased quantity must be charged to new money, and this is not affected by the fact that the need for that increased quantity may in effect be a 'continuing need' that arose during the prior period.

Another illustration is B-226198, July 21, 1987. In late FY 1986, the U.S. Geological Survey ordered certain microcomputer equipment to be delivered in early FY 1987, charging the purchase to FY 1986 funds. The equipment was delivered and accepted but was stolen before reaching the ordering office. The decision held that a reorder, placed in FY 1987, had to be charged to FY 1987 funds. As with the thermal viewers in B-207433, the fact that the need for the equipment arose in 1986 was immaterial. See also B-286929, April 25, 2001 (agency could not use expired funds for a project even if there was a bona fide for the project during the period of availability of the expired appropriation because the agency did not create an obligation to satisfy that need during the fiscal year by contracting).

Discussion Problem 4-3

In FY 2000, an agency awards a contract for declassification of information. The contract describes a three-phase project, stating: "This Contract addresses Phase I. Phases II and III will be addressed upon completion of Phase I." The agency obligates $17.5 million of FY 2000 funds for Phase I. The contractor completes Phase I in May 2001 at a cost of $8.5 million. The agency wants to use the unexpended, but now-expired, balance of $9 million to start work on Phase II of the declassification project. The agency contends that Phases II and III are bona fide needs of FY 2000 and that the expired budget authority should remain available to fund these additional phases. Is the agency correct? (Reference B-286929, April 25, 2001.)

Application of the Bona Fide Needs Rule to Supply Contracts

As a general rule, agencies must obligate funds that are current in the fiscal year in which the supplies will be used. B-287619, July 5, 2001; B-156161, 44 Comp. Gen. 695 (1965); B-155876, 44 Comp. Gen. 399 (1965); B-130815, 37 Comp. Gen. 155 (1957). In a 1901 opinion, the Comptroller General addressed the applicability of the bona fide needs rule and stated:

> An appropriation should not be used for the purchase of an article not necessary for the use of a fiscal year in which ordered merely in order to use up such appropriation. This would be a plain violation of the law.

8 Comp. Dec. 346,348 (1901).

Thus, where an obligation is made toward the end of a fiscal year and it is clear from the facts and circumstances that the need relates to the following fiscal year, the bona fide needs rule has been violated. The obligation is not a proper charge against the earlier appropriation, but must be charged against the following year's funds.

This was the result, for example, in 1 Comp. Gen. 115 (1921), in which an order for gasoline had been placed three days before the end of FY 1921 (the fiscal year ended in June at that time), with the gasoline to be delivered in monthly installments in FY 1922. The Comptroller General stated:

> It is not difficult to understand how the need for an article of equipment, such as a typewriter, might arise during the fiscal year 1921 and its purchase be delayed until the latter part of June, but as to supplies that are consumed as used, such as gasoline, it can not be held that they were purchased to supply a need of the fiscal year 1921 when the contract is made late in the month of June and expressly precludes the possibility of delivery before July 1, 1921.

This opinion makes a useful distinction between consumable supply items that an agency will use gradually over time (e.g., gasoline) and supply items that an agency can fully use immediately (e.g., typewriter). If the agency has a bona fide need for a typewriter (or a personal computer) in the year it is purchased, then it must fully charge the appropriation current at the time of purchase. Unlike the typewriter, however, the gasoline will be used in partial quantities, and such use will cross fiscal years. In this situation, unless an exception applies, the bona fide needs rule requires the agency to use funds current when the gasoline is consumed. Thus, although the agency will own and use the typewriter for more than one fiscal year (ideally), the typewriter cannot be allocated to different fiscal years, as could a consumable item, such as gasoline. As indicated in 1 Comp. Gen. 115, this difference affects the fiscal year to which an obligation should be charged.

> **Discussion Problem 4-4**
>
> An agency awards a contract on August 1, 2002 (citing FY 2002 funds) for furniture to be used in a building that is under construction at the time the furniture contract is awarded. The completion date for the building is November 15, 2002. The furniture supplier advises that it can make delivery within 30 days. Can the agency use the FY 2002 funds for this purchase?

As discussed, agencies must generally obligate funds that are current in the fiscal year in which the supplies will be used. Practical necessity, however, has resulted in two exceptions to this general rule: (1) the lead-time exception and (2) the stock-level exception.

The Lead-Time Exception

The lead-time exception recognizes that causes beyond an agency's control may result in delivery in the fiscal year subsequent to the year in which the bona fide need for the item arose. This delayed delivery typically results from either delivery lead time or production lead time.

The delivery lead-time exception recognizes that an agency may have a need for an item but may not be able to receive it in the current fiscal year. In this situation, if an agency has a bona fide need for an item in the year in which it is purchased, delivery in the next fiscal year does not violate the bona fide needs rule. For the exception to apply, the delivery lead time must be caused by factors beyond the agency's control, e.g., the contractor has many other orders to fill and does not have enough delivery personnel. Further, the time between contracting and delivery must not be excessive and the procurement must not be for standard, commercial items readily available from other sources. B-138574, 38 Comp. Gen. 628, 630 (1959). In other words, if the agency can obtain the items from another source in the same fiscal year in which the obligation was created, then accepting delivery in the subsequent year would indicate that the item was a bona fide need of the subsequent, and not the current, fiscal year.

The production lead-time exception permits the agency to consider the normal production lead-time in determining the bona fide needs for an acquisition. Thus, an agency may contract in one fiscal year for delivery of an item in the subsequent fiscal year if the intervening period is necessary for the production of the item. See B-130815, 37 Comp. Gen. 155, 159 (1957). As in the case of the delivery lead-time exception, the critical factor is the existence of a bona fide need for the item at the time the obligation is created. For example, if an agency needs an item in FY 2001, but the normal lead time between order and delivery of the item is 45 days, an obligation of FY 2001 funds is appropriate if delivery occurs on or before November 14, 2001. (Remember October 1, 2001, is the beginning of FY 2002). This obligation represents a bona fide need of FY 2001. However, if the contractor can deliver sooner, but the agency directs the contractor to withhold delivery until *after* November 14, 2001, there is no bona fide need for the item in FY 2001 because the necessary production lead-time would allow delivery in FY 2001.

Although delivery lead time and production lead time have been analyzed separately for the sake of clarity, in an actual procurement, the production time and the delivery time would be combined. Thus, assume that an agency has a bona fide need for an item in fiscal year 2001 and awards a contract for the item on September 30, 2001. If the production lead time is 45 days and the delivery lead time is 15 days, these periods could be combined to allow for obligation of FY 2001 funds if the delivery date is 60 days or less after the start of the new fiscal year.

The Stock-Level Exception

Under the stock-level exception, an agency may purchase stock items in one fiscal year even though it will not use the items until the subsequent fiscal year if the purchase is necessary to maintain adequate and normal stock levels. For example, an agency may award a contract to maintain the normal, authorized stock levels of repair parts in August 2001 and may require delivery in September 2001, using FY 2001 funds, even if the agency knows that it will not *use* the repair parts until FY 2002. The stock-level exception recognizes that, although an agency may not have bona fide need to use the item at the time of obligation, it does have a bona fide need to maintain a certain stock level at the time of obligation. It is this latter need that justifies the use of the FY 2001 funds in the example.

To use this exception properly, agencies must ensure that they are *maintaining* a stock level based on historical usage rates, and not exceeding that level. It would be a violation of the bona fide needs rule for an agency to stockpile supplies at the end of the fiscal year in a manner that exceeds the traditional stock level. B-134277, Dec. 18, 1957 (unpub.). The bona fide needs rule would be violated by such stockpiling even if the agency could obtain greatly reduced prices for the item. Note that stockpiling items at the *beginning* of a fiscal year is not as likely to violate the bona fide needs rule because it is more likely that the agency will take delivery and use the items within the same fiscal year. It is the purchase of items in one fiscal year and the delivery or use of the items in the next fiscal year that must be justified by one of the exceptions.

Application of the Bona Fide Needs Rule to Service Contracts

As a general rule, services are considered to be a bona fide need of the fiscal year in which the services are rendered. B-277165, January 10, 2000; B-237180, Jan. 17, 1990, 90-1 CPD ¶ 64; B-214597, 65 Comp. Gen. 154 (1985). Consequently, when the general rule applies, an agency would have to fund services from an appropriation that is current when the services are rendered. Thus, to avoid a break in services, an agency would have to fund its service contracts on a fiscal year cycle (i.e., incurring obligations with a period of performance that commences on October 1 and ends on September 30). However, there are many situations in which the general rule does not apply.

Severable vs. Nonseverable Services

To facilitate analysis under the bona fide needs rule, it is useful to categorize services as either severable or nonseverable.

A service is *severable* if it can be separated into components that independently meet a separate need of the government. For example, a typical custodial services contract is a severable contract because each day the government receives a benefit (e.g., a clean building) that is independent of the services that have been performed and the services that will be performed in the future. The determination of whether services are severable or nonseverable does not depend on the type of contract under which the services are procured. See *Funding for Air Force Cost Plus Fixed Fee Level of Effort Contract*, B-277165, January 10, 2000 (nature of the work determines whether a service is severable or nonseverable for obligational purposes, not the type of contract).

As a general rule, severable services are the bona fide needs of the fiscal year in which performed. *Matter of Incremental Funding of Multiyear Contracts*, B-241415, 71 Comp. Gen. 428 (1992); *EPA Level of Effort Contracts*, 65 Comp. Gen. 154 (1985). Thus, funding of severable service contracts generally may not cross fiscal years and must be funded from an appropriation that is available for obligation on the date the contractor performs the services.

A service is *nonseverable* if the service produces a single or unified outcome that cannot be subdivided for separate performance in different fiscal years. For example, a contract to perform an environmental impact assessment and submit a report of the contractor's findings would be a nonseverable contract because the final product (the report) is the result of all of the contractor's prior interdependent efforts. If a service is nonseverable, the agency must fund the entire effort with dollars available for obligation at the time the contract is awarded, and the contract performance may cross fiscal years. *Incremental Funding of U.S. Fish and Wildlife Service Research Work Orders*, B-240264, 73 Comp. Gen. 77 (1994); *Proper Appropriation to Charge Expenses Relating to Nonseverable Training Course*, B-238940, 70 Comp. Gen. 296 (1991); *Proper Fiscal Year Appropriation to Charge for Contract and Contract Increases*, B-219829, 65 Comp. Gen. 741 (1986); *Comptroller General to W.B. Herms, Department of Agriculture*, B-37929, 23 Comp. Gen. 370 (1943).

Discussion Problem 4-5

The Veterans Administration (VA) awards a contract on September 1, 2002, for a national needs assessment study of Vietnam-era veterans. The contract cites the agency's "expenses" appropriation, which has a period of availability of one year. The statement of work (SOW) requires the contractor to submit a final report 42 months after award. In addition, the SOW requires the contractor to provide interim reports at one-month intervals during the first six months and subsequently at three-month intervals. Can the VA use its one-year appropriation for work that will span 42 months? (Refer to B-219829, Jul. 22, 1986, 65 Comp. Gen. 741.)

The Air Force case cited above, B-277165, contained a useful analysis that advanced the level of guidance that had been previously available on the severable vs. nonseverable services distinction. In that case, the contract was for launch vehicle integration (LVI) services (i.e., the integration of the satellite with launch vehicle). The contractor was required to conduct a variety of tests, review integration documents, attend working group meetings, track and report agency interface verification activities, and perform various other ongoing, repetitive functions. The agency contended that this was a nonseverable contract because all of the contractor's efforts were aimed at a particular result, the successful launch of the satellite. GAO did not agree, however, and concluded that the contract was severable, stating:

> We agree that the scope and objective of CLIN 006 in Contract 0050 (and Contract 0029 for that matter) was in a general sense the successful launch of the satellite on Flight 17. However, this is not dispositive of the severability issue since most services have some identifiable goal to be achieved by their completion. For example, while we view employee services as severable for bona fide need purposes, the result of employee services are always directed towards the accomplishment of some goal that often includes identifiable end products that meet the needs of the government. While the SOW generally may state that contract 0050 is intended to insure a successful launch and orbiting of the satellites, such a general goal does not in and of itself make the required repeat LVI effort a completion, as opposed to a term, contract. Nor does it constitute an end product requiring the contract be treated as nonseverable for obligating purposes.

Thus, merely stating a general objective, such as a "clean building," will not transform a severable services contract into one that is nonseverable. In the launch vehicle integration case, the agency received incremental elements of completed performance. Although these increments led to a larger end result, the contract was considered severable because each incremental element of performance conferred a benefit.

Statutory Exception

A fairly recent change to the general rule regarding severable services contracts authorizes agencies to obligate funds current at the time of contract award to fund a severable service contract that crosses fiscal years, provided the period of performance does not exceed 12 months. See, 10 U.S.C. § 2410a; 41 U.S.C. § 253l. This authority enables agencies to avoid the end-of-fiscal-year increase in contracting workload because it can spread the award of its services contracts throughout the fiscal year. Further, this authority makes it possible to fund more than 12 months of services from an annual appropriation. For example, assume that an agency awards an 11-month severable services contract on October 1, 2001. This contract would be funded with funds current on the date of award (i.e., FY 2002 funds). Assume further that the agency awards a follow-on contract for 12 months when the first contract ends (September 1, 2002). Although this contract will be performed almost entirely in FY 2003, under the statutory authority discussed, the agency can use FY 2002 funds to fund the entire contract. In this example, the agency was able to fund 23 months of severable services from an annual appropriation because each contract was for a period of 12 months or less. See, e.g., *Funding of Maintenance Contract Extending Beyond Fiscal Year*, B-259274, May 22, 1996, 96-1 CPD ¶ 247 (the "Kelly Air Force Base" case). This statutory authority is significant only in the context of severable service contracts. Nonseverable contracts may cross fiscal years and are not limited to a 12-month period of performance.

Application of the Bona Fide Needs Rule to Training Contracts

Training courses that begin shortly after the start of the fiscal year would constitute a bona fide need of the prior fiscal year if the scheduling of the course is beyond the control of the agency and the time between award of the contract and performance is not excessive. *Proper Appropriation to Charge for Expenses Relating to Nonseverable Training Course*, B-238940, 70 Comp. Gen. 296 (1991); *Proper Appropriation to Charge for Expenses Relating to Nonseverable Training Course*, B-277886.2, Aug. 3, 1989 (unpub.).

Application of the Bona Fide Needs Rule to Construction Contracts

Contracts for construction must fulfill a bona fide need arising within the funds' period of availability. A determination of what constitutes a bona fide need of a particular year depends upon the facts and circumstances of a particular year. *Associate General Counsel Kepplinger*, B-235086, Apr. 24, 1991 (unpub.). Construction contracts may constitute a bona fide need of the fiscal year in which the contract is awarded even though performance is not completed until the following fiscal year.

In analyzing bona fide needs for construction contracts, the agency should consider all factors that relate to the timing of the project. For example, the agency should obviously consider when it actually needs the construction project to be completed. If an agency will not be prepared to occupy an office building on its scheduled completion date, it may not have a bona fide need to award a contract for the project until a subsequent fiscal year.

The agency should also consider the normal weather conditions for the area. A project that cannot reasonably be expected to commence before the onset of winter weather is not the bona fide need of the prior fiscal year. For example, if the construction will be performed in a northern location where weather conditions generally preclude construction work between November and March, it is unlikely that the agency will be able to demonstrate that it has a bona fide need to award a construction contract in September.

Finally, the agency should always consider when it will be able to make facilities, sites, or tools available to the contractor. To illustrate, if the agency must occupy a building until December, award of a demolition contract in the prior fiscal year (ending on September 30) would violate the bona fide needs rule, unless there were unusual circumstances necessitating the award at that time. Such circumstances could exist, for example, if the contractor needed three months to study the building to determine the most appropriate demolition method. Thus, when analyzing a bona fide needs issue, the agency should consider the *entire* requirement and identify any preliminary activities that the contractor must perform, as well as any long lead-time activities. This analysis may indicate the need for an earlier start time and, consequently, an earlier obligation date.

USE OF EXPIRED APPROPRIATIONS

Annual funds that remain unobligated at the end of the fiscal year for which they were appropriated are said to "expire" for obligational purposes. In other words, they cease to be available for new obligations. The same principle applies to multiple-year appropriations as of the end of the last fiscal year of their period of availability. For purposes of this discussion, annual and multiple-year appropriations are referred to cumulatively as "fixed appropriations." 31 U.S.C. § 1551(a)(3).

For five years after the time an appropriation expires for incurring new obligations, both the obligated and unobligated balances of that appropriation are available for recording, adjusting, and liquidating obligations properly chargeable to that account. 31 U.S.C. § 1553(a). Appropriations retain their complete accounting classification identifiers throughout the entire five-year period. Since expired funds are no longer available for new obligations, agencies generally prefer to use expired funds rather than current funds and often devise novel justifications for doing so. Many of these novel justifications are highlighted in various Inspector General reports and GAO audits as violations of the bona fide needs rule. The following, however, are situations in which an agency may properly record obligations against expired funds.

Bid Protests

When an agency receives a bid protest, it is prohibited from awarding or authorizing commencement of performance of the contract that is the subject of the protest. This prohibition remains in effect until the protest is resolved (except in limited circumstances that are not relevant to this fiscal discussion). 31 U.S.C. § 3553(c); 4 C.F.R. § 21.6 (1998); FAR 33.104(b); *McDonald Welding v. Webb*, 829 F.2d 593 (6th Cir. 1987); *Survival Technology Inc. v. Marsh*, 719 F. Supp. 18 (D.D.C. 1989); *Florida Professional Review Org.*, B-253908.2, Jan. 10, 1994, 94-1 CPD ¶ 17.

If the funds intended for the contract have expired while the protest is being litigated, application of the general rule would prohibit the agency from using those funds for a new obligation after the protest is resolved. However, a statutory exception, 31 U.S.C. § 1558, enables agencies to avoid this result. Section 1558 provides that funds available to an agency for obligation at the time that a GAO protest is filed, or at the time a judicial or administrative action is commenced, will remain available for obligation for 100 days after the date on which the final ruling is made on the protest or other action. However, this rule applies only if the action involves a challenge to (1) a contract solicitation (2) a proposed contract award, (3) an actual contract award, or (4) the eligibility of an offeror, a potential offeror, or the awardee to receive the contract. In addition, the commencement of the protest or other action must prevent the agency from awarding the contract or proceeding with the procurement. See also FAR 33.102(c).

To illustrate, if an agency issues a request for proposals (RFP) in one fiscal year and receives a protest challenging the terms of the solicitation, it is prohibited from awarding a contract under the challenged solicitation until the protest is resolved. If the protest is resolved in the subsequent fiscal year and the agency still has a need for the goods or services solicited, it can use the now expired funds to award the contract. Such an award would generally be prohibited because it is a new obligation and is citing expired funds. The statutory exception allows the agency and the protester to fully address the protest issues without concern regarding the imminent expiration of funds.

> **Discussion Problem 4-6**
>
> An agency releases an RFP on August 1, 2002, for 100 desktop computers and reserves funds in its one-year "operations" appropriation. On August 15 a prospective bidder files a bid protest with GAO, alleging that the RFP improperly restricts competition. GAO issues a decision denying the protest on November 1, 2002. The agency still needs the computers. Can it use the now-expired FY 2002 operations funds to make this purchase?
>
> Assume that, due to an expansion in its work force, the agency now needs 25 more computers and would like to simply add them to the original contract rather than start the paperwork for a new contract. The contracting officer asks the fund certification official if she could provide additional funds from the FY 2002 operations appropriation for the additional 25 computers. Is this permissible?

Terminations for Default

If an agency terminates a contract for default in one fiscal year and a bona fide need still exists for the supplies or services in the subsequent fiscal year, then the originally obligated funds remain available for obligation for a reprocurement contract, even if they have otherwise expired. The Comptroller General articulated the rationale for this rule as follows:

> If all replacement contracts were treated as new contracts, an agency whose contractor defaults would be required to deobligate prior year's funds which support the defaulted contract, and reprogram and obligate current year funds, even though the particular expenditure was budgeted for the prior year. Because contractor defaults can neither be anticipated nor controlled, a great deal of uncertainty would be introduced into the budgetary process. In some cases agencies would have to request supplemental appropriations to cover these unplanned and unprogrammed deficits which could result in costly

program overruns. The rule, therefore, avoids many administrative problems that cause procurement delays.

Funding of Replacement Contracts, B-198074, July 15, 1981, 60 Comp. Gen. 591, 81-2 CPD ¶ 33.

Requirements

Three requirements that must be met to allow for the use of expired funds for the reprocurement contract. *Lawrence W. Rosine Co.*, B-185405, 55 Comp. Gen. 1351 (1976).

First, a bona fide need for the work, supplies, or services must have existed when the original contract was executed, and it must continue to exist up to the award of the replacement contract. E.g., 55 Comp. Gen. 1351, 1353 (1976); 34 Comp. Gen. 239, 240 (1954). If it is determined that the terminated contract was awarded to fulfill a bona fide need of a fiscal year other than the year against which the obligation was recorded, it would also be improper to charge the replacement contract to the same appropriation. 35 Comp. Gen. 692 (1956). In other words, this exception does not confer upon an agency the authority to do something it could not have properly done when it awarded the terminated contract.

The second requirement is that the replacement contract cannot exceed the scope of the terminated contract. To the extent that the replacement contract does exceed the scope of the terminated contract, it constitutes a new obligation and must be charged to funds available for obligation at the time the replacement contract is awarded. E.g., 44 Comp. Gen. 399 (1965); B-181176-O.M., June 26, 1974. The scope of the terminated contract can be exceeded, for example, by ordering more supply items or additional hours (in a labor-hour contract) than were initially purchased. These types of costs are to be distinguished from additional costs to perform the same work, which are referred to as excess costs of reprocurement in the context of terminations for default. The agency may use funds from the appropriation originally charged under the contract to cover the excess costs of reprocurement. Most default termination clauses permit the agency to seek reimbursement from the defaulted contractor for these excess costs.

Finally, the replacement contract must be awarded within a reasonable time after termination of the original contract. E.g., 60 Comp. Gen. 591, 593 (1981). Excessive delay raises the presumption that the original contract was not intended to meet a bona fide need existing at the time of award. The same result may follow if there is unwarranted delay in terminating the original contract. 32 Comp. Gen, 565 (1953). There are no firm rules concerning how much time an agency has to award a replacement contract, and the determination of what constitutes an "excessive delay" will depend on the facts of each situation. Relevant factors include the length of time it took the agency to award the terminated contract, the availability of personnel to perform the administrative tasks necessary to make award (including evaluators, advisors, and contracting personnel), whether the contractor has challenged the termination for default and external conditions affecting the requirement (e.g., seasonal availability of materials, the effects weather on contract performance).

General Continuing Needs Distinguished

The first requirement states that the bona fide need addressed by the terminated contract must continue to exist in the fiscal year in which the replacement contact is awarded. This situation differs from the "continuing bona fide need" discussed earlier. Under the general bona fide need rule, if an agency has a continuing need (e.g., a leaky roof), it can elect to satisfy the requirement as long as the need exists, but it would have to use funds current when the obligation is created. If the roof repair contract is awarded in FY 2001, then FY 2001 funds would have to be used (assuming an annual appropriation). An agency could not award a roof repair contract in FY 2001, citing FY 2000 funds, on the theory that the roof started leaking in FY 2000 and is therefore a FY 2000 bona fide need. The termination for default situation is actually an exception to this general rule because it allows an agency to create a new obligation that cites expired funds.

Thus, in the termination for default situation, there is also a "continuing need" in the sense that the agency had a requirement last fiscal year that continues into the subsequent fiscal year because the agency terminated the contract. However, if the agency wants to use the now-expired prior year funds, it must comply with the requirements of the exception and award the reprocurement contract without undue delay. In the more conventional continuing need situation, the agency is obligating current funds and there is no requirement to make the award promptly, provided of course that the award is made during the period of availability of the appropriation cited.

Discussion Problem 4-7

On August 1, 2001, an agency awards a cost-reimbursement contract to develop inventory control software for $500,000. The contract cites FY 2001 annual appropriations. On November 15 the contracting officer properly terminates the contract because the contractor has informed the contracting officer that it was spending too much time on this contract and will not continue working on it. On November 30 the contracting officer issues a solicitation for a replacement contract; on January 15, 2002, the contracting officer awards a contract. Unfortunately, the cost of the replacement contract is $100,000 more than the terminated contract.

Since the replacement contract was awarded in FY 2002, should the agency use FY 2002 funds? Can the agency use the now-expired FY 2001 funds up to the original contract cost of $500,000? Can it also use FY 2001 funds for the additional cost ($100,000)?

Mandatory vs. Discretionary Use of Expired Funds after Default Termination

The GAO decisions applying this rule state that, if the conditions discussed are met, the funds obligated to the terminated contract remain "available" for obligation. It is not clear, however, whether this means that an agency *may* use the expired funds to award the replacement contract or that an agency *must* use the expired funds to award the replacement contract. It would seem that an agency would always be authorized to obligate currently available funds to meet a valid and current bona fide need. However, some of the GAO decisions cited use language that suggests that the agency *must* use the funds cited on the terminated contract.

For example, in B-198074, July 15, 1981, 60 Comp. Gen. 591, the Comptroller General explained that, when a contract is terminated for default, "the obligation established for the original contract is not extinguished because the replacement contract is considered to represent a continuation of the original obligation rather than a new contract." If the replacement contract is not a new contract, then it could be argued that the agency can use *only* the funds that were used to fund the terminated contract. Although this precise issue has not been addressed by the Comptroller General, it seems unlikely that GAO, by this language, intended to require that agencies use prior-year funds exclusively. Since it is well established that agencies can use current funds to award a contract for an existing bona fide need, even if that need arose in a prior fiscal year, if GAO intended to limit this authority, one would have expected that it would have done so more explicitly. Consequently, it would seem that an agency may use *either* current funds or prior-year funds (if the conditions are met) to fund a replacement contract.

Terminations for Convenience of the Government

The right of the federal government to terminate a contracts for its own convenience is a right that does not have a direct counterpart in the commercial sector. In the commercial sector, such a unilateral rejection of a contract would be regarded as a breach of contract (unless the other party has first breached the contract). To avoid placing excessive risk and hardship on the contractor, the standard termination for convenience clauses (see, e.g., FAR 42.249-2) require the agency to reimburse the contractor for its allowable costs of performance prior to the termination, the costs of responding to the termination, plus a reasonable profit.

Fiscal Effect of Termination for Convenience

As a general rule, termination of a contract for the convenience of the government will extinguish the availability of prior-year funds obligated to the terminated contract. Consequently, in most instances, such funds are not available to fund a replacement contract in a subsequent year. The inability to use the expired funds for a replacement contract in this situation is generally not a problem: When an agency terminates a contract for its convenience, it typically does so because it cannot fund continued performance or there is no longer a need for the goods or services to be provided under the terminated contract. In either situation, the agency is not interested in awarding a replacement contract.

There is one situation, however, in which the agency is interested in awarding a replacement contract after it has terminated a contract for convenience. If an agency receives a protest to the award of a contract and it is determined that the contract award was improper, the agency may terminate the improperly awarded contract for convenience. In this situation, it is likely that the agency will still need the goods or services for which it contracted and will be interested in awarding a replacement contract. If the funds obligated to the improperly awarded contract have expired, an issue arises as to the availability of those funds for the replacement contract.

Funds originally obligated for an improperly awarded contract may be used in a subsequent fiscal year to fund a replacement contract if the original contract is terminated for convenience pursuant to a court order or to a determination by GAO or other competent authority that the award was improper. *Funding of Replacement Contracts*, B-232616, 68 Comp. Gen. 158 (1988). In 1991, this exception was extended to situations in which the contracting officer, instead of a judicial or administrative forum, determines that a contract award was improper and that the contract should be terminated for convenience. See *Navy, Replacement Contract*,

B-238548, Feb. 5, 1991, 70 Comp. Gen. 230, 91-1 CPD ¶ 117 (holding that funds are available after contracting officer's determination that original award was improper).

Requirements

As with the exception applicable to terminations for default, several requirements must be satisfied before an agency can obligate expired funds to award a contract to replace a contract terminated for convenience: (1) the original award must have been made in good faith; (2) the agency has a continuing bona fide need for the goods or services involved; (3) the replacement contract is of the same size and scope as the original contract; and (4) the contracting officer executes the replacement contract without undue delay after the original contract is terminated for convenience. If these requirements are satisfied, then the agency may award a replacement contract and obligate the funds that were initially obligated to the terminated contract, even if those funds have expired.

This exception only applies to convenience terminations necessitated by a determination that the terminated contract was awarded improperly. If an agency terminates a contract for some other reason, it cannot use expired funds to procure the goods or services that would have been provided under the terminated contract.

> **Discussion Problem 4-8**
>
> On September 15, 2001, an agency awards a 12-month contract for facility maintenance services at its aging administrative headquarters building. On October 15, 2001, the agency determines that the aging building should be demolished and a new building constructed. The agency starts moving people out of the building on October 30, 2001. On November 1, 2001, the contracting officer terminates the contract for convenience, since the building will no longer be occupied. In an unforeseen turn of events, the agency determines on January 15, 2002, that the old building has great historic value and decides not to demolish it. The agency decides to move people back into the building, which triggers a need for facility maintenance services. The contracting officer would like to use the now-expired FY 2001 funds, using the "replacement contract" theory discussed in a 1988 GAO case (*Funding of Replacement Contracts*, B-232616, 68 Comp. Gen. 158).
>
> Are the FY 2001 funds available for the award of the facility maintenance contract in FY 2002? Did the agency have authority to award a severable services contract that crosses fiscal years using FY 2001 funds?

Contract Modifications That Reduce Scope

When an agency executes a contract modification that reduces the scope of the contract, the result is generally a reduction in the agency's liability. If the funds obligated on the contract exceed the amount of the agency's known liability, the agency is generally required to deobligate the excess funds. If the agency still has a need for the goods or services deleted from the contract, an issue arises regarding the availability of the deobligated funds for the replacement contract.

This situation may arise when the contractor's overall performance is satisfactory, but is unsatisfactory in a some areas. In such a situation, an agency may not be able to terminate the entire contract for default (or may not want to do so), but wants to have another contractor perform those aspects of the work that are not being performed satisfactorily by the current contractor. If the funds are deobligated while they are still available for obligation, then the agency may use the current funds just as it would when creating any new obligation. However, if the funds have expired, the agency may want to use the expired funds by analogizing to the termination for convenience exception. In other words, the issue is whether a deductive change could be viewed as a termination for convenience on a smaller scale and, if so, whether the termination for convenience funding exception would apply to allow use of expired funds for the replacement contract.

The Comptroller General has considered this type of situation and concluded that an agency may not use expired funds deobligated as a result of a modification to fund a replacement contract. B-200692.2, September 1, 1987, 66 Comp. Gen. 625. The basis for distinguishing deductive modifications from terminations for convenience is the degree of agency discretion. In the termination for convenience situation, recall that an agency may obligate expired funds for a replacement contract only if the termination results from a determination that the underlying contract award was improper. In such a case, the agency is required to terminate the contract to ensure the integrity of the contract award process. However, in the deductive modification situation, the agency is not required to modify the contract and has the discretion to use a variety of other contract administration procedures to address the contractor's performance problems.

This distinction was illustrated in B-200692.2, September 1, 1987, 66 Comp. Gen. 625. In that case, the Navy had awarded a contract for the construction of 12 ships. The contractor filed for bankruptcy and was authorized under the Bankruptcy Act to reject the entire contract. To avoid this possibility, the Navy agreed to a contract modification reducing the number of ships to be provided from 12 to 10. The question was whether the now-expired funds originally obligated for the two ships deleted by the modification were available to fund a reprocurement. GAO concluded that they were not because there had been no default, nor was there an actual rejection under the Bankruptcy Act. GAO reasoned: "[T]he modification was an essentially voluntary act on the part of the Navy, and as such is beyond the scope of the replacement contract rule." 66 Comp. Gen. 625, 627. Therefore, any replacement contract for the two deleted ships would have to be charged to appropriations current at the time it was made. Thus, although a deductive modification may be similar to a partial termination for convenience in some respects, since it is a voluntary agency action, an agency cannot use expired deobligated funds to procure the goods or services that were deleted from the modified contract.

Contract Modifications That Increase Amount Obligated

The period of contract performance may extend over several fiscal years, and modifications to the contract may occur for a variety of reasons. If a contract modification increases the amount the government owes the contractor, and the modification occurs after the expiration of the appropriation used to fund the contract, the question from the bona fide needs perspective is which fiscal year to charge with the modification. The determination of which fiscal year funds must be used in this situation requires application of the general rules of obligation discussed in Chapter 2. The basic rule is that new obligations can be charged only to funds that are available for obligation at the time the obligation is created. Thus, the critical issue is whether the modification creates a new liability (use current appropriation) or satisfies a pre-existing liability (use appropriation obligated for contract award).

Situations in Which Modifications May Be Charged to Expired Appropriations

When a contract modification does not represent a new requirement or liability, but instead only quantifies the amount of the government's pre-existing liability, then such a price adjustment is a bona fide need of the same year in which funds were obligated for the original contract. Most government contracts contain provisions that, under certain conditions, render the government liable to make equitable adjustments in the contract price. Such liability may arise due to changes in specifications, government-caused delay, changed conditions, increased overhead rates, or any one of a number of other similar causes. These bases for the government's liability are set out in standard contract clauses such as the "changes" clause, "government property" clause, "negotiated overhead rates" clause, and many other remedy-granting clauses that apply to particular situations.

Since the government cannot know at the time of contract award whether it will incur any liability under the contract's remedy-granting clauses and, if so, the amount of such liability, it cannot obligate funds to cover this potential liability at the time of award. Nevertheless, when an upward price adjustment is necessitated in a subsequent year, the general approach is to ask whether the adjustment is attributable to "antecedent liability," that is, whether it arises and is enforceable under a provision in the original contract. If the government's liability is based on antecedent liability, then a within-scope price adjustment executed in a subsequent fiscal year must generally be charged against the appropriation current at the time the contract was awarded. (There is one exception to this general rule that will be discussed later in this chapter.) See B-224702, Aug 5, 1987, 87-2 CPD ¶ 128; 59 Comp. Gen. 518 (1980); 23 Comp, Gen, 943 (1944); 21 Comp. Gen. 574 (1941); 18 Comp. Gen. 363 (1938); B-146285 -O. M., September 28, 1976. Thus, under this rule, if an agency owes a contractor money for providing the contractor with defective government property, the costs will be charged to the appropriation initially cited on the contract. This is true even if the liability is not determined until a fiscal year subsequent to the year of contract award. B-203074, August 6, 1981 (holding that the appropriation initially obligated on a contract is the correct appropriation to use to fund termination settlement costs). This principle is often referred to as the "relation back" doctrine. E.g., 37 Comp. Gen. 861,863 (1958).

The rationale for the relation-back doctrine is that a within-scope contract modification based on a remedy-granting clause in the contract does not give rise to a new liability, but instead only renders fixed and certain the amount of the government's pre-existing liability under the contract. In other words, at the time of contract award, the government agreed to be liable to the contractor if certain conditions arose during the period of contract performance. As noted, the government property clauses (FAR 52.245-2 and FAR 52.245-5) are examples of such liability. Under these clauses, the contractor is entitled to an equitable adjustment if the government delivers defective government-furnished property (GFP) to the contractor. Although the *amount* of the government's liability is unknown at the time of contract award, the basis for the liability was established by the terms of the contract. Since that liability arose at the time the contract was awarded, the subsequent price adjustment is considered a bona fide need of the year of contract award. The concept was stated as follows in 23 Comp. Gen. 943, 945 (1944):

> It is true that at the time the contract was executed it was not known that there would, in fact, be any changes ordered for which the contractor would be entitled to be paid an amount in addition to amounts otherwise payable under the contract. Also, it is true that [the Changes clause] contemplates the execution of amendments to the contract from time to time covering such changes. However, the fact remains that the obligations and liabilities of the parties respecting such changes are fixed by the terms of the original contract, and the various amendments merely render definite and liquidated the extent of the Government's liability in connection with such changes.

See also B-245856.7, 71 Comp. Gen. 502 (1992) (since it is the original contract that makes the government liable for a price increase under specified conditions and the subsequent contract change merely makes that liability fixed and certain, the liability relates back to the original contract and the price increase is charged to the appropriation initially obligated by the contract).

Of course, if and when the government becomes liable to a contractor under a remedy-granting clause, it must be able to identify a source of funds to satisfy that liability. To avoid over-obligating the original appropriation, the contracting officer must estimate the expected net additional obligations to ensure that available appropriations are not committed to other purposes. E.g., 61 Comp. Gen. 609,612 (1982); B-192036, September 11, 1978. The agency (generally the financial management office) must frequently review the contracting officer's estimates of potential liability to ensure that appropriations do not remain encumbered in excess of the amounts that will actually be needed to meet the total liability under the contract.

For example, the NASA Financial Management Manual 9000, provides the following guidance to ensure that funds will be available to liquidate contingent liabilities that will be finalized as modifications to the contract:

> i. **CONTRACT AMENDMENTS AND MODIFICATIONS.** An authorization to amend or modify a non-incrementally funded contract shall be recorded as a commitment at the time of certification of fund availability in the amount of the estimated cost of such amendment or modification. Where the authorization is to amend or modify an incrementally funded contract, only those amendments or modifications which add funds in addition to the previously funded increment shall be certified for fund availability and committed. The commitment recorded shall be in the amount of the additional funding.

Chapter 9030, para. 9031-9.

This is an important preliminary step. If the contracting officer executes the modification prior to ensuring the availability of adequate funding, an Antideficiency Act violation would result if funding is not available.

If an agency must charge the appropriation initially used to fund the contract, but the unobligated balance in that appropriation is not sufficient, the agency cannot charge current funds. The general rule is that, absent statutory authority, current appropriations are not available to fund an obligation or liability of a prior obligational period. If insufficient funds remain in the prior year's appropriation, the agency must seek a supplemental or deficiency appropriation and must further consider the possibility that the Antideficiency Act has been violated.

In an early case, for example, an agency had contracted for repairs to a building toward the end of fiscal year 1904. Since it was clear that the repairs were needed at the time they were ordered, they were chargeable to FY 1904 appropriations, and the exhaustion of the 1904 appropriation did not permit use of 1905 funds. 11 Comp. Dec. 454 (1905). (The contract constituted a valid obligation against the 1904 appropriation.). See also 21 Comp. Dec. 822 (1915).

Situations in Which Modifications May Not Be Charged to Expired Appropriations

If a contract modification adds capability, expands performance, or increases quantities in response to new or amended requirements, then the original funds are not be available for obligation even if such modification is authorized under the changes clause. Thus, if a modification exceeds the general scope of the original contract, for example, by increasing the quantity of items to be delivered, the modification amounts to a new obligation and is chargeable to funds current at the time the modification is made. 25 Comp. Gen. 332 (1945) (purported change order issued after completion of contract, covering work contractor was not legally bound to do under original contract, amounted to new contract). 37 Comp. Gen. 861 (1958); B-207433, September 16, 1983. See also *Modification to Contract Involving Cost Underrun*, B-257617, 1995 U.S. Comp. Gen. LEXIS 258 (April 18, 1995); *Magnavox—Use of Contract Underrun Funds*, B-207433, 83-2 CPD ¶ 401 (1983); *Memorandum, Department of the Army Office of General Counsel,* subject: Antecedent Liabilities (4 October 2000).

In the case of a contract for services that are severable, a modification providing for increased services must be charged to the fiscal year or years in which the services are rendered. 61 Comp. Gen. 184 (1981), aff'd upon reconsideration, B-202222, August 2, 1983; B-224702, August 5, 1987. The basis for this rule is that severable services are, by their nature, a bona fide need of the period in which they are performed. Thus, if an agency awards a severable services labor-hour contract (e.g., help desk support) in one fiscal year and modifies the contract in the subsequent fiscal year to add hours, the additional hours are considered new work and must be charged to the fiscal year that is current when the modification is executed.

In 61 Comp, Gen. 184, for example, a contract to provide facilities and staff to operate a project camp was modified in the last month of FY 1980. The modification called for work to be performed in FY 1981. Regardless of whether the contract was viewed as a service contract or a contract to provide facilities, the modification did not meet a bona fide need of FY 1980. The modification amounted to a separate contract and could be charged only to FY 1981 funds, notwithstanding that it purported to modify a contract properly chargeable to FY 1980 funds.

> **Discussion Problem 4-9**
>
> On August 1, 2001, an agency awards a severable services contract for custodial maintenance services to cover a period of eight months, ending on March 31, 2002. The agency uses FY 2001 annual funds and is able to cross fiscal years under the authority of 10 U.S.C. § 2410a, which allows agencies to use current funds for severable services contracts that cross fiscal years, provided that the period of performance does not exceed 12 months. In February 2002, the agency wants to extend the services for an additional four months and wants to use the now-expired funds (FY 2001). The agency's rationale is that, since it could have initially used the FY 2001 funds to award the contract for 12 months under 10 U.S.C. § 2410a, it can use the same funds to extend the period of performance from eight months to 12 months. Discuss the merits of the agency's position.

As noted, there is an important exception to the antecedent liability rule. The exception applies to cost-reimbursement contracts, specifically to increases to the cost ceiling. Cost-reimbursement contracts include a standard clause that authorizes the contractor to stop working once the cost ceiling is reached unless the contracting officer obligates additional funds. (The clauses referenced are the limitations of cost clause, FAR 52.232-20, which is used in fully funded cost-reimbursement contracts, and the limitation of funds clause, FAR 52.232-22, which is used in incrementally funded cost-reimbursement contracts.) However, the clause does not require the contracting officer to add funding and leaves this decision to the contracting officer's discretion.

The exception to the antecedent liability rule is that *discretionary* cost increases (i.e., increases that are not enforceable by the contractor) that exceed funding ceilings established by the contract must be charged to funds currently available when the discretionary increase is granted by the contracting officer. 61 Comp. Gen. 609 (1982). It would be unreasonable, the decision pointed out, to require the contracting officer to reserve funds in anticipation of increases beyond the contract's ceiling. Id. at 612. For example, assume that an agency has awarded a cost-plus-fixed-fee contract with a cost ceiling of $1 million. The agency would obligate the estimated cost plus the fixed fee. It would neither obligate nor commit funds in excess of $1 million because the limitation of cost clause limits the agency's liability to the cost ceiling of $1 million. Thus, the "antecedent liability" rule would not apply in this situation because the contract does not require the contracting officer to increase the cost ceiling. See *Proper Fiscal Year Appropriation to Charge for Contract and Contract Increases*, B-219829, 65 Comp. Gen. 741 (1986) (finding proper the use of current funds to fund increase to CPFF contract). It follows that, if the contractor is *entitled* to an above-ceiling modification, then the rule regarding discretionary increases would not apply and the agency would have to charge the increase to the appropriation initially used to fund the contract.

There have been only two situations in which contractors have been found *entitled* to funds in excess of the fund ceiling specified in the contract. The first situation is where the overrun was unforeseeable. Overruns have been deemed unforeseeable in some cases where the contractor's overhead rates were higher than could have been reasonably expected. *RMI, Inc. v. United States*, 800 F.2d 246 (Fed. Cir. 1986); *General Elec. Co. v. United States*, 194 Ct. Cl. 678, 440 F.2d 420 (1971). The other situation in which contractors have recovered amounts in excess of the contract ceiling is where a government official encouraged the contractor to continue working even though contract funds had run out. This situation, referred to as an estoppel, has been applied when the agency has received a benefit from the contractor's continued performance and it would be inequitable to deny recovery. *American Elec. Labs., Inc. v. United States*, 774 F.2d 1110 (Fed. Cir. 1985) (successfully asserted); *Hydrothermal Energy Corp. v. United States*, 26 Cl. Ct. 7 (1992). If either of these situations applies and the adjustment causes the contract ceiling to be exceeded, then the agency would have to charge the increase to the appropriation initially used to fund the contract.

If a contract modification does not increase the ceiling amount, then the general rules applicable to modifications apply. Thus, within-scope modifications based on antecedent liability are charged to the appropriation used to initially fund the contract. Conversely, out-of-scope modifications (i.e., modifications that add capability, expand performance, or increase quantities) are to the appropriation that is current when the modification is executed.

CLOSED APPROPRIATIONS

Once an appropriation account has closed (generally five fiscal years after the expiration of the period of obligational availability), questions of antecedent liability or relation back are no longer relevant since account balances cease to be available for any purpose and only current funds may be used, up to specified limits, for such obligations, 31 U.S.C.§§ 1552 and 1553, as amended by Pub. L. No. 101-510, § 1405(a), 104 Stat. 1485, 1676 (1990). The statute states:

> [O]bligations and adjustments to obligations that would have been properly chargeable to that account, both as to purpose and in amount, before closing and that are not otherwise chargeable to any current appropriation account of the agency may be charged to any current appropriation account of the agency available for the same purpose.

31 U.S.C. § 1553(b)(1).

This is a major exception to the rule that current appropriations are not available to satisfy obligations properly chargeable to a prior year.

There are limitations, however, to an agency's ability to obligate current appropriations to fund a liability properly chargeable to a closed account. When a currently available appropriation is used to pay an obligation that otherwise would have been properly chargeable both as to purpose and amount to a canceled appropriation, the total of all such payments by that current appropriation may not exceed the lesser of: (1) the unexpended balance of the canceled appropriation, (2) the unexpired unobligated balance of the currently available appropriation, or (3) one percent of the total original amount appropriated to the current appropriation being charged. For annual accounts, the one percent limitation is of the annual appropriation for the applicable account—not total budgetary resources (e.g., reimbursable authority). For multi-year accounts, the one percent limitation applies to the total amount of the appropriation. For contract changes, charges made to currently available appropriations will have no impact on the one percent limitation rule. The one percent amount will not be decreased by the charges made to current appropriations for contract changes.

The purpose of the one percent limitation is to ensure that an agency does not obligate more than it could have from the closed appropriation. For example, assume that an agency must modify a contract to recognize an antecedent liability of $100,000. Since the modification liquidates an antecedent liability, the relation-back doctrine applies and the agency must charge the appropriation used initially to fund the contract. Assume further that this appropriation has closed and had an unexpended balance of $90,000 at the time it closed. Since the agency cannot charge the modification to the closed account (regardless of the unexpended balance at the time of closing), it will charge the current appropriation. If the current appropriation has a balance of $1 million, how much can the agency use for this modification?

One percent of $1 million (i.e., $100,000) would be sufficient to cover the modification. However, the agency is limited to the *lesser* of the unexpended balance of the canceled appropriation or one percent of the total original amount appropriated to the current appropriation being charged.

Since the closed appropriation had only $90,000, this is the amount that is available in the current appropriation to fund the modification. The agency will have to make up the difference through a reprogramming, transfer, supplemental appropriation, or some other means, in order to avoid an Antideficiency Act violation.

Another issue that arises with regard to closed appropriations is the disposition of amounts received by an agency that would normally be credited to the appropriation if it were still available for obligation or in an expired status. As noted, agencies may credit appropriations when they recover excess reprocurement costs, liquidated damages, or costs incurred to cure defective work. The rule in such situations is clear: Agencies must deposit collections authorized or required to be credited to an account, but received after an account is closed, in the Treasury as miscellaneous receipts. 31 U.S.C. § 1552(d); *Appropriation Accounting—Refunds and Uncollectibles*, B-257905, Dec. 26, 1995, 96-1 CPD ¶ 130.

> This chapter addressed the second of the three limitations imposed by Congress on the use of appropriated funds: the time limitation. Agencies must incur obligations within the "period of availability" of the appropriation charged. This chapter discussed how to determine the period of availability as well as the duration of any restrictions contained in an appropriations act.
>
> Next, the application of the bona fide needs rule was discussed in various contexts to emphasize the importance of aligning the timing of the obligation with the existence of a valid, i.e., bona fide, need. The lawful use of expired funds was discussed, and the "relation-back" doctrine was explained to assist the reader in determining the proper fiscal year to charge.
>
> Finally, this chapter closed with a discussion of the consequences of the account closure rules and the availability of current appropriations to liquidate obligations chargeable to a closed appropriation account.

CHAPTER 5
Limitations on the Use of Appropriated Funds: Amount

This chapter will discuss the various statutes that, collectively, are referred to as the Antideficiency Act. Preceding chapters discussed the fiscal rules pertaining to the time and purpose limitations. Violation of these limitations, however, does not necessarily constitute a violation of the Antideficiency Act. The Antideficiency Act is generally violated only when an agency obligates or expends (or authorizes the obligation or expenditure of) an amount that exceeds what is available in an appropriation, apportionment, or formal administrative subdivision of funds. (As will be discussed later in this chapter, sections of the Antideficiency Act also prohibit accepting voluntary services and requesting an apportionment at a rate that would require a deficiency appropriation).

The Comptroller General summarized the interrelationship of the purpose, time, and amount restrictions as follows:

> These statutes evidence a plain intent on the part of the Congress to prohibit executive officers, unless otherwise authorized by law, from making contracts involving the Government in obligations for expenditures or liabilities beyond those contemplated and authorized for the period of availability of and within the amount of the appropriation under which they are made; to keep all the departments of the Government, in the matter of incurring obligations for expenditures, within the limits and purposes of appropriations annually provided for con-

ducting their lawful functions, and to prohibit any officer or employee of the Government from involving the Government in any contractor or other obligation for the payment of money for any purpose, in advance of appropriations made for such purpose; and to restrict the use of annual appropriations to expenditures required for the service of the particular fiscal year for which they are made.

42 Comp. Gen. 272, 275 (1962).

Since the correction of every violation of the purpose rules or the time rules will not result in the over-obligation or over-expenditure of funds, the Antideficiency Act will not be violated in every instance in which the purpose or time rules are violated. Instead, the Antideficiency Act should be viewed as a third limitation on an agency's use of funds that is independent of the purpose and time restrictions. Thus, each of these limitations must be considered when analyzing fiscal law.

OVERVIEW OF THE ANTIDEFICIENCY ACT

The Antideficiency Act is one of the principal means by which Congress exercises its constitutional control of public funds. The Antideficiency Act is not really a single congressional enactment, but evolved over a period of time in response to various abuses. Indeed, the evolution of the entire body of fiscal law could be viewed as a repeated story of congressional limitations, followed by executive branch circumvention, followed by additional congressional limitations, and so on.

During the mid-to-late nineteenth century, for example, it was not uncommon for agencies to incur obligations in excess or in advance of appropriations. In other cases, agencies would spend their entire appropriations during the first few months of the fiscal year, continue to incur obligations, and then return to Congress for appropriations to fund these "coercive deficiencies." Since the government had incurred obligations and received the benefit of the contractor's performance, it incurred at least a moral duty (and in some cases a legal duty) to provide compensation. Congress felt it had no choice but to appropriate funds to enable the agency to fulfill these commitments, but the frequency of these deficiency appropriations interfered with the orderly management of the federal budget. Congress eventually tired of being "greenmailed" by agencies that mismanaged their funds; the congressional response was, and continues to be, the Antideficiency Act.

The Senate Committee on Government Operations summarized the history of the Antideficiency Act as follows:

> Control in the execution of the Government's budgetary and financial programs is based on the provisions of section 3679 of the Revised Statutes, as amended . . . commonly referred to as the Antideficiency Act. As the name . . . implies, one of the principal purposes of the legislation was to provide effective control over the use of appropriations so as to prevent the incurring of obligations at a rate which will lead to deficiency (or supplemental) appropriations and to fix responsibility on those officials of Government who incur deficiencies or obligate appropriations without proper authorization or at an excessive rate. "The original section 3679 . . . was derived from legislation enacted in 1870 [16 Stat. 251] and was designed solely to prevent expenditures in excess of amounts appropriated. In 1905 [33 Stat. 1257] and 1906 [34 Stat. 48], section 3679 . . . was amended to provide specific prohibitions regarding the obligation of appropriations and required that certain types of appropriations be so apportioned over a fiscal year as to 'prevent expenditures in one portion of the year which may necessitate deficiency or additional appropriations to complete the service of the fiscal year for which said appropriations are made.' Under the amended section, the authority to make, waive, or modify apportionments was vested in the head of the department or agency concerned. By Executive Order 6166 of June 10, 1933, this authority was transferred to the Director of the [Office of Management and

Budget]. . . . During and following World War II, with the expansion of Government functions and the increase in size and complexities of budgetary and operational problems, situations arose highlighting the need for more effective control and conservation of funds. In order to effectively cope with these conditions it was necessary to seek Legislation clarifying certain technical aspects of section 3679 of the Revised Statutes, and strengthening the apportionment procedures, particularly as regards to agency control systems. Section 1211 of the General Appropriation Act, 1951 [64 Stat. 765], amended section 3679 . . . to provide a basis for more effective control and economical use of appropriations. Following a recommendation of the second Hoover Commission that agency allotment systems should be simplified, Congress passed legislation in 1956 [70 Stat. 783] further amending section 3679 to provide that each agency work toward the objective of financing each operating unit, at the highest practical level, from not more than one administrative subdivision for each appropriation or fund affecting such unit. In 1957 [71 Stat. 440] section 3679 was further amended, adding a prohibition against the requesting of apportionments or reapportionments which indicate the necessity for a deficiency or supplemental estimate except on the determination of the agency head that such action is within the exceptions expressly set out in the law. The revised Antideficiency Act serves as the primary foundation for the Government's administrative control of funds systems.

Senate Committee on Government Operations, *Financial Management in the Federal Government*, S. Doc. No. 11, 87th Cong., 1st Sess. 45-46 (1961). (At the time of the report, the Antideficiency Act was referred to as "section 3679 of the Revised Statutes." That designation that is now obsolete.)

The various statutory provisions that make up the Antideficiency Act each impose a different type of restriction on the use of funds. In this chapter each aspect of the Antideficiency Act will be discussed and illustrated with examples from actual cases.

APPORTIONMENT OF APPROPRIATIONS

Through several statutes, Congress requires agencies to effectively manage the budget authority it provides in appropriations acts. Apportionment is one means by which Congress expects agencies to manage its appropriations.

An apportionment is a distribution of appropriated funds into amounts available for specified time periods, activities, projects, or objects. The President is required, by 31 U.S.C. § 1513(b), to apportion executive branch appropriations to ensure that agencies have sufficient funds to conduct their operations throughout the fiscal year. The President has delegated this authority to the Office of Management and Budget (OMB). OMB has issued OMB Cir. A-34, Article II (November 3, 2000) to implement its apportionment responsibilities. OMB Cir. A-34 describes the purpose of apportionments as follows:

> 20.2 What is the purpose of the apportionment process?
> The purpose of the apportionment process is to centralize the Administration approval of agency spending plans to:
> • Prevent agencies from obligating funds in a manner that would require deficiency or supplemental appropriations. In certain specified instances (see section 21.18), OMB may approve apportionments and reapportionments that indicate the necessity for a deficiency or supplemental appropriation. However, these instances must be reported to Congress.
> • Achieve the most effective and economical use of amounts made available.
> Apportionments also may reflect any legal limitations imposed by Congress.

The effect of the apportionment requirement is that, at the start of the fiscal year, agencies do not have access to the full amount appropriated. Instead, agencies must obligate funds within the amount apportioned.

On July 13, 2001, the Director of OMB announced that all apportionments will be electronic by FY2003. That announcement (Transmittal Memorandum No. 17) stated in relevant part that OMB plans to: "[I]mplement an electronic signature capability that agencies can use to sign their electronic apportionment requests and OMB can use to legally approve the apportionments returned to the agencies. Our target for having this capability available is August 2002, for use with the initial FY 2003 apportionments."

Time limits are established for (1) the various agency heads to submit information to OMB to enable it to make reasonable apportionments, and (2) for OMB to issue the apportionment. Although primary responsibility for a violation of section 1512 lies with the director of OMB, the head of the agency concerned may also be found responsible if he or she fails to send the director accurate information on which to base an apportionment. Executive agencies must submit their apportionment requests to OMB not later than the later of: (1) 40 days before the beginning of the fiscal year for which the appropriation is available, or (2) 15 days after the date of enactment of the appropriations act. 31 U.S.C. § 1513(b)(1). The director of OMB then has up to 20 days before the start of the fiscal year or 30 days after enactment of the appropriation act, whichever is later, to make the actual apportionment and notify the agency of the action taken. Again, the apportionments must be in writing. 31 U.S.C. § 1513(b)(2).

It is important to recognize the relationship among apportionments, administrative subdivision of funds, and obligation of funds. The Comptroller General described this complex relationship in *Appropriation Accounting—Refunds and Uncollectibles*, B-257905, 96-1 CPD ¶ 130, December 26, 1995:

> Once an appropriation is enacted, it is usually made available to the agency to spend through the apportionment and allotment process. Generally, accounting for the use of appropriations occurs in a sequential order. Apportionments authorized by the Office of Manage-

ment and Budget (for executive branch agencies) are charged to related appropriations. Authorized allotments are charged to the apportionment and obligations are charged to the related allotments. Obligations, such as purchase orders tendered or contracts entered into, constitute a formal charge for which an agency expects to expend funds. Recording the obligation reduces the unobligated portion of the allotment that is available for incurring obligations. As a contract is performed and payments made, the obligation is liquidated without effecting the charges to the allotment. Payments are generally intended to equal the related obligation. However, when payments total either more or less than the amount obligated, the allotment is adjusted. The allotment balance is increased if the total payment is less than the amount obligated and is reduced if the total payment is more than amount obligated. The allotment balance should reflect the actual amount of payments charged to the allotment, and thus also charged to the appropriation. These budgetary accounting procedures are intended to ensure that government agencies and officials comply with the limits on their authority to spend funds as set forth in appropriation acts.

Thus, an apportionment can be exceeded in a variety of ways. For example, administrative subdivisions (e.g., allotments) can be issued in a total amount that exceeds the amount apportioned; the total amount of obligations can exceed the amount apportioned; or the total amount of expenditures can exceed the amount apportioned. Effective management of appropriated funds requires accurate distribution of funds and recording of obligations, as well as disbursement procedures that ensure that amounts disbursed do not exceed amounts obligated.

Requirement to Avoid Apportionments That Indicate a Need for Additional Appropriations

Apportionment is statutorily required by 31 U.S.C. § 1512, which states:

(a) Except as provided in this subchapter, an appropriation available for obligation for a definite period shall be apportioned to prevent obligation or expenditure at a rate that would indicate a necessity for a deficiency or supplemental appropriation for the period. An appropriation for an indefinite period and authority to make obligations by contract before appropriations shall be apportioned to achieve the most effective and economical use. An apportionment may be reapportioned under this section.
(b)(1) An appropriation subject to apportionment is apportioned by -
(A) months, calendar quarters, operating seasons, or other time periods;
(B) activities, functions, projects, or objects; or
(C) a combination of the ways referred to in clauses (A) and (B) of this paragraph.

Thus, although Congress has conferred to agencies the discretion to request the apportionment of funds in various ways, agencies must ensure that their apportionment requests do not indicate the need "for a deficiency or supplemental appropriation."

Implementing the Statutory Requirement

Section 1512(b) makes it clear that apportionments need not be made strictly on a monthly, quarterly, or other fixed time basis, nor must they be for equal amounts in each time period. The apportioning officer is free to take into account the "activities, functions, projects, or objects" of the program being funded and the usual pattern of spending for such programs in deciding how to apportion the funds. Absent some statutory provision to the contrary, OMB's apportionment determination must be followed by all agencies. Thus, for example, in *Maryland Department of Human Resources v. Department of Health and Human Services*, 854 F.2d 40 (4th Cir. 1988), the court upheld OMB's quarterly apportionment of social services block grant funds, rejecting the state's contention that it should receive its entire annual allotment at the beginning of the fiscal year.

In addition to requiring that agencies request apportionments in a manner that does not indicate a need for additional appropriations, section 1512 also requires that agencies ensure that they will have sufficient funds to continue operations throughout the fiscal year without a drastic reduction of activities. An agency violates the apportionment statute if it must curtail its activites drastically to enable it to complete the fiscal year without exhausting its appropriation. *To John D. Dingell*, B-218800, 64 Comp. Gen. 728 (1985); *To the Postmaster Gen.*, B-131361, 36 Comp. Gen. 699 (1957). Congress clearly does not want to be in a position midway through the fiscal year where it has the unenviable choice of either appropriating additional funds to a fiscally irresponsible agency or allowing the agency to drastically reduce operations.

For example, in the *Postmaster General* case, the director of OMB reapportioned Postal Service funds in such a way that the agency's fourth quarter funds were substantially less than its third quarter funds. The Comptroller General stated:

> A drastic curtailment toward the close of a fiscal year of operations carried on under a fiscal year appropriation is a prima facie indication of a failure to so apportion an appropriation 'as to prevent obligation or expenditure thereof in a manner which would indicate a necessity for deficiency or supplemental appropriations for such period.' In our view, this is the very situation the amendment of the [apportionment] law in 1950 was intended to remedy."

36 Comp. Gen. at 703.

Therefore, the very fact that a deficiency or supplemental appropriation is necessary or that services in the last quarter must be drastically cut suggests that the apportioning authority has violated 31 U.S.C. § 1512(a).

However, an agency is not required to reduce the activity level of every program or activity for the full fiscal year to avoid a drastic reduction in any specific program or activity. Section 1512(a) applies to amounts made available in an appropriation or fund and does not apply to specific programs or activities.

To illustrate, the Veterans Administration (VA) nursing home program was funded from moneys made available in a general, lump-sum VA medical care appropriation. The agency could discontinue the nursing home program and reprogram the balance of its funds to other programs also funded under that heading without violating the apportionment statute. B-167656, June 18, 1971. This is because, under a lump-sum appropriation, an agency generally has discretion to allocate funds in a way that effectively allows it to fulfill its mission. Conversely, if Congress had appropriated a specific amount for the nursing home program, the VA would not have had the flexibility to discontinue or drastically curtail the program.

The requirement to apportion applies not only to "one-year" appropriations and other appropriations limited to a fixed period of time, but also to "no-year" money and even to contract authority (i.e., authority to contract in advance of appropriations). 31 U.S.C. §§ 1511(a), 1512(a). In the case of no-year money and contract authority, the statute states only that the apportionment is to be made in such a way as "to achieve the most effective and economical use" of the appropriation. 31 U.S.C. § 1512(a).

> **Discussion Problem 5-1**
>
> On September 15, an agency receives its salary appropriation of $40 million. Under 31 U.S.C. 1513(b)(1), what is the last day on which the agency may submit its apportionment request to OMB? If the agency waits until the last day, what is the day by which OMB must apportion the funds? The agency's apportionment request seeks a quarterly distribution of funds as follows:
> 1st Quarter: $12 million
> 2nd Quarter: $12 million
> 3rd Quarter: $12 million
> 4th Quarter: $4 million
> Since the agency's apportionment amounts do not exceed the $40 million appropriated, is there any fiscal problem with its request?

Exceptions

There are several exceptions to the requirement of section 1512(a) that apportionments be made in a manner that ensures that the funds will last throughout the fiscal year such that there will be no need for a deficiency appropriation. One of the exceptions authorized under 31 U.S.C. § 1515(a) is that deficiency apportionments are permissible if necessary to pay salary increases granted pursuant to law to federal civilian and military personnel. Such a deficiency apportionment may become necessary because the agency, when it submitted its budget request, did not anticipate the magnitude of salary increases included within the appropriation act that was passed several months later. In such a case, the agency's expenditure rate will be higher than expected and it would have to request an apportionment that covers its increased expenditures. Under this exception, such an apportionment request would be lawful, even though it would indicate the need for additional appropriations later in the fiscal year.

Another exception is provided at 31 U.S.C. § 1515(b). Under that section, apportionments can be made in an unbalanced manner (e.g., an entire appropriation could be obligated by the end of the second quarter) if the apportioning officer determines that (1) a law enacted subsequent to the transmission of budget estimates for the appropriation requires expenditures beyond administrative control, or (2) there is an emergency involving safety of human life, protection of property, or immediate welfare of individuals in cases where an appropriation for mandatory payments to those individuals is insufficient.

Although the exception for expenditures "beyond administrative control" required by a statute enacted after submission of the budget estimate is broad enough to include statutory increases in compensation, these cases would be specifically covered by subsection (a), discussed in the first paragraph of this subsection (2). This section would apply to situations in which Congress imposes mandatory responsibilities upon an agency that require expenditures in excess of amounts appropriated.

For example, in *Department of Educ.: Recording of Obligations Under the Guaranteed Student Loan Program*, B-219161, 65 Comp. Gen. 4 (1985), Congress enacted legislation that required the Department of Education to make expenditures to satisfy student loan guarantees. When the number of student defaults was higher than expected, the Department of Education was required to make expenditures in excess of amounts appropriated. The Comptroller General held that such expenditures did not violate the Antideficiency Act. Although this case dealt with that section of the Antideficiency Act that applies to the amount available in an *appropriation*, since that section was not violated under the circumstances, one could make a sound argument that the Department of Education could have requested an *apportionment* of funds that was sufficient to cover its mandatory expenditures, even if such request indicated a need for additional appropriations later in the fiscal year.

The third exception to the rule in 31 U.S.C. § 1512 prohibiting apportionments "that would indicate a necessity for a deficiency or supplemental appropriation" is the emergency exception provided in 31 U.S.C. § 1515(b), which states:

(b)(1) Except as provided in subsection (a) of this section, an official may make, and the head of an executive agency may request, an apportionment under section 1512 of this title that would indicate a necessity for a deficiency or supplemental appropriation only when the official or agency head decides that the action is required because of –
(A) . . . ; or
(B) an emergency involving the safety of human life, the protection of property, or the immediate welfare of individuals when an appropriation that would allow the United States Government to pay, or contribute to, amounts required to be paid to individuals in specific amounts fixed by law or under formulas prescribed by law, is insufficient.

The exceptions in subsection 1515(b)(l)(B) do not appear to have been discussed in any federal court or GAO decision. However, since the exceptions for safety of human life and protection of property appear to be patterned after the "emergency exception" under 31 U.S.C. §1342 (the prohibition against accepting voluntary services), the case law under that section should be equally relevant for construing the scope of the exceptions under section 1515(b). (The voluntary services rule and the emergency exception will be discussed later in this chapter.)

Requirement to Avoid Obligations or Expenditures That Exceed the Amount Available in an Apportionment

As discussed, 31 U.S.C. § 1512 (a) prohibits agencies from requesting an apportionment at a rate that indicates a need for a supplemental or deficiency appropriation later in the fiscal year (unless one of the exceptions applies). In this section, we will discuss the prohibition against making or authorizing obligations or expenditures in excess of an amount apportioned.

Overview

It is important to note that the exceptions in 31 U.S.C. § 1515(b) are exceptions only to the prohibition against making or requesting apportionments requiring deficiency estimates; they are not exceptions to the basic Antideficiency Act against obligating or spending in excess or advance of appropriations (31 U.S.C. § 1341). In other words, although section 1515(b) may authorize an agency to request an apportionment that indicates a deficiency toward the end of the fiscal year, the agency still must ensure that its obligations do not exceed the amount appropriated. It may meet this requirement in a variety of ways, such as by reducing operations, transferring or reprogramming funds, or requesting that Congress appropriate additional funds.

The Comptroller General reached this conclusion in a case in which legislation had been proposed in the Senate to repeal 41 U.S.C. § 11, which prohibits awarding a contract unless there is an appropriation "adequate to its fulfillment," except in the case of contracts made by a military department for "clothing, subsistence, forage, fuel, quarters, transportation, or medical and hospital supplies." B-167034, September 1, 1976. The question was whether, if 41 U.S.C. §11 were repealed, the military departments would have essentially the same authority under section 1515(b). The Comptroller General expressed the view that section 1515(b) would *not* be an adequate substitute for the 41 U.S.C. § 11 exception, which allows obligations to be incurred for limited purposes even though the applicable appropriation is insufficient to cover the expenses at the time the obligation is made. The Comptroller General decision stated:

> [Section 1515(b)] in no way authorizes an agency of the Government actually to incur obligations in excess of the total amount of money appropriated for a period. It only provides an exception to the general apportionment rule set out in [31 U.S.C. § 1512(a)] that an appropriation be allocated so as to insure that it is not exhausted prematurely. [Section 1515(b)] says nothing about increasing the total amount of the appropriation itself or authorizing the incurring of obligations in excess of the total amount appropriated. On the contrary, as noted above, apportionment only involves the subdivi-

sion of appropriations already enacted by Congress. It necessarily follows that the sum of the parts, as apportioned, could not exceed the total amount of the appropriations being apportioned.

The significance of this case can be illustrated by the following example. Assume that an agency, in its apportionment request, asks for all of its salary appropriation to be distributed in the first three quarters. Normally, this would violate 31 U.S.C. § 1512(a) because the agency is requesting an apportionment at a "rate that would indicate a necessity for a deficiency or supplemental appropriation for the period." Now assume that one of the exceptions applies. For example, the reason that the agency is requesting distribution of its entire salary appropriation in the first three quarters is because Congress has increased the salaries of federal employees. Since an exception applies, the agency would not violate 31 U.S.C. § 1512(a) by requesting an apportionment that indicates a need for a deficiency or supplemental appropriation. However, this does not entirely solve the agency's problem, because it still must find a way to pay its employees in the fourth quarter. This is because the exception to the apportionment statute does not authorize an agency to obligate or expend more than was appropriated. Consequently, the agency would have to seek additional funds to cover its salary expenses in the fourth quarter.

Statutory Requirement

Although Congress has provided the executive branch the discretion to determine how appropriated funds should be apportioned, it also expects that agencies will not obligate or expend amounts that exceed the amounts apportioned. This expectation is reflected in the mandatory requirements of 31 U.S.C. § 1517(a) as follows:

> (a) An officer or employee of the United States Government or of the District of Columbia government may not make or authorize an expenditure or obligation exceeding -
> (1) an apportionment;

This statute imposes essentially four different types of restrictions. An officer or employee of the United States government or the District of Columbia cannot: (1) make an expenditure, (2) make an obligation, (3) authorize an expenditure, or (4) authorize an obligation that exceeds the amount in an apportionment.

Each of these restrictions may be illustrated by the following example: Assume that an agency receives a one-year operations appropriation of $10 million. Of this amount, the agency has requested and received an apportionment of $5 million for the first quarter of the fiscal year. If the agency incurs obligations (e.g., awards contracts) that exceed $5 million in the first quarter, it will violate the second restriction ("make an obligation"). If the agency then goes on to liquidate those obligations, then it will violate the first restriction ("make an expenditure"). Generally, when the expenditure restriction is violated, the obligation restriction is also violated. Thus, if the agency disbursed $6 million, it is likely that it had previously incurred obligations that total $6 million. This is not always the case, however. For example, if the agency's obligations were within the $5 million apportionment limit, but it disbursed more than $5 million, it would be in violation of the "make an expenditure" restriction but not the "make an obligation" restriction.

The problem of disbursing more than the amount obligated has been documented in various audits. [See, e.g., Department of Defense, Office of the Inspector General, *Recording Obligations in Official Accounting Records*, Report No. D-2000-030 (November 4, 1999); Department of Defense, Office of the Inspector General, *Trends and Progress in Reducing Problem Disbursements and In-Transit Disbursements*, Report No. 99-135 (April 16, 1999).] For example, in its 1999 financial report, the Comptroller General made the following finding:

> **Cash Disbursement Activity**
> Several major agencies are not effectively reconciling cash disbursements. These reconciliations are intended

to be a key control to detect and correct errors and other misstatements in financial records in a timely manner—similar in concept to individuals reconciling personal checkbooks with a bank's records each month. Although improvements in some agency reconciliation processes have been noted, there continued to be billions of dollars of unreconciled differences between agencies' and Treasury records of cash disbursements as of the end of fiscal year 1999. As a result, the government is unable to ensure that all disbursements are properly recorded. Improperly recorded disbursements could result in misstatements in the financial statements and in certain data provided by agencies for inclusion in the President's budget concerning fiscal year 1999 obligations and outlays.

General Accounting Office, *1999 Financial Report of the United States Government*, GAO/AIMD-00-131 (March 2000), pp. 25–26.

Thus, while overdisbursement generally results from overobligation, it is possible, because of faulty disbursing procedures, that an agency may overdisburse funds even when its obligations are within the applicable limitation.

As stated in 31 U.S.C. § 1517(a), an agency employee or official may also violate the statute by *authorizing* an expenditure or obligation that exceeds an apportionment. An expenditure may be authorized when an agency employee or official approves a voucher for payment or annotates on a receiving report that goods have been received and accepted. An obligation may be authorized when a fund certification official signs funding documentation indicating that sufficient funds are available for obligation. If the employee or official authorizes an expenditure or obligation in an amount that exceeds the applicable apportionment, then such action violates 31 U.S.C. 1517(a). Since the statute specifically makes the *authorization* of an expenditure or obligation an offense that is distinct from the actual making of the expenditure or obligation, the statute would be violated even if no actual expenditure or obligation is made. For example, if a fund certification official certifies that $1 million is available for obligation and less than this amount is available in the apportionment, then the official has violated 31 U.S.C. 1517(a), even if the contracting officer never obligates the funds.

> **Discussion Problem 5-2**
>
> Recall that in the previous discussion problem the agency submitted an apportionment request that apportioned its $40 million salary appropriation as follows:
> 1st Quarter: $12 million
> 2nd Quarter: $12 million
> 3rd Quarter: $12 million
> 4th Quarter: $4 million.
> There is a general prohibition against requesting an apportionment that requires drastic curtailment of activity. Which exception to this rule would be most likely to apply in this case? What are some of the ways in which the agency could continue operating without drastically reducing the level of its operations in the fourth quarter?

ADMINISTRATIVE SUBDIVISION OF APPROPRIATIONS

In addition to the requirement regarding apportionment of funds, Congress requires agency heads to establish administrative controls that (1) restrict obligations or expenditures to the amount of apportionments and (2) enable the agency to fix responsibility for exceeding an apportionment. 31 U.S.C. § 1514. This statute reads as follows:

> Sec. 1514. Administrative division of apportionments
> (a) The official having administrative control of an appropriation available to the legislative branch, the judicial branch, the United States International Trade Commission, or the District of Columbia government, and, subject to the approval of the President, the head of each executive agency (except the Commission) shall pre-

scribe by regulation a system of administrative control not inconsistent with accounting procedures prescribed under law. The system shall be designed to -
(1) restrict obligations or expenditures from each appropriation to the amount of apportionments or reapportionments of the appropriation; and
(2) enable the official or the head of the executive agency to fix responsibility for an obligation or expenditure exceeding an apportionment or reapportionment.
(b) To have a simplified system for administratively dividing appropriations, the head of each executive agency (except the Commission) shall work toward the objective of financing each operating unit, at the highest practical level, from not more than one administrative division for each appropriation affecting the unit.

This statutory requirement is implemented by OMB Cir. A-34, *Instructions on Budget Execution*, as well as by regulations promulgated by each executive agency. OMB Circular A-34 explains the goals of an agency's administrative fund control system as follows:

50.1 Why must my agency have a fund control system?
The Antideficiency Act requires that your agency head prescribe, by regulation, a system of *administrative control of funds*. The system is also called *the fund control system* and the regulations are called *fund control regulations*.

50.2 What is the purpose of my agency's fund control system?
The purpose of your agency's fund control system is to:
• Restrict *both* obligations and expenditures (for example, outlays or disbursements) from each appropriation or fund account to *the lower of* the amount apportioned by OMB or the amount available for obligation and/or expenditure in the appropriation or fund account.
• Enable the head of your agency to identify the person responsible for any obligation or expenditure exceeding the amount available in the appropriation or fund account, the OMB apportionment or reapportionment, the

allotment or sub-allotments made by your agency, any statutory limitations, and any other administrative subdivision of funds made by your agency.

Under the authority of 31 U.S.C. § 1514 and OMB Circular A-34, each executive agency must issue regulations describing how the agency will administratively subdivide its apportioned funds to achieve these objectives. See, e.g., DoD Dir. 7200.1, *Administrative Control of Appropriations*; DoD 7000.14-R, vol. 14, app. A. This process will ensure that funds will be available throughout the agency so that each organizational subdivision has sufficient funds to operate.

As with apportionments, however, Congress expects agencies to control their obligations and expenditures so that they do not exceed the amount of funds available in a formal subdivision. This expectation is described in 31 U.S.C. § 1517, which states:

> **Sec. 1517. Prohibited obligations and expenditures**
> (a) An officer or employee of the United States Government or of the District of Columbia government may not make or authorize an expenditure or obligation exceeding -
> . . .
> (2) the amount permitted by regulations prescribed under section 1514(a) of this title.

Subsection (a)(2) makes it a violation to obligate or expend in excess of an administrative subdivision of an apportionment to the extent provided in the agency's fund control regulations. The statutory language of 31 U.S.C. § 1514 must be read in conjunction with that of 31 U.S.C. 1517. Section 1514(b) becomes much clearer when it is read in conjunction with 31 U.S.C. § 1517(a)(2). Section 1514(b) does not prescribe the level of fiscal responsibility for violations below the apportionment level. It merely recommends that the agency set the level at the highest practical point and suggests no more than one subdivision below the apportionment level. The agency thus, under the statute, has a measure of discretion. If it chooses to elevate overobligations or overexpenditures of lower-tier subdivisions to the level of Antideficiency Act violations, it is free to do so in its fund control regulations. This is the effect of 31 U.S.C. § 1517(a)(2), which states that exceeding an administrative subdivision constitutes an Antideficiency Act violation, and 31 U.S.C. § 1514(b), which gives agencies the discretion to determine at which level Antideficiency Act violations may be triggered.

A typical example of how an agency may exercise this discretion is found in NASA's Financial Management Manual, at paragraph 9231-3, which states:

> **9231-3 NATURE OF ALLOTMENT ACCOUNTING**
> The NASA allotment accounting system is designed to record and control documents and transactions in order to prevent overcommitment, overobligation, and overexpenditure of appropriations and other funds controlled by allotments. General ledger allotment accounts are an integral part of the overall NASA accounting system, which provide:
> a. A control technique for commitments, obligations, and expenditures incurred against appropriations and funds within authorized fund availability, and to ensure compliance with the provisions of 31 USC 1341-1351 and as amended, and as implemented by NPD 9050.3.

Under the NASA manual, Antideficiency Act violations occur at the allotment level. The Department of Defense extends the range of potential Antideficiency Act violations to multiple levels, designated as allotments, suballotments, allocations, and suballocations. See DoD Financial Management Regulation, vol.14, app. A (March 2001) (available at www.dtic.mil/comptroller/fmr/14/index.html).

At this point, it is important to return to a discussion of OMB Circular No. A-34. Since agency fund control regulations must be approved by OMB, OMB has a role in determining what levels of administrative subdivision should constitute Antideficiency Act violations. Under A-34, overobligation or overexpenditure of an allotment or suballotment are always violations. Overobligation or overexpenditure of lower-level administrative subdivisions are violations only if and to the extent specified in the agency's fund control regulations. OMB Circular No. A-34, § 40.2 and 40.5. This distinction is reflected in numerous decisions of the Comptroller General.

In 37 Comp. Gen. 220 (1957), GAO considered proposed fund control regulations of the Public Housing Administration. The regulations provided for allotments as the first subdivision below the apportionment level. They then authorized the further subdivision of allotments into "allowances" but retained responsibility at the allotment level. The allowances were intended to be a means of meeting operational needs rather than an apportionment control device. GAO advised that this proposed structure conformed to the purposes of 31 U.S.C. § 1514. For further illustration, see 35 Comp. Gen. 356 (1955) (overobligation of allotment stemming from misinterpretation of regulations constitutes a violation of the Antideficiency Act); B-95136, August 8, 1979 (overobligation of regional allotments would constitute reportable violation unless sufficient unobligated balance existed at central account level to adjust the allotments); B-179849, December 31,1974 (overobligation of allotment held a violation of section 15 17(a) where agency regulations specified that allotment process was the "principal means whereby responsibility is fixed for the conduct of program activities within the funds available"); B-114841.2-O.M., January 23,1986 (no violation in exceeding allotment subdivisions termed "work plans").

The distinction between formal subdivisions (e.g., an allotment or an allocation) and an informal subdivision (e.g., an allowance) may be illustrated by an example. Suppose an agency has created an allotment of $1 million. From this allotment, the agency comptroller distributes $400,000 each to the two subdivisions within the agency. If one of the subdivisions obligates or expends more than its allowance of $400,000, it will *not* violate the Antideficiency Act unless the total amount obligated or expended by the agency causes it to exceed the $1 million allotment. In the example, the agency comptroller held back $200,000. (The allotment was $1,000,000, but only $800,000 was distributed to the subdivisions.) Consequently, unless the subdivisions grossly exceed their allowances, there should be a sufficient unobligated balance to cover the obligations or expenditures that exceed the allowances.

Of course, the fact that the subdivisions did not violate the Antideficiency Act does not mean that exceeding an allowance is a sound financial management practice. If both of the subdivisions in the example obligated or expended $600,000, the agency would have violated the Antideficiency Act since it would have exceeded the $1 million allotment. Exceeding an allowance makes such violations more likely.

Discussion Problem 5-3

An agency receives a procurement appropriation of $50 million. The agency comptroller allots $14 million to each of the agency's three major subdivisions, A, B, and C. At the end of the appropriation's period of availability, it is discovered that subdivisions A and B each fully obligated the $14 million they had been allotted. However, subdivision C obligated $15 million. Since the total obligations ($43 million) do not exceed the amount appropriated ($50 million), has an Antideficiency Act violation been committed?

ANTIDEFICIENCY ACT VIOLATIONS AT THE APPROPRIATIONS LEVEL

We have discussed Antideficiency Act violations in the context of apportionments and administrative divisions of apportioned funds. In this section, we will focus on Antideficiency Act violations that involve overobligation or overexpenditure of the amount available in the appropriation.

Scope of the Statutory Limitation

The applicable statute states:

> Sec. 1341. Limitations on expending and obligating amounts
> (a)(1) An officer or employee of the United States Government or of the District of Columbia government may not -
> (A) make or authorize an expenditure or obligation exceeding an amount available in an appropriation or fund for the expenditure or obligation;
> (B) involve either government in a contract or obligation for the payment of money before an appropriation is made unless authorized by law;

Section 1341(a)(l) is not only the key provision of the Antideficiency Act, but it was also the original Antideficiency Provision. All of the other sections were subsequently added to ensure enforcement of the basic prohibitions of section 1341.

Section 1341 is not limited to the executive branch, but applies to any "officer or employee of the United States Government" and thus extends to all branches. Examples of legislative branch applications are B-107279, January 9, 1952 (Office of Legislative Counsel, House of Representatives); B-78217, July 21, 1948 (appropriations to Senate for expenses of Office of Vice President); 27 Op. Att'y Gen. 584 (1909) (Government Printing Office). Within the judicial branch, it applies to the Administrative Office of the United States Courts. 50 Comp. Gen. 589 (1971).

Some government corporations are also classified as agencies of the United States government, and their officials are therefore "officers and employees of the United States." To the extent that they operate with funds, which are regarded as appropriated funds, they too are subject to 31 U.S.C. § 1341(a)(l). See, e.g., B-286661, January 19, 2001 (United States Enrichment Corporation); B-285725, September 29, 2000 (District of Columbia Health and Hospitals Public Benefit Corporation); B-223857, February 27, 1987 (Commodity Credit Corporation); B-135075-O.M., February 14, 1975 (Inter-American Foundation). It follows that section 1341(a)(l) does not apply to a government corporation that is not an agency of the United States government. B-175155, July 26, 1976 (Amtrak). The determination of whether a government corporation is subject to the Antideficiency Act is, of course, also affected by the language provided in the relevant legislation that created the government corporation.

This section applies also to funds other than "appropriated" funds. Note that the statute refers to overspending the amount available in an appropriation "or fund." The use of "or" between the terms "fund" and "appropriation" indicates the intent of Congress to apply the restrictions of 31 U.S.C. § 1341(a) to funds other than "appropriated" funds. Thus, this section would also apply to revolving funds.

OMB Circular No. A-34 states:

> **40.4 Do the requirements for reporting violations differ for revolving funds?**
> No. The incurring of obligations in excess of apportioned budgetary resources in a revolving fund is a violation of the Antideficiency Act, whether or not a fund has unapportioned budgetary resources or non-budgetary assets greater than the amount apportioned.

In addition, the Antideficiency Act applies to Indian trust funds managed by the Bureau of Indian Affairs. It also includes appropriations not subject to apportionment, e.g., expired appropriations. B-253623, Sept. 28, 1994 (unpub.); B-245856.7, 71 Comp. Gen. 502 (1992). However, the investment of these funds in certificates of deposit with federally insured banks under authority of 25 U.S.C. § 162a does not, in GAO's opinion, constitute an obligation or expenditure for purposes of 31 U.S.C. §1341. Accordingly, overinvested trust funds do not violate the Antideficiency Act unless the overinvested funds, or any attributable interest income, are obligated or expended by the Bureau. B-207047-0. M., June 17, 1983.

There are two distinct prohibitions in section 1341(a)(l). Unless otherwise authorized by law, no officer or employee of the United States may (1) make expenditures or incur obligations in *excess* of available appropriations or (2) make expenditures or incur obligations in *advance* of appropriations.

The distinction between obligating in excess of an appropriation and obligating in advance of an appropriation is clear in the majority of cases, but can occasionally become blurred. For example, an agency that tries to meet a current shortfall by "borrowing" from (i.e., obligating against) an unenacted appropriation for the next fiscal year is clearly obligating in advance of an appropriation. See, e.g., B-236667, January 26, 1990. However, it is also obligating in excess of the currently available appropriation. Since both are equally illegal, determining precisely which subsection of 31 U.S.C. § 1341(a) has been violated is of secondary importance.

In any event, the point is that the law is violated not only if there are insufficient funds in an account when a *payment* becomes due. The very act of obligating the United States to make a payment when the necessary funds are not already in the account also violates 31 U.S.C. § 1341(a).

Obligations in Excess of Appropriations

Incurring an obligation in excess of the available appropriation violates 31 U.S.C. § 1341 (a)(l)(A). In 1903, the Comptroller of the Treasury explained the nature of this limitation to an agency head by stating, "your authority in the matter was strictly limited by the amount of the appropriation . . . otherwise there would be no limit to your power to incur expenses for the service of a particular fiscal year. . . ." 9 Comp. Dec. 423, 425 (1903). Similarly, the Supreme Court has stated that, absent statutory authorization, "it is clear that the head of the department cannot involve the government in an obligation to pay anything in excess of the appropriation." *Bradley v. United States*, 98 U.S. 104, 114 (1878). See also B-286661, Jan. 19, 2001; B-245541, 71 Comp. Gen. 402 (1992). For example, the statute was violated by an agency's acceptance of an offer to install automatic telephone equipment for $40,000 when the unobligated balance in the relevant appropriation was only $20,000. 35 Comp. Gen. 356 (1955).

In a 1969 case, the Air Force wanted to purchase computer equipment but did not have sufficient funds available at the time of contract award. It devised an arrangement by which it made an initial down payment, with the balance of the purchase price to be paid in installments over several years. The contract would continue unless the government took some affirmative action to terminate it. Since the contract obligated the Air Force to make payments that exceeded the amount of funds available, it violated the Antideficiency Act. 48 Comp. Gen. 494 (1969). This type of arrangement could also be considered an obligation in *advance* of appropriations since payment of the balance of the purchase price would be charged to appropriations that had not been enacted at the time the obligation was created.

Determining the Amount Available in an Appropriation

Since 31 U.S.C. § 1341(a)(1)(A) makes it a violation to obligate or expend more than the amount "available" in an appropriation, it is important to know how to determine the amount "available." The most obvious scenario is one in which the relevant appropriation act appropriates a specific sum, e.g., $1 million. In such a case, an agency will violate 31 U.S.C. § 1341(a)(1)(A) if it obligates or expends (or authorizes obligations or expenditures) in excess of $1 million. Unfortunately, most Antideficiency Act issues are not so straightforward. In many cases, one must know how to interpret language in the appropriation that limits the amount available within the appropriation. Over the course of time, certain forms of appropriation language have become standard and have a well-established meaning. This section will highlight the more commonly used language with respect to amount.

Congress may want to specifically designate, or "earmark," part of a more general lump-sum appropriation for a particular object as either a maximum or a minimum (or both). For example, assume that an agency has a lump-sum appropriation of $1 million for "research projects," and a particular paragraph within that appropriation is titled "ale brewing research." If the appropriation specifies "not to exceed" $10,000 for ale brewing research or "not more than" $10,000 for ale brewing research, then $10,000 is the maximum available for ale brewing research. See, e.g., 64 Comp. Gen. 263 (1985). A specifically earmarked maximum may not be augmented with funds from the general appropriation. Thus, in this example, it does not matter that there is a large unobligated balance that will soon expire if not obligated. The most the agency may obligate and expend for ale brewing research is $10,000.

Since the earmark is treated as a statutory ceiling on the amount available, if an agency needs to obligate or expend funds in excess of the earmarked amount, statutory transfer authority is required. In 12 Comp. Gen. 168 (1932), the Comptroller General held that general transfer authority could be used to increase maximum earmarks for personal services, subject to the percentage limitations specified in the transfer statute. The rationale for this exception is that the purpose of the general transfer authority is to provide the agency with such authority with the flexibility to transfer funds for higher priority needs that may not have been anticipated when the agency submitted its budget request. If the amount available in an earmark (or in the entire appropriation) could not be augmented via general transfer authority, then the purpose for which Congress provided the transfer authority would be thwarted.

Similarly, in 36 Comp. Gen. 607 (1957), funds transferred to an operating appropriation from a civil defense appropriation could be used to exceed an administrative expense limitation in the former that had been calculated without including the increased administrative expenses the added civil defense functions would entail. However, transfer authority is not always a solution. In 33 Comp. Gen. 214 (1953), the Comptroller General held that general transfer authority could not be used to exceed a maximum earmark on an emergency assistance program where it was clear that Congress, aware of the emergency, intended that the program be funded *only* from the earmark. See also 18 Comp. Gen. 211 (1938).

Under a "not to exceed" earmark, the agency is not required to spend the entire amount on the object specified. See *Brown v. Ruckelshaus*, 364 F. Supp. 258, 266 (C.D. Cal. 1973) ("the phrase 'not to exceed' connotes limitation, not disbursement"). If, in our hypothetical example, the entire $10,000 is not used for ale brewing research, unobligated balances may be obligated for other purposes, provided that such obligation complies with all the time, purpose, and amount restrictions applicable to any obligation. 31 Comp. Gen. 578, 579 (1952); 15 Comp. Dec. 660 (1909); B-4568, June 27, 1939. Consequently, since the ale brewing research earmark was included in the more general "research projects" appropriations, the funds may be used for research projects but could not be used for purposes unrelated to research.

Taking the ale brewing example a step further, assume that later in the fiscal year a supplemental appropriation is made for "beer brewing research." The funds provided in the supplemental appropriation may not be used to increase the $10,000 earmark limitation for "ale brewing research" unless the appropriations act specifically authorizes such an increase. This is an example of the rule against repeal by implication discussed in Chapter 1. Under this rule, an appropriation will not be interpreted to repeal a previously enacted law unless it is clear from the language of the appropriation that such was the intent of Congress. The intent to repeal is most clearly manifested by specific reference to the law intended to be repealed. In the example, since the supplemental appropriation applied broadly to "beer brewing" and did not reference the prior earmark applicable to "ale brewing," the earmark stands and the agency could not spend more than $10,000 for ale brewing research.

Words like "not to exceed" are not the only way to establish a maximum limitation. If the appropriation includes a specific amount for a particular object (such as "for ale brewing research, $10,000"), then the appropriation is a maximum that may not be exceeded. 36 Comp. Gen. 526 (1957); 19 Comp. Gen. 892 (1940); 16 Comp. Gen. 282 (1936). Another method Congress has used to designate earmarks as maximum limitations is the following general provision:

> Whenever in this Act, an amount is specified within an appropriation for particular purposes or objects of expenditure, such amount, *unless otherwise specified*, shall be considered as the maximum amount that may be expended for said purpose or object rather than an amount set apart exclusively therefore (emphasis added).

District of Columbia Appropriations Act, 1992, Pub. L. No. 102-111, at 103, 105 Stat. 559, 567 (1991).

By virtue of the "unless otherwise specified" clause, the provision does not apply to amounts within an appropriation that have their own specific earmarking "words of limitation," such as "exclusively." 31 Comp. Gen. 578 (1952). For example, if an appropriation included a statement that "not less than $1,000 shall be available for lab equipment," then the general rule that would limit the amount available to $1,000 would be superseded by the "not less than" language.

If a lump-sum appropriation includes several particular objects and provides further that the appropriation "is to be accounted for as one fund" or "shall constitute one fund," then the individual amounts are not limitations, the only limitation being that the total amount of the lump-sum appropriation cannot be exceeded. However, individual items within that lump-sum appropriation that include the "not to exceed" language will still constitute maximum limitations. 22 Comp. Dec. 461 (1916); 3 Comp. Dec. 604 (1897); A-79741, August 7, 1936. Although the "one fund" language is still occasionally encountered, it has become uncommon.

If Congress wants to specify a minimum for the particular object but not a maximum, the appropriation act may provide "beer brewing research, $100,000, of which not less than $10,000 shall be available for ale brewing research." See, e.g., B-137353, December 3, 1959. See also 64 Comp. Gen. 388 (1985); B-131935, March 17, 1986. If the phrase "not less than" is used, portions of the $10,000 not obligated for ale brewing research may *not* be applied to the other objects of the appropriation, in this case beer brewing research in general. 64 Comp. Gen. at 394–95; B-128943, September 27, 1956. Note that this is a different result than applies when a "not to exceed" earmark is applied. In that scenario, the agency *is* authorized to obligate and expend the unobligated balance of the $10,000 maximum appropriated for "ale brewing research."

Another phrase Congress often uses to earmark a portion of a lump-sum appropriation is "shall be available." There are variations in the phrases that Congress may elect to use. For example, our hypothetical $100,000 "beer brewing research" appropriation may provide that, out of the $100,000, $10,000 "shall be available," "shall be available only," or "shall be available exclusively" for ale brewing research. Still another variation is "$100,000, including $10,000 for ale brewing research."

Use of the word "exclusively" is somewhat more precise. The earmark "shall be available exclusively" is generally considered to be both a maximum that cannot be augmented from the general appropriation and a minimum that cannot be diverted to other objects within the appropriation. B-102971, August 24, 1951. Once again, however, this is the general interpretation of these terms, and a clearly expressed congressional intent could produce a different result. B-113272-O. M., May 21, 1953; B-111392-O. M., October 17, 1952 (language indicated that earmark was intended to be a minimum only). Similarly, the term "including" has been held to establish both a maximum and a minimum. For example, an appropriation may state: "$100,000 for beer brewing research, *including* $10,000 for ale brewing research." See e.g., A-99732, January 13, 1939. Consequently, the $10,000 for ale brewing research in the example cannot be augmented from a more general appropriation, 19 Comp. Gen.

892 (1940), or diverted to other uses within the appropriation, 67 Comp. Gen. 401 (1988).

Thus, the most effective way to establish a maximum (but not minimum) earmark is by the words "not to exceed" or "not more than." The words "not less than" are the most effective way to establish a minimum (but not maximum). These are all phrases with well-settled plain meanings. The phrase "shall be available" presumptively "fences in" the earmarked sum (establishing both a maximum and a minimum), but is more subject to variation based upon the underlying congressional intent, which may be discerned through a review of the applicable legislative history.

Finally, earmarking language may be found in authorization acts as well as appropriation acts. The same rules of interpretation apply. Several of the cases cited involve authorization acts, e.g., 64 Comp. Gen. 388 (1985) and B-131935, March 17, 1986.

Determining if an Obligation or Expenditure Exceeds the Amount Available

Once the amount "available" in an appropriation is determined, it must be determined whether an obligation or expenditure will exceed or has exceeded it.

First, to determine if the amount obligated exceeds the amount available in an appropriation, one must ensure that the amount obligated is accurate. Reliance solely on the recording of obligations can result in two types of errors: It can suggest violations that do not in fact exist, and it can overlook violations that do exist. If it appears that the total amount of recorded obligations exceeds the available appropriation, there may be several reasons other than an Antideficiency Act violation. For example, if obligations had been recorded in amounts that exceed the government's actual liability, a new obligation could appear to violate the Antideficiency Act. If the obligations had been recorded accurately, no Antideficiency Act violation would exist. Similarly, transactions may have been incorrectly posted or improperly recorded as obligations. Or, accounts receivable that should be credited to the appropriation may not have been properly identified and taken into consideration. Thus, although an amount of recorded obligations that exceeds available appropriations may suggest an Antideficiency Act violation, it is not conclusive. B-134474-O.M., December 18, 1957. Similarly, GAO has cautioned that an Antideficiency Act violation should not be determined solely on the basis of year-end reports prior to reconciliation and adjustment. B-114841.2-O. M., January 23, 1986.

Just as an examination of recorded obligations can be misleading by indicating violations that do not exist, the converse is also true, i.e., violations may exist that recorded obligations alone will not disclose. For example, obligations may have been underrecorded such that the full amount of the government's liability is not reflected in the amount recorded. However, inaccurately recording obligations will not excuse a violation of the Antideficiency Act.

Thus, before one can conclude that the amount available in an appropriation has been exceeded, the agency must accurately determine the amount available—taking into account overobligations, underobligations, and unrecorded credits existing at the time of the act that gave rise to the suspected violation.

Discussion Problem 5-4

On August 1, 2002, Contracting Officer A receives a funding document properly indicating that $5 million is available for obligation. On the same day, another contracting officer in the agency (Contracting Officer B) awards a $1 million firm-fixed-price contract citing funds from the same appropriation. However, on August 5, 2002, this $1 million obligation is erroneously recorded in the amount of $2 million. On September 15, 2002, Contracting Officer A awards a contract for $5 million. When the agency comptroller tries to record this obligation, the fund control system indicates an unobligated balance of only $4 million. Did the agency necessarily violate the Antideficiency Act in this case?

In many situations, the amount of the government's liability is not definitely fixed at the time the obligation is incurred. Some common examples are contracts with provisions for economic price adjustments, award fees, or incentive fees. In such situations the government's liability is contingent on factors that cannot be known until after award. Consequently, the government is not required to record any obligation unless and until the contingency materializes. Because of such fluctuations in the extent of the government's liability, it is possible that there are sufficient funds to cover the initial obligation, but because of increases in the extent of the government's liability during contract performance, sufficient funds are not available when needed to make an upward adjustment. Thus, while examining the actual recording of obligations is a necessary first step, it is also essential to look at what happens as the contract is performed.

Finally, the possibility exists that there are valid obligations that the agency has failed or neglected to record. Incurring an obligation in excess or advance of appropriations violates the Antideficiency Act, and the agency's failure to record the obligation will not excuse the violation. 65 Comp. Gen. 49 (1985); 62 Comp. Gen. 692, 700 (1983). In 55 Comp. Gen. 812 (1976), GAO held:

> [T]he recording of obligations under 31 U.S.C. $ [1501] is not the sole consideration in determining violations of 31 U.S.C. § [1341]. . . . We believe that the words 'any contract or other obligation' as used in [the predecessor of 31 U.S.C. § 1341] encompass not merely recorded obligations but other actions which give rise to Government liability and will ultimately require the expenditure of appropriated funds.

55 Comp. Gen. 812, 824 (1976). See also 42 Comp, Gen. 272, 277 (1962) (Act forbids not only the incurring of obligations beyond the period of availability but also "any other obligation or liability that may arise thereunder and ultimately require the expenditure of funds"); B-163058, March 17, 1975;

B-133170, January 29, 1975. An example would be conduct by an agency that, under the relevant case law, would result in government liability to a contractor through claims proceedings. 55 Comp. Gen. at 824; B-163058, March 17, 1975. To ensure that adequate funds are available to meet contingent liabilities, many agencies will administratively reserve an amount of funds. Such "fencing" helps ensure that the fenced funds are not made available for other obligations.

Exhausted Appropriations

An obligation will exceed the amount "available" in an appropriation when the balance of the appropriation is exhausted. Expenditures from an exhausted appropriation usually will not violate the Antideficiency Act because expenditures are generally preceded by obligations, and the obligation ensures that adequate funding is available to liquidate the obligation. This would not be true, however, once the appropriation closes. At that point any remaining balance reverts back to the Treasury and is longer available for disbursement.

An appropriation may become "exhausted" in several ways. The most obvious example is where the amount appropriated has been fully obligated or expended. The appropriation is fully *obligated* when the unobligated balance is zero. Expenditures may still be lawfully made from a fully obligated appropriation provided the expenditures are within the amounts obligated. However, once the appropriation is fully *expended*, no further expenditures can be lawfully made from that appropriation unless it receives additional funds.

Another example of the exhaustion of the amount available is where a maximum amount specifically earmarked in a more general lump sum appropriation has been fully obligated or expended (e.g., "not more than $20,000 shall be paid in overtime to any employee of Agency X"). See, e.g., *Customs Serv. Payment of Overtime Pay in Excess of Limit in Appropriation Act*, B-201260, 60 Comp. Gen. 440 (1981). Similarly, exhaustion of the amount available in an appropriation may occur through depletion of an amount subject to a monetary ceiling imposed by some other statute (e.g., 10 U.S.C. § 2805 prohibits the Department of Defense from using operations and maintenance funds for construction projects over $750,000).

When the appropriation is fully expended, further payments will violate the Antideficiency Act, even if the funds had been previously obligated. Since the lack of funds is not a legal basis to refuse to pay proper contractor invoices or other financial obligations, an agency in this position must obtain the necessary funds to make the expenditure. It may do this under general transfer authority (if available); it may seek special transfer authority; it may seek deficiency or supplemental appropriations from Congress; or it can use specific statutory authority (if applicable) that permits the agency to make expenditures in excess of available appropriations. Alternatively, the agency may be able to avert an Antideficiency Act violation by curtailing its operations to reduce expenditures. E.g., 61 Comp. Gen. 661 (1982); 38 Comp. Gen. 501 (1959). If the exhausted appropriation account has expired but has not yet been closed, the agency can ask Congress for authority to use current appropriations to liquidate the obligations; this option may enable more prompt liquidation. B-123964, November 27, 1956.

Thus, the mere fact that an obligation complies with the Antideficiency Act at the time it is created is no guarantee against future violations. Determination of Antideficiency Act violations is not frozen at the point when the obligation is created. Certainly the act is violated if unobligated balances are insufficient to support the obligation at the time it is incurred. However, even if the initial obligation was well within available funds, the act can still be violated if insufficient funds remain to liquidate the obligation when actual payment is due or if upward adjustments cause the obligation to exceed available funds. E.g., 55 Comp. Gen. 812, 826 (1976).

Examples of Violations of 31 U.S.C. § 1341(a)(1)(A)

The following cases illustrate some of the many types of violations of 31 U.S.C. § 1341(a)(1)(A) that have occurred.

(See paragraph 40.2 of Attachment 5-1 at the end of this chapter for a complete listing of types of violations, along with the corresponding statutory reference.) In one case, the Navy overobligated and overspent nearly $110 million from its "Military Personnel, Navy" appropriation during the years 1969–1972. These violations were initially discovered in an internal audit, and GAO summarized the violation in a letter report, B-177631, June 7, 1973. However, GAO concluded that the violation was not intentional; rather, the "basic cause of the violation was the separation of the authority to create obligations from the responsibility to control them." The authority to create obligations had been decentralized, while control was centralized in the Bureau of Naval Personnel. Although the violation was not caused intentionally, it was nevertheless a reportable Antideficiency Act violation.

In another case, in November 1975, the Department of the Army discovered that, for a variety of reasons, it had overobligated four procurement appropriations in the aggregate amount of more than $160 million and consequently had to halt payments to approximately 900 contractors. The Army requested and received the Comptroller General's advice on a number of potential courses of action it was considering. The resulting decision was 55 Comp. Gen. 768 (1976). The Army acknowledged that there were adequate funds available when all the contracts were signed, and therefore the contractors generally had valid, enforceable obligations. However, the Army also recognized its duty to mitigate the Antideficiency Act violation. It was clear that without a deficiency appropriation, all the contractors could not be paid. The Army could not use current funds because there is no authority to apply current funds to pay off debts incurred in a previous year.

This rule applies to appropriations that have expired but have not yet closed. 71 Comp. Gen. 502, B-245856.7, August 11, 1992. Once an account has been closed, typically 5 fiscal years after expiration, obligations chargeable to that account must, within certain limits, be charged to current appropriations. 31 U.S.C. § 1553(b). One solution that GAO approved of was to reduce the amount of the deficiencies by terminating some of the contracts for convenience, although the termination costs would still have to come from a deficiency appropriation unless there was enough left in the appropriation accounts to cover them.

Compare, for example, the situation in 55 Comp. Gen. 812 (1976). In this case, the exercise of a contract option required the Navy to furnish various items of government-furnished property (GFP), but another contract clause authorized the Navy to unilaterally delete items of GFP. If the entire quantity of GFP had to be treated as a firm obligation at the time the option was exercised, the obligation would have exceeded available appropriations, resulting in an Antideficiency Act violation. However, since the Navy was not absolutely obligated to furnish all the GFP items at the time the option was exercised, it was inappropriate to use the full value of all GFP items under the contract to assess a violation of 31 U.S.C. § 1341 at that time. The Navy could avert a violation if it were able to delete enough GFP to stay within the available appropriation; if it found that it could not do so, the violation would then exist.

This rationale worked in this case because the Navy could stay within the appropriation by deleting a relatively small percentage of GFP. If the amount of GFP to be deleted were so large as to effectively preclude contractor performance, the analysis might well have been different since the agency could not have a valid obligation within the amount appropriated. In a 1964 report, for example, GAO found the Antideficiency Act violated where the Air Force, to keep within a "minor military construction" ceiling, deleted needed plumbing, heating, and lighting from a building alteration contract, resulting in an incomplete facility, and subsequently charged the deleted items to operation and maintenance appropriations. *Continuing Inadequate Control Over Programming: Financing of Construction*, B-133316, July 23, 1964, at 12-15. See also B-134474-O. M., December 18, 1957.

In 47 Comp, Gen. 155 (1967), GAO considered an Air Force contract for mobile generator sets that specified minimum and maximum quantities to be purchased over a 12-month period. Since the contract committed the Air Force to purchase only the minimum quantity, it was necessary to obligate only sufficient funds to cover that minimum. Subsequent orders for additional quantities up to the maximum were not legally objectionable as long as the Air Force had sufficient funds to cover the cost when it placed those orders. See also 19 Comp. Gen. 980 (1940). The fact that the Air Force did not, at the time it entered into the contract, have sufficient funds available to cover the maximum quantity was, for Antideficiency Act purposes, irrelevant. Similarly, in a 1983 case, GAO found no Antideficiency Act problems with a General Services Administration multiple award schedule contract under which no minimum purchases were guaranteed and no binding obligation would arise unless and until a using agency placed an order for an item with a vendor on the schedule. 63 Comp, Gen. 129 (1983).

Regardless of whether we are dealing with a requirements contract, indefinite quantity contract, or some variation, the determination of whether or not there is an Antideficiency Act violation depends on the extent of the government's liability created by the contract. In other words, the extent of the government's liability determines the extent of the obligation that is recorded, which ultimately determines whether there has been a violation of the Antideficiency Act. Even if there is no violation at the time the contract is entered into, a violation may occur later if the government subsequently incurs an obligation under the contract in excess of available funds, for example, by electing to order a maximum quantity without sufficient funds to cover the quantity ordered.

A related situation is a contract, which gives the government the option of two performances at different prices. The government can enter into such a contract without violating the Antideficiency Act provided it has sufficient appropriations available at the time the contract is entered into to pay the lesser amount. Since the government can elect to create an obligation in either the higher or lower amount, it avoids an Antideficiency Act violation if it has at least enough to cover the lesser amount.

For example, the Defense Production Act of 1950 authorizes the President to contract for synthetic fuels, but the contract must give the President the option to refuse delivery and instead pay the contractor the amount by which the contract price exceeds the prevalent market price at the time the delivery is made. Such a contract would not violate the Antideficiency Act at the time it is entered into as long as sufficient appropriations are available to pay any anticipated difference between the contract price and the estimated market price at the time of performance. 60 Comp. Gen. 86 (1980). Of course, if the government elects to accept delivery, it has to ensure that sufficient appropriations are available at that time to cover the full cost of the fuel under the contract.

Discussion Problem 5-5

On August 1, 2001, an agency awards a fixed-price contract to purchase three pieces of equipment that will be used to test aircraft engines. The equipment is priced at $2 million each. The total contract amount of $6 million is charged to a three-year appropriation titled "FY 01 – General Procurement." In FY 02, the agency decides it needs two additional pieces of test equipment. The agency modifies the contract to add the two additional pieces of equipment and charges the FY 01 general procurement appropriation. However, the contracting officer signs the modification prior to obtaining a certificate of fund availability. When the contracting officer reports the upward obligation to the comptroller, the comptroller advises that there is an insufficient unobligated balance in the cited appropriation to cover the modification.

Has there been a violation of the Antideficiency Act? If the contracting officer learned, prior to signing the modification, that there were insufficient funds in the FY 01 procurement appropriation, could he or she have charged this purchase to another fiscal year?

Finally, another type of violation under 31 U.S.C. § 1341(a)(1)(A) arises when an agency charges an obligation to an appropriation or fund that is not within the scope of that appropriation or fund and cannot properly be charged to any other appropriation or fund. GAO was presented with this situation in B-286661, January 19, 2001. In that case, the United States Enrichment Corporation (USEC) Privatization Act of 1996 (Pub. L. No. 104-134, Title III, Chapter 1, Subchapter A, 110 Stat. 1321-355, Apr. 26, 1996) authorized the Department of Energy (DOE) to use USEC funds to pay the expenses of privatizing the USEC. DOE took the position that it could also use USEC funds to pay for expenses resulting from the privatization, such as providing a backup capability plan for operations that were transferred to the USEC in the privatization. However, GAO disagreed, holding:

> "[W]e conclude that the costs of the DOE plan here in question do not constitute 'expenses of privatization' within the meaning of the Privatization Act and therefore are not payable from the USEC Fund. Consistent with this opinion, unless DOE can identify other available funds to cover such an obligation, such an obligation would constitute a violation of the Antideficiency Act, which prohibits officers or employees of the government from making or authorizing an expenditure 'exceeding an amount available in an appropriation or fund for the expenditure or obligation.' If DOE has obligated funds from the USEC Fund for the costs of its plan, it should report a violation of the Antideficiency Act to the President and the Congress.

If this were a simple case of charging the wrong appropriation, DOE could have corrected the error by deobligating the funds charged to the wrong appropriation and obligating the funds to the correct appropriation. In this situation, the Antideficiency Act would not be violated if the correct appropriation contained an unobligated balance sufficient to cover the obligation. However, in cases in which there is no correct appropriation, as indicated in the DOE case, then the mischarge is uncorrectable. Since the obligation exceeds the amount available in any appropriation, the agency has violated the Antideficiency Act.

Obligations in Advance of Appropriations

The second prohibition of section 1341(a)(1) states that an officer or employee may not involve the government in a contract or obligation for the payment of money before an appropriation is made unless authorized by law. 31 U.S.C. § 1341(a)(1)(B); B-225039, 66 Comp. Gen. 556 (1987) (20-year agreement violated this provision because the agency had only a one-year appropriation); B-144641, 42 Comp. Gen. 272 (1962) (three-year maintenance contract funded with annual appropriation violated provision). This section of the Antideficiency Act has been applied to a variety of situations in which an agency incurs an obligation in one fiscal year that would have to be funded with appropriations to be enacted in one or more subsequent fiscal years.

Obligations Citing Future Year's Appropriations

An agency violates 31 U.S.C. § 1341(a)(1)(B) if it creates an obligation in one fiscal year and cites funds that are not to be appropriated until one or more subsequent fiscal years. For example, if an agency creates an obligation by awarding a contract on September 15 and cites funds that will become available for obligation on October 1, it has violated this section of the Antideficiency Act unless the obligation falls under a specific statutory exception. Of course, if the award of the contract does not create an obligation, then this section of the Antideficiency Act would not be violated.

As discussed, requirements contracts do not obligate funds at the time of award. It is also possible for an agency to award a contract contingent on the availability of funds in the subsequent fiscal year. FAR 32.703-2 states:

32.703-2 Contracts conditioned upon availability of funds.

(a) Fiscal year contracts. The contracting officer may initiate a contracting action properly chargeable to funds of the new fiscal year before these funds are available; provided, that the contract includes the clause at 52.23218, Availability of Funds (see 32.7051(a)). This authority may be used only for operation and maintenance and continuing services (e.g., rentals, utilities, and supply items not financed by stock funds)-
(1) Necessary for normal operations and
(2) For which Congress previously had consistently appropriated funds, unless specific statutory authority exists permitting applicability to other requirements.

The reason that such a contract would not violate the prohibition against obligations in advance of appropriations is because the effect of FAR 52.252-18 is that no obligation is created unless and until the cited funds become available for obligation. B-140850, 39 Comp. Gen. 340 (1959); B-20670, 21 Comp. Gen. 864 (1942). FAR 52.252-18 states:

> **FAR 52.232-18, Availability Of Funds (Apr 1984)**
> Funds are not presently available for this contract. The Government's obligation under this contract is contingent upon the availability of appropriated funds from which payment for contract purposes can be made. No legal liability on the part of the Government for any payment may arise until funds are made available to the Contracting Officer for this contract and until the Contractor receives notice of such availability, to be confirmed in writing by the Contracting Officer.
> (End of clause)

Thus, an agency may initiate certain contracting actions prior to an appropriation if the solicitation and contract include the clause FAR 52.232-18, Availability of Funds. Conversely, if the agency has failed to include the availability of funds clause and awards a contract citing next year's funds, it will violate the Antideficiency Act. For example, the Comptroller General held that an agency violated the Antideficiency Act when it awarded a contract in one fiscal year, citing next year's appropriation without including the availability of funds clause. To Charles R. Hartgraves, B-235086, Apr. 24, 1991 (unpub.). The agency contended that it did not violate the Antideficiency Act because the availability of funds clause should be read into the contract under the Christian Doctrine [which states that "a mandatory provision required by law that a contracting officer failed to include in a government contract, either intentionally or unintentionally, will be read into the contract by operation of law." G.L. Christian Associates v. United States, 160 Ct.Cl. 1, 312 F.2d 418 (1963), cert. denied, 375 U.S. 954 (1963)]. GAO rejected this contention, holding:

> Traditionally, the courts and the Comptroller General have only discussed the "Christian Doctrine" in situations involving the administration of government contracts to prevent a private contractor from avoiding certain legal requirements. See, e.g., General Services Administration v. Benson, 415 F.2d 878, 880 (1969); and 47 Comp. Gen. 457 (1968). We know of no authority to apply the doctrine to relieve a government official of his responsibility under the law.

Thus, while the availability of funds clause will allow an agency to award a contract citing next year's funds without violating the Antideficiency Act, the agency must ensure that the solicitation contains the clause.

Multi-year Contracts

A multi-year contract is a contract covering the needs or requirements of more than one fiscal year. FAR 17.103 notes that the key distinguishing difference between multi-year contracts and multiple-year contracts is that multi-year contracts buy more than one year's requirement (of a product or service) without establishing and having to exercise an option for each program year after the first.

Multi-year contracts raise issues pertaining to obligations in advance of appropriations in two contexts: (1) the period of performance and (2) termination liability.

A multi-year contract raises issues regarding obligations in advance of appropriations because a fixed-term appropriation (fiscal-year or multiple-year) may be obligated only during its period of availability. This is because a fixed-term appropriation may be validly obligated only for the bona fide needs of that fixed term. For example, in the absence of statutory authority, an agency could not award a five-year contract using annual funds if the contract will be funded with future years' appropriations. A multi-year contract funded from a fixed-term appropriation can violate the Antideficiency Act because the Act prohibits the making of contracts that purport to obligate appropriations not yet made.

The rule that has evolved from many GAO decisions is that a multi-year procurement is permissible only in two limited circumstances: (1) when multi-year or no-year appropriations are available at the time the contract is executed, covering the entire period of the government's commitment, or (2) when permitted by specific statutory authority. FAR 17.102-1(a).

A leading case discussing the Antideficiency Act ramifications of "multi-year" contracts is 42 Comp. Gen. 272 (1962). That decision considered a three-year contract the Air Force had awarded to a firm to provide any service or maintenance work necessary for government aircraft landing on Wake Island. GAO questioned the legality of entering into a multi-year contract, since the Air Force had charged the obligation to an appropriation with a one-year period of availability. The Air Force argued that this was a "requirements" contract and was not an obligation in excess of currently available appropriations because no obligation arises under a requirements contract until work is ordered.

Although this is an accurate description of how funds are obligated under a requirements contract, GAO disagreed that this was a valid requirements contract because the services covered were "automatic incidents of the use of the air field." Orders were not issued for each task, and no one was making a true administrative determination that the services were or were not needed. Accordingly, the contract was not a true requirements contract but amounted to a firm obligation for the needs of three years that was funded with a one-year appropriation. It was, therefore, an unauthorized multi-year contract. As such, it violated the Antideficiency Act because years two and three would be charged to appropriations that were not yet appropriated at the time the contract was awarded.

If the contract had been a legitimate requirements contract in which each task was preceded with a task order, there would have been no Antideficiency Act violation. This is because no obligation would have been recorded until a task order was issued, and application of standard procurement procedures would ensure that adequate funding was available at that time. Since no obligation would be recorded unless and until adequate funding was available, the obligation would not be in advance of or in excess of available appropriations, and the violation would have been averted.

There are various situations in which performance may lawfully extend into a subsequent fiscal year. As noted in Chapter 3 (Time Limitations), an agency may fund a contract for nonseverable services with funds current when the contract is awarded, even though performance may continue into subsequent fiscal years. In addition, Congress has provided statutory authority for the award of severable services contracts that cross fiscal years, provided the period of performance is 12 months or less (see 10 U.S.C. § 2410a; 41 U.S.C. § 253l). Also, as long as a contract is properly obligated against funds for the year in which it was made, actual payment can extend into subsequent years.

Apart from these situations, and unless the agency either has specific multi-year contracting authority [e.g., 62 Comp. Gen. 569 (1983)] or is operating under a no-year appropriation [see 43 Comp. Gen. 657 (1964)], the Antideficiency Act, together with the bona fide needs rule, prohibits contracts purporting to bind the government beyond the obligational duration of the appropriation. This is because the current appropriation is not available for future needs, and appropriations for those future needs have not yet been enacted by Congress. The rationale for this rule is that Congress does not want to be in the position of being coerced into making an appropriation because the agency had created a liability by entering into an obligation in a prior year charging a future year's appropriation. The Comptroller General's decisions over the years have consistently supported this rule. E.g., 67 Comp. Gen. 190 (1988); 66 Comp. Gen. 556 (1987); 61 Comp. Gen.184,187 (1981); 48 Comp. Gen. 471, 475 (1969); 42 Comp. Gen. 272 (1962); 37 Comp. Gen. 60 (1957); 36 Comp. Gen. 683 (1957); 33 Comp. Gen. 90 (1953); 29 Comp. Gen. 91 (1949); 27 Op. Att'y Gen. 584 (1909).

The guiding principle still followed today stems from a 1925 decision of the United States Supreme Court. In that case an agency had entered into a long-term lease for office space with one-year money, but the lease specifically provided that payment for periods after the first year was subject to the availability of future appropriations. In *Leiter v. United States*, 271 U.S. 204 (1925), the Supreme Court specifically rejected that theory. The Court held that the lease was binding on the government only for one fiscal year, and it ceased to exist at the end of the fiscal year in which the obligation was incurred. It would take some type of affirmative action, such as a determination that appropriated funds were available, to bring the obligation back to life. The Court stated its position as follows:

> It is not alleged or claimed that these leases were made under any specific authority of law. And since at the time they were made there was no appropriation available for the payment of rent after the first fiscal year, it is clear that in so far as their terms extended beyond that year they were in violation of the express provisions of the [Antideficiency Act]; and, being to that extent executed without authority of law, they created no binding obligation against the United States after the first year. . . . A lease to the Government for a term of years, when en-

tered into under an appropriation available for but one fiscal year, is binding on the Government only for that year.... And it is plain that, to make it binding for any subsequent year, it is necessary, not only that an appropriation be made available for the payment of the rent, but that the Government, by its duly authorized officers, affirmatively continue the lease for such subsequent year; thereby, in effect, by the adoption of the original lease, making a new lease under the authority of such appropriation for the subsequent year.

Id. at 206–07.

GAO has relied heavily on the Leiter case in its subsequent decisions. For example, GAO refused to approve an automatic, annual renewal of a contract for repair and storage of automotive equipment, even though the contract provided that the government had a right to terminate. The reservation of a right to terminate does not save the contract from the prohibition against binding the government in advance of appropriations. 28 Comp. Gen. 553 (1949). This is because the Leiter case required some type of affirmative action to continue the obligation. Although the contracting could terminate the contract if sufficient funds did not become available, the effect of this arrangement would be that the contract would continue unless terminated. The Supreme Court in *Leiter* held that a multi-year contract funded from an annual appropriation must automatically end after the first year unless affirmatively continued.

In another case, the Post Office wanted to enter into a contract for services and storage of government-owned highway vehicles for periods of up to four years because it could obtain a more favorable flat rate per mile of operations instead of an item-by-item charge required if the contract was for one year only. GAO held that any contract for continuous maintenance and storage of the vehicles would be prohibited by 31 U.S.C. § 1341 because it would obligate the government beyond the period of availability of the existing appropriation. However, there would be no legal objection to including a provision that gave the government an affirmative option to renew the contract from year to year, not to exceed four years. 29 Comp. Gen. 451 (1950). See also, 67 Comp. Gen. 190 (1988); 66 Comp. Gen. 556 (1987); 42 Comp. Gen. 272, 276 (1962); 37 Comp. Gen. 155,160 (1957); 37 Comp. Gen. 60, 62 (1957); 36 Comp. Gen. 683 (1957); 9 Comp. Gen. 6 (1929); B-116427, September 27, 1955. See also B-97718, October 9,1950 (similar point but *Leiter* not cited).

The difference between the situation in the *Leiter* case and a situation in which the contract is extended by exercising an option is that in the *Leiter* case, the lease automatically continued from year to year, unless the government took affirmative steps to terminate it. If Congress did not enact an appropriation and the agency continued to occupy the premises, there would be at least a moral obligation to pay rent, even if the "subject to availability" provision technically relieved the agency of any legal duty to pay. Conversely, where a contract gives the government a renewal option, the contract ends unless the government takes the affirmative step of continuing the contract. Thus, the agency has the opportunity to consider the availability of funds prior to exercising the option and can ensure that no services or supplies are accepted unless funds have been appropriated.

This arrangement is less likely to involve the government in situations in which it has received some benefit prior to enactment of the appropriation that would be used to pay for that benefit. See, e.g., 61 Comp. Gen. 184, 187 (1981). Of course, the fact that funds become available in subsequent years does not place the government under any obligation to exercise the renewal option. *Government Systems Advisors, Inc. v. United States*, 13 Cl. Ct. 470 (1987), aff'd, 847 F.2d 811 (Fed. Cir. 1988).

Note that in *Leiter*, the inclusion of a contract provision conditioning the government's obligation on the subsequent availability of funds was not sufficient to avoid violation of the "in advance of" limitation of the Antideficiency Act. See also 67 Comp. Gen. 190, 194 (1988); 42 Comp. Gen. 272, 276 (1962); 36 Comp. Gen. 683 (1957). The rationale is that if a "subject to availability" clause were sufficient to permit multi-year contracting, the effect would be automatic continuation from year to year unless the government terminated the contract. As noted, if funds were not available and the government nevertheless permitted or acquiesced in the continuation of performance, the contractor would obviously expect to be paid for its performance. This is another example of a "coercive deficiency" that the Antideficiency Act was intended to prohibit. Thus, it is not enough for the government to retain the option to terminate at any time if sufficient funds are not available.

Under *Leiter* and later cases applying *Leiter*, the general rule is that the contract must end at the end of the period of availability of the appropriation charged and may be extended into subsequent fiscal years only by affirmative action by the government. See, e.g., *Cray Research, Inc. v. U.S.*, 44 Fed.Cl. 327, No. 95-564C (Jun 16, 1999) (to comply with the Antideficiency Act, "each renewal option must be (1) contingent on future congressional appropriations, and (2) exercised only by the government's affirmative action."). This "new" contract is then chargeable to appropriations for the subsequent year. Finally, if an agency can use multi-year statutory authority, then the contract would not be subject to the *Leiter* rule and could continue beyond the period of availability of the appropriation.

Nevertheless, the "subject to availability" clauses serve a useful function and are required by the Federal Acquisition Regulation in several situations: (1) contract actions initiated prior to the availability of funds, (2) certain requirements and indefinite-quantity contracts, (3) fully funded cost-reimbursement contracts, (4) facilities acquisition and use, and (5) incrementally funded cost-reimbursement contracts. FAR Subpart 32.7. These contract clauses all have in common that they require the contracting officer to specifically notify the contractor of the availability of funds and to confirm the notification in writing. This requirement is intended to ensure that contractors do not interpret government silence to constitute authorization to continue performance in the absence of funds. See *ITT Federal Laboratories*, ASBCA No. 12987, 69-2 BCA 117849 (1969).

> **Discussion Problem 5-6**
>
> In FY 2002, an agency enters into a contract to purchase a parcel of land for $10 million using annual funds. The seller asks that the payment period be extended over a period of four years to minimize the tax impacts of the sale. The entire purchase price of $10 million is recorded against the FY 2002 appropriation. Does the extended payment period violate the "in advance of" prohibition of the Antideficiency Act?

When the government decides not to exercise an option, the contractor may suffer a loss if it had to incur substantial capital costs at the outset of the period of performance. Thus, contractors have a legitimate concern over recovering these costs if the government does not exercise an option. One method sometimes used to address this problem is a clause requiring the government to pay separate termination charges if the government elects not to exercise an option under contracts in which the contractor has incurred significant nonrecurring startup costs. However, the Comptroller General has opined that separate charges violate the bona fide needs rule to the extent that they do not reasonably relate to the value of current fiscal year requirements. See, e.g., 36 Comp. Gen. 683 (1957), affd, 37 Comp. Gen. 155 (1957). As such, whether we regard such separate charges as obligations against funds not yet appropriated or obligations against current funds for the needs of future years, they violate the "in advance of" section of the Antideficiency Act (31 U.S.C. § 1341(a)(1)(B)).

The leading case in this area is 56 Comp. Gen. 142 (1976), affd, 56 Comp. Gen. 505 (1977). In that case, the Burroughs Corporation protested the award of a contract to the Honeywell Corporation to provide information technology (IT) equipment to the Mine Enforcement and Safety Administration. If all renewal options were exercised, the contract would run for 60 months after equipment installation. The contract included a "separate charges" provision under which, if the government failed to exercise any renewal option or otherwise terminated the contract prior to the end of the 60-month systems life, the government would pay a percentage of all future years' rentals based on Honeywell's "list prices" at the time of discontinuance or termination.

GAO determined that this provision violated the Antideficiency Act for two reasons. First, it created an obligation of fiscal-year funds for the requirements of future years. Second, it would commit the government to indeterminate liability because the contractor could raise its list or catalog prices at any time and the government would be liable to pay the higher amount. The government had no way of knowing the amount of its commitment. Similar cases involving separate charges are 56 Comp. Gen. 167 (1976), B-216718.2, November 14, 1984, and B-190659, October 23, 1978.

The Burroughs decision also offers guidance on when separate charges may be acceptable. One instance is where the use of separate charges is the only way the government can meet its requirements. Cited in this regard was 8 Comp. Gen. 654 (1929), a case involving the installation of equipment and the procurement of a water supply from a town. There, however, the town was the only source of a water supply, a situation clearly unlike the competitive IT industry at issue in the Burroughs case. 56 Comp. Gen. 142, 157. In addition, separate charges are permissible if they, together with payments already made, reasonably represent the value of requirements actually performed. Thus, where the contractor has discounted its price based on the government's stated intent to exercise all renewal options, separate charges may be based on the "reasonable value" (e.g., the reasonable full market price of the IT) of the work actually performed at termination based upon the shortened term." Id. at 158.

When a contract is terminated for the convenience of the government, the contractor is entitled to a settlement that typically includes payment for costs incurred, a reasonable profit (unless the contractor is in a loss status at time of termination), and reasonable costs of settlement of the terminated work. See, e.g., FAR 52.249-1, Termination for the Convenience of the Government (Fixed-Price). As is the case when the government does not exercise an option, a contractor with a multi-year contract may have incurred significant nonrecurring startup costs to enable it to perform the contract. If the government terminates a multi-year contract for convenience, the contractor will attempt to recover these costs. However, termination charges may not be inconsistent with the termination for convenience clause remedy; for example, they may not exceed the value of the contract or include costs not cognizable under a termination for convenience (e.g., expectancy profits).

Thus, if and when an agency decides to terminate a multi-year contract for convenience, the Antideficiency Act requires that the agency have sufficient funds available to pay the full amount of allowable termination costs. E.g., 62 Comp. Gen. 143 (1983). See also 8 Comp. Gen. 654, 657 (1929) (same point but Antideficiency Act not cited). This requirement is sometimes specified in multi-year contracting legislation. An example is 40 U.S.C. § 757(c)(1), the Information Technology Fund, which states:

> (c)(1) In the operation of the Fund, the Administrator is authorized to enter into multi-year contracts for the provision of information technology hardware, software, or services for periods not in excess of five years, if -
> (A) funds are available and adequate for payment of the costs of such contract for the first fiscal year and any costs of cancellation or termination;

Even if this requirement was not specified in the multi-year legislation, the same requirement would apply because of the Antideficiency Act requirement that obligations and expenditures not exceed the amount available in an appropriation.

Congress may also, of course, provide exceptions. See, e.g., B-174839, March 20, 1984. Congress sometimes designates fund sources for terminated multi-year contracts. For example, 10 U.S.C. § 2306b states the following with regard to multi-year contracts within DoD:

> **Sec. 2306b. Multi-year contracts: acquisition of property**
> . . .
> (f) Cancellation or Termination for Insufficient Funding. – In the event funds are not made available for the continuation of a contract made under this section into a subsequent fiscal year, the contract shall be canceled or terminated. The costs of cancellation or termination may be paid from -
> (1) appropriations originally available for the performance of the contract concerned;
> (2) appropriations currently available for procurement of the type of property concerned, and not otherwise obligated; or
> (3) funds appropriated for those payments.

Similarly, Congress has granted generally applicable authority extending the normal period of availability of funds needed to pay termination costs. Section 254c of Title 41 of the United States Code states:

> **Sec. 254c. Multi-year contracts**
> . . .
> (b) Termination clause
> A multi-year contract entered into under the authority of this section shall include a clause that provides that the contract shall be terminated if funds are not made available for the continuation of such contract in any fiscal year covered by the contract. Amounts available for paying termination costs shall remain available for such purpose until the costs associated with termination of the contract are paid.

In the absence of specific authority allowing the use of either prior year or current year funds (10 U.S.C. § 2306b) or extending the period of availability (41 U.S.C. § 254c), agencies must, of course, comply with the general fiscal rules pertaining to time, purpose, and amount.

Unlimited Indemnification Clauses

Under an indemnification agreement, one party promises, in effect, to cover another party's losses. When the government is asked to indemnify another party, the general rule is that it may not agree to indemnify where the amount of the government's liability is indeterminate. There are limited statutory exceptions to this general rule.

Applicability of the Antideficiency Act. An agreement that provides for indeterminate liability would violate both the Antideficiency Act, 31 U.S.C. § 1341, and the Adequacy of Appropriations Act, 41 U.S.C. § 11, since it could not be determined with certainty that sufficient funds have been appropriated to cover the contingency. This rule has been applied by GAO as well as numerous courts. For example, the Court of Claims stated in *California-Pacific Utilities Co. v. United States*, 194 Ct. Cl. 703, 715 (1971):

> The United States Supreme Court, the Court of Claims, and the Comptroller General have consistently held that absent an express provision in an appropriation for reimbursement adequate to make such payment, [the Antideficiency Act] proscribes indemnification on the grounds that it would constitute the obligation of funds not yet appropriated. [Citations omitted].

In an early case, the Interior Department, as licensee, entered into an agreement with the Southern Pacific Company under which Interior was to lay telephone and telegraph wires on property owned by the licensor in New Mexico. The agreement included a provision that Interior was to indemnify the company against any liability resulting from the operation. Upon reviewing the indemnity provision, the Comptroller General found that it purported to impose indeterminate contingent liability on the government. By including the indemnity provision, the contracting officer had exceeded his authority, and the provision was held void. 16 Comp. Gen. 803 (1937).

Similarly, an indefinite and unlimited indemnification provision in a lease entered into by the General Services Administration without statutory authority was held to be beyond the authority of the contracting officer and, therefore, imposed no legal liability on the government. 35 Comp. Gen. 85 (1955).

Perhaps the most comprehensive case discussing this issue is 59 Comp. Gen. 369 (1980), in which the National Oceanic and Atmospheric Administration (NOAA) sought to undertake a series of hurricane seeding experiments off the coast of Australia in cooperation with its Australian counterpart. The Australians were understandably concerned that this adventure could result in significant property damage and personal injury should the hurricane seeding experiments succeed. The State Department, as negotiator, sought GAO'S opinion on an Australian proposal under which the United States would agree to indemnify Australia against all damages arising from the activities. The State Department recognized that an unlimited agreement would violate the Antideficiency Act and asked whether the proposal would be acceptable if it specified that the government's liability would be subject to the appropriation of funds by Congress for that purpose. GAO conceded that an agreement expressly providing that the United States would not be obligated unless Congress chooses to appropriate the funds would not violate the letter of the law. However, it would violate the spirit of the law because, even though it would impose no legal obligation, it would impose a moral obligation on the United States to make good on its promise. This is still another example of the so-called "coercive deficiency" whereby Congress would feel that it had no choice but to appropriate funds to compensate the victims of the government's activities.

GAO did provide a possible solution, however. Since the government's policy of self-insurance did not apply here, NOAA could purchase private insurance, with the premiums perhaps shared by the government of Australia. NOAA's share of the insurance premium would simply be a necessary expense of the project.

Another decision applying the general prohibition against indeterminate liability held that the Federal Emergency Management Agency (FEMA) could not agree to provide indeterminate indemnification to agents and brokers under the National Flood Insurance Act, B-201394, April 23, 1981. If FEMA considered indemnification necessary to the success of its program, it could either insert a provision limiting the government's liability to available appropriations or seek broader authority from Congress.

In another GAO case, B-201072, May 3, 1982, the Department of Health and Human Services questioned the use of a contract clause titled "Insurance–Liability to Third Persons," found in the Federal Procurement Regulations (predecessor to the FAR). The clause purported to permit federal agencies to agree to reimburse contractors, without limit, for liabilities to third persons for death, personal injury, or property damage arising out of performance of the contract and not compensated by insurance, whether or not caused by the contractor's negligence. Since the clause purported to commit the government to an indefinite liability that could exceed available appropriations, the Comptroller General found it in violation of the Antideficiency Act and the Adequacy of Appropriations Act. This decision was affirmed upon reconsideration in 62 Comp. Gen. 361 (1983), another one of GAO'S more comprehensive discussions of the indemnification problem. For other cases applying or discussing the general rule, see 20 Comp. Gen. 95, 100 (1940); 7 Comp. Gen. 507 (1928); 15 Comp. Dec. 405 (1909); B-1 17057, December 27, 1957; A-95749, October 14, 1938; 2 Op. Off. Legal Counsel 219, 223–24 (1978). The clause has since been rewritten and now effectively limits the government's liability to the amount available in the appropriation funding the contract.

In addition to these GAO cases, numerous court cases have found that open-ended indemnification provisions violate fiscal law and are invalid. See, e.g., *Frank v. United States*, 797 F.2d 724,727 (9th Cir. 1986); *Lopez v. Johns Manville*, 649 F. Supp. 149 (W.D. Wash. 1986), aff'd on other grounds, 858 F.2d 712 (Fed. Cir. 1988); *In re All Asbestos Cases*, 603 F. Supp. 599 (D. Hawaii 1984); *Wm. T. Thompson Co. v. United States*, 26 Cl. Ct. 17,29 (1992); *Hercules Inc. v. United States*, 25 Cl. Ct. 616 (1992); *Johns-Manville Corp. v. United States*, 12 Cl. Ct. 1 (1987). (Several of these are asbestos cases in which the courts rejected claims of an implied agreement to indemnify.) In *Johns-Manville Corp. v. United States*, the court stated:

> Contractual agreements that create contingent liabilities for the Government serve to create obligations of funds just as much as do agreements creating definite or certain liabilities. The contingent nature of the liability created by an indemnity agreement does not so lessen its effect on appropriations as to make it immune to the limitations of [the Antideficiency Act].

12 CL Ct. at 25.

The Federal Labor Relations Authority has also applied the anti-indemnity rule in *National Federation of Federal Employees and U.S. Department of the Interior*, 35 F. L.R.A. 1034 (No. 113, 1990) (proposal to indemnify union against judgments and litigation expenses resulting from drug testing program held contrary to law and therefore nonnegotiable); *American Federation of State, County and Municipal Employees and U.S. Department of Justice*, 42 F. L.R.A. 412, 515–17 (No. 33, 1991) (same).

A limited exception to the rule was recognized in 59 Comp. Gen. 705 (1980). In that case, the Comptroller General held that the General Services Administration could agree to certain indemnity provisions in procuring public utility services for government agencies under the Federal Property and Administrative Services Act. The rationale for the exception was necessity. GSA needed to acquire utility services, and the public utility insisted on an open-ended indemnity provision; there was no other source from which the government could obtain the needed utility services. The Comptroller General agreed to permit the indemnity clause, but carefully pointed out that the case provides a very narrow exception to the general rule.

GAO's decision in 59 Comp. Gen. 705 was later discussed in B-197583, January 19, 1981. There, GAO once again applied the general rule and held that the Architect of the Capitol could not agree to indemnify the Potomac Electric Power Company (PEPCO) for loss or damages resulting from PEPCO's performance of tests on equipment installed in government buildings or from certain other equipment owned by PEPCO that could be installed in government buildings to monitor electricity use for conservation purposes. GAO pointed to two distinguishing factors that limited the exception applied in 59 Comp. Gen. 705. First, in 59 Comp. Gen. 705, there was no other source from which the government could obtain the needed utility services. Here, the testing and monitoring could be performed by government employees. The second factor is summarized in the following excerpt from B-197583:

> An even more important distinction, though, is that unlike the situation in the GSA case [59 Comp. Gen. 705], the Architect has not previously been accepting the testing services or using the impulse device from PEPCO and has therefore not previously agreed to the liability represented by the proposed indemnity agreements. In the GSA case [59 Comp. Gen. 705], GSA merely sought to enter a contract accepting the same service and attendant liability, previously secured under a non-negotiable tariff, at a rate more advantageous to the Government. Here, however, the Government has other means available to provide the testing and monitoring desired.

Thus, the case did not fall within the "narrow exception created by the GSA decision," and the proposed indemnity agreement was improper.

Lawful indemnification provisions. Indemnification agreements may be lawful because of the way they are structured or because they have been specifically authorized by Congress.

Indemnification agreements may be proper if they are limited to available appropriations and are otherwise authorized. Thus, the first question, before determining whether the indemnification is limited to available appropriations, is whether the indemnity agreement is authorized. Such agreements may be authorized either expressly or under a necessary expense theory (i.e., the indemnification agreement is necessary to enable the agency to fulfill its mission). For example, in 1958, the National Gallery of Art (a federal agency) asked if it could enter into an agreement to indemnify a corporation that was providing air conditioning equipment maintenance training to members of the National Gallery's engineering staff. Under the proposal, the National Gallery would indemnify the corporation for losses resulting from death or injury to its employees caused by the negligence of the corporation or its employees. In reviewing the proposal, GAO did not find it necessary to determine whether the indemnification provided for definite or indefinite liability. There was simply no authority for the National Gallery to use appropriated funds to pay claims of this type. B-137976, December 4, 1958. See also 63 Comp. Gen. 145, 150 (1984); 59 Comp. Gen. 369 (1980); B-201394, April, 23, 1981.

Once the necessary expense requirement of the purpose statute (31 U.S.C. § 1301) is satisfied, i.e., once the agency has determined that the indemnification proposal it is considering is a legitimate object on which to spend its appropriations, then the unlimited liability issue may be addressed. One way to deal with this issue is, of course, to specifically limit the amount of the liability assumed to available appropriations. Such a limitation of an indemnity agreement may come about in either of two ways: (1) it may follow necessarily from the nature of the agreement itself, or (2) it may be expressly written into the agreement. The latter alternative is the only acceptable one where the government's liability would otherwise be potentially unlimited.

An example of the first type of limitation, i.e., one that follows from the nature of the agreement, is the agreement at issue in 48 Comp. Gen. 361 (1968), where the government rented buses to transport Selective Service registrants for physical examination or induction. The Comptroller General did not object to an indemnity provision, which was a standard provision in the applicable motor carrier charter coach tariff. Potential liability was not indefinite since it was necessarily limited to the value of the motor carrier's equipment. Similarly, under a contract for the lease of aircraft, the Federal Aviation Administration could agree to indemnify the owner for loss or damage to the aircraft to eliminate the need to reimburse the owner for the cost of "hull insurance" and thereby secure a lower rental rate. This indemnification agreement satisfied fiscal requirements because the liability could properly be viewed as a necessary expense incident to hiring the aircraft, FAA had no-year appropriations available to pay for any such liability, and, as in the Selective Service case, the agreement was not indefinite because maximum liability was measurable by the fair market value of the aircraft. 42 Comp. Gen. 708 (1963). See also 22 Comp. Gen. 892 (1943) (Maritime Commission could amend contract to agree to indemnify contractor against liability to third parties, in lieu of reimbursing contractor for cost of liability insurance premiums, to the extent of available appropriations, and provided liability was limited to coverage of existing insurance policies).

In B-114860, December 19, 1979, GAO determined that the Farmers Home Administration (FmHA) could lawfully enter into an indemnity agreement to obtain the release of deeds of trust for borrowers where the original promissory notes had been lost while in FmHA's custody. GAO concluded that the indemnity agreement was permissible because it was limited to an amount not to exceed the original principal amount of the trust deed. Regarding the need to administratively reserve funds to cover the potential liability under the indemnity agreement, GAO determined that administrative reservation of funds would not be necessary because under the particular circumstances involved, GAO could not foresee situations in which the government might be required to indemnify the public trustee. Thus, since the possibility of indemnification liability was remote, administrative reservation of funds was not required. In other cases where the possibility of indemnification is more likely, prudent fiscal management would suggest that the agency administratively reserve some amount of funds.

In cases like the Selective Service bus case (48 Comp. Gen. 361) and the FAA aircraft case (42 Comp. Gen, 708), even though the government's potential liability is limited and determinable, this fact alone does not guarantee that the agency will have sufficient funds available should the contingency ripen into an obligation. This concern is met in one of two ways. The first is the obligation or administrative reservation of sufficient funds to cover the potential liability. In particular cases, such as the FmHA case (B-198161), reservation may be determined unnecessary. Of course, administrative reservation is not required if an agency has specific congressional authority to enter into an indemnification agreement and there is clear congressional indication that reservation of funds is not required. See B-159141, August 18, 1967.

The second way to ensure that adequate funds will be available for indemnification is for the agreement to expressly limit the agency's liability to appropriations available at the time of the loss with no implication that Congress will appropriate funds to make up any deficiency. This second method—the express limitation of the government's liability to available appropriations—avoids an Antideficiency Act violation based on unlimited indemnification. GAO has considered this type of provision in several contexts. For example, the government may in limited circumstances assume the risk of loss to contractor-owned property. While the maximum potential liability would be determinable, it could be very large, and the "administrative reservation" of funds is not feasible. Thus, without a provision limiting the government's liability to some specific dollar amount, such an agreement could result in obligations in excess of available appropriations.

In 54 Comp. Gen. 824, the Comptroller General set forth the following guidance: If it is administratively determined to be in the best interest of the government, the government may assume the risk for contractor-owned property that is used solely in the performance of government contracts. However, the government may not assume the risk for contractor-owned property that is used solely for nongovernment work. If the property is used for both government and nongovernment work and the nongovernment portion is separable, the government may not assume the risk relating to the nongovernment work. Finally, where the amount of a contractor's commercial work is so insignificant when compared to the amount of the contractor's government work that the government is effectively bearing the entire risk of loss by in essence paying the full insurance premiums, the government may assume the risk if administratively determined to be in the best interest of the government.

These rules are simply applications of the necessary expense rule discussed in Chapter 3. Thus, the greater the connection between the contractor's property and its performance of a government contract, the greater the authority of the government to indemnify the contractor for the loss of such property.

Any agreement for the assumption of risk by the government under these rules must clearly provide that, in the event the government has to pay for losses, payments may not exceed appropriations available at the time of the losses. Moreover, nothing in the contract may be considered as implying that Congress will at a later date appropriate funds sufficient to meet deficiencies. Within the context of government contracts, a FAR clause applies to this situation. FAR 52.228-7 Insurance-Liability to Third Persons, provides:

FAR 52.228-7, Insurance-Liability To Third Persons (Mar 1996)
. . .
(c) The Contractor shall be reimbursed-
(1) For that portion-
(i) Of the reasonable cost of insurance allocable to this contract; and

(ii) Required or approved under this clause; and
(2) For certain liabilities (and expenses incidental to such liabilities) to third persons not compensated by insurance or otherwise without regard to and as an exception to the limitation of cost or the limitation of funds clause of this contract. These liabilities must arise out of the performance of this contract, whether or not caused by the negligence of the Contractor or of the Contractor's agents, servants, or employees, and must be represented by final judgments or settlements approved in writing by the Government. These liabilities are for-
(i) Loss of or damage to property (other than property owned, occupied, or used by the Contractor, rented to the Contractor, or in the care, custody, or control of the Contractor); or
(ii) Death or bodily injury.
(d) The Government's liability under paragraph (c) of this clause is subject to the availability of appropriated funds at the time a contingency occurs. Nothing in this contract shall be construed as implying that the Congress will, at a later date, appropriate funds sufficient to meet deficiencies.

This clause, which is required for cost reimbursement contracts, legally avoids an Antideficiency Act violation because the obligation to indemnify cannot exceed the amount of appropriated funds available.

GAO has applied the rules applicable to contractor-owned property in cases where the government has made an installment purchase of property. In 60 Comp. Gen. 584 (1981), the General Services Administration agreed to an "installment purchase plan" for information technology equipment. Under the plan, GSA would make monthly payments until the entire purchase price was paid, at which time GSA would take title to the equipment. GSA's obligation was conditioned on its exercising an option at the end of each fiscal year to continue payments for the next year. The contract contained a risk of loss provision under which GSA would be required to pay the full price for any equipment lost or damaged during the term of the contract. GAO concluded that the equipment should be treated as contractor-owned property for purposes of the risk of loss provision, and that the provision would be improper unless the contract included the provisions specified in 54 Comp. Gen. 824 limiting GSA's liability to appropriations available at the time of the loss and expressly precluding any inference that Congress would appropriate sufficient funds to meet any deficiency. If the contract did not include these provisions, then GSA must obligate sufficient funds to cover its possible liability under the risk of loss provision. If neither of these conditions were met, the assumption of risk clause could potentially violate the Antideficiency Act by creating an obligation in excess of available appropriations if the contingency occurs.

The Comptroller General upheld a limitation of liability provision used by the Department of Defense in a 1982 case. In that case, the DoD and the state of New York entered into a contract for New York to provide certain support functions for the 1980 Winter Olympic Games at Lake Placid, New York. The contract provided for federal reimbursement of any disability benefits that New York might be required to pay in case of death or injury of persons participating in the operation. The contract specified that the government's liability could not exceed appropriations for assistance to the games available at the time of a disabling event, and that the contract did not imply that Congress would appropriate funds sufficient to meet any deficiencies. Since these provisions satisfied the test of 54 Comp. Gen. 824, the indemnity agreement was legally unobjectionable. B-202518, January 8, 1982. See also, B-201394, April 23, 1981; B-201072, May 3, 1982; *National Railroad Passenger Corp. v. United States*, 3 Cl. Ct. 516, 521 (1983) (indemnification agreement between Federal Railroad Administration and Amtrak did not violate Antideficiency Act where liability was limited to amount of appropriation).

> **Discussion Problem 5-7**
>
> The Federal Aviation Administration (FAA) has a contract with Pacific Gas and Electric Company (PG&E) whereby PG&E will connect various FAA facilities to the PG&E power line. PG&E wants the FAA to include the following provision in the contract:
>
>> [FAA] shall indemnify and hold harmless PG&E, its officers, agents, and employees against all loss, damage, expense, and liability, resulting from injury to or death of any person, including but not limited to employees of PG&E, [FAA], or any third party, or for loss, destruction, damage to property, including but not limited to, property of PG&E, [FAA], or any third party, arising out of or in any way connected with the performance of this Agreement and any and all construction activities, however caused, except to the extent caused by the active negligence or willful misconduct of PG&E, its officers, agents and employees.
>
> Does this provision violate the Antideficiency Act?

Congressionally Authorized Indemnification. An open-ended indemnification agreement will not violate the Antideficiency Act if it is specifically authorized by Congress, i.e., by statute. For example, one statutory exception to the indemnification rules exists for certain defense-related contracts by virtue of 50 U.S.C. § 1431, often referred to as Public Law 85-804. The implementing details on indemnification are found in Executive Order No. 10789, as amended. Another statutory exception is 42 U.S.C. § 2210, the Price-Anderson Act, which authorizes indemnification agreements with Nuclear Regulatory Commission licensees and Department of Energy contractors to pay claims resulting from nuclear accidents.

Some GAO decisions, however, have suggested that indemnity agreements, even with limiting language, should not be entered into without congressional approval in view of their potentially disruptive fiscal consequences to the agency. 63 Comp. Gen. 145,147 (1984); 62 Comp. Gen. 361, 368 (1983); B-242146, August 16, 1991. Precisely what form this approval should take in cases where the contractual language is sufficient to minimally satisfy the Antideficiency Act is not entirely clear. In 1986, the Chairman of the Subcommittee on Nuclear Regulation, Senate Committee on Environment and Public Works, in connection with proposed Price-Anderson amendments the committee was considering, asked GAO to identify possible funding options for a statutory indemnification provision. GAO'S response, B-197742, August 1, 1986, lists several options and notes the benefits and drawbacks of each from the perspective of con gressional flexibility. The options range from creating a statutory entitlement with a permanent indefinite appropriation for payment (indemnity guaranteed but no congressional flexibility), to making payment fully dependent on the appropriations process (full congressional flexibility but no guarantee of payment). In between are various other devices such as contract authority, use of contract provisions such as those in 54 Comp. Gen. 824, and various forms of limited funding authority.

The discussion in B-197742 highlights the essence of the indemnification funding problem:

> An indemnity statute should generally include two features—the indemnification provisions and a funding mechanism. Indemnification provisions can range from a legally binding guarantee to a mere authorization. Funding mechanisms can similarly vary in terms of the degree of congressional control and flexibility retained. It is impossible to maximize both the assurance of payment and congressional flexibility. Either objective is enhanced only at the expense of the other. . . . If payment is to be assured, Congress must yield control over funding, either in whole or up to specified ceilings. . . . Conversely, if Congress is to retain funding control, payment cannot be assured in any legally binding form and the indemnification becomes less than an entitlement.

The decision stresses (to Congress) the importance of legislation that clearly and specifically describes the nature of the indemnification that is authorized and the source of funding to be used.

Thus, unless an agency has specific statutory authority, it generally may not enter into an indemnification agreement that would impose an indeterminate or potentially unlimited liability on the government. Since the obligation or administrative reservation of funds is not a feasible option in the indeterminate liability situation, the only cure is for the agreement to expressly limit the government's liability to available appropriations with no implication that Congress will appropriate the money to meet any deficiencies. If the government's potential liability is limited and determinable, an agreement to indemnify will be lawful, assuming it is otherwise authorized and appropriate safeguards are taken to protect against violation of the Antideficiency Act. These safeguards may be either the obligation or administrative reservation of sufficient funds to cover the potential liability or the inclusion in the agreement of a clause expressly limiting the government's liability to available appropriations.

Although following these rules will enable the agency to avoid Antideficiency Act violations, they present other, practical problems. For example, limiting an indemnification agreement to appropriations available at the time of the loss, as in the New York Winter Olympics case, may remove the "unlimited liability" objection, but it remains entirely possible that liabilities incurred under such an agreement could exhaust the agency's appropriation and either cause other Antideficiency Act violations or force Congress to appropriate additional funds to enable the agency to continue to function. Also, from the standpoint of the contractor or other "beneficiary," indemnification under these circumstances can prove largely illusory, as it will obviously make a big difference whether the incident giving rise to the claim occurs at the beginning or the end of a fiscal year. If the liability-causing event occurs toward the end of the source appropriation's period of availability, a very small unobligated balance may be available for indemnification.

Obligations in Advance of Apportionments

As discussed, 31 U.S.C. § 1341(a)(1)(B) prohibits obligations in advance of appropriations. Although an agency's appropriation may have been enacted and signed by the President, it is possible that the funds are not apportioned for some period of time thereafter. An issue arises regarding whether an agency may lawfully charge obligations against an appropriation that has been enacted by Congress and signed by the President but that has not yet been apportioned by the Office of Management and Budget (OMB)—in other words, whether it is a violation of the Antideficiency Act to incur obligations in advance of apportionments.

The Antideficiency Act itself does not prohibit obligations in advance of apportionments. It does, however, prohibit obligations in *excess* of apportionments. 31 U.S.C. § 1517(a). It could be argued, therefore, that an obligation in *advance* of an apportionment is unlawful because, prior to apportionment, the amount available in an apportionment is zero, and any obligation would exceed it. While this argument has some persuasiveness, it did not persuade the Court of Appeals for the Federal Circuit, which rejected the argument in a 1997 decision.

In that case, a contractor (Cessna Aircraft) did not want to perform an option, presumably because it could use its resources more profitably outside the contract. To avoid its duty to perform under the option, Cessna contended that the contracting officer lacked the authority to exercise the option because, although the funds cited by the agency had been appropriated, they had not been apportioned as of the effective date of the option. *Cessna Aircraft Co. v. Dalton*, 126 F.3d 1442 (Fed. Cir. Oct. 6, 1997). The court rejected this contention, stating:

> We reject Cessna's arguments. As noted above, 31 U.S.C. Sec. 1341(a) prohibits the government from making expenditures or incurring obligations before funds have been appropriated. However, as for the apportionment process, addressed by 31 U.S.C. Sec. 1511-1519, no such timing limitation exists. For example, section 1512 merely requires appropriations to be apportioned to pre-

vent obligations at rates that could result in the need for a deficiency or supplemental appropriation. Section 1513 provides a timetable for carrying out the apportionment process, but is silent on the issue of whether the apportionment process must be carried out before obligations can be incurred. For its part, section 1517 prohibits government officials or employees from authorizing obligations that exceed apportionments, but says nothing about incurring obligations prior to carrying out the apportionment process. In sum, the relevant statutory provisions do not prohibit government agencies from incurring contractual obligations before completing the apportionment process. The remaining sections pertaining to apportionments are similarly silent.

The effect of this decision is that an obligation in advance of an apportionment will not *automatically* violate the Antideficiency Act. However, if the total amount of obligations exceeds the apportionment that is eventually received, then the agency has violated 31 U.S.C. § 1517, which prohibits obligations in excess of apportionments. Careful financial management should enable the agency to avoid such violations, since OMB's apportionment is based on the request submitted by the agency. Consequently, the agency should know the amount it will receive through the apportionment process.

Lastly, although an obligation in advance of apportionments does not violate the Antideficiency Act, most agency financial management regulations require that, prior to incurring obligations, the funds cited be both appropriated and apportioned. For example, the DoD Financial Management Regulation states:

> 130204. Apportionments and Reapportionments
> A. An apportionment or reapportionment is a distribution made by the OMB of amounts available for obligation in an appropriation or fund account. Except in certain instances, as specified in OMB Circular No. A-34, apportionments and reapportionments by the OMB are required before funds maybe obligated.

Thus, although the agency may not violate the Antideficiency Act by obligating in advance of apportionment, it may be violating its own financial management regulations, which could result in negative audit reports and adverse personnel actions for the individuals responsible.

VOLUNTARY SERVICES PROHIBITION

In addition to the limitations pertaining to the amount and timing of obligations and expenditures, the Antideficiency Act also prohibits accepting or employing certain types of services, generally referred to as "voluntary services."

The voluntary services prohibition of the Antideficiency Act is located at 31 U.S.C. § 1342, which states:

> Sec. 1342. Limitation on voluntary services
> An officer or employee of the United States Government or of the District of Columbia government may not accept voluntary services for either government or employ personal services exceeding that authorized by law except for emergencies involving the safety of human life or the protection of property. This section does not apply to a corporation getting amounts to make loans (except paid in capital amounts) without legal liability of the United States Government. As used in this section, the term "emergencies involving the safety of human life or the protection of property" does not include ongoing, regular functions of government the suspension of which would not imminently threaten the safety of human life or the protection of property.

This provision first appeared, in almost identical form, in a deficiency appropriation act enacted in 1884 (23 Stat. 17). The original prohibition read "hereafter, no department or officer of the United States shall accept . . ." and appeared to apply to all departments and officers of the United States. However, it was included in an appropriation for the (then existing) Indian Office of the Interior Department, and the

Court of Claims held that it was applicable only to that office of the Interior Department. *Glavey v. United States*, 35 Ct. Cl. 242, 256 (1900). In contrast to the interpretation of the Court of Claims, the Comptroller of the Treasury continued to apply the statute to all departments and officials of the United States. See, e.g., 9 Comp. Dec. 181 (1902).

The applicability of the 1884 statute soon became academic because Congress reenacted it as part of the Antideficiency Act in 1905 (33 Stat. 1257) and again in 1906 (34 Stat. 48). Prior to the 1982 recodification of Title 31, section 1342 was subsection (b) of the Antideficiency Act, while the basic prohibitions of section 1341 constituted subsection (a). (Recall that the prohibitions of section 1341(a) pertain to making or authorizing obligations or expenditures in excess of appropriations, and to obligations in advance of appropriations.) The proximity of the two provisions in the United States Code reflects their relationship: Section 1342 (voluntary services prohibition) supplements and is a logical extension of section 1341 (prohibition of obligations in advance of and in excess of appropriations). If an agency cannot directly obligate in excess or advance of its appropriations, it should not be able to accomplish the same thing indirectly by accepting ostensibly "voluntary" services and then presenting Congress with the bill, in the hope that Congress will recognize a "moral obligation" to pay for the benefits conferred.

Congress has repeatedly expressed its displeasure with such tactics, informally referred to as "greenmailing," and more formally as a "coercive deficiency." For example, the chairman of the House committee responsible for what became the 1906 reenactment of the voluntary services prohibition stated:

> It is a hard matter to deal with. We give to Departments what we think is ample, but they come back with a deficiency. Under the law they can [not] make these deficiencies, and Congress can refuse to allow them; but after they are made it is very hard to refuse to allow them. . . .

39 Cong. Rec. 3687 (1906), quoted in 30 Op. Att'y Gen. 51, 53-54 (1913).

In addition, since the Antideficiency Act was intended to keep an agency's level of operations within the amounts Congress appropriates, the unrestricted ability to use voluntary services would permit circumvention of that objective. Thus, without section 1342, a large legal loophole would exist and section 1341 would not be fully effective.

There are two situations in which 31 U.S.C. § 1342 does not apply. First, the section 1342 prohibition against accepting voluntary services or employing personal services does not apply to or prohibit the receipt of funds. The acceptance and retention of funds is addressed under the rule prohibiting augmentation of appropriations in the absence of statutory authority.

For example, in 59 Comp. Gen. 294 (1980), the United States Customs Service wanted to alleviate delays in clearing Customs at Miami International Airport by using funds received from the airport, airlines, and Dade County, Florida, to hire and compensate additional personnel for inspection services during regular business hours. The Comptroller General noted that there is no statutory authority for the Customs Service to accept and use funds for the proposed purpose. The Comptroller General concluded that, in the absence of statutory authority, funds for administering regular Customs services must come from Customs appropriations; reimbursement from outside sources for services on behalf of the general public would constitute augmentation of customs appropriations. This, even though the funds would eventually be used to hire services personnel, the Comptroller General applied the augmentation of appropriations rule because *funds*, and not *services*, were being accepted by the agency.

The second situation in which the voluntary services prohibition does not apply is when the services are not provided for the primary benefit of the government, but are provided for the benefit of the person(s) rendering the service. For example, in a 1905 decision, a vendor asked permission to install an appliance on Navy property for trial purposes at no expense to the Navy. Presumably, if the Navy liked the appliance, it would then buy it. In concluding that this arrangement did not violate the voluntary services prohibition, the Comptroller pointed out an easily overlooked phrase in the voluntary service prohibition: The services that are prohibited are voluntary services "for the United States." Here, temporary installation by the vendor for trial purposes amounted to service for its own benefit and on his own behalf, "as an incident to or necessary concomitant of a proper exhibition of his appliance for sale." Therefore, the Navy could grant permission without violating the voluntary services prohibition or the Antideficiency Act, provided that the vendor agreed to remove the appliance at its own expense if the Navy chose not to buy it. 11 Comp. Dec. 622 (1905).

This case seems to mean that a "primary benefit" test should be used. Clearly the Navy received *some* benefit from the vendor's installation of the appliance and the Navy's free use of it. Nevertheless, because the Comptroller General found that the vendor received the greater benefit, the Navy did not violate the voluntary services prohibition.

Finally, note that 31 U.S.C. § 1342 contains two distinct although closely related prohibitions: It bans (1) the employment of personal services "exceeding that authorized by law" and (2) the acceptance of any type of voluntary services for the United States.

Employment of Personal Services

One of the evils that the "personal services" prohibition was designed to correct was a practice that was controversial in 1884 but is much less so today. Lower-grade government employees were being forced to "volunteer" their services for overtime periods in excess of the periods allowed by law, thus enabling the agency to economize at the employees' expense, which often resulted in claims by the employees. See, e.g., 15 Cong. Rec. 3410-11 (1884), quoted in 30 Op. Att'y Gen. 51, 54-55 (1913). Although the practice that this part of the statute was enacted to address is not as prevalent today, the applicability of 31 U.S.C. § 1342 remains relevant in a number of other contexts involving services by government employees or services rendered by others that would otherwise have to be performed by government employees.

One of the earliest questions to arise under 31 U.S.C. § 1342 (and the issue that seems to have generated the greatest number of cases) was whether a government officer or employee, or an individual about to be appointed to a government position, could voluntarily work for nothing or for a reduced salary. Initially, the Comptroller of the Treasury was able to avoid directly answering the question on the grounds that the practice did not involve a payment from the Treasury, and suggested that the question was appropriate to take to the Attorney General. 19 Comp. Dec. 160, 163 (1912).

The following year, the Attorney General addressed the question when asked whether a retired Army officer could be "employed" as superintendent of an Indian school without compensation beyond his retirement pay. In what has become the leading case construing 31 U.S.C. § 1342, the Attorney General replied that the appointment would not violate the voluntary services prohibition. 30 Op. Att'y Gen. 51 (1913). In reaching this conclusion, the Attorney General drew a distinction that the Comptroller of the Treasury thereafter adopted and that GAO and the Justice Department continue to follow to this day. This is the distinction between "voluntary services" and "gratuitous services."

The key passages from the Attorney General's opinion are as follows:

> [I]t seems plain that the words "voluntary service" were not intended to be synonymous with "gratuitous service" and were not intended to cover services rendered in an official capacity under regular appointment to an office otherwise permitted by law to be non-salaried. In their ordinary and normal meaning these words refer to service intruded by a private person se a "volunteer" and not rendered pursuant to any prior contractor obligation. . . . It would be stretching the language a good deal

> to extend it so far as to prohibit official services without compensation in those instances in which Congress has not required even a minimum salary for the office. The context corroborates the view that the ordinary meaning of "voluntary services" was intended. The very next words "or employ personal service in excess of that authorized by law" deal with contractual services, thus making a balance between "acceptance" of "voluntary service" (i.e., the cases where there is no prior contract) and "employment" of "personal service" (i.e., the cases where there is such prior contract, though unauthorized by law).
>
> . . . .
>
> Thus it is evident that the evil at which Congress was aiming was not appointment or employment for authorized services without compensation, but the acceptance of unauthorized services not intended or agreed to be gratuitous and therefore likely to afford a basis for a future claim upon Congress. . . ."

Id. at 52–53, 55.

The Comptroller of the Treasury agreed with this interpretation and, in 1920, stated:

> [The statute] was intended to guard against claims for compensation. A service offered clearly and distinctly as gratuitous with a proper record made of that fact does not violate this statute against acceptance of voluntary service. An appointment to serve without compensation which is accepted and properly recorded is not a violation of [31 U.S.C. § 1342], and is valid if otherwise lawful.

27 Comp. Dec. 131, 132–33 (1920).

Two main rules, applicable today, emerge from the Attorney General's 1913 legal opinion (30 Op. Att'y Gen. 51) and the cases that later interpreted it. First, if compensation for a position is fixed by law, an appointee may not agree to serve without compensation or to waive that compensation in whole or in part. Id. at 56. See, e.g., *To Tom Tauke*, B-206396, Nov. 15, 1988 (unpub.); *The Agency for Int'l Dev.—Waiver of*

Compensation Fixed by or Pursuant to Statute, B-190466, 57 Comp. Gen. 423 (1978) (AID employees could not waive salaries); *In the Matter of Waiver of Compensation, Gen. Servs. Admin.,* B-181229, 54 Comp. Gen. 393 (1974); *To the President, United States Civil Serv. Comm'n,* B-66664, 26 Comp. Gen. 956 (1947).

This portion of the Attorney General's opinion did not create a new rule. The courts had already held, based on public policy, that compensation fixed by law could not be waived. See, e.g., *Glavey v. United States,* 182 U.S. 595 (1901); *Miller v. United States,* 103 F. 413 (C.C.S.D.N.Y. 1900). See also 9 Comp. Dec. 101 (1902); *MacMath v. United States,* 248 U.S. 151 (1918); and *United States v. Andrews,* 240 U.S. 90 (1916). Second, if the level of compensation is discretionary, or if the relevant statute prescribes only a maximum (but not a minimum), the compensation can be set at zero, and an appointment without compensation or a waiver, entire or partial, would be permissible. See 27 Comp. Dec. at 133.

Both GAO and the Justice Department have had frequent occasion to address these issues, and numerous decisions illustrate and apply the rules. See, e.g., 32 Comp. Gen. 236 (1952); 23 Comp. Gen. 109, 112 (1943); 14 Comp. Gen. 193 (1934); 34 Op. Att'y Gen. 490 (1925); 30 Op. Att'y Gen. 129 (1913); 3 Op. Off. Legal Counsel 78 (1979). In a 1988 opinion, the Justice Department's Office of Legal Counsel (OLC) considered whether the Iran-Contra Independent Counsel could appoint Professor Laurence Tribe as Special Counsel under an agreement to serve without compensation. Applying the rules set forth in 30 Op. Att'y Gen. 51, the OLC concluded that the appointment would not contravene the Antideficiency Act since the statute governing the appointment set a maximum salary but no minimum. *Independent Counsel's Authority to Accept Voluntary Services—Appointment of Laurence H. Tribe,* Op. Off. Legal Counsel, May 19, 1988. Similarly, the Comptroller General held in 58 Comp. Gen. 383 (1979) that members of the United States Metric Board could waive their salaries since the relevant statute merely prescribed a maximum rate of pay. In addition, since the board had statutory authority to accept gifts, a member who chose to do so could accept compensation and then return it to the board as a gift.

Both cases make the point that compensation is not "fixed by law" for purposes of the "no waiver" rule if the statute merely sets a maximum limit for the salary. In such cases, the employee can waive any or all compensation.

An example of the kind of situation 31 U.S.C. §1342 is designed to prevent is 54 Comp. Gen. 393 (1974). Members of the Commission on Marijuana and Drug Abuse had, apparently at the chairman's urging, agreed to waive their statutory entitlement to $100 per day while involved on commission business. The year after the commission ceased to exist, one of the former commissioners changed his mind and filed a claim for a portion of the compensation he would have received but for the waiver. Since the $100 per day had been a statutory entitlement, the purported waiver was invalid and the former commissioner was entitled to be paid. Similar claims by any or all of the other former members would also have to be allowed. If insufficient funds remained in the commission's now-expired appropriation, a deficiency appropriation would be necessary.

Since such a situation would violate the basic Antideficiency Act prohibition against incurring obligations in excess of appropriations, one may wonder why Congress felt it necessary to enact 31 U.S.C. § 1342, which imposes additional liability on government officials who accept voluntary services. The underlying rationale is Congress's aversion to coercive deficiencies. Since Congress has no alternative but to appropriate funds to cover the liability, its control over the appropriations process is undermined whenever it is presented with a coercive deficiency situation. By prohibiting the acceptance of voluntary services in the first place, Congress hoped to minimize the occurrence of such situations.

A few earlier cases deal with fact situations similar to that considered in 30 Op. Att'y Gen. 51, i.e., when someone already on the federal payroll performs additional duties without additional compensation. In 23 Comp. Gen. 272 (1943), for example, GAO concluded that a retired Army officer could serve, without additional compensation, as a courier for the State Department. The voluntary services prohibition, said the decision, does not preclude "the assignment of persons holding office under the Government to the performance of additional duties or the duties of another position without additional compensation." Id. at 274. The retired officer was considered to be "holding office" by virtue of his status as a reemployed annuitant and his receipt of federal funds.

Acceptance of Voluntary Services

"Employment of personal services" cases differ from cases that involve the appointment of an individual to an official government position, permanent or temporary. Services rendered prior to such an appointment or in the complete absence of an appointment are considered purely voluntary and, by virtue of 31 U.S.C. § 1342, cannot be accepted or compensated. *Lee v. United States*, 45 Ct. Cl. 57, 62 (1910); B-181934, October 7, 1974. These types of cases generally involve situations in which members of the general public and various civic groups offer to render services to government agencies without compensations, ostensibly motivated by patriotism and a sense of civic duty.

While the acceptance of such services would seem to be harmless, they enable the receiving agency to do more than it could otherwise have done within the amount Congress appropriated to it. Although this would seem to be a benefit to the government, it upsets the constitutional balance between the executive and the legislative branches because the voluntary services enable the agency to operate somewhat independently of congressional appropriations and outside of congressional control. The enactment of 31 U.S.C. § 1342, prohibiting executive agencies from accepting voluntary services, helps restore this balance and mitigates the need for deficiency appropriations to pay claims submitted by the "volunteers."

This category of voluntary services also includes post-retirement services that are rendered apart from appointment as a reemployed annuitant. Thus, under the general prohibition, such services cannot be lawfully accepted or compensated.

In a case that illustrates how many of these situations arise, a retired civil service employee claimed entitlement to compensation in addition to his annuity for temporary full-time duties he allegedly performed following his retirement. 65 Comp. Gen. 21 (1985). He stated that he was never formally appointed to a position following his retirement, but contended that his former supervisor accepted his offer to continue working after retirement and said that he would find a way to pay him. GAO denied the retiree's claim and noted that, under 31 U.S.C. § 1342, an officer or employee of the government is prohibited from accepting the voluntary services of an individual. Thus, the former supervisor violated section 1342 when he accepted the services of the retiree. Further, the retiree was not entitled to payment because the government cannot be bound by the unauthorized acts of the former supervisor, even if the former supervisor was unaware of the limitations on his authority.

Many voluntary services cases involve the two issues presented in this case: (1) Did a government official violate section 1342 by accepting voluntary services? and (2) Is the "volunteer" entitled to compensation? Generally, the cases hold that, if the government employee has violated section 1342, the "volunteer" will not be entitled to compensation for the services rendered.

Most of the voluntary services cases have been resolved by applying the "voluntary vs. gratuitous" distinction first enunciated by the Attorney General in 30 Op. Att'y Gen. 51. In essence, if a service is rendered based on a written agreement that the service provider will not be compensated, then the services can generally be accepted.

The underlying rationale of the distinction between prohibited voluntary services and lawful gratuitous services is well articulated in the following statement by the Justice Department's Office of Legal Counsel:

> Although the interpretation of § [1342] has not been entirely consistent over the years, the weight of authority

does support the view that the section was intended to eliminate subsequent claims against the United States for compensation of the "volunteer," rather than to deprive the government of the benefit of truly gratuitous services.

6 Op. Off. Legal counsel 160, 162 (1982).

Accordingly, the voluntary services provision of 31 U.S.C. § 1342 covers any type of service that has the effect of creating a legal or moral obligation to pay the person rendering the service. In an early interpretation of the voluntary services rule, the Comptroller General noted that:

> The voluntary service referred to in [31 U.S.C. § 1342] is not necessarily synonymous with gratuitous service, but contemplates service furnished on the initiative of the party rendering the same without request from, or agreement with, the United States therefor. Services furnished pursuant to a formal contract are not voluntary within the meaning of said section.

7 Comp.Gen.810,811 (1928).

Thus, if the service provider has a written agreement waiving compensation, or a contract whereby the contractor agrees to perform without pay, such services would not be considered "voluntary services" and would not violate 31 U.S.C. § 1342.

Several of the cases addressing gratuitous services agreements require that the agreement to serve without compensation be in writing. Proper documentation is important for evidentiary purposes in the event that the volunteer later submits a claim. See, e.g., 27 Comp. Gen. 194, 195 (1947); 26 Comp. Gen. 956, 958 (1947); 27 Comp. Dec. 131,132-33 (1920); 2 Op. Off. Legal Counsel 322,323 (1977). The contract, instead of stating that the service provider will work without pay, could also provide for a nominal amount, for example, $1. In either case, the amount of compensation is fixed, and the risk of subsequent valid claims for additional compensation is minimal.

An example of lawful gratuitous services rendered under a contract is 7 Comp. Gen. 810 (1928). In that case, a contractor had agreed to prepare stenographic transcripts of Federal Trade Commission (FTC) public proceedings and to furnish copies to the FTC without cost, in exchange for the exclusive right to report the proceedings and to sell transcripts to the public. The decision noted that consideration under a contract does not have to be monetary consideration, and held that the contract in question was supported by sufficient legal consideration and did not, therefore, violate the prohibition against acceptance of voluntary services.

In another case, B-13378, November 20, 1940, the Comptroller General held that the Secretary of Commerce could accept gratuitous services from a private agency, created by various social science associations, that had offered to assist in the preparation of official monographs analyzing census data. The services were to be rendered under a cooperative agreement that specified that they would be provided at no cost to the government.

Applying the same approach, GAO found no violation of 31 U.S.C. § 1342 for the Commerce Department to accept services by the Business Advisory Council, agreed in advance to be gratuitous. B-125406, November 4, 1955. Likewise, the Commission on Federal Paperwork could accept free services from the private sector as long as they were agreed in advance to be gratuitous. B-182087-0. M., November 26, 1975. In a 1982 decision, the American Association of Retired Persons wanted to volunteer services to assist in crime prevention activities (distribute literature, give lectures, etc.) on Army installations. GAO found no Antideficiency Act problem as long as the services were agreed in advance, and so documented, as gratuitous. B-204326, July 26, 1982.

In some cases, the existence of a contractual relationship does not preclude the performance of voluntary services by the contractor in violation of 31 U.S.C. § 1342. Thus, section 1342 may be violated when government contracting officers solicit or permit a contractor to continue performance on a "temporarily unfunded" basis while the agency, which has exhausted its appropriations and can't pay the contractor immediately, seeks additional appropriations.

This was one of the options considered in 55 Comp. Gen. 768 (1976), in which the Army proposed a contract modification that would explicitly recognize the government's obligation to pay for any work performed under the contract, including reasonable interest, subject to subsequent availability of funds. The government promised to use its best efforts to obtain a deficiency appropriation and agreed to issue certificates to this effect to the contractor, including a statement that any additional work performed would be done at the contractor's own risk. In return, the contractor would be asked to defer any action against the government for breach of contract.

GAO found this proposal "of dubious validity at best." Although the certificate given to the contractor would say that continued performance was at the contractor's own risk, it was clear that both parties expected the contract to continue. The government expected to accept the benefits of the contractor's performance, and the contractor expected to be paid for it. This is certainly not an example of a clear written understanding that work for the government is to be performed gratuitously.

This type of situation can arise in any contract that contains either the limitation of cost or limitation of funds clause. FAR 32.704 provides the following guidance:

> **32.704 Limitation of cost or funds.**
> (a)(1) When a contract contains the clause at 52.23220, Limitation of Cost; 52.23221, Limitation of Cost (Facilities); or 52.23222, Limitation of Funds, the contracting officer, upon learning that the contractor is approaching the estimated cost of the contract or the limit of the funds allotted, shall promptly obtain funding and programming information pertinent to the contract's continuation and notify the contractor in writing that
> (i) Additional funds have been allotted, or the estimated cost has been increased, in a specified amount;
> (ii) The contract is not to be further funded and that the contractor should submit a proposal for an adjustment of fee, if any, based on the percentage of work completed in

relation to the total work called for under the contract;
(iii) The contract is to be terminated; or
(iv)(A) The Government is considering whether to allot additional funds or increase the estimated cost-
(B) The contractor is entitled by the contract terms to stop work when the funding or cost limit is reached; and
(C) Any work beyond the funding or cost limit *will be at the contractor's risk*. [Emphasis added]

If the funds initially available for the contract have been exhausted, the contracting officer has the choices delineated in (a)(1)(i) thru (iv) in FAR 32.704. If a contracting officer directs the contractor to continue performing prior to obtaining the additional funds, the services would be voluntary and the acceptance of such services would violate 31 U.S.C. § 1342. Note that the GAO decision in 55 Comp. Gen. 768 (1976) goes even further. In that decision, even if the contractor elected to perform at its own risk, without direction or request from the contracting officer, GAO would consider such an arrangement "of dubious validity at best," because the contractor would expect to be paid, which could create a moral obligation to pay.

Despite GAO's concerns, the limitation of cost and limitation of funds clauses specifically allow the contactor to perform at its own risk when contract funds have been exhausted, and agencies may include those clauses in their contracts. However, agency personnel must be careful not to say or otherwise indicate that the contractor should continue working because the agency will obtain the necessary funding.

> **Discussion Problem 5-8**
>
> Bob, an experienced claims examiner for the Department of Federal Programs, has retired after 30 years of outstanding service. His services were so outstanding, in fact, that his former supervisor cannot get by without him. The supervisor calls Bob and, after an exchange of pleasantries, asks if Bob would like to examine claims again on a voluntary basis, three days per week. Bob has been getting bored playing golf and fishing, so he agrees. After Bob has been working under this arrangement for a year, his supervisor (who has just returned from a federal appropriations law course) decides that Bob should sign a "gratuitous services agreement." Bob says "sure" and signs the agreement.
>
> Did the supervisor violate 31 U.S.C. § 1341? What is the effect of the gratuitous services agreement?

Exceptions

There are several exceptions to the prohibition against accepting voluntary services.

The Emergency Exception

The principal statutory exception to the prohibition against accepting voluntary services is the one included within 31 U.S.C. § 1342 itself. This exception authorizes a government employee or official to accept voluntary services in cases of "emergencies involving the safety of human life or the protection of property." Over the years, there have been relatively few GAO decisions interpreting the scope of this exception. However, in 1981, the Attorney General considered the exceptions in the context of funding gaps and articulated a somewhat broader standard than that applied in the early GAO decisions. The opinion, published at 5 Op. Off. Legal Counsel 1 (1981), is discussed in Continuing Resolution and Funding Gaps chapter at paragraph I.B.3.e. Perhaps to counter the fairly expansive definition of what constitutes an emergency articulated in the 1981 opinion, in 1990 Congress amended 31 U.S.C. § 1342 (see Pub. L. 101-508) by adding the following language:

> As used in this section, the term "emergencies involving the safety of human life or the protection of property" does not include ongoing, regular functions of government the suspension of which would not imminently threaten the safety of human life or the protection of property.

In 1995, when the Attorney General next had an opportunity to issue an opinion on the meaning of the emergency exception to 31 U.S.C. § 1342, the opinion was much more restrictive than the 1981 opinion, due mainly to the 1990 amendment. The 1995 Attorney General Opinion stated:

> Under the formulation of the 1981[Attorney General] Opinion, government functions satisfy § 1342 if . . . the safety of human life or the protection of property would be "compromised, in some degree." It is conceivable that some would interpret this phrase to be satisfied even if the threat were de minimis, in the sense that the increased risk to life or property were insignificant, so long as it were possible to say that safety of life or protection of property bore a reasonable likelihood of being compromised at all. This would be too expansive an application of the emergency provision. The brief delay of routine maintenance on government vehicles ought not to constitute an "emergency," for example, and yet it is quite possible to conclude that the failure to maintain vehicles properly may "compromise, to some degree" the safety of the human life of the occupants or the protection of the vehicles, which are government property. We believe that the revised articulation clarifies that the emergencies exception applies only to cases of threat to human life or property where the threat can be reasonably said to [be] . . . near at hand and demanding of immediate response.

DOJ Memorandum for Alice Rivlin, Office of Management and Budget, Aug. 16, 1995.

Interestingly, just a few months after this opinion was issued, the government was confronted with a funding gap at the beginning of FY 1996. To avoid a large-scale government shutdown, Congress passed a temporary amendment to 31 U.S.C. § 1342. That amendment, contained in Pub. L. 104-92, temporarily amended section 1342 by inserting the following language:

> All officers and employees of the United States Government or the District of Columbia government shall be deemed to be performing services relating to emergencies involving the safety of human life or the protection of property.

Section 310(a) of Pub. L. 104-92.

This amendment was in effect only for the period of December 15, 1995, through January 26, 1996. The effect of the amendment was that *all* government employees were authorized to perform their government duties, even though no appropriation had been enacted. Acceptance of such services in the absence of an appropriation would have otherwise constituted a violation of 31 U.S.C. § 1342. Thus, although the law was amended to make clear that routine functions will not qualify for the emergency exception, when a funding gap threatened to shut down the federal government, Congress provided relief from the restrictive language it added in 1990. The following subsections address some situations in which special statutory relief was not available and the emergency exception was an issue.

Safety of Human Life. To qualify for the exception, the services provided to protect human life must have been rendered in a true emergency situation. Several decisions discuss what constitutes an emergency. In 12 Comp. Dec. 155 (1905), a municipal health officer disinfected several government buildings to prevent the further spread of diphtheria. Several cases of diphtheria had already occurred at the government compound, including four deaths. The Comptroller of the Treasury found that the services had been rendered in an emergency involving the loss of human life, and held accordingly that the doctor could be reimbursed for the cost of materials used and the fair value of his services. This decision highlights the two-fold nature of the voluntary services cases. One issue is whether a government employee had improperly accepted voluntary services; the other issue is whether the volunteer is entitled to payment.

In another case, the S.S. Rexmore, a British vessel, deviated from its course to London to answer a call for help from an Army transport ship carrying over 1,000 troops. The ship had sprung a leak and appeared to be in danger of sinking, even though its pumps were working at full capacity to discharge the incoming water. The Comptroller General allowed a claim for the vessel's actual operating costs plus lost profits attributable to the services performed. The Rexmore had rendered a tangible service to save the lives of the people aboard the Army transport, as well as the transport vessel itself. 2 Comp. Gen. 799 (1923).

In contrast, GAO denied payment to a man who was boating in the Florida Keys and saw a Navy seaplane make a forced landing. He offered to tow the aircraft over two miles to the nearest island, and did so. His claim for expenses was denied. GAO noted that the aircraft had landed intact, the pilot was able to radio for help before the forced landing, and the pilot was in no immediate danger. Rendering service to overcome mere inconvenience or even a potential future emergency is not enough to overcome the statutory prohibition. 10 Comp. Gen. 248 (1930).

It is clear that the emergency exception will not apply when the emergency is created by the agency's own mismanagement of its funds. In *Matter of: Anti-Deficiency Act Violation Involving the District of Columbia Health and Hospitals Public Benefit Corporation*, B-285725, September 29, 2000, the District of Columbia Health and Hospitals Public Benefit Corporation (PBC) continued to incur obligations after exhausting its appropriation. It claimed that it did not violate the Antideficiency Act because, since it was a hospital, it was regularly engaged in the protection of human life. GAO rejected this argument, stating:

PBC's failure to regulate its activities and spending so as to operate within its available budget resources is not the type of "emergency" covered either by the Attorney General's earlier opinions or 31 U.S.C. Sec. 1342. . . . The PBC (like a number of federal agencies, e.g., U.S. Secret Service, U.S. Capitol Police, Bureau of Prisons, Veterans Administration) requests and receives appropriations to cover the costs of providing services essential to the protection of life. Like other similarly situated federal entities, the Congress may reasonably expect the PBC and the District to consider this fact when preparing the budget request for submission to the Congress. Once the Congress enacts appropriation, it is incumbent on the PBC (and similarly situated federal agencies) to manage its resources to stay within the authorized level. Nothing in the District's Submission demonstrates that the PBC's exhaustion of appropriations prior to the end of the fiscal year was caused by some unanticipated event or events (e.g., mass injuries resulting from hurricane, flood or other natural disasters) requiring PBC to provide services for the protection of life beyond the level it should have reasonably been expected to anticipate when it prepared its budget. Moreover, to accept the District and PBC's argument that everything the PBC does qualifies under the section 1342 exception for "emergency" service would nullify the oversight and control provided by the appropriation process and would provide the PBC with unlimited authority to incur obligations to fund its operations. While the PBC may have to confront emergencies that qualify under the section 1342 exception, we are unwilling, for obvious reasons, to agree with PBC's expansive reading of its authority under this provision of law.

Thus, the emergency exception would apply if there is some unanticipated event for which the agency could not have budgeted, which caused the agency's costs of operations to exceed the amount of funds available. The emergency exception would not apply simply because the agency is involved, in a general way, in the protection of human life. Further, as indicated in the District of Columbia case, the emergency exception is unavailable to shield an agency from an Antideficiency Act violation when overobligations are attributable to the agency's mismanagement of its funds. *Protection of Property.* When considering the applicability of the emergency exception for the protection of property, the key factor is that the property must be either government-owned property or property for which the government has some responsibility. This standard was articulated by the Comptroller of the Treasury in 9 Comp. Dec. 182, 185 (1902) as follows:

> I think it is clear that the statute does not contemplate property in which the Government has no immediate interest or concern; but I do not think it was intended to apply exclusively to property owned by the Government. The term "property" is used in the statute without any qualifying words, but it is used in connection with the rendition of services for the Government. The implication is, therefore, clear that the property in contemplation is property in which the Government has an immediate interest or in connection with which it has some duty to perform.

In this decision, an individual had gathered up mail scattered in a train wreck and delivered it to a nearby town. Although the government did not "own" the mail, it did have a responsibility to deliver it. Therefore, the services came within the statutory exception, and the individual could be paid for the value of his services. Applying this same approach, the Comptroller General held in B-152554, February 24, 1975, that section 1342 did not permit the Agency for International Development to make expenditures in excess of available funds for disaster relief services in foreign countries, since the government did not have an immediate interest or a duty to protect foreign property.

A case clearly within the exception is 3 Comp. Gen. 979 (1924), which allowed reimbursement to a municipality that had rendered firefighting assistance to prevent the destruction of federal property that was not within the territory for which the municipal fire department was responsible. An exception was also recognized in 53 Comp. Gen. 71 (1973), where a government employee brought in food for a group of security personnel responding to the unlawful occupation of a federal building. GAO found that these circumstances would justify a determination that the expenditure was incidental to the protection of government property in an extreme emergency.

Statutorily Authorized Waivers of Compensation Fixed by Statute

The rule that compensation fixed by statute may not be waived does not apply if the waiver or appointment without compensation is itself authorized by statute. The Comptroller General stated the principle as follows in 27 Comp. Gen. 194,195 (1947):

> [E]ven where the compensation for a particular position is fixed by or pursuant to law, the occupant of the position may waive his ordinary right to the compensation fixed for the position and thereafter forever be estopped from claiming and receiving the salary previously waived, if there be some applicable provision of law authorizing the acceptance of services without compensation." (Emphasis in original.)

In B-139261, June 26, 1959, GAO reiterated this principle and gave several examples of statutes sufficient for this purpose. Another example may be found in 2 Op. Off. Legal Counsel 322 (1977) and 32 Comp. Gen. 236 (1952).

The rules for waiver of salary or appointment without compensation may be summarized as follows: If compensation is *not* fixed by statute, i.e., if it is fixed administratively or if the statute merely prescribes a maximum but not a minimum, it may be waived as long as the waiver qualifies as "gratuitous." There should be an advance written agreement waiving all claims for compensation. If compensation *is* fixed by statute, it may not be waived, even under a gratuitous services agreement, unless there is specific statutory authority. Of course, even in the absence of specific statutory authority, if a government employee whose salary is fixed by statute really wants to work for nothing, he or she can accept the statutorily fixed salary and donate it to the agency (if the agency is authorized to accept gifts) or directly to the United States Treasury.

Experts and Consultants

Experts and consultants employed under authority of 5 U.S.C. § 3109 may serve without compensation without violating the Antideficiency Act as long as it is clearly understood and agreed that no compensation is expected. The statute states:

> Sec. 3109. Employment of experts and consultants; temporary or intermittent.
> . . .
> (b) When authorized by an appropriation or other statute, the head of an agency may procure by contract the temporary (not in excess of 1 year) or intermittent services of experts or consultants or an organization thereof, including stenographic reporting services. Services procured under this section are without regard to -
> (1) the provisions of this title governing appointment in the competitive service;
> . . .

Since the provisions pertaining to appointment in the competitive service are inapplicable to experts and consultants, the salary of such individuals is not fixed by statute and can be waived. This was the conclusion reached by the Comptroller General in 27 Comp. Gen. 194 (1947):

> When the temporary (not in excess of one year) or intermittent services of an expert or consultant are authorized in an appropriation or other act to be procured by contract, the Procurement of such service may be had without regard to the civil service and classification laws. In the absence of some act specifically fixing the amount to be paid an expert or consultant, there is no law other than the classification law which would require that a rate of compensation be fixed for a position occupied by an expert or consultant. Since the classification law particularly is made inapplicable to the procuring of services of experts or consultants on a temporary or intermittent

basis in accordance with [5 U.S.C. 3109] it follows that, generally, an expert or consultant whose services are thus used temporarily or intermittently, may agree to serve without compensation, or at any compensation up to the maximum. . . . Accordingly, an expert or consultant whose services are procured on a temporary or intermittent basis, may Agree to serve without compensation, and thereafter he would be estopped from asserting any valid claim for Compensation on account of the service performed.

See also 6 Op. Off. Legal Counsel 160 (1982).

Services in Support of Alternative Dispute Resolution
Section 593 of Title 5 of the United States Code establishes the Administrative Conference of the United States. Among other responsibilities, the Conference may:

> (1) study the efficiency, adequacy, and fairness of the administrative procedure used by administrative agencies in carrying out administrative programs, and make recommendations to administrative agencies, collectively or individually, and to the President, Congress, or the Judicial Conference of the United States, in connection therewith, as it considers appropriate;

These duties include participation in alternative dispute resolution (ADR) procedures. ADR refers to any means of settling disputes outside of the courtroom and typically includes arbitration, mediation, early neutral evaluation, and conciliation. Title 9 of the U.S. Code establishes federal law supporting arbitration.

Regarding the authority to accept voluntary services, 5 U.S.C. § 593(c) states:

> (c) Members of the Conference, except the Chairman, are not entitled to pay for service. Members appointed from outside the Federal Government are entitled to travel expenses, including per diem instead of subsistence, as authorized by section 5703 of this title for individuals serving without pay.

This express statutory authority to accept voluntary services from members of the Conference provides a clear exception to the prohibition of 31 U.S.C. § 1342 and typifies the degree of statutory specificity that one should look for when attempting to justify an exception.

Student Intern Programs
Section 3111 of Title 5 states:

> Sec. 3111. Acceptance of volunteer service
> . . .
> (b) Notwithstanding section 1342 of title 31, the head of an agency may accept, subject to regulations issued by the Office, voluntary service for the United States if the service -
> (1) is performed by a student, with the permission of the institution at which the student is enrolled, as part of an agency program established for the purpose of providing educational experiences for the student;
> (2) is to be uncompensated; and
> (3) will not be used to displace any employee.

This statute has the classic "notwithstanding" language that overrides the statute referenced, in this case 31 U.S.C. § 1342. As noted in the discussion pertaining to "repeals by implication" in Chapter 1, when Congress wants to override a statute, it must do so expressly and specifically. The use of the term "notwithstanding" and the specific reference to 31 U.S.C. § 1342 satisfy this requirement.

To illustrate why the exception is necessary, in 26 Comp, Gen. 956 (1947), the (then) Civil Service Commission asked the Comptroller General whether an agency could accept the uncompensated services of college students as part of a college's internship program. The students "would be assigned to productive work, i.e., to the regular work of the agency in a position which would ordinarily fall in the competitive civil service." The answer was no. The students would be used in positions for which the compensation was fixed by law, and compensation fixed by law cannot be waived; therefore, the proposal would require legislative authority. Without statutory authority, uncompensated student services that furthered the agency's mission, i.e., "productive work," could not be accepted. See also 2 Op. Off. Legal Counsel 185 (1978).

In view of the long-standing rule, supported by decisions of the Supreme Court, prohibiting the waiver of compensation for positions required by law to be salaried, GAO and the Justice Department had little choice but to respond as they did. The consequence of these decisions, however, is that uncompensated student interns could be used only for essentially "non-productive work," a result that benefits neither the students nor the agencies.

The solution to this dilemma was legislative authority, which Congress provided later in 1978 by the enactment of 5 U.S.C. § 3111. The statute authorizes agencies (subject to regulations of the Office of Personnel Management) to accept the uncompensated services of high school and college students, "notwithstanding section 1342 of Title 31," if the services are part of an agency program designed to provide educational experience for the student and will not be used to displace any employee. In a 1981 decision, GAO held that 5 U.S.C. § 3111 does not authorize the payment of travel or subsistence expenses for the students. 60 Comp. Gen. 456 (1981). Section 3111 of Title 5 continues to provide the requisite statutory authority.

Medical Care, Museums, Natural Resources Programs, and Family Support Programs

Section 1588 of Title 10 provides specific authority to the Department of Defense to accept certain designated voluntary services. That statute states:

> Sec. 1588. Authority to accept certain voluntary services
> (a) Authority To Accept Services. - Subject to subsection (b) and notwithstanding section 1342 of title 31, the Secretary concerned may accept from any person the following services:
> (1) Voluntary medical services, dental services, nursing services, or other health-care related services.

(2) Voluntary services to be provided for a museum or a natural resources program.
(3) Voluntary services to be provided for programs providing services to members of the armed forces and the families of such members . . .

This statute, like 5 U.S.C. § 3111, uses the preferred "notwithstanding" language that clearly indicates a congressional intent to override 31 U.S.C. § 1342 in the areas designated. The statute is quite broad, especially subparagraph (3), which authorizes acceptance of any voluntary services that provide support to "members of the armed forces and the families of such members."

Red Cross Volunteers

Section 2602 of Title 10 allows the President, and by delegation, executive agencies, to accept voluntary services from the Red Cross. That statute states:

> **Sec. 2602. American National Red Cross: cooperation and assistance**
> (a) Whenever the President finds it necessary, he may accept the cooperation and assistance of the American National Red Cross, and employ it under the armed forces under regulations to be prescribed by the Secretary of Defense.

This statute, like 5 U.S.C. § 3111, is quite broad and allows executive agencies to accept virtually any services that are considered "necessary" and are within the operating charter of the Red Cross.

Reserve Officers

Section 10212 of Title 10 authorizes the military departments to accept services of reserve officers as consultants or in furtherance of enrollment, organization, or training of reserve components. The statute states:

Sec. 10212. Gratuitous services of officers: authority to accept
(a) Notwithstanding section 1342 of title 31, the Secretary of Defense may accept the gratuitous services of an officer of a reserve component (other than an officer of the Army National Guard of the United States or the Air National Guard of the United States) in consultation upon matters relating to the armed forces.
(b) Notwithstanding section 1342 of title 31, the Secretary of a military department may accept the gratuitous services of an officer of a reserve component under the Secretary's jurisdiction (other than an officer of the Army National Guard of the United States or the Air National Guard of the United States) -
(1) in the furtherance of the enrollment, organization, and training of that officer's reserve component or the Reserve Officers' Training Corps; or
(2) in consultation upon matters relating to the armed forces.

This statute also specifically references 31 U.S.C. § 1342 and uses the preferred "notwithstanding" language. Note that this statute refers to acceptance of "gratuitous services" rather than voluntary services. As discussed, gratuitous services generally are performed under the terms of a written gratuitous services agreement whereby the person(s) performing the services waive any claim to compensation.

Statutory Training Programs

Statutes authorizing training programs are enacted from time to time to provide job training assistance to various classes of individuals. The training is intended to enable participants to enter the labor market at a higher level of skill and thereby avoid the need for public assistance. Questions have arisen under programs of this nature as to the authority of federal agencies to accept services from participants in these programs and the applicability of 31 U.S.C. § 1342, as well as other fiscal rules, such as the augmentation of appropriations rules.

For example, a 1944 case, 24 Comp. Gen. 314, considered a vocational rehabilitation program for disabled war veterans. GAO concluded that 31 U.S.C. § 1342 did not preclude federal agencies from providing on-the-job training, without payment of salary, to program participants. The decision is further discussed in 26 Comp. Gen. 956, 959 (1947).

In 1975, GAO held that a federal agency could accept the free services of trainees sponsored and paid by nonfederal organizations from federal grant funds under the Comprehensive Employment and Training Act of 1973. 54 Comp. Gen. 560 (1975). The decision stated:

> [Considering that the services in question will arise out of a program initiated by the Federal Government, it would be anomalous to conclude that such services are proscribed as being voluntary within the meaning of 31 U.S.C. § [1342]. That is to say, it is our opinion that the utilization of enrollees or trainees by a Federal agency under the circumstances here involved need not be considered the acceptance of "voluntary services" within the meaning of that phrase as used in 31 U.S.C. § [1342].

Id. at 561.

Under the rationale of this decision, an agency can accept services performed in accordance with a statutory training program because the enactment of the statute indicates an intent not to apply the prohibition against accepting voluntary services established by 31 U.S.C. § 1342. This decision seems to contravene the generally applicable rule against repeals by implication. If the statute establishing a particular training program does not reference 31 U.S.C. § 1342 or use the phrase "notwithstanding any other law" (or equivalent), then application of the "no repeals by implication" rule would seem to apply. Application of that rule would mean that 31 U.S.C. § 1342 would prohibit acceptance of voluntary services, even if such services are provided under the auspices of a statutory training program.

Although 54 Comp. Gen. 560 (1975) allows for an implied override of 31 U.S.C. § 1342, this decision must be read against the backdrop of the well-established rule against repeals by implication. In such cases where section 1342 is not specifically mentioned in the statutory training program, affected agencies may consider seeking an advance opinion from the Comptroller General regarding their authority to accept the services.

Several other issues have arisen when agencies have accepted services under a statutory training program. In B-211079.2, January 2, 1987, GAO considered services performed and accepted under the Community Work Experience Program. The relevant program legislation expressly authorized program participants to perform work for federal agencies "notwithstanding section 1342 of title 31," thereby avoiding the "no repeal by implication" issue. 42 U.S.C. § 609(a)(4)(A). However, the decision goes on to say that the statutory authority was necessary, not because of the voluntary services prohibition, but to avoid an impermissible augmentation of appropriations. This is because acceptance of otherwise authorized voluntary services may be an improper augmentation of an appropriation if federal employees normally would perform the work, unless a statute authorizes gratuitous services. *Community Work Experience Program — State Gen. Assistance Recipients at Fed. Work Sites*, B-211079.2, Jan. 2, 1987 (unpub.).

The decisions in this area are not entirely consistent because other cases hold that augmentation occurs when funds, not services, are accepted. See, e.g., *Senior Community Serv. Employment Program*, B-222248, Mar. 13, 1987 (unpub.) (acceptance of services not an augmentation or appropriations) and *Federal Communications Comm'n*, B-210620, 63 Comp. Gen. 459 (1984) (noting that augmentation entails receipt of funds). The important point, regardless of whether analyzed as an augmentation or a voluntary service, is that the agency should ensure that the statutory authority establishing the training program specifically indicates that acceptance of the services is authorized.

Other Statutory Exceptions

These are a small sample of the statutory exceptions to the voluntary services prohibition of 31 U.S.C. § 1342. A word search in the LEXIS™ United States Code database returned 235 "hits" in which statutory exceptions to 31 U.S.C. § 1342 are cited. See, e.g., 2 U.S.C. § 175 (Library of Congress may accept services of voluntary and uncompensated personnel); 2 U.S.C. § 475 (Office of Technology Assessment may accept and utilize the services of voluntary and uncompensated personnel as necessary); 5 U.S.C. § 3161 (head of a temporary organization may accept volunteer services appropriate to the duties of the organization without regard to section 1342 of title 31); and 7 U.S.C. § 911 (Secretary of Agriculture may accept voluntary services of federal, state, and local officers and employees in support of rural electrification). Agencies and prospective volunteers should consult these and other statutes to ensure that the performance of voluntary services is authorized.

REPORTING ANTIDEFICIENCY ACT VIOLATIONS

When an agency official determines that an Antideficiency Act violation has occurred, the official must report the violation to the head of the agency, generally through agency comptroller channels. 31 U.S.C. §§ 1351, 1517. The agency head must then submit a transmittal letter to the President through the Director of OMB. See OMB Circular A-34, Section 40 (included as Attachment 5-1 at the end of this chapter.) Factors such as mistake, inadvertence, lack of intent, or the minor nature of a violation do not affect the duty to report. Of course, if the agency feels there are extenuating circumstances, it may include them in the report. 35 Comp. Gen. 356 (1955).

OMB Circular A-34 requires that the letter to the President contain the following information:

- The title and Treasury symbol (including the fiscal year) of the appropriation or fund account, the amount in-

volved for each violation, and the date on which the violation occurred.
• The name and position of the officer(s) or employee(s) responsible for the violation.
• All facts pertaining to the violation, including the type of violation (for example, overobligation of an appropriation, overobligation of an apportionment, overobligation of an allotment or suballotment), the primary reason or cause, any statement from the responsible officer(s) or employee(s) with respect to any circumstances believed to be extenuating, and any germane report by the agency's Inspector General and/or the agency's counsel.
• A statement of the administrative discipline imposed and any further action(s) taken with respect to the officer(s) or employee(s) involved in the violation.
• In the case where an officer or employee is suspected of willfully and knowingly violating the Antideficiency Act, confirm that all information has been submitted to the Department of Justice for determination of whether further action is needed.
• A statement regarding the adequacy of the system of administrative control prescribed by the head of the agency and approved by OMB, if such approval has been given. If the head of the agency determines a need for changes in the regulations, such proposals will be submitted as provided in section 50.7.
• A statement of any additional action taken by, or at the direction of, the head of the agency, including any new safeguards provided to prevent recurrence of the same type of violation.
• If another agency is involved, a statement concerning the steps taken to coordinate the report with the other agency.

The agency must submit the same letter to the Speaker of the House of Representatives and the President of the Senate.

These reporting requirements apply even if the violation is discovered by GAO or OMB, instead of an official within the agency. If GAO has discovered the violation, the report to the President must indicate whether the agency agrees that a violation has occurred, and if so, the report must contain an explanation of why the violation was not discovered and previously reported by the agency. If the agency does not agree that a violation has occurred, the report to the President and the Congress will explain the agency's position. If OMB has discovered a violation, it may request that the agency conduct an investigation or audit. In such cases, a report describing the results of the investigation or audit must be submitted to OMB through the head of the agency. If the report indicates that no violation of the Antideficiency Act has occurred, the agency head must so inform OMB and forward a copy of the report to OMB. If the report indicates that a violation of the Antideficiency Act has occurred, the agency head must report to the President and the Congress as soon as possible. If the agency head does not agree that a violation has occurred, the report to the President and to the Congress will explain the agency's position.

CONSEQUENCES OF ANTIDEFICIENCY ACT VIOLATIONS

Antideficiency Act violations have both criminal and administrative consequences. If an agency has properly implemented a sound financial management system, identifying the person responsible for a violation should not be difficult in most cases. However, even if an agency has a sound financial management system, if numerous individuals are involved in a complex transaction, and particularly when the actions producing the violation occurred over a long period of time, identifying the responsible person(s) can be much more difficult. In such cases, the investigation must focus on the person who was in the best possible position to avoid the violation. This will generally be the person who was aware of the actions that triggered the violation (e.g., disbursement, obligation) and knew or should have known that such actions were questionable.

For example, if a contracting officer relies on a fund certification document that indicates that $1 million is available for obligation, and awards a contract for $2 million, the contracting officer is the responsible party. However, what if a contracting officer relies on a fund certification document indicating that $2 million is available for obligation, when only $1 million is actually available? If the contracting officer awards a contract for $2 million, he or she would generally not be identified as the responsible party because the contracting officer may rely on the amount of funding indicated on the fund certification document. In this case, the likely responsible party would be the fund certification official who (incorrectly) indicated that $2 million was available for obligation.

Criminal Penalties

The applicability of criminal penalties for Antideficiency Act violations are established by 31 U.S.C. §§ 1350, 1519. A knowing and willful violation of the Antideficiency Act is a Class E felony under 18 U.S.C. § 3559(a)(5), and the maximum punishment per violation is a $5,000 fine, confinement for two years, or both. It is also a felony to knowingly and willfully conceal an Antideficiency Act violation. 18 U.S.C. § 4. See B-245856.7, August 11, 1992 (the knowing and willful failure to record an overobligation in an account to *conceal* a violation of the Antideficiency Act would be an offense under 18 U.S.C. § 4). Thus, failing to report a violation or devising an overly creative justification for an obligation or expenditure that appears to violate the act could result in prosecution under the concealment prohibition.

Although factors such as the absence of bad faith or the lack of intent to commit a violation are irrelevant for purposes of determining whether a violation has occurred, they are relevant in determining whether one may be held criminally liable for an Antideficiency Act violation. A prerequisite to criminal liability is a determination that the law was "knowingly and willfully" violated.

Administrative Sanctions

Adverse administrative actions may be taken pursuant to 31 U.S.C. §§ 1349(a), 1518. Most agencies implement this authority through regulation. For example, DoD officers or employees who authorize or make prohibited obligations or expenditures are subject to administrative discipline, including suspension without pay and removal from office. DOD Dir. 7200.1; DOD 7000.14-R, vol. 14, ch. 9; Memorandum, Comptroller, Dep't of Defense, subject: Violations of the Antideficiency Act (19 Dec. 1994).

Good faith or mistake of fact does not relieve an individual from responsibility for a violation. As with any adverse personnel action, supervisors should consider the surrounding facts and circumstances that led to the violation. Factors such as a lack of intent, workload, and the employee's past duty record are relevant in determining the appropriate level of discipline. However, such factors do not negate the violation or the need to impose *some* disciplinary action. For a case in which an official was reduced in grade and reassigned to other duties, see *Duggar v. Thomas*, 550 F. Supp. 498 (D.D.C. 1982) (upholding the agency's action against a charge of discrimination).

EFFECT OF EXHAUSTION OF APPROPRIATION ON CONTRACTORS' RIGHT TO PAYMENT

Since an agency cannot lawfully disburse funds from an exhausted appropriation, issues occasionally arise regarding whether contractors are nevertheless entitled to payment. The answer seems to depend on the type of appropriation involved and whether or not the contractor knew or should have known of the limitations of the appropriation.

Where a contractor is but one party out of several to be paid from a general appropriation, the contractor would not be expected to know the status or condition of the appropriation account on the government's books. This is the situation commonly encountered under an agency's general operations appropriations, which are usually enacted as a lump sum on an annual basis. Such appropriations are used to fund ongoing, routine functions of the agency for a particular fiscal year. If the appropriation becomes exhausted, the Antideficiency Act may prevent the agency from making any further payments, but valid obligations will remain enforceable in the courts.

For example, in *Ferris v. United States*, 27 Ct. Cl, 542 (1892), the plaintiff had a contract with the government to dredge a channel in the Delaware River. The Corps of Engineers made him stop work halfway through the job because it had run out of money. In discussing the contractor's rights in a breach of contract suit, the court said:

> A contractor who is one of several persons to be paid out of an appropriation is not chargeable with knowledge of its administration, nor can his legal rights be affected or impaired by its maladministration or by its diversion, whether legal or illegal, to other objects. An appropriation *per se* merely imposes limitations upon the Government's own agents; it is a definite amount of money intrusted to them for distribution; but its insufficiency does not pay the Government's debts, nor cancel its obligations, nor defeat the rights of other parties.

Id. at 546.

The rationale for this rule is that "a contractor cannot justly be expected to keep track of appropriations where he is but one of several being paid from the fund." *Ross Construction Corp. v. United States*, 392 F.2d 984, 987 (Ct. Cl. 1968). Other cases reaching the same conclusion include *Dougherty ex rel. Slavens v. United States*, 18 Ct. Cl. 496 (1883) (the Antideficiency Act may "apply to the official, but [does] not affect the rights in this court of the citizen honestly contracting with the Government"); and *Joplin v. United States*, 89 Ct. Cl. 345 (1939). See also *Wetsel-Oviatt Lumber Co. v. U.S.*, 38 Fed.Cl. 563, No. 96-323C (August 12, 1997), where the agency claimed that it should be relieved of its responsibility to pay its contractor monies owed under the contract because it lacked adequate funds. The court, in rejecting this contention, considered the applicability of the statutory judgment fund and stated:

> [A]ssuming the Forest Service does not have appropriations from which to compensate Wetsel, there exists a statutory appropriation from which the government is permitted to pay Wetsel. Pursuant to 41 U.S.C. Sec. 612(a), "[a]ny judgment against the United States on a claim under . . . [the Contract Disputes Act] shall be paid promptly in accordance with the procedures provided by section 1304 of Title 31." . . . Title 31 U.S.C. Sec. 1304(a) provides, in pertinent part, that "[n]ecessary amounts are appropriated to pay final judgments, awards, compromise settlements, and interest and costs specified in the judgments or otherwise authorized by law when . . . (1) payment is not otherwise provided for. . . ." Thus, if the Forest Service has no funds from which to pay Wetsel, this Court may enter judgment for plaintiff and require payment to Wetsel. . . . In sum, notwithstanding the Appropriations Clause and the Anti-deficiency Act, the Court finds that, where the government lawfully contracts with another, the government cannot avoid liability—and must compensate the party with whom the government lawfully contracts—if there is found to be a government breach of contract. Further, in this case, there exists a statutory source of appropriations to pay final judgments against—and compromise settlements with—the United States, for which payment is not otherwise provided.

It is important to distinguish between situations in which a contractor claim is settled between the parties and situations in which the claim results in a judgment from a court or a board. In the former situation, the settlement is considered a matter of contract administration, and the agency must have adequate funding to cover the settlement modification or it will violate the "amount" section of the Antideficiency Act (1341(a)(1)(A)). However, if the claim results in a judgment and the judgment is in excess of an amount available in an appropriation or a subdivision of funds, there is no violation. *Bureau of Land Management, Reimbursement of Contract Disputes Act Payments*, B-211229, 63 Comp. Gen. 308 (1984); *Availability of Funds for Payment of Intervenor Attorney Fees*, B-208637, 62 Comp. Gen. 692 (1983). The rationale for these decisions is that a judicial or quasi-judicial judgment or award does not involve a deficiency created by an administrative officer of the agency, and therefore does not trigger liability under the Antideficiency Act.

Thus, the well-settled rule is that contractors paid from a general appropriation are not barred from recovering for breach of contract even though the appropriation is exhausted. This rule applies regardless of whether the contractor's right to payment is based on a routine voucher for performance, settlement of a claim, or a formal determination of liability by a court or board of contract appeals. To liquidate its liability to the contractor, the agency, in such cases, would have to obtain additional funds. It could do so, for example, by requesting additional funds from Congress, requesting a transfer of funds from another appropriation, or reprogramming funds within the same appropriation.

The ability of a contractor to recover is far more limited, however, under a specific line-item appropriation. Since an appropriations act is a public law, everyone has constructive knowledge of its contents. Thus, a contractor in this situation is deemed to have notice of the limits on the spending power of the government official with whom he contracts. A contract under these circumstances is valid only up to the amount of the available appropriation. Exhaustion of the appropriation will generally bar any further recovery beyond that limit. See, e.g., *Sutton v. United States*, 256 U.S. 575

(1921); *Hooe v. United States*, 218 U.S. 322 (1910); *Shipman v. United States*, 18 Ct. Cl. 138 (1883); *Dougherty ex rel. Slavens v. United States*, 18 Ct. Cl. 496 (1883).

The distinction between the rules that apply under a general appropriation compared to a specific appropriation stems logically from the old maxim that ignorance of the law is no excuse. If Congress appropriates a specific dollar amount for a particular contract, that amount is specified in the appropriation act and the contractor is deemed to know it. It is certainly not difficult to locate. If, on the other hand, a contract is but one activity under a larger appropriation, it is not reasonable to expect the contractor to know how much of that appropriation remains available for it at any given time.

> This chapter addressed the second of the three limitations imposed by Congress on the use of appropriated funds: the amount limitation. The various sections of the Antideficiency Act were analyzed, and the application of the act to apportionments, appropriations, and administrative subdivisions was discussed.
>
> The chapter also discussed the voluntary services prohibition and the two recognized exceptions: specific statutory authority and the existence of an emergency. Next, the administrative and criminal consequences of violating the Antideficiency Act were discussed. The chapter closed with a discussion of the effect of exhaustion of an appropriation on a contractor's right to payment.

Attachment 5-1

360 APPROPRIATIONS LAW: PRINCIPLES AND PRACTICE

SECTION 40 -- REQUIREMENTS FOR REPORTING
ANTIDEFICIENCY ACT VIOLATIONS

SECTION 40 -- REQUIREMENTS FOR REPORTING ANTIDEFICIENCY ACT VIOLATIONS

Table of Contents
40.1 What is the Antideficiency Act? 40.2 What violations must I report? 40.3 How do the requirements for reporting violations differ for credit programs? 40.4 Do the requirements for reporting violations differ for revolving funds? 40.5 Do the requirements for reporting violations differ for closed and expired accounts? 40.6 How do I report a violation? 40.7 What if the GAO reports a violation? 40.8 What if OMB suspects a violation? Ex-40A Antideficiency Act Violation Sample Letter to the Director Ex-40B Antideficiency Act Violation Sample Letter to the President

40.1 What is the Antideficiency Act?

The Antideficiency Act consists of provisions of law that were passed by Congress (beginning in the nineteenth century and later incorporated into Title 31 of the United States Code) to prevent departments and agencies from spending their entire appropriations during the first few months of the year. The Act *prohibits* you and any other Federal employee from:

- Entering into contracts that *exceed* the enacted appropriations for the year.

- Purchasing services and merchandise *before* appropriations are enacted.

The Act:

- Requires that OMB *apportion* the appropriations, that is, approve a plan that spreads out spending over the fiscal period for which the funds were made available.

- Restricts *deficiency apportionments* to amounts approved by the agency heads only for "extraordinary emergency or unusual circumstances."

- Establishes *penalties* for Antideficiency Act violations. Violations are obligations or expenditures in excess of the lower of the amount in the affected account, the amount apportioned, or the amount allotted.

- Requires the agency head to report any Antideficiency Act violations to the President, through the OMB Director, and Congress.

Under the Act, if you obligate or expend more than the amount in the appropriation or fund or the amount apportioned or any other subdivision of funds, you shall be subject to appropriate administrative discipline, including -- when circumstances warrant -- a written reprimand, suspension from duty without pay, or removal from office.

OMB Circular No. A-34 (2000)   131

SECTION 40 -- REQUIREMENTS FOR REPORTING ANTIDEFICIENCY ACT VIOLATIONS

In addition, if you are convicted of willfully and knowingly overobligating or overexpending the amount, then you shall be fined not more than $5,000, imprisoned for not more than 2 years, or both.

In 1982, Congress reworded and reorganized the language of the Antideficiency Act along with the rest of Title 31 of the United States Code. The intent of Congress was to modernize the language of the Act, without changing its meaning. You will find a crosswalk between the provisions of law that made up the Antideficiency Act before it was modernized and the current language in Appendix A.

40.2 What violations must I report?

If you . . .	The amount . . .	Then, you must report of violation of . . .
Authorize or make an obligation exceeding	In an appropriation or fund.	31 U.S.C. 1341(a)
	In an apportionment or reapportionment (a type of administrative subdivision of funds).	31 U.S.C. 1317(a)(1)
	In an allotment or a suballotment (a type of administrative subdivision of funds).	31 U.S.C. 1517(a)(2)
	In any other administrative subdivision of funds, if the overobligation results in the overobligation of one of the previous amounts.	31 U.S.C. 1517(a)
Authorize or make a disbursment exceeding	In an appropriation or fund.	31 U.S.C. 1341(a)
	In an apportionment or reapportionment (a type of administrative subdivision of funds).	31 U.S.C. 1517(a)(1)
	An allotment or a suballotment (a type of administrative subdivision of funds).	31 U.S.C. 1517(a)(2)
	In any other administrative subdivision of funds if the overexpenditure results in the overexpenditure of one of the previous amounts.	31 U.S.C. 1517(a)
Obligate or Expend	Funds required to be sequestered.	31 U.S.C. 1341(a)
Involve the Government in a contract or obligation	Before you receive the appropriation, unless such contract or obligation is authorized by law.	31 U.S.C. 1341(a)
Accept voluntary service	In excess of that authorized by law.	31 U.S.C. 1342

40.3 How do the requirements for reporting violations differ for credit programs?

In addition to the violations specified in section 40.2, report overobligation or overexpenditure of:

- The subsidy -- where an officer or employee of the United States has made or authorized a direct loan obligation or loan guarantee commitment that requires a subsidy cost obligation or expenditure in excess of amounts appropriated and/or apportioned for such purposes. Modifications of direct

362 APPROPRIATIONS LAW: PRINCIPLES AND PRACTICE

SECTION 40 -- REQUIREMENTS FOR REPORTING
ANTIDEFICIENCY ACT VIOLATIONS

loans or loan guarantees (or of direct loan obligations or loan guarantee commitments), as defined in section 70, that result in obligations or expenditure in excess of apportioned unobligated balances of subsidy amounts are violations. (31 U.S.C. 1341(a), 31 U.S.C. 1517(a))

- The credit level supportable by the enacted subsidy -- where an officer or employee of the United States has made or authorized a direct loan obligation or loan guarantee commitment, that is in excess of the level specified by law. This includes, for example, obligations or expenditures that are in excess of a limitation on direct loan obligations or guaranteed loan commitments. (31 U.S.C. 1341(a))

- The amount appropriated for administrative expenses -- where an officer or employee of the United States has made or authorized an expenditure or created or authorized an obligation that is in excess of the amount appropriated for administrative expenses. (31 U.S.C. 1341(a))

- The expired unobligated balance of the subsidy -- where an officer or employee of the United States has made or authorized an expenditure or created or authorized an obligation, including a commitment, against unobligated subsidy balances after the period of obligational authority has expired. Correction of mathematical or data input errors up to the amount of the expired unobligated balance of the subsidy are not violations. Corrections of these errors in excess of the amount of the expired unobligated balance of the subsidy are violations. (31 U.S.C. 1341(a))

40.4 Do the requirements for reporting violations differ for revolving funds?

No. The incurring of obligations in excess of apportioned budgetary resources in a revolving fund is a violation of the Antideficiency Act, whether or not a fund has unapportioned budgetary resources or non-budgetary assets greater than the amount apportioned.

40.5 Do the requirements for reporting violations differ for closed and expired accounts?

No. You are required to report violations when:

- Obligations and expenditures or adjustments to obligations and expenditures exceed the original appropriations.

- There are obligations or expenditures in closed accounts.

- Obligations and expenditures or adjustments to obligations and expenditures exceed the amount apportioned or allotted.

40.6 How do I report a violation?

Transmittal letter to the Director of OMB. You will transmit the letter from your agency head to the President through the Director of OMB. A sample transmittal letter is provided in Exhibit 40A.

Letter to the President. You will report a violation of the Antideficiency Act violation in the form of a letter (original and three copies) from your agency head to the President. A sample letter is provided in Exhibit 40B.

OMB Circular No. A-34 (2000)   133

Limitations on the Use of Appropriated Funds: Amount 363

SECTION 40 -- REQUIREMENTS FOR REPORTING ANTIDEFICIENCY ACT VIOLATIONS

The letter will set forth the following:

- The title and Treasury symbol (including the fiscal year) of the appropriation or fund account, the amount involved for each violation, and the date on which the violation occurred.

- The name and position of the officer(s) or employee(s) responsible for the violation.

- All facts pertaining to the violation, including the type of violation (for example, overobligation of an appropriation, overobligation of an apportionment, overobligation of an allotment or suballotment), the primary reason or cause, any statement from the responsible officer(s) or employee(s) with respect to any circumstances believed to be extenuating, and any germane report by the agency's Inspector General and/or the agency's counsel.

- A statement of the administrative discipline imposed and any further action(s) taken with respect to the officer(s) or employee(s) involved in the violation.

- In the case where an officer or employee is suspected of willfully and knowingly violating the Antideficiency Act, confirm that all information has been submitted to the Department of Justice for determination of whether further action is needed.

- A statement regarding the adequacy of the system of administrative control prescribed by the head of the agency and approved by OMB, if such approval has been given. If the head of the agency determines a need for changes in the regulations, such proposals will be submitted as provided in section 50.7.

- A statement of any additional action taken by, or at the direction of, the head of the agency, including any new safeguards provided to prevent recurrence of the same type of violation.

- If another agency is involved, a statement concerning the steps taken to coordinate the report with the other agency.

Letters to Congress. You will report identical letters to the Speaker of the House of Representatives and the President of the Senate.

If the letters to Congress are identical to the letter to the President, include a statement to this effect in the letter to the President. If the letters to Congress are not identical to the letter to the President, you will submit a copy of the letter to Congress with your letter to the President.

40.7 What if the GAO reports a violation?

You should report to the President and Congress on violations reported by the General Accounting Office in connection with audits and investigations.

In these cases, the report to the President will indicate whether the agency agrees that a violation has occurred, and if so, it will contain an explanation as to why the violation was not discovered and previously reported by the agency. If the agency does not agree that a violation has occurred, the report to the President and the Congress will explain the agency's position.

SECTION 40 -- REQUIREMENTS FOR REPORTING
ANTIDEFICIENCY ACT VIOLATIONS

40.8 What if OMB suspects a violation?

Whenever OMB determines that a violation of the Antideficiency Act may have occurred, OMB may request that an investigation or audit be undertaken or conducted by the agency. In such cases, a report describing the results of the investigation or audit will be submitted to OMB through the head of the agency. If the report indicates that no violation of the Antideficiency Act has occurred, the agency head will so inform OMB and forward a copy of the report to OMB. If the report indicates that a violation of the Antideficiency Act has occurred, the agency head will report to the President and the Congress in accordance with section 40.6 as soon as possible. If the agency head does not agree that a violation has occurred, the report to the President and to the Congress will explain the agency's position.

Exhibit 40A

SECTION 40 -- REQUIREMENTS FOR REPORTING
ANTIDEFICIENCY ACT VIOLATIONS

Antideficiency Act Violation
Sample Letter to the Director

Honorable Director
Office of Management and Budget
Washington, D.C. 20503

Dear Mr. Director:

Enclosed is a letter transmitting a violation report of section [1341 or 1517] of Title 31, United States Code to the President.

The Antideficiency Act violation totaled $XXXX.XX. This violation report is required by section [1351 or 1517] of Title 31, United States Code, to be submitted to the President; it is being submitted through the Director of the Office of Management and Budget.

To comply with the aforementioned provisions, copies of the report are also being submitted to the President of the Senate and the Speaker of the House of Representatives.

Sincerely,
Agency Head

Enclosure

SECTION 40 -- REQUIREMENTS FOR REPORTING
ANTIDEFICIENCY ACT VIOLATIONS   Exhibit 40B

Antideficiency Act Violation
Sample Letter to the President

The President
The White House
Washington, D.C. 20500

Dear Mr. President:

This letter is to report a violation of the Antideficiency Act, as required by section [1351 or 1517] of Title 31, United States Code.

A violation occurred in account [Treasury symbol and title]. The violation occurred on [date] in connection with [identify the affected program or activity] for FY XXXX. Mr./Ms. _____ (rank/grade/title) was [were] the officer(s) responsible for the violation(s).

[Describe the nature of the violation (see section 40.2). Then state the primary reason or cause. Include any statement from the responsible officer(s) or employee(s) as to any circumstances believed to be extenuating. Include any germane report by the agency's Inspector General.]

[State which administrative discipline was imposed as well as any further action(s) taken with respect to the officer(s) or employee(s) involved. (see section 40.1)]

[In the case where an officer or employee is suspected of willfully and knowingly violating the Antideficiency Act, confirm that all information has been submitted to the Department of Justice.]

[State whether the adequacy of the system of administrative control has been approved by OMB. (see section 21)]

[State whether any additional action need be taken to prevent recurrence of the same type of violation.]

[If another agency is involved, state what steps are being taken to coordinate the report with the other agency.]

[Identical reports will be submitted to the presiding officer of each House of Congress. If identical to the report to the President, so state. (see section 40.6)]

Respectfully,
Agency Head

CHAPTER 6
Fiscal Law Issues Related to Interagency Transactions

When one agency provides goods or services to another agency and funds are transferred, the arrangement could violate the rules pertaining to augmentation and transfer of appropriations. In various situations, however, the authority to transfer funds between agencies could achieve significant economies and benefits. This chapter will discuss the various statutory bases of authority that allow such transactions.

THE ECONOMY ACT

The best-known and most widely used statute authorizing interagency transfers is the Economy Act, 31 U.S.C. §§ 1535 and 1536.

Overview of the Economy Act

In 1932, Congress enacted the first government-wide statutory authorization for federal agencies to provide work, services, or materials to other federal agencies on a reimbursable basis. Although interagency transactions offer many advantages, widespread use had been discouraged by the "well established rule that one Government activity may not be reimbursed for services performed for another except to the extent that it is shown that increased costs have been incurred." A-31040, May 6, 1930. GAO explained the rationale for this rule as follows:

> [O]ne government activity may not be reimbursed for services performed for another except to the extent that it is shown that increased costs have been incurred. . . . [U]nless increased costs have actually been incurred by the performing activity, there is nothing to be paid and if payment is made merely on some theoretical, or hypothetical, or estimated basis, where no actual increased costs are shown to have been incurred, the effect is to augment the appropriation of the performing activity at the expense of the appropriation of the requesting activity, and thus to apply the appropriation of the requesting activity to the purposes of the performing activity in contravention of [the Purpose statute].

See also, e.g., 10 Comp. Gen. 193 (1930); 10 Comp. Gen. 131 (1930); 8 Comp. Gen. 600 (1929); 6 Comp. Gen. 81 (1926).

Under this rule, the performing agency could not recover costs that it would have incurred regardless of whether it performed on behalf of another agency. For example, the salaries of agency personnel used in providing the service would have been incurred whether the services were performed for the agency employing the personnel or another agency.

The bill that would become known as the "Economy Act" was introduced in 1930. The purpose of the legislation was "to permit the utilization of facilities and personnel belonging to one department by another department or establishment and to enact a simple and uniform procedure for effecting the appropriation adjustments involved." Interdepartmental Work: Hearings on H.R. 10199 Before the Committee on Expenditures in the Executive Departments, 71st Cong., 2d Sess. 3 (1930), quoted in 57 Comp. Gen. 674, 678 (1978). The relationship between interagency transactions and general principles of fiscal law were explained by the Comptroller General as follows:

> It is also a requirement of law, in using appropriations for the support of any activity that the appropriation be ex-

pended only for the objects specified therein. This requires that when one department obtains work, materials or services from another department it should pay the full cost of such work, materials or services. If full cost is not paid, then such part of the cost as is not reimbursed must fall upon the department doing the work, which is contrary to [the Purpose statute, 31 U.S.C. § 1301(a)] and the appropriation of the department for which the work was done will be illegally augmented because it does not bear all of the cost of the work done for it. Id. at 4.

57 Comp. Gen. at 678.

In other words, it would violate the purpose statute for Agency A to use its funds to perform or acquire goods or services for Agency B. Congress could have handled this matter by simply prohibiting one agency from performing or acquiring goods or services for another agency. However, Congress recognized that various economies and benefits could be realized if such transactions were authorized. In 1932, Congress enacted the law authorizing interagency transactions, officially designated as section 601 of the Legislative Branch Appropriation Act for 1933, ch. 314, 47 Stat. 382, 417 (1932), but which became popularly known as the Economy Act.

Section 601 of the Economy Act has been amended several times, receiving its current structure and designation in the 1982 recodification of Title 31, and is now found at 31 U.S.C. §§ 1535 and 1536. The basic authority is set out in 31 U.S.C. § 1535(a):

> (a) The head of an agency or major organizational unit within an agency may place an order with a major organizational unit within the same agency or another agency for goods or services if—
> (1) amounts are available;
> (2) the head of the ordering agency or unit decides the order is in the best interest of the United States Government;
> (3) the agency or unit to fill the order is able to provide or get by contract the ordered goods or services; and

(4) the head of the agency decides ordered goods or services cannot be provided by contract as conveniently or cheaply by a commercial enterprise.

The introductory portion of 31 U.S.C. § 1535(a) delineates who can use the authority and what they can use it for. The numbered subsections establish four basic conditions for use of the authority.

The first condition is the obvious requirement that funds are available. Since the Economy Act does not create a general exception to the purpose statute (31 U.S.C. § 1301(a)), the ordering agency must have funds that are available for the contemplated purpose. 26 Comp. Gen. 545, 548 (1947); 16 Comp. Gen. 3, 4 (1936); 15 Comp. Gen. 704 (1936); 15 Comp. Gen. 5 (1935); B-259499, August 22, 1995. Thus, although the ordering agency does not need specific authority in its appropriation language to use the Economy Act, it must adhere to any monetary limits Congress may choose to impose. 19 Comp. Gen. 585 (1939). Further, the ordering agency cannot take advantage of any special statutory authorities that the performing agency has but that the ordering agency lacks. In other words, the Economy Act does not authorize an agency to use another agency to do anything it could not lawfully do itself. See, e.g., 5 Comp. Gen. 757 (1926).

This prohibition against the transfer of funds to another agency being used to circumvent 31 U.S.C. § 1301(a) is not limited to Economy Act transactions but applies to all transfers, whether in advance or by reimbursement, to working funds or otherwise, unless authorized under a statute that expressly provides differently. See, e.g., 7 Comp. Gen. 524, 526 (1928), emphasizing that since the appropriation in question "is not available for direct expenditure for such purpose . . . it can not be made available for such purpose by transfer" to another agency. See also 30 Comp. Gen. 453 (1951); 28 Comp. Gen. 365 (1948); 22 Comp. Gen. 462 (1942); 19 Comp. Gen. 774 (1940).

The second requirement is that the head of the ordering agency must determine that the interagency order is in the best interests of the government. This requirement confers very broad authority on the agency, and there is apparently no GAO decision in which an interagency transaction under the Economy Act was rejected for this reason.

The third condition is that the performing agency is "able to provide" the goods or services or can obtain them "by contract." This requirement goes to the essence of the Economy Act. The objective of the statute is to permit an agency to take advantage of another agency's expertise, not merely to offload work, funds, or both or to avoid legislative restrictions. A good example is 13 Comp. Gen. 138 (1933), in which the Comptroller General recognized that, under the Economy Act, a government corporation issuing its own securities could seek assistance from the forerunner of the Bureau of the Public Debt. If necessary, the agency may, as long as the work or service is within the scope of activities it normally performs, procure additional supplies or equipment or hire additional temporary personnel to enable it to provide or acquire goods and services for the requesting agency. B-197686, December 18, 1980.

For example, in 13 Comp. Gen. 138 the fact that the Public Debt Service had to hire additional personnel to perform for the requesting agency did not render the agreement objectionable. If property is purchased incident to an Economy Act transaction, upon completion of the work it is "an asset of the agency bearing the cost of its acquisition." 33 Comp. Gen. 565, 567 (1954). If the ordering agency has paid through an advance of funds to the performing agency, then whatever remains when performance is complete should be returned to the ordering agency for use or disposal as appropriate. If several agencies have contributed to the cost, the property is regarded as "owned" by all of the agencies on a pro rata basis. 38 Comp. Gen. 36 (1958).

Whether an agency "is able to provide or get by contract the ordered goods or services" to do Economy Act work is primarily the agency's own determination, and GAO will generally defer to the agency's discretion. 23 Comp. Gen. 935, 937 (1944). However, what an agency is able to do includes legal as well as factual considerations. The legal considerations include whether any statutory prohibitions or restrictions would obstruct performance. Id. at 937–938. For example, if the performing agency is statutorily prohibited from performing certain functions, it could not perform those functions on behalf of the ordering agency. This is true even if the ordering agency is legally authorized to perform those functions. In other words, the Economy Act does not give a performing agency any authority that it would not otherwise have. 18 Comp. Gen. 262, 266 (1938).

The fourth condition is that the ordering agency must determine that it cannot obtain the goods or services "as conveniently or cheaply" from a private contractor. See *USA Info. Sys., Inc., and Dataware Techs., Inc. v. Government Printing Office*, GSBCA Nos. 13535-P, 13560-P, 96-2 BCA ¶ 28,315; *Dictaphone Corp.*, B-244691.2, Nov. 25, 1992. The effect of this requirement is to enable agencies to function more like commercial buyers by having them compare the costs and benefits of contracting with another agency versus a commercial vendor.

In making the "lower cost" determination, it is permissible to solicit bids and then reject all bids if they exceed the cost of dealing with another agency. 37 Comp. Gen. 16 (1957). Even if an agency determines that the "ordered goods or services cannot be provided by contract as conveniently or cheaply by a commercial enterprise," it is not *required* to accomplish the procurement through another agency. The authority to use the Economy Act is permissive rather than mandatory. Id.

Conversely, if the agency *cannot* determine that the "ordered goods or services cannot be provided by contract as conveniently or cheaply by a commercial enterprise," then use of the Economy Act is improper. This requirement is reflected in the procurement regulations of most agencies. For example, paragraph 17.503 of the Defense Federal Acquisition Regulation Supplement states:

Determinations and Findings Requirements.
(a) Each Economy Act order shall be supported by a Determination and Finding (D&F). The D&F shall state that —
(1) Use of an interagency acquisition is in the best interest of the Government; and
(2) The supplies or services cannot be obtained as conveniently or economically by contracting directly with a private source.

Note that the regulation tracks with the Economy Act. Further agency supplements provide additional detail regarding who must prepare and sign the determination and findings. See, e.g., AFFARS 5317.503-90, Air Force Determination Requirements (providing detailed guidance and a model Determination and Findings).

The cost comparison of 31 U.S.C. § 1535(a)(4) is required only if the agency is contemplating an Economy Act transaction. It does not apply where the agency chooses to perform a function in-house in lieu of renewing an existing commercial contract. *Techniarts Engineering v. United States*, 51 F.3d 301 (D.C. Cir. 1995). The Economy Act itself does not require that agencies document the two determinations called for by 31 U.S.C. § 1535(a) (interest of the government and lower cost). However, GAO regards documenting the determinations as "sound practice" and a desirable internal control. *Interagency Agreements: Fiscal Year 1988 Agreements at Selected Agencies Were Proper*, GAO/AFMD-88-72 (September 1988), p. 8. As noted, many agency regulations require that the determinations be documented.

Regarding the order issued by the ordering agency, although not specifically required by the Economy Act, GAO has emphasized that an Economy Act transaction should be evidenced by a "written order or agreement in advance, signed by the responsible administrative officer of each of the departments or offices concerned." 13 Comp. Gen. 234, 237 (1934). A written agreement is important because, as in any contract situation, the terms to which the parties agree, as reflected in the writing, establish the scope of the undertaking and the rights and obligations of the parties. For example, the DoD Financial Management Regulations, Vol. 11A, Ch. 3, states:

> 030501. Ordering Procedures. An Economy Act order may be placed on any form that is acceptable to both the requesting and servicing agencies involved based upon the documentation standards in Chapter 1, paragraph 010204, of this Volume. Typically, between DoD components, a DD Form 448, MIPR is used to place the order. A DD Form 448-1, "Acceptance of MIPR," is used to show acceptance.

Also, the written agreement can establish a ceiling on the ordering agency's financial obligation. 22 Comp. Gen. 74 (1942).

While an advance agreement normally "should be regarded as essential . . . the lack of a specific agreement does not necessarily preclude reimbursement" in appropriate cases. B-39297, January 20, 1944. An "appropriate case" would seem to be one in which the facts are sufficient to establish an implied contract or an express contract that was not finalized. For example, in A-85201, April 15, 1937, an agreement had been in effect for several years and the facts showed that both agencies intended to continue the agreement for the year in question.

GAO recommends that the agreement specify at least the following: (1) legal authority for the agreement; (2) terms and conditions of performance; (3) cost of performance, including appropriate ceilings when cost is based on estimates; (4) mode of payment (advance or reimbursement); (5) any applicable special requirements or procedures for assuring compliance; and (6) approvals by authorized officials. GAO, *Policy and Procedures Manual for Guidance of Federal Agencies*, Title 7, § 2.4.C.2e.

Finally, it would be useful for the agreement to set forth a requirement and procedures for the performing agency to notify the ordering agency if it appears that performance will exceed estimated costs and to cease or curtail performance as may be necessary. This is an important safeguard to protect the performing agency against Antideficiency Act violations. See 7 GAO-PPM § 2.4.C.2g; B-234427, August 10, 1989 (non-decision letter).

Scope of the Economy Act

The coverage of the Economy Act is broad, and there is no distinction between who can place an order and who can perform one. The statute says that "[t]he head of an agency or major organizational unit within an agency may place an order with a major organizational unit within the same agency or another agency." 31 U.S.C. § 1535(a). This embraces all three branches of the federal government. Within the legislative branch, for example, one of the earliest Economy Act decisions applied the statute to the Architect of the Capitol. 12 Comp. Gen. 442 (1932). Financial audits conducted by GAO of legislative branch agencies include the Economy Act as one of the laws tested for compliance. See, e.g., *Financial Audit: First Audit of the Library of Congress Discloses Significant Problems*, GAO/AFMD-91-13 at 29 (August 1991). GAO has also viewed the law as applicable to itself. B-156022-O.M., January 6, 1972; B-130496-O.M., March 13, 1957; B-13988, January 7, 1941. See also, A-31068, March 25, 1930 (Economy Act's 1920 predecessor applicable to Botanic Garden). The court in *United States v. Mitchell*, 425 F. Supp. 917, 918 (D.D.C. 1976), regarded the law as applicable to the judicial branch.

The Economy Act also applies to government corporations. 13 Comp. Gen. 138 (1933); B-116194, October 5, 1953; B-39199, January 19, 1944; B-27842, August 13, 1942; A-46332, January 9, 1933. These decisions involve a variety of government corporations in the capacity of both ordering agency and performing agency. Although the specific corporations in those cases are now defunct, the rationale applying the Economy Act to government corporations remains valid.

The common thread of applicability is that the entity in question must be an agency or instrumentality of the United States government. Accordingly, the Economy Act does not apply to the District of Columbia government. 50 Comp. Gen. 553, 556 (1971); B-107612, February 8, 1952. Nor does it apply to the National Guard, except possibly when the Guard is called into federal service. B-152420, October 3, 1963, aff'd on recons., B-152420, February 25, 1964. It does not apply to Indian tribes (B-44174, September 6, 1944), agencies of the United Nations (23 Comp. Gen. 564 (1944)), American Samoa (B-194321, August 7, 1979), or a presidential inaugural committee (62 Comp. Gen. 323, 330 (1983)).

Finally, it is important to note that the Economy Act authorizes intra-agency, as well as inter-agency, transactions. E.g., 57 Comp. Gen. 674 (1978); 25 Comp. Gen. 322 (1945); B-77791, July 23, 1948. While the decisions had consistently taken this position, this is one instance in which the recodified language of 31 U.S.C. § 1535(a) (which included "major organizational unit within the same agency" within the coverage of the Economy Act) is more precise than the original language. While the two bureaus or offices may be part of the same department or agency, they must be funded under separate appropriations. 38 Comp. Gen. 734, 738 (1959); B-60609, September 26, 1946.

Agency regulations often emphasize this limitation. For example, the DoD Financial Management Regulation states:

> 030104. Limitations. Because of previous instances of abuse of Economy Act
> . . .
> An Economy Act order cannot be used by one organizational unit to order work or services from another organizational unit under the same activity commander where the activity commander is in a position to fund the required goods or services through the use of direct funds.

Further, the Economy Act does not apply with respect to separate appropriations of a single bureau or office. 38

Comp. Gen. at 737–738. Thus, an official of a bureau or office of a federal agency could not properly issue an Economy Act order to another subdivision of that same bureau or office, even if the ordering and performing subdivisions are funded from different appropriations. Such a transaction would constitute an unauthorized transfer of appropriations. Further, it is unlikely that the ordering official would be able to make the required determination that the "other" entity could perform more effectively than the requiring entity when the transaction is between subdivisions of the same office.

Discussion Problem 6-1

The Office of Advanced Project Research (OAPR) within the Department of Defense consists of two branches: the Airplane Research Branch and the Helicopter Research Branch. The OAPR is headed by General Farhout I. Dears. The specific programs of each branch receive specific, line-item appropriations. The airplane branch is planning to award a contract for airplane engine research. The helicopter branch believes that the research conducted under the airplane engine research contract would be applicable to helicopter engines as well. The helicopter branch would like to issue an Economy Act order to the airplane branch so the contractor could conduct related experiments applicable specifically to helicopter engines. Would this be a proper Economy Act transaction?

Fiscal Issues Related to Implementation of the Economy Act

Fiscal issues related to implementation of the Economy Act deal with (1) making and accounting for payments, (2) calculating the "actual cost" to be reimbursed, (3) obligation and deobligation of funds, (4) applicability of general restrictions and limitations, and (5) exception to the requirement for certification in advance of payment.

Making and Accounting for Payments

The payment provision of the Economy Act (31 U.S.C. § 1535(b)) states:

> Payment shall be made promptly by check on the written request of the agency or unit filling the order. Payment may be in advance or on providing the goods or services ordered and shall be for any part of the estimated or actual cost as determined by the agency or unit filling the order. A bill submitted or a request for payment is not subject to audit or certification in advance of payment. Proper adjustment of amounts paid in advance shall be made as agreed to by the heads of the agencies or units on the basis of the actual cost of goods or services provided.

Advance Payments and Reimbursements. This provision authorizes two types of payment: payments made in advance and payments made to reimburse the performing agency for costs it incurred on the ordering agency's behalf. The decision of which payment method to use is made by the performing agency.

Performing agencies will often use one procedure for non-federal procedures and the other procedure for federal customers. For example, the NASA Financial Management Manual states:

> **(1)Non-Federal Customers.** Non-Federal customers will be billed and pay in advance except where otherwise authorized by law and approved by the Center DCFO or Headquarters, Chief, Accounting, Reporting & Analysis Branch, Code BFB, in writing.
> **(2)Federal Customers.** Federal customers shall pay billed expenses by Treasury's On-line Payment and Collection System (OPAC) in order to streamline the payment of interagency reimbursable costs.

Payment may be in a lump sum or in installments, and a pre-audit is not required.

Payments made in advance will often necessarily be based on estimates; if so, the amounts should be adjusted appropriately once the actual cost becomes known. Any excess (the amount by which the advance exceeds actual cost) should be returned to the ordering agency. Retention of the excess amount by the performing agency is an improper augmentation of its funds. 72 Comp. Gen. 120 (1993). If the account to which the excess would otherwise be returned has been closed, the money must be deposited in the Treasury as miscellaneous receipts. 31 U.S.C. § 1552(b). If the excess is determined while the appropriation charged with the advance is still available for obligation, the performing agency should pay special attention to returning the funds in time for the ordering agency to be able to use them. GAO, Policy and Procedures Manual for Guidance of Federal Agencies, tit. 7, § 2.4.C.2d (May 1993). Note that the Economy Act requires that payment be made "promptly."

The authority to pay by reimbursement is essentially an exception to the purpose statute (31 U.S.C. § 1301(a)) because it allows the performing agency to temporarily use its own funds to do the ordering agency's work. See B-234427, August 10, 1989 (nondecision letter); B-6124-O.M., October 11, 1939.

Accounting for payments is addressed in 31 U.S.C. § 1536. Subsection (a) sets forth general requirements, and subsection (b) deals with goods provided from stock. Subsection (a) provides:

> An advance payment made on an order under section 1535 of this title is credited to a special working fund that the Secretary of the Treasury considers necessary to be established. Except as provided in this section, any other payment is credited to the appropriation or fund against which charges were made to fill the order.

This provision provides an exception to the so-called "miscellaneous receipts" statute, 31 U.S.C. § 3302(b). 56 Comp. Gen. 275, 278 (1977). Advance payments must be credited to special working funds created for that purpose. A working fund is a type of intragovernmental revolving fund. The intent of the original Economy Act was that Treasury would establish a working capital fund when requested by the performing agency. H.R. Rep. No. 1126, 72d Cong., 1st Sess. 16 (1932).The language of the 1982 recodification would appear to give Treasury the final decision on the need to create such a fund. When the work is completed, the amount of the advance is adjusted.

Payments made as reimbursements are credited to the appropriations of the performing agency "against which charges were made" in effecting performance. This means that the reimbursement must be credited to the fiscal year in which it was "earned," that is, the fiscal year actually charged by the performing agency, without regard to when the reimbursement is made. If the appropriation that earned the reimbursement is still available for obligation at the time of reimbursement, the money may be used for any authorized purposes of that appropriation. 31 U.S.C. § 1536(b). This would be true as a matter of general appropriations law even if the statute did not specifically address it. If the appropriation is no longer available for new obligations, the reimbursement must be credited to the appropriate expired account or, if the account has been closed, to miscellaneous receipts. B-260993, June 26, 1996; 31 U.S.C. § 1552(b). See also B-211953, n.8, December 7, 1984; B-194711-O.M., January 15, 1980.

A significant exception to 31 U.S.C. § 1536(b) exists for the Department of Defense. By virtue of 10 U.S.C. § 2210(a), DoD may, at its option, credit Economy Act reimbursements to the appropriations that earned them or, if those appropriations have expired, to appropriations current at the time of collection. See *Reimbursements to Appropriations: Legislative Suggestions for Improved Congressional Control*, GAO/FGMSD-75-52 (November 1, 1976); B-179708-O.M., December 1, 1975 at 16. This authority applies only to working capital funds (i.e., a type of revolving fund) that receive proceeds from the sale or disposal of certain categories of DoD property.

> **Discussion Problem 6-2**
>
> An ordering agency issues an Economy Act order for supplies in August 2002, and the (non-DoD) performing agency uses its 2002 appropriation to perform the order. If the ordering agency reimburses the performing agency in the next fiscal year (e.g., October 2002), which appropriation must the performing agency credit, FY 2002 or FY 2003?

Items Provided From Stock. Items that the performing agency provides from its stock or inventory are subject to special rules. Section 1536(b) states:

> (b) An amount paid under section 1535 of this title may be expended in providing goods or services or for a purpose specified for the appropriation or fund credited. Where goods are provided from stocks on hand, the amount received in payment is credited so as to be available to replace the goods unless -
> (1) another law authorizes the amount to be credited to some other appropriation or fund; or
> (2) the head of the executive agency filling the order decides that replacement is not necessary, in which case, the amount received is deposited in the Treasury as miscellaneous receipts.

Thus, 31 U.S.C. § 1536(b) limits the performing agency's authority to retain payment to situations in which replacement is necessary. This limitation illustrates the Economy Act's approach of structuring the transaction so that the performing agency neither profits nor is penalized. It does not say merely that payments are available for replacement, but limits their *availability* to cases where replacement is necessary. B-36541, September 9, 1943. The rationale is that retaining payment when replacement is not necessary would amount to a form of profit. 41 Comp. Gen. 671, 674 (1962) (purpose of provision is "to preclude augmentation of the appropriations involved").

The law does not require replacement in the same fiscal year as delivery but does require, in general terms, that "agency accounting systems . . . be able to relate credits from the use of stocks on hand in Economy Act transactions to replacement needs." B-179708-O.M., July 10, 1975 (see fn. 8). In this connection, B-179708-O.M. states, beginning on page 15:

> The crucial factor with respect to implementation of the statute is the determination that replacement is necessary—or, more precisely, not unnecessary—rather than the actual replacement transaction. Thus we believe that the statutory requirement is satisfied by some mechanism for screening out payments for stocks not in need of replacement and insuring that such payments are treated as miscellaneous receipts rather than credits. Once this is accomplished, we think the timing of replacements, including fiscal year differences, is essentially immaterial, except perhaps to the extent that time lapses are so great as to be relevant from an audit standpoint in terms of the validity of the determination that replacement was necessary. Finally, we perceive no objection to the fact that replacement items might not be identical to the materials furnished from stocks so long as there is sufficient similarity to justify a bona fide replacement relationship.

More recently, the GAO Office of General Counsel interpreted this decision to allow crediting the reimbursement to the appropriation that is current when the reimbursement is received, even if the appropriation used to perform the order has expired. The GAO Office of General Counsel has written:

> It follows that if the appropriation which earned the reimbursement has expired and the performing agency has made the replacement decision but has not implemented it prior to expiration, the payment may be credited to the corresponding appropriation current at the time of collection, since this is the only way it can be "credited so as to be available to replace the goods," as required by section 1536(b)(2).

Principles of Federal Appropriations Law, Vol. IV, p. 15–35 (March 2001).

Receipt of payment too late in the fiscal year to permit conducting a procurement for the replacement items poses a problem, but there is no authority to put the payment in some sort of holding account to be credited to next year's appropriation when it shows up. A-92491, April 5, 1938. Thus, if the payment arrives in the same fiscal year as the replacement decision is implemented, it effectively becomes the budgetary resource for purposes of the obligation; if the payment arrives in the following year, it is credited to the expired account.

While the replacement items need not be identical, the Economy Act does not authorize exchange of dissimilar items. 41 Comp. Gen. 671 (1962). That case involved a proposal by the Public Health Service and the Defense Supply Agency to exchange lists of medical goods and equipment in long supply or available for rotation and to, in effect, swap supplies and equipment not presently needed, making necessary appropriation adjustments periodically. GAO recognized that the proposal had merit and suggested that the agencies seek legislative authority, but was forced to conclude that 31 U.S.C. § 1536(b) does not authorize what amounts to "program replacements," i.e., replacements of excess materials with other materials within the general area covered by the appropriation.

Calculating the "Actual Cost" To Be Reimbursed

To avoid unlawful augmentation of appropriations, payments under the Economy Act, whether by advance with subsequent adjustment or by reimbursement, must be based on "the actual cost of goods or services provided." 31 U.S.C. § 1535(b). This applies to both intra-agency and interagency transactions under the Act. 57 Comp. Gen. 674, 684 (1978). Unfortunately, as the decisions from GAO have pointed out, neither the statute nor its legislative history address the meaning of the term "actual cost." Id. at 681.

The starting point is the general rule that agencies, including those using the Economy Act, must avoid the unauthorized augmentation of appropriations. B-250377, January 28, 1993. In the context of the Economy Act, an augmentation could typically occur in one of two ways. First, charging too much augments the appropriations of the performing agency. B-45108/B-48124, February 3, 1955; B-101911-O.M., April 4, 1951. Alternatively, charging too little augments the appropriations of the ordering agency. 57 Comp. Gen. at 682.

To avoid violation of the augmentation of appropriations rule, both parties to the Economy Act transaction must determine the "actual cost" of the transaction, consistent with the statutory objectives and legislative history, if any. The following passage from 57 Comp. Gen. 674, at 681 describes this approach:

> While the law and its legislative history are silent as to what was meant by the term 'actual cost' . . . the legislative history does indicate that . . . Congress intended to effect savings for the Government as a whole by: (1) generally authorizing the performance of work or services or the furnishing of materials pursuant to inter- and intra-agency orders by an agency of Government in a position to perform the work or service; (2) diminishing the reluctance of other Government agencies to accept such orders by removing the limitation upon reimbursements imposed by prior [GAO] decisions [footnote omitted]; and (3) authorizing inter- and intra-departmental orders only when the work could be as cheaply or more conveniently performed within the Government as by a private source. Thus in determining the elements of actual cost under the Economy Act, it would seem that the only elements of cost that the Act requires to be included in computing reimbursements are those which accomplish these identified congressional goals. Whether any additional elements of cost should be included would depend upon the circumstances surrounding the transaction.

Thus, the universe of costs may be divided into (1) direct costs and (2) indirect costs. Direct costs are expenditures incurred by the performing agency that are specifically identifiable and attributable to performing the transaction in question. Quoting from 57 Comp. Gen. at 682:

> The Economy Act clearly requires the inclusion as actual cost of all direct costs attributable to the performance of a service or the furnishing of materials, regardless of whether expenditures by the performing agency were thereby increased.

One element of direct cost is the salary of employees engaged in doing the work. 12 Comp. Gen. 442 (1932). This means gross compensation. 14 Comp. Gen. 452 (1934). Thus, in addition to salaries, it includes, for example, the accrual of annual leave. 32 Comp. Gen. 521 (1953); 17 Comp. Gen. 571 (1938). Another common element of direct cost is the cost of materials or equipment furnished to the ordering agency or consumed in the course of performance. "Actual cost" in this context means historical cost and not current replacement or production cost. B-130007, December 7, 1956. See also 58 Comp. Gen. 9, 14 (1978). This does not necessarily have to be the original acquisition cost, but may be the most recent acquisition cost of the specific kind of item provided to the requesting agency. B-250377, January 28, 1993. Related transportation costs are another reimbursable direct cost item. Id.

Not every identifiable direct cost is reimbursable under the "actual cost" formulation. An illustration was provided in 39 Comp. Gen. 650 (1960). The Maritime Administration was activating several tankers for use by the Navy. In the course of performing this activity, an employee of a Maritime Administration contractor was injured, sued the United States under the Suits in Admiralty Act, and recovered a judgment that the Maritime Administration paid from a revolving fund. While this was a cost that was incurred in the course of performance, the judgment was not "necessary or required in order to condition the tanker for use by the Navy" (id. at 653), and therefore was properly payable as a judgment and not as a reimbursable Economy Act cost that could be billed to the Navy.

In addition to direct costs, it has long been recognized that "actual cost" for Economy Act purposes includes certain indirect costs (overhead) proportionately allocable to the transaction. E.g., 22 Comp. Gen. 74 (1942). Indirect costs are those "incurred for common objectives and therefore cannot be directly charged to any single cost objective." A Glossary of Terms Used in the Federal Budget Process, GAO/PAD-81-27, 87 (3d ed. March 1981). Indirect costs that (1) are funded out of currently available appropriations, and (2) bear a significant relationship to the service or work performed or the materials furnished, are recoverable in an Economy Act transaction the same as direct costs. 56 Comp. Gen. 275 (1977), as modified by 57 Comp. Gen. 674 (1978), as modified in turn by B-211953, December 7, 1984. Examples of indirect costs include administrative overhead applicable to supervision (56 Comp. Gen. 275) and rent paid to GSA attributable to space used in the course of performing Economy Act work (B-211953).

It is clear from GAO decisions that agencies have some flexibility in determining how to calculate their costs. In B-257823, January 22, 1998, GAO stated:

> Agencies possess some flexibility in applying the Act's "actual cost" standard to specific situations, so long as there is reasonable assurance that the performing agency is reimbursed for its costs without the ordering or the performing agency augmenting its appropriations. B-250377, Jan. 28, 1993. Thus, we have not objected to the use of a standard cost for items provided out of inventory (B-250377, Jan. 28, 1993), or to a standard level user cost for the use of storage space (B-211953, Dec. 7, 1984). From a fiscal law perspective, our concern is whether reimbursements are based on reasonable standard cost determinations that do not augment appropriations or otherwise run afoul of the Economy Act.

In this case, the Financial Management Service (FMS) of the Treasury Department developed a unique approach that GAO determined was reasonable. Specifically, FMS recognized that a portion of time spent by its employees in performing Economy Act orders was not directly chargeable to any particular customer and had to be accounted for as indirect costs. To compute these costs, FMS estimated that each billable employee devoted, on average, 1,400 hours per year to directly working on Economy Act orders. FMS noted that OMB had determined that of the 2,088 hours attributable on an annual basis to a federal employee, each employee actually works only 1,744 hours per year. OMB Cir. No. A-76 (Revised), Performance of Commercial Activities, p. IV-8 (Aug. 1983). The difference is attributable to the average amount of annual, sick, holiday, and administrative leave used. FMS determined that the difference between the 1,400 hours of directly chargeable hours and the 1,744 total hours worked (i.e., 344 hours) was attributable to administrative and other matters that do not directly relate to specific projects. Accordingly, FMS treated those costs as indirect costs and included them in the standard hourly rates as an indirect cost. GAO concluded that, "based on our review of FMS's methodology, we have no basis to conclude that FMS's estimate is inconsistent with the requirements of the Economy Act." Id.

The costs discussed thus far are those that the Economy Act can fairly be said to require. In addition, there may be others, so-called "situational costs." This category of costs could be either direct or indirect in nature and arise based on the unique circumstances of a particular transaction. To be reimbursable, the costs must generally be incurred to advance the intent of Congress or a well-established public policy. This concept was discussed in 57 Comp. Gen. 674, which stated:

> [The Economy Act] is not so rigid and inflexible as to require a blanket rule for costing throughout the Government . . . . Certainly neither the language of the Economy Act nor its legislative history requires uniform costing beyond what is practicable under the circumstances. This is not to say that costing is expected to be different in a substantial number of circumstances. We

are merely recognizing that in some circumstances, other competing congressional goals, policies or interests might require recoveries beyond that necessary to effectuate the purposes of the Economy Act

. . . .

"[T]he term ['actual costs'] has a flexible meaning and recognizes distinctions or differences in the nature of the performing agency, and the purposes or goals intended to be accomplished.

Id. at 683, 685.

For example, depreciation is not normally recoverable because it is not funded out of currently available appropriations. 57 Comp. Gen. 674; 72 Comp. Gen. 159, 162 (1993). (Under prior decisions, actual cost could include depreciation. E.g., 38 Comp. Gen. 734 (1959). This is one of the aspects of the earlier cases superseded by 57 Comp. Gen. 674 and later cases citing it.) However, in 57 Comp. Gen. 674, in view of the congressionally established goal that the performing agency (the government entity that operated Washington National and Dulles International Airports) be self-sustaining and recover its operating costs and a fair return on the government's investment, it was appropriate to include depreciation and interest as indirect costs. The amounts so recovered were deposited in the general fund of the Treasury as miscellaneous receipts. Id. at 685-86.

Since agencies have discretion to determine how to structure their recovery, it is important to consult the particular performing agency's regulations to understand the particular procedures that will be applied. For example, the NASA Financial Management Manual addresses recovery of depreciation as follows:

> (3) **Depreciation.** Centers will charge all non-Federal customers depreciation except as otherwise provided by law. Such charges should be calculated based upon the specific property, plant and equipment used to support the reimbursable agreement. All collections of deprecia-

tion charges will be deposited to the Treasury miscellaneous receipts account (803220, General Fund Proprietary Receipts).

As in the Comptroller General case, the depreciation amount recovered must be deposited in the United States Treasury's miscellaneous receipts account. This approach illustrates an important distinction between funds that the performing agency may *recover* and funds that it may *retain*. Thus, because depreciation costs are actual costs, the performing agency may collect them. However, because depreciation costs do not represent costs incurred against current appropriations, they cannot be retained.

Another example of permissible "situational costs" is where the performing activity is funded by a statutorily authorized stock, industrial, or similar fund that provides for "full cost" recovery, i.e., beyond what the Economy Act would otherwise require, and the fund's Economy Act work is an insignificant portion of its overall work. In such a situation, there might be sound reasons for charging all customers alike. B-250377, January 28, 1993.

While particular circumstances might authorize some indirect costs beyond what the Economy Act requires, their inclusion in the performing agency's charges is not required but is discretionary. Failure to recover them is not legally objectionable, except in the unlikely event it could be shown to be an abuse of discretion. B-198531, September 25, 1980.

The Economy Act was intended to promote interagency cooperation, not interagency disagreements, over billings. Hence, the statutory scheme emphasizes the role of agreement. It contemplates that application of the "actual cost" standard in a given case should be "primarily for administrative consideration, to be determined by agreement between the agencies concerned." 22 Comp. Gen. 74, 78 (1942). In the interest of intragovernmental harmony, GAO has held that the Economy Act does not require a detailed cost audit by the ordering agency. 32 Comp. Gen. 479 (1953); 39 Comp. Gen. 548, 549-50 (1960). Nor does the Economy Act require the performing agency to provide a detailed breakdown unless the agreement provides otherwise. B-116194, October 5, 1953. Payment is authorized "at rates established by the servicing agency so long as they are reported to be based upon the cost of rendition of the service and do not appear to be excessive." 32 Comp. Gen. at 481.

While at times actual cost can be computed with precision, the Economy Act does not require that the determination be an exact science. GAO cases involving reimbursable transactions have long recognized the acceptability of a reasonable and appropriate methodology over "absolutely accurate ascertainment," which might entail considerable burden and expense. 3 Comp. Gen. 974 (1924). As stated in B-133913, January 21, 1958, "[a]s long as the amount agreed upon results from a bona fide attempt to determine the actual cost and, in fact, reasonably approximates the actual cost," the Economy Act is satisfied.

Agency financial management regulations will typically address how the agency will calculate "actual costs" under Economy Act transactions. The DoD FMR, Vol. 11A, Ch. 3, for example, states:

> 030601. The requesting agency must pay the servicing agency the actual costs of the goods or services provided. Actual costs include all direct costs attributable to providing the goods or services, regardless of whether the servicing agency's expenditures are increased. Actual costs also include indirect costs (overhead) to the extent they have a significant relationship to providing the goods or services and benefit the requesting agency. DoD activities not funded by working capital funds normally do not charge indirect costs to other DoD activities.

Another methodology GAO has found to be reasonable and "consistent with the minimum legal requirements of the Economy Act" is billing on the basis of "standard costs" derived from documented costs of the last acquisition or production. B-250377, January 28, 1993 (containing a detailed discussion); Iran Arms Sales: DoD's Transfer of Arms to the Central Intelligence Agency, GAO/NSIAD-87-114, 8 (March 1987).

There are limits, however, and the calculation must have some reasonable basis and relationship to the actual costs incurred. Thus, a cost allocation in which some customers are paying excessive amounts and effectively subsidizing others is improper. 70 Comp. Gen. 592 (1991). Also improper are situations in which an allocation is based on the availability of appropriations (B-114821-O.M., November 12, 1958) or a per capita funding arrangement is not related to the goods or services actually received (67 Comp. Gen. 254, 258 (1988)).

Agencies may waive the recovery of small amounts where processing would be uneconomical. An agency wanting to do this should set a minimum billing figure based on a cost study. B-156022, April 28, 1966. The case for waiver is even stronger when the account to be credited with the payment is no longer available for obligation. See B-120978-O.M., October 19, 1954. Another approach is the delay and accumulation of small amounts until the end of the fiscal year. See, e.g., DoD FMR, Vol. 11A, Ch. 3, para. 030503, which states:

> When an appropriated fund activity is the performer and the amount to be billed within the same DoD Component or to another DoD Component is less than $1,000, the billing may be suspended by the billing organization until the end of the fiscal year, or until the total billed exceeds $1,000. However, no later than the end of the fiscal year, all suspended amounts must be billed even though the amount to be billed is less than $1,000.

Finally, while the Economy Act talks about the "actual cost of goods or services provided," there is one situation in which payment of actual costs will have no relationship to anything "provided." For example, an agency may find it necessary to terminate an Economy Act contract before it is completed. It can terminate the contract "for convenience," the same as it could with a commercial contract, in which case the performing agency should not have to bear the loss for any expenses it has already incurred.

The Comptroller General addressed this situation as follows in B-61814, January 3, 1947:

> [W]here an order issued pursuant to [the Economy Act] is terminated after the establishment receiving said order has incurred expenses incident thereto the amount of such expenses or costs is for determination and adjustment by agreement between such agencies. . . . [T]here would appear to be ample authority for an agreement between the agencies . . . to effect an adjustment of the appropriations and/or funds of said agencies on the basis of the actual amount of the costs or expenses incurred.

Thus, even though no goods or services may have been provided, the Comptroller General would apparently not oppose use of the ordering agency's appropriations to reimburse the performing agency for the costs of termination paid. As a practical matter, this will generally be accomplished by the performing activity using the funds intended for the purchase to pay the termination costs and then returning the balance to the ordering agency.

Obligation and Deobligation of Funds

The obligational treatment of Economy Act transactions is addressed in 31 U.S.C. § 1535(d) as follows:

> An order placed or agreement made under this section obligates an appropriation of the ordering agency or unit. The amount obligated is deobligated to the extent that the agency or unit filling the order has not incurred obligations, before the end of the period of availability of the appropriation, in—
> (1) providing goods or services; or
> (2) making an authorized contract with another person to provide the requested goods or services.

The first sentence of section 1535(d) recognizes that an Economy Act agreement is sufficient to obligate the ordering agency's appropriations even though the agency's liability is not subject to enforcement the same as a contract with a private party. This sentence must be read in conjunction with 31 U.S.C. § 1501(a)(1), which recognizes interagency agreements and prescribes the requirements for a valid obligation. (See Chapter 2 for more details.) Under section 1501(a)(1), an obligation is recordable when supported by documentary evidence of:

(1) a binding agreement between an agency and another person (including an agency) that is—
(A) in writing, in a way and form, and for a purpose authorized by law; and
(B) executed before the end of the period of availability for obligation of the appropriation or fund used for specific goods to be delivered, real property to be bought or leased, or work or service to be provided[.]

Thus, an Economy Act agreement is recordable as an obligation under 31 U.S.C. § 1501(a)(1) if it meets the requirements specified in that section. 34 Comp. Gen. 418, 421 (1955); 39 Comp. Gen. 317, 318- 19 (1959). It must, for example, involve a definite commitment for specific equipment, work, or services. See, e.g., 15 Comp. Gen. 863 (1936). Also, the recording statute reinforces a point in the Economy Act itself, namely, that the order or agreement must be for a purpose the ordering agency is authorized to accomplish.

In addition, a valid Economy Act obligation must satisfy the basic fiscal requirements applicable to obligations in general. For example, orders under the Economy Act must comply with the bona fide needs rule, 58 Comp. Gen. 471 (1979); B-195432, July 19, 1979, and the ordering agency must have sufficient obligational authority to satisfy the Antideficiency Act. Therefore, an Economy Act order must be recorded as an obligation under 31 U.S.C. § 1501(a)(l) when the performing agency accepts the order. While the order must be placed or the agreement entered into before the ordering agency's appropriation expires for obligational purposes, actual payment to the performing agency may occur in a later fiscal year. However, if payment does not take place until after the obligated account has closed pursuant to 31 U.S.C. § 1552, the payment must be charged to a current appropriation of the ordering agency available for the same purpose. 31 U.S.C. § 1553(b); B-260993, June 26, 1996.

The second sentence of section 1535(d) establishes the deobligation requirement by stating that the performing agency must incur obligations to fill the order within the period of availability of the appropriation being used. Otherwise the ordering agency must deobligate the funds. This requirement is unique to interagency orders under the Economy Act. See, e.g., *National Park Service Soil Surveys*, B-282601, September 27, 1999 (because the National Park Service entered into interagency agreements for soil surveys with the Department of Agriculture pursuant to a statute other than the Economy Act, it was not required to deobligate funds at the end of the period of availability since section 1535(d) only applies to interagency agreements under the Economy Act).

Agency regulations often provide specific guidance on this deobligation requirement. For example, the DoD Financial Management Regulation provides:

> B. Economy Act Order. An Economy Act order is an intragovernmental order that does not qualify as a project order on another federal agency or on another DoD Component. It shall be recorded as an obligation in the amount stated in the order when it is accepted in writing. Undelivered Economy Act orders issued against annual or multiple-year appropriations, or both, shall be adjusted downward when the appropriation is no longer available for obligation . . . The amount of the adjustment shall be the difference between the value of the order or orders and the obligations incurred by the performing agency.

Vol. 3, Ch. 8, para. 080703. See also, The NASA Financial Management Manual, Vol. 9000, Ch. 9040, para. 9041-8, Interagency Orders ("For orders chargeable to those appropriations expiring in the current year and placed under the authority of the Economy Act, a deobligation is required at the end of the fiscal year to the extent that the performing agency has not incurred a valid obligation.")

The deobligation requirement differs also from transactions between an agency and a contractor. In the case of a contract with a contractor (as discussed in Chapter 3), obligated funds remain available to fund work performed in a subsequent fiscal year provided that the obligation satisfied the bona fide needs rule when the obligation was created. Some statutes authorizing interagency transactions specifically provide for obligations to be treated the same as obligations with private contractors. E.g., 41 U.S.C. § 23. Subsection (c) of the original Economy Act contained similar language (47 Stat. 418). However, a concern soon arose that the Economy Act was being used to effectively extend the obligational life of appropriations beyond what Congress had provided. To avoid such abuses, Congress amended the Economy Act to add the deobligation requirement. The apparent purpose of this requirement was to prevent agencies from using the Economy Act to continue the availability of appropriations beyond the period provided in the appropriating act. See 31 Comp. Gen. 83, 85 (1951); B-95760, June 27, 1950. Thus, funds obligated under the Economy Act must be deobligated at the end of their period of availability (fiscal-year or multiple-year period) to the extent the performing agency has not performed or itself incurred valid obligations as part of its performance (34 Comp. Gen. 418, 421-422 (1955)).

The deobligation requirement is not limited to advance payments but applies as well to payment by way of reimbursement. 31 Comp. Gen. 83 (1951). Accordingly, as stated in 31 Comp. Gen. at 86, "where work is performed or services rendered on a reimbursable basis by one agency for another over a period covering more than one fiscal year, the respective annual appropriations of the serviced agency must be charged pro tanto with the work performed or services rendered in the particular fiscal year." The following example illustrates the difference between a commercial contract and an Economy Act contract.

Suppose that, toward the end of fiscal year 2001, an agency develops the need for a statistical study. It enters into a contract with a contractor a few days before the end of the fiscal year, obligating fiscal year 2001 appropriations, expecting that most of the work will be performed in the following year. Assuming the need was legitimate when the contract was awarded, the obligated funds remain available to pay for the work. In contrast, if the same transaction was between agencies under the Economy Act and the work was to be done by personnel of the performing agency, the 2001 funds could be used only for work actually performed in the remaining days of that fiscal year. The remainder would have to be deobligated. The agency would have to charge the balance of the Economy Act order to FY 2002 appropriations. See B-223833, November 5, 1987; B-134099, December 13, 1957.

The deobligation requirement of 31 U.S.C. § 1535(d) applies only to obligations under the Economy Act and has no effect on obligations for interagency transactions under other statutory authorities. E.g., 55 Comp. Gen. 1497 (1976); 51 Comp. Gen. 766 (1972); B-108332, March 26, 1952; B-95760, June 27, 1950. As would be expected, the deobligation requirement of 31 U.S.C. § 1535(d) does not apply where the appropriation originally obligated is a no-year appropriation. 39 Comp. Gen. 317 (1959).

Discussion Problem 6-3

On September 25, 2002, federal Agency A issues two Economy Act orders to federal Agency B: one for 100 desktop computers and the other for 50 laptop computers. Agency B accepts both orders in writing on September 28, 2002. On September 30, 2002, Agency B enters into a contract for the 100 desktop PCs but cannot locate a suitable laptop supplier until October 15, 2002, at which time it awards a contract for 50 laptops on behalf of Agency A. Based on these facts, when did Agency A's orders become recordable obligations? Is either order subject to the deobligation requirement?

Applicability of General Restrictions and Limitations

Every agency is subject to a variety of authorities, limitations, restrictions, and exemptions. Some are government-wide; others are agency-specific; still others may be specific to a branch, division, or even a program. These provisions relate to an Economy Act transaction in a variety of ways.

In analyzing these relationships, it is important to recall the purpose of the Economy Act. In essence, the law is designed to permit an agency to accomplish some authorized task more simply and economically by using another agency's expertise. It is not intended to permit an agency to avoid legislative restrictions on the use of its funds, nor is it intended to permit an agency running short of money to use another agency's appropriations. This rule was stated in 18 Comp. Gen. 189, 190-491 (1938):

> Funds transferred from the appropriations under one department to another department for the performance of work or services under authority of [the Economy Act], or similar statutory authority, are available for the purposes for which the appropriation from which transferred are available, and also subject to the same limitations fixed in the appropriations from which the funds are transferred.

Under the first part of this rule, the purpose availability of the funds is determined by reference to the purpose availability of the source appropriation. In other words, an Economy Act transfer cannot expand the purposes for which the source appropriation was provided. In making this determination, the agency should apply the "necessary expense" rule and all the rules of interpretation discussed in Chapter 4, which discusses the purpose statute in depth.

The second part of the rule is that funds transferred under the Economy Act remain subject to limitations and restrictions applicable to the ordering agency. One example is an expenditure limitation applicable to the source appropriation. 17 Comp. Gen. 900 (1938); 17 Comp. Gen. 73 (1937); 16 Comp. Gen. 545 (1936). In 31 Comp. Gen. 109, it was held that appropriation language limiting the number of vacancies that the ordering agency could fill applied to the funds after they were advanced to the performing agency's working fund. Another decision applied the same rule to payments made by reimbursement. B-106101, November 15, 1951.

> **Discussion Problem 6-4**
>
> The National Institute for Allergies and Infectious Diseases (NIAID) is interested in conducting biological research in a zero-gravity environment. Assume that NIAID's appropriations acts have included language stating: "None of the funds appropriated by this act may be used for biological research in a zero-gravity environment." NASA is seeking suggestions for biological research experiments to be conducted on the Space Station (in a zero-gravity environment). NIAID prepares a Determination and Findings concluding that it could save millions of dollars and greatly advance progress toward development of a new anthrax vaccine if it could conduct an experiment on the Space Station.
>
> Can NIAID properly use the Economy Act to conduct this research?

On the positive side, if there is an *exemption* from a restriction that is applicable to the ordering agency or the funds cited on the Economy Act order, the exemption also applies to the performing agency. For example, a statute long since repealed prohibited what GAO's decisions referred to as "the employment of personal services" in the District of Columbia without express authority. The Navy had a statutory exemption. The Army had one too, but it was much more limited. In a case where the Army was doing Economy Act work for the Navy, GAO held that the exemption applicable to the Navy controlled. Therefore, the Army could proceed without regard to the restriction it would have had to follow when making direct expenditures for its own work. 18 Comp. Gen. 489 (1938).

In a similar case, the Commerce Department needed to procure supplies for use in Economy Act work it was doing for the Army. Both agencies had exemptions from the advertising requirement of 41 U.S.C. § 5 for small dollar amounts—$500 for the Army but only $25 for Commerce. The Comptroller General advised that even though Commerce was doing the purchasing, it could do so under the Army's more liberal exemption because it would be using Army money to make the purchase. 21 Comp. Gen. 254 (1941). See also B-54171, December 6, 1945.

Discussion Problem 6-5

Modifying the facts in the preceding discussion problem, assume that the appropriations act for NIAID stated: "Not to exceed $2,000,000 shall be available to conduct biological research in a zero-gravity environment." Assume further that NASA's appropriations acts have included language stating: "None of the funds appropriated by this act may be used for biological research in a zero-gravity environment." After coordinating with NASA, NIAID issues an Economy Act order to NASA to conduct biological research in a zero-gravity environment.

Is NASA prohibited from performing this order?

There have been a number of exceptions to the rule that Economy Act transfers are subject to the limitations of the source appropriation. The substantive aspects of the exceptions are not as important as their rationale. Ordering agencies may be able to avoid restrictions applicable to the agency or its funds by carefully applying the rationales used in certain cases. For example, in B-106002, October 30, 1951, GAO concluded that funds advanced or reimbursed in Economy Act transactions were not subject to a monetary limit on personal services contained in the ordering agency's appropriation because it could be clearly demonstrated that the ceiling was based on the cost of employees on the ordering agency's payroll, which did not include the estimated cost of Economy Act services either performed by the agency or reimbursed to it.

A similar limitation for the Bureau of Reclamation was the subject of another exception in B-79709, October 1, 1948. Legislative history clearly indicated that the limitation stemmed from a congressional concern over an excessive number of administrative and supervisory personnel employed by the bureau (the ordering agency). Thus, the limitation was aimed at the bureau's staffing level and not at the funds. The limitation was not intended to limit funds that could be transferred to some *other* agency and spent by that agency to pay its own personnel used in performing Economy Act work requested by the bureau. Thus, the bureau could pay for Economy Act work without regard to the ceiling.

Still another group of exceptions involved the authority to employ (and pay) personnel without regard to certain civil service laws. The issue first arose in 21 Comp. Gen. 749 (1942), in connection with Economy Act work being performed by the Bureau of the Census for various national defense agencies. The question was whether the Census Bureau was bound by limitations in the source appropriations of the defense agencies. The decision noted the line of cases applying the general rule that the transaction is subject to the limitations applicable to the source appropriation, e.g., 18 Comp. Gen. 489 and 21 Comp.Gen. 254, and summarized these cases as follows:

> [S]uch decisions involved cases in which it was sought to employ transferred funds for purposes for which the funds would not have been available in the transferring agency; or where it was sought to use transferred funds to employ personal services when such services could not have been employed (regardless of the method of appointment or the rates of pay) by the transferring agency; or where the transferred funds were directly subject to restrictions regarding the amount expendable therefrom for passenger-carrying automobiles, or for procurements without advertising, etc.

Id. at 752.

The decision then went on to distinguish the prior cases on the following grounds:

> What is involved in the instant matter is essentially different being the accomplishment of certain object for which the funds of the transferring agency are available and which the agency to which the transfer is made is equipped to accomplish by the use of personnel and equipment it already has or is otherwise authorized to procure. Under such circumstances, the charge to be made by the performing agency against the funds of the agency desiring the services—whether under a reimbursement or advance-of-funds procedure—should be on the basis of the rates of compensation which the performing agency is otherwise authorized by law to pay to its personnel used in the performance of the services.

Id. See also B-38515, December 22, 1943, B-43377, August 14, 1944, and B-76808, July 29, 1948.

Since the limitation regarding salaries did not apply to the performing agency (Bureau of the Census), the limitations applicable to the ordering agency (DoD) did not affect the performing agency's authority to pay whatever rates it is authorized to pay.

A similar rationale was applied by GAO in B-259499, August 22, 1995, advising the Central Intelligence Agency (CIA) on the extent to which it could use its own personal services contractors to perform Economy Act orders when the ordering agency lacks authority to contract for personal services. If the CIA is merely using the contractors along with its own employees to perform otherwise authorized work, there is no violation. This is merely "a means to an otherwise authorized end, and not an end in itself." Id. at 8. However, GAO noted, the Economy Act would be violated if the contractors were placed under the direct supervision and control of the ordering agency, or if the CIA awarded the contracts solely in response to the ordering agency's needs. The latter two situations would amount to using the Economy Act to circumvent limitations on the ordering agency's authority.

One of the Economy Act's objectives is to avoid improper augmentations. An Economy Act transaction carried out in accordance with law serves this purpose because, as the Comptroller General has held, Economy Act agreements "do not increase or decrease the appropriation of the requisitioned agency." A-99125, November 21, 1938. That case held that Economy Act transactions would not violate an appropriation proviso that limited the amounts available to a particular agency to the funds appropriated in that act. This is because the funds transferred under the authority of the Economy Act did not affect the amount available in the appropriation accounts of the performing agency.

Similarly, unless there is some indication of a contrary intent, a monetary limit on general transfer authority is aimed at transfers that supplement the appropriation in question, and does not apply to credits to that appropriation incident to otherwise proper Economy Act transactions. B-120414, June 17, 1954. For example, if the performing agency was subject to a restriction that stated that the agency could not receive more than $50 million through general transfer authority in any fiscal year, the amounts it receives through Economy Act transfers would not be counted toward the $50 million limit.

Similarly, in 31 Comp. Gen. 190 (1951), an agency whose appropriation contained a monetary ceiling on personal services asked the Comptroller General whether the ceiling applied to reimbursements it received from ordering agencies for services it provided for them. Viewing the limitation as applicable to expenses incurred for the agency itself, and noting the point from A-99125, November 21, 1938, that Economy Act transactions do not increase or decrease the performing agency's appropriation, GAO decided that the reimbursements did not count against the ceiling. Absent evidence of a contrary intent, the rationale of 31 Comp. Gen. 190 would presumably apply as well to other types of limitations on the performing agency.

Exception to the Requirement for Certification in Advance of Payment

Economy Act payments by the ordering agency to the performing agency are not subject to the general requirement for advance certification. In general, prior to disbursement of public funds to a private party, the payment must be certified to ensure that all necessary preconditions have been satisfied. See 31 U.S.C. § 3528. However, a payment to another federal agency differs from a payment to a private party in that an overpayment or erroneous payment to another agency does not result in an actual loss of funds to the United States. 24 Comp. Gen. 851, 853 (1945); B-156022, April 28, 1966; B-116194, October 5, 1953; B-44293, September 15, 1944. As stated in 24 Comp. Gen. at 853:

> The question here presented does not involve the discharge of a Government obligation to a non-Government agency or individual where an excess payment might result in a loss to the United States. In case of an overpayment by one department to another, the matter can be adjusted upon discovery.

Accordingly, the Economy Act includes in its payment provision the statement that a "bill submitted or a request for payment is not subject to audit or certification in advance of payment." 31 U.S.C. § 1535(b). Agency regulations incorporate this practice. For example, the DoD Financial Management Regulation states:

> 030502. Payment Procedures. Payment shall be made promptly upon the written request (or billing) of the agency or unit filling the order. Payment may be made in advance or upon delivery of the goods or services ordered and shall be for any part of the estimated or actual cost as determined by the agency or unit filling the order. A bill submitted or a request for payment is not subject to audit or certification in advance of payment. Proper adjust-

ment of amounts paid in advance shall be made as agreed to by the heads of the agencies or units on the basis of the actual cost of goods or services provided.

DoD Financial Management Regulation, Vol. 11A, Ch. 3, para. 030502.

The language of 31 U.S.C. § 1535(b) (excusing the need for certification in advance of Economy Act payments) is narrower and more specific than 31 U.S.C. § 3528 (requiring advance certification). Application of the rule of statutory construction that the specific controls the general means that an ordering agency is not required to certify vouchers prior to making an Economy Act payment to another federal entity, whether in advance or by reimbursement.

There are some cases that seem to require certification in advance of payment, notwithstanding the language of 31 U.S.C. § 1535(b) that plainly exempts payments under the Economy Act. The editors of Volume IV of *Principles of Federal Appropriations Law*, GAO-01-179SP (March 2001) considered this inconsistency and state:

> To the extent it supports a contrary proposition, the editors view 39 Comp. Gen. 548 (1960) as incorrect. It inexplicably fails to consider the no advance certification language, and is inconsistent with the plain terms of the Economy Act itself (see 37 Op. Att'y Gen. 559 (1934)), and with applications of similar language in other statutes, such as 44 U.S.C. § 310 (payments for printing and binding). See also 56 Comp. Gen. 980 (1977); A-30304-O.M., February 10, 1930.

Id. at p. 50, note 24.

Nevertheless, since the ordering agency "remains accountable to the Congress for activities under appropriations made to it" (46 Comp. Gen. 73, 76 (1966)), it would be expected that ordering agencies would, as a matter of sound financial management, pass vouchers through some form of limited certification process. 16 Comp. Gen. 3, 4-5 (1936). Of course, the no advance certification language has no application to disbursements by the performing agency's payment to any contractor it selected to perform the work. Consequently, the performing agency must comply with the general requirement for certification in advance of disbursement.

This assumes that the agencies are following the typical two-step payment process—that is, payment by the ordering agency to the performing agency is either preceded or followed by obligation and payment by the performing agency. There is an approach, described and approved in 44 Comp. Gen. 100 (1964), that consolidates these into a single step and, thereby, removes the "no advance certification" language from consideration. In that case, the former Department of Health, Education, and Welfare (HEW) was performing Economy Act services for the Agency for International Development (AID). Under the terms of the arrangement, AID would establish appropriate fund limitations, and HEW certifying officers would certify vouchers directly against AID appropriations for direct payment of costs incurred in performing, with HEW being responsible for staying within the established fund limitations. Once the agencies reached agreement to this process, the primary legal obstacle was that certifying officers are normally supposed to be employees of the agency whose funds they are certifying. The solution was an innovative approach that could be referred to as "cross-certification." Under this procedure, the ordering agency appoints the performing agency's certifying officer as an officer or employee of the ordering agency, without compensation, and then designates him or her as one of its own certifying officers. This concept of "cross-certification" could apply where financial services are themselves the subject of an Economy Act agreement.

For example, GSA sometimes enters into Economy Act "support agreements" with smaller agencies, boards, or commissions to provide administrative support services, including the processing of payment vouchers. In 55 Comp. Gen. 388 (1975), GSA inquired about the potential liability of its certifying officers in such a situation. The answer is that it depends on exactly what has preceded the GSA certifying officer's actions. Certainly, GSA could provide full certification under the agreement, in which event the GSA certifying officer would be the equivalent of the HEW certifying officer in 44 Comp. Gen. 100. However, if an official of the client agency certifies the voucher before it gets to GSA, GSA's administrative processing is not "certification" for purposes of the accountable officer laws, and the GSA official will be liable only for errors made during his or her final processing.

The cross-certification concept has also been applied to overseas Economy Act transactions. For example, State Department officials may perform certifying and disbursing functions for military departments overseas, charging payments directly to the applicable military appropriations. 44 Comp. Gen. 818 (1965); 22 Comp. Gen. 48 (1942). Similarly, when the Department of Education was created and took over responsibility for the Defense Department's Overseas Dependents' Schools, Education wanted to retain Defense's financial support services, which had been in place for decades. It could accomplish this with an Economy Act agreement, applying guidance from decisions such as 44 Comp. Gen. 100 and 55 Comp. Gen. 388. B-200309-O.M., April 3, 1981.

Authorized Services

Various types of interagency services have been authorized under the Economy Act, including details of personnel, loans of property, and common services. This section will discuss the history and current rules applicable to such interagency services.

Details of Personnel

A common type of interagency service is the loan or detail of personnel. The Comptroller General has defined a detail as "the temporary assignment of an employee to a different position or a specified period, with the employee returning to regular duties at the end of the detail." 64 Comp. Gen. 370, 376(1985).

Some of the earliest administrative decisions deal with details of personnel, but have allowed for reimbursement by the gaining agency only in the most limited circumstances. For example, in 14 Comp. Dec. 294 (1907), the Comptroller of the Treasury was asked to advise the Secretary of the Treasury on a proposal to lend an employee to another agency, with the "borrowing agency" to reimburse only the employee's travel and incidental expenses, but not basic salary. The Comptroller recognized that such arrangements could be prohibited by the purpose statute (31 U.S.C. § 1301(a)), but upheld the practice because interagency loans of personnel had a very long history. He held as follows:

> If these were questions of first impression I would be impelled to answer each of them in the negative, because of that provision in the statute [31 U.S.C. § 1301(a)] which requires all appropriations to be used exclusively for the purposes for which made. . . . [However] they are not questions of first impression.

14 Comp. Dec. 294 (1907) at pp. 294-295.

The Comptroller went on to explain that the practice had developed in the executive branch of lending employees without reimbursement except for extra expenses incurred on account of the detail. This practice had been around for so long, according to the Comptroller, that it was virtually "etched in stone." Id. at 295-96. The Comptroller concluded by reasoning that as long as the agency could spare the employee for the requested time, it would be:

> [I]n the interest of good government and economy to so utilize his services. His regular salary would be earned in any event, and in all probability without rendering in his own Department adequate services therefor. Therefore reimbursement has never, to my knowledge, been made on such details for regular salaries. But where additional expenses have accrued because of such detail such expenses have always been reimbursed to the regular appropriation from which originally paid.

Id. at 296.

In other words, although a government employee could be detailed to another agency, the gaining agency could not reimburse the lending agency unless the lending agency incurred some "additional expenses" because of the detail. This rationale was quite remarkable because it assumed that the detailed employee would otherwise be idle and also seemed to overlook the possibility that the nonreimbursable detail could have the effect of augmenting the appropriations of the gaining agency. Not surprisingly, subsequent comptrollers have struggled with the rationale's weakness and were careful not to expand the rule of the 1907 case. Thus, if the lending agency had to employ someone else to do the detailed employee's job while he was gone, then the salary was reimbursable (because the detail resulted in an "extra" expense). 22 Comp. Dec. 145 (1915).

Interestingly, with regard to *intra*-agency details, the early decisions allowed for reimbursement. Thus, if an employee worked for different divisions or bureaus within the same agency, the agency could prorate the salary among the appropriations involved or could pay the entire salary from one appropriation and seek reimbursement from the others. 5 Comp. Gen. 1036 (1926).

The Economy Act, enacted in 1932, superseded the restrictive approach taken in the earlier cases and authorized fully reimbursable details of personnel. 13 Comp. Gen. 234 (1934). However, after enactment of the Economy Act, the early decisions held that agencies had a choice. If they chose not to enter into a written Economy Act agreement expressly providing for full reimbursement, they could continue to operate under the old rules. Id. at 237. However, these cases overlooked two fundamental fiscal issues involved in the nonreimbursable detail situation: First, the lending agency is using its appropriation to benefit another agency, which would seem to violate the purpose statute (31 U.S.C. § 1301(a)); second, the gaining agency was, in effect, augmenting its appropriations by receiving services without providing for reimbursement. Thus, the question of how an agency could lawfully make nonreimbursable details in light of these fiscal issues remained unanswered.

It was not until 1985, however, that the Comptroller General directly addressed the applicability of the purpose statute in the context of nonreimbursable details. In 64 Comp. Gen. 370 (1985), after reviewing the prior decisions and the legislative history of the Economy Act, the Comptroller General held:

> Although Federal agencies may be part of a whole system of Government, appropriations to an agency are limited to the purposes for which appropriated, generally to the execution of particular agency functions. Absent statutory authority, those purposes would not include expenditures for programs of another agency. Since the receiving agency is gaining the benefit of work for programs for which funds have been appropriated to it, those appropriations should be used to pay for that work. Thus, a violation of the purpose law does occur when an agency spends money on salaries of employees detailed to another agency for work essentially unrelated to the loaning agency's functions.

64 Comp. Gen. at 379.

Accordingly, absent specific statutory authority to the contrary, details of personnel between agencies or between separately funded components of the same agency may not be done on a nonreimbursable basis but must be done in accordance with the Economy Act, which requires full reimbursement of actual costs, one of which is the employee's salary. See, e.g., B-283510, September 27, 1999 ("the Economy Act requires reimbursement to the agency providing the detailee for the 'actual costs' of the services provided, unless the detail falls within one of the recognized exceptions"). The fact that the lending agency pays the employee from a revolving fund changes nothing; a nonreimbursable detail still creates an unauthorized augmentation of the receiving agency's appropriation, as well as violates the purpose limitations of 31 U.S.C. § 1301(a). B-247348, June 22, 1992.

There are two nonstatutory exceptions to the rule against nonreimbursable details of federal employees. First, nonreimbursable details are permissible "where they involve a matter similar or related to matters ordinarily handled by the loaning agency and will aid the loaning agency in accomplishing a purpose for which its appropriations are provided." 64 Comp. Gen. at 380. This rationale satisfies the purpose statute concern because the detail benefits the lending agency and is, therefore, a proper use of the lending agency's salary appropriation. The issue of augmentation of the gaining agency's appropriation remains, however. This exception could allow for innovative cost sharing by the agencies involved in the transaction.

For example, since completely nonreimbursable details are authorized if the lending agency receives some benefit from the transaction, would it be permissible for the agencies to agree that the detail be partially nonreimbursable? If the agencies agree that the detail benefits both agencies, but primarily benefits the lending agency, why couldn't the agencies agree to a reimbursement arrangement that reflects the relative benefit received from the detailee's services? If the lending agency receives 90 percent of the benefit and the borrowing agency only 10 percent, it may be possible for the borrowing agency to reimburse only 10 percent of the salary. Recall that under the Economy Act, full reimbursement of actual cost is required. The GAO-created exception allows for nonreimbursable details when the lending agency receives a benefit. An approach that splits the reimbursement cost is actually less of an exception than the fully nonreimbursable arrangement approved by GAO. Of course, prior to attempting such an arrangement, agency personnel should consult with legal counsel.

Second, details "for brief periods when the numbers of persons and cost involved are minimal" and "the fiscal impact on the appropriation is negligible" do not require reimbursement. Id. at 381. GAO has declined to attempt to specify the limits of the "de minimis" exception, but it could not, for example, be stretched to cover a detail of 15–20 people. 65 Comp. Gen. 635 (1986). The Department of Justice's Office of Legal Counsel (OLC) has taken essentially the same position as 64 Comp. Gen. 370. 13 Op. Off. Legal

Counsel 188 (1989) (United States Attorney's Office for the District of Columbia must reimburse Defense Department for year-long detail of 10 lawyers).

While the agreement should normally precede the detail, an agreement entered into after the detail has started can include the services already performed. B-75052, May 14, 1948. Reimbursement should include accrued annual and sick leave. 17 Comp. Gen. 571 (1938). It should also include travel expenses incurred in connection with the detail work. 15 Comp. Gen. 334 (1935); B-141349, December 9, 1959. If the detail is to be for a substantial period of time, the lending agency should change the employee's official duty station to the location of the detail and then restore it when the assignment is done. If applicable to the distances involved, the employee may then become entitled to allowances incident to a permanent change of station, such as shipment of household goods. 24 Comp. Gen. 420 (1944). This was done in B-224055, May 21, 1987.

Discussion Problem 6-6

The borrowing agency and the lending agency enter into an Economy Act agreement whereby the lending agency will detail an attorney to the borrowing agency for one year. The annual salary of the attorney is $60,000/year. The nature of the duties that the lawyer will be performing will benefit both the lending agency and the borrowing agency equally. Consequently, the agencies agree that the borrowing agency will pay only half of the lawyer's annual salary, or $30,000.

Is there a problem with this arrangement? Under the Economy Act, what is the general rule regarding reimbursement by the agency to which the employee is detailed? When are completely nonreimbursable details authorized? Where does this case fit?

If interagency details are authorized under statutory authority other than the Economy Act, whether or not they are reimbursable will naturally depend on the terms of the statute. A statute that is silent on the issue will generally be construed as permitting reimbursement unless a contrary intent is manifested.

For example, 5 U.S.C. § 3341 authorizes intra-agency details within the executive branch for renewable periods of not more than 120 days. The statute says nothing about reimbursement, and GAO has interpreted the statute as authorizing the details and permitting reimbursement. 64 Comp. Gen. at 381-82. The same applies to 5 U.S.C. § 3344, which authorizes detailing of administrative law judges but is similarly silent on the issue of reimbursement. 65 Comp. Gen. 635 (1986). The Justice Department has reached the same conclusion with respect to "temporary reassignments" under the Anti-Drug Abuse Act of 1988. 13 Op. Off. Legal Counsel 188 (1989). An example of a statute that addresses reimbursement is 3 U.S.C. § 112, which authorizes details of executive branch employees to various White House offices and requires reimbursement for details exceeding 180 calendar days in any fiscal year. See 64 Comp. Gen. at 380; B-224033, May 26, 1987 (internal memorandum). A different type of statute, discussed and applied in B-247348, June 22, 1992, is 44 U.S.C. § 316, which prohibits details of Government Printing Office employees "to duties not pertaining to the work of public printing and binding . . . unless expressly authorized by law." This type of statute prohibits the detail altogether in the absence of other authority, so the issue of whether the detail can be nonreimbursable is never reached.

The applicability of civil service limitations must be considered in the interagency detail scenario, as it was in the more traditional fee for services arrangement. The issue in this context is: If the gaining agency is limited in the amount it can pay people performing certain positions, how much can it pay if the lending agency pays the detailed employee more than the gaining agency is authorized to pay? For example, assume that the lending agency pays a supervisor $60,000 per year. Assume further that this person is detailed to the gaining agency to fill the position of "supervisor of accounting," a position that the gaining agency is limited by statute to pay no more than $50,000 per year. How can the detail be accomplished? Note that this detail probably could not be accomplished under the Economy Act because that act requires that the performing agency (here, the lending agency) be reimbursed for its actual cost. Since the actual cost of the detailee is $60,000 and the gaining agency is limited to paying only $50,000, the "actual cost" requirement could not be satisfied without violating the statutory pay limitation. The arrangement would be permissible, however, if there were another source of statutory authority for the detail that did not require reimbursement of actual cost.

For example, the Section 127 of the Trade Deficit Review Commission Act, Pub. L. No. 105-277, Div. A, section 127, 112 Stat. 2681-547 (1998), authorizes the chairperson of the commission to appoint an executive director, "except that the rate of pay for the executive director . . . may not exceed the rate payable for Level V of the Executive Schedule." Section 127 further provides that "[a]ny Federal Government employee may be detailed to the Commission without reimbursement." In B-283510, September 27, 1999, the Trade Deficit Review Commission wanted to accept a detailee from the Export-Import Bank to fill the position of Executive Director. The bank paid the individual at Executive Level IV, which is a higher rate than the maximum rate (Level V) that the commission is authorized to pay. If this transaction were conducted under the Economy Act, the commission would have to reimburse the bank for full actual cost of the detailee (Level IV salary), which would cause it to exceed the statutory maximum salary of Level V. However, the agency contended that it did not have to proceed under the Economy Act because the applicable statute authorized details and authorized them to be made on a nonreimbursable basis. The commission asked GAO whether it would be permissible for it to pay the bank a portion of the detailee's salary (an amount equal to the Level V rate) and for the bank to pay the difference between Level V and Level IV. This arrangement ensured that the detailee received full compensation and enabled the commission to avoid a violation of its funding limitation.

GAO allowed this arrangement, reasoning:

> [T]he fact that the detail may be made without reimbursement does not prevent it being effected with partial reimbursement, if the Commission finds that to be in its interests. This appears to satisfy both the language and intent of the limitation on the use of Commission funds to pay its personnel at no more than the rate applicable for level V of the Executive Schedule and the provision authorizing a detail to the Commission of "any Federal Government employee" without loss of civil service status or privilege.

Thus, when the detail is authorized by a statute other than the Economy Act, the agencies involved in the transaction may have greater flexibility to develop innovative reimbursement arrangements that are tailored to the circumstances of the particular situation.

Finally, it is not uncommon for agencies to detail employees to congressional committees. Two 1942 decisions, 21 Comp. Gen. 954 and 21 Comp. Gen. 1055, addressed this situation and held essentially that the details could be nonreimbursable if the committee's work for which the detail was sought could be said to help the agency accomplish some purpose of its own appropriations. These cases were the source of the "commonality of function" exception that, in 64 Comp. Gen. 370, GAO expanded to all federal agency details. See 64 Comp. Gen. at 379. The second 1942 decision emphasized that "mutuality of interest" is not enough to authorize a nonreimbursable detail. "[I]t must appear that the work of the committee to which the detail or loan of the employee is made will actually aid the agency in the accomplishment of a purpose for which its appropriation was made such as by obviating the necessity for the performance by such agency of the same or similar work." 21 Comp. Gen. at 1058. A 1988 decision applied these precedents to conclude that the Treasury Department could detail two employees to the House Committee on Government Operations on a nonreimbursable basis to work with the committee on the oversight and review of the FTS-2000 telecommunications project. B-230960, April 11, 1988.

As to reimbursable details, section 202(f) of the Legislative Reorganization Act of 1946, 2 U.S.C. § 72a(f), provides that "[n]o committee [of the Congress] shall appoint to its staff any experts or other personnel detailed or assigned from any department or agency of the Government, except with the written permission of "specified committees. The Justice Department's Office of Legal Counsel regards this as implicit authority for reimbursable details of executive branch personnel to congressional committees, the theory being that a restriction like 2 U.S.C. § 72a(f) would be pointless if the authority didn't already exist. 12 Op. Off. Legal Counsel 184, 185 (1988). See also 1 Op. Off. Legal Counsel 108 (1977). However, the OLC cautions that agencies should have due regard for potential ethics and separation-of-powers concerns. 12 Op. Off. Legal Counsel at 186-89. GAO has pointed out that 2 U.S.C. § 72a(f) is a limitation on the authority of congressional committees, not a limitation on the lending agency, and that compliance is not the lending agency's responsibility. B-129874, January 4, 1971.

Loans of Personal Property

Another area where the Economy Act significantly changed prior practice was reimbursement for interagency loans of equipment and other personal property.

Prior to the enactment of the Economy Act in 1932, there was no authority to charge another government agency for the use of borrowed property. E.g., 9 Comp. Gen. 415 (1930). Also, the borrowing agency could not use its appropriations to repair the borrowed property unless the repairs were necessary for its own continued use, the theory being that the property belonged to the United States and not to any individual agency. (For additional discussion on this point, see *Principles of Federal Appropriations Law*, vol. III, chap. 12, under the Interagency Claims heading.) To some extent at least, the Economy Act amounts to "tacit recognition of property ownership rights in the various departments and agencies possessing such property." 30 Comp. Gen. 295, 296 (1951). Thus, one early case held that the Economy Act authorized the Civil Aeronautics Board to lease surplus aircraft from another government agency. 24 Comp. Gen. 184 (1944). It also authorized the Soil Conservation Service to borrow a shallow draft riverboat from the Bureau of Land Management for certain work in Alaska. 30 Comp. Gen. 295 (1951). The logic of this decision is simple. Since the Economy Act authorizes the permanent transfer of equipment, then it must also authorize "lesser transactions between departments on a temporary loan basis." Id. at 296.

Another case is 38 Comp. Gen. 558 (1959), in which the Maritime Administration wanted to lend a tug to the Coast Guard and asked GAO if the transaction was within the scope of 24 Comp. Gen. 184. GAO answered affirmatively, finding that there was no "essential difference" between the lease in the 1944 case and the loan in this one (Id. at 559), and therefore no reason not to follow 24 Comp. Gen. 184 and 30 Comp. Gen. 295.

In addition, several judicial decisions have confirmed that the Economy Act authorizes interagency loans of personal property. The cases arose out of the 1973 occupation of the village of Wounded Knee, South Dakota, by members of a group called the American Indian Movement. Various law enforcement agencies had been called in, including the United States Marshals and the Federal Bureau of Investigation. The Army provided substantial amounts of equipment, such as sniper rifles, protective vests, and armored personnel carriers. Defendants charged with obstructing law enforcement officers tried to argue that the Army's involvement violated 18 U.S.C. § 1385, the so-called Posse Comitatus Act, which prohibits use of the Army or Air Force for law enforcement unless specifically authorized. With one exception, the courts held that the Posse Comitatus Act applies to personnel, not to equipment, and in any event providing the equipment was authorized by the Economy Act. *United States v. McArthur,* 419 F. Supp. 186, 194 (D.N.D. 1976), aff'd sub nom. United States v. Casper, 541 F.2d 1275 (8th Cir. 1976), cert. denied, 430 U.S. 970; *United States v. Red Feather,* 392 F.Supp. 916, 923 (D.S.D. 1975); *United States v. Jaramillo,* 380 F. Supp. 1375, 1379 (D. Neb. 1974), appeal dismissed, 510 F. 2d 808 (8th Cir. 1975). As the court in the McArthur case noted, borrowing "highly technical equipment . . . for a specific, limited, temporary purpose is far preferable" to having to maintain the equipment permanently. 419 F. Supp. at 194. However, one court disagreed, holding that the Economy Act applies "only to sales, and not to loans." *United States v. Banks,* 383 F. Supp. 368, 376 (D. S.D. 1974). However, this case goes against the clear weight of authority in this respect.

Subsequent to the Wounded Knee litigation, Congress enacted 10 U.S.C. § 372, which expressly authorizes the Secretary of Defense to make equipment available to law enforcement organizations. At first, reimbursement was discretionary. See Pub. L. No. 97-86, § 905(a)(1), 95 Stat. 1099, 1116 (1981); 6 Op. Off. Legal Counsel 464 (1982). The reimbursement provision, 10 U.S.C. § 377, was amended in 1988 to require reimbursement, with certain exceptions, "[t]o the extent otherwise required" by the Economy Act or other applicable law.

The reimbursement of "actual costs" is somewhat different for loans of personal property than for other Economy Act transactions. If an agency lends a piece of equipment to another agency and the borrowing agency returns it in as good condition as when lent, the lending agency has not incurred any direct costs. Thus, the decision at 24 Comp. Gen. 184 (lease of surplus aircraft) said merely that the borrowing agency should agree "to reimburse the department for the cost, if any, necessarily incurred by it in connection with such transaction," plus repair costs. Id. at 186. Although depreciation is an identifiable indirect cost, the recovery of depreciation is normally inappropriate because it is not a cost that is funded out of currently available appropriations of the performing agency. See 57 Comp. Gen. 674 (1978) at pp.682–683.

Reimbursable costs (or costs the borrowing agency should pay directly) include such costs as transportation, activation, operation, maintenance, and repair. See, e.g., 38 Comp. Gen. 558, 560 (1959). Another permissible item of "cost" is a refundable deposit on containers. B-125414, September 30, 1955.

When one agency lends property for which it is responsible to another agency and the borrowing agency damages or destroys the property, as a general rule, the lending agency cannot assert a damage claim against the borrowing agency. E.g., 65 Comp. Gen. 464 (1986); 25 Comp. Gen. 49 (1945); 6 Comp. Dec. 74 (1899). The rule is sometimes referred to as the "interdepartmental waiver doctrine." See, e.g., 60 Comp. Gen. 406 (1981); 59 Comp. Gen. 93 (1979). The term seems to have evolved from language in 25 Comp. Gen. 49, 55 (1945), approving a "mutual waiver" of damage claims by the Navy and two government corporations. The rule also applies to loans of property between components of a single agency funded under separate appropriations. See 65 Comp. Gen. 910, 911 (1986); 3 Comp. Gen. 74 (1923); B-35478, July 24, 1943.

The rule is based in large measure on the premise that ownership of public property is in the United States as a single entity and not in the individual departments or agencies. 41 Comp. Gen. 235, 237 (1961); 22 Comp. Dec. 390 (1916). Therefore, a claim by one agency against another for damage to borrowed property would amount to the government asserting a claim against itself.

A number of cases also rely in part on the purpose statute (31 U.S.C. § 1301(a)), which restricts the use of appropriations to the purposes for which they were made. 26 Comp. Gen. 235, 239 (1946); 6 Comp. Gen. 171, 172 (1926). The theory is that an agency that is authorized to acquire property is also authorized to maintain or repair that property to keep it suitable for its intended use; its appropriations, if not expressly available for repairs, are nevertheless available by necessary implication without regard to how the property was damaged or who damaged it. See 6 Comp. Dec. at 75. Thus, under the rationale of these cases, it would violate the purpose statute for the borrowing agency to use its appropriation to repair the lending agency's property. Further, if, as these cases indicate, payment by the agency causing the damage would be a payment for an unauthorized purpose, it follows that it would also improperly augment the appropriations of the claimant agency. 29 Comp. Gen. 470, 471 (1950); 6 Comp. Gen. at 172.

One of the earliest cases addressing the interdepartmental waiver doctrine is 10 Comp. Gen. 288 (1930), holding that the Bureau of the Census was not authorized to reimburse the Marine Corps for the cost of replacing and repairing furniture borrowed by the bureau, notwithstanding an under standing between the parties that the furniture would be returned to the corps in as good condition as when lent. The decision stated:

> The rule has long been established that where one department loans property or equipment to another it is not entitled to charge for its use or depreciation, or to have lost property replaced or damaged property repaired upon its return to the loaning establishment. . . . [T]he ownership of public property is in the Government and not in a department or branch thereof having possession of the property, and, accordingly, an executive department may not lawfully be reimbursed for the value of such property loaned to, and lost by, another department. . . . If appropriations of an establishment to which property is loaned are not chargeable with the cost of replacing articles lost or for use and depreciation of the property, obviously they are not chargeable with the costs of repairs to restore the property to its former condition upon its return to the loaning establishment. Such repairs are not for the benefit of the borrowing establishment but are for the future use and benefit of the establishment to which the property is returned.

Thus, at least since 1930, the general rule has been that when an agency lends property to another agency, it cannot assert a damage claim if the property is destroyed or damaged while in the possession of the borrowing agency. Note also that the existence of an agreement, whether written or oral, was not considered sufficient to overcome the purpose statute. Agency personnel do not have the authority to grant themselves exceptions to fiscal limitations imposed by Congress simply by signing a memorandum of agreement.

One of the major exceptions to this rule are transactions under the Economy Act where the agreement requires the borrowing agency to pay for repairs. The earliest case to discuss the Economy Act authority in this context appears to be 30 Comp. Gen. 295 (1951). The Bureau of Land Management of the Interior Department lent a motorboat to the Agriculture Department's Soil Conservation Service under a written agreement stating that the Soil Service would "return the boat in as good condition as when received, normal wear and tear excepted." Repairs to the boat's motor were necessary to satisfy this agreement, and the question was whether the repair cost was a proper charge against Soil Service appropriations. Responding in the affirmative, the Comptroller General stated:

> [Since the Economy Act permits] for a consideration, the total transfer between departments of material, supplies, and equipment on a permanent basis, [it] would appear to sanction, as well, lesser transactions between departments on a temporary loan basis. . . . [N]o good reason appears why the loaning department may not provide by agreement with the borrowing department that the property be returned in as good condition as when loaned and that the expense of placing the property in such condition be borne by the latter department provided, of course, that its appropriation is available therefor.

Id. at 296.

In another case, the Air Force lent two planes to the Army under an agreement that provided that the Army would be liable for damage to or destruction of the property from any cause. One plane was completely destroyed in a crash. In B-146588, August 23, 1961, GAO held that the Army could legally reimburse the Air Force for the lost property, stating:

[T]he rule prohibiting replacements of or repairs to property generally, no longer applies to loans of personal property as between Government agencies when the loan agreement provides that the borrowing agency must return the property in as good condition as when loaned and that the expense of placing the property in such condition would be borne by that agency, subject, of course, to the availability of its appropriations.

In the absence of an agreement under the Economy Act or similar statutory authority that the borrowing agency will reimburse the lending agency for the use, repair, or replacement of the property, the "interdepartmental waiver" rule continues to apply and would prohibit the lending agency from asserting a claim against the borrowing agency for repair or replacement costs. For example, in 25 Comp. Gen. 322 (1945), the Army lost a 50-ton ball-bearing jack borrowed from another Defense establishment. The parties had not entered into an Economy Act agreement providing for reimbursement, although they could have done so. Therefore, the general rule applied, and the Army was not authorized to pay for the lost property.

Discussion Problem 6-7

The borrowing agency needs to borrow several pieces of road repair equipment that belong to the lending agency. The two agencies enter into an Economy Act agreement whereby the borrowing agency agrees to: "Return the property in as good a condition as received, except for normal wear and tear. In the event that the property is not returned in as good a condition as received, the borrowing agency shall be liable for the repair or replacement of the property." Through no fault of its own, the property is stolen while in the possession of the borrowing agency.

The lending agency asserts a claim for the property, and the borrowing agency makes an argument in opposition to the claim. First, it contends that the "interdepartmental waiver" doctrine prohibits one federal agency from sub-

> mitting a claim against another federal agency for damage or loss of lent property. Second, the borrowing agency contends that it cannot be liable for the replacement of the property because it was not at fault. How should these issues be decided?

GAO has generally held that the Economy Act may not be used for loans for indefinite periods that amount to permanent, cost-free transfers. The reason is that a permanent transfer, while authorized under the Economy Act, requires payment for the property. 59 Comp. Gen. 366, 368 (1980); 38 Comp. Gen. 558, 560 (1959). In 16 Comp. Gen. 730 (1937), for example, an agency had lent office equipment to another agency. When the borrowing agency's need for the property continued to the point where the lending agency had to replace it for its own use, the borrowing agency paid for the equipment. Agencies seeking a permanent transfer without reimbursement should seek statutory authority. 38 Comp. Gen. at 560.

A permanent transfer raises the question of how to value the property. The same question arises when property lent under the Economy Act is totally destroyed. The decision at 16 Comp. Gen. 730 does not specify how the amount of the payment was calculated. In a case where property was destroyed, the question was whether value should be set at acquisition value or the value of similar property being disposed of as surplus property. GAO declined to choose, advising that the amount to be billed "is primarily a matter for adjustment and settlement" between the agencies concerned. B-146588, August 23, 1961.

In 25 Comp. Gen. 322 (1945), however, a case involving lost property, the adjustment amount was zero. The parties could have provided for adjustment in an Economy Act agreement but did not. Consequently, the "interdepartmental waiver" rule applied, which precluded a claim by the lending agency against the borrowing agency for the lost property. Id. at 325.

Common Services

When one segment of an agency performs services or purchases items that benefit other segments of the agency, questions often arise regarding the propriety of reimbursement of the performing agency segment by the segments benefited. Issues concerning the provision and funding of common services arise most frequently in the case of larger agencies made up of component bureaus or offices funded under separate appropriations. It often makes sense, economically as well as operationally, to provide certain common services (e.g., procurement) centrally. How the agency goes about doing this depends primarily on its appropriations structure.

One approach agencies use is to budget specifically for common services from a single, centralized appropriation. For example, a department might receive an appropriation that is available for certain specified department-wide services such as personnel, information resources management, and "other necessary expenses for management support services to offices of the department." Under this type of structure, questions of reimbursement should not arise. Indeed, requiring reimbursement from the component bureaus when Congress has provided funding in the departmental appropriation would be an improper augmentation of the receiving appropriation. B-202979-O.M., September 28, 1981.

A different approach is illustrated by 43 U.S.C. § 1467, which establishes a working capital fund for the Interior Department, to be available for specified common services—document reproduction, communication, supply, library, and health—plus "such other similar service functions as the Secretary determines may be performed more advantageously on a reimbursable basis." The receiving components are required to reimburse the fund "at rates which will return in full all expenses of operation, including reserves for accrued annual leave and depreciation of equipment." Under this structure, services within the scope of the working fund are provided centrally, but each component bureau must budget for its own needs, much as agencies budget for and pay rent to GSA. If each bureau receives its own appropriations for support services and there is no further statutory guidance, the agency may centralize the provision of common services on a reimbursable basis under authority of the Economy Act—provided the reimbursements correspond to the value actually received. 70 Comp. Gen. 592, 595 (1991) (executive computer network); B-77791, July 23, 1948 (procurement of office supplies); B-202979-O.M., September 28, 1981 (legal services).

The centralization of common services may provide for efficiencies in the case of a single bureau with more than one operating appropriation, or a smaller agency that is not divided into component entities but that nevertheless receives several separate appropriations. The Economy Act would not apply in these situations, since the transactions would not be between agencies or even between departments within an agency. Consequently, because transfers between separate appropriations are involved, specific statutory authority is necessary. 38 Comp. Gen. 734, 737-738 (1959).

Following this 1959 decision, the Bureau of the Census, to which that decision had been addressed, sought and received specific authority to charge common services to any available appropriation, provided the benefiting appropriation(s) reimbursed the financing appropriation no later than the end of the fiscal year. Pub. L. No. 87-489, 76 Stat. 104 (1962). Other agencies sought similar authority, and GAO supported the enactment of government-wide legislation. See B-136318, December 20, 1963. The legislation was enacted a few years later, and today may be found at 31 U.S.C. § 1534. This statute states:

> 1534. Adjustments between appropriations
> (a) An appropriation available to an agency may be charged at any time during a fiscal year for the benefit of another appropriation available to the agency to pay costs -
> (1) when amounts are available in both the appropriation to be charged and the appropriation to be benefited;

and (2) subject to limitations applicable to the appropriations.

(b) Amounts paid under this section are charged on a final basis during, or as of the close of, the fiscal year to the appropriation benefited. The appropriation charged under subsection (a) of this section shall be appropriately credited.

Thus, for intra-bureau services, or intra-agency services for agencies not divided into component entities, 31 U.S.C. § 1534 provides the necessary authority.

For agencies composed of separately funded bureaus or offices, 31 U.S.C. § 1534 exists side-by-side with the Economy Act, and the agency would appear to have discretion in choosing which authority to use, although 31 U.S.C. § 1534 seems somewhat broader. The difference was illustrated in 17 Comp. Gen. 748 (1938).

The Bureau of Prisons entered into a contract for safety inspections and evaluations of all federal prisons. It proposed charging the contract price to the appropriation for one penitentiary, subject to proportionate reimbursement by the others. GAO concluded that this arrangement could not be authorized under the Economy Act; at the time, the only option was for the voucher to list and charge all contributing accounts. Although the contractor would be paid with one check, the funds of each prison would be charged individually. Id. at 751. Today, under authority of 31 U.S.C. § 1534, one agency subdivision could pay the contractor the entire amount owed and seek reimbursement from the benefited subdivisions.

Services Not Authorized under the Economy Act

Limitations on what can be done under the Economy Act derive largely from common sense and the requirements of the appropriations process. One limitation frequently encountered is that the Economy Act may not be used for services that the performing agency is required by law to provide and for which it receives appropriations. As the

Department of Justice has noted, this rule "is required in order to prevent agencies from agreeing to reallocate funds between themselves in circumvention of the appropriations process." 9 Op. Off. Legal Counsel 96, 98 (1985) (preliminary print). See also 61 Comp. Gen. 419, 421 (1982) (charging the receiving agency "would compromise the basic integrity of the appropriations process" and would amount to a "usurpation of the congressional prerogative").

For example, if a GAO audit enables an agency to recover overcharges, the amounts recovered may not be paid over to GAO to help defray the cost of conducting the audit. B-163758-O.M., December 3, 1973. The reason is that conducting audits is GAO's job, and it receives appropriations for that purpose. Similarly, the Social Security Administration is not authorized to charge the Railroad Retirement Board for information it is required to furnish under 45 U.S.C. § 231f (b)(7). 44 Comp. Gen. 56 (1964).

Nor may the Justice Department, which is required by law to conduct the government's litigation and which receives appropriations for its litigation functions, pass the costs on to the "client agency." 16 Comp. Gen. 333 (1936). However, if the client agency provides litigation support to the Justice Department, an Economy Act agreement whereby the Justice Department reimburses the client agency would be permissible. The client agency would even be authorized to hire additional attorneys to perform the work for the Justice Department, provided that the attorneys will be performing work that the client agency is authorized to do itself. 9 Op. Off. Legal Counsel 96 (1985) (preliminary print); 2 Op. Off. Legal Counsel 302 (1978). Thus, the types and extent of support depend in part on the breadth of the client agency's own statutory authority. 2 Op. Off. Legal Counsel at 305-06.

A situation may arise in which an agency that is required by law to provide a service (e.g., the duty of the Justice Department to provide litigation services) does not have adequate funding available. In this situation, the performing agency would be interested in obtaining reimbursement for rendering the required services. However, GAO has held that, if a service is required to be provided on a nonreimbursable basis, then the inadequacy of the providing agency's appropriations is legally irrelevant and does not permit reimbursement by the receiving agency. 18 Comp. Gen. 389, 391 (1938). However, if the service is authorized but not required, there may be circumstances under which reimbursement is permissible.

GAO discussed one such situation in B-194711-O.M., January 15, 1980. Each agency is required by 44 U.S.C. § 3102 to have a records management program. In addition, the National Archives and Records Administration (NARA) has oversight and assistance responsibilities, which include conducting surveys and inspections. When NARA is performing its oversight function or conducts a study on its own initiative, the general rule applies and NARA's appropriations must bear the cost. However, if an agency wants to conduct an "internal" study of its own program and asks NARA to do it, and NARA's appropriations are insufficient, nothing precludes a reimbursable arrangement under the Economy Act. Also, if Congress has provided appropriations for a particular activity for an initial start-up period and later discontinues funding with the intent that the activity become self-sufficient, reimbursement under the Economy Act is authorized. B-165117-O.M., December 23, 1975.

Another situation in which an agency may be reimbursed for performing the type of services that it is required to provide is when it is providing services that are over and above what is required by law. In such situations, the performing agency may invoke the Economy Act to recover the actual costs of the non-required services. For example, 44 U.S.C. § 1701 requires the Government Printing Office to provide addressing, wrapping, and mailing services for certain public documents. It cannot charge for these required services. 29 Comp. Gen. 327 (1950). However, section 1701 specifically excludes certain documents from its mandate. Since GPO was in a position to provide those services in an efficient and economical manner with respect to the excluded documents, it could do so on a reimbursable basis under the

Economy Act. Id. Similarly, the Secret Service is statutorily required to provide protective services to specified officials. Officials other than those specified may obtain the services only by "purchasing" them under the Economy Act. 54 Comp. Gen. 624 (1975), modified on other grounds, 55 Comp. Gen. 578 (1975).

An important variation to the rule that the performing agency may not be reimbursed for services that it is required by law to provide occurred in 34 Comp. Gen. 340 (1955). A series of decisions in the early 1950s had held that the Patent and Trademark Office could not charge fees to other government agencies for services performed in administering the patent and trademark laws. 33 Comp. Gen. 559 (1954), modified, 34 Comp. Gen. 340 (1955); 33 Comp. Gen. 27 (1953), amplified, 33 Comp. Gen. 559 (1954); 32 Comp. Gen. 392 (1953). However, an exception was created in 34 Comp. Gen. 340 (1955). In that case, the Army had entered into an agreement with the United Kingdom for a royalty-free license to an invention. Under this agreement the Army was to bear all costs associated with filing a patent application in the United States. The issue was whether the Army could reimburse the Patent Office for the costs of reviewing the patent application, since that was the type of task that the Patent Office was generally required to perform.

GAO held that the general rule that an agency cannot be reimbursed for performing a mandatory function would not apply in this situation because the services were not really being rendered to another government agency, but were being rendered for the United Kingdom. The fees were essentially part of the consideration for the license that the United Kingdom paid to the Army and that the Army could, in turn, pay to the Patent Office. (The law was changed in 1965 to authorize the Patent Office to charge fees to other government agencies, subject to discretionary waiver in the case of an "occasional or incidental request." 35 U.S.C. § 41(e).)

This same rationale could be applied to any situation in which it could be demonstrated that the service is being rendered for an entity other than another federal agency. Note that this rationale would even apply in situations like that in 34 Comp. Gen. 340, where two federal agencies were directly involved in the transaction. In that case, and presumably in future cases involving similar facts, GAO will look beyond the parties directly involved in the transaction and will consider who the real party in interest is. If the real party in interest is a non-federal entity, then the performing agency should be able to obtain reimbursement for performing services that it would be required to perform for a federal agency.

Discussion Problem 6-8

The primary mission of the General Services Board of Contract Appeals (GSBCA) is to adjudicate claims arising under or related to contracts awarded by GSA. The GSBCA becomes interested in supporting alternative dispute resolution (ADR) initiatives and decides to make its judges available to serve as ADR neutrals.

If NASA and one of its contractors would like to use the services of the GSBCA, can the GSBCA provide this service under the Economy Act on a reimbursable basis? Why or why not? Would the answer be different if the GSBCA wants to charge GSA divisions for adjudicating claims arising under or relating to GSA contracts?

Another issue that arises in the context of Economy Act transactions is based on the principle that an agency may not transfer administrative functions to another agency under the authority of the Economy Act. This principle was applied in B-45488, November 11, 1944, in which GAO explained:

> The theory . . . is that there is inherent in a grant of authority to a department or agency to perform a certain function, and to expend public funds in connection therewith, a responsibility which, having been reposed specifically in such department or agency by the Congress, may not be transferred except by specific action of the Congress. The soundness of this principle is without question.

The difficulty in applying the rule is that no one has ever attempted to define the vague term "administrative function" in this particular context. Certainly it would prohibit transfer of an entire appropriation from one agency to another with a request to essentially perform all of the ordering agency's missions. Decision of July 7, 1923 (no file designation), 23A MS 101. In this decision, the Comptroller General stated the following very fundamental proposition:

> The intent of the Congress in requiring estimates and the making of appropriations thereon is the imposition of a duty upon the department to which [the appropriations are] made to act and be responsible for the expenditures made under the appropriations.

Such an arrangement, in addition to undermining the intent of the appropriation, would also undermine the purpose of the Economy Act, which is to enable agencies to avail themselves of the services of other agencies with greater expertise. When an ordering agency, in effect, transfers its core mission functions to another agency, it has acted in a manner that is inconsistent with the clear intent of the Economy Act.

The rule that an agency cannot use the Economy Act to transfer to another agency its core mission responsibilities has been held to include functions with respect to which an agency has authority to make "final and conclusive" determinations. Thus, the Veterans Administration (VA) could not transfer to the Federal Housing Administration management and disposal functions with respect to property that the VA acquired through its credit programs. B-156010-O.M., March 16, 1965. Equally unauthorized is the transfer of debt collection responsibilities under the Federal Claims Collection Act. While debt collection services can be provided under the Economy Act, they may not include the taking of final compromise or termination action. B-117604(7)-O.M., June 30, 1970. Both of these cases involve functions that GAO considered to be subject to "final and conclusive" authority of the ordering agency.

Although the earlier decisions seemed to emphasize the permanency of the proposed transfer, e.g., 14 Comp. Gen. 455 (1934), the later decisions recognize that the crucial factor is who ends up exercising ultimate control. The first case to adopt this approach appears to have been B-45488, November 11, 1944. The Civil Service Commission proposed, at least for the duration of wartime conditions, to advance to the Army funds from the Civil Service Retirement and Disability Fund. The Army would hold the money in a trust account and treat it as a working fund from which to make refunds of retirement deductions to certain separating civilian employees. All concerned seemed to accept, as a starting premise, that the proposal amounted to performance by the Army of an administrative function of the Civil Service Commission.

However, the proposal also contemplated that the commission would audit all cases of refunds, and this, said the decision, "must be considered as a retention of a certain degree of supervision and control." Thus, while the Army would be actually making the refunds, "responsibility for the performance of the function generally would remain" in the commission. Therefore, the proposal was authorized under the Economy Act, since the ordering agency (the commission) retained a level of supervision and control GAO considered to be appropriate.

Thus, if an agency is contemplating an Economy Act transaction in which it will be asking another agency to perform functions that relate closely to the ordering agency's core mission areas, the ordering agency must be sure to structure the agreement so that it retains a significant degree of supervision and control over the performing agency's work. In sum, the lesson of B-45488 is that, for purposes of applying the "administrative function" rule, the allocation of ultimate responsibility is more important than the determination of what does or does not constitute an administrative function. An agency can acquire services under the Economy Act but cannot turn over the ultimate responsibility for administering its programs or activities.

Use of Contractors to Perform Economy Act Orders

As originally enacted, the Economy Act made no provision for the performing agency to contract out all or any part of its performance. Indeed, the law authorized only work or services the performing agency was "in a position" to provide, and GAO construed this as precluding performance by contractors. 20 Comp. Gen. 264 (1940); 19 Comp. Gen. 544 (1939).

Amendments to the Economy Act

Notwithstanding this limitation, it soon became clear that the use of commercial contractors in performing Economy Act orders could, in certain circumstances, be advantageous. Accordingly, in 1942, Congress considered a bill that would have amended the Economy Act to authorize all agencies to use private contractors to perform Economy Act orders. GAO found the proposal unobjectionable in B-18980, February 13, 1942. However, the legislation as enacted (Act of July 20, 1942, ch. 507, 56 Stat. 661) authorized the use of contractors only if the ordering agency was one of five specified agencies: the Army, Navy, Treasury, Federal Aviation Administration, and Maritime Administration. The only explanation for reducing the scope of coverage appeared to be a comment in the legislative history expressing concern about "trading going on among too many departments." See 52 Comp. Gen. 128, 133 (1972). For the next forty years (1942–1982) the only agencies authorized to use contractors to perform Economy Act orders were the five agencies specified in the statute.

In 1982, Congress amended the Economy Act to authorize all agencies to obtain goods and services by contract in fulfilling Economy Act orders. Pub. L. No. 97–332, 96 Stat. 1622. The legislative history described some of the potential advantages as follows:

> Since 1942, when the Economy Act was amended to allow agencies to contract out for goods and services on behalf of only 5 specified agencies, numerous areas of

agency expertise have been developed. With the authority extended to allow agencies to contract out on behalf of any other Federal agency, an agency having only an occasional requirement in a specific area could turn to an agency with substantial experience in the area for assistance. This would eliminate the need to duplicate the requisite expertise. For instance, if the Immigration and Naturalization Service has a requirement for night sensors for border protection, that agency could seek assistance from the Department of Defense which presumably has already developed expertise in that area. Or, if the Coast Guard had a requirement for navigational equipment, it could seek assistance from the Department of the Navy to acquire such, rather than duplicate research and development already under way or completed. Various statutes now permit such interagency requisitioning in specific areas; however, removal of the general restriction allows the maximum utilization by the Government of valuable expertise developed over the years in the various Government agencies. In addition, such generally available authority creates the potential for wider use by the Government of quantity discounts or other benefits which may not have been available in the past. It will also permit an agency to use another agency which has some, though not all, of the capability to do the requisitioned work by allowing the requisitioned agency to simply contract out the part of the work that it cannot do.

H.R. Rep. No. 97–456, 4 (1982), reprinted in 1982 U.S.C.C.A.N. 3182, 3185.

The 1982 amendment changed the Economy Act in three ways. First, it amended 31 U.S.C. § 1535(a)(3) to generally authorize performing agencies to obtain ordered goods and services by contract and deleted the limitation to the five named agencies. Second, it amended 31 U.S.C. § 1535(a)(4) to replace the specific reference to competitive bids with a more general reference to providing the goods or services simply "by contract." The intent of this change was to permit the performing agency to use whatever methods of procurement are available to it. H.R. Rep. No. 97-456 at 5; 1982 U.S.C.C.A.N. at 31, 86. This change became significant in light of the myriad types of contracting vehicles that have been developed through various acquisition reform initiatives in the last several years. Finally, the amendment added 31 U.S.C. § 1535(c), which states:

> A condition or limitation applicable to amounts for procurement of an agency or unit placing an order or making a contract under this section applies to the placing of the order or the making of the contract.

This provision is designed to preclude use of the Economy Act to avoid legal restrictions applicable to the funds of the ordering agency. This approach was originally recommended by GAO, Reorganization Act of 1981; Amend Economy Act to Provide That All Departments and Agencies Obtain Materials or Services from Other Agencies by Contract; and Amend the Federal Grant and Cooperative Agreement Act: Hearings on H.R. 2528 et al. Before a Subcomm. of the House Comm. on Government Operations, 97th Cong., 1st Sess. 78 (1981) (statement of Milton J. Socolar, Special Assistant to the Comptroller General of the United States). It "prevents the ordering agency from accomplishing under the guise of an Economy Act transaction, objects or purposes outside the scope of its authority." B-259499, August 22, 1995, at 8.

Applicability of the Competition in Contracting Act

The Competition in Contracting Act (CICA) requires that procuring agencies obtain full and open competition "except in the case of procurement procedures otherwise expressly authorized by statute." 41 U.S.C. § 253(a)(1) (civilian procurements); 10 U.S.C. § 2304(a)(1) (military procurements). For purposes of this provision, the Economy Act is one of the otherwise authorized procedures. *National Gateway Telecom. Inc. v. Aldridge*, 701 F. Supp. 1104, 1113 (D.N.J. 1988), aff'd mem., 879 F.2d 858 (3d Cir. 1989) (10 U.S.C. §

2304); 70 Comp. Gen. 448, 453-54 (1991) (41 U.S.C. § 253). Thus, an agency can obtain its needs under another agency's requirements contract, as long as the transaction is in compliance with the Economy Act and the action is permissible under the performing agency's contract. *National Gateway*, 701 F. Supp. at 1114; 70 Comp. Gen. at 454; B-244691.2, November 25, 1992, recons. denied, B-244691.3, January 5, 1993.

The ordering agency is not required to "compete" its requirement between the performing agency and the general commercial marketplace. However, the performing agency must comply (or must have complied) with the requirements of CICA in the award of the contract that will be used to perform the work of the ordering agency. This is required by CICA itself at 10 U.S.C. 2404(f)(5)(B) and 41 U.S.C. § 253(f)(5)(B).

One of the Economy Act requirements that the ordering agency must satisfy is the "lower cost" determination, 31 U.S.C. § 1535(a)(4). However, agencies have some discretion in deciding what data to consider in making this determination. For example, in B-244691.2, November 25, 1992, the ordering agency made the determination without performing market research because the price under the performing agency's requirements contract was lower than the current Federal Supply Schedule price, and agencies are permitted to purchase from a supply schedule contract without seeking further competition. This, GAO found, was perfectly reasonable. As long as the various requirements of the Economy Act are satisfied, the ordering agency may also legitimately take into consideration such factors as administrative convenience or procurement risks, 70 Comp. Gen. at 454 n.5, or the need to obligate funds to avoid future funding cuts, *National Gateway*, 701 F. Supp. at 1111.

Economy Act Abuses and "Off-Loading"

In the late 1980s and early 1990s, congressional concerns regarding reported abuses under the Economy Act resulted in a detailed report by the Subcommittee on Oversight of

Government Management, Senate Committee on Governmental Affairs: *Off-Loading: The Abuse of Inter-Agency Contracting to Avoid Competition and Oversight Requirement*, S. Rept. No. 61, 103d Cong., 2d Sess. (1994). The report's title reflects the birth of a new term, off-loading, defined (on page 1 of the Senate report) as "when one agency buys goods or services under a contract entered and administered by another agency." The report found that government agencies "off-load billions of dollars of contracts every year," and that "improper off-loads total at least in the hundreds of millions of dollars and losses to the taxpayers are at least in the tens of millions of dollars." Id. at 5. Among the abuses the report cited were the use of off-loading to avoid competition, to direct contracts to favored contractors, to improperly obligate expiring year-end appropriations, and to make a variety of inappropriate purchases. Id. at 6. The report recommended that off-loading be limited and subject to stronger regulatory controls. Id. at 44-46.

Congress responded with two pieces of legislation: for military procurements, section 844 of the National Defense Authorization Act for Fiscal Year 1994, Pub. L. No. 103-160, 107 Stat. 1547, 1720, enacted into law as the Senate report was being written; and for civilian procurements, section 1074 of the Federal Acquisition Streamlining Act of 1974, Pub. L. No. 103-355, 108 Stat. 3243, 3271. The two provisions are virtually identical and require that the governing procurement regulations be amended to: (1) permit off-loading only if the performing agency (a) has an existing contract for the same or similar goods or services, (b) is better qualified to enter into or administer the contract by reason of capabilities or expertise the ordering agency does not have, or (c) is specifically authorized by law to act in that capacity; (2) require that off-loads be approved in advance by an authorized official of the ordering agency; and (3) prohibit the payment of any fee in excess of the performing agency's actual costs or, if not known, estimated costs. Implementing regulations are found in the Federal Acquisition Regulation, 48 C.F.R. Subpart 17.5 (60 Fed. Reg. 49720, September 26, 1995).

OTHER INTERAGENCY TRANSACTIONS

Although the best-known statute authorizing interagency transactions is the Economy Act, there are many others. Some are mandatory, but most are optional. Two examples of authorized interagency transactions that are covered by statutes other than the Economy Act include printing by GPO and the various services provided by GSA.

If a more specific statute is applicable to an interagency transaction, the Economy Act will not apply. 44 Comp. Gen. 683 (1965); 6 Op. Off. Legal Counsel 464 (1982); *Integrated Systems Group, Inc. v. GSA and Department of the Army*, GSBCA No. 13108-P, 95-1 B.C.A. ¶ 27, 484 (1995). However, there are often situations where the Economy Act may be consulted for guidance even though it cannot be used to conduct the transaction. One example would be where the statute prescribes reimbursement only in general terms, and the parties want to look to the procedures under the Economy Act to see how reimbursement would be handled under that statute. For example, in 72 Comp. Gen. 159 (1993), GAO referred to the Economy Act to determine that the term "reimbursable basis" in statute directing agencies to furnish certain services to Nuclear Regulatory Commission can include "added factor" for overhead.

Although the Economy Act is often consulted for guidance, the statute that specifically applies to the transaction is controlling with respect to what services can be provided, who the customers may be, and who bears the costs. Several other statutes authorize interagency transactions.

The Project Order Statute

The project order statute, 41 U.S.C. § 23, provides DoD with interdepartmental authority to order goods and services, separate and distinct from the Economy Act. (14 U.S.C. § 151 provides similar authority to the Coast Guard.) The statute applies to transactions between military departments and DoD government-owned, government-operated (GOGO) establishments for work related to military projects.

B-246773, May 5, 1993, 72 Comp. Gen. 172. If DoD is issuing the order to a non-DoD agency, then the Economy Act, and not the project order statute, would apply. GOGO facilities include shipyards, arsenals, ordnance plants, manufacturing or processing plants or shops, equipment overhaul or maintenance shops, research and development laboratories, testing facilities, and proving grounds that are owned and operated within DoD. DoD Financial Management Regulation, Vol. 11A, Ch. 2, para. 020303.

Orders placed with GOGOs are treated as if placed with a commercial entity. Consequently, as with a contract with a commercial entity, there is no requirement that the requesting agency deobligate funds if the performing activity has not incurred an obligation before the funds expire. Thus, if the performing agency accepts the requesting agency's order prior to the end of the period of availability of the funds cited, the funds remain available for payment in the subsequent fiscal year regardless of whether the performing agency commenced performance or awarded a contract prior to the end of the fiscal year.

Regarding the recording of obligations under the Project Order statute, the DoD Financial Management Regulation states:

> A project order is treated as a contract. When it is accepted in writing by the performing activity, the amount of the project order shall be recorded as an obligation in the amount stated in the order.

Id. at Vol. 11I, Ch. 8, para. 080703.

Of course, as with any other obligation, project orders must serve a bona fide need existing in the fiscal year in which issued; otherwise, a valid obligation is not created. When work does not commence until the fiscal year following the fiscal year in which the order was issued, the GOGO must commence work within 90 days of accepting the project order. If work does not commence within 90 days of acceptance, "the project order shall be returned by the performing activity for cancellation unless it is documented that the delay is unavoidable and could not have been foreseen at the time of project order acceptance and that documentation is retained for audit review." DoD Financial Management Regulation, Vol. 11A, Ch. 2, para. 020510B.

The rationale for this requirement is that if work commences more than 90 days after the order is accepted and there is no valid reason for the delay, the requirement does not appear to be a bona fide need of the year in which the order was issued. In such cases, the ordering agency should charge funds current when the work commences.

Discussion Problem 6-9

On September 29, a DoD agency issues a project order to a government-owned government-operated (GOGO) facility for equipment overhaul and maintenance. On September 30, the GOGO accepts the order. However, the GOGO does not commence performance until December 1. The fund certification officer, who has recently been reassigned from a job in which he worked exclusively with Economy Act orders, believes that the agency must deobligate the funds on the project order because work did not commence within the fiscal year in which the order was issued. Is deobligation required in this case?

The project order statute does not require the special determinations required for Economy Act orders, i.e., that the use of an interagency acquisition is in the best interest of the government and the supplies or services cannot be obtained as conveniently or economically by contracting directly with a private source. General Regulatory Guidance. DoD Financial Management Regulation, Vol. 11A, Ch. 2.

Examples of typical goods and services that DoD activities may order under the project order statute include: (1) production, maintenance, or overhaul of missiles and other weapons, vehicles, ammunition, clothing, and machinery, and other military supplies or equipment; (2) research, development, test, and evaluation; and (3) minor construction or maintenance of real property. However, DoD activities may not use the project order statute to order: (1) major construction; (2) education, training, subsistence, storage, printing, laundry, welfare, transportation, travel, or communications; or (3) any requirement where a contractual relationship cannot exist.

The Government Employees Training Act

Under the Government Employees Training Act (GETA), an agency covered by the act (as defined in 5 U.S.C. § 4101) can extend its training to employees of other government agencies. Since GETA provides independent fund transfer authority, the requirements and restrictions of the Economy Act are inapplicable. *Army Corps of Engineers - Disposition of Fees Received from Private Sector Participants in Training Courses*, B-271894, July 24, 1997 (unpub.); *To Walter L. Jordan*, B-241269, Feb. 28, 1991 (unpub.). The key statutory provision is 5 U.S.C. § 4104, which states:

> An agency program for the training of employees by, in, and through Government facilities under this chapter shall . . .
> (2) provide for the making by the agency, to the extent necessary and appropriate, of agreements with other agencies in any branch of the Government, on a reimbursable basis when requested by the other agencies, for—
> (A) use of Government facilities under the jurisdiction or control of the other agencies in any branch of the Government; and
> (B) extension to employees of the agency of training programs of other agencies.

The legislative history of this provision, discussed in B-193293, November 13, 1978, makes clear that training can be reimbursable or nonreimbursable, at the discretion of the agency providing it. This is different from the Economy Act, which requires that the ordering agency reimburse the performing agency its actual costs of performance. Thus, NASA may, at its discretion, make its procurement training courses available on a space-available and tuition-free basis to employees of civilian agencies. Id. An agency choosing to charge a fee for its training is equally free to do so and may credit fees received from other government agencies to the appropriation that financed the training. B-241269, February 28, 1991. However, an agency may not obtain reimbursement for training if funds are already provided for interagency training in its appropriation. This would be the case, for example, if it is the responsibility of the agency to provide interagency training. Charging and retaining fees under these circumstances would constitute an unauthorized augmentation of appropriations. Lastly, GETA does not authorize charging or retaining fees for training nongovernment personnel.

The Clinger-Cohen Act of 1996

Section 5112(e) of the FY 1996 National Defense Authorization Act (Pub. L. No. 104-106) (permanently codified at 40 U.S.C. § 1412(e)) instructed the Director of OMB to designate one or more heads of executive agencies as executive agent for government-wide acquisitions of information technology. To implement this requirement, OMB has designated GSA as the executive agent for certain government-wide acquisitions of information technology (IT).

The scope of the designation is limited to programs that are funded on a reimbursable basis through the Information Technology Fund established by 40 U.S.C. § 757. These programs include the Federal Systems Integration and Management Center (FEDSIM) and the Federal Computer Acquisition Center (FEDCAC), as well as other existing government-wide IT acquisition programs. The OMB designation, in combination with 40 U.S.C. § 757, provides separate authority for acquisition from these GSA programs and states in relevant part:

Sec. 757. Information Technology Fund
(1) There is established on the books of the Treasury an Information Technology Fund (hereinafter referred to as the "Fund"), which shall be available without fiscal year limitation.

Current issues with the Information Technology Fund involve the general requirement that orders represent a bona fide need of the ordering agency at the time the order is issued. Although the fund is, by statute, "available without fiscal year limitation," the appropriations of the *ordering* agencies remain subject to the periods of availability applicable to their respective appropriations. Thus, an ordering agency cannot cite expired funds on its order under FEDSIM or FEDCAC. See B-286929, April 25, 2001, in which GAO held: "as with other contractual obligations, once the agency liquidates the obligation, any remaining balances are not available to enter into a new obligation after the account has expired (i.e., if fiscal year funds, after the end of the fiscal year)."

Similarly, an agency cannot "park" or "dump" about-to-expire funds at the end of the fiscal year by issuing orders that do not state a specific and definite requirement. Such orders may not be sufficiently definite to satisfy the requirements for recording obligations. Section 1501 of Title 31 of the United States Code states the requirements for a valid obligation as follows:

31 U.S.C. 1501(a)(1)
(a) An amount shall be recorded as an obligation . . . only when supported by documentary evidence of -
(l) a binding agreement . . . that is–
(B) executed before the end of the period of availability
. . . for *specific* goods to be delivered

If an ordering agency issues a general order (e.g., "Provide 100 personal computers"), it may not satisfy the requirement for specificity. The consequence of failing to create a recordable obligation prior to the expiration of the funds cited would be that the funds would become unavailable at the end of the fiscal year and could not be thereafter used once the requirement becomes better defined.

> **Discussion Problem 6-10**
>
> On September 30, 2002, Agency ABC submits an order to GSA for "100 desktop computers" through the "Information Technology Fund." The ABC agency cites FY 2002 operation and maintenance funds. GSA accepts the order the same day. Two months later, ABC provides GSA with specific details and specifications, and GSA purchases the computers for ABC. Any problems here?

The Federal Property and Administrative Services Act of 1949

The Federal Property and Administrative Services Act (FPASA) authorizes GSA to "procure and supply personal property and nonpersonal services for the use of executive agencies in the proper discharge of their responsibilities." See 40 U.S.C. Sec. 481(a)(3) (1994). GSA manages the Federal Supply Schedule (FSS) program pursuant to the Section 201 of FPASA. The Federal Supply Schedule is referred to as the Multiple Award Schedule (MAS). The MAS provides federal agencies with a simplified process for obtaining commercial supplies and services at prices associated with volume buying. The FSS program provides over four million commercial off-the-shelf products and services, at stated prices, for given periods of time.

Interagency orders placed against the MAS are not subject to the procedures applicable to the Economy Act. Thus, for example, GAO will deny a protest based on an allegation that an agency failed to prepare the Determination and Findings required under the Economy Act when issuing an order under the MAS. Thus, in B-285451.3, October 25, 2000, GAO denied such a protest, reasoning:

> GSA has the authority to conduct this procurement to fulfill the Army's requirements under the Federal Prop-

erty and Administrative Services Act of 1949, under which GSA is authorized to "procure and supply personal property and nonpersonal services for the use of executive agencies in the proper discharge of their responsibilities. . . . We think this broad authority encompasses the requirement being procured here, so that the Economy Act is not applicable to this transaction.

See also, B-285164.2, August 31, 2000 (MAS order for travel services under FPASA is not subject to terms of the Economy Act).

The Tennessee Valley Authority

The Tennessee Valley Authority (TVA) is authorized to "provide and operate facilities for the generation of electric energy for the use of the United States or any agency thereof." 16 U.S.C. § 831h-1. Rates charged are calculated to produce sufficient revenue to cover the operation, maintenance, and administration of the power system, payments to states and counties in lieu of taxes, required payments to the United States Treasury, and commitments to bondholders. 16 U.S.C. § 831n-4(f). This is an example of a statute that is sufficiently specific and detailed to wholly displace the Economy Act. 44 Comp. Gen. 683 (1965). Since electric power is a utility service, GSA can, under 40 U.S.C. § 481(a)(3), contract with TVA for periods of up to 10 years and can delegate this authority to other agencies.

District of Columbia

Enacted as part of the 1973 District of Columbia home rule legislation, 31 U.S.C. § 1537 authorizes the United States government and the District of Columbia government to provide reimbursable services to each other. Services provided under this authority are to be documented in an agreement negotiated by the respective governments and approved by the Director of OMB and the Mayor of the District of Columbia. Subsection (c) of the legislation states:

(1) costs incurred by the United States Government may be paid from appropriations available to the District of Columbia government officer or employee to whom the services were provided; and
(2) costs incurred by the District of Columbia government may be paid from amounts available to the United States Government officer or employee to whom the services were provided.

Charges are to be "based on the actual cost of providing the services." 40 U.S.C. § 1537(b)(2). Under this authority, for example, the Bureau of Prisons could provide personnel to the District of Columbia Department of Corrections in the event of a strike by District employees. 4B Op. Off. Legal Counsel 826 (1980). Another example is printing done for the District of Columbia by GPO. 60 Comp. Gen. 710 (1981). That decision pointed out that, since the District is not a federal agency, the federal agency providing the services can charge interest on overdue accounts and can collect a debt by administrative offset, but not against amounts withheld from the salaries of federal employees for D.C. income tax.

National Academy of Sciences

A statute dating back to 1863 provides that the National Academy of Sciences (NAS) "shall, whenever called upon by any department of the Government, investigate, examine, experiment, and report upon any subject of science or art, the actual expense of such investigations, examinations, experiments, and reports, to be paid from appropriations which may be made for the purpose, but the academy shall receive no compensation whatever for any services to the Government of the United States." 36 U.S.C. § 253.

This statute authorizes NAS to be reimbursed for its "actual expenses," but nothing beyond that. A formal contract is not required, although the documentation used should adequately describe the services to be provided and the payment terms. B-37018, October 14, 1943. An agreement calling for a fixed price that is not limited to reimbursement of actual expenses has been found to violate the statute. B-4252, June 21, 1939. However, the Academy has been permitted to recover the excess where its actual expenses exceeded the fixed price. 39 Comp. Gen. 71 (1959), as modified by 39 Comp. Gen. 391 (1959).

GAO's suggestion is that the agreement should provide for the reimbursement of actual expenses up to a stipulated maximum, and should also provide that no costs be incurred above that amount unless authorized by some form of supplemental agreement. 39 Comp. Gen. at 392. A flat surcharge for overhead also violates the statute (because it is not based on actual expenses), but if the interagency work causes NAS to increase its normal overhead, the amount of the increase (or a reasonable approximation) constitutes part of the actual expenses. B-19556, August 28, 1941.

Cases like these do not stand for the proposition that NAS's cost recovery cannot be subjected to contractual limits. Thus, a 1977 decision held that NAS's recovery of independent research and development costs were limited by provisions in procurement regulations to which it had agreed to be bound. B-58911, August 1, 1977.

> Since Congress appropriates funds to specific agencies, any transfer of funds between federal agencies must be based on statutory authority. It does not matter that the transfer will save money or otherwise is the best course of action. Each of the major statutory authorities for interagency transactions is somewhat different. When an agency is contemplating an interagency transaction, it must ensure that it fully complies with the unique requirements that are applicable to the statutory authority being relied upon.

CHAPTER 7
Funding Gaps and Continuing Resolution Authority

For the most part, we have thus far addressed fiscal law within the context of regularly enacted appropriations acts. However, Congress does not always complete action on all appropriations bills by the start of the fiscal year. (See Table 1 in Attachment 7-1 at the end of this chapter.) In these situations, one or more agencies may have to conduct operations under a temporary appropriation referred to as a "continuing resolution." On occasion Congress has not been able to pass a continuing resolution *or* a regular appropriations act. When this happens, a funding gap exists, and most agencies are required to curtail their operations significantly or even shut down completely. This chapter will discuss the unique and special rules that apply when an agency must operate under either a funding gap or a continuing resolution.

FUNDING GAPS

The term "funding gap" refers to a period of time between the expiration or exhaustion of an appropriation and the enactment of a new one. Since an agency is without annual budget authority during a funding gap, significant questions arise regarding what an agency may and may not do during this period. Funding gaps occur most commonly at the end of a fiscal year when new appropriations (or a continuing resolution) have not yet been enacted. In this context, a gap may affect only a few agencies (if, for example, only one appropriation act remains unenacted as of October 1) or the entire federal government. A funding gap may also occur if a particular appropriation becomes exhausted before the end of the fiscal year, in which case it may affect only a single agency or a single program, depending on the scope of the appropriation. Attachment 1 to this chapter is a report prepared by the Congressional Research Service, entitled *Preventing Federal Government Shutdowns: Proposals for an Automatic Continuing Resolution* (October 18, 1999). Table 1 illustrates the number and duration of funding gaps between 1977 and 1999.

A funding gap may occur under two circumstances. First, as noted, a funding gap will result if Congress fails to pass either an appropriations act or a continuing resolution. A funding gap will also result if the President vetoes an appropriations act or a continuing resolution. See General Accounting Office, *Principles of Federal Appropriations Law*, 2d ed., GAO/OGC 91-5 (July 1991), at pp. 6-92 thru 6-99. In either case, the result is the same: One or more federal agencies will not have budget authority to conduct operations.

In the absence of annual budget authority, as during a funding gap, an agency generally may not incur new obligations. Although there are some limited exceptions to this rule, most agency operations must be reduced during a funding gap.

Legal Framework for Agency Operations during a Funding Gap

Most of the legal analysis pertaining to agency operations during a funding gap can be traced back to 1980. In that year, President Jimmy Carter requested a legal opinion from the Attorney General, Mr. Benjamin Civiletti, as to whether an agency may lawfully permit its employees to continue work after the expiration of the agency's appropriation for the prior fiscal year and prior to any appropriation for the current fiscal year. Although the legal opinion provided in response to the President's question was quite restrictive, subsequent legal opinions have interpreted and, in general, mitigated the harsh effects of a literal interpretation of the 1980 opinion. In addition, Comptroller General opinions, as well as guidance issued by OMB, have contributed to the body of law and policy that must be considered in assessing what an agency can and cannot do during a funding gap.

The 1980 Attorney General Opinion

In response to President Carter's inquiry in anticipation of a funding gap at the start of fiscal year 1981, the Attorney General responded by stating that:

> It is my opinion that, during periods of "lapsed appropriations," no funds may be expended except as necessary to bring about the orderly termination of an agency's functions, and that the obligation or expenditure of funds for any purpose not otherwise authorized by law would be a violation of the Antideficiency Act.

43 U.S. Op. Atty. Gen. No., 43 U.S. Op. Atty. Gen. No. 24, 4A U.S. Op. Off. Legal Counsel 16.

The Attorney General opinion went on to state:

> It follows first of all that, on a lapse in appropriations, federal agencies may incur no obligations that cannot lawfully be funded from prior appropriations unless such obligations are otherwise authorized by law. There are no exceptions to this rule under current law, even where obligations incurred earlier would avoid greater costs to the agencies should appropriations later be enacted. Second, the Department of Justice will take actions to enforce the criminal provisions of the Act in appropriate cases in the future when violations of the Antideficiency Act are alleged.

Although the Attorney General opinion clearly prohibited agencies from creating new obligations in advance of the enactment of the appropriation to be charged, it also indicated two situations in which an agency may lawfully continue operations and incur obligations. First, the opinion recognized that an agency may incur obligations that will be funded from a prior multiple-year appropriation, if that appropriation is still available for obligation and has a sufficient unobligated balance to cover the obligation.

For example, assume that, on October 1, 2001, an agency received a two-year appropriation to conduct research and development (an FY02 appropriation). Assume further that, on October 1, 2002, Congress had not enacted a new appropriation or continuing resolution. If an unobligated balance remained in the FY 2002 appropriation, the agency could use those funds to incur new obligations in FY 2003, since the appropriation is available for obligation throughout fiscal years 2002–2003.

Agency regulations may not permit obligating funds after their first year of availability, even though Congress authorized the agency to incur obligations at any time during the appropriation's period of availability. This situation illustrates the difference between fiscal law and fiscal policy. In matters of fiscal policy, an official within the agency may generally grant a waiver. In a contract, because of the constitutional separation of powers doctrine, an agency official could not waive a statutory restriction unless Congress specifically granted waiver authority to the agency.

Second, an agency may continue operations and incur obligations during a funding gap if "otherwise authorized by law." As will be discussed, several statutes and constitutional provisions authorize executive branch agencies to perform certain activities. These exceptions must be viewed within the context of the general requirements addressed in the Attorney General's opinion, which greatly restrict what an agency can lawfully do during a period of lapsed appropriations.

The 1980 Comptroller General Opinion

The limited nature of an agency's operations during a period of lapsed appropriations was also emphasized in a Comptroller General opinion issued shortly before the 1980 Attorney General opinion, B-197841, March 3, 1980. In the GAO opinion, the Comptroller General stated:

[I]t is our opinion that any supervisory officer or employee, including the head of an agency, who directs or permits agency employees to work during any period for which the Congress has not enacted an appropriation for the pay of these employees violates the antideficiency act. . . . In the absence of express statutory authority to the contrary, we have held that unless there is an agreement in writing that the person rendering the services does so gratuitously (a term not necessarily synonymous with "voluntarily") with no expectation of ever being paid, acceptance of such services is a violation of [31 U.S.C. § 1342]. See 26 Comp. Gen. 956 (1947); 7 Comp. Gen. 810, 811 (1928). . . . During a period of expired appropriations, the only way the head of an agency can avoid violating the antideficiency act is to suspend the operations of the agency and instruct employees not to report to work until an appropriation is enacted.

Opinion of the Attorney General, Apr. 25, 1980.

The underlying rationale for the Comptroller's General's opinion is that any government official who allows a government employee to work during a period of lapsed appropriations violates the prohibition against acceptance of voluntary services (31 U.S.C. § 1342) as well as the prohibition against incurring obligations in advance of appropriations (31 U.S.C. § 1341(a)(1)(B)).

The 1995 Attorney General Opinion

In anticipation of a potential funding gap, the Clinton Administration requested updated guidance from the Attorney General on the scope of permissible government activity during a funding gap. In response, the Department of Justice issued what is known as the "Dellinger Memo," which reemphasized the restricted level of allowable government activity. However, the memo mitigated the harsh effects of a literal interpretation of the 1980 Attorney General opinion and noted that a lapse in appropriations would not result in a total "government shut-down." DOJ Memorandum for Alice Rivlin, Office of Management and Budget, Aug. 16,

1995. The 1995 opinion then went on to identify several aspects of government operations that would not have to be terminated during a funding gap:

Multi-Year Appropriations and Indefinite Appropriations. The 1995 Attorney General opinion recognized that a funding gap primarily affects those agency operations that are funded with annual appropriations. However, not all government functions are funded with annual appropriations. Some operate under multi-year appropriations and others operate under indefinite appropriations provisions that do not require passage of annual appropriations legislation.

Social security is a prominent example of a program that operates under an indefinite appropriation. In such cases, benefit checks continue to be honored by the Treasury, because there is no lapse in the relevant appropriation. Similarly, operations funded by no-year appropriations, which are available until expended without any limitation as to time, would not be directly affected by a funding gap.

Thus, if Congress has not enacted an agency's appropriations act as of October 1, 2002, the agency could lawfully continue activities that are funded by multi-year appropriations, no-year appropriations, permanent indefinite appropriations, or revolving funds (i.e., working capital funds). Of course, the fund source would have to have a sufficient unobligated balance to cover the anticipated obligation(s).

Contracting Authority and Borrowing Authority. Congress often expressly authorizes agencies to enter into contracts or borrow funds to accomplish some of their functions. Contract authority (discussed in Chapter 1) permits an agency to incur obligations in advance of the enactment of the appropriation that will eventually be used to liquidate the obligation. However, the agency may not make expenditures until Congress has passed and the President has signed the appropriations act.

An example of contract authority is the "food and forage" authority given to the Department of Defense and the Department of Transportation, which authorizes contracting for necessary "clothing, subsistence, forage, fuel, quarters, transportation, or medical and hospital supplies, which, however, shall not exceed the necessities of the current year." 41 U.S.C. § 11(a). In such cases, the agency may obligate funds for the specified purposes, even though there is no appropriation available, because the Antideficiency Act does not bar such activities when they are authorized by law.

Contract authority must be specific, and the mere authorization or even direction to perform a certain action that is referenced in an agency's enabling legislation is insufficient to provide contract authority. In other words, there must be some additional indication of an evident intention to have the activity continue despite an appropriation lapse.

Discussion Problem 7-1

The Defense Operational Testing Agency (DOTA) receives annual appropriations to fulfill its mission to "test and evaluate state-of-the-art weapons systems to ensure maximum operational availability for the warfighters." Assume that on October 1, 2001, Congress has not enacted the agency's appropriation and it does not seem likely that the appropriation will be enacted within the next few weeks. DOTA is scheduled to test the Navy's new stealthy "invisible hull" submarine on October 10.

DOTA determines that it is essential to conduct the test on schedule, because a slip in schedule will impact a big naval exercise in early spring 2002. While DOTA is trying to figure out a way to conduct the test on schedule, the agency civil engineer discovers that the temporary quarters housing the visiting test personnel (also DOTA employees) has suffered a burst water pipe, which has caused flooding and made several rooms uninhabitable. Thus, DOTA needs funding to: (1) conduct the test on October 15; (2) repair the damaged pipe and related damage to the quarters; and (3) find temporary alternate quarters for the visiting test personnel. Which, if any, of these requirements may DOTA contract for prior to enactment of its FY 2002 appropriation?

Authority to Obligate That Is Necessarily Implied by Statute. The 1995 Attorney General opinion noted that a limited number of government functions funded through annual appropriations must continue despite a funding gap because the lawful continuation of other activities necessarily implies that these functions will continue as well. The 1995 opinion specifically identified the following examples:

> Examples include the check writing and distributing functions necessary to disburse the social security benefits that operate under indefinite appropriation. Further examples include contracting for materials essential to the performance of the emergency services that continue under that separate exception. In addition, in a 1980 opinion, Attorney General Civiletti opined that agencies are by necessary implication authorized "to incur those minimal obligations necessary to closing [the] agency."

Most agencies rely on annual appropriations to conduct their daily operations, typically a "salary and expense" or "operations and maintenance" type of appropriation. These types of appropriations are generally used to pay employee salaries. The 1995 Attorney General opinion would allow agency employees to work if such work is directly related to a function that is authorized to continue, even though Congress has not yet enacted the annual appropriation that would eventually be used to pay the employees' salaries.

Although not specifically identified as one of the examples in the 1995 opinion, the rationale used to support those examples could be applied in many other situations. The rationale for allowing the continuation of functions funded through annual appropriations was that "the lawful continuation of other activities necessarily implies that these functions will continue as well." As noted, activities that are funded by multi-year, indefinite year, or no-year appropriations, or working capital funds, may continue notwithstanding a lapse in the availability of annual appropriations. Since many of these functions would be administered by government personnel whose salaries are funded through annual appropriations, it would seem that application of the "necessary implication" rationale would authorize allowing government employees to support functions that are otherwise authorized to continue.

For example, assume that an agency receives no-year funds to conduct research and development and uses these funds to award several incrementally funded multi-year research contracts. At the start of each fiscal year, the agency allots an amount to these contracts from the no-year appropriation. If Congress fails to enact annual appropriations by the start of the fiscal year, these contracts could continue, since the no-year appropriation provides the necessary budget authority. However, the administration of the contracts would generally require work by annually funded government employees, such as a government contracting officer, one or more program managers and technical support personnel, disbursement personnel, and anyone else whose services are essential to the lawful administration of the contracts. Although the salaries of these government employees would most likely be paid from annual appropriations, it would seem that the authority for their continued services is "necessarily implied" because of their essential role in the administration of contracts that may lawfully continue during the lapse of annual appropriations.

The "necessarily implied" authority may also apply in the context of revolving fund activities. A revolving fund activity is authorized to generate and retain funds earned through its activities. Often referred to as working capital funds, there are many such funds throughout the government. For example, within DoD, the Transportation Working Capital Fund (TWCF) provides transportation services for DoD customers for a fee. These fees are retained and may be used for purposes reasonably related to supporting the TWCF mission. Since revolving fund activities are generally not dependent on annual appropriations, a lapse in annual appropriations will generally not have a direct effect on operations (although an indirect effect may be that income falls during the lapse because the customers may depend on annual appropriations). If a revolving fund activity requires support from government employees whose salaries are paid from annual appropriations, the authority for their performance during a funding gap may be necessarily implied by their relationship to the revolving fund activity.

There are no doubt many other similar examples. The relevant point is that, if an activity may lawfully continue during a lapse in annual appropriations and if certain government personnel are essential to the continuation of that activity, then an agency could determine that its employees may lawfully perform services in support of the activity even though the appropriation from which they will be paid is not available for obligation at the time the services are rendered. Similarly, the agency should also be permitted, under the rationale of the 1995 opinion, to award services contracts deemed necessary to support continuation of any activity that lawfully may continue.

For example, assume that an agency has historically awarded a contract on October 1 for services to support a working capital fund activity. Since the working capital fund activity is not dependent on enactment of an appropriation, it may lawfully continue. The agency should be able to lawfully incur obligations, under the "necessarily implied" rationale of the 1995 opinion, for continued contractor support of the working capital fund activity. Of course, during a lapse of appropriations, each agency must establish its own response plan, and that plan must be consistent with the law and other applicable directives, such as those typically issued by OMB in anticipation of a funding gap.

Discussion Problem 7-2

Each year an agency receives two appropriations. One is a "salary and expense" appropriation with a one-year period of availability; the other is a "program" appropriation that funds specific major agency programs and has a three-year period of availability. One of the programs funded under the program appropriation is the production of ten communications satellites. Assume that it is October 1 and Congress has not yet enacted an appropriations act or continuing resolution. However, the agency has a sufficient unobligated balance in its program appropriations from the last two fiscal years to enable it to continue activity on its communications satellite program.

Can the agency apply the unobligated balances of its program appropriation to continue work on the program in the absence of a new appropriation? How can the agency manage the work on the program prior to the enactment of its annual salary and expense appropriation?

Obligations Necessary to the Discharge of the President's Constitutional Duties and Powers. The United States Constitution vests in the President of the United States certain exclusive duties and powers. Although the 1995 Attorney General opinion does not identify any such duties and powers, the Constitution describes several of these duties and powers as follows:

> Clause 2: He shall have Power, by and with the Advice and Consent of the Senate, to make Treaties, provided two thirds of the Senators present concur; and he shall nominate, and by and with the Advice and Consent of the Senate, shall appoint Ambassadors, other public Ministers and Consuls, Judges of the Supreme Court, and all other Officers of the United States, whose Appointments are not herein otherwise provided for, and which shall be established by Law: but the Congress may by Law vest the Appointment of such inferior Officers, as they think proper, in the President alone, in the Courts of Law, or in the Heads of Departments.

In considering the effect of a funding gap on the exercise of the President's constitutional duties and powers, the 1995 Attorney General opinion stated:

> Efforts should be made to interpret a general statute such as the Antideficiency Act to avoid the significant constitutional questions that would arise were the Act read to critically impair the exercise of constitutional functions assigned to the executive. In this regard, [a prior Attorney General] Opinion noted that when dealing with the functions instrumental in the discharge of the President's constitutional powers, the "President's obligational authority . . . will be further buttressed in connection with any initiative that is consistent with statutes . . . that are more narrowly drawn than the Antideficiency Act and that would otherwise authorize the President to carry out his constitutionally assigned tasks in the manner he contemplates.

Thus, if a specific statute addresses the discharge of the President's constitutional duties or powers, then a statute of general application, such as the Antideficiency Act, should not be interpreted to limit the discharge of the duties or the exercise of the powers, even during a funding gap.

Constitutionally mandated activities of the other branches of government may also be authorized. See, e.g., *Armster v. United States District Court*, 792 F.2d 1423 (9th Cir. 1986) (suspension of jury trials for more than the "most minimal" time would violate the 7th Amendment; note that the court did not specifically say that incurring an obligation to pay jurors would not violate the Antideficiency Act).

Personal or Voluntary Services For Emergencies Involving the Safety of Human Life or the Protection of Property. One of the sections of the Antideficiency Act, specifically 31 U.S.C.§ 1342, states that:

> An officer or employee of the United States Government or of the District of Columbia government may not accept voluntary services for either government or employ personal services exceeding that authorized by law ex-

cept for emergencies involving the safety of human life or the protection of property. This section does not apply to a corporation getting amounts to make loans (except paid in capital amounts) without legal liability of the United States Government. *As used in this section, the term "emergencies involving the safety of human life or the protection of property" does not include ongoing, regular functions of the government the suspension of which would not imminently threaten the safety of human life or the protection of property* (emphasis added).

The italicized text was added by amendment in 1990, apparently to emphasize that, during a period of lapsed appropriations, agencies may not simply continue their normal level of activity through blanket application of the emergency exception. Thus, the amendment specifically excluded "ongoing, regular functions of the government" from the emergency exception.

Interpretations of this law have significantly impacted agency operations during periods of lapsed appropriations. Since the salaries of most government employees are paid from annual appropriations, if such employees perform their jobs during a funding gap, they are essentially serving as "volunteers," and the government would be employing "personal services exceeding that authorized by law." (As noted, employees whose salaries are funded from annual appropriations may perform their duties in support of activities and programs that may lawfully continue during a period of lapsed appropriations. This is an exception that is distinct and separate from the emergency exception to the voluntary services prohibition of 31 U.S.C. § 1342.)

The major exception states that the limitation does not apply during "emergencies involving the safety of human life or the protection of property." Thus, during a period of lapsed appropriations, a government employee may perform duties that, in some way, protect life or property during an emergency. This broad wording of the statute left agencies much room for interpretation.

In response to what the Attorney General perceived to be overly broad interpretations, he wrote in his 1995 opinion:

> Under the formulation of the 1981 [Attorney General] Opinion, government functions satisfy § 1342 if . . . the safety of human life or the protection of property would be "compromised, in some degree." It is conceivable that some would interpret this phrase to be satisfied even if the threat were de minimis, in the sense that the increased risk to life or property were insignificant, so long as it were possible to say that safety of life or protection of property bore a reasonable likelihood of being compromised at all. This would be too expansive an application of the emergency provision. The brief delay of routine maintenance on government vehicles ought not to constitute an "emergency," for example, and yet it is quite possible to conclude that the failure to maintain vehicles properly may "compromise, to some degree" the safety of the human life of the occupants or the protection of the vehicles, which are government property. We believe that the revised articulation clarifies that the emergencies exception applies only to cases of threat to human life or property where the threat can be reasonably said to [be]. . . near at hand and demanding of immediate response.

Although the 1995 opinion stresses that the emergency exception would only apply when the danger to life or property is real and imminent, there is still much room for interpretation. At one end of the spectrum would be firefighters, police officers, and air traffic controllers, all of whom are involved on a daily basis in the protection of life or property. At the other end of the spectrum are administrative support personnel at agencies that are not directly involved in the protection of life or property, e.g., the Library of Congress or the Bureau of Public Debt. In between these two extremes are innumerable government employee positions that allow for the exercise of agency discretion.

During the FY 1996 funding gap, for example, OMB required agencies to categorize their personnel as either "essential" or "non-essential." Non-essential employees were prohibited from performing their government jobs during the funding gap, while essential government employees were required to report to work. This is still an evolving area of the law and one in which agencies must necessarily retain the discretion to identify which positions qualify for the emergency exception.

Discussion Problem 7-3

The Air Force operates an installation responsible for acquiring and testing aircraft engines. The installation employs 1,000 people. If there was a funding gap, which of the following categories of workers would be likely to satisfy the "emergency" exception?
  1. Custodial workers involved in routine cleaning duties
  2. Security personnel assigned to guard the highly classified $10 million engines
  3. Personnel clerk assigned to perform quality assurance of performance appraisals
  4. On-site nurse to provide immediate medical care in case of accidents during the more hazardous phases of testing
  5. Golf course groundskeeper.

OMB Bulletin No. 80-14

OMB has issued guidance concerning actions that agencies must take during funding gaps. On August 28, 1980, OMB issued OMB Bulletin No. 80-14, *Shutdown of Agency Operations Upon Failure by the Congress to Enact Appropriations*. The OMB bulletin requires all federal agencies to develop contingency plans to conduct an orderly shutdown of operations. In response to this requirement, when a funding gap is anticipated, agency comptrollers will generally issue guidance to the various agency subdivisions on how to plan for the "orderly shutdown" of operations and how to identify whether an exception applies to any particular office functions.

The OMB bulletin is consistent with the Comptroller General decision and the Attorney General opinions in that they all require some sort of shutdown of agency operations during a period of lapsed appropriations, unless there is a specific exception. The OMB bulletin also recognizes that agencies may continue to incur obligations (e.g., award contracts) to continue activities during a funding gap if the obligations: are otherwise authorized by law (e.g., activities funded with multi-year or no-year appropriations); are authorized through specifically granted contract authority (e.g., 41 U.S.C § 11, Feed and Forage Act); protect life and property in an emergency situation (e.g., 31 U.S.C. § 1342); or are necessary to begin phase-down of other activities.

Problems Associated with Operating during a Funding Gap

Thus, a number of exceptions to the Antideficiency Act permit certain activities to continue during a funding gap. However, for activities not covered by any of the exceptions, the agency must proceed with prompt and orderly shutdown of its operations or violate the act and risk invocation of the criminal sanctions.

Within this legal framework, GAO and the Justice Department have addressed a number of specific problems that agencies have encountered when operating during a funding gap. For example, toward the end of FY 1982, the President vetoed a supplemental appropriations bill. As a result, the Defense Department did not have sufficient funds to meet the military payroll. The total payroll obligation consisted of (1) the take-home pay of the individuals, and (2) various items the employing agency was required to withhold and transfer to someone else, such as federal income tax and Social Security contributions. The Treasury Department published a change to its regulations permitting a temporary deferral of the due date for payment of the withheld items, and the Defense Department, relying on the "safety of human life or protection of property" exception, used the funds that had thereby become available to pay military personnel their full take-home pay. The Attorney General upheld the legality of this action. 6 Op. Off. Legal Counsel 27 (1982).

The Comptroller General agreed, but questioned the blanket assumption that all military personnel fit within the emergency exception. B-208985, October 5, 1982; B-208951, October 5, 1982. The extent to which this same rationale might be available to non-DoD agencies would depend on (1) Treasury's willingness to grant a similar deferral, and (2) the extent to which the agency could legitimately invoke the emergency exception.

Over the years, GAO has issued several reports on funding gaps. The first was titled *Funding Gaps Jeopardize Federal Government Operations*, PAD-81-31 (March 3, 1981). In that report, GAO noted the costly and disruptive effects of funding gaps and recommended the enactment of permanent legislation to permit federal agencies to incur obligations, but not disburse funds, during a funding gap.

In the second report, *Continuing Resolutions and an Assessment of Automatic Funding Approaches*, GAO/AFMD-86-1 6 (January 1986), GAO compared several possible options, including the automatic availability of budget authority to the extent that regular appropriations or a continuing resolution had not been enacted. OMB had pointed out, and GAO agreed, that automatic funding legislation could have the undesirable effects of (1) reducing pressure on Congress to make timely funding decisions, and (2) permitting major portions of the government to operate for extended periods without action by either house of Congress or the President. See also *Considerations for Updating the Budget Enforcement Act*, GAO-01-99IT (July 19, 2001).

As noted in *Principles of Federal Appropriations Law*, GAO/OGC-92-13, p. 6-99, after the comments received by OMB to its 1986 report, GAO continued to support the concept of an automatic continuing resolution, but in a form that does not reduce the incentive to complete action on the regular appropriation bills. See, e.g., *Managing the Cost of Government: Proposals for Reforming Federal Budgeting Practices*, GAO/AFMD-90-1 (October 1989) at 28-29. A 1991 report analyzed the impact of a funding gap that occurred over the 1990 Columbus Day weekend and again renewed the recommendation for permanent legislation to, at a minimum, allow agencies to incur obligations to compensate employees during temporary funding gaps but not pay them until enactment of the appropriation. *Government Shutdown: Permanent Funding Lapse Legislation Needed*, GAO/GGD-91-76 (June 1991). The report stated:

> In our opinion, shutting down the government during temporary funding gaps is an inappropriate way to encourage compromise on the budget. Beyond being counterproductive from a financial standpoint, a shutdown disrupts government services. In addition, forcing agency managers to choose who will and will not be furloughed during these temporary funding lapses severely tests agency management's ability to treat its employees fairly. Id. at 9.

To date, Congress has not enacted legislation that would provide for an automatic continuing resolution. Consequently, the potential for funding gaps remains, and federal agencies, as well as government contractors, must be familiar with the rules applicable during such periods.

Permissible Activities during a Funding Gap

The various activities that may continue during a funding gap must be analyzed together in the event of an actual funding gap. Typically, an agency will be able to combine several exceptions and thereby continue to perform its core mission. Thus, although each agency will develop its own contingency plan in anticipation of a funding gap, several general categories of operations could continue.

For example, during a funding gap, national security activities may continue based on the President's constitutional power to conduct foreign policy and serve as Commander in Chief of the Armed Forces. Under this authority (as well as several specific statutes in Title 10 of the United States Code), agencies may support deployments, contingency operations, and wars, notwithstanding a lapse in appropriations. Similarly, both strategic and tactical intelligence-gathering activities in support of national security could continue. For example, a funding gap should not result in the cessation of activities in support of the launch and operation of reconnaissance satellites, nor in the receipt and processing of the data they produce.

Another general category of activities that may continue during a funding gap would be payments and the performance of contract obligations under no-year and multi-year authority or expenditures from other funds still available for those purposes. As discussed, an agency may incur obligations against multi-year or no-year appropriations even during a lapse in annual appropriations, since the multi-year and no-year appropriations provide budget authority that is independent of the enactment of annual appropriations. This same rule would apply to revolving fund activities for the same reason. Under the "necessarily implied" authority referenced in the 1995 Attorney General opinion, personnel essential to the administration of these lawfully created obligations would be authorized to perform their government duties, even during a funding gap.

There is one other category of contracts that would also seem to qualify for this exception. As noted in Chapter 4, an agency may award a services contract in one fiscal year that crosses into the subsequent fiscal year in at least two situations. One situation involves contracts for nonseverable services, and the other involves severable contracts with a period of performance up to 12 months. In both of these situations, the agency fully funds the contract with funds current when the obligation is created. Since these contracts are fully funded, they are not dependent on the enactment of annual appropriations and may lawfully continue into the subsequent fiscal year. Just as in the situations in which multi-year, no-year, or revolving funds are used, personnel essential to the administration of these lawfully created obligations are authorized to perform their government duties, even during a funding gap.

Finally, an agency may continue activities considered essential to the protection of life and property (31 U.S.C. §

1342). Such activities include: the medical care of inpatients and emergency outpatient care; activities essential to ensuring continued public health and safety, including safe use of food, drugs, and hazardous materials; border and coastal protection and surveillance; protection of federal lands, buildings, waterways, equipment, and other government property; care of prisoners and other persons in the custody of the United States; law enforcement and criminal investigations; emergency and disaster assistance; activities essential to the preservation of the essential elements of the money and banking system of the United States, including borrowing and tax collection activities of the Treasury; activities that ensure production of power and maintenance of the power distribution system; and activities necessary to maintain government-owned research property.

In these general categories of activities, agencies will identify specific activities within their areas of responsibility that may continue during a funding gap. This determination is generally made during the development of the contingency plan required by OMB Bulletin 80-14. For example, in September 1995, DoD issued detailed guidance addressing what activities the military departments and other DoD agencies could perform during a funding gap.

Among the activities deemed exempt from a government suspension or shut-down are: units and the administrative, logistical, and maintenance functions required in support of major contingency tasking; units and personnel supporting ongoing international treaties, commitments, essential peacetime engagement, and counter-drug operations; units and personnel preparing for or participating in operational exercises; functions or activities necessary to protect life and property or to respond to emergencies (including fire protection, physical security, law enforcement, air traffic control and harbor control, utilities, housing and food services for military personnel, trash removal, and food supply and service inspections); educational activities deemed necessary for immediate support of permissible activities; educational activities not otherwise allowed if undertaken by active duty military personnel for other active military personnel only;

negotiation, preparation, execution, and administration of new/existing contracts for permissible activities/functions; litigation activities associated with imminent legal action, only so long as courts and administrative boards remain in session; legal support for any permitted activities; and child care activities.

This list illustrates the extensive planning and analysis that an agency must perform when planning for a funding gap. It also illustrates that it is impossible to establish specific government-wide direction regarding which activities may or may not continue during a funding gap. Consequently, it is important that agency personnel, as well as contractors working with government agencies, be aware of the policies and guidance implemented by their respective agencies, since there will certainly be variations on the level of authorized activity based on the mission of the agency and the interpretive latitude exercised.

Impact of Funding Gaps on Agency Operations

Planning for and working during a funding gap can significantly impair the efficiency of agency operations. For example, in 1995, I was teaching a contracting procedures class to mostly government personnel. Although the class was only four days long, it crossed over into fiscal 1996, which many readers may recall was the year of one of the longest fund gaps in history for many agencies. On the morning of October 1, the 30-person class had been reduced to a five-person class, as most agencies recalled their personnel when it was certain that a funding gap existed.

The agencies had already paid for the class with FY 1995 funds, even though the class crossed over into FY 1996. This is authorized because the agencies had a bona fide need for the class when they contracted for it, and the class was nonseverable in nature. As discussed in Chapter 4, an agency may fully fund nonseverable services contracts with funds current when the obligation is created, even if some of the services are performed in the subsequent fiscal year. It would seem that, since the class was already fully paid for, then the lapse of FY 1996 appropriations should not have required the return of the students. However, it was not the class tuition that demanded this result, but the salaries of the government employees, which were funded from the unenacted annual appropriations bills. The effect of this difference was that the agency paid for the class, but the students could not attend it in its entirety because of the funding gap.

This result was required (at least for the DoD attendees) by the following paragraph of the DoD Financial Management Regulation:

> 020601. Split Year Funding. In the event of a trip that is initiated using currently available fiscal year funding, but which requires new fiscal year funding to continue or complete the travel, the traveler shall return to his or her official duty station if no appropriation act has been signed or no continuing resolution has been passed to make available new fiscal year funds. Expenses incurred in returning to the traveler's duty station will be posted in the new fiscal year as necessary costs to close down operations.

DoD Financial Management Regulation, Vol. 9, Ch. 2 para. 020601.

This is but one real-life example of the many types of inefficiencies that result when agencies must operate during a lapse in annual appropriations.

A closely related problem involves the planning process that is required when a funding gap is anticipated. Toward the end of the fiscal year, federal agency comptrollers and legislative liaison personnel closely monitor the progress of their appropriations bills and continuing resolutions. Nevertheless, this is a highly political process with many competing interests, and agencies generally cannot predict whether a funding gap will occur or estimate its duration. Consequently, it is difficult for agencies to plan for such gaps.

Similarly, if a funding gap does materialize, agencies must implement their shutdown plans. During this period, there are always questions regarding which activities must continue and which must be curtailed. Although during the planning process agencies are required to be restrictive (see, e.g., discussion of OMB Bulletin 80-14), during the actual implementation, mission requirements often result in a more expansive view of which activities may continue.

Agencies may actually be encouraged to take this more expansive view by the ratification language that is typically included in the appropriations acts or continuing resolutions that follow a funding gap. For example, the FY 1994 DoD Appropriations Act contained the following statement: "All obligations incurred in anticipation of this Act are hereby ratified and confirmed if otherwise in accordance with this Act." Department of Defense Appropriations Act, 1993, § 9049, Pub. L. No. 102-396, 106 Stat. 1876. Similarly, the first fiscal year 1980 continuing resolution, Public Law 96-86, provided as follows in section 117: "All obligations incurred in anticipation of the appropriations and authority provided in this joint resolution are hereby ratified and confirmed if otherwise in accordance with the provisions of the joint resolution." Since an obligation that is authorized does not have to be ratified, this language would seem to apply principally to obligations incurred during a funding gap that are not clearly authorized. This recurring ratification language may, therefore, encourages agencies to take a more expansive view of which activities should continue during a funding gap, since Congress has historically ratified obligations incurred during that period.

There are various other indications that Congress does not intend for the government to simply shut down during a funding gap. The Comptroller General, in B-197841, March 3, 1980, stated:

> However, we do not believe that the congress intends that federal agencies be closed during periods of expired appropriations. For example, at the start of the period of expired appropriations at the beginning of the current fiscal year, Senator Magnuson, the chairman of the senate committee on appropriations, cited with approval a memorandum to employees from GAO's Director of General Services and Controller. Senator Magnuson re-

quested that the memorandum be printed in the congressional record as a guide to other agencies. The memorandum began as follows:

> Even though Congress has not yet passed an FY 1980 GAO appropriation or continuing resolution, we do not believe that it is the intent of congress that GAO close down until an appropriate measure has been passed. (125 Cong. Rec. 13784 (daily ed., October 1, 1979)).
>
> It thus appears that the congress expects that the various agencies of the government will continue to operate and incur obligations during a period of expired appropriations.

Similarly, GAO, in its authoritative *Principles of Federal Appropriations Law*, 2d ed., GAO/OGC 91-5 (July 1991), stated: "Whatever might be the cause of a particular funding gap, it seem[s] clear that it was not the intent of Congress that the federal government simply shut down." See p. 6-93.

This situation leaves agencies in a dilemma. On the one hand, agencies must prepare and implement a contingency plan that provides for at least a partial shutdown of their operations. On the other hand, the uncertain nature of a funding gap, both in terms of the probability of its occurrence and its duration, make it reasonable for an agency to take a wait-and-see approach to the problem before commencing a large-scale shutdown. This latter approach may actually be encouraged by the ratification language that typically appears in appropriations acts and continuing resolutions that follow a period of lapsed appropriations.

Perhaps the best that agencies can do in such an uncertain situation it to carefully analyze their functions and prepare written determinations to support decisions regarding which activities may continue. The determinations must be in accordance with OMB guidance, opinions of the Attorney General and GAO, and internal agency instructions.

Forunately, funding gaps of more than a few days' duration are rare occurrences. However, this means that agencies must develop unique responses when they occur, which has resulted in a documented loss of efficiency. See General Accounting Office, *Government Shutdown: Permanent Funding Lapse Legislation Needed*, GAO/GGD-91-76, B-241730, June 6, 1991; General Accounting Office, *Funding Gaps Jeopardize Federal Government Operations*, No. PAD-81-31, Mar. 3, 1981.

Finally, to assess whether a funding gap is likely, agency personnel can check on the status of their agency's appropriations act by checking the Thomas Register website at: http://thomas.loc.gov/home/approp/app03.html.

CONTINUING RESOLUTIONS

Since a funding gap results when Congress has been unable to pass all of the appropriations bills by the start of the fiscal year, it is not uncommon for Congress to agree to a continuing resolution while action continues on the appropriations bills. A continuing resolution is a temporary appropriation intended to serve as an interim measure to keep existing federal programs functioning after the expiration of previous budget authority and until regular appropriations acts are enacted. Congress resorts to the continuing resolution when there is no regular appropriation for an agency or program. This situation may arise for various reasons, for example, because the two houses are unable to agree on common language, authorizing legislation has not yet been enacted, or the President has vetoed an appropriation act passed by Congress. 58 Comp. Gen. 530, 532 (1979).

When Congress enacts the typical (i.e., temporary) continuing resolution, it is clear that Congress intends and expects that the normal authorization and appropriation process will eventually produce appropriation acts that will replace or terminate the budget authority provided by the continuing resolution. Thus, the typical continuing resolution will state that funds appropriated for an activity by the resolution will no longer be available for obligation if the activity is later funded by a regular appropriation act or if Congress indicates its intent to end the activity by enacting an applicable appropriation act without funding the activity. 58 Comp. Gen. 530, 532 (1979). Obligations already incurred under the resolution may be liquidated pursuant to the authority provided by the continuing resolution.

Continuing resolutions are enacted as joint resolutions that continue appropriations for a certain fiscal year. Although enacted in this form rather than as an "act," once passed by both houses of Congress and approved by the President, a continuing resolution is a statute that has the force and effect of law. See *Oklahoma v. Weinberger*, 360 F. Supp. 724 (W.D. Okla. 1973). Accordingly, the continuing resolution may impose mandatory requirements upon agencies and place conditions on the agencies' use of funds provided.

Discussion Problem 7-4

An agency is annually funded with appropriations with a one-year period of availability. At the start of FY 2002, Congress has not enacted the agency's regular appropriation act. However, on September 30, Congress does manage to pass a continuing resolution providing budget authority to the agency until October 15, 2001. The agency comptroller has recently taken a fiscal law refresher course and recalls some rule holding that, in the absence of an appropriation, an agency must immediately commence shutting down its operations, unless an exception applies.

Is the agency comptroller's recollection accurate? What is the legal effect of a continuing resolution? How does this situation differ from an agency's authority during a funding gap?

Definitions

The Comptroller General defines continuing resolution authority as "[l]egislation enacted by Congress to provide budget authority for Federal agencies and/or specific activities to continue in operation until the regular appropriations are enacted. Continuing resolutions are enacted when action on appropriations is not completed by the beginning of the fiscal year." GAO, *Glossary of Terms Used in the Federal*

Budget Process, PAD-81-27 (3d ed. March 1981), at p. 44. Agency financial management regulations often contain supplemental definitions of continuing resolutions. For example, the DoD Financial Management Regulation defines a continuing resolution as follows:

> Legislation enacted by the Congress to provide budget authority for specific ongoing activities in cases where the regular fiscal year appropriation for such activities has not been enacted by the beginning of the fiscal year. The continuing resolution usually specifies a maximum rate at which the agency may incur obligations, based on the rate of the prior year, the President's budget request, or an appropriation bill passed by either or both Houses of the Congress.

DoD Financial Management Regulation, Vol. 2A Ch. 1, para. 010107.B.16.

Key Aspects of Continuing Resolutions

Continuing resolutions are generally worded in very broad terms and, since they are enacted in haste, there is typically very little legislative history that an agency can analyze to determine congressional intent. Nevertheless, various rules of interpretation and procedures have evolved over time that should be used to ensure that agency actions are consistent with the authority conferred by the continuing resolution. These rules and procedures generally apply within the context of several specific aspects of continuing resolutions, including how to determine the amount provided by the continuing resolution, the duration of the continuing resolution, and what agencies may and may not do under a continuing resolution.

Amount Provided by a Continuing Resolution

Unlike regular appropriation acts, continuing resolutions in their traditional form do not usually appropriate specified sums of money. Rather, they usually appropriate "such amounts as may be necessary" for continuing projects or activities at a certain "rate for operations." The rate for operations has no generally applicable meaning, and each continuing resolution can, and often does, describe the term differently. For example, the continuing resolution may describe the "rate for operations" as: the amount provided for the activity in an appropriation act that has passed both houses but has not become law; the lower of the amounts provided when each house has passed a different act; the lower of the amounts provided either in an act that has passed only one house or in the administration's budget estimate; the amount specified in a particular conference report; the lower of either the amount provided in the budget estimate or the "current rate." Accordingly, to determine the sum of money appropriated for any given activity by this type of continuing resolution, it is necessary to examine not only the continuing resolution itself, but also other documents referenced in the resolution.

Continuing resolutions generally limit agencies to the smallest amount specified by the various reference points. For example, if the current rate is $1,000,000, the agency had requested $1,200,000 in its budget, and the Senate bill would provide $900,000, the continuing resolution will generally limit the agency to the smallest amount, i.e., $900,000. This approach represents an attempt by Congress to maintain the "status quo" of existing programs and rates of operation or production during the time frame between the appropriation that expired on September 30 and the appropriation acts that Congress is working on.

Continuing resolutions use what is referred to as the "current rate" to establish the upper limit at which agencies may continue to fund a project or activity. The following language from the FY 1996 continuing resolution illustrates this approach:

> [Sec. 101](c) Whenever an Act listed in this section has been passed by only the House or only the Senate as of October 1, 1995, the pertinent project or activity shall be

continued under the appropriation, fund, or authority granted by the one House *at a rate for operations not exceeding the current rate or the rate permitted by the action of the one House, whichever is lower,* and under the authority and conditions provided in applicable appropriations Acts for the fiscal year 1995. FY 1996 Continuing Resolution (emphasis added).

Discussion Problem 7-5

An agency is operating under a continuing resolution containing the language above. The agency has properly determined that its "current rate" is $10 million. However, the House version of the agency's appropriation bill indicates that the House committees intend to cut back the agency's funding, and the current version of the bill would appropriate only $7 million. The agency needs to start obligating funds immediately to keep its programs running smoothly. How much is available for obligation under this scenario?

Sometimes, Congress will specify a more mathematical approach for determining the amount available under a continuing resolution. For example, Congress has authorized agencies to use the average of the amounts being discussed in the House and Senate versions of the appropriations bills. The FY 1996 continuing resolution stated:

> [Sec. 101](b) Whenever the amount which would be made available or the authority which would be granted under an Act listed in this section as passed by the House as of October 1, 1995, *is different* from that which would be available or granted under such Act as passed by the Senate as of October 1, 1995, the pertinent project or activity shall be continued at a rate for operations *not exceeding the average of the rates permitted by the action of the House or the Senate* under the authority and conditions provided in the applicable appropriations Act for the fiscal year 1995. . . . (emphasis added).

Under this language, if the House version of an agency's appropriations bill would appropriate $10 million and the Senate version of the bill would appropriate $20 million, the authorized rate for operations would be the average of the two figures, or $15 million. Occasionally, a program will be funded in one House of Congress but not the other. When this occurs, Congress is inclined to severely restrict the amount available under a continuing resolution. This was illustrated in the FY 1996 continuing resolution, which stated:

> Sec. 101](b) . . . [W]here an item is included in only one *version of the Act as passed by both Houses* as of October 1, 1995, the pertinent project or activity shall be continued under the appropriation, fund, or authority granted by the one House *at a rate for operations that is one-half of that permitted by the action of the one House* under the authority and conditions provided in the applicable appropriations Act for the fiscal year 1995. (emphasis added).

Since the "current rate" generally sets the upper limit on the amount of budget authority provided by a continuing resolution, it is critical to calculate this amount as accurately as possible.

The current rate, as the term is used in continuing resolutions, is equivalent to the total amount of budget authority that was available for obligation for an activity during the fiscal year preceding the one for which the continuing resolution is enacted. The method for determining the amount available for obligation in the prior fiscal year will differ based on whether the relevant appropriation is an annual or multiple-year type. When the program in question has been funded by one-year appropriations in prior years, the current rate is equal to the total funds appropriated for the program for the previous fiscal year. See 64 Comp. Gen. 21,22 (1984); 58 Comp. Gen. 530 (1979); B-194362, May 1, 1979. Thus, if an agency received an annual appropriation that provided $1 million for a particular program in the preceding fiscal year, then the "current rate" for that program under a continuing resolution would be $1 million. The agency would, therefore, be authorized to obligate and expend up to $1 million for the program, unless the continuing resolution specified another reference point (e.g., the agency's budget request or a House or Senate bill) as the relevant limitation and that reference point establishes a lesser amount. In either case, the term "current rate" is used in continuing resolutions to indicate the level of funding that Congress wants to establish for a program.

A resolution may appropriate sufficient funds to enable a program to operate at a rate for operations "not in excess of the current rate," or at a rate "not in excess of the lower of the current rate" or the rate provided in a certain bill. It is possible to read the term "current rate" as referring to either the amount of money available for the program in the preceding year or an amount of money sufficient to enable continuation of the program at the level of the preceding year. For example, if an agency buys ten cars each year for its motor pool and last fiscal year received an annual appropriation that provided $100,000 to purchase ten cars, would the "current rate" under a continuing resolution provide $100,000 or an amount sufficient to purchase ten similar cars? This question becomes relevant if the per-car cost had increased or decreased since the last fiscal year. If it cost the same to buy nine cars this fiscal year as it cost to buy ten cars last fiscal year, the issue is whether the agency can follow its prior practice of buying ten cars per year or is limited to $100,000, which would only allow for the purchase of nine cars.

As a general proposition, GAO regards the term "current rate" as referring to a sum of money rather than a program level. 58 Comp. Gen. 530,533 (1979); B-194362, May 1, 1979. Thus, in the car example, the agency would be limited to obligating $100,000, which, because of the increased price per car, will require the agency to buy nine cars instead of ten. When a continuing resolution appropriates in terms of the current rate, the amount of money available under the resolution will be limited by that rate, even though cost increases may force the agency to purchase fewer units than it purchased in the prior fiscal year. Similarly, an increase in the minimum wage may force a reduction in the number of people participating in an employment program (B-194063, May 4, 1979), or an increase in the mandatory level of assistance will reduce the number of meals provided under a "meals for the elderly" program (B-194362, May 1, 1979).

The term "current rate" refers to the rate of operations carried on *within the appropriation* for the prior fiscal year. B-152554, December 6, 1963. The current rate is equivalent to the total appropriation, or the total funds that were available for obligation, for an activity during the previous fiscal year. *Edwards v. Bowen*, 785 F.2d 1440 (9th Cir. 1986); 64 Comp. Gen. 21 (1984); 58 Comp. Gen. 530, 533 (1979); B-194063, May 4, 1979; B-194362, May 1, 1979; B-164031(1), December 13, 1972. This means that if an agency received a general salary and expense appropriation of $50 million in the preceding year, the "current rate" under a continuing resolution in the following year would provide $50 million. The amount that the agency administratively subdivides to subordinate divisions of the agency is left to the discretion of the agency. This is because the current rate is determined at the appropriation level and not at the level of lower-level administrative subdivisions of funds.

> **Discussion Problem 7-6**
>
> Each year an agency receives a lump-sum capital expense appropriation of $10 million. A subdivision of this agency, the Automobile Purchasing Unit (APU), has historically purchased ten new cars per year for the motor pool. The agency comptroller administratively provides $100,000 per year so the APU can make these purchases. This year, however, the agency is operating under a continuing resolution that requires the agency to continue operations at the "current rate." Because of inflation, the APU can only purchase nine cars for the $100,000 it had been provided in past years. The APU asks the agency comptroller to provide $111,111, which will enable the APU to purchase ten vehicles at the higher price.
>
> Can the comptroller provide the APU with $111,111 without violating the "current rate" limitation in the continuing resolution? Does the "current rate" apply at the appropriation level, the administrative subdivision level, or both?

There are exceptions to the rule that "current rate" means a sum of money rather than a program level. For example, GAO construed the FY 1980 continuing resolution as appropriating sufficient funds to support an increased number of Indochinese refugees in view of explicit statements by both the Appropriations and the Budget Committees that the resolution was intended to fund the higher program level. B-197636, February 25, 1980. Also, the legislative history of the FY 1981 continuing resolution (Pub. L. No. 96-369, 94 Stat. 1351) indicated that in some instances "current rate" must be interpreted so as to avoid reducing existing program levels. This conclusion was based on clear and unambiguous legislative history. In the absence of such a clear indication of congressional intent, the general rule would apply, and the current rate would be interpreted as referring to an amount and not an operating level. For this reason, it is always preferable for the exception to be specified in the continuing resolution itself.

Starting with the first continuing resolution for fiscal year 1983 (Pub. L. No. 97-276, 96 Stat. 1186 (1982)), Congress began appropriating for the continuation of certain programs "at a rate to maintain current operating levels." GAO has construed this language as meaning sufficient funds to maintain the program in question at the same operating level as at the end of the immediately preceding fiscal year. B-209676, April 14, 1983; B-200923, November 16, 1983 (non-decision letter).

Since the "current rate" is based on the amount the agency had available for obligation in the preceding fiscal year, an issue arises regarding the treatment of amounts transferred into or out of the particular appropriation. For example, if Congress appropriated a salary and expense appropriation of $50 million, but the agency transfers $10 million from that appropriation into another one, is the current rate $50 million or $40 million? The rule GAO established in such cases is that funds administratively transferred from the account during the fiscal year, under authority contained in substantive legislation, should not be deducted in determining the current rate. B-197881, April 8, 1980; B-152554, November 4, 1974. This is because the relevant point in time for determining the current rate is the point at which the appropriation became law since that is the amount that Congress intended to make available for obligation as a result of the appropriations process. Conversely, it follows that funds transferred *into* the account during the fiscal year pursuant to statutory authority should be excluded. B-197881, April 8, 1980.

Finally, if the funding for the preceding fiscal year covered only a part of that year, it may be appropriate to "annualize" the previous year's appropriation in order to determine the current rate. This was the result in 61 Comp. Gen. 473 (1982), where the 1981 appropriation for a particular program had been contained in a supplemental appropriation act and was intended to cover only the last quarter of the fiscal year. The current rate for purposes of the FY 1982 continuing resolution was four times the FY 1981 figure, which equals the annualized amount.

In those instances in which the program has been funded by multiple-year or no-year appropriations in prior years, the current rate is equal to the total funds appropriated for the previous fiscal year plus the total unobligated budget authority carried over into that year from prior years. 58 Comp. Gen. 530 (1979); B-152554, October 9, 1970. For example, assume that an agency receives a two-year appropriation each year in the amount of $1,000,000. Assume further that the agency always obligates $800,000 in the first year and carries forward an unobligated balance of $200,000 into the next fiscal year. Thus, the amount available for obligation at the start of the fiscal year is typically $1,200,000 ($1,000,000 of newly appropriated funds and $200,000 carried forward from the prior year appropriation). If the agency starts the fiscal year with a continuing resolution, the starting point for calculating the current rate will be the amount available for obligation in the prior fiscal year (i.e., $1,200,000).

However, in the case of multi-year appropriations, one additional calculation must be made to account for any unobligated balance that is carried forward into the year covered by the continuing resolution. As noted, Congress generally intends that the continuing resolution provide no more budget authority than necessary to maintain the status quo. If the current rate under a continuing resolution were interpreted to authorize an agency to obligate the total amount it had available for obligation in the prior fiscal year, *plus* the unobligated balance carried forward into the year covered by the continuing resolution, the current rate would provide *more* than the agency had available in the prior fiscal year.

Following up with the preceding example, recall that the agency had $1,200,000 available for obligation in the prior fiscal year ($1,000,000 newly appropriated in the prior year and $200,000 carried forward from the year before that). Assume that the agency, following its pattern, has an unobligated balance of $200,000 left over from the $1,000,000 appropriated in the prior year that is still available for obligation in the year covered by the continuing resolution.

If the current rate were interpreted to be $1,200,000, then the agency would actually have $1,400,000 available for obligation under the continuing resolution. This is because it can carry forward the $200,000 unobligated balance from the fiscal year. Since this represents an *increase* in the amount the agency had available in the prior fiscal year, the continuing resolution would not be maintaining the status quo. Consequently, when there is a balance of unobligated funds that can be carried over into the present fiscal year, this unobligated balance must be deducted from the current rate in determining the amount of funds appropriated by the continuing resolution. If this were not done, the program would be funded at a higher level in the present year than it was in the preceding year, which is generally not permitted by the language of the resolution. 58 Comp. Gen. 530, 535 (1979).

Thus, in the example, the agency would start with the total amount available for obligation in the preceding year ($1,200,000) and subtract the $200,000 unobligated balance from the prior year. This means that the amount provided by the continuing resolution would be $1,000,000 (i.e., $1,200,000–$200,000).

Discussion Problem 7-7

Each year an agency receives a two-year appropriation to conduct research. In FY 2002, the agency receives $10 million under this two-year appropriation. In addition, it has an unobligated balance from the FY 2001 appropriation of $3 million. In FY 2003, the agency is operating under a continuing resolution that limits the amount of its obligations to the "current rate." At the start of FY 2003, the agency has an unobligated balance of $1 million from the FY 2002 appropriation. How much is provided by the continuing resolution?

Continuing resolutions often state that the agency is limited to the current rate or some other specified reference point, whichever is less. When the reference point is not the current rate, an issue arises regarding how to account for any unobligated balance carried forward from a prior multiple-year appropriation. The reference point may be an unenacted bill, a conference report, the President's budget estimate, or any other item specified in the continuing resolution.

When the current rate is the lower figure, the general rule applies and any unobligated carryover balance must be deducted to determine the amount appropriated by the continuing resolution, as required by 58 Comp. Gen. 530. However, when the current rate is not the lower of the two referenced points, the general rule does not necessarily apply. This situation was addressed by the Comptroller General in 64 Comp. Gen. 649 (1985). In that case, a continuing resolution appropriated funds for the Office of Refugee Resettlement at a rate for operations not in excess of the lower of the current rate or the rate authorized by a bill as passed by the House of Representatives. The rate under the House-passed bill was $50 million. The current rate was $77.5 million, of which an unoblgated balance of $39 million was carried over into the fiscal year covered by the continuing resolution.

If the continuing resolution had simply specified a rate not in excess of the current rate, application of the general rule would have required deduction of the $39 million carryover balance from the $77.5 million current rate to determine the funding provided by the continuing resolution. This same adjustment would have been required if the rate in the House-passed bill had been greater than the current rate, since this would have made the current rate the relevant reference point. If, however, the rate in the House-passed bill was the lower of the two, the Comptroller General determined that no adjustment is required to account for the unobligated balance. The rationale for this result is that the "current rate," which is the amount available for obligation in the prior fiscal year, includes the unobligated balance that is carried forward into the fiscal year covered by the continuing resolution. Consequently, if the resolution is interpreted to provide the full current rate without a deduction for the balance carried forward, the continuing resolution would be providing an amount that duplicates the amount carried forward. Conversely, since the rate in the House-passed bill did not include a prior year's balance, and supported by the legislative history of the continuing resolution, the Comptroller General concluded that the amount available for the current year was the amount appropriated by the resolution (i.e., the $50 million provided by the House bill), plus the unobligated carryover balance of $39 million, for a total of $89 million.

The decision distinguished this case from 58 Comp. Gen. 530, which applied the general rule, stating that "the rule with respect to deduction of unobligated balances in 58 Comp. Gen. 530 is not applicable where the lower of two referenced rates is not the current rate." 64 Comp. Gen. 649, at 652-53. The case was appealed to federal court, and the Ninth Circuit Court of Appeals reached the same result. *Edwards v. Bowen*, 785 F.2d 1440 (9th Cir. 1986).

This distinction could result in a significant difference in the amount available to an agency based on insignificant differences between the current rate and the specified reference item. This may be illustrated by comparing the results when a small difference affects whether the current rate or the specified reference point is the lower figure.

For example, assume that the specified reference point is the amount provided in a House bill (e.g., $100 million) and the current rate is $101 million, of which $30 million may be carried over into the current fiscal year. In this situation the House bill is the relevant reference point because it is lower than the current rate. Applying the rule stated in 64 Comp. Gen. 649, the agency would have the $100 million provided by the House bill, *plus* the unobligated balance of $30 million, for a total of $130 million. If, however, the current rate were $99 million instead of $101 million, the agency would have only $69 million available for obligation under the continuing resolution. This is because a current rate of $99 million is lower than the amount in the House bill ($100 million), which would trigger the requirement to deduct the unobligated balance carried forward. 58 Comp. Gen. 530. Thus, the agency would subtract the $30 million unobligated balance from the

$99 million current rate, leaving only $69 million available for obligation under the continuing resolution.

Although the basis for the distinction is understandable (i.e., the House bill does not contain an unobligated balance and therefore no adjustment is necessary to account for an unobligated balance when the House bill is the lower reference point), the large disparity illustrated by this example suggests a need for an alternative analysis. It may be more effective to *always* account for any unobligated balance carried forward from a prior fiscal year. Taking this approach in the example would have resulted in comparing $70 million (the $100 million from the House bill minus $30 million) with $69 million (the current rate of $99 million minus $30 million) and using the lower figure.

Duration of a Continuing Resolution and the Pattern of Obligation

A continuing resolution is generally enacted to provide budget authority for a specified time (a week, month, or year), until a fixed cut-off date specified in the continuing resolution, until an appropriations act replaces it, or for an entire fiscal year (if no appropriations act is passed). In describing the duration of a continuing resolution, Congress will typically use language similar to that used in the FY 1996 continuing resolution, which stated:

> Sec. 106. Unless otherwise provided for in this joint resolution or in the applicable appropriations Act, appropriations and funds made available and authority granted pursuant to this joint resolution shall be available until (a) enactment into law of an appropriation for any project or activity provided for in this joint resolution, or (b) the enactment of the applicable appropriations Act by both Houses without any provision for such project or activity, or
> (c) November 13, 1995, whichever first occurs.

This time period is the length of time that the funds provided by the continuing resolution remain available for obligation. It is important to note that this limited period of availability does not affect the *amount* of funds available for obligation. The continuing resolution, regardless of its duration, generally is considered to appropriate the full annual amount. See B-152554, November 4, 1974 and B-271304, March 19, 1996 (GAO held: "Standard continuing resolution language makes it clear that the appropriations are available to the extent and in the manner which would be provided by the pertinent appropriations act that has yet to be enacted (unless otherwise provided in the continuing resolution)").

For example, if Congress passes a continuing resolution with a duration of 10 days, the agency is not required to limit the period of performance of its contractual obligations to only 10 days. Within the 10-day duration of the continuing resolution, the agency may obligate sufficient funds to ensure that performance will continue for the entire fiscal year, if such has been the pattern of obligation followed by the agency in prior fiscal years.

An agency may determine the pattern of its obligations under a continuing resolution, provided that it operates under a plan that will keep it within the rate for operations limit set by the resolution. If an agency usually obligates most of its annual budget in the first month or first quarter of the fiscal year, it may continue that pattern under the resolution. If an agency usually obligates funds uniformly over the entire year, it will be limited to that pattern under the resolution, unless it presents convincing reasons why its pattern must be changed in the current fiscal year.

Thus, under a continuing resolution with a duration of one month, and which appropriates funds at a rate for operations not in excess of the current rate, the agency is not necessarily limited to incurring obligations at the same rate it incurred them in the corresponding month of the preceding year. B-152554, December 6, 1963. The same principle applies when the resolution appropriates funds at a rate to maintain current operating levels. B-209676, April 14, 1983.

However, the pattern of obligations in prior years does provide a framework for determining the proper pattern of obligations under the continuing resolution. For example, if the activity is a formula grant program in which nearly all appropriated funds are normally obligated at the beginning of the fiscal year, then the full annual amount should be made available to the agency under the resolution, even though the resolution may be in effect for only one month. However, if the activity is salaries and expenses, in which funds are normally obligated uniformly throughout the fiscal year, then the amount made available to the agency should be only one-twelfth of the annual amount under a one-month resolution or one-fourth of the annual amount under a calendar-quarter resolution. B-152554, February 17, 1972.

Congress can, of course, alter the pattern of obligations by providing direction in the continuing resolution. For example, if the resolution limits obligations in any calendar quarter to one-fourth of the annual rate, the agency is limited to that one-fourth rate regardless of its normal pattern of obligations, B-152554, October 16, 1973. Further, even if the resolution itself does not have such limitations, but the legislative history clearly shows the intent of Congress that only one-fourth of the annual rate be obligated each calendar quarter, only this amount should be made available unless the agency can demonstrate a real need to exceed that rate. B-152554, November 4, 1974.

Agency Actions under a Continuing Resolution

Agencies may take various actions under a continuing resolution, given the limitations imposed by the typical continuing resolution.

Liquidation of Contract Authority. As discussed in Chapter 1, contract authority is the authority that Congress may provide to an agency to incur obligations in advance of the enactment of the appropriation that will eventually be used to liquidate that obligation. For example, assume that an agency is operating under a funding gap and awards a contract based upon a statutory grant of "contract authority." Since the agency has properly incurred an obligation, there must be a fund source to liquidate that obligation and pay the contractor. Recall that contract authority is authority to incur obligations, but does not provide authority to disburse funds. Thus, when Congress has failed to enact an appropriation on time and passes a continuing resolution instead, the continuing resolution provides the funds to liquidate the contract authority to the extent that amount becomes due during the period covered by the continuing resolution.

As noted, agencies must ensure that their obligations do not exceed the "current rate" established by a continuing resolution. The agency must include obligations incurred under contract authority if those obligations were incurred in the fiscal year covered by the continuing resolution. B-114833, November 12, 1974. Thus, once the "rate for operations" is determined (based on the amount of funding available for obligation in the prior fiscal year), the agency must ensure that its obligations, whether incurred through budget authority or contract authority, are within any applicable "rate for operations" limitation. However, if the agency incurred an obligation under contract authority in the fiscal year preceding that covered by the continuing resolution, then those obligations are not counted against the current rate limitation. Contract authority provides statutory authority to incur contractual obligations. The liquidation of contract authority represents the discharge of a prior year obligation and, therefore, does not affect the "rate for operations" conducted in the fiscal year covered by the continuing resolution.

Effect of Passage of the Appropriations Act. When the appropriations act becomes law, expenditures made pursuant to a continuing resolution must be charged against the appropriations act. This rule is designed to ensure that the agency does not consider the appropriations act to provide funding in *addition* to that provided by the continuing resolution. For example, if the "current rate" under the continuing resolution is $1,000,000 and the appropriation eventually enacted is $1,000,000, the agency does not have authority to obligate $2,000,000. The obligations incurred under the continuing resolution are merely charged to the applicable appropriation, when enacted. This accounting method was addressed in the text of the FY 1996 continuing resolution as follows:

Sec. 108. Expenditures made pursuant to this joint resolution shall be charged to the applicable appropriation, fund, or authorization whenever a bill in which such applicable appropriation, fund, or authorization is contained is enacted into law.

Final Appropriation Insufficient to Fully Liquidate Valid Obligations Incurred Under the Continuing Resolution. If an agency operating under a continuing resolution incurs obligations within the rate for operations limit, but Congress subsequently appropriates a total annual amount that is *less* than the amount of these obligations, the obligations remain valid. B-152554, February 17, 1972. For example, assume that a one-month continuing resolution prohibits an agency from incurring obligations in excess of the current rate, which for this example is $1 million. Assume further that the agency historically obligates the full annual amount in the first month of the fiscal year and it follows that pattern under the continuing resolution. However, when Congress enacts the regular appropriation act, the agency discovers that Congress had appropriated only $800,000. Now the agency has obligations of $1 million and an appropriation of $800,000. Under these circumstances, the obligations incurred by the agency remain valid obligations of the United States. This is because the obligations were within the current rate and were, therefore, valid when incurred.

If an obligation validly incurred under a continuing resolution remains valid even if the subsequently enacted appropriation act cannot cover it, the next question is how such obligations are to be paid. Continuing resolutions typically include a section that states:

> Appropriations made and authority granted pursuant to this joint resolution shall cover all obligations or expenditures incurred for any program, project, or activity during the period for which funds or authority for such projector activity are available under this joint resolution.

GAO has interpreted this language to mean that funds made available by a continuing resolution remain available to pay validly incurred obligations that exceed the amount of the final appropriation. 62 Comp. Gen. 9 (1982). See also 67 Comp. Gen. 474 (1988); B-207281, October 19, 1982. Thus, obligations under a continuing resolution are treated as follows:

> When an annual appropriation act provides sufficient funding for an appropriation account to cover obligations previously incurred under the authority of a continuing resolution, any unpaid obligations are to be charged to and paid from the applicable account established under the annual appropriation act. Similarly, to the extent the annual act provides sufficient funding, those obligations that were incurred and paid during the period of the continuing resolution must be charged to the account created by the annual appropriation act. On the other hand, to the extent the annual appropriation act does not provide sufficient funding for the appropriation account to cover obligations validly incurred under a continuing resolution, the obligations in excess of the amount provided by the annual act should be charged to and paid from the appropriation account established under authority of the continuing resolution.

62 Comp. Gen. 9, 11–12 (1982).

However, to comply with the intent of the lower appropriation, OMB requires that agencies "reduce obligations in the most cost-effective way and to the maximum extent possible." OMB Circular No. A-34, § 22.1. Thus, agencies are required to make their best efforts to remain within the amount of the final appropriation. However, to the extent an agency is unable to do so, the appropriation made by the continuing resolution remains available to liquidate the "excess" obligations.

This is the situation when obligations were *properly* incurred under a continuing resolution, i.e., the obligations did not exceed the "current rate" or other applicable limitation. However, an obligation incurred under a continuing resolution that is in *excess* of the amount authorized by the continuing resolution could not be "saved" by the rule allowing the continuing resolution to be the fund source to cover the obligations.

For example, if an agency obligated more than was authorized under a continuing resolution, and the amount eventually appropriated is less than what is required to liquidate these obligations, the agency cannot charge the excess amount to the continuing resolution. As discussed, if the appropriation eventually enacted is insufficient to cover obligations incurred under the continuing resolution, the excess amount can be charged to the continuing resolution. However, this rule applies *only* if the obligations incurred under the continuing resolution were authorized. If the obligations incurred under the continuing resolution exceed the amount provided by the continuing resolution, they would not become valid under this rule.

Such an obligation would become valid if ratified by Congress. Nevertheless, since the agency incurred an obligation that was in excess of the amount available at the time, it is likely that the obligation has violated the Antideficiency Act, specifically 31 U.S.C. § 1341(a)(1)(A).

Discussion Problem 7-8

An agency is operating under a continuing resolution. It has properly determined that the amount available for obligation under the continuing resolution is $10 million. Because of an administrative oversight, however, after the agency has obligated the full $10 million, it awards a firm-fixed price contract for $2 million, which causes the agency to obligate more than was provided by the continuing resolution. When the regular appropriations act is finally enacted, it provides only $8 million.

To which appropriation should the agency charge the first $8 million in obligations? How about the amount between $8 million and $10 million? Finally, how should the agency charge the amount over $10 million?

Limitations on Initiation or Expansion of Programs. Continuing resolutions generally do not allow agencies to initiate new programs or expand the scope of existing programs, projects, and activities. For example, the FY 1996 continuing resolution stated:

> Sec. 102. *No appropriation or funds* made available or authority granted pursuant to section 101 for the Department of Defense *shall be used for new production of items not funded for production in fiscal year 1995 or prior years, for the increase in production rates above those sustained with fiscal year 1995 funds, or to initiate, resume, or continue any project, activity, operation, or organization . . . for which appropriations, funds, or other authority were not available during the fiscal year 1995. . . .*

This language reflects the intent of Congress that the continuing resolution serve only to maintain the status quo. An agency should not increase the level of its operations under a continuing resolution unless there is clear direction in the continuing resolution itself directing such increase.

There is, however, some flexibility in the application of this rule. Under a lump-sum appropriation, when a continuing resolution authorizes continuation of projects or activities at the current rate, it generally refers to the amount appropriated in the prior fiscal year and not the amount of funding provided to each individual program. B-204449, November 18, 1981. Thus, if a resolution appropriates funds to continue projects or activities at a rate for operations not exceeding the current rate, the agency is operating within the limits of the resolution so long as the total of obligations under the appropriation does not exceed the current rate, i.e., the amount provided in the lump-sum appropriation in the prior fiscal year.

Within the appropriation, an agency may fund a particular activity at a higher rate than that activity was funded in the previous year and still not violate the current rate limitation, assuming of course that the resolution itself does not provide to the contrary. Of course, if the appropriation for the preceding fiscal year was a line-item appropriation, then the requirement to continue the project or activity at the current rate will be limited to the *amount* available for obligation in the prior fiscal year for that particular project or activity. See 66 Comp. Gen. 484 (1987).

For example, assume that an agency receives two appropriations. One is a lump-sum appropriation for operations and the other is an appropriation titled "procurement," which identifies the specific programs for which funds have been appropriated. The agency, in its budget request for the upcoming fiscal year, stated that it would fund ten activities from its operations appropriation and needed $1 million for each activity (total = $10 million). Similarly, the agency's budget request pertaining to its procurement appropriation stated that it planned to acquire five new procurement items and needed $2 million to acquire each (total = $10 million). In the prior fiscal year, the agency requested the same amounts for the same activities and procurement items.

In the new fiscal year, the agency is operating under a continuing resolution that states that it may continue operations at the "current rate." In the case of the procurement appropriation, the agency has $5 million to fund each of the five programs it funded last year. In the case of the operations appropriation, the agency has $10 million that it can use to fund the 10 activities, but it is not required to obligate $1 million for each program and has the flexibility to obligate other amounts, provided the total amount does not exceed $10 million.

Recent continuing resolutions have required agencies to reduce operations by a stated percentage applied to the current rate. For example, the FY 1996 continuing resolution stated:

> Sec. 115. Notwithstanding any other provision of this joint resolution, except section 106, the rates for operation for any continuing project or activity provided by section 101 that have not been increased by the provisions of section 111 or section 112 *shall be reduced by 5 percent but shall not be reduced below the minimal level de-*

fined in section 111 or below the level that would result in a furlough. FY 1996 Continuing Resolution (emphasis added).

Such language reflects the intent of Congress that agencies exercise fiscal constraint while Congress continues work on the appropriations acts. To implement this restriction, the agency would first use the techniques discussed to determine the current rate and then reduce that amount by the stated percentage. This will generally be accomplished at the headquarters level of the agency, and funds distributed to lower organizational levels will reflect the reduced level of funding.

> This chapter discussed two unusual appropriations situations: funding gaps and continuing resolutions. Each involves the application of unique rules that both agency personnel and contractors must be familiar with. The objective of this chapter was to provide a thorough and practical discussion of the applicable rules so that agency and contractor operations may continue with minimal disruption while awaiting enactment of the regular appropriations acts.

Attachment 7-1

Order Code RL30339

CRS Report for Congress
Received through the CRS Web

Preventing Federal Government Shutdowns: Proposals for an Automatic Continuing Resolution

Updated May 19, 2000

Robert Keith
Specialist in American National Government
Government and Finance Division

Congressional Research Service ❖ *The Library of Congress*

ABSTRACT

For several decades, difficulties in enacting regular appropriations acts and continuing resolutions in a timely manner periodically have resulted in funding gaps. In 1980 and 1981, revised interpretations of the law governing agency behavior during funding gaps led to more aggressive enforcement of the law, causing the federal government to shut down affected agencies during funding gaps. In an effort to ameliorate the consequences of the tardy enactment of appropriations, some Members have proposed that an automatic continuing resolution be set in place so that funding gaps would not occur and federal government shutdowns would be prevented. Congressional interest in automatic continuing proposals was spurred by two especially troublesome funding gaps that occurred in late 1995 and early 1996. This report examines the concept of the automatic continuing resolution, outlines legislative action on such proposals in the 105th and 106th Congresses, and provides background information on the incidence of continuing resolutions and funding gaps.

This report will be updated as developments warrant. (For related information, see CRS Report 98-844: *Shutdown of the Federal Government: Causes, Effects, and Process*, by Sharon S. Gressle.)

Preventing Federal Government Shutdowns: Proposals for an Automatic Continuing Resolution

Summary

Over the past several decades, the tardy enactment of regular appropriations bills has been a persistent problem in the annual appropriations process. When action on such bills is delayed, Congress turns to one or more *continuing resolutions* (CRs) to provide interim funding. The interval during the fiscal year when agency appropriations are not enacted into law, either in the form of a regular appropriations act or a CR, is referred to as a *funding gap*. When a funding gap occurs, the federal government begins a *shutdown* of the affected agencies, as required by the Antideficiency Act, which entails the furlough of "non-emergency" employees.

During the 24 fiscal years from FY1977 through FY2000, there were 17 funding gaps. In order to avoid the occurrence of funding gaps and government shutdowns, proposals have been made to establish an *automatic continuing resolution* (ACR) that would provide a fallback source of funding for activities, at a restricted level, in the event the timely enactment of appropriations is disrupted. The funding would become available automatically and remain available as long as needed so that a funding gap would not occur and the furlough of federal employees would be avoided (or at least severely limited).

During the 105th Congress, an ACR proposal was included in a supplemental appropriations bill (H.R. 1469), but the bill was vetoed by President Clinton on June 9, 1997, in part because he objected to the inclusion of the ACR provision. The proposal would have provided automatic continuing appropriations for activities, during FY1998 only, at 100 percent of the FY1997 level.

So far during the 106th Congress, ACR proposals have been reported in both the House and Senate, but only the House has considered one on the floor. House bill 853, the leading proposal in the House, was reported by the House Appropriations, Budget, and Rules Committees (H.Rept. 106-198, Part 1, June 24, 1999, and Parts 2 and 3, August 5, 1999, respectively); the House Appropriations Committee filed an adverse report and recommended that the ACR proposal be dropped from the bill. On May 16, 2000, the House considered and failed to pass H.R. 853 by a vote of 166-250. Under the terms of consideration set by a special rule (H.Res. 499), the ACR proposal was stripped from base text but was made in order as an amendment. Representative Gekas offered the ACR amendment, but it was defeated by a vote of 173-236.

Senate bill 558, the leading proposal in the Senate, was reported by the Senate Governmental Affairs Committee on March 16, 1999 (S.Rept. 106-15).

The two bills represent different approaches to establishing an automatic continuing resolution (as part of Title 31 of the *United States Code*). While H.R. 853 proposed a permanent ACR, S. 558 would limit its application to two fiscal years only. Second, S. 558 would fund activities at the lower of the prior-year level or the amount proposed in the President's budget, unlike H.R. 853, which would have funded activities only at the prior-year level.

Contents

Background 1
    The Annual Appropriations Process 1
    The Legal Underpinning for Funding Gaps and Shutdowns 2
    History of Recent Funding Gaps 3
Automatic Continuing Resolution 5
    Features of ACRs 6
    Arguments For 6
    Arguments Against 7
Recent Congressional Action on ACR Proposals 8
    Action in the 105th Congress 8
    ACR Proposals in the 106th Congress 9

List of Tables

Table 1. Appropriations Funding Gaps: FY1977-2000 4

Preventing Federal Government Shutdowns: Proposals for an Automatic Continuing Resolution

For several decades, difficulties in enacting regular appropriations acts and continuing resolutions in a timely manner periodically have resulted in funding gaps. In 1980 and 1981, revised interpretations of the law governing agency behavior during funding gaps led to more aggressive enforcement of the law, causing the federal government to shut down affected agencies during funding gaps. In an effort to ameliorate the consequences of the tardy enactment of appropriations, some Members have proposed that an automatic continuing resolution be set in place so that funding gaps would not occur and federal government shutdowns would be prevented. Congressional interest in automatic continuing proposals was spurred by two especially troublesome funding gaps that occurred in late 1995 and early 1996. This report examines the concept of the automatic continuing resolution, outlines legislative action on such proposals in the 105th and 106th Congresses, and provides background information on the incidence of continuing resolutions and funding gaps.

Background

The Annual Appropriations Process. The routine activities of most federal agencies are funded by means of annual appropriations provided in one or more of the 13 regular appropriations acts. When action on the regular appropriations acts is delayed, Congress turns to a *continuing resolution* (CR) to provide stop-gap funding.[1] The CR is so named because it provides continuing appropriations in the form of a joint resolution. (Occasionally, however, continuing appropriations are provided in bill form.)

CRs usually fund activities under a formula-type approach that provides spending at a restricted level, such as the lesser of the amount passed by the House or the Senate in appropriations bills not ready for transmittal to the President. In many instances, the amount of funding available for particular activities is increased when the regular appropriations act is subsequently enacted. Congress is not bound by these conventions in determining funding levels, however, and there have been many variations in practice in recent CRs. Further, CRs usually do not allow new activities to be initiated—funding is available only for activities conducted during the past year—and existing conditions and limitations on program activity are retained.

---

[1]For general information, see: U.S. Library of Congress. Congressional Research Service. *Continuing Appropriations Acts: Brief Overview of Recent Practices*, by Sandy Streeter, CRS Report RL30343 (Washington: December 14, 1999), 10 p.

CRS-2

Over the past several decades, the timing patterns for congressional action on regular appropriations acts have varied considerably, but tardy enactment has been a persistent problem. Congress and the President were not able to enact all of the regular appropriations acts on time in any year during the 25-year period running from FY1952 through FY1976. As a result, one or more CRs were enacted each year during this period, except for FY1953.[2]

In an effort to reduce the reliance on CRs, the Congressional Budget Act of 1974 lengthened the time available for Congress to act on annual appropriations measures by moving the start of the fiscal year back three months, from July 1 to October 1.[3] Notwithstanding this change, there have been only four instances beginning with FY1977 (when procedures under the 1974 Congressional Budget Act first were implemented fully) in which all of the regular appropriations acts were enacted on time—FY1977, 1989, 1995, and 1997. Consequently, one or more CRs were needed each year during this period, except for FY1989, 1995, and 1997.[4]

In most years, more than one CR was needed as Congress worked to complete action on the regular appropriations acts. The number of CRs enacted during the period ranged from zero to seven, except for FY1996, when 14 separate measures providing continuing appropriations were enacted.[5] In some years, especially during the 1980s, the final CR provided funding for one or more of the regular appropriations acts for the remainder of the fiscal year.

The Legal Underpinning for Funding Gaps and Shutdowns. The Antideficiency Act (31 *U.S.C.* 1341-1342, 1511-1519) generally bars agencies from continued operation in the absence of appropriations.[6] Exceptions are made under the act for certain activities, primarily those involving "the safety of human life or the protection of property." The interval during the fiscal year when agency appropriations are not enacted into law, either in the form of a regular appropriations act or a CR, is referred to as a *funding gap*. Although funding gaps may occur on

---

[2]Although regular appropriations measures for FY1953 were enacted into law after the start of the fiscal year on July 1, 1952, no continuing appropriations were provided. Section 1414 of P.L. 82-547 (July 15, 1952), a supplemental appropriations measure for FY1953, resolved technical legalities arising from the tardy enactment of appropriations for that year.

[3]Section 501 (88 *Stat.* 321) of P.L. 93-344; July 12, 1974. This section later was replaced by the Federal Credit Reform Act of 1990, but the start of the fiscal year remains October 1.

[4]Although all of the regular appropriations acts were enacted on time for FY1977, two continuing resolutions were needed to fund certain unauthorized programs that had been omitted from one of the regular appropriations acts.

[5]See the following two reports: U.S. Library of Congress. Congressional Research Service: (1) *Continuing Appropriations Acts: Summary Data for Fiscal Years 1977-1995*, by Edward Davis and Robert Keith, CRS report 95-78 GOV (Washington: December 30, 1994), 5 p.; and (2) *FY1996 Continuing Resolutions: List of Measures, Chronology, Citations*, by Sandy Streeter, CRS Report 96-652 GOV (Washington: July 25, 1996), 5 p.

[6]For a discussion of the features and legislative history of the Antideficiency Act, see: U.S. Library of Congress. Congressional Research Service. *General Management Laws: A Selective Compendium*, CRS report RL30267 (Washington: July 28, 1999) pages 127-131.

CRS-3

October 1, at the beginning of the fiscal year, they may occur any time a CR expires and another CR (or the regular appropriations act) is not enacted immediately thereafter. Also, multiple funding gaps may occur for a fiscal year.

In 1980 and 1981, Attorney General Benjamin Civiletti issued opinions regarding the Antideficiency Act clarifying the need for federal agencies to begin terminating regular activities immediately upon the occurrence of a funding gap.[7] The narrowness of the exceptions allowed under the act was reaffirmed by the Budget Enforcement Act of 1990, which in part stated that the exceptions do not include "ongoing, regular functions of government the suspension of which would not imminently threaten the safety of human life or the protection of property."[8]

Accordingly, when a funding gap occurs, the federal government begins a *shutdown* of the affected agencies. A shutdown entails the prompt furlough of non-emergency personnel[9] and curtailment of agency activities, including the provision of most services to the public.[10] The general practice of the federal government over the years has been to pay furloughed employees, after the shutdown has ended, for time missed, even when no work was performed.

When a funding gap is expected to occur, the affected agencies are given guidance on the preparation for a shutdown by the Office of Management and Budget (usually in the form of a *bulletin*) and the Office of Personnel Management.

History of Recent Funding Gaps. As shown in **Table 1**, there were 17 funding gaps during the 24 fiscal years covering FY1977 through FY2000. One or more funding gaps occurred in 12 of these years, but there were no funding gaps in the remaining 12 years. In three instances (for FY1983, FY1985, and FY1996), there were two funding gaps for one fiscal year, and in one instance (for FY1978) there were three funding gaps.

The gaps ranged in duration from one to 21 full days. Six of the seven lengthiest funding gaps, lasting from 8 to 17 days, occurred between FY1977 and FY1980, before the Civiletti opinions were issued. In general, the duration of funding gaps shortened considerably after the issuance of these opinions (ranging from one to three days, with the longer gaps occurring over a weekend). However, a five-day and a 21-day funding gap for FY1996 occurred between mid-November of 1995 and early January of 1996.

---

[7]See, in particular, 43 *Op. Atty. Gen.* 293—January 16, 1981.

[8]See Section 13213 of P.L. 101-508 (104 *Stat.* 1388-621), the Omnibus Budget Reconciliation Act of 1990 (Title XIII of the act, which contains this section, is known as the Budget Enforcement Act of 1990).

[9]Until recently, such personnel were usually referred to as "non-essential," but this term has come to be regarded as demeaning.

[10]See U.S. Library of Congress. Congressional Research Service. *Shutdown of the Federal Government: Causes, Effects, and Process*, by Sharon S. Gressle, CRS report 98-844 GOV (Washington: November 8, 1999), 6 p.

Funding Gaps and Continuing Resolution Authority 503

CRS-4

Table 1. Appropriations Funding Gaps: FY1977-2000

Fiscal year	Date gap commenced[1]	Full day(s) of gaps	Date gap terminated[2]
1977	Thursday, 09-30-76	10	Monday, 10-11-76
1978	Friday, 09-30-77 Monday, 10-31-77 Wednesday, 11-30-77	12 8 8	Thursday, 10-13-77 Wednesday, 11-09-77 Friday, 12-09-77
1979	Saturday, 09-30-78	17	Wednesday, 10-18-78
1980	Sunday, 09-30-79	11	Friday, 10-12-79
1981	---	---	---
1982	Friday, 11-20-81	2	Monday, 11-23-81
1983	Thursday, 09-30-82 Friday, 12-17-82	1 3	Saturday, 10-02-82 Tuesday, 12-21-82
1984	Thursday, 11-10-83	3	Monday, 11-14-83
1985	Sunday, 09-30-84 Wednesday, 10-03-84	2 1	Wednesday, 10-03-84 Friday, 10-05-84
1986	---	---	---
1987	Thursday, 10-16-86	1	Saturday, 10-18-86
1988	Friday, 12-18-87	1	Sunday, 12-20-87
1989	---	---	---
1990	---	---	---
1991	Friday, 10-05-90	3	Tuesday, 10-09-90
1992	---	---	---
1993	---	---	---
1994	---	---	---
1995	---	---	---
1996	Monday, 11-13-95 Friday, 12-15-95	5 21	Sunday, 11-19-95 Saturday, 01-06-96
1997	---	---	---
1998	---	---	---
1999	---	---	---
2000	---	---	---

[1] Gap commenced at midnight of the date indicated.
[2] Gap terminated during the date indicated due to the enactment of regular appropriations or further continuing appropriations measures.

CRS-5

In six cases (two occurring after the Civiletti opinion), the funding gaps were due to the failure to enact the initial continuing resolution by the start of the fiscal year on October 1. In the remaining 11 cases (nine occurring after the Civiletti opinion), the funding gaps occurred between continuing resolutions, as the fiscal year already was underway. Although nine funding gaps occurred at the start of the fiscal year or during October, another eight occurred as late as November or December.

In some instances, funding gaps resulted in the widespread furlough of federal employees and the shutdown of federal agencies. The disruption was minimized most of the time because the funding gap occurred during a weekend.

One of the most dramatic of the earlier shutdowns occurred in November 1981.[11] A funding gap began at midnight on Friday, November 20, when a continuing resolution expired. President Reagan vetoed a further continuing resolution on the morning of Monday, November 23, prompting a shutdown. The budgetary confrontation between the President and Congress was resolved later that day and a further continuing resolution was signed into law that evening, ending the shutdown. Another notable shutdown occurred during the Columbus Day weekend in October of 1990.[12]

Perh`aps the most dramatic of all shutdowns involved a five-day and 21-day shutdown for FY1996 occurring between late 1995 and early 1996. The shutdowns were due to unusually difficult and protracted negotiations between President Clinton and Congress over appropriations and other budgetary issues.[13] During the first of the two shutdowns, about 800,000 federal employees were furloughed.

Automatic Continuing Resolution

Extensive reliance on CRs, and the occurrence of funding gaps and federal government shutdowns, have been persistent features of the annual appropriations process. Proposals have been made from time to time over the years to alleviate these

---

[11] The circumstances surrounding the shutdown are discussed in detail in the *Congressional Quarterly Weekly Report* of November 28, 1981 (Vol. 39, No. 48); see "Weekend Contest Produces 3-Week Funding Accord; Government Shutdown Ends" and "Funding Gap Led to Sweeping Shutdown . . . But No Lapse in Essential U.S. Services," pages 2324-2327.

[12] Information on the consequences of the Columbus Day shutdown is provided in the following two reports of the General Accounting Office: (1) *Data on Effects of 1990 Columbus Day Weekend Funding Lapse*, GAO/GGD-91-17FS, October 19, 1990, 36 pages; and (2) *Permanent Funding Lapse Legislation Needed*, GAO/GGD-91-76, June 6, 1991, 56 pages.

[13] For a discussion of these funding gaps, see the *1995 Congressional Quarterly Almanac*, "Government Shuts Down Twice Due to Lack of Funding," pages 11-3 through 11-6. Also, a lengthier and more colorful discussion of the political circumstances surrounding the funding gaps may be found in *Mirage: Why Neither Democrats Nor Republicans Can Balance the Budget, End the Deficit, and Satisfy the Public*, by George Hager and Eric Pianin, Random House (New York: 1997), see especially pages 258-303.

CRS-6

problems by establishing an *automatic continuing resolution* (ACR).[14] The common feature of these proposals is the establishment of a mechanism to ensure a fallback source of funding for activities, at a restricted level, in the event the timely enactment of appropriations is disrupted. The funding would become available automatically and remain available as needed so that a funding gap would not occur and the furlough of federal employees would be avoided (or at least severely limited).

Features of ACRs. The two major variables in the design of an automatic continuing resolution are funding level and duration. With regard to funding level, most ACR proposals would set funding for the new fiscal year at a level consistent with the rate of operations for the prior fiscal year or some percentage of that rate. This would allow agencies to continue operating at close to the "status quo," without prejudging which programs should be increased or scaled back.

On the issue of duration, ACR proposals range from providing continuing appropriations for a short interval, like a month, to the full fiscal year, or even indefinitely (so that continuing appropriations would become available automatically year after year as needed). Some proposals stop short of providing comprehensive automatic continuing appropriations and instead focus on continuing only basic civilian and military pay and benefits.

Arguments For. Proponents of ACR proposals identify several categories of problems that could, they assert, be avoided if funding gaps and the ensuing federal government shutdowns were not allowed to occur. First, shutdowns may incur significant costs to the federal government for various reasons, including program inefficiencies that arise from the disruption and from making payments to federal employees, after the shutdown has ended, for a period when work was not performed. If the shutdown is fairly large in scale, as occurred in late 1995 and early 1996, the cost to the federal government runs into hundreds of millions of dollars. In addition, federal employees themselves may have to contend with delayed or reduced paychecks, the interruption of official travel, and similar problems.

Second, shutdowns may incur significant costs to private sector entities that have business arrangements with the federal government or otherwise are closely aligned with federal activities. A lengthy shutdown may impede the timely payment of federal contractors, for example. Less directly, businesses dependent on federally sponsored activities, such as hotels and restaurants that service visitors to national parks and monuments, may suffer economic losses when these facilities shut down.

Third, shutdowns may disrupt the provision of services to program beneficiaries and the general public. Certain benefit payments, involving such programs as veterans' assistance and Medicare payments to health maintenance organizations, may not be paid when a shutdown lasts for any significant period. Citizens intending to

---

[14]See, for example, the report of the General Accounting Office, *Funding Gaps Jeopardize Federal Government Operations* (PAD-81-31), March 3, 1981; the print of the House Government Operations Committee, *Reform of the Federal Budget Process: An Analysis of Major Proposals*, June 1987 (pages 4-7); and the print of the Senate Governmental Affairs Committee, *Proposed Budget Reforms: A Critical Analysis*, April 1988 (pages 32-35).

CRS-7

travel overseas may not be able to obtain passport services; tourists making long-planned vacations may be barred from entry at many public sites.

Fourth, many ACR proponents believe that shutdowns create a strong, negative perception regarding the ability of elected officials to govern effectively and that the onus falls principally on Congress rather than the President.

Finally, an ACR, in the view of some, may promote an atmosphere at the end of the session more conducive to the constructive resolution of negotiations over legislation. Too often, they assert, the crisis atmosphere surrounding funding gaps late in the year pressures Members into accepting less-than-desirable solutions to break legislative impasses.

Arguments Against. The major concern of opponents of ACR proposals is that they could serve as a disincentive to enact the regular appropriations bills in a timely manner, or even at all. By knowing that a "fail-safe" funding mechanism in the form of an ACR exists, which would prevent the disruption from a government shutdown, negotiations over annual appropriations could slow down considerably as different sides see an advantage in taking more time to pursue their goals. If negotiations extended weeks past the beginning of the fiscal year without clear signs of impending agreement, an acceptance of the status quo, or something near to it, and adjournment might be the most appealing option to many at that time. In this view, an ACR, therefore, could offer Congress a convenient "escape hatch" from a difficult situation when time has run out.

Further, ACR critics maintain that supporters of reduced funding levels for annual appropriations might very well see thwarting action on the regular appropriations bills (at least those that would increase spending) as an important means of achieving their goal. A funding formula set much lower than 100 percent of the prior year's level probably would encourage a congressional majority to seek enactment of the regular bills; but the 98-percent or 100-percent formula may be seen by many as an adequate funding level given the interest in constraining spending growth. Reliance upon an ACR could allow Congress to achieve this goal without actually taking any "tough votes" to cut discretionary spending significantly.

Finally, the chief drawback to a formula-based approach, opponents of an ACR assert, is that it may engender inequities and undermine accountability. Many would argue that the notions of congressional accountability and responsibility in exercising the "power of the purse" entail the exercise of deliberate choice. The development of annual appropriations bills through the regular legislative process entails making thousands of separate decisions. The effects of increasing funding or decreasing funding for each account, and the programs, projects, and activities within those accounts, are carefully weighed according to various criteria. All Members have an opportunity to take part in this process at some level. Resort to a formula-based approach, however, treats all items the same. Programs in need of significant increases are treated in the same manner as programs that can be cut significantly, if not eliminated altogether. From this perspective, when Members are denied the opportunity to influence outcomes for particular programs, they may not be held as clearly accountable for them.

CRS-8

Recent Congressional Action on ACR Proposals

Action in the 105th Congress. During the 105th Congress, the House and Senate acted on an ACR proposal included in legislation providing supplemental appropriations for FY1997. The legislation was vetoed by President Clinton on June 9, 1997. A subsequent supplemental appropriations measure, which did not contain an ACR provision, was enacted into law (P.L. 105-18).

The Senate initiated consideration of the supplemental appropriations bill, S. 672. An ACR provision, pegged at 98-percent of the prior year's funding level and effective for the duration of FY1998, was included in the bill as developed in the Senate Appropriations Committee.[15] The provision was sponsored by Senators John McCain and Kay Bailey Hutchison and was based upon a free-standing ACR proposal they had introduced earlier, S. 547. Pursuant to the provision, the 98-percent funding level could remain in effect for as long as the entire fiscal year, but would have no effect beyond FY1998. Several provisions, dealing with such matters as the terms and conditions, coverage, and charging of expenditures under continuing appropriations also were included in the proposal; these provisions essentially were "boilerplate" from recent continuing resolutions. According to Senators McCain and Hutchison, the funding formula—98 percent of the prior year's level—was consistent with past budget resolution policy aimed at balancing the budget by FY2002. Accordingly, if circumstances dictated that the funding formula remain in effect for all programs during the entire fiscal year, that action would not undermine balanced-budget efforts.

An unsuccessful motion to strike the provision was made in committee by Senator Robert Byrd. On May 5, 1997, during Senate consideration of S. 672, Senator Byrd again offered an amendment (#59) to strike the provision from the bill. During discussion of the proposal, Senator McCain obtained unanimous consent to modify the provision, raising the funding formula from 98 percent to 100 percent. He explained that the recent budget summit agreement, which provided for modest increases in discretionary spending, made the adjustment reasonable. The Byrd amendment was tabled the next day by a vote of 55-45 and the modified provision was retained in the bill.

The House considered its version of the supplemental appropriations measure, H.R. 1469, on May 15. Representative George Gekas offered an amendment (#7) proposing an ACR that was identical to the Senate provision. The Gekas amendment was adopted by the House by a vote of 227-197.

The ACR proposal, as passed by both the House and Senate, was included in the final version of H.R. 1469 (as Title IX), which passed both chambers on June 5.[16] President Clinton vetoed the measure on June 9, 1997. The President cited several objections to the measure, the first being the inclusion of the ACR proposal. He indicated that the ACR, if it funded all appropriations for the entire fiscal year, would

---

[15]See Title VII, the *Government Shutdown Prevention Act*, on pages 81-85 of S. 672 as reported on April 30, 1997 (S.Rept. 105-16).

[16]See the conference report on H.R. 1469 (H.Rept. 105-119, June 4, 1997), pages 67-69 (legislative text) and 125 (brief explanation).

CRS-9

have resulted in funding levels $18 billion below the levels contained in the budget agreement he had reached earlier with Congress.[17]

In the House, other measures dealing with ACRs and related issues included H.R. 342 (Stearns), H.R. 638 and H.R. 1916 (Gekas), H.R. 987 (J. Peterson), H.R. 1326 (Bunning), H.R. 1372 (Cox), H.R. 1537 (Meek), H.R. 1785 (Kleczka), and H.R. 1912 (T. Davis). Similar proposals in the Senate included S. 228 and S. 547 (McCain) and S. 396 (Mikulski).

ACR Proposals in the 106th Congress. So far during the 106th Congress, ACR proposals have been reported in both the House and Senate, but only the House has considered one on the floor. Two of the leading proposals—H.R. 853 and S. 558— are discussed separately below.

H.R. 853. In the House, H.R. 853 (the Comprehensive Budget Process Act of 1999) was introduced on February 25, 1999 by Representatives Jim Nussle and Benjamin Cardin.[18] The measure was cosponsored by a bipartisan coalition of Members that includes, among others, Representative John Kasich (chairman of the House Budget Committee), Representative David Dreier (chairman of the House Rules Committee), and Representative Porter Goss (chairman of the Legislative and Budget Process Subcommittee of the House Rules Committee). It represented the culmination of efforts begun in the 105th Congress by the Task Force on the Budget Process (the so-called Nussle-Cardin task force) of the House Budget Committee and concurrent efforts by the House Rules Committee.

The Budget and Rules Committees marked up H.R. 853 on June 17 and June 23, respectively, and reported it on August 5 (H.Rept. 106-198, Parts 2 and 3). In addition, H.R. 853 also was referred to the House Appropriations Committee for consideration of that portion of the bill setting forth an automatic continuing resolution. The Appropriations Committee filed an adverse report on June 24 (H.Rept. 106-198, Part 1), recommending that the ACR provision be dropped from the bill.

As reported by the Budget and Rules Committees, Section 641 of H.R. 853 would have permanently established an automatic continuing resolution as part of Title 31 (Money and Finance) of the *United States Code*. The ACR would have providee funding at the prior year's level (*i.e.*, the amount provided in annual appropriations acts enacted for the preceding fiscal year).[19] The proposals of the two committees essentially were the same, except that the Rules Committee's proposal

---

[17]For the text of the President's veto message, see the *Congressional Record* of June 10, 1997, at pages H3633-34.

[18]For a detailed summary of H.R. 853, see: U.S. Library of Congress. Congressional Research Service. *H.R. 853, The Comprehensive Budget Process Reform Act: Summary of Provisions*, by James V. Saturno, CRS report RL30236 (Washington: May 4, 2000), 17 pages.

[19]The ACR proposal is discussed in detail in the reports of the Budget and Rules Committees (H.Rept. 106-198)on pages 74-79 (in Part 2) and on pages 101-103 (in part 3), respectively.

CRS-10

would have excluded designated emergency spending from the calculation of the prior-year level.

On May 16, 2000, the House considered and failed to pass H.R. 853 by a vote of 166-250. Under the terms of consideration set by a special rule (H.Res. 499), the ACR proposal was stripped from the base text but was made in order as an amendment. Representative George Gekas offered the ACR amendment, but it was defeated by a vote of 173-236.

S. 558. On March 16, 1999, the Senate Governmental Affairs Committee reported S. 558, the Government Shutdown Prevention Act (S.Rept. 106-15). As in the case of the House bill discussed above, S. 558 built upon ACR proposals considered in the preceding several years. In particular, Senator Pete Domenici, the chairman of the Senate Budget Committee, had introduced a comprehensive budget process reform measure, S. 93 (the Budget Enforcement Act of 1999), on January 19, 1999. On January 27, the Budget and Governmental Affairs Committees held a joint hearing on S. 93 (and S. 92, Senator Domenici's biennial budgeting proposal). Subsequently, the Governmental Affairs Committee decided to report the ACR proposal in Title IV of S. 93 as a free-standing measure, S. 558.

Senate bill 558, like H.R. 853, establishes an automatic continuing resolution as part of Title 31 of the *United States Code.* However, S. 558 differs from H.R. 853 in two fundamental ways. First, while H.R. 853 proposed a permanent ACR, S. 558 limits the application of the ACR to FY2000 and FY2001 only (although in this session, the FY2000 funding is now moot). The Senate Governmental Affairs Committee indicated that its duration should be limited because the procedure is untried. Second, S. 558 would fund activities at the lower of the prior-year level or the amount proposed in the President's budget (unlike H.R. 853, which would have funded activities only at the prior-year level).

Implication of CBO Scoring of H.R. 853 and S. 558. In addition to issues pertaining to the advantages or disadvantages of particular approaches to framing an ACR, cost estimates for the two proposals developed by the Congressional Budget Office (CBO) raise important implications.

Under traditional scoring practices, CBO regarded both bills as providing direct spending in the form of a permanent appropriations. Accordingly, CBO estimated FY2000 budget authority for H.R. 853 and S. 558 at $566 billion and $550 billion, with FY2000 outlays of $338 billion and $330 billion, respectively.[20]

Under current budget enforcement procedures,[21] the enactment of measure containing significant direct spending would require a significant sequester of spending for such programs at the end of the session in which enactment occurred,

---

[20] The CBO cost estimates are included in the committee reports on H.R. 853 and S. 558 (see H.Rept. 106-198, Part 2, pages 142-143, and S.Rept. 106-15, pages 7-9, respectively).

[21] Current budget enforcement procedures are described in: U.S. Library of Congress. Congressional Research Service. *Manual on the Federal Budget Process*, by Robert Keith and Allen Schick, CRS report 98-720 (Washington: August 24, 1998), 184 p.

CRS-11

unless the costs were not offset by comparable reductions in other direct spending programs, increases in revenues, or a combination of the two.

CHAPTER 8
Liability and Relief of Accountable Officers

This chapter will address the liability and relief of government officers and employees who are entrusted with public funds or who have certain specific responsibilities in the disbursement of public funds. Such government employees are referred to as "accountable officers." As the Comptroller General once stated, "A special trust responsibility exists with regard to public monies and with this special trust goes personal financial responsibility." B-161457, October 30, 1969. If government funds are lost because of a government employee's misconduct or carelessness, and if the responsible employee is not required to make up the loss, the result is that the taxpayer ends up paying twice for the same thing—or paying for nothing.

HISTORICAL PERSPECTIVE

This section provides an historical perspective on the liability of accountable officers and relief from liability.

Historical Bases of Accountable Officer Liability

The concept of accountability for public funds in the form of strict personal liability evolved during the 19th century. So-called "strict liability" is a type of legal liability that does not require proof of fault or intent. Strict liability is generally applied when there is an overriding policy that justifies assessing liability in the absence of fault. Accountable officer liability is an example of this type of strict liability and is premised on the need to safeguard public funds. In 1846, Congress mandated that all government officials safeguard public funds in their custody. The statute provided that:

> [A]ll public officers of whatsoever character, be, and they are hereby, required to keep safely, without loaning, using, depositing in banks, or exchanging for other funds than as allowed by this act, all the public money collected by them, or otherwise at any time placed in their possession and custody, till the same is ordered, by the proper department or officer of the government, to be transferred or paid out . . .

Act of August 6, 1846, ch. 90, § 6, 9 Stat. 59,60.

This statute still exists, as amended, at 31 U.S.C. § 3302(a). The clear intent of this statute is to prohibit government officials from taking any action with regard to public funds other than actions that have been specifically authorized.

These laws are civil provisions. Congress also addressed fiscal accountability in a variety of criminal statutes that also limit the uses of public funds to those purposes authorized by law. An important one is the Act of June 14, 1866, ch. 122, 14 Stat. 64, which declared it to be the duty of disbursing officers to use public funds entrusted to them "only as . . . required for payments to be made . . . in pursuance of law," and made it a felony for a disbursing officer to, among other things, "apply any portion of the public money intrusted [sic] to him" for any purpose not prescribed by law.

This statute still exists and is found at 18 U.S.C. § 653. Other provisions of the Criminal Code relevant to accountable officers include 18 U. S.C. § 643 (failure to render accounts), 648 (misuse of public funds), and 649 (failure to deposit). These four provisions of Title 18 apply to "all persons charged with the safe-keeping, transfer, or disbursement of the public money." 18 U.S.C. § 649(b).

The strict liability of accountable officers became firmly established in a series of early Supreme Court decisions. In 1845, the Court upheld liability in a case where money had been stolen with no fault or negligence on the part of the accountable officer. The Court said:

> Public policy requires that every depositary of the public money should be held to a strict accountability. Not only that he should exercise the highest degree of vigilance, but that 'he should keep safely' the moneys which come to his hands. Any relaxation of this condition would open a door to frauds, which might be practiced with impunity.

United States v. Prescott, 44 U.S. (3 How.) 578, 588–89 (1845).

This decision makes the important point that the laws relating to the liability and relief of accountable officers are intended not only to give the officers incentive to guard against theft by others, but also to protect against dishonesty by the officers themselves. In an 1872 case, *United States v. Thomas*, 82 U.S. (15 Wall.) 337, the Supreme Court recognized that the liability announced in *Prescott*, while strict, was not absolute. In that case, the Court refused to hold a customs official liable for funds that had been forcibly taken by Confederate forces during the Civil War. In formulating its conclusion, the Court recognized two exceptions to the strict liability rule:

> [N]o rule of public policy requires an officer to account for moneys which have been destroyed by an overruling necessity, or taken from him by a public enemy, without any fault or neglect on his part.

Id. at 352.

The exceptions, however, are limited. In *Smythe v. United States*, 188 U.S. 156 (1903), the Court reviewed its prior decisions, including *Prescott* and *Thomas*, and upheld the liability of an employee of the United States Mint for funds that had been destroyed by fire, finding the loss attributable neither to "overruling necessity" nor to a public enemy.

In effect, an accountable officer is an "insurer" of the funds in his or her charge. See, e.g., 64 Comp. Gen. 303, 304 (1985); 54 Comp. Gen. 112, 114 (1974); 48 Comp. Gen. 566,567 (1969); 6 Comp. Gen. 404,406 (1926); United States v. Heller, 1 F. Supp. 1, 6 (D. Md. 1932). The liability is automatic and arises by operation of law at the moment a physical loss occurs or an erroneous payment is made. 70 Comp. Gen. 12, 14 (1990); 54 Comp. Gen. at 114. In addition to the statutory provisions, an accountable officer's strict liability is based on public policy. See, *Prescott*, 44 U.S. at 587–88 ("The liability of the defendant . . . arises out of . . . principles which are founded upon public policy"); *Heller*, 1 F. Supp. at 6 (strict liability "is imposed as a matter of public policy").

Historical Bases for Relief of Liability

The early cases and statutes made no mention of *relief* from liability. It is important to distinguish between relief from liability and situations in which there is no liability in the first place. In the *Thomas* case, the Court held that an accountable officer is not liable when the loss is caused by "overruling necessity" or the "public enemy." This is not relief from liability, because there was no liability to begin with. Relief from liability starts out with a determination that the accountable officer is liable, but is relieved from liability in accordance with applicable rules. "Relief" in this context means an action, taken by someone with the legal authority to grant relief, that absolves an accountable officer from liability for a loss.

Prior to World War II, with limited exceptions for certain accountable officers of the armed forces, an accountable officer had only two relief options. First, the accountable officer could file a request for relief in what was then the Court of Claims under 28 U.S.C. § 52512. This tactic could be costly because the accountable officer would probably need legal representation and would have to pay all necessary expenses, none of which were reimbursable. Second, the accountable officer could seek private relief legislation, which required formal congressional action. Although this is a burdensome process for amounts that were often relatively small, this became the more popular method of obtaining relief.

There was no procedure for providing relief at the administrative level, regardless of how meritorious the case may have been. 4 Comp. Gen. 409 (1924); 27 Comp. Dec. 328 (1920). However, starting in 1941, Congress enacted a series of relief statutes that created a comprehensive statutory scheme for the administrative relief of accountable officers who are found to be without fault.

ACCOUNTABLE OFFICER DEFINED

To adequately address the issues of accountable officer liability and relief from liability, it is important to start out by defining the term "accountable officer." An accountable officer is any government officer or employee who by reason of his or her employment is responsible for or has custody of government funds. B-287043, May 29, 2001; 62 Comp. Gen. 476, 479 (1983); 59 Comp. Gen. 113, 114 (1979); B-188894, September 29, 1977. For non-DoD agencies, the term "accountable officer" is broad and encompasses such officials as certifying officers, disbursing officers, and any other government officer or employee who is responsible for or has custody of government funds. Other officials who may have a role in authorizing expenditures and creating obligations (contracting officers, for example) are not accountable officers for purposes of the laws discussed in this chapter.

DoD uses the term "accountable individual" to define this broad category of personnel, which includes DoD disbursing officers, certifying officers, and "accountable individuals." DoD Financial Management Regulation, Vol. 5, Definitions, para. 2. DoD defines the term "accountable official" as any person, not otherwise accountable under applicable law, who provides information, data, or services to a certifying or disbursing officer in support of the payment process. An "accountable official" is not a certifying or disbursing officer. DoD Financial Management Regulation, Vol. 5, Ch. 33, paras. 330302 and 331001. For example, a DoD accountable official includes personnel involved with the purchase card program, temporary duty (TDY) travel authorizations, contract and vendor payments, and military and civilian payments.

The training and appointment of accountable officers is carefully controlled by most federal agencies to ensure that only highly qualified personnel have access to public funds. For example, Department of Defense regulations urge that the number of accountable officers be minimized for security reasons. The DoD Financial Management Regulation (available at www.dtic.mil/comptroller/fmr), Vol. 5, Ch. 2 (2001), states:

> 020601 . . . Officers, enlisted members, or civilian employees satisfactory to the appointing officer, may be appointed to the position of disbursing agent, cashier, or paying agent. From a security standpoint, it is undesirable to allow excessive numbers of individuals to have access to public funds. Commanders and the Directors of DFAS sites shall take appropriate steps to ensure that only the minimum number of accountable positions are authorized at activities under their jurisdictions. Examination and inspection teams should review the number of accountable positions in use at disbursing activities and include comments and recommendations, as appropriate, in the report of examination or inspection.

Maintaining the smallest effective number of accountable officers is intended to ensure accountability and control of public funds.

The Comptroller General has held that an agency cannot, by agency regulation, designate an individual an "accountable officer" in the absence of statutory authority. In *Authority to Impose Pecuniary Liability by Regulation*, B-280764, May 4, 2000, GAO considered a DoD regulation that authorized DoD certifying officers to designate persons who approve time and attendance (T&A) records, receiving officials, and system administrators as "accountable officials." DoD Financial Management Regulation, DoD 7000.14-R, Vol. 5, Ch. 33, para. 330505 (August 1998). The regulation provided that these officials shall be pecuniarily liable for erroneous payments resulting from the negligent performance of their duties. GAO determined that the regulation could not impose such liability and stated:

> In our opinion, absent statutory authority, an agency may not administratively impose pecuniary liability on federal employees for the negligent performance of their duties. Since we are aware of no statutory authority in DoD to support this extension of pecuniary liability to "accountable officials," we would not view such officials as personally liable for any losses that result from the negligent performance of their duties.

GAO held that this decision overruled any of its prior decisions that upheld the imposition of liability based solely on an agency's designation of a government employee as an "accountable officer." This rationale for this decision could arguably also be applied as a defense to strict liability in cases involving use of the IMPAC card and the Government Travel Card.

Current law specifies certain bases for determining liability for each of the traditional types of accountable officers:

- Certifying officers
- Disbursing officers
- Cashiers
- Collecting officers
- Other custodians of federal funds.

Certifying Officers

Accountability for public funds in civilian agencies rests primarily with the certifying officer, a government officer or employee whose duties include certifying vouchers (including voucher schedules or invoices used as vouchers) for payment. Essentially, the certifying officer's duty is to ensure that vouchers and resulting payments comply with all applicable requirements and are otherwise proper. The Treasury Financial Manual, which is applicable to all federal agencies, defines a certifying officer as follows:

> Section 1145 - Designation of Certifying Officer
> Certifying Officers are individuals to whom authority to approve disbursal of agency funds has been delegated, by a properly authorized designating official. The designating official must have a valid FMS Form 2958 on file with FMS, providing authority to designate Certifying Officers for the agency. Officials, other than Head of Agency, delegated designation authority for Certifying Officers, MAY NOT designate themselves as Certifying Officers. (When it is necessary for such an individual to be designated as a Certifying Officer, the designation must be made by an official one level, or more, higher in the designation chain.)

A certifying officer differs from other accountable officers in that the certifying officer has no public funds in his or her physical custody. Consequently, certifying officer accountability is based on the nature of the function of certifying officers and not the physical loss of funds. The statutory basis for a certifying officer's liability is 31 U.S.C. § 3528. This statute makes certifying officers responsible for the legality of proposed payments and makes them liable for the amount of illegal or improper payments resulting from their certifications.

Although many government officials make official "certifications" of one type or another, this does not make them "certifying officers" for purposes of fiscal accountability and liability. The concepts of accountability and relief in this context apply only to authorized certifying officers who certify vouchers that will thereafter result in payments by disbursing officers to discharge a debt or obligation of the government. 23 Comp. Gen. 953 (1944). In rare circumstances, the head of a department or agency may serve as a certifying officer. 31 U.S.C. § 3325(a)(l); 21 Comp. Gen. 976, 979

(1942); 40 Op. Att'y Gen. 284 (1943), which states that "A disbursing official in the executive branch of the United States Government shall (1) disburse money only as provided by a voucher certified by (A) the head of the executive agency concerned. . . ."

An authorized certifying officer must be designated in writing. 31 U.S.C. § 3325(a)(1). Thus, an employee who "certified" overtime assignments, verifying that employees worked the hours of overtime claimed, could not be held liable for resulting overpayments as an accountable officer. B-197109, March 24, 1980. Similarly, an official who certifies that long-distance telephone calls are necessary for official business as required by 31 U.S.C. § 1348(b) is not an accountable officer. 65 Comp. Gen. 19, 20–21 (1985).

The same approach applies to various post-certification administrative actions, the rule being that once a voucher has been certified by an authorized official, subsequent administrative processing does not constitute certification for purposes of 31 U.S.C. § 3528. 55 Comp. Gen. 388, 390 (1975). For example, the Comptroller General has held that 31 U.S.C. § 3528 does not apply to an "approving officer" who merely approves vouchers after they have been duly certified. 21 Comp. Gen. 841 (1942).

Disbursing Officers

A disbursing officer is an officer or employee of a federal department or agency, civilian or military, designated to disburse moneys and render accounts in accordance with laws and regulations governing the disbursement of public funds. The term is essentially self-defining. As one court has stated:

> We do not find the term 'disbursing officer' statutorily defined, probably because it is self-definitive. It can mean nothing except an officer who is authorized to disburse funds of the United States.

Romney v. United States, 167 F.2d 521, 526 (D.C. Cir. 1948), cert. denied, 334 U.S. 847.

Whether an employee is a "disbursing officer" depends more on the nature of the person's duties than on the title of his or her position. In some cases, the job title will actually be "disbursing officer." This is the title for the disbursing officers of the Treasury Department who disburse for most civilian agencies under 31 U.S.C. § 3321. For the Department of Defense, which generally does its own disbursing, the applicable section of the DoD Financial Management Regulation (2001) states:

> 020301.B. Accountable Positions. Except as otherwise specifically provided, the function of regularly receiving and maintaining custody of public funds shall be performed only by DOs and their duly appointed deputies, agents and cashiers with respect to all public funds;
> The vast majority of disbursements within the Department of Defense are performed by the Defense Finance and Accounting Service (DFAS).

As a general rule, any employee to whom public funds are entrusted for the purpose of making payments from those funds will be regarded as a disbursing officer. See B-151156, December 30, 1963. There may be more than one disbursing officer for a given transaction. At military disbursing operations, for example, the account is often held in the name of a supervisory official such as a finance and accounting officer, with the actual payment made by someone else (agent, cashier, deputy, etc.). Both are regarded as disbursing officers for purposes of liability and relief, although the standards for relief differ. E.g., 62 Comp. Gen. 476, 479–80 (1983); B-245127, September 18, 1991.

Cashiers

A cashier is an officer or employee of a federal department, agency, or corporation who, having been recommended by the head of the activity, has been designated as a cashier by the officer responsible for making disbursements and is thereby authorized to perform limited cash disbursing functions or other cash operations. Cashier's Manual, Section II (available at www.fms.treas.gov/imprest). For example, the selection process within DoD is as follows:

> 020603. Cashiers
> A. Selection Procedure. An officer, enlisted member, or a civilian employee, with working knowledge of the cash functions and operations, may be designated as cashier. The DO or disbursing agent should make a thorough investigation of the selectee to ensure that the individual is of unquestionable integrity. To accomplish this the DO or disbursing agent should examine personnel records and talk to the individual and other persons as necessary. In addition, a credit report should be obtained if access to a credit reporting service is available.

An agency-designated Approving Office may appoint a cashier by completing OF 211, Request for Change or Establishment of Imprest Fund (Request for Change form) or a comparable agency-approved form. Cashiers must be employees of the agency for which they will perform cashier functions. Cashier's Manual, Section III. (The Treasury defines an "imprest fund" as: "A fixed-cash or petty-cash fund in the form of currency or coin that has been advanced as Funds Held Outside of Treasury. Federal agencies are required to report their imprest funds in General Ledger Account 1120 - Imprest Funds, on their annual financial statements. See Treasury Department Policy Directive at www.fms.treas.gov/imprest/policy.html.)

With respect to disbursing functions under 31 U.S.C. § 3321, cashiers are divided into three categories: (1) a Class A Cashier is a cashier who is authorized to make disbursements but may not advance an imprest fund to another cashier, except to an alternate cashier; (2) a Class B Cashier is a cashier who is authorized to make disbursements and may also advance funds to an alternate cashier or subcashier; and (3) a Class D Cashier is a cashier designated solely for change-making purposes. (When the Treasury Department issued the Cashier's Manual in April 2001, see http://www.fms

.treas.gov/imprest/, it deleted Class C Cashiers but retained the traditional Class A, B, and D categories.)

The role of imprest fund cashiers has diminished significantly in recent years. The Treasury Department issued a Policy Directive in November 1999 (www.fms.treas.gov/imprest/policy.html) that required all federal agencies to eliminate imprest funds unless a waiver was obtained. The rationale for this decision was stated as follows:

> The Federal government is increasingly relying on electronic payment mechanisms to streamline the payment process and reduce administrative and transaction costs. Legislation requiring the Federal government to make payments electronically has spurred the use of electronic alternatives to cash, particularly government purchase cards and, increasingly, debit cards, to eliminate cash payments from imprest funds. Many forms of payments historically made by cash have been converted to Direct Deposit to an individual's bank account, including travel advances and travel reimbursement. This changing payment environment has resulted in the formulation of new policy requiring, with some exceptions, that agencies eliminate their imprest funds. On November 9, 1999, the Financial Management Service published the Imprest Fund Policy Directive (Policy Directive) and other supporting documentation on the Internet at www.fms.treas.gov/imprest. The Policy Directive requires that all Federal agencies eliminate agency use of imprest funds by October 1, 2001, except where waived.

Regarding waivers, the Directive states:

> Imprest funds may only be used when:
> (a) A payment by [electronic funds transfer] EFT is waived in accordance with the provisions of 31 C.F.R. 208, Management of Federal Agency Disbursements, at §208.4 Waivers, and,
> (b) Payments involve national security interests, military operations, or national disasters;
> (c) Payments are made in furtherance of a law enforcement action;

(d) The amount owed is less than $25;
(e) The political, financial, or communications infrastructure of a foreign country does not support payment by a non-cash mechanism; or
(f) Payments are made in emergencies, or in mission critical circumstances, that are of such an unusual and compelling urgency that the Government would otherwise be seriously injured, unless payment is made by cash.

Note that the waivers will generally permit the use of imprest funds only in situations in which electronic fund transfers are not practical.

Cashiers are personally liable for any loss or shortage of funds in their custody unless relieved by proper authority. The Cashier's Manual states:

> As a cashier, you are liable for all funds advanced to you from the time you receive the funds until an acceptable and correct accounting is made and/or your designation as a cashier has been revoked or transferred.

For the most part, a cashier will be operating with funds advanced by his or her own employing agency. In some situations, however, such as an authorized interagency agreement, the funds maybe advanced by another agency. Liability and relief are the same in either case. 65 Comp. Gen. 666, 675–77 (1986).

Collecting Officers

Collecting officers are responsible for receiving or collecting money for the government, such as IRS collectors or Customs collectors. Collecting officers are accountable for all money collected. 59 Comp. Gen. 113, 114 (1979); 3 Comp. Gen. 403 (1924); 1 Comp. Dec. 191 (1895); B-201673 et al., September 23, 1982. For example, an IRS collector is responsible for the physical safety of taxes collected, must pay over to the government all taxes collected, and must make restitution for any money lost or stolen while in his or her custody unless relieved of liability. E.g., 60 Comp. Gen. 674 (1981). Similarly, the clerk of a bankruptcy court, if one has been appointed under 28 U.S.C. § 156(b), is the accountable officer with respect to fees paid to the court, as prescribed by 28 U.S.C. §1930, by parties commencing a case under the Bankruptcy Code. 28 U.S.C. § 156(b).

This provision, added in 1986, essentially codified the result of two GAO decisions issued the previous year, 64 Comp. Gen. 535 (1985) and B-217236, May 22, 1985. However, under an arrangement whereby tax payments are mailed to a financial institution at a post office box and then wired to a Treasury account, IRS officials are not accountable for funds in the possession of the financial institution since they do not gain custody or control over those funds. B-223911, February 24, 1987. Thus, a significant factor in establishing liability is whether the collecting officer had custody or control over the funds at the time they were lost or stolen.

In some situations, government funds may be collected by a contractor. Since the contractor is not a government officer or employee, the various accountable officer statutes do not apply, and the contractor's liability is governed by the terms of the contract. For example, a parking service contract with the General Services Administration required the contractor to collect parking fees at certain government buildings and to remit those fees to GSA on a daily basis. One day, instead of remitting the receipts, a contractor employee took the money home in a paper bag and claimed to have been robbed in a parking lot near her residence. When GSA withheld the amount of the loss from contract payments, the contractor tried to argue that the risk of loss should fall upon the government. The Claims Court disagreed. Since the contract terms were clear and the contractor failed to comply, the contractor was held responsible for the loss. *Miracle Contractors, Inc. v. United States*, 5 Cl. Ct. 466 (1984).

When the government uses volunteers to collect funds, such volunteers (unlike contractor personnel) have been treated as government employees for purposes of liability for public funds and relief from liability. For example, the Department of Agriculture has statutory authority to use volunteers to collect user fees in national forests. The volunteers, private individuals, must be bonded, and the cost of the bonds is paid by the Agriculture. 16 U.S.C. § 4601-6a(k). In 68 Comp. Gen. 470 (1989), GAO concurred with the Department of Agriculture's contention that the volunteers could be regarded as agents of the Forest Service and, as such, eligible for relief for non-negligent losses. The practical significance of this decision is that it would be difficult to recruit volunteers if they could not be relieved from liability for non-negligent losses, a possibility that would exist even under a surety bond.

Other Custodians of Federal Funds

Even if a government officer or employee does not fall into any of the preceding categories of accountable officers, they still may become liable for federal funds placed in their custody. This liability is based on the broad responsibilities imposed by 31 U.S.C. § 3302(a), which states:

> Sec. 3302. Custodians of money
> (a) Except as provided by another law, an official or agent of the United States Government having custody or possession of public money shall keep the money safe without -
> (1) lending the money;
> (2) using the money;
> (3) depositing the money in a bank; and
> (4) exchanging the money for other amounts.

This statute applies to any government employee, regardless of job description, to whom public funds are entrusted in connection with the performance of government business. See, e.g., B-170012, February 3, 1972. Examples of employees in this general custodial category include: a special messenger delivering cash to another location, B-188413, June 30, 1977; a messenger sent to the bank to cash checks,

B-226695, May 26, 1987; State Department employees responsible for packaging and shipping funds to an overseas embassy, B-193830, October 1, 1979; an officer in charge of a laundry operation on an Army base who had been advanced public funds to be held as a change fund, B-155149, October 21, 1964; and a Department of Energy Special Counsel with control over petroleum overcharge refunds, B-200170, April 1, 1981. More recently, the use of the government credit card (the IMPAC card) could result in violations of 31 U.S.C. § 3302 if a government employee uses the credit card to make personal purchases.

As with disbursing officers, there may be more than one accountable officer in a given case. The concept of accountability is not limited to the person in whose name the account is officially held, nor is it limited to the person or persons for whom relief is officially requested. B-247708, November 3, 1992, 72 Comp. Gen. 49 ("There may be more than one accountable officer in a given case and may include, in addition to the person in whose name an account is held, any other government employee who by reason of employment physically handles or otherwise takes custody of the funds.")

For example, accounts in the regional offices of the U.S. Customs Service are typically held in the name of the Regional Commissioner. While the Regional Commissioner is therefore an accountable officer with respect to that account, subordinate employees who actually handle the funds are also accountable officers. B-197324, March 7, 1980; B-193673, May 25, 1979. The same principle applies to the various service centers of the IRS. E.g., 60 Comp. Gen. 674 (1981).

As demonstrated by the Customs and IRS situations, as well as the many cases involving military finance and accounting officers, a supervisory official will be an accountable officer if that official has actual custody of public funds or if the account is held in the official's name, regardless of who has physical custody. Unless these factors are present, however, a supervisor is not an accountable officer and does not become one merely because he or she supervises an accountable officer. E.g., B-214286, July 20, 1984; B-194782, August 13, 1979.

In each case, it is necessary to examine the particular facts and circumstances to determine who had responsibility for or custody of the funds at the time of the occurrence or transaction. In some cases, more than one person may be held liable. Thus, in B-193830, October 1, 1979, money shipped from the State Department to the American Embassy in Paraguay never reached its destination. While the funds were chargeable to the account of the Class B cashier at the Embassy, the State Department employees responsible for packaging and shipping the funds were also accountable officers with respect to that transaction. In another case, a new Class B cashier had been recommended at a Peace Corps office in Western Samoa, and had in fact been doing the job, but his official designation was not made until after the loss in question. Since the new cashier, even though not yet formally designated, had possession of the funds at the time of the loss, he was an accountable officer. However, since the former cashier retained responsibility for the imprest fund until formally replaced, he too was an accountable officer. B-188881, May 8, 1978.

In sum, any government officer or employee who physically handles government funds, even if only occasionally, is accountable for those funds while they are in his or her custody. However, in the unlikely situation in which it cannot be determined who was responsible for the funds when the loss occurred, no one will be held liable for the loss.

For example, the Drug Enforcement Administration used a flash roll (see next section for definition of a flash roll) of 650 $100 bills and discovered that 15 bills had been replaced by counterfeits scattered throughout the roll. The roll had been used in a number of investigations, and in each instance, the transactions (transfers from cashier to investigators, returns to cashier, transfers between different groups of investigators) were recorded on receipts and the money was counted. While it was possible to determine precisely who had the roll on any given day, there was no way to determine when the substitution took place and hence to establish to whom the loss should be attributed. B-191891, June 16, 1980.

Discussion Problem 8-1

How do the responsibilities of a disbursing officer differ from those of a certifying officer?

In terms of accountable officer liability, what is the difference between a contractor employee who collects public funds and a non-contractor volunteer who collects public funds on behalf of the government?

What is the citation of the statute that imposes liability for misuse of public funds on personnel who are not "accountable officers"?

FUNDS FOR WHICH ACCOUNTABLE OFFICERS ARE RESPONSIBLE

Accountable officers are responsible for "public funds." Public funds comprise three categories of funds: (1) appropriated funds; (2) funds received by the government from nongovernment sources; and (3) funds held in trust for others. If funds do not fall within any of these categories, the funds are not subject to the laws governing the liability and relief of accountable officers. However, liability for losses may still arise on some other basis.

Appropriated Funds

Appropriated funds are accountable funds that typically remain in the Treasury until they are disbursed. However, appropriated funds may also be advanced to a government cashier or employee for some authorized purpose. Specific rules apply to determine if several different types of appropriated funds are "accountable" funds.

Imprest Funds

Imprest fund cashiers are liable for all funds advanced to them from the time they receive the funds until an acceptable and correct accounting is made and/or the cashier's designation as a cashier has been revoked or transferred. See Cashiers Manual, p. 8.

Flash Rolls

Law enforcement officers on undercover assignments frequently need a supply of cash to support their operations, for example, to purchase contraband or to use as a gambling stake. This money, often advanced from an imprest fund, is called a "flash roll." A flash roll in the hands of a law enforcement agent retains its status as government funds. *Garcia v. United States*, 469 U.S. 70 (1984) (flash roll held to be money of the United States for purposes of 18 U.S.C. § 2114, which makes it a criminal offense to assault a custodian of government money). However, if the flash roll is lost because of a risk that is inherent in the law enforcement operation (e.g., the criminal suspect steals the money), then the loss is not viewed as an "accountable officer" loss but may be handled internally by the agency. See, e.g., 61 Comp. Gen. 313 (1982); B-238222, February 21, 1990 (suspect stole flash roll during drug arrest); B-232253, August 12, 1988 (informant stole money provided to rent undercover apartment); and B-205426, September 16, 1982 (federal agent robbed at gunpoint while trying to purchase illegal firearms).

Travel Advances

Travel advances to government personnel are regarded as nonaccountable funds and hence are not governed by the accountable officer laws. Rather, they are treated as loans for the personal benefit of the traveler. Consequently, if the funds are lost or stolen while in the traveler's custody, regardless of the presence or absence of fault attributable to the traveler, the funds must be recovered as provided by 5 U.S.C. § 5705, and the accountable officer relief statutes do not apply. 54 Comp. Gen. 190 (1974); B-206245, April 26, 1982; B-183489, June 30, 1975.

5 U.S.C. § 5705 provides:

> Sec. 5705. Advancements and deductions
> An agency may advance, through the proper disbursing official, to an employee entitled to per diem or mileage allowances under this subchapter, a sum considered advisable with regard to the character and probable duration of the travel to be performed. A sum advanced and not used for allowable travel expenses is recoverable from the employee or his estate by -
> (1) setoff against accrued pay, retirement credit, or other amount due the employee;
> (2) deduction from an amount due from the United States; and
> (3) such other method as is provided by law.

The same principle applies to traveler's checks. 64 Comp. Gen. 456, 460 (1985). In many cases, a messenger or some other clerical employee picks up the advanced funds for the traveler. If the funds are lost or stolen while in the intermediary's custody, and use of the intermediary was the traveler's choice, the intermediary is the agent of the traveler and since the traveler has constructively received the funds, the traveler is liable. B-204387, February 24, 1982; B-200867, March 30, 1981. However, if use of the intermediary is required by the agency or local policy, then the intermediary is the agent of the government and the traveler would not be liable. 67 Comp. Gen. 402 (1988).

As a result of the enactment the Travel and Transportation Reform Act of 1998 (TTRA), Public Law 105-264, government employees are generally required to use the government-sponsored, contractor-issued travel card to pay for costs incident to official business travel. Cardholders may use the card to obtain travel advances at automated teller machines (ATMs). Since the travel cards are issued in the name of the individual employee, liability for payment falls on the employee and not the government. Consequently, the travel advances do not constitute "public funds" and do not trigger accountable officer liability. Of course, agencies may determine that it is appropriate to impose other sanctions for misuse of the travel card. The DoD Financial Management Regulation, Vol. 9, Ch. 3 (2000) addresses this point as follows:

> 030607. Misuse. Commanders or supervisors shall not tolerate misuse of the DoD travel card and cardholders who do misuse their DoD travel cards shall be subject to appropriate administrative or disciplinary action. These cards shall be used only for reimbursable expenses associated with official travel.

The misuse of the government travel card has been addressed in several government studies. See, e.g., a study conducted by the Department of Justice (www.usdoj.gov/oig/ 1200101/findings.htm); a presentation by the Navy (www.fmo.navy.mil/docs/comp_05mar02_chargeprog.pdf); and a House Subcommittee Hearing (www.house.gov/reform/gefmir/hearings/2001hearings/ 0730_creditcards/ 0730_grassley.htm). Continued delinquency problems could cause commercial contractor banks to cease their support for the program. If this were to happen, agencies might go back to the traditional travel advance system, and the prior rules would once again apply.

Funds Received from Nongovernment Sources

A government agency may receive funds from nongovernment sources from the exercise of its sovereign powers (e.g., tax collections, customs duties, court fees) and from a variety of business-type activities (e.g., sale of publications). These collections, whether they are to be deposited in the Treasury as miscellaneous receipts or credited to some agency appropriation or fund, are accountable funds from the moment of receipt. See, e.g., 64 Comp. Gen. 535 (1985) (fees paid to bankruptcy court); 60 Comp. Gen. 674 (1981) (tax collections); B200170, April 1, 1981 (petroleum overcharge refunds); B-194782, August 25, 1980 (recreational fee collections). Since such funds are "accountable," accountable officers may be held liable for their loss.

Funds Held in Trust for Others

When the government holds private funds in a trust capacity, it must, by virtue of its fiduciary duty, transfer those funds to the rightful owners at the proper time. Thus, although the funds are not appropriated funds, they are nevertheless accountable funds. This principle has been stated as follows:

> [T]he same relationship between an accountable officer and the United States is required with respect to trust funds of a private character obtained and held for some particular purpose sanctioned by law as is required with respect to public funds.

6 Comp. Gen. 515, 517 (1927).

The Court of Claims reached the same conclusion in *Woog v. United States*, 48 Ct. Cl. 80 (1913).

An example in which an agency holds funds for others is the Department of Veterans Affairs "Personal Funds of Patients" (PFOP) account. Upon admission to a VA hospital, patients may deposit personal funds in this account for safekeeping and use as needed. Upon release, the balance is returned to the patient. Patient funds in the PFOP account have been consistently treated as accountable funds. 68 Comp. Gen. 600 (1989); 68 Comp. Gen. 371 (1989); B-226911, October 19, 1987; B-221447, April 2, 1986; B-215477, November 5, 1984; B-208888, September 28, 1984.

Another example is private funds of litigants deposited in a registry account of a court of the United States, to be held pending distribution by order of the court in accordance with 28 U.S.C. §§ 2041-2042. These are also accountable funds under the trust fund concept. 64 Comp. Gen. 535 (1985); 6 Comp. Gen. 515 (1927); B-200108iB-198558, January 23, 1981. See also *Osborn v. United States*, 91 U.S. 474

(1875) (court can summarily compel restitution of funds improperly withdrawn from registry account by former officers). Other situations applying the trust fund concept are 67 Comp. Gen. 342 (1988) (Indian trust accounts administered by Bureau of Indian Affairs); 17 Comp. Gen. 786 (1938) (United States Naval Academy laundry fund); B-190205, November 14, 1977 (foreign currencies accepted in connection with accommodation exchanges authorized by 31 U.S.C. § 3342; and A-22805, November 30, 1929 (funds taken from prisoners at the time of their confinement, to be held in their behalf. See also 69 Comp. Gen. 314 (1990) (agency may contract with private bank for ministerial aspects of trust fund disbursements, but government disbursing officer must retain responsibility for managerial and judgmental aspects).

However, not all nongovernment funds in the custody of a government official are held in a trust capacity. For example, in B-164419 -O.M., May 20, 1969, GAO distinguished between funds of a foreign government held by the United States incident to a cooperative agreement (trust funds) and funds of a private contractor held by a government official for safekeeping as a favor to the contractor. The latter situation was a mere bailment for the benefit of the contractor, and not one in which the funds were being held in trust for another. In such cases, the official is not an accountable officer with respect to those funds.

EVENTS THAT CAN RESULT IN ACCOUNTABLE OFFICER LIABILITY

There are two broad categories of events that can result in accountable officer liability: (1) physical loss or deficiency, and (2) illegal, improper, or incorrect payment. Recall that there is a distinction between how the term "accountable officer" is defined by non-DoD agencies and DoD. Within non-DoD agencies, the term "accountable officer" is very broad and includes certifying officers and disbursing officers. Although DoD has certifying officers and disbursing officers, it has created a third category, "accountable officials," which covers any person who is not a certifying officer or a disbursing officer, but who provides information, data, or services to a certifying or disbursing officer in support of the payment process. This section discusses the liability of civilian and military certifying and disbursing officers.

Since the statutes that authorize relief are expressly tied to these categories, the proper classification of a fiscal irregularity is the essential first step in determining which statute to apply when attempting to grant relief.

Physical Loss or Deficiency

A useful definition of "physical loss or deficiency" was provided by the Comptroller General in B-202074, July 21, 1983, which stated:

> In sum, "physical loss or deficiency" includes such things as loss by theft or burglary, loss in shipment, and loss or destruction by fire, accident, or natural disaster. It also includes the totally unexplained loss, that is, a shortage or deficiency with absolutely no evidence to explain the disappearance. . . . Finally . . . losses resulting from fraud or embezzlement by subordinate finance personnel may . . . be treated as physical losses.

This definition has been repeated in several subsequent decisions, including 70 Comp. Gen. 616, 621 (1991) and 65 Comp. Gen. 881, 883 (1986).

Illegal, Improper, or Incorrect Payment

The second type of fiscal irregularity is the "illegal, improper, or incorrect payment." 31 U.S.C. §§ 3527(c), 3528(a)(4). The key word here is "payment," which is the disbursement of public funds by a disbursing officer or his subordinate. B-202074, July 21, 1983. Improper payments include payments obtained by fraud, whether by non-government persons or by government employees other than subordinate finance personnel; erroneous payments or overpayments resulting from human or mechanical error attributable to the government; payments prohibited by statute; and disbursements for unauthorized purposes. The legislative history of the statute pertaining to relief for disbursing officers who have made improper payments, 31 U.S.C. § 3527(c), describes an improper payment as a payment "which the Comptroller General finds is not in strict technical conformity" with the law.

Comparison of the Two Bases for Liability

It is sometimes difficult to distinguish between the two bases for liability. For example, a loss resulting from an uncollectible personal check may be an improper payment or a physical loss, depending on the circumstances. If the loss results from an authorized check-cashing transaction, it is an improper payment because government funds were disbursed to the bearer. 70 Comp. Gen. 616 (1991). However, if the check is tendered to pay an obligation owed to the United States or to purchase something from the government, the loss, to the extent an accountable loss exists, would be a physical loss.

In some situations, a bad check may not trigger accountable officer liability at all. In this connection, the Treasury Financial Manual states:

> Checks received by Government officers are accepted subject to collection. If a check cannot be collected in full or is lost or destroyed before collection, the administrative agency concerned is responsible for obtaining the proper payment. Payment by check is not effective until the full proceeds are received.

Treasury Financial Manual, Vol. I, § 5-2010.

Thus, if a personal check is accepted subject to collection, and if the government does not exchange value for the check, any resulting loss is not a loss within the scope of the accountable officer laws and may be adjusted administratively by the agency. An example would be a personal check submitted to pay a fine to the IRS. Since the IRS did not sell anything to the payor or otherwise exchange something of value, if the check is partly or entirely uncollectible, the loss would not be an accountable officer loss.

Typically, the agency will seek collection from the payor. If, however, an accountable officer accepts a personal check in satisfaction of an obligation due the United States (rather than for collection only), or if the government parts with something of value in exchange for the check (e.g., sale of government property), any resulting loss would be treated as a physical loss. B-215194, Feb. 25, 1985, 64 Comp. Gen. 303; B-201673, September 23, 1982. See also 3 Comp. Gen. 403 (1924); A-44019, March 15, 1934. GAO summarized the distinction in B-201673 as follows:

> If a check tendered in payment of a fine, duty, or penalty becomes uncollectible, it may be argued that the Government incurs a loss in the sense that it does not have money to which it was legally entitled, but it has not lost anything that it already had. When the check is in exchange for property, the Government has lost the property, the value of which is measured by the agreed-upon sales price. Of course, recovery of the property will remove or mitigate the loss.

The concept of B-201673 was applied to a check seized as forfeiture under the Currency and Foreign Transactions Reporting Act and subsequently returned as uncollectible. B-208398, September 29, 1983. Since the government had not exchanged value for the check, the situation was not considered a "physical loss" within the scope of the accountable officer laws. In contrast, in B-216279, October 9, 1984, a teller at a Customs Service auction gave a receipt to a customer who had purchased agency property but had negligently failed to collect the tendered funds. It was suggested that there was no loss because the teller never had physical possession of the funds. However, the applicable relief statute (31 U.S.C. § 3527) uses the terms "physical loss *or* deficiency" [emphasis added], and there was clearly a deficiency in the teller's account to the extent of the property turned over in exchange for the lost payment.

While every fiscal irregularity by definition involves a loss or deficiency for which someone is accountable, not every loss or deficiency is a fiscal irregularity that will trigger accountable officer liability. For example, an accountable officer is not liable for interest lost on collections that should have been deposited promptly but were not. 64 Comp. Gen. 303 (1985) (failure to deposit collections in designated depositary); B-190290, November 28, 1977 (increased interest charges on funds borrowed from Treasury, no net loss to United States). Similarly, losses resulting from the imperfect exercise of judgment in routine business operations, where no law has been violated, do not create accountable officer liability. 65 Comp. Gen. 881 (1986) (loss to Internal Revenue Service Tax Lien Revolving Fund caused by sale of property for substantially less than amount for which it had been redeemed).

The distinction between these cases and cases in which liability arises is that, in the "no liability" cases, the government did not physically possess the funds "lost" or otherwise have a right to them. Although the failure to promptly deposit funds caused the government to lose interest, the government never possessed or had a right to the interest payments. Consequently, for accountable officer purposes, the non-receipt of interest is not considered a "loss or deficiency."

> **Discussion Problem 8-2**
>
> The Bureau of Land Management (BLM) is responsible for the operation of several copper and silver mines for the United States. It is authorized to sell excess ore and can fine trespassers on mine property. The BLM cashier is responsible for the funds received for the sale of excess ore and also collects the fines from the trespassers. Which of the following situations, if any, give rise to accountable officer liability?
> 1. There is a shortage of $1,000 in the account for funds received for the sale of excess ore.
> 2. A check received as payment for the sale of excess ore is uncollectible.
> 3. A check received as payment for a fine from a trespasser is uncollectible.

RELIEF FROM LIABILITY

As discussed, there are two statutory bases for accountable officer liability: (1) physical loss or deficiency, and (2) illegal, improper, or incorrect payment. Each of the statutes imposing liability also provides for relief from liability under certain circumstances. Differences arise depending on whether the individual is an employee of a DoD agency or a non-DoD agency. This section will separately discuss the circumstances under which relief may be granted under each of the two statutory bases of liability, who may grant such relief, and the procedures that must be followed.

Relief in Physical Loss or Deficiency Cases

The two principal statutes authorizing administrative relief from liability for the physical loss or deficiency of public funds are 31 U.S.C. §§ 3527(a) and 3527(b). In general, subsection (a) applies to accountable officers in non-DoD agencies, and subsection (b) applies to DoD disbursing officers and, as a result of 1996 legislation, Pub. L. No. 104-106, § 913(c), to DoD certifying officers. The relief statute, as it pertains to physical losses or deficiencies, states:

> **Sec. 3527. General authority to relieve accountable officials and agents from liability**
> (a) Except as provided in subsection (b) of this section, the Comptroller General may relieve a present or former accountable official or agent of an agency responsible for the physical loss or deficiency of public money, vouchers, checks, securities, or records, or may authorize reimbursement from an appropriation or fund available for the activity in which the loss or deficiency occurred for the amount of the loss or deficiency paid by the official or agent as restitution, when -
> (1) the head of the agency decides that -
>   (A) the official or agent was carrying out official duties when the loss or deficiency occurred, or the loss or deficiency occurred because of an act or failure to act by a subordinate of the official or agent; and
>   (B) the loss or deficiency was not the result of fault or negligence by the official or agent;
> (2) the loss or deficiency was not the result of an illegal or incorrect payment; and
> (3) the Comptroller General agrees with the decision of the head of the agency
> (b)(1) The Comptroller General shall relieve an official of the armed forces referred to in subsection (a) responsible for the physical loss or deficiency of public money, vouchers, or records, or a payment described in section 3528(a)(4)(A) of this title, or shall authorize reimbursement, from an appropriation or fund available for reimbursement, of the amount of the loss or deficiency paid by or for the official as restitution, when -
>   (A) in the case of a physical loss or deficiency -
> (i) the Secretary of Defense or the appropriate Secretary of the military department of the Department of Defense (or the Secretary of Transportation, in the case of a disbursing official of the Coast Guard when the Coast Guard is not operating as a service in the Navy) decides that the official was carrying out official duties when the loss or deficiency occurred;

(ii) the loss or deficiency was not the result of an illegal or incorrect payment; and
(iii) the loss or deficiency was not the result of fault or negligence by the official; or
(B) in the case of a payment described in section 3528(a)(4)(A) of this title, the Secretary of Defense or the Secretary of the appropriate military department (or the Secretary of Transportation, in the case of a disbursing official of the Coast Guard when the Coast Guard is not operating as a service in the Navy), after taking a diligent collection action, finds that the criteria of section 3528(b)(1) of this title are satisfied.
(2) The finding of the Secretary involved is conclusive on the Comptroller General.

The rules authorizing relief for physical losses and deficiencies are slightly different for civilian and military accountable officers.

Civilian Agency Accountable Officers

The physical loss or deficiency relief statute applicable to accountable officers generally, 31 U.S.C. § 3527(a), was originally enacted in 1947 (61 Stat. 720). Its justification, similar to that for all relief statutes, was to provide a streamlined administrative process for granting relief instead of the more formal procedures that had historically been used. This justification was summarized by the Senate Committee on Expenditures in the Executive Departments as follows:

> The justification . . . is that, at the present time, relief of the kind with which this bill is concerned is required to be granted either through passage of a special relief bill by the Congress or by the filing of suit by the responsible person in the United States Court of Claims, the latter to be done at the personal expense of the responsible person. Both methods are costly and time consuming.

S. Rep. No. 379, 80th Cong., 1st Sess., reprinted in 1947 U.S. Code Cong. Service 1546.

Before the actual relief mechanism is triggered, two threshold issues must be satisfied: (1) the loss must be a physical loss or deficiency and not an improper payment, 31 U.S.C. § 3527(a)(2); and (2) the person for whom relief is desired must be an "accountable officer." (This statute will generally not apply to certifying officers since they do not have actual custody of funds. However, a certifying officer could conceivably have other duties or supervisory responsibilities and thus be accountable and therefore eligible for relief under 31 U.S.C. § 3527(a) based on those supervisory responsibilities.) The legislative history confirms that the definition of accountable officer includes persons who have custody of public funds, even if they are not "disbursing officers." The Senate Report stated:

> There are many agents of the Government who do not disburse but who, nevertheless, are fully responsible for funds . . . entrusted to their charge and, for that reason, the committee bill has been broadened to include that class of personnel.

S. Rep. No. 379, 1947 U.S. Code Cong. Service at 1547.

Once it has been determined that there has been a physical loss or deficiency of "public money, vouchers, checks, securities, or records" for which an accountable officer is liable, the statute authorizes the Comptroller General to grant relief from that liability if the head of the agency involved makes two administrative determinations (31 U.S.C. § 3527(a)(1)) and if the Comptroller General agrees with those determinations (§ 3527(a)(3)). First, the agency head must determine that the accountable officer was carrying out official duties at the time of the loss *or* that the loss was attributable to the act or omission of a subordinate of the accountable officer. The latter part, loss attributable to a subordinate, is designed to cover the situation, found in several agencies such as the IRS and the Customs Service, in which the account is in the name of a supervisory official who does not actually handle the funds. In this situation, both persons are accountable, and relief of one does not necessarily merit relief of the other. The second administrative determination that the head of the agency must make is that the loss was not attributable to fault or negligence on the part of the accountable officer. Thus, while lack of fault does not affect the automatic imposition of liability, it does provide the basis for relief.

Generally, the requirement that the accountable officer must have been acting in the discharge of official duties does not present problems. Thus, in the typical case, the central question becomes whether GAO is able to concur with the administrative determination that the loss or deficiency occurred without fault or negligence on the part of the accountable officer. Many factors may bear on the determination of whether a loss or deficiency was without the fault or negligence of the accountable officer, and GAO's assessment will be based on the interrelationship of these factors.

Finally, note that section 3527(a) applies to accountable officers of "an agency," which is defined in 31 U.S.C. § 101 as any "department, agency, or instrumentality of the United States Government." Thus, section 3527(a) has been construed as applicable to the judicial branch (B-200108/B-198558, January 23, 1981; B-197021, May 9, 1980; B-191440, May 25, 1979; B-185486, February 5, 1976), and to agencies of the legislative branch, such as the GAO (B-192503 -O. M., January 8, 1979, denying relief to a GAO employee).

Department of Defense Disbursing Officers and Certifying Officers

The physical loss and deficiency statute applicable to DoD disbursing and certifying officers is 31 U.S.C. § 3527(b). The statute applies to both civilian and military personnel of the various military departments who serve as either disbursing or certifying officers. B-151156, December 30, 1963.

Section 3527(b) and section 3527(a) are similar in at least one regard: Once it has been determined that a loss is properly cognizable under the statute, the applicable agency head must determine that (1) the disbursing or certifying officer was carrying out official duties at the time of the loss or deficiency; (2) the loss or deficiency was not the result of an illegal or incorrect payment; and (3) the loss occurred without fault or negligence on the part of the disbursing or certifying officer.

The first determination, 31 U.S.C. § 3527(b)(l)(A), does not expressly include the "loss attributable to subordinate" clause found in section 3527(a). However, GAO cases have included such losses in the same manner as in section 3527(a). See B-155149, October 21, 1964; B-151 156, December 30, 1963. An administrative determination to relieve a DoD disbursing or certifying officer from liability is conclusive on GAO. 31 U.S.C. § 3527(b)(1). Thus, once the determinations are made, the granting of relief is mandatory. Thus, unlike section 3527(a), if the situation is properly cognizable under section 3527(b), GAO has no discretion in the matter. Consequently, GAO does not require that the DoD determination be forwarded to GAO. See *GAO Policy and Procedures Manual for Guidance of Federal Agencies*, Title 7, § 8.10; B-271859, Sep. 26, 1996 (unpub.). This distinction is reflected in the wording of section 3527(a) ("the Comptroller General *may* relieve"), as compared to section 3527(b) ("the Comptroller General *shall* relieve").

The Secretary of Defense has delegated the authority to make relief determinations as follows:

> The Secretary of Defense has delegated authority to the Director, DFAS, to act for the Secretary of Defense to make the required determinations and to grant or deny relief for all requests for relief of liability for physical losses submitted under the provisions of this volume. The Director, DFAS, has delegated this authority to the Director for Finance, DFAS.

DoD Financial Management Regulation, Vol. 5, Ch. 6, para. 060902 (2000).

For purposes of granting relief, the DoD definition of disbursing officials includes deputy disbursing officers, disbursing agents, cashiers, agent cashiers, collection agents, paying agents, imprest fund cashiers, and change fund custodians. DoD Financial Management Regulation, Vol. 5, Ch. 6, para. 060902 (2000). Although DoD's determination is final regarding whether to grant relief from liability for physical loss, determinations on the threshold issues (e.g., what is a physical loss and who is a disbursing officer) are not conclusive on GAO. B-151156, December 30, 1963.

Discussion Problem 8-3

The rules applicable to relief of accountable officers for losses and deficiencies differ in at least two significant respects for non-DoD accountable officers as compared to DoD accountable officers. What are these two differences?

Officials Authorized to Grant Relief

The rules regarding officials authorized to grant relief are also slightly different for civilian and military accountable officers.

Civilian Agency Accountable Officers
Section 3527(a) of Title 31 confers the authority to grant relief on the Comptroller General. However, in 1969, GAO initiated the practice of setting a dollar amount, initially $150, below which agencies could apply the standards and grant or deny relief accordingly without the need to obtain formal concurrence from GAO. GAO has raised the amount several times over the years and has used various formats to announce the increase. The current ceiling is $3,000. See GAO, *Policy and Procedures Manual for Guidance of Federal Agencies*, Title 7, § 8.9.C; *Mr. Frank Palmer*, B-252809, Apr. 7, 1993 (unpub.); *Mr. Thomas M. Vapniarek*, B-249796, Feb. 9, 1993 (unpub.); *Mr. Melvin L. Hines*, B-247708, 72 Comp. Gen. 49 (1992). B-243749, October 22, 1991. The authorization applies to physical losses or deficiencies but not to improper payments (with a few exceptions to be noted later). 61 Comp. Gen. 646 (1982); 59 Comp. Gen. 113 (1979).

As GAO stated in 61 Comp. Gen. at 647:

> For the most part, the law governing the physical loss or deficiency of Government funds is clear, and most cases center around the determination of whether there was

any contributing negligence on the part of the accountable officer. Our numerous decisions in this area should provide adequate guidance to agencies in resolving most smaller losses.

The $3,000 limitation applies to "single incidents or the total of similar incidents which occur about the same time and involve the same accountable officer." GAO, *Policy and Procedures Manual for Guidance of Federal Agencies*, title 7, § 8.9.C (1990). Thus, two losses arising from the same theft, one under the limit and one over, should be combined for purposes of relief. B-189795, September 23, 1977.

For example, in B-193380, September 25, 1979, an imprest fund cashier discovered a $300 shortage while reconciling her cash and subvouchers. A few days later, her supervisor, upon returning from vacation, found an additional $500 missing. Since the losses occurred under very similar circumstances, GAO agreed with the agency that they should be treated together for purposes of seeking relief.

Another case, B-187139, October 25, 1978, involved losses of $1,500, $60, and $50. Since there was no indication that the losses were related, the agency was advised to resolve the $60 and $50 losses administratively. The ceiling was $500 at the time B-193380 and B-187139 were decided.

Thus, in cases of physical loss or deficiency, it is necessary to request relief from GAO only if the amount involved is $3,000 or more. For below-ceiling losses, GAO's concurrence is, in effect, granted categorically provided the matter is properly cognizable under the statute, the agency makes the required determinations, and the administrative resolution is accomplished in accordance with the standards set forth in the GAO decisions. See, e.g., B-206817, February 10, 1983; B-204740, November 25, 1981. GAO recommends that each agency maintain a central control record of its below-ceiling resolutions, document the basis for its decisions, and retain that documentation for subsequent internal or external audit or review. 7 GAO-PPM § 8.9.C (1990).

As a practical matter, GAO's authorization for below-ceiling agency resolution affects the relief procedures only where the agency believes relief should be granted. If the agency believes relief should not be granted, its refusal to support relief effectively ends the matter regardless of the amount, because GAO will not review an agency's refusal to grant relief in a below-ceiling case. 59 Comp. Gen. 113, 114 (1979).

Department of Defense Disbursing and Certifying Officers

Like 31 U.S.C. § 3527(a), section 3527(b) also specifies the Comptroller General as the relieving authority. However, since the determination by DoD to grant relief is binding on GAO, the monetary ceiling concept used in civilian relief cases has much less relevance to military disbursing and certifying officer losses. By circular letter B-198451, February 5, 1981, GAO notified the military departments of a change in procedures under 31 U.S.C. § 3527(b). In a 1996 decision, GAO declined to consider a request for relief from liability and stated:

> Relief of military disbursing officers for physical losses is governed by 31 U.S.C. Sec. 3527(b). Section 3527(b) requires that the Secretary of Defense or the appropriate Secretary of the military department determine that the loss (1) occurred in the line of duty, (2) without fault or negligence on the part of the disbursing officer, and (3) was not the result of an improper payment. In military physical loss relief requests in which these administrative determinations are made, the granting of relief follows automatically. In a 1981 letter, we advised the heads of military departments that they do not need to submit physical loss relief requests to GAO.

Although this case applied to "disbursing officers," the addition of certifying officers to 31 U.S.C. 3527(b) in 1996 presumably make this procedure equally applicable to DoD certifying officers in physical loss or deficiency cases. Thus, since GAO has no discretion with respect to the agency determinations and relief is mandatory as long as the determinations are made, there is no need for GAO to review any of those determinations on a case-by-case basis.

Thus, there is no need for the agency to submit a formal request for relief regardless of the amount involved. As long as the case is properly cognizable under 31 U.S.C. § 3527(b) (i.e., it involves a disbursing officer and a physical loss or deficiency), it is sufficient for purposes of compliance with the statute for the agency to make the required determinations and to retain the documentation on file for audit purposes.

Standard for Granting Relief in Physical Loss or Deficiency Cases

Accountable officers are strictly liable for all losses but may be relieved if found to be free from fault or negligence. In other words, if there is a loss or deficiency of public funds, the responsible accountable officer is automatically liable. Consequently, it is the accountable officer who must prove that relief from liability is appropriate, and it is not the burden of the agency to prove liability. This section discusses what the accountable officer must prove to be relieved of liability.

Absence of Negligence

In evaluating the facts to determine whether or not an accountable officer was negligent, GAO applies the standard of "reasonable care." 54 Comp. Gen. 112 (1974); B-196790, February 7, 1980. This is the standard of simple or ordinary negligence, not gross negligence. 54 Comp. Gen. at 115; B-158699, September 6, 1968. The standard has been described as what the reasonably prudent and careful person would have done to take care of his or her own property under similar circumstances. B-209569, April 13, 1983; B-193673, May 25, 1979; *Malone v. United States*, 5 Ct. Cl. 186, 189 (1869). This is an objective standard, that is, it does not change based on the age and experience of the particular accountable officer.

GAO has consistently held that the doctrine of comparative negligence (allocating the loss based on the degree of fault) does not apply under the relief statutes. B-211962, July

20, 1983; B-190506, November 28, 1977. Thus, the accountable officer is either responsible for the full amount of the loss or relieved of liability entirely.

Discussion Problem 8-4

A federal agency cashier office employs two cashiers, Ima Olde and Justa Newbe. Ima has been a cashier for 28 years and is considered the most knowledgeable cashier in the federal government. Justa has been on the job only three weeks. Each has been assigned one account, and each is responsible for maintaining a ledger for their own account. During a routine audit, it was discovered that both accounts had a loss, apparently attributable to a failure to record receipts properly. Both cashiers requested relief from liability. The agency determined that Ima should have known better and denied relief. However, in consideration of Justa's lack of experience, the agency recommended relief as a "one-time good deal." Were the agency's determinations based on appropriate considerations?

Accountable officers trying to prove the absence of negligence have a difficult burden because the mere fact that a loss or deficiency has occurred creates a presumption of negligence on the part of the accountable officer. The presumption may be rebutted by evidence to the contrary, but it is the accountable officer's burden to produce the evidence, i.e., that he or she exercised the requisite degree of care.

This rule originated in decisions of the Court of Claims under 28 U.S.C. § 2512, before any of the administrative relief statutes existed, and has been consistently followed. An early and often quoted statement is the following from *Boggs v. United States*, 44 Ct. Cl. 367, 384 (1909), where the court stated:

> [T]here is at the outset a presumption of liability, and the burden of proof must rest upon the officer who has sustained the loss.

See also *O'Neal v. United States*, 60 Ct. Cl. 413 (1925); *Serrano v. United States*, 612 F.2d 525, 532–33 (Ct. Cl. 1979). GAO follows the same rule, stating it in literally dozens of relief cases. See, e.g., 67 Comp. Gen. 6 (1987); 65 Comp. Gen. 876 (1986); 54 Comp. Gen. 112 (1974); 48 Comp. Gen. 566 (1969).

The amount and types of evidence that will suffice to rebut the presumption vary with the facts and circumstances of the particular case. However, there must be affirmative evidence. It has not been enough for the accountable officer to simply rely on the absence of implicating evidence, nor is the mere administrative determination that there was no fault or negligence, unsupported by evidence, sufficient to rebut the presumption. See, e.g., 70 Comp. Gen. 12, 14 (1990); B-204647, February 8, 1982; B-167126, August 9, 1976.

For example, if the record clearly establishes that the loss resulted from burglary or robbery, the presumption is easily rebutted. However, the evidence does not have to explain the loss with absolute certainty, and even if the evidence is not all that clear, the accountable officer may still be able to rebut the presumption by presenting evidence tending to corroborate the likelihood of theft or showing that some factor beyond his control was responsible for the loss. If such evidence exists, and if the record shows that the accountable officer complied fully with all applicable regulations and procedures, the agency's determination of no fault or negligence will usually be accepted by GAO and relief granted.

GAO has considered polygraph results as an additional factor but has not regarded those results, standing alone, as dispositive. This applies whether the results are favorable (B-206745, August 9, 1982; B-204647, February 8, 1982; B-142326, March 31, 1960; B-182829 -O. M., February 3, 1975) or unfavorable (B-209569, April 13, 1983; see also B-192567, August 4, 1983, aff'd upon reconsideration, B-192567, June 21, 1988).

Another situation in which the presumption is easily rebutted is where the accountable officer does not have control of the funds at the time of the loss. An example is losses occurring while the accountable officer is on leave or other authorized duty absence. As a practical matter, relief will be granted unless there is evidence of actual contributing negligence on the part of the accountable officer. B-196960, November 18, 1980; B-184028, March 2, 1976; B-175756-0. M., June 14, 1972. Of course, where contributing negligence exists (e.g., prior to departing on leave, the accountable officer left the cash drawer open), relief will be denied. B-182480, February 3, 1975.

Although the presumption of negligence may seem harsh, GAO and various courts have determined that it is necessary to preserve the concept of accountability and to protect the government against dishonesty as well as negligence. See B-167126, August 28, 1978; B-191440, May 25, 1979. As stated in one decision, the presumption of negligence:

> [I]s a reasonable and legal basis for the denial of relief where the accountable officers have control of the funds and the means available for their safekeeping but the shortage nevertheless occurs without evidence of forcible entry or other conclusive explanation which would exclude negligence as the proximate cause of the loss.

B-166519, October 6, 1969.

If the facts indicate that the accountable officer was negligent, and if it appears that the negligence was the proximate cause of the loss, then relief must be denied. To illustrate, one group of GAO cases involves the accountable officer's failure to lock a safe. It is negligence for an accountable officer to place money in a safe in an area that is accessible to others and then leave the safe unlocked for a period of time when he or she is not physically present. See, e.g., B-190506, November 28, 1977; B-139886, July 2, 1959. It is also negligence to leave a safe unattended in a "day lock" position. B-199790, August 26, 1980; B-188733, March 29, 1979, aff'd, B-188733, January 17, 1980; B-187708, April 6, 1977. Thus, an accountable officer who leaves a safe unlocked (either by leaving the door open or by closing the door but not rotating the combination dial) and then leaves the office for lunch or for the night will be denied relief. B204173, January 11,

1982, aff'd, B-204173, November 9, 1982; B-183559, August 28, 1975; B-180957, Apr. 24, 1975; B-142597, Apr. 29, 1960; B-181648 -O.M., August 21, 1974.

Merely being physically present while the safe is unlocked may not be enough to justify relief from liability. A degree of attentiveness, dictated by the circumstances and common sense, is also required. In B-173710-O.M., December 7, 1971, relief was denied where the cashier did not lock the safe while a stranger, posing as a building maintenance man, entered the cashier's cage ostensibly to repair the air conditioning system and erected a temporary barrier between the cashier and the safe.

The GAO cases indicate that a good rule-of-thumb for the accountable officer is: Do the best you can with what is available to you. Failure to avail yourself of available safeguards, without a compelling justification, does not meet the standard of reasonable care. Some examples of cases of actual negligence are: B-192567, June 21, 1988 (funds missing from bar-locking file cabinet; combination safe was available but not used); B-177730-O.M., February 9, 1973 (cashier left funds overnight in locked desk drawer instead of safe provided for that purpose); B-161229-O. M., April 20, 1967 (cashier left funds in unlocked drawer while at lunch instead of locked drawer provided for that purpose); B-172614-O.M., May 4, 1971, and B-167596-O.M., August 21, 1969 (accountable officer left unlocked cash box in safe to which several other persons had access).

GAO has considered inattentiveness or simple carelessness that facilitates a loss to constitute negligence, thereby precluding relief. 64 Comp. Gen. 140 (1984) (shoulder bag with money left unattended on airport counter for several minutes); B-233937, May 8, 1989 (bag with money set on ledge in crowded restaurant); B-208888, September 28, 1984 (evidence suggested that funds were placed on desk and inadvertently knocked into trash can); B-127204, April 13, 1956 (pay envelopes left on top of desk in cashier's cage 19 inches from window opening on hallway to which many persons had access). Similarly, the best way to know how much cash you have is to count it. Failure to do so in situations where reasonable care would require it constitutes negligence. B-247581, June 4, 1992 (alternate cashier failed to count cash upon receipt from principal or upon return to principal); B-206820, September 9, 1982 (accountable officer handed money over to another employee without counting it or obtaining receipt); B-193380, September 25, 1979 (cashier cashed checks at bank and failed to count the cash received).

Another category of cases involves counterfeit currency. GAO considers a deficiency in an accountable officer's account caused by the acceptance of counterfeit money to be a physical loss for purposes of 31 U.S.C. § 3527(a). B-140836, October 3, 1960; B-108452, May 15, 1952; B-101301, July 19, 1951. Whether accepting counterfeit money is negligent depends on the facts of the particular case, primarily whether the counterfeit was readily detectable. B-239724, October 11, 1990; B-191891, June 16, 1980; B-163627-O. M., March 11, 1968. (Relief was granted in these three cases.) If the quality of the counterfeit is such that a prudent person in the same situation would question the authenticity of the bill, relief should not be granted. B-155287, September 5, 1967. Also, failure to check a bill against a posted list of serial numbers will generally be viewed as negligence. B-155287, September 5, 1967; B166514-O.M., July 23, 1969. Finally, GAO has held that failure, without compelling justification, to use an available counterfeit detection machine is negligence. B-243685, July 1, 1991. The increased anti-counterfeiting technology used to print bills, as well as the technology available to detect counterfeits, is likely to make it increasingly difficult to grant relief from liability when an accountable officer accepts counterfeit currency.

The Concept and Application of Proximate Cause

An essential element of liability under a negligence theory of liability is proximate cause. An accountable officer may be relieved from liability if it can be shown that the negligence was not the "proximate cause" of the loss or shortage. The concept means that, first, there must be a cause-and-effect relationship between the negligence and the loss. In other words, the negligence must have contributed to the loss. This does not mean that *any* connection between the negligence and the loss will be sufficient to create liability. Instead, the negligence must be related to the loss in such a way that the cause-and-effect relationship is reasonably foreseeable; that is, a reasonably prudent person should have anticipated that a given consequence could reasonably follow from a given act.

Since the accountable officer has the burden of proving eligibility for relief, it is the accountable officer who must show that some factor other than his negligence, or some combination of factors other than his negligence, was the proximate cause of the loss.

Certain techniques for analyzing proximate cause have evolved over the years. First, if the accountable officer had not been negligent, would the loss have occurred anyway? If the answer to this question is yes, the negligence of the accountable officer is not the proximate cause of the loss, and relief will probably be granted. However, if this question cannot be answered with a reasonable degree of certainty, the next question to ask is whether the negligence of the accountable officer was a "substantial factor" in bringing about the loss. If this question is answered yes, relief will probably be denied.

For example, if an accountable officer leaves cash visible and unguarded on a desk while away at lunch and the money disappears during this time, there can be no question that the accountable officer's negligence was the proximate cause of the loss. Compare that situation with one in which an accountable officer failed to count cash received, which is negligent. If the accountable officer is attacked and robbed at gunpoint after returning to work, the failure to count the cash would not be the proximate cause of the loss since presumably the robbers would have taken the money regardless of whether it had been counted. In such a case, the absence of proximate cause between the accountable officer's negligence and the loss would support relieving the accountable officer of liability.

Thus, in B-229587, January 6, 1988, an accountable officer left the combination to a safe in an unlocked desk drawer. Burglars found the combination and looted the safe. However, since the burglars pried open locked desk drawers throughout the office, locking the desk drawer would most likely not have prevented the theft; therefore, leaving the drawer unlocked was not the proximate cause of the loss.

Discussion Problem 8-5

Twelve armed men in two vans break into the American Embassy in Lagos, Nigeria. They forcibly enter the cashier's office and proceed to carry the safe down the stairs. The burglars drop the safe while carrying it, the safe opens upon being dropped, and the burglars take the money and flee. The reason the safe opens when dropped is that the cashier had not locked it, clearly an act of negligence. Was the cashier's negligence the proximate cause of this loss? Do these facts support granting relief from liability? (Scenario based on B-201173, August 18, 1981.)

Unexplained Losses

Because an accountable officer is liable for losses of funds under his or her control, there is no requirement that there be actual evidence of negligence. Thus, an accountable officer may be held liable even without evidence of negligence (e.g., unlocked safe, failure to count money). Accountable officer liability may be established if there is an unexplained loss or shortage. In the typical case, money is found missing or an internal audit reveals a shortage in an account. There is no evidence of negligence or misconduct on the part of the accountable officer, nor is there evidence of burglary or any other reason for the disappearance. All that is known with any certainty is that the money is gone. In other words, the loss or shortage is totally unexplained.

The significance of the presumption of negligence is perhaps most apparent in the unexplained loss situation. Since the burden of proof is on the accountable officer to establish eligibility for relief, the denial of relief will generally result from any loss that cannot be adequately explained. Since there is no evidence to rebut the presumption, there is no basis on which to grant relief. The presumption and its application to unexplained losses were discussed in 48 Comp. Gen. 566, 567-68 (1969) as follows:

> While there is no positive or affirmative evidence of negligence on the part of [the accountable officer] in connection with this loss, we have repeatedly held that positive or affirmative evidence of negligence is not necessary, and that the mere fact that an unexplained shortage occurred is, in and of itself, sufficient to raise an inference or presumption of negligence. A Government official charged with the custody and handling of public moneys . . . is expected to exercise the highest degree of care in the performance of his duty and, when funds . . . disappear without explanation or evident reason, the presumption naturally arises that the responsible official was derelict in some way. Moreover, granting relief to Government officials for unexplained losses or shortages of this nature might tend to make such officials lax in the performance of their duties.

The rationale for such a rule is obvious. The loss is most likely attributable to one of two scenarios: Either the accountable officer failed to exercise the requisite degree of care and someone else took the money, or the accountable officer took the money. In either situation, the unexplained loss raises the presumption of (at least) negligence and imposes liability on the accountable officer.

The denial of relief in an unexplained loss case does not imply dishonesty by the particular accountable officer; it means merely that there was insufficient evidence to rebut the legal presumption of negligence. See B-122688, September 25, 1956. Nor is the legal presumption of liability overcome by the fact that the accountable officer could not exercise due care because of poor health or because the classified nature of the work made it difficult to account for funds. For example, GAO has held:

> You assert that the unspecified but yet classified nature of some of his activities could "possibly" have affected his record keeping. This, however, has no bearing on Dr. Jones' responsibilities as [an accountable officer] to properly record dollar amounts and dates of expenditures. Likewise, your second assertion, that his health affected his abilities to account for the funds, does not absolve Dr. Jones of his responsibilities as a custodian of public funds.

B-272613, October 16, 1996.

Despite the strictness of the rule, in many unexplained loss cases the presumption can be rebutted and relief granted. To determine whether the evidence is sufficient to rebut the presumption, it is necessary to evaluate all of the evidence, including statements by the accountable officer and other agency personnel, investigation reports, and any relevant circumstantial evidence. In some cases, for example, it may be possible to reasonably conclude that any negligence that may have occurred was not the proximate cause of the loss.

For example, if the agency has systemic security weaknesses that are beyond the individual accountable officer's ability to control, then the security weaknesses could be the proximate cause of the loss. The evidence of security weaknesses, in conjunction with the lack of any evidence that the accountable officer caused the loss, would support the granting of relief.

Since the burden of proof always rests with the accountable officer, the accountable officer's own statements are particularly relevant in establishing due care, and relief should not be denied without considering them. Naturally, the more specific and detailed the statement is, and the more closely tied to the time of the loss, the more helpful it will be.

While the accountable officer's statement may be motivated by self-interest, it has been enough to tip the balance in favor of granting relief when combined with other evidence. See, e.g., B-288014, May 17, 2002 (cashier's statement that she followed a process of reconciling accounts prior to the destruction of the records by political dissidents corroborated by electronic evidence of reconciliations); B-242830, September 24, 1991 (cashier's statement supported by another employee that safe had been opened for only one transaction in early afternoon); B-214080, March 25, 1986 (cashier made sworn and unrefuted statement to local police and Secret Service); B-210017, June 8, 1983 (cashier's statement corroborated by witness); B-188733, March 29, 1979 (forcible entry to office but not to safe itself; cashier's statement that he locked safe on day of robbery accepted).

Effect of Regulatory Violations

If a particular activity of an accountable officer is governed by a regulation, failure to follow that regulation will be considered negligence. If that failure is the proximate cause of a loss or deficiency, relief will be denied. 70 Comp. Gen. 12 (1990); 54 Comp. Gen. 112, 116 (1974). The relationship of this rule to the standard of reasonable care is the presumption that the prudent person exercising the requisite degree of care will become familiar with, and will follow, applicable regulations. Indeed, it has been stated that accountable officers have a duty to familiarize themselves with pertinent Treasury Department and agency rules and regulations. B-229207, July 11, 1988; B-193380, September 25, 1979.

Treasury Department regulations on disbursing, applicable to all agencies for which Treasury disburses under 31 U.S.C. § 3321, are found in the Treasury Financial Manual (available at www.fms.treas.gov/tfm/vol1/index.html). Treasury regulations governing disbursements are found in I TFM Part 4 and in the Treasury Department's TFM supplement entitled *Manual of Procedures and Instructions for Cashiers* (issued in April 2001; see www.fms.treas.gov/imprest/). The Treasury Manuals establish general requirements for proper cash control, and failure to comply has resulted in denial of relief. See 70 Comp. Gen. 12 (1990) (cashier, contrary to Cashiers' Manual, kept copy of safe combination taped to underside of desk pull-out panel).

The same principle applies with respect to violations of individual agency regulations and written instructions. B-193380, September 25, 1979 (cashier violated agency regulations by placing the key to a locked cash box in an unlocked cash box and then leaving both in a locked safe to which more than one person had the combination). The decision further pointed out that oral instructions to the cashier to leave the cash box unlocked could not be considered to supersede published agency regulations. However, if agency regulations are ambiguous, relief may be granted if the accountable officer's interpretation was reasonable. B-169848-O.M., December 8, 1971.

Negligence will not be imputed to an accountable officer who fails to comply with regulations where full compliance is prevented by circumstances beyond his or her control. This recognizes the fact that compliance is sometimes up to the agency and beyond the control of the individual. For example, violating a regulation that requires that funds be kept in a safe is not negligence where the agency has failed to provide the safe. B-78617, June 24, 1949. Also, as with other types of negligence, failure to follow regulations will not prevent the granting of relief if the failure was not the proximate cause of the loss or deficiency. B-229207, July 11, 1988; B-229587, January 6, 1988; B-185666, July 27, 1976; *Libby v. United States*, 81 F. Supp. 722, 727 (Ct. Cl. 1948).

In B-185666, for example, a cashier kept her cash box key and safe combination in a sealed envelope in an unlocked desk drawer, in violation of the Treasury Cashiers' Manual. Relief was nevertheless granted because the seal on the envelope had not been broken and the negligence could therefore not have contributed to the loss.

> **Discussion Problem 8-6**
>
> The regulation that establishes cash control procedures for DoD states:
>
> > The combination of all vaults, safes, and fund containers is changed at least once every 6 months and upon relief, transfer, separation, or discharge of the accountable individual.
>
> Tarrybul Luk is the cashier at a DoD disbursing center. The combinations on the two small safes have not been changed for 12 months. Tarrybul has asked his supervisor several times to have the combinations changed, but his supervisor has told him that the change would have to wait until the next fiscal year when additional funding becomes available. One day, three armed robbers enter the disbursing center when only Tarrybul is present and physically remove both safes. The safes contain $50,000. Could Tarrybul be relieved of liability even though the cash control regulation was violated?

Earthquakes, Fires, and Other Unfortunate Events

The Supreme Court's conclusion in *United States v. Thomas*, 82 U.S. (15 Wall.) 337, 352 (1872), that strict liability for loss of funds would not be imposed in two situations (i.e., where the funds were destroyed by an "overruling necessity" and where the funds were taken by a "public enemy") provided that there is no contributing fault or negligence by the accountable officer. The Court gave only one example of an "overruling necessity," an earthquake. Id. at 348. There have been no subsequent judicial attempts to further define "overruling necessity," although some administrative decisions have used the term "acts of God." See, e.g., 48 Comp. Gen. 566, 567 (1969).

Thus, at the very least, assuming no contributing fault or negligence, an accountable officer would not be liable for funds lost or destroyed in an earthquake, and hence there is no need to seek relief. Contributing negligence might occur, for example, if an accountable officer failed to periodically deposit collections and funds were therefore on hand that should not have been. See B-71445, June 20, 1949.

Whatever the scope of the "overruling necessity" exception, it is clear that it does not extend to destruction by fire. In *Smythe v. United States*, 188 U.S. 156, 173–74 (1903), the Supreme Court declined to apply *Thomas* and expressly rejected the argument that an accountable officer's liability for notes destroyed by fire should be limited to the cost of printing new notes. See also 1 Comp. Dec. 191 (1895) (relief not granted for loss caused by fire). Thus, a loss by fire is a physical loss for which the accountable officer is liable.

As in any case of liability, however, relief may be granted (31 U.S.C. § 3527) if the statutory conditions are met. Examples are B-212515, December 21, 1983, and B-203726, July 10, 1981. Beyond the earthquake cases, one could surmise that events of similar magnitude could justify exceptions to liability. Thus, hurricanes, tornados, mudslides, and other like scenarios that cause a loss or destruction of public funds could justify non-application of the strict liability rule.

Theft by Third Parties

Closely related to the "overruling necessity" cases are cases in which the loss is attributable to theft in circumstances in which the accountable officer could not reasonably be expected to prevent the theft. The rule that has evolved through GAO decisions is that if money is taken in a burglary, robbery, or other form of theft, the accountable officer will be relieved of liability if the following conditions are met: (1) there is sufficient evidence that a theft took place; (2) there is no evidence implicating, or indicating contributing negligence by, the accountable officer; (3) the agency has made the administrative determinations required by the relief statute.

GAO has consistently stated: "In losses involving theft, we generally grant relief if the evidence presented shows that the theft cannot be attributed to fault or negligence on the part of the accountable officer, on the ground that such evidence rebuts the presumption of negligence." B-260862 June 6, 1995. The second condition is often the basis for denying relief. In a 1994 opinion, GAO held:

> While the record confirms that a theft occurred, we believe the record shows that [the accountable officer] was negligent, and that this negligence enabled the theft to occur, and was, thus, the proximate cause of the loss. . . . Accountable officers are held to a standard of reasonable care. . . . Placing $3,978.69 in cash under the front seat of an automobile cannot be characterized as an action that a reasonably prudent and careful person would have taken to safeguard the funds. We note your concern that lack of adequate training contributed to the loss; we cannot grant relief on the basis of inexperience or inadequate training or supervision. Based on the record, we find that [the accountable officer] was negligent.

B-257120 December 13, 1994.

The cases upon which these rules are based fall into several well-defined categories:

Burglary: Forced Entry. In the typical case, a government office is broken into while the office is closed, and money is stolen. Evidence of the forced entry is clear. As long as there is no evidence implicating the accountable officer, no other contributing fault or negligence, and the requisite administrative determinations are made, relief will be granted. See, e.g., B-265856 November 9, 1995 (GAO held: "Since there is evidence of forcible entry into the office where the safe was located and there is no evidence in the record to implicate these two employees, we agree with your administrative finding that the loss was not a result of fault or negligence on the part of these two employees"); B-242773, February 20, 1991 (burglars broke into the welding shop at a government laboratory, took a blowtorch and acetylene tanks to the administrative office and used them to cut open the safe); B-193174, November 29, 1978 (cashier's office was robbed over a weekend and although there was evidence that the office had been forcibly entered, there was no evidence of forced entry into the safe, and FBI found no evidence of negligence or breach of security by any government personnel associated with the office); B-182590, February 3, 1975 (persons unknown broke front door lock of Bureau of Indian Affairs office in Alaska and removed the safe on sled; sled tracks led to an abandoned building in which the safe was found with its door removed); B-202290, June 5, 1981 (unsecured bolt cutters found on premises used to remove safe padlock, but no contributing negligence because there was no separate facility in which to secure the tools).

Armed Robbery. In this category of cases, one or more individuals, armed or credibly pretending to be armed, rob an accountable officer. As in the burglary cases, as long as there is no evidence implicating the accountable officer and no contributing negligence, relief is readily granted. The accountable officer is not expected to risk his or her life by resisting. See, e.g., B-260915 April 3, 1995 (Haitian Army Sergeant assigned to provide security shot and killed two government officials and severely wounded another before taking the payroll); B-235458, August 23, 1990 (gunman entered cashier's office, knocked cashier unconscious, and robbed safe); B-191579, May 22, 1978 (man claiming to be armed entered cashier's office in a veterans hospital and handed cashier a note demanding all of her $20 bills). Depending on the circumstances, it is not necessary that the thief be, or pretend to be, armed. An example is the common purse-snatching incident. B-197021, May 9, 1980; B-193866, March 14, 1979.

Evidence of Theft Uncertain. In many cases, the evidence of theft is not all that clear. The losses are unexplained in the sense that what happened cannot be determined with any certainty. The problem then becomes whether the evidence of theft is sufficient to classify the loss as a theft and to rebut the presumption of negligence.

Recognizing that complete certainty is impossible in many cases, GAO gives weight to the agency's administrative determination and to statements of the individuals concerned, but these factors cannot be conclusive and the decision will be based on all of the evidence. Other relevant factors include how and where the safe combination was stored, when it was last changed, whether the combination dial was susceptible of observation while the safe was being opened, access to the safe and to the facility itself, and the safeguarding of keys to cash boxes. For example, in B-198836, June 26, 1980, funds were kept in the bottom drawer of a four-drawer file cabinet. Each drawer had a separate key lock, and the cabinet itself was secured by a steel bar and padlock. Upon arriving at work one morning, the cashier found the bottom drawer slightly out of alignment, with several pry marks on its edges. A police investigation was inconclusive. GAO viewed the evidence as sufficient to support a conclusion of burglary and, since the record contained no indication of negligence on the part of the cashier, granted relief.

In another case, a safe was found unlocked with no signs of forcible entry. However, there was evidence that a thief had entered the office door by breaking a window. The accountable officer stated that he had locked the safe before going home the previous evening, and there was no evidence to contradict this or to indicate any other negligence. GAO accepted the accountable officer's uncontroverted statement and granted relief, B-188733, March 29, 1979. See also B-210017, June 8, 1983

In B-170596-O.M., November 16, 1970, the accountable officer stated that she had found the padlock on and locked in reverse from the way she always locked it. Her statement was corroborated by the agency investigation. In addition, the lock did not conform to agency specifications, but this was not the cashier's responsibility. Since she had used the facilities officially provided for her and was not otherwise negligent, relief was granted.

Relief was also granted in B-170615-O.M., November 23, 1971, reversing upon reconsideration B-170615-O.M., December 2, 1970. In that case, there was some evidence that the office lock had been pried open, but there were no signs of forcible entry into the safe. This suggested the possibility of negligence either in failing to lock the safe or in not adequately safeguarding the combination. However, the accountable officer's supervisor stated that he (the supervisor) had locked the safe at the close of business on the preceding workday, and two safe company representatives provided statements that the safe was vulnerable and could have been opened by anyone with some knowledge of safe combinations.

The occurrence of more than one loss under similar circumstances within a relatively short time will tend to corroborate the likelihood of theft. B-199021, September 2, 1980; B-193416, October 25, 1979. In B-199021, two losses occurred in the same building within several weeks of each other. All agency security procedures had been followed, and the record indicated that the cashier had exercised a very high degree of care in safeguarding the funds. In B-193416, the first loss was totally unexplained, and the entire cash box disappeared a week later. The safe combination had been kept in a sealed envelope in a "working safe" to which other employees had access. Although the seal on the envelope was not broken, an investigation showed that the combination could be read by holding the envelope up to a strong light. In neither case was there any evidence of forcible entry or of negligence on the part of the accountable officer. Balancing the various relevant factors in each case, GAO granted relief.

Discussion Problem 8-7

The regulation that establishes cash control procedures for a federal agency states:

Keys to the work space or disbursing office are strictly controlled. A record shall be maintained that identifies who has keys, when they were issued, and when they were surrendered.

Miss Plaste Keyes is the cashier at the agency's disbursing center. Several days ago she misplaced the spare set of keys to the cashier cage. Miss Keyes did not maintain a record of the keys as required, nor did she report that she was unable to locate the keys. One morning, before the spare set of keys could be found, Miss Keyes noticed upon entering the cashier cage that the safe had been removed. There was no sign of forced entry into the cashier cage and, in fact, the lost key was found in the cashier cage door. The safe contained $50,000. Could Miss Keyes be relieved of liability in this case, since the theft occurred while she was gone and not in control of the funds?

Embezzlement

Embezzlement is the fraudulent misappropriation of property by someone to whom it has lawfully been entrusted. Black's Law Dictionary 522 (6th ed. 1990). Losses due to embezzlement or fraudulent acts of subordinate finance personnel, acting alone or in concert with others, are treated as physical losses, and relief will be granted only if the statutory conditions are met. B-202074, July 21, 1983, at 6; B-21 1763, July 8, 1983; B-133862-O.M., November 29, 1957; B-101375-O.M., April 16, 1951.

As would be expected, agencies have fairly strict policies for dealing with cases of embezzlement (or any other intentional act of wrongdoing by a government employee). For example, the applicable DoD regulation states:

> [L]osses resulting from wrongful conduct, such as theft, robbery, burglary, embezzlement, or fraudulent acts of

disbursing personnel, acting alone or in collusion with others, are treated as major physical losses regardless of the amount involved.

The effect of treating such cases as "major physical losses" is to trigger formal reporting and investigation requirements. It is the misconduct of the employee, rather than the amount involved, that warrants the increased procedural requirements.

Many of these cases involve the embezzlement of tax collections, under various schemes, by employees of the IRS. In each case the IRS pursued the perpetrators, and most were prosecuted and convicted. The IRS recovered what it could from the employees and sought relief for the balance from the pertinent supervisor in whose name the account was held. In each case involving a supervisor, GAO applied the "no fault or negligence" determination and granted relief. B-260563 March 31, 1995; B-244113, November 1, 1991; B-226214, June 18, 1987; B-215501, November 5, 1984. The accountable officer in each of the IRS cases was a supervisor who did not actually handle the funds.

The approach consistently applied by GAO when evaluating the presence or absence of negligence when the accountable officer is a supervisor is to review the adequacy of internal controls and ask whether the accountable officer provided reasonable supervision. If internal controls and management procedures are reasonable and were being followed, relief has generally been granted.

Losses resulting from the fraudulent acts of other than subordinate finance personnel (e.g., payments on fraudulent vouchers) are not physical losses but must be treated as improper payments. 2 Comp. Gen. 277 (1922); B-202074, July 21, 1983; B-76903, July 13, 1948; B-133862 -O.M., November 29, 1957.

Adequacy of Security Measures

When evaluating the cause of a physical loss of funds, the existence, adequacy, and use of security measures and facilities is a significant consideration. The Treasury Department's *Manual of Procedures and Instructions for Cashiers* (available at http://www.fms.treas.gov/imprest/) sets forth many of these security requirements, which are often supplemented by internal agency regulations. For example, the Cashiers' Manual provides that safe combinations should be changed annually, whenever there is a change of cashiers, or when the combination has been compromised, and prescribes procedures for safeguarding the combination. It also reflects what is perhaps the most fundamental principle of sound cash control—that an employee with custody of public funds should have exclusive control over those funds. DoD regulations impose an even stricter standard, requiring that combinations be changed every six months. DoD Financial Management Regulation, Vol. 5, Ch. 3., para. 030392 (1999).

The first step in analyzing the effect of a security violation or deficiency is to determine whether the violation or deficiency is attributable to the accountable officer or to the agency. Two fundamental premises drive this analysis: (1) the accountable officer is responsible for safeguarding the funds in his or her custody, and (2) the agency is responsible for providing adequate means to do so. Adequate means includes both physical facilities and administrative procedures. Basically, if the accountable officer fails to use the facilities and procedures that have been provided, this failure will most likely be considered negligent and, unless some other factor appears to be the proximate cause of the loss, will preclude the granting of relief.

Another element of the accountable officer's responsibility is the duty to report security weaknesses to appropriate supervisory personnel. See 63 Comp. Gen. 489, 492 (1984), rev'd on other grounds; 65 Comp. Gen. 876 (1986). If the agency fails to respond, a loss attributable to the reported weakness is not the accountable officer's fault. See B-235147.2, August 14, 1991; B-208511, May 9, 1983. Ultimately, an accountable officer can do no more than use the best that has been made available, and relief will not be denied for failure to follow adequate security measures that are beyond the accountable officer's control. Thus, relief was granted in the following cases: B-226947, July 27, 1987 (U.S. Mint employees stole coins from temporarily leased facility that could not be adequately secured); B-207062, May 12, 1983 (agent kept collections in his possession because, upon returning to office at 4:30 p.m., he found all storage facilities locked and all senior officials gone for the day); B-210245, February 10, 1983 (lockable gun cabinet was the most secure item available); B-186190, May 11, 1976 (funds kept in safe with padlock because combination safe, which had been ordered, had not yet arrived); B-7861 7, June 24, 1949 (agency failed to provide safe).

In each of these cases, correction of the security weaknesses was beyond what could be reasonably expected of the accountable officer. If, however, correction of the weaknesses was within the accountable officer's control, the accountable officer is expected to make the corrections and is likely to be denied relief for failing to do so. B-127204, April 13, 1956.

The basis for granting relief in these cases is that the proximate cause of the loss is the agency's failure to provide adequate security, and not any action or inaction by the accountable officer. This principle manifests itself in a variety of contexts.

One group of cases involves multiple security violations. For example, in B-182386, April 24, 1975, imprest funds were found missing when a safe was opened for audit. The accountable officer was found to be negligent for failing to follow approved procedures. However, the agency's investigation disclosed a number of security violations attributable to the agency. Two cashiers operated from the same cash box; transfers of custody were not documented; the safe combination had not been changed despite several changes of cashiers; and at least five persons knew the safe combination. The agency, in recommending relief, concluded that the loss was caused by "pervasive laxity in the protection and administration of the funds . . . on all levels." GAO agreed, noting that the lax security "precludes the definite

placement of responsibility" for the loss, and granted relief.
In several other unexplained loss cases (no sign of forcible entry, no indication of fault or negligence on the part of the accountable officer), GAO granted relief because it determined that the proximate cause of the loss was the overall lax security on the part of the agency, which could not be attributed to the accountable officer. B-243324, April 17, 1991; B-229778, September 2, 1988; B-226847, June 25, 1987; B-217876, April 29, 1986; B-21 1962, December 10, 1985; B-21 1649, August 2, 1983. All these cases involved numerous security violations beyond the accountable officer's control, and several used the "pervasive laxity" characterization used in B-182386. However, it is not necessary in order to grant relief that the security weaknesses rise to the level of "pervasive laxity." Relief will usually be granted where several persons other than the accountable officer have access to the funds through knowledge of the safe combination since "multiple access" makes it impossible to attribute the loss to the accountable officer. B-235072, July 5, 1989; B-228884, October 13, 1987; B-214080, March 25, 1986; B-21 1233, June 28, 1983; B-209569, April 13, 1983; B-196855, December 9, 1981; B-199034, February 9, 1981.

> **Discussion Problem 8-8**
>
> Norma Lee Kayreful is a cashier at a federal agency disbursing office. Each night, prior to departing, Norma must lock the safe and then lock the door of the vault that contains the safe. One day Norma notices that the key used to lock the vault door is becoming worn, and it takes her several tries to secure the door. Norma immediately reports this problem to the appropriate person and requests that the lock be replaced.
>
> After 30 days have passed and the agency still has not replaced the lock, the key has become so worn that it is now impossible to lock the vault door. Although Norma could wheel the safe to a secure location down the hall, she figures that she has done her part by promptly reporting the problem and that she should not have to physically move the safe because of the agency's failure to act promptly. Consequently, at the end of the day, Norma locks the safe and closes the vault door, which now cannot be locked.
>
> One morning, the safe is missing, apparently wheeled out of the building. Security experts assigned to the case opine that the theft could have been prevented if the vault door had been locked. Is this an appropriate case for granting relief from liability?

Standard for Granting Relief in Improper Payments Cases

From the perspective of accountability for improper payments, the modern legal structure of federal disbursing evolved in three major steps. First, Congress enacted legislation in 1912 (37 Stat. 375), the remnants of which are found at 31 U.S.C. § 3521(a), to prohibit disbursing officers from preparing and auditing their own vouchers. With this newly mandated separation of voucher preparation and examination from actual payment, payment was accomplished by having some other administrative official "certify" the correctness of the voucher to the disbursing officer. The 1912 legislation was thus the genesis of what would later become a new class of accountable officer, i.e., the certifying officer.

Prior to a 1996 legislative change (Public Law 104-106, § 913) the Department of Defense did not have certifying officers, and only disbursing officers were pecuniarily liable for fiscal irregularities, including erroneous payments. The 1996 legislation required DoD to appoint certifying officers. DoD has determined that "Sound financial management and internal control practices dictate that such certifying officers be independent and organizationally separate from disbursing officers, whenever practicable." DoD Financial Management Regulation, Vol. 5, Ch. 33, para. 330101.

Disbursing officers remained accountable for improper payments. However, since the 1912 law was intended to prohibit the disbursing officer from duplicating the detailed voucher examination already performed by the "certifying officer," disbursing officers were held liable only for errors apparent on the face of the voucher, as well as, of course, payments prohibited by law or for which no appropriation was available. 20 Comp. Dec. 859 (1914). In effect, the 1912 statute operated in part as a relief statute, since a disbursing officer would be relieved from liability except in the limited circumstances in which the error was apparent on the face of the voucher. See, e.g., 4 Comp. Gen. 991 (1925); 3 Comp. Gen. 441 (1924).

The second major step in the evolution of the legal structure was section 4 of Executive Order No. 6166, signed by President Roosevelt on June 10, 1933. The first paragraph of section 4, later codified at 31 U.S.C. § 3321(a), consolidated the disbursing function in the Treasury Department, thereby eliminating the separate disbursing offices of the other executive departments. The second paragraph, 31 U.S.C. § 3321(b), authorized the Treasury Department to delegate disbursing authority to other executive agencies for purposes of efficiency and economy. The third paragraph gave new emphasis to the certification function, stating:

> The Division of Disbursement [Treasury Department] shall disburse moneys only upon the certification of per-

sons by law duly authorized to incur obligations upon behalf of the United States. The function of accountability for improper certification shall be transferred to such persons, and no disbursing officer shall be held accountable therefor.

The following year, Executive Order No. 6728, May 29, 1934, exempted the military departments, except for salaries and expenses in the District of Columbia, from the centralization. This exemption is codified at 31 U.S.C. § 3321(c) and authorizes the Department of Defense to "designate personnel of the agency as disbursing officials to disburse public money available for expenditure by the agency." Executive Order 6166 provided the framework for the disbursing system still in effect today. Apart from specified exemptions, the certifying officer is now an employee of the spending agency and the disbursing officer is an employee of the Treasury Department.

Disbursing officers continued to be liable for their own errors, as under the 1912 legislation. See 13 Comp. Gen. 469 (1934). However, a major consequence of Executive Order 6166 was to make the certifying officer an accountable officer as well. The certifying officer became liable for improper payments "caused solely by an improper certification as to matters not within the knowledge of or available to the disbursing officer." 13 Comp. Gen. 326, 329 (1934). See also 15 Comp. Gen. 986 (1936); 15 Comp. Gen. 362 (1935).

Over the next few years, it became apparent that there was confusion and disagreement as to the precise relationship of certifying officers and disbursing officers with respect to liability for improper payments. In the Annual Report of the Comptroller General of the United States for the Fiscal Year Ended June 30, 1940, at pages 63–66, GAO summarized the problem and recommended legislation to specify the allocation of responsibilities "to provide the closest possible relationship between liability and fault" (Id. at 64).

The third major evolutionary step was the enactment of Public Law 77-389, 55 Stat. 875 (1941), to implement GAO'S recommendation. Section 1, 31 U.S.C. § 3325(a), codified the substance of Executive Order 6166. It requires that a disbursing officer disburse money only in accordance with a voucher certified by the head of the spending agency or an authorized certifying officer who, except for some interagency transactions, will also be an employee of the spending agency. Section 3325(a) does not apply to disbursements of the military departments except for salaries and expenses in the District of Columbia. 31 U.S.C. § 3325(b). The rest of the statute describes the responsibilities of certifying and disbursing officers and provides a mechanism for the administrative relief of certifying officers.

It should be apparent that control of public funds must be the responsibility of federal officials. However, this does not mean that every task in the disbursement process must be performed by a government employee. For example, GAO has advised that the Bureau of Indian Affairs may contract with a private bank to perform certain ministerial or operational aspects of disbursing Indian trust fund money, such as printing checks, delivering checks to payees, and debiting amounts from accounts. However, to comply with 31 U.S.C. §§ 3321 and 3325, a federal disbursing officer must retain managerial and judgmental responsibility. 69 Comp. Gen. 314 (1990). The decision concluded:

> [W]e see no reason to object to a contractual arrangement whereby a private contractor provides disbursement services, so long as a government disbursing officer remains responsible for reviewing and overseeing the disbursement operations through agency installed controls designed to assure accurate and proper disbursements.

Id. at 278.

To intrude further into this responsibility would require clear statutory authority. B-210545-O.M., June 6, 1983 (Indian Health Service would need statutory authority to use fiscal intermediaries to pay claims by providers; memorandum cites examples of such authority in Medicare Legislation).

Impact of Automated Disbursing Systems on Relief from Liability

The vast majority of disbursements involve the use of computerized systems that did not exist when the statutory structure was developed. It has been a challenge implementing the liability and relief provisions of these statutes within the ever-evolving electronic data management environment. The fact that the accountable officer relied on an automated system does not, in itself, relieve the accountable officer from liability. For example, the DoD Financial Management Regulation states:

> Certifying officers are accountable for illegal, improper or incorrect payments made as a result of their certification even though they may have relied on other accountable officials or automated payment systems. Certifying officers may request relief of liability for such payments as provided in chapters 6 and 33 of this volume.

Id. at Vol. 5, Ch. 1, para. 010501.C (1999).

Note that the certifying officer is liable for improper or incorrect payments, even though he or she relied on an approved automated payment system. If, however, such reliance was reasonable, the certifying officer may be relieved of liability.

Thus, in considering requests for relief for improper payments made through an automated payment system where verification of individual transactions is impractical, the basic question will be the reasonableness of the certifying officer's reliance on the system to continually produce legal and accurate payments. GAO explained its approach to analyzing these situations as follows:

> Authorized certifying officers located at [the agency's] automated finance centers rely on the integrity of the automated payment system as a whole and do not physically examine hard copy payment documentation (vouchers) in each and every case. Although the use of an automated payment system does not alter the basic con-

cepts of accountability for certifying officers, the reasonableness of a certifying officer's reliance on an automated payment system to continually produce legal and accurate payments is a factor that we consider when addressing the officer's liability for illegal or improper payments. 69 Comp. Gen. 85 (1989). Further, we have set forth criteria that agencies whose certifying officers rely on automated payment systems should satisfy. Specifically, certifying officers should be provided with information showing that the system on which they rely is functioning properly and reviews should be made at least annually to determine that the automated system is operating effectively and can be relied upon to make accurate and legal payments.

B-247563.3, April 5, 1996. See also, B-178564, January 27, 1978 (confirming the conceptual feasibility of using automated systems to perform pre-audit functions under various child nutrition programs); B-201965, June 15, 1982.

Contexts in which system reliance is relevant are discussed in 69 Comp. Gen. 85 (1989) (automated "ZIP plus 4" address correction system) and 59 Comp. Gen. 597 (1980) (electronic funds transfer program). Regardless of what automated system is used, there is, of course, no authority to intentionally make improper or incorrect payments. B-205851, June 17, 1982; B-203993-O.M., July 12, 1982.

Relief of Certifying Officers

Generally referred to as the Certifying Officers' Relief Act, 31 U.S.C. § 3528(b) establishes a mechanism for the administrative relief of non-DoD certifying officers governed by 31 U.S.C. § 3528(a). Section 3528(b) states:

> (b)(1) The Comptroller General may relieve a certifying official from liability when the Comptroller General decides that -
> (A) the certification was based on official records and the official did not know, and by reasonable diligence and inquiry could not have discovered, the correct information; or

(B)(i) the obligation was incurred in good faith;
(ii) no law specifically prohibited the payment; and
(iii) the United States Government received value for payment.
(2) The Comptroller General may deny relief when the Comptroller General decides the head of the agency did not carry out diligently collection action under procedures prescribed by the Comptroller General.

Although this section does not expressly apply to DoD certifying officers, it has been used as the standard for granting relief within DoD. See DoD Financial Management Regulation, Vol. 5, Ch. 6, para. 060903B. As in the physical loss cases, the determination by the designated DoD official is binding on the Comptroller General. The DoD Financial Management Regulation states as follows in this regard:

As provided in 31 U.S.C. 3527 and 31 U.S.C. 3528 (reference (e)), the Comptroller General shall relieve DOs and certifying officers of the Armed Forces of liability for deficiencies upon a finding that the following statutory standards are met. The determination of the Secretary of Defense that relief should be granted is binding on the Comptroller General.

Id. at Vol. 5, Ch. 6., para. 060903.

There are two standards for relief under this statute. (The standards for granting relief are the same for both non-DoD and DoD certifying officers.) The Comptroller General may relieve a certifying officer from liability for an illegal, improper, or incorrect payment upon determining that: (1) the certification was based on official records and the certifying officer did not know, and by reasonable diligence and inquiry could not have discovered, the actual facts (this standard is (b)(1)(A) of the statute); or (2) the obligation was incurred in good faith, the payment was not specifically prohibited by statute, and the United States received value for the payment (this standard is (b)(1)(B) of the statute). Under either standard, relief may be denied if the agency fails to diligently pursue collection action against the recipient of the improper payment. 31 U.S.C. § 3528(b)(2).

Unlike the physical loss relief statutes, 31 U.S.C. § 3528(b) does not require an administrative determination by the agency as a prerequisite to relief. The determinations under section 3528(b) are made by the Comptroller General. Also, the relief standards under section 3528(b) are stated in the alternative; relief may be granted if either of the two standards can be established. Relief is discretionary (the statute says "may relieve"), but no case has been discovered in which a certifying officer who met either of the standards was denied relief.

Section 3528 does not prescribe any special format for requesting relief. Relief may be requested by the agency on behalf of the certifying officer, or directly by the certifying officer. See, 31 Comp. Gen. 653 (1952) for an example of the latter. Relief requests must present sufficient information to permit GAO to make one of the findings required by section 3528(b). See B-191900, July 21, 1978.

Certifying Officer Unaware of Actual Facts. The first relief standard, 31 U.S.C. § 3528(b)(l)(A), relates essentially to the certification of incorrect facts and permits relief if the certification was based on official records and if the certifying officer did not know, and could not reasonably have learned, the actual facts. GAO has never attempted to formulate a general rule as to what acts may support relief from the certification of incorrect facts. GAO's approach was described in 55 Comp. Gen. 297, 299–300 (1975), as follows:

> [W]e have sought to apply the relief provisions by considering the practical conditions and procedures under which certifications of fact are made. Consequently, the diligence to be required of a certifying officer before requests for relief under the act will be considered favorably is a matter of degree dependent upon the practical conditions prevailing at the time of certification, the sufficiency of the administrative procedures protecting the interest of the Government, and the apparency of the error.

For example, Social Security Administration certifying officers who certify large numbers of awards each month may, apart from obvious errors, rely on the award documents presented for certification. B-119248-O.M., April 14, 1954. Similarly, in B-237419, December 5, 1989, GAO granted relief to a Forest Service certifying officer who certified the refund of a timber purchaser's cash bond deposit without knowing that the refund had already been made. The certifying officer had followed proper procedures by checking to see if the money had been refunded, but did not discover the prior payment because it had not been properly recorded.

Another case in which relief was granted under subsection (b)(l)(A) is B-246415, July 28, 1992. A certifying officer paid a contract invoice to a financing institution to which payments had been assigned under the Assignment of Claims Act without discovering that the contract file contained a prior assignment. The contracting officer had erroneously acknowledged the second assignment when he should have either rejected it or invalidated the first one. The agency remained liable to the first assignee and was unable to recover the improper payment from the second assignee. The certifying officer had checked the contract file, and neither agency procedures nor reasonable diligence required her to keep looking once she found what appeared to be a properly acknowledged assignment.

The case also illustrates how an agency (the Panama Canal Commission in this case) should respond to a loss, i.e., by reviewing its procedures to determine if they can be improved, within reason, to prevent recurrence. In this instance, the agency began requiring that contract files include a "milestone" log and that assignments be tabbed in the file and reviewed prior to acknowledgment.

As a general rule, a certifying officer may not escape liability for losses resulting from improper certification merely by stating either that he was not in a position to determine that each item on a voucher was correctly stated, or that he must depend on the correctness of the computations of his subordinates. A certifying officer who relies upon statements and computations of subordinates must assume responsibility for the correctness of their statements and computations, unless it can be shown that neither the certifying officer nor his or her subordinates, in the reasonable exercise of care and diligence, could have known the true facts. 55 Comp. Gen. 297, 299 (1975); 26 Comp. Gen. 578 (1947); 20 Comp. Gen. 182 (1940).

Similarly, certifying officers are accountable for illegal, improper, or incorrect payments made as a result of their certification even though they may have relied on automated payment systems. See, e.g., the DoD Financial Management Regulation, Vol. 5, Ch. 1, Para. 010501. (1999).

When the record indicates that the certifying officer exercised care and diligence, relief will generally be granted. For example, in B-287043 May 29, 2001, GAO granted relief where four certifying officers relied on original receipts approved and receipted by the agency's facilities maintenance supervisor. The record indicated that they did not know, and by reasonable diligence and inquiry could not have discovered, that fraudulent petty cash vouchers had been submitted for reimbursement. In this situation, the certifying officers and the cashier satisfied the statutory standard for relief. Further, the record indicated that the cashier followed the prescribed procedures for disbursing funds, and nothing in the record indicates that the cashier should have been suspicious of the fraudulent receipts. Finally, GAO found that there was no indication that the improper payments were proximately caused by bad faith or lack of reasonable care on the cashier's part.

In 49 Comp. Gen. 486 (1970), a certifying officer asked GAO for an advance opinion regarding whether he would be held accountable where his own agency would not tell him exactly what he was being asked to certify. The agency took the position that the expenses in question were confidential and could be disclosed only to those with a need to know, which did not include the certifying officer. GAO disagreed and distinguished this case from cases in which the agency was operating under "unvouchered expenditure" authority such as 31 U.S.C. § 3526(e)(2). Under that type of specific statutory authority, a certifying officer who is not informed of the object or purpose of the expenditure is not accountable for its legality. 24 Comp. Gen. 544 (1945). In the 49 Comp. Gen. 486 case, however, the agency had no such authority. Therefore, the certifying officer would be liable if he certified a voucher without knowing what it represented.

As GAO pointed out in a later case, any other answer would defeat the purpose of the certification requirement, which is to protect the United States against illegal or erroneous payments. 55 Comp. Gen. 297, 299 (1975). However, if the certifying officer is otherwise without fault or negligence, the agency's failure to inform the certifying official of the nature of the expenses would support a grant of relief from liability.

Certifying Officer Acted in Good Faith. The second relief standard, 31 U.S.C. § 3528(b)(l)(B), contains three elements, all of which must be satisfied: (1) the obligation was incurred in good faith; (2) the payment is not specifically prohibited; and (3) the United States received value for the payment. If a certifying officer qualifies for relief under this standard, it becomes irrelevant whether he or she could also have qualified under the first standard.

The first element requires that the obligation supporting the payment was incurred in "good faith." There is no simple formula for determining good faith. Black's Law Dictionary defines the term as follows:

> Good faith is an intangible and abstract quality with no technical meaning or statutory definition, and it encompasses, among other things, an honest belief, the absence of malice and the absence of design to defraud. . . . Honesty of intention, and freedom from knowledge of circumstances which ought to put the holder upon inquiry.

Black's Law Dictionary 693 (6th ed. 1990).

An important factor in evaluating good faith for purposes of 31 U.S.C. § 3528 is whether the certifying officer had, or reasonably should have had, doubt regarding the propriety of the payment and, if so, what he or she did about it. Whether the certifying officer reasonably should have been in doubt depends on a weighing of all surrounding facts and circumstances and cannot be resolved by any "hard and fast rule." 70 Comp. Gen. 723, 726 (1991).

In several cases, GAO has held that the failure to obtain an advance decision from GAO on questionable payments was considered to indicate a lack of good faith. See 14 Comp. Gen. 578, 583 (1935). Depending on the circumstances, following the advice or instructions of an agency administrative official in lieu of seeking an advance decision may not constitute "reasonable inquiry" under the first relief standard of 31 U.S.C. § 3528.31 Comp. Gen. 653 (1952). For example, in B-184145, September 30, 1975, 55 Comp. Gen. 297, GAO stated:

> Thus, we have held that a certifying officer, who accepts the advice and instruction of an administrative or legal officer concerning a doubtful payment instead of exercising his right to obtain a decision by the Comptroller General, may not be relieved of responsibility for making an erroneous payment. . . . Where there is doubt as to the legality of a payment, the certifying officer's only complete protection from liability for an erroneous payment is to request and follow the Comptroller General's advance decision under 31 U.S.C. 82D (1972).

Although not as conclusive as seeking an advance opinion from the Comptroller General, consulting agency counsel has been considered a relevant factor in demonstrating good faith under the second standard. B-191900, July 21, 1978; B-127160, April 3, 1961.

To understand the second element, i.e., "no law specifically prohibited the payment," it is helpful to note the language of the original 1941 statute, which stated "the payment was not contrary to any statutory provision specifically prohibiting payments of the character involved" (55 Stat. 875–76). GAO interpreted this language to mean that the statute expressly prohibits payments for specific items or services. 70 Comp. Gen. 723, 726 (1991); B-191900, July 21,1978. An example would be 40 U.S.C. § 34, which prohibits the rental of space in the District of Columbia without specific authority. 46 Comp. Gen. 135 (1966). Other examples are 31 U.S.C. § 1348(a) (telephones in private residences) and 44 U.S.C. § 3702 (newspaper advertisements). This interpretation was good news for certifying officers seeking relief from liability, since it would satisfy the second element unless their actions were in direct conflict with a specific statutory prohibition.

GAO's interpretation of the current language ("payment prohibited by law") is much broader than its interpretation of the earlier language ("no law specifically prohibited the payment"). GAO has interpreted the current language, for example, to include violations of general fiscal statutes such as the Antideficiency Act (31 U.S.C. § 1341) or the general purpose statute (31 U.S.C. § 1301(a)). B-142871-O.M., September 15, 1961. The practical effect of this broader interpretation is that the certifying officer will be unable to satisfy the second element of the three-part test if the payment violated any statute, however general. As a result, a request for relief from liability would probably be denied in such a case.

The third element—that the United States received value for the payment—generally refers to the receipt of goods or services with a readily determinable dollar value. See B-241879, April 26, 1991 (services performed under an information technology maintenance contract extended without proper authority). However, in appropriate circumstances, an intangible item may constitute value received where the payment in question has achieved a desired program result. B-191900, July 21, 1978; B-127160, April 3, 1961. For example, in a consulting services contract, the expertise and advice of the contractor would constitute value if it enabled the agency to accomplish an objective, even if no tangible "deliverable" could be identified. If all three elements of the second test are met, GAO has granted relief in prior cases.

Liability and Relief of Accountable Officers 583

> **Discussion Problem 8-9**
>
> Ima Violaytor is a certifying officer with an unblemished 20-year career. Ima receives a contractor payment voucher and, as is her practice, carefully ensures that the voucher is in proper form and that the goods purchased under the contract have been inspected and accepted by the contracting officer. Ima does not, however, check the funding documentation in the file to verify that adequate funds are available for payment. Ima makes the payment.
>
> It turns out that the funding document indicated that $50,000 was available, while the voucher was for $100,000, causing an Antideficiency Act violation. Since Ima carefully ensured that the voucher was in proper format, should Ima be relieved of liability?

Relief of Disbursing Officers

The administrative relief statute for disbursing officers, (31 U.S.C. § 3527(c)), was enacted in 1955 (69 Stat. 687). The statute states:

> (c) On the initiative of the Comptroller General or written recommendation of the head of an agency, the Comptroller General may relieve a present or former disbursing official of the agency responsible for a deficiency in an account because of an illegal, improper, or incorrect payment, and credit the account for the deficiency, when the Comptroller General decides that the payment was not the result of bad faith or lack of reasonable care by the official. However, the Comptroller General may deny relief when the Comptroller General decides the head of the agency did not carry out diligently collection action under procedures prescribed by the Comptroller General.

Under this statute, the Comptroller General is authorized to relieve present or former disbursing officers from liability for deficiencies in their accounts resulting from illegal, improper, or incorrect payments, upon determining that the payment was not the result of bad faith or lack of reasonable care by the disbursing officer. The determination may be made by the agency and concurred in by GAO, or it may be made by GAO on its own initiative. A relief request must contain sufficient information to enable an independent evaluation to be conducted by the agency and, if necessary, GAO. B-235037, September 18, 1989.

As in the case of relief for certifying officers for improper payment, within DoD the agency's determination to grant relief is binding on the Comptroller General. In making this determination, DoD will consider the same factors that the Comptroller General would have to consider in a non-DoD disbursing officer case.

Relief may be denied if the agency concerned fails to diligently pursue collection action against the recipient of the improper payment. The statute further provides that granting relief under section 3527(c) does not affect the liability or authorize the relief of the beneficiary or recipient of the improper payment, nor does it diminish the government's duty to pursue collection action against the beneficiary or recipient. 31 U.S.C. § 3527(d)(2).

However, in contrast with the certifying officer relief statute, 31 U.S.C. § 3527(c) is not limited to the executive branch. The Comptroller General has held that it applied also to the judicial branch. See, e.g., B-200108/B-198558, January 23, 1981. Within the executive branch, it applies to military and civilian agencies alike. Thus, the relief authority of 31 U.S.C. § 3527(c) is not limited only to those disbursing officers whose duties are prescribed by 31 U.S.C. § 3325(a) (which does not apply to military disbursing officers).

The relief statute is intended to provide relief based on the circumstances of individual cases and does not authorize the blanket relief of unknown disbursing officers for unknown amounts. B-165743, May 11, 1973. Once it is determined that there has been an improper payment for which a disbursing officer is accountable, and that relief has been requested, the primary issue is whether the payment was the result of bad faith or lack of reasonable care on the part of the disbursing officer. "Bad faith," like "good faith," is difficult to define with any precision. It is generally considered to be somewhere between negligence and actual dishonesty, and closer to the latter. Black's Law Dictionary provides the following definition:

> The opposite of "good faith," generally implying or involving actual or constructive fraud, or a design to mislead or deceive another, or a neglect or refusal to fulfill some duty or some contractual obligation, not prompted by an honest mistake as to one's rights or duties, but by some interested or sinister motive. Term "bad faith" is not simply bad judgment or negligence, but rather it implies the conscious doing of a wrong because of dishonest purpose or moral obliquity. . . .

Black's Law Dictionary, p. 139 (6th ed. 1990).

Cases involving bad faith of a disbursing officer are relatively uncommon. Far more common are cases invoking the reasonable care standard. This standard, which looks at whether the disbursing officer exercised reasonable care, is the legal definition of negligence and is the same standard applied in the physical loss cases. 65 Comp. Gen. 858, 861–62 (1986); 54 Comp. Gen. 112 (1974).

The determination of whether a payment was or was not the result of bad faith or lack of due care must be made on the basis of the facts and circumstances surrounding the particular payment in question. A high error rate in the disbursing office involved does not automatically establish lack of due care in the making of a particular payment, nor does a low error rate and a record of an exemplary operation automatically establish due care. B-141038-O.M., November 17, 1959; B-136027-O.M., June 13, 1958. GAO has found, however, that the continued existence of an "inherently dangerous" procedure does indicate a lack of due care on the part of the responsible disbursing officer. B-162629-O.M., November 9, 1967.

Although it is not possible to define precisely what is and what is not "good faith," the relevant GAO decisions indicate that, as a general matter, GAO is more likely to grant relief where: (1) the agency has made proper efforts to collect from the recipient of the improper payment, (2) the agency has determined that the payment was not the result of bad faith or lack of due care on the part of the disbursing officer, and (3) there is no evidence to the contrary. Also, relief may be granted without the agency's administrative determination where due care and the absence of bad faith are evident from the facts.

Actual negligence that contributes to an improper payment demonstrates a lack of good faith and due care and will preclude the granting of relief. For example, making a payment on the basis of documents that have obviously been altered, without first seeking clarification, does not evidence good faith or due care. B-233276, October 31, 1989, aff'd upon reconsideration, B-233276, June 20, 1990; B-138593-O.M., February 18, 1959; B-13591 O-O.M., July 14, 1958. Similarly, GAO denied relief where the disbursing officer made duplicate payments even though the voucher schedule indicated that payment had already been made. In this case, GAO determined that the payment could only have been made as a result of a lack of due care. B-142051, March 22, 1960.

In another case, GAO denied relief where the disbursing officer continued to pay a New Mexico gasoline tax after the State Attorney General and Judge Advocate General had both concluded that the United States was not liable for the tax. Although the disbursing officer was aware of the rulings, he claimed that he had not received specific instructions to stop paying. B-135811, May 29, 1959.

As with physical losses, failure to follow applicable regulations is generally regarded as negligent, and if an improper payment is attributable to that failure, relief has been denied. 54 Comp. Gen. 112, 116 (1974); 44 Comp. Gen. 160 (1964). Conversely, compliance with regulations will help establish due care. However, the mere fact that a disbursing officer complied with regulations may not always satisfy the standard if the regulations themselves are clearly insufficient. B-192558, December 7, 1978.

As is the case with certifying officers, the concept of proximate cause is also applicable when granting relief to disbursing officers. Accordingly, relief is appropriate where any negligence that may have existed was not the proximate cause of the improper payment. For example, GAO considered a situation in which local operating procedures at a military installation were found inadequate because they permitted personal checks to be cashed without checking identification cards. However, GAO granted relief because the cashier checked ID cards on his own initiative, and did so in the case for which relief was sought. Therefore, the inadequacy of the procedures could not have contributed to the loss. B-221415, March 26, 1986. For other examples, see B-227436, July 2, 1987, and B-217663, July 16, 1985.

The essence of negligence is the existence of a duty to exercise reasonable care in a particular situation and the violation of that duty. In B-188744, July 15, 1977, a Bureau of Indian Affairs disbursing officer erroneously made a payment to the wrong heir. Unknown to him, the probate and title determinations on which he had based the payment had been reopened and revised. Under established procedures, the disbursing officer was neither required nor expected to verify inheritance determinations. Since the verification was not within the scope of his duty, and was not something anyone in his position would reasonably be expected to do, there was no lack of due care. See also B-137223-O.M, January 18, 1960.

Thus, negligence will generally not be imputed to a disbursing officer where payment is made on the basis of information upon which the disbursing officer may properly rely, even though the information turns out to be inaccurate. This assumes that there is nothing on the face of the documents presented to the disbursing officer that should reasonably have alerted him or her that something might be wrong.

Although a disbursing officer is accountable for payments made by his or her subordinates, relief may be granted under 31 U.S.C. § 3527(c) if the improper payment was not the result of bad faith or lack of due care attributable to the disbursing officer personally. B-141038-O.M., November 17, 1959. Within DoD, the liability of a supervisor is described as follows:

> 060303. Major Physical Losses by Deputies, Disbursing Agents, Paying Agents, Cashiers, and Collection Agents. Agents are pecuniarily liable for all funds entrusted to them. The DO, however, maintains overall responsibility for the funds and is jointly and severally liable for any agent losses unless relieved of pecuniary liability under section 0609. Since agent losses are essentially DO losses, the agent shall report losses to his or her principal immediately upon discovery.

DoD Financial Management Regulation, Vol. 5, Ch. 6, para. 060303 (2000).

Thus, as with any accountable officer, a supervisory disbursing officer is presumed to be liable for improper payment by a subordinate but, in appropriate circumstances, may be relieved of liability. Where the actual disbursement is made by a subordinate, relief for the supervisory disbursing officer requires a showing that the disbursing officer exercised adequate supervision. Adequate supervision in this context means that the disbursing officer: (1) maintained an adequate system of controls and procedures to avoid errors and (2) took appropriate steps to ensure that the system was effective and was being followed at the time of the improper payment. See B-271608, June 21, 1996 (relief denied to disbursing officer for actions of subordinate because record demonstrated that disbursing officer failed to exercise adequate supervision); 62 Comp. Gen. 476, 480 (1983).

GAO has not attempted to define the elements of an adequate supervisory system and, as a practical matter, there can be no universally applicable formula. Each supervisory system will necessarily vary based on the size of the disbursing operation and the types of payments or transactions involved. Nevertheless, GAO has identified several elements that commonly appear in good systems.

The first element is compliance with agency regulations. For example, a military disbursing office will need to ensure compliance with any pertinent directives of the Defense Department, the particular military department involved, and the parent command.

The second element is locally developed instructions (often called standard operating procedures or SOPS) tailored to the needs of the particular disbursing office. Relief requests should include copies of any relevant SOPS. While SOPS are extremely helpful, the lack of a written SOP will not in and of itself cause a system to "flunk" the relief standard. See B-215226, April 16, 1985.

Third is training. This includes both initial training for new personnel and periodic refresher training, again tailored to the needs of the particular office. Training in this context does not necessarily mean formal classroom training, but includes on-the-job training and such devices as "Read Files," which are circulated periodically and especially when pertinent changes occur.

The fourth element is periodic review or inspection by the supervisor. The forms this may take will vary with the size and nature of the operation.

To establish due care, it is not necessary for the supervisory system to be perfect. Many cases have made the point that a skillfully executed criminal scheme can occasionally overcome even the best supervised system. See B-241880, August 14, 1991; B-202911, June 29, 1981. Similarly, human error will occur even in the most carefully established and supervised system. The best system cannot be expected to eliminate or detect every clerical error by a subordinate. See B-224961, September 8, 1987; B-212336, August 8, 1983.

The cases also recognize that, in a large operation, the supervisory disbursing officer cannot reasonably be expected to personally review every check that is issued or every cash payment that is made. See B-215734, November 5, 1984 (check cashed with fraudulent endorsement); B-194877, July 12, 1979 (amounts of two payments inadvertently switched, resulting in overpayment to one payee); B-187180, September 21, 1976 (wrong amounts inserted on checks).

Thus, it is possible for a supervisor to be relieved for an error by a subordinate which, if attributable to the disbursing officer personally, would have resulted in the denial of relief. For example, if a disbursing officer made a payment based on an obviously altered document, he or she would most likely be denied relief. In these cases, the disbursing officer saw or should have seen the documents. However, relief has been granted for similar losses occurring in otherwise adequate systems under which the supervisor was not required to see, and in fact did not see, the altered document. B-141038-O.M., November 17, 1959. These cases illustrate that the likelihood of relief is related to the level of personal involvement of the individual whose liability is at issue.

Where the subordinate who made the payment is also an accountable officer (a cashier, for example), the standard for relieving the subordinate is whether the individual complied with established procedures and whether anything occurred that should reasonably have made the individual suspicious that something was wrong. See B-233997.3, November 25, 1991; B-241880, August 14, 1991.

Discussion Problem 8-10

D.A. Boss is the disbursing officer in a large payments office that employs 20 assistant disbursing officers and 50 cashiers. Boss rose up through the ranks and likes to make payments occasionally just to keep up her skills. As part of the officer quality control program, each week she randomly selects 10 vouchers, reviews them, and pays them. In one particular week, of the 1,000 payments made, two were discovered to be improper. There were obvious inconsistencies in the documents that the cashier making the payments did not notice. Boss did not personally review these vouchers as part of the quality assurance process.

Is she accountable for this loss? Is this a proper case for relief of D.A. Boss? Is this a proper case for relief of the cashier who made the payments?

Depending on the particular facts, in cases involving two disbursing officers accountable for a payment, one a supervisor and the other a subordinate, it is possible for relief to be granted to both, denied to both, or granted to one and denied to the other. The key factor is the relative level of personal involvement of the accountable officers involved. Examples of cases applying these standards in which relief was granted to the supervisor but not the subordinate are B-231503, June 28, 1988 (cashier failed to observe annotations on voucher), and B-214436, April 6, 1984 (agency declined to seek relief for subordinate who had failed to follow established procedures).

As noted in the discussion of the physical loss cases, statements by the accountable officer are important to the determination of whether relief should be granted. The principle also applies to improper payment cases. The existence of adequate controls and procedures is usually documented, but this is not always the case, and the passage of time may make it impossible to locate a copy of the specific version of the SOPS in effect at the time of the improper payment. Also, testimony of the accountable officer(s) and others is often the only way of establishing how the controls and procedures were being implemented at the time of the payment.

While the disbursing officer's own statement is obviously not disinterested and cannot be regarded as conclusive, it is always given appropriate weight by GAO and, as with unexplained loss cases, has often been enough to tip the balance in favor of relief where the record contains no controverting evidence or where documentary evidence is no longer available. Examples are B-234962, September 28, 1989; B-215226, April 16, 1985; B-217637, March 18, 1985; B-216726, January 9, 1985; B-215833, December 21, 1984; and B-212603 et al., December 12, 1984.

Finally, a disbursing officer has the same statutory right as a certifying officer to obtain an advance decision from the Comptroller General. 31 U.S.C. § 3529. Obviously, for the decision to protect the disbursing officer, the request must include all of the relevant facts relating to the proposed transaction. 20 Comp. Gen. 759 (1941). Following administrative advice in lieu of seeking a GAO decision may, depending on the circumstances, be relevant to the determination of whether the disbursing officer exercised due care. See 49 Comp. Gen. 38 (1969).

As noted in the discussion relating to relief of certifying officers, consulting agency counsel will often help a certifying officer establish good faith. There is no reason why it should not also help a disbursing officer establish good faith and due care, although this may not be enough if the advice received is obviously inconsistent with other applicable guidance of which the disbursing officer is or should be aware. See 65 Comp. Gen. 858 (1986), affd upon reconsideration, B-217114.5, June 8, 1990.

Whichever course of action is chosen, the disbursing officer faced with a doubtful payment needs to do something. It will be very difficult for a disbursing officer to be granted relief if he or she makes a payment, even though in doubt regarding the propriety of the payment, without consulting either GAO or appropriate agency officials. See 23 Comp. Gen. 578 (1944).

> The rule of strict liability makes accountable officers automatically liable for improper payment or loss of public funds for which they are responsible. Evidence of fault or negligence is not required. However, relief from liability may be granted if the accountable officer acted in accordance with applicable procedures and otherwise exercised due care under the circumstances.

Student Exam

1. The constitutional basis for fiscal law states:
   a. "The Executive Branch of Government shall have the power of the purse."
   b. "No money shall be drawn from the Treasury, but in consequence of appropriations made by law."
   c. "If necessary, the Government may expend funds in excess of the amount appropriated by Congress."
   d. None of the above.

2. A federal agency must generally expend appropriated funds for the purposes specified by Congress in appropriations acts, even if the federal agency believes the expenditure to be unwise.
   True or False (underline one)

3. The authority to incur a legal obligation to pay a sum of money from the U.S. Treasury is called:
   a. Spending authority
   b. Contract authority
   c. Obligation authority
   d. Budget authority.

4. Name a congressional enactment that provides a federal agency with budget authority.

   _____

5. Identify the three limitations that Congress imposes on the use of appropriated funds.

   1. _____

   2. _____

   3. _____

6. A "commitment" of funds is defined as:
   a. Any act that legally binds the government to make payment
   b. An administrative reservation of an allotment or other funds in anticipation of their obligation
   c. Payment of funds based on valid obligations
   d. The expiration of funds at the end of their period of availability.

7. How much should be obligated for a firm-fixed-price contract awarded at a price of $500,000?
   a. $500,000
   b. $500,000 plus a reasonable estimate for contingent liabilities
   c. Nothing. Funds should be obligated only when disbursement is made, not at the time of award.
   d. 50% of the award amount.

8. How much should an agency obligate upon award of an indefinite-delivery/indefinite-quantity contract with a maximum of $2 million, an estimate of $1 million, and a guaranteed minimum of $100,000?
   a. $2 million
   b. $1 million
   c. $100,000
   d. Nothing (too indefinite).

9. A three-part test is used to identify the purpose of an appropriation. Identify each of the parts of the three-part test.

   1. _____

   2. _____

   3. _____

10. Any limitation on the use of appropriated funds that is included in a conference report or committee report will always be binding on executive branch agencies.
    True or False (underline one)

11. If an agency includes in its budget a request for funds for an unlawful purpose, and Congress enacts the appropriations act without specifically objecting to the request, the agency may expend the funds for the unlawful purpose.
    True or False (underline one)

12. According to the necessary expense doctrine, an expenditure is permissible if it is:
    a. Expedient and reasonable to accomplish the agency's mission
    b. Reasonably necessary in carrying out an authorized function or will contribute materially to the effective accomplishment of that function
    c. Made to pay a claim under a contract
    d. Approved in advance by the contracting officer.

13. Change the following sentence so that it is a true statement:
    In determining whether an agency charged the proper appropriation, GAO will always substitute its own judgment.

14. In general, a restriction included in an appropriations act:
    a. Can be ignored because an appropriations act is not a valid law
    b. Should always be appealed by the agency
    c. Applies only to the fiscal year covered by the act
    d. Applies to the fiscal year covered by the act and all future fiscal years.

15. A general appropriation may always be used as a backup for a more specific appropriation.
    True or False (underline one)

16. The use of appropriated funds to buy clothing is generally:
    a. Prohibited because it is considered a personal expense
    b. Prohibited specifically in the appropriations act
    c. Authorized if purchased under a contract
    d. Authorized specifically in the appropriations act.

17. An agency may use appropriated funds to pay for meals at formal meetings or conferences if:
    a. The meals are incidental to the meeting
    b. Attendance of the employees at the meals is necessary for full participation in the meeting
    c. The employees are not free to take meals elsewhere without being absent from the essential business of the meeting
    d. All of the above.

18. Change the following sentence so that it is a true statement:
    Appropriated funds generally are always available to pay for entertainment.

19. What are the circumstances in which an agency may use appropriated funds to purchase business cards for its employees?

_____

_____

_____

20. If an agency uses one appropriation to pay expenses that should be charged to another appropriation, it has violated which of the following fiscal rules?
    a. The alternative source rule
    b. The doctrine of mischarged expenses
    c. The Antideficiency Act
    d. The augmentation of appropriations rule.

21. Agencies must obligate appropriations during this period of availability, or the authority to obligate expires. True or False (underline one)

22. Change the following sentence so that it is a true statement:
    Unless stated otherwise in the appropriations act, funds are presumed to be available for obligation for five years.

23. The rule that an appropriation may be obligated only to meet a legitimate need existing during the appropriation's period of availability is referred to as:
    a. The legitimate need rule
    b. The bona fide need rule
    c. The purpose statute
    d. The Antideficiency Act.

24. Explain why the following statement is not accurate: Under supply contracts, the bona fide need is always determined by when the government actually requires (i.e., will be able to use) the supplies being acquired. Thus, agencies must always obligate funds that are current in the fiscal year in which the supplies will actually be used.

_____

_____

_____

_____

_____

25. Which of the following is a proper method for funding service contracts?
    a. Use funds that are current when the severable services are performed
    b. Use funds to fund the entire period of a nonseverable service contract
    c. Use funds to fund up to 12 months of severable services, even if the contract crosses fiscal years
    d. All of the above.

For 26–28, match the term with the correct definition.

26. ___ Current appropriations
    a. Appropriations whose availability for new obligations has expired, but which retain their fiscal identity and are available to adjust and liquidate previous obligations

27. ___ Expired appropriations
    b. Appropriations whose availability for new obligations has not expired under the terms of the applicable appropriations act

28. ___ Closed appropriations
    c. Appropriations that are no longer available for any purpose

29. Under the "relation back" doctrine:
   a. Expired appropriations cannot be used for recording, adjusting, and liquidating prior obligations properly chargeable to the account
   b. Closed appropriations remain available for recording, adjusting, and liquidating prior obligations properly chargeable to the account
   c. Expired appropriations remain available for recording, adjusting, and liquidating prior obligations properly chargeable to the account
   d. None of the above

30. After an account is closed, agencies may, within certain limitations, charge obligations formerly chargeable to the closed account to any current agency account available for the same general purpose.
   True or False (underline one)

31. An "apportionment" is defined as:
    a. An administrative division of funds from higher to lower levels within an agency
    b. A distribution by the Office of Management and Budget of amounts available in an appropriation into amounts available for specified time periods, activities, projects, or objects
    c. A transfer of funds from one agency to another agency to accomplish mission-essential requirements
    d. An enactment by Congress that specifies how an agency may expend appropriated funds.

32. An Antideficiency Act violation will result if an agency obligates or expends funds in excess of the amount available in an:
    a. Apportionment
    b. Administrative division of funds
    c. Appropriation
    d. All of the above.

33. It is never a violation of the Antideficiency Act to obligate funds in advance of the enactment of the appropriation, provided there are sufficient funds available to pay the obligation when the appropriations act becomes effective.
    True or False (underline one)

34. Which of the following clauses allows an agency to initiate contracting actions in advance of enactment of the appropriation cited?
    a. Changes clause
    b. Initiation of contracting action clause
    c. Fiscal exception clause
    d. Subject to availability of funds clause.

35. Fill in the blanks in the following sentence so that it is a true statement:
    Obligation of funds for an improper purpose does not create an Antideficiency Act violation if _____

    _____

    _____

36. A contract stating that the government will indemnify the contractor for "any and all damages arising from performance of this contract" violates the Antideficiency Act even if no damages actually occur.
    True or False (underline one)

37. An agency may accept voluntary services if:
    a. The volunteer agrees in writing to waive any right to compensation
    b. A law authorizes the acceptance of voluntary services
    c. The services are accepted in an emergency situation
    d. All of the above.

38. A government employee cannot be disciplined for causing an Antideficiency Act violation if the violation resulted from a simple, innocent mistake.
    True or False (underline one)

39. Violation of the Antideficiency Act could result in a maximum criminal punishment of:
    a. Two years imprisonment, a $5,000 fine, or both
    b. Five years imprisonment or a $5,000 fine
    c. Two years imprisonment or a $2,000 fine
    d. None of the above

40. Which of the following is not one of the four determinations that an agency must make prior to placing an order under the Economy Act?
   a. Funds are available.
   b. The interagency order is in the best interests of the government.
   c. The ordering agency has determined that it cannot obtain the goods or services "as conveniently or cheaply" from a private contractor.
   d. The transaction is with a government-owned government-operated (GOGO) facility.

41. The Economy Act authorizes inter-agency transactions, but not intra-agency transactions.
   True or False (underline one)

42. Under the rules of obligation applicable to Economy Act transactions, if the performing agency does not obligate the funds cited on an order within their period of availability:
   a. There is no obligational impact, and the funds may be obligated by the performing agency after they expire.
   b. It must pay the ordering agency a penalty.
   c. The ordering agency must deobligate the funds.
   d. None of the above.

43. The Economy Act authorizes interagency transactions for the:
   a. Purchase of supplies
   b. Loan of equipment and personal property
   c. Purchase of services
   d. All of the above.

44. The Clinger-Cohen Act of 1996 has resulted in:
    a. Designation of the General Services Administration as the executive agent for certain government-wide acquisitions of information technology
    b. Designation of the Department of Defense as the executive agent for certain government-wide acquisitions of information technology
    c. Elimination of the Information Technology Fund
    d. All of the above.

45. The term "funding gap" refers to:
    a. The failure of an agency to budget for a contingency (hence, "gap" in funding)
    b. A period of time between the expiration or exhaustion of an appropriation and the enactment of a new one
    c. A budget surplus that authorizes the agency to cross fiscal years
    d. The period between the end of a contract period of performance and the exercise of an option.

46. Continuing resolutions generally:
    a. Provide funds in excess of the amount appropriated in the prior fiscal year (to account for inflation)
    b. Automatically authorize agencies to commence "new starts"
    c. Limit agencies to the smallest amount specified by various reference points
    d. Authorize agencies to obligate and expend amounts equal to the greatest amount specified by various reference points.

47. The duration of a continuing resolution is generally:
    a. A time period specified in the continuing resolution (e.g., a week, month, or year)
    b. Until a fixed cut-off date specified in the continuing resolution
    c. Until an appropriations act replaces it
    d. All of the above.

48. A certifying officer differs from other accountable officers in that the certifying officer:
   a. Generally does not have physical custody of public funds
   b. Is the only accountable officer authorized to have physical custody of public funds
   c. Must be a college graduate
   d. Must also serve as a contracting officer or program manager.

49. Accountable officers are generally responsible for:
   a. Appropriated funds
   b. Funds held in trust for others
   c. Receipts
   d. All of the above.

50. An accountable officer may not be held liable if public funds are lost due to factors beyond his or her control. True or False (underline one)

Index

A

accountability, certifying officers, 518
accountable funds, 528
accountable officer, 515–517
accountable officer liability
  absence of negligence, 547–552
  accountable officials, 534
  automated disbursing systems, 574–575
  civil agency, 540–542, 544–546
  disbursing officers and certifying officers, DoD, 542–544, 546–547
  embezzlement, 565–566
  fiscal irregularity, 537
  history, 511–514
  illegal, improper, or incorrect payment, 533–535, 570–573
  negligence, 558
  overruling necessity, 559–560
  physical loss or deficiency, 533–534
  proximate cause, 552–554
  regulatory violation, 557–558
  relief of liability, 514–515, 538–540
  security measures, 566–569
  theft by third parties, 560–564
  uncollectible personal check, 535–536
  unexplained losses, 554–557
accountable official, 516, 534
accounting classification codes, 14
Accounting Principles and Standards, General Accounting Office (GAO), 49
actual cost, 386
ADA. *See* Antideficiency Act
Administrative Control of Appropriations, 270
administrative division of apportionments, 268–269
Administrative Procedures Act (APA), 132
administrative sanctions, Antideficiency Act violations, 354
administrative subdivision of funds, 13
ADR. *See* alternative dispute resolution
advance certification, 403–405
adversary adjudication, 134
Age Discrimination in Employment Act, 28
agency discretion
  fairs and expositions, 118–120
  necessary expense rule, 114–115

605

range of discretion, variability, 115–117
Agency for International Development (AID), 405
agency membership fees, 193–195
agency mission, changing scope of, 28
AID. *See* Agency for International Development
Air Force, 224, 289, 295–296, 420
Airport and Airway Development Act of 1970, 36
alcoholic beverages, 142
allocations, 13, 272
allotments, 13, 44, 272
allowance, 272
alternative dispute resolution (ADR), 343–344, 429
American Association of Retired Persons, 332
American Hospital Association, 193
American Indian Movement, 416
American Management Association, 194
American Samoa, 376
amount, of appropriation. *See* Antideficiency Act
amount available, determining, 277–282
antecedent liability rule, 245–246, 248
Antideficiency Act (ADA). *See also* multi-year contracts; unlimited indemnification clause; voluntary services prohibition
administrative subdivision of appropriations, 268–273
amount available, determining, 277–282
apportionment indicates need for additional appropriations, 257–263

apportionment of appropriations, 255–257
appropriations-level violations, 273–276
consequences of violations, 352–354
contractor's right to payment, 354–358
exhausted appropriations, 285–286
expenditures exceed apportionment, 263–268
importance of, 4, 20, 48, 242
obligation citing future year's appropriation, 292–294
obligation exceeds amount available, 276–277, 282–285
obligation in advance of apportionment, 319–321
obligation in advance of appropriation, 292
overview, 252–254
reporting violations, 350–352
Requirements for Reporting Antideficiency Act Violations, 360–366
statutory limitation, 274–276
violation examples, 286–292
APA. *See* Administrative Procedures Act
appointment without compensation, 327, 341–342
apportionment of appropriations, 13, 255–257
appropriated amount
exceeds previously authorized amount, 34–36
is less than previously authorized amount, 36–38
appropriated funds, 528–531
appropriation, determining purpose of
appropriation act, 98–100

budget request, 107–109
  importance of, 97–98
  legislative history, 100–107
  program termination, 110–112
Appropriation Accounting–Refunds and Uncollectibles, 249, 256–257
  appropriation amount, 251–252.
    See also Antideficiency Act
appropriations act, 7
Approving Office, 521
armed robbery, 562
Army, 180, 216, 333, 399, 420
Assignment of Claims Act, 578
ATM. *See* automatic teller machine
attorneys' fees, incurred during contract litigation
  bid protests, 131–133
  contract disputes, 133–134
augmentation, unauthorized, 384
authorization act
  failure to enact, 7, 40–41
  funds appropriated prior to enactment of, 38–40
automatic teller machine (ATM), 530
automobile telephone calls, 190
availability of appropriations, 93, 293. *See also* purpose statute
award ceremonies,
  nongovernment personnel attendance at, 130–131

B

Bankruptcy Act, 238
banquets, 142
below-ceiling loss, 545
bid protests, 131–133
binding agreement, 56–58
blanket purchase agreement (BPA), 51
bona fide needs rule
  construction contracts, 226–227
  continuing needs, 215–218
  definition, 202, 211–212
  fact-sensitive nature of, 212–213
  lead-time exception, 220–221
  multiple-year appropriation, 213–215
  nonseverable service, 223–225
  one-year concept, 212
  service contracts, 222–223
  severable service, 223–225
  statutory basis, 212
  statutory exception, 225–226
  stock-level exception, 221–222
  supply contracts, 218–220
  training contracts, 226
BPA. *See* blanket purchase agreement
budget authority, 7
budget execution, 12
Budget Issues: The President's Budget Submission, 9
budget preparation and review, federal budget process, 8
budget resolution, passage of, 10–11
Bureau of Census, 401, 419, 424
Bureau of Indian Affairs, 275, 562, 573
Bureau of Land Management, 416
Bureau of Narcotics and Dangerous Drugs, 192
Bureau of Prisons, 425
Bureau of Public Debt, 371
Bureau of Reclamation, 400
burglary, 549, 561–562
Business Advisory Council, 332
business cards for government employees, 196

C

carelessness, 551
cash disbursement activity, 266–267

cashiers, 520–523
CBO. *See* Congressional Budget Office
cellular telephone, 190
Central Intelligence Agency (CIA), 401
certification of fund availability, 44
certifying officer
  acted in good faith, 580–583
  definition, 43, 517–519
  non-DoD compared to DoD, 575–576
  relief, 576–577
  unaware of actual facts, 577–580
Certifying Officers' Relief Act, 575–576
Cessna Aircraft, 319–320
CFTC. *See* Commodity Futures Trading Commission
check-cashing transaction, 535
Chief Financial Officers Act of 1990, 13
CIA. *See* Central Intelligence Agency
CICA. *See* Competition in Contracting Act
Civil Aeronautics Administration, 181
Civil Aeronautics Board, 416
civilian agency accountable officers, 544–546
civil provisions, 512
civil service laws, 400–401
Civil Service Retirement and Disability Fund, 431
Class A Cashier, 521
Class B Cashier, 521
Class C Cashier, 522
Class D Cashier, 521
Clean Air Act, 169–170
Clinger-Cohen Act of 1996, 441–443
closed appropriation, 203, 247–249

clothing
  authorized purchase, 135–136
  Federal Employees Uniform Act, 136–137
  necessary expense, 134–135, 138–140
  Occupational Safety and Health Act of 1970, 137–138
Coast Guard, 179, 416
coercive deficiency, 252–253, 300, 322
coffee breaks, 149
collecting officers, 523–525
Commerce Department, 194
Commission on Federal Paperwork, 332
Commission on Marijuana and Drug Abuse, 328
commitment, 44
commitment accounting, 45–46
commitment data, 46
commitment of funds
  contingent liabilities, 47–50
  contractual liabilities, 50–51
  importance of, 44–45
  purpose, 45
  responsibilities, 46–47
commitment register, 47
Commodity Futures Trading Commission (CFTC), 187
Communication Services Administration, 207
comparative negligence, 547
Competition in Contracting Act (CICA), 132, 434–435
Competitive Equality Banking Act of 1987, 32
Comptroller General, 16–18, 544, 591–592
Computer Data Authentication Standard, 59
computer-related media, satisfying in writing requirement with, 59
computers manufactured in foreign countries, purchasing, 15

concurrent resolution, 11
Congress
   general appropriations act, 1789, 5–6
   power of the purse, 2–3
   power to tax and spend, 2
   restrictions imposed by, 3
Congressional Budget Act
   deadline for budget process completion, 12
   government-wide budget totals, 9–10
Congressional Budget Office (CBO), 10
construction contracts, 226–227
contingent liabilities, 47–50
continuing needs, 215–218
continuing resolution. See also funding gap
   amount provided, 473–474
   current rate, 474–478
   definition, 471–473
   effect of appropriations act passage, 488–489
   insufficient final appropriation, 489–491
   limitations on initiation or expansion of programs, 492–494
   liquidation of contract authority, 487–488
   multiple-year appropriations, 481
   no-year appropriations, 481–482
   pattern of obligation, 485–487
   program level, 479–480
   rate of operations, 474
   unobligated carryover balance, 482–485
   wording, 473
contract authority, 7, 260
Contract Disputes Act of 1978, 61, 87, 133–134

contract modifications
   increasing amount obligated, 239–247
   reducing scope, 237–239
contractor's right to payment, 354–358
Corps of Engineers, 355
cost ceiling, 245
cost-plus award fee contract (CPAF), 50, 69–70
cost-plus fixed fee contract (CPFF), 50, 68
cost-plus incentive fee contract (CPIF), 68–69
cost-reimbursement contract, 50, 245
counterfeit currency, 552
Court of Claims, 514
CPAF. See cost-plus award fee contract
CPFF. See cost-plus fixed fee contract
CPIF. See cost-plus incentive fee contract
Criminal Code, 512
criminal penalties, Antideficiency Act violations, 353–354
cross-certification, 405–406
CRS Report for Congress, 496–510
Currency and Foreign Transactions Reporting Act, 536
current appropriations, 203
custodians, 525–528
Customs Service, 178–179, 523, 536

D

Defense Federal Acquisition Regulation Supplement, 372
Defense Logistics Agency, 215
Defense Operational Testing Agency (DOTA), 453
Defense Production Act of 1950, 194, 290

deferrals, 16
delivery lead time, 221
delivery order (DO), 71
deobligations, 89–91
Department of Agriculture, 525
Department of Commerce, 399
Department of Defense (DoD), 179
　accountable officers, 516
　Antideficiency Act violations, 271
　disbursing officers, 571
　Economy Act reimbursements, 380
　federal reimbursement of disability benefits, 315
　Financial Management Regulation, 45, 48–49, 55, 320–321, 576
　FY 1987 Appropriations Act, 3–4
　Overseas Dependents' Schools, 406
　project order statute, 437–440
　relief from liability, 542–544
Department of Education, 262
Department of Energy (DOE), 111, 139, 316, 526
Department of Health, Education, and Welfare (HEW), 405
Department of Housing and Urban Development (HUD), 120, 194
Department of Justice, 29, 531
Department of Labor Appropriations Act, 113–114
Department of State, 526–527
Department of the Interior, 305–306, 423
Department of the Treasury, 40, 557
Department of Veterans Affairs, 532
deserters, 179
detail of personnel
　actual cost requirement, 413
　additional expenses, reimbursement of, 407–408
　annual and sick leave, 411
　congressional committees, 414–415
　definition, 406
　nonreimbursable, 409–410
　renewable periods, 412
　revolving fund, 409
　written agreement, 408
direct cost, 384–385
disbursing more than amount obligated, 266–267
disbursing officer
　administrative relief statute, 583–584
　agency counsel, consulting, 592
　agency regulations, compliance with, 589
　bad faith, 588
　definition, 519–520
　good faith, 585
　judicial branch, 584
　level of personal involvement, 591
　negligence, 586
　periodic review, 589
　proximate cause, 587
　standard operating procedures, 589
　subordinates, 590
　supervisory, 588
　training, 589
discretionary cost, 245–246
District of Columbia, 376, 444–445, 572
District of Columbia Health and Hospitals Public Benefit Corporation (PBC), 338–339
DO. *See* delivery order
DoD. *See* Department of Defense
DOE. *See* Department of Energy

DOTA. *See* Defense Operational
   Testing Agency
Drug Enforcement Administration,
   527

E

EAJA. *See* Equal Access to Justice
   Act
earmarking appropriations,
   277–282
Economic Stabilization Agency,
   193
Economy Act. *See also* detail of
   personnel; personal property,
   loaning
 abuses, 435–436
 actual cost, calculating, 383–392
 administrative functions,
   transfer of, 429–431
 advance certification, 403–405
 advance payments and
   reimbursements, 378–380
 amendment, 432–433
 American Samoa, 376
 appropriate cases, 374
 augmentation, unauthorized,
   384
 authority, 370
 branches of government, 375
 Bureau of Public Debt, 371
 civil service laws, 400–401
 common services, 423–425
 Competition in Contracting Act,
   434–435
 competitive bids, 433
 cost comparison, 373
 cross-certification, 405–406
 deobligation of funds, 394–396
 Department of Defense, 380
 depreciation, 388–389
 direct cost, 384–385
 District of Columbia
   government, 376
 exemptions, 398–399
 Financial Management Services,
   386–387
 fiscal issues, 377
 full cost recovery, 389
 general restrictions and
   limitations, 397–402
 government corporations, 375
 government-owned,
   government-operated facility,
   437–438
 history, 367–369
 improper augmentation, 402
 Indian tribes, 376
 indirect cost, 384–385
 interagency transactions, 369,
   376
 intra-agency transactions, 369,
   376
 items provided from stock,
   381–383
 limitations, 425
 lower cost determination, 372,
   435
 miscellaneous receipts statute,
   379
 National Guard, 376
 non-required services, 427
 obligation of funds, 392–394
 off-loading, 436
 overcharges, 426
 patent and trademark laws,
   428
 presidential inaugural
   committee, 376
 recovery of small amounts,
   waiving, 391
 scope, 375–377
 situational cost, 387–388
 standard costs, 390–391
 support agreements, 405–406

United Nations, 376
written agreement, 373–375
EEOC. *See* Equal Employment Opportunity Commission
electronic apportionment, 256
Electronic Data Interchange (EDI), 59
emergency exception, 262–263, 335–341
Endangered Species Act of 1973, 30
entertainment, 141–142
Environmental Protection Agency (EPA), 23, 172
Equal Access to Justice Act (EAJA), 132, 209
Equal Employment Opportunity Commission (EEOC), 28
Equal Pay Act, 28
estoppel, 246
evidence of theft uncertain, 562–564
exception for safety of human life, 263
exempt activities, government shutdown, 466
exhausted appropriations, 285–286
expenditures beyond administrative control, 262
expenditures that exceed apportionment, 263–268
experts and consultants, 342–343
expired appropriations
  bid protests, 228–229
  contract modifications that increase amount obligated, 239–247
  contract modifications that reduce scope, 237–239
  definition, 203
  general continuing needs, 232–233
  mandatory *versus* discretionary use, 233–234
  reprocurement contract, 231–232
  termination for convenience of the government, 234–236
  termination for default, 230–231
  time limits, 228
Export Control Act, 177
expositions, 118–120

F

fairs, 118–120
family support programs, 345–346
Farmers Home Administration (FmHA), 311
FBI. *See* Federal Bureau of Investigation
FEDCAC. *See* Federal Computer Acquisition Center
Federal Acquisition Regulation (FAR)
  availability of funds, 293
  electronic data transmission methods, 59
  prohibited actions, assumptions regarding, 4–5
Federal Acquisitions Streamlining Act, 436
Federal Aviation Administration, 208
Federal Bureau of Investigation (FBI), 167–168, 416
Federal Claims Collection Act, 430
Federal Computer Acquisition Center (FEDCAC), 441
Federal Emergency Management Agency (FEMA), 307
Federal Housing Administration (FHA), 430
Federal Information Processing Standard (FIPS), 59

Federal Labor Relations Authority, 308
Federal Mediation and Conciliation Service, 192
Federal Property and Administrative Services Act (FPASA), 308, 443–444
Federal Property Management Regulations, 138, 198
federal reimbursement of disability benefits, 315
Federal Secure Telephone Service, 188–189
Federal Supply Schedule (FSS), 443
Federal Systems Integration and Management Center (FEDSIM), 441
Federal Trade Commission (FTC), 332
FEDSIM. See Federal Systems Integration and Management Center
FEMA. See Federal Emergency Management Agency
fencing, 45
FFP. See firm fixed-price contract
FHA. See Federal Housing Administration
Financial Management in the Federal Government, 254
Financial Management Service (FMS), 386–387
fines and penalties
  general rule, 165–167
  levied against an agency, 169–170
  protecting government interest, 167–169
FIPS. See Federal Information Processing Standard
firm fixed-price contract (FFP), 62–63
fiscal irregularity, 537

fiscal law, 1
fiscal year, 7, 20, 204, 293
fish tags, 180
fixed-cash fund, 521
fixed-price award fee contract (FPAF), 65–66
fixed-price contract, 50
fixed-price incentive contract (FPIF), 64–65
fixed-price with economic price adjustment contract (FP/EPA), 63–64
flash roll, 527
flexiplace program, 189
FmHA. See Farmers Home Administration
food, purchasing for government employees
  award ceremonies, 154–157
  cultural and ethnic programs, 157–158
  meetings and conferences, 147–153
  no free food rule, 143–144
  training, 153–154
  unusual conditions at employee's usual duty location, 144–146
Forest Service, 177
formal subdivision, 272
FPAF. See fixed-price award fee contract
FPASA. See Federal Property and Administrative Services Act
FP/EPA. See fixed-price with economic price adjustment contract
FPIF. See fixed-price incentive contract
fraudulent voucher, 566
FSS. See Federal Supply Schedule
FTC. See Federal Trade Commission

fund cite, 14
fund control system, 269–270
Funding Air Force Cost Plus Fixed Fee Level of Effort Contract, 223
funding gap. *See also* continuing resolution
    Attorney General opinions, 449–452
    authority to obligate, 454–456
    automatic continuing resolution, 464
    background, 448–449
    borrowing authority, 452–453
    Comptroller General opinion, 450–451
    contracting authority, 452–453
    definition, 447–448
    emergencies, 458–461
    impact on agency operations, 467–471
    indefinite appropriations, 452
    multi-year appropriations, 452
    OMB Bulletin No. 80-14, 461–462
    permissible activities, 464–467
    Presidential constitutional duties and powers, 457–458
    supplemental appropriations bill, 462–464
Funding of Maintenance Contract Extending Beyond Fiscal Year, 226
Funding of Replacement Contracts, 235
fund managers, 44
funds
    appropriated prior to enactment of authorization act, 38–40
    availability of, 293
    held in trust for others, 532–533
    received from nongovernment sources, 531–532
Funds Held Outside of Treasury, 521

G

General Accounting Office (GAO), 1, 6, 9, 49
general appropriation, 20–22
general continuing needs, 232–233
General Services Administration (GSA), 289, 306, 405
General Services Board of Contract Appeals (GSBCA), 429
GETA. *See* Government Employees Training Act
GFP. *See* government furnished property
gifts and awards
    agency objectives, linking to, 173–175
    examples, 171–173
    necessary expense doctrine, 170–171
Glossary of Terms Used in the Federal Budget Process, 6
GOGO. *See* government-owned, government-operated
good faith, 580–581
Government Employees Incentive Award Act, 155–157
Government Employees Training Act (GETA), 154, 440–441
government furnished property (GFP), 241, 288
government-owned, government-operated (GOGO), 437–438
Government Printing Office (GPO), 427, 437
government property clause, 51
government travel card, 517, 531
GPO. *See* Government Printing Office
gratuitous membership, 195
gratuitous services, 325–326
greenmailing, 253, 322

Index 615

GSBCA. *See* General Services Board of Contract Appeals

H

help desk support, 244
HEW. *See* Department of Health, Education, and Welfare
House Appropriations Committee, 11
HUD. *See* Department of Housing and Urban Development

I

IDIQ. *See* indefinite-delivery/ indefinite-quantity contract
Immigration and Naturalization Service (INS), 39, 118
IMPAC card, 517, 526
Impoundment Control Act, 16–18
Impoundment Control Act of 1974, 15–18
imprest fund, 521, 545
improper augmentation, 402
incentive clause, 50
Incremental Funding of U.S. Fish and Wildlife Service Research Work Orders, 224
indefinite-delivery/indefinite-quantity contract (IDIQ), 71
Indian tribes, 376
indirect cost, 384–385
individual membership fees, 191–193
informal subdivision, 272
informants, 176 179
Information Technology Fund, 441–442
information technology (IT), 301, 441

initiation, 44
INS. *See* Immigration and Naturalization Service
Institute of Electrical and Electronic Engineers, 192
Instructions on Budget Execution, 12–13, 269
Insurance-Liability to Third Persons, 313–314
Integrated Services Digital Network (ISDN), 189
interagency transaction, 77
interdepartmental waiver doctrine, 419
Internal Revenue Service (IRS), 178, 189, 523, 537, 566
ISDN. *See* Integrated Services Digital Network
IT. *See* information technology

L

lack of funds, 286
last in time rule, 36, 40
lead-time exception, 220–221
legal duty, 253
legislative history
 appropriation, determining purpose of, 100–101
 committee reports, 102–103
 definition, 25–26, 101–102
 floor debates, 104–106
 hearings, 106–107
letter contract, 50, 73–74
Library of Congress, 350
limitations, on use of appropriated funds
 amount limitations, 20
 expending and obligating amounts, 274
 purpose limitations, 19
 time limitations, 19–20

line-item appropriation, 36
liquidated damages, 85
liquor, 142
litigation, 86–88
live artistic performances, 142
lower cost determination, 435
lump-sum appropriation, 27–28, 205, 277

M

Magnavox–Use of Contract Underrun Funds, 243
Marine Corps, 419
Maritime Administration, 416
market research, 435
MAS. *See* Multiple Award Schedule
Matter of Incremental Funding of Multiyear Contracts, 223
meals, reimbursement for, 146
medical care, 345–346
meetings and conventions, attendance
  military personnel, 128
  nongovernment personnel, 128–131
  sponsored by federal government, 127–128
  sponsored by nongovernment entities, 124–126
membership fees
  agency membership, 193–195
  appropriated funds, 191
  individual membership, 191–193
Mine Enforcement and Safety Administration, 301–302
miscellaneous receipts, 249, 379
Modification to Contract Involving Cost Underrun, 243
moral duty, 253

Multiple Award Schedule (MAS), 443
multiple-year appropriation, 8, 213–215
multiple-year period, 206
multi-year contracts
  acquisition of property, 304
  Air Force, 295–296
  coercive deficiency, 300
  definition, 294
  liability, 297–298
  obligations in advance of appropriation, 295
  Post Office, 298–299
  right to terminate, 298
  subject to availability clause, 300
  termination charges, 301–303
museums, 345–346
music, 142
mutuality of intent to be bound, 60

N

NARA. *See* National Archives and Records Administration
NAS. *See* National Academy of Sciences
NASA. *See* National Aeronautics and Space Administration
NASA Financial Management Manual, 46, 57–58, 242, 271, 378
National Academy of Sciences (NAS), 445–446
National Aeronautics and Space Administration (NASA), 17–18, 34
National Archives and Records Administration (NARA), 427

National Capital Park and
Planning Commission, 209
National Defense Authorization
Act for Fiscal Year 1994, 436
*National Endowment for the Arts–
Time Availability for
Appropriations,* 208
National Environmental Policy
Act, 31
National Guard, 376
National Institute of Standards
and Technology (NIST), 59
National Oceanic and
Atmospheric Administration
(NOAA), 192, 306–307
National Security Agency (NSA), 155
natural resources programs,
345–346
Navy, 33, 181, 287–288, 324, 398
necessary expense doctrine
agency discretion, 114–121
expenditure, relationship to
appropriation, 113
expenditure otherwise provided
for, 123
expenditure prohibited by law,
121–123
importance of, 112–113
specifically stated purpose,
113–114
negligence, absence of, 547–552
NIST. *See* National Institute of
Standards and Technology
NOAA. *See* National Oceanic and
Atmospheric Administration
nonseverable service, 223–225
non-vested mandatory
authorization, 37
not less than phrase, 281
not to exceed earmark, 279
no-year appropriation, 8, 207–210,
260

*No-Year Appropriations in the
Department of Agriculture,* 210
Nuclear Regulatory Commission
(NRC), 189, 209, 316

O

obligation, 8, 44
obligation amount, determining
cost-plus award fee contract, 69–70
cost-plus fix fee contract, 68
cost-plus incentive fee contract,
68–69
cost-reimbursement contract,
66–68
delivery order, 71
firm fixed-price contract, 62–63
fixed-price award fee contract,
65–66
fixed-price contract, 62
fixed-price incentive contract,
64–65
fixed-price with economic price
adjustment contract, 63–64
indefinite-delivery/indefinite-
quantity contract, 71
interagency agreement required
by law, 81–83
interagency transaction, 77
letter contract, 73–74
option, 76
orders from stock, 83
purchase order, 75–76
rental agreement, 76–77
requirements contract, 71–73
task order, 71
variable quantity contracts, 70–71
voluntary interagency
agreement, 81–83

obligation citing future year's
 appropriation, 292–294
obligation in advance of
 appropriation, 276, 292
obligation in excess of
 appropriation, 276–277
obligation of appropriations
 binding agreement, 56–58
 contract obligations, 55–56
 importance of, 51–53
 in writing requirement, 58–61
 requirement of specificity, 61–62
 statutory requirement for
  recording obligations, 53–55
obligation subject to availability of
 funds, 88–89
Occupational Safety and Health
 Act of 1970 (OSHA), 137–138
office decorations, 197–200
Office of Economic Opportunity
 (OEO), 110–111
Office of Management and Budget
 (OMB)
 apportionment of
  appropriations, 255
 budget preparation and review,
  8–9
 bulletins and circulars issued by,
  1
 Instructions on Budget Execution,
  12–13
 *Preparation and Submission of
  Budget Estimates*, 9
Office of Personnel Management
 (OPM), 121, 155
Office of Technology Assessment,
 350
off-loading, 436
OMB Bulletin No. 80-14, 461–462
Omnibus Budget Reconciliation
 Act of 1990, 10
one percent limitation, 248

one-year appropriations, 8, 204,
 260
OPM. *See* Office of Personnel
 Management
option, 76
OSHA. *See* Occupational Safety
 and Health Act of 1970
out-of-scope modification, 247
overdisbursement, 266–267
overexpenditure, 272
overinvested trust fund, 27
overobligation, 267, 272
overrecording obligations, 51
overruling necessity, 559–560
overruns, unforeseeable, 246
overtime, volunteering for,
 324–325

P

Panama Canal Commission, 578
Patent and Trademark Office, 428
payment prohibited by law, 582
PBC. *See* District of Columbia
 Health and Hospitals Public
 Benefit Corporation
PBS. *See* Public Buildings Service
PEPCO. *See* Potomac Electric
 Power Company
period of availability
 authorization acts, effect upon,
  210–211
 definition, 202–203
 determining, 203–204
 multiple-year, 206
 no-year appropriation, 207–210
 presumption of one year, 204–
  205
 specified by Congress, 206
permanent legislation, 23–27
permanent transfer, 422

permissible activities, funding gap, 464–467
Personal Funds of Patients (PFOP), 532
personal property, loaning
  actual cost, 417
  Economy Act, impact upon, 415–416
  interdepartmental waiver doctrine, 419
  lost property, 421
  permanent transfer, 422
  reimbursable cost, 418
  repairs, paying for, 420
personal services prohibition, 324–329
petty-cash fund, 521
PFOP. See Personal Funds of Patients
point of order, 35
Posse Comitatus Act, 416
Postmaster General, 29
Post Office, multi-year contracts, 298–299
Potomac Electric Power Company (PEPCO), 309
power of the purse, 2
presidential constitutional duties and powers, 457–458
presidential inaugural committee, 376
presidential reorganization, 28
Presidential Transition Act of 1963, 211
President's budget, submission of, 9
presumption of negligence, 548
price adjustment, 240–241
Price Anderson Act, 316
price escalation clause, 50
price redetermination clause, 50
private insurance, 306–307

production lead time, 221
programmatic delay, 18
prohibited obligations and expenditures, 270
project order statute, 437–440
Proper Appropriation to Charge Expenses Relating to Nonseverable Training Course, 224
Proper Fiscal Year Appropriation to Charge for Contract and Contract Increases, 224, 246
protection of property, 340–341
proximate cause, 552–554
Public Buildings Service (PBS), 174–175
public enemy, 514
public funds, 528
Public Housing Administration, 272
purchase order, 75–76
purpose statute
  application of, 94–97
  importance of, 93–94

R

ratification by appropriation, doctrine of, 27–29
ratification of unauthorized commitments, 84–85
reasonable care, 551
receptions, 142
reconciliation directives, 11
recordable obligation, 47
recording obligations, 53–55
recreational facilities, 142
Red Cross volunteers, 346
reduction by appropriation, 37
Regional Commissioner, Customs Service, 526
regulatory violation, 557–558

relation-back doctrine, 88, 241, 248
relief determination, 543
relief of liability, accountable officer, 514–515, 538–540
remedy-granting clauses, 240–242
rental agreement, 76–77
repairs, paying for, 420
repeal by implication, rule against, 30–33, 36, 279
representation funds
  emergency and extraordinary expenses, 159
  foreign dignitaries, entertaining, 160
  official reception and representation, 161
  scope, 162–165
reprocurement contract, 231–232
request for proposals (RFP), 229
requirements contract, 71–73
Requirements for Reporting Antideficiency Act Violations, 360–366
rescissions, 16
reservation and notification letter, 52
reserve officers, 346–347
Resource Conservation and Recovery Act, 172
revolving funds, 275
rewards
  contractual bases for, 181–183
  finders of lost government property, 180–181
  informants, 176–179
  missing government employees, 179
  necessary expense, 180
  statutory authority, 175–176
RFP. *See* request for proposals
right to payment, contractor's, 354–358

rule against repeal by implication, 30–33, 36
rule of election, 22
Rules of the House of Representatives, 35

S

safety of human life, 337–340
secure communications, 189
security weaknesses, correcting, 568
Senate Committee on Expenditures, 540
Senate Committee on Government Operations, 253
separate termination charges, multi-year contracts, 301–303
service contracts, 222–223
severable service, 223–225
severable services labor-hour contract, 244
shall be available phrase, 281
Small Business Administration (SBA), 171
Social Security Administration, 578
Soil Conservation Service, 416
Solar Energy and Energy Conservation Bank Act, 211
SOPS. *See* standard operating procedures
sovereign immunity, doctrine of, 169
specific appropriation, 20–22
standard operating procedures (SOPS), 589
standing offer, 182
statutorily authorized waivers of compensation, 341–342
statutory training programs, 347–349

stock-level exception, 221-222
strict liability, 511-512
student intern program, 344-345
subject to availability clause,
  multi-year contracts, 300
subordinates, liability of, 590-591
subsequent legislation, 34
supplemental appropriation, 259
supplemental appropriations bill,
  462-464
supply contracts, 218-220
surplus, 10

T

T&A. *See* time and attendance
  records
task order (TO), 71
Tax Lien Revolving Fund, 537
telephones in private residences of
  government employees
  appropriated funds, 183-184
  exceptions, 185-191
  Federal Secure Telephone
    Service, 188-189
  military family housing, 184-
    185
  necessity, 188
Tellico Dam and Reservoir Project,
  30
temporarily unfunded basis, 332
Ten-Day Rule, 55
Tennessee Valley Authority (TVA),
  29, 444
termination charges, multi-year
  contracts, 301-303
termination for convenience of
  the government, 234-236
termination for default, 230-231
termination liability, 49
time and attendance (T&A)
  records, 516

time-and-material contract, 50
time limitations, placing on
  appropriated funds, 201-202
TO. *See* task order
Trade Deficit Review Commission
  Act, 413
training contracts, 226
training programs, 347-349
transitory legislation, 23-27
Transportation Working Capital
  Fund (TWCF), 455
Travel and Transportation Reform
  Act of 1998 (TTRA), 530
traveler's checks, 530
Treasury Financial Manual, 518
trust fund, 275, 533
TTRA. *See* Travel and
  Transportation Reform Act of
  1998
TVA. *See* Tennessee Valley
  Authority
TWCF. *See* Transportation
  Working Capital Fund

U

underrecording obligations, 52
unexplained losses, 554-557
United Nations, 376
United States Constitution
  appropriations clause, 2-3
  power to tax and spend, 2
United States Custom Service, 323
United States Enrichment
  Corporation (USEC), 291
United States Information Agency
  (USIA), 147
United States Marshals, 416
United States Metric Board, 327
United States Mint, 513
unless otherwise specified clause,
  280

unlimited indemnification clause
  Architect of the Capitol, 309
  Congressionally authorized
    indemnification, 316–318
  contractor-owned property, 312
  definition, 305
  Department of the Interior,
    305–306
  Farmers Home Administration,
    311
  Federal Emergency Management
    Agency, 307
  Federal Labor Relations
    Authority, 308
  Federal Property and
    Administrative Services Act,
    308
  federal reimbursement of
    disability benefits, 315
  indemnification funding
    problem, 317–318
  Insurance-Liability to Third
    Persons, 313–314
  lawful indemnification
    provisions, 309–315
  National Gallery of Art, 310
  National Oceanic and
    Atmospheric Administration,
    306–307
  Potomac Electric Power
    Company, 309
  Price-Anderson Act, 316
  Selective Service, 311
unvouchered expenditure,
  579–580
U.S. Geological Survey, 217
USEC. *See* United States
  Enrichment Corporation
USIA. *See* United States
  Information Agency

V

variable quantity contracts, 70–71
Veterans Administration (VA),
  146, 193, 260, 430
violations, 275, 286–292
voluntary interagency agreement,
  81–83
voluntary services
  acceptance of, 329–334
  alternative dispute resolution,
    343–344
  American Association of Retired
    Persons, 332
  appointment without
    compensation, 327
  coercive deficiency, 322
  Commission on Federal
    Paperwork, 332
  Commission on Marijuana and
    Drug Abuse, 328
  District of Columbia Health and
    Hospitals Public Benefit
    Corporation, 338–339
  emergency exception, 335–341
  employment of personal
    services, 324–329
  experts and consultants, 342–
    343
  family support programs, 345–
    346
  Federal Trade Commission, 332
  gratuitous services, 325–326
  greenmailing, 322
  Library of Congress, 350
  medical care, 345–346
  museums, 345–346
  natural resources programs,
    345–346
  Navy, 324

Office of Technology
  Assessment, 350
 overview, 321–322
 protection of property, 340–341
 Red Cross volunteers, 346
 reserve officers, 346–347
 safety of human life, 337–340
 statutorily authorized waivers of
  compensation, 341–342
 statutory training programs,
  347–349
 student intern program,
  344–345

United States Custom Service, 323
United States Metric Board, 327
vouchers, certifying, 517–519

W

waiver of salary, 341–342
within-scope price adjustment,
 240–241
words of futurity, 24–26
work plans, 272
Wounded Knee, South Dakota, 416